Irene Hanson Frieze • Christina E. Newhill
Rachel Fusco

Dynamics of Family and Intimate Partner Violence

Springer

Irene Hanson Frieze
Department of Psychology
University of Pittsburgh
Pittsburgh, PA, USA

Christina E. Newhill
University of Pittsburgh School
of Social Work
Pittsburgh, PA, USA

Rachel Fusco
School of Social Work
University of Georgia
Athens, GA, USA

ISBN 978-3-030-42606-4 ISBN 978-3-030-42608-8 (eBook)
https://doi.org/10.1007/978-3-030-42608-8

This Springer imprint is published by the registered company Springer Nature Switzerland AG
The registered company address is: Gewerbestrasse 11, 6330 Cham, Switzerland

Preface

We have written this book primarily for those working with clients experiencing violence from someone in their family or in a close relationship. Such service providers include social workers, counselors, nurses, teachers, or people in other helping professions. We also believe that students in these fields as well as in psychology or other social sciences will also find the book of interest. It is written to also be readable by the general public who might want to know more about the issues we discuss. Throughout the book, we have relied heavily on the empirical and theoretical body of research, drawing from psychology, social work, sociology, nursing, criminal justice, and many other fields. We look at those experiencing violence as well as at those who are perpetrating the violence, attempting to understand what is being done, who is doing it, how common it is, and what is being done to help those involved. We have also tied these published studies to our own clinical experiences in an attempt to provide context and make the situations we describe more vivid and real.

The body of relevant research and theory has grown tremendously since first initiated in the 1960s. In this book we draw on this long history, and also attempt to focus on current research findings and note how the field and even the things previously thought to be true have changed over time. In doing this, we draw heavily on our own work as well as the work of many others in the field. Another major goal is to integrate clinical findings into the review of published theory and empirical research. The Appendix contains actual cases from the clinical practice experiences of coauthors Christina Newhill and Rachel Fusco. We also include cases contributed by social workers Allison Little and Elizabeth Mulvaney based on their work in child welfare and gerontology, respectively. These case vignettes are based on actual client cases, but all identifying information have been removed or disguised and some cases are composite, meaning they have aspects from several clients combined. Other brief case examples have also been added throughout the book that are drawn from our personal practice experience with clients we worked with. Some published cases from the newspaper have also been used.

Irene Frieze's work on intimate partner violence (IPV) began in the early 1970s when a student in Dr. Frieze's Psychology of Women class came to her to talk about being beaten by her husband, wondering what, if anything, she could do about this.

At that time, there was very little research on this topic that she could look to in giving suggestions. As she and her student talked more about her situation, Dr. Frieze realized how important this was for many women's daily lives, and suggested that she and the student might try to do some research on her situation and that of other women. Other students were also interested in this project, and they formed a small research group to talk about marital violence against women and to design a research project. This led to Dr. Frieze writing a formal research proposal which was submitted to and funded by the National Institutes of Mental Health in 1977. The proposal involved in depth interviews with women who had identified as being battered either through seeking help at one of the new battered women's shelters being developed in the Pittsburgh region or by looking at court filings of women seeking protection from an abusive partner, as well as volunteers solicited from posted notices in public restrooms. The researchers attempted to find a comparison sample by matching each battered woman with a randomly selected married woman from her same neighborhood. (Of course, they did not tell this potential comparison to woman why she had been selected). The women were paid a small amount for their participation. Many wanted to talk to the interviewers and told detailed stories. The longest interview lasted for 15 h, done over three sessions. To the great surprise of the researchers, about one-third of the women in the comparison group also reported receiving some type of violence from their partner, and many of the women in both the comparison and battered samples told the interviewers that they had also used violence against their partners. Following this major study, Dr. Frieze conducted many other interview and survey studies, primarily using college students as her sample, looking at intimate partner violence. An earlier book about her work as well as a review of other research, called *Hurting the One You Love: Violence in Relationships*, was published in 2005 by Thompson Wadsworth publishers. This present book builds on and elaborates this earlier book.

The collaboration between the three authors that initiated this book began with discussion of mutual interests between Dr. Frieze and Dr. Newhill. Incorporating her personal clinical experiences and body of written cases based on this work seemed like a major addition to the book that Dr. Frieze had been thinking of. The two began working together on the book. As we did this, we realized that since much of our work focused on victims of intimate partner violence than on other forms of maltreatment in the family, we needed a collaborator working on child abuse. We decided to ask Dr. Fusco to join the collaboration. This allowed us to include cases based on her practice experience in child welfare and in a domestic violence service agency. Both Dr. Newhill and Dr. Fusco added important perspectives to the book based on their experiences in the School of Social Work. This was an important aspect of the book and greatly enhanced the more theoretical and research-based experience of Dr. Frieze.

Preparing this book has been a process that builds on the body of research our colleagues have published in a variety of fields, as well as on our own research and clinical experience. In addition, we would like to thank an anonymous reviewer for feedback on early drafts of some of the chapters. Additional thanks go to Melinda Ciccocioppo for her helpful comments about language. Lauren Hallion was especially helpful in discussions about PTSD and current clinical views about trauma. Her feedback was highly relevant for Chap. 3. We would also like to thank Nancy Grote for her feedback about an early draft of Chap. 9. Dr. Frieze also wants to include special thanks to the Department of Psychology at the University of Pittsburgh for providing ongoing support for her work after she formally retired from the university.

In preparing this book, we would especially like to thank Elizabeth (Beth) Mulvaney, MSW, LCSW, for contributing several cases and case vignettes illustrating situations involving elder abuse based on her 14 years of practice experience as a gerontological social worker providing medical, care management, and program administration services, with experience in long-term care including behavioral care planning, dementia care, and end of life care. Beth earned her MSW from the University of North Carolina at Chapel Hill and a BA in psychology from the University of Virginia.

Pittsburgh, PA, USA — Irene Hanson Frieze
Pittsburgh, PA, USA — Christina E. Newhill
Athens, GA, USA — Rachel Fusco

Contents

About the Authors

Irene Hanson Frieze is an Emeritus Professor of Psychology at the University of Pittsburgh. She has received awards for her research from the Association for Women in Psychology, and the Society for Psychology of Women (Division 35 of the American Psychological Association). Her research has resulted in her being appointed as a Fellow in five different divisions of the American Psychological Association as well as in the Association for Psychological Science. She has taught courses on violence and victimization, psychology of gender, psychology of women, social motivation, close relationships, and human sexuality. She has received national awards for her mentoring of graduate students and has coauthored papers with many of them. She received her PhD and MS in Psychology from UCLA.

Dr. Frieze's research interests include violence in close relationships, looking both at marital relationships and dating partnerships. She has also published on career issues for professional women, social motivation, and psychological factors in migration and emigration decision-making as well as place attachment. She has published several books, including *Hurting the one you love: Violence in relationships*, in 2005 by Thomson Wadsworth publishers.

Christina E. Newhill is Professor of Social Work at the University of Pittsburgh with a joint appointment with the Clinical and Translational Science Institute, and teaches in the MSW and PhD programs. In 2008, she received the Chancellor's Distinguished Teaching Award, Pitt's highest teaching honor. She earned a PhD in social welfare from the University of California, Berkeley; a master's degree in social work from Syracuse University; and a BA in sociology from the State University of New York, Binghamton. Dr. Newhill's primary research interests are violence risk markers and psychopathology, improving risk assessment of violent clients and social worker safety, intervention development for individuals with serious mental illness and their families, emotion regulation problems and borderline personality disorder, psychiatric emergency services, and racial disparities in mental health services. Her "Families as Partners in Reducing Violence" project, funded by the National Institute of Mental Health, lays the groundwork for the development of an innovative refinement of existing family psychoeducation interventions that will assist family members/caretakers in coping successfully with potentially violent situations involving their ill relative.

Dr. Newhill has more than 10 years of community mental health practice experience, primarily in psychiatric emergency and inpatient settings. She has conducted training workshops on client violence and social worker safety at the local, state, and national levels for many years and authored *Client violence in social work practice: Prevention, intervention and research*, published in 2003 by Guilford Press; other books include *Interventions for serious mental disorders: Working with individuals and their families* published by Pearson/Allyn & Bacon in 2015 and, most recently, *Skill development for generalist practice: Exercises for real-world application* released by Sage in 2019.

Rachel Fusco is an associate professor at the University of Georgia's School of Social Work where she is the Georgia Athletic Association Endowed Chair in Health and Well-Being. Dr. Fusco was previously on the faculty at the University of Pittsburgh School of Social Work where she taught courses in the BASW, MSW, and PhD programs including an advanced practice graduate course on intimate partner violence. She earned a PhD in social welfare from the University of Pennsylvania and an MSSW from the University of Texas at Austin.

Dr. Fusco's research focuses on the mental health and well-being of children, adolescents, and their mothers especially in families experiencing child maltreatment and/or intimate partner violence. Her current research involves supporting new mothers with opioid use disorders to increase treatment adherence, so they can engage in loving and safe parenting. The primary goal of this work is to promote attachment and decrease the likelihood of child welfare system entry. In addition, she conducts research on sleep problems in foster care youth and how that correlates with marijuana use. Prior to receiving her PhD, Dr. Fusco was a social worker in the child welfare system, in a center for battered women, and in adolescent mental health services.

Chapter 1
Introduction: Examining Family and Relationship Violence in U.S. Society

Case Example: Multiple Forms of Violence Occurring in a Single Family

Andy is a 20 year old unemployed single white male brought to the psychiatric emergency room by the city police for evaluation following an argument with his stepfather and his mother (all three had been drinking for several hours). At one point Andy pulled a knife and threatened to kill his parents and when police arrived, he had already cut himself and was now threatening to kill himself, stating he has nothing to live for. Andy was subsequently hospitalized involuntarily on the psychiatric inpatient unit on the basis of danger to self and others.

A few days later, after Andy was sufficiently detoxed from alcohol, he met with the inpatient social worker for a psychosocial assessment. Andy reports that he has never had a good relationship with his mother and stepfather and that the stepfather, who has a history of incarceration for assault, beats his mother regularly and was abusive to Andy when Andy was younger. However, once Andy turned 16, he fought back and his stepfather never laid a hand on him again.

The family lives in a rural area of the county and has six cats and five dogs living in the house with them. Andy doesn't see the animals as pets but, rather, as targets for discharging his frustration and aggression. He admits that several years ago, he set one of their cat's tails on fire using lighter fluid and enjoyed watching the cat suffer. His two younger siblings—both boys—fight a lot and Andy enjoys teasing them and behaving in ways that the social worker perceived as bullying.

The parents are well aware of their sons' behaviors but do nothing to intervene. Andy's maternal grandmother, who lives with them, has tried to stop the fighting but to no avail. Andy's mother and the grandmother also argue and fight and once someone broke the grandmother's arm but nobody in the family would admit to it. The police are frequently called to the house by concerned

I. H. Frieze et al., *Dynamics of Family and Intimate Partner Violence*,
https://doi.org/10.1007/978-3-030-42608-8_1

neighbors and the family has been involved with child welfare services for years but the various forms of family violence have continued and actions taken by the various agencies involved with the family have seemed to have had no positive effect. When the social worker asked Andy how he could help him and his family, Andy just shrugged.

This composite case example illustrates how various forms of violence—intimate partner violence, child physical abuse, sibling violence, animal cruelty, elder abuse and criminal behavior—can co-occur in a single multigenerational family. [We have combined parts of several actual cases to develop a composite case here to provide a concrete example and to preserve confidentiality. Throughout the book, we present cases from actual practice to demonstrate the general points being made]. Each of these forms of family and partnership violence and abuse and their dynamics will be explored in depth throughout this book.

In this first chapter of the book, we begin with a general overview of violent interpersonal behavior in the U.S., focusing on criminal violence. This provides a larger context for a more detailed examination in the remainder of the book of intimate partner violence, as well as parental abuse of children and other forms of violence in the family. As will be discussed below, violent crime rates have generally been dropping although they showed a slight rise in 2017. Reasons for this are suggested. This same trend can be seen looking more directly at partner violence (see Chaps. 4 and 5), one of the many types of crimes monitored by the U.S. Department of Justice, as well as child maltreatment (see Chap. 6). Not surprisingly, along with changes in criminal *behavior*, there is also evidence for changes in attitudes about interpersonal violence. This chapter includes an analysis about changing attitudes about the acceptability of intimate partner violence (IPV) and about spanking and other forms of parental violence toward children. We also discuss some methodological issues relating to research on family violence.

1.1 Crime in the United States and Other Countries

1.1.1 The National Crime Victimization Survey

The United States Department of Justice puts much effort into to collecting comprehensive data about all types of crimes, and the *victims* (*survivors?*) of those crimes (see Box 1.1 for discussion of these terms). These data are available to the public on the Bureau of Justice website at https://www.bjs.gov/. One very important source of information about experiences of those victimized by crimes is an annual national survey (the National Crime Victimization Survey or NCVS) of a representative sample of the U.S. population. This survey is conducted by the U.S. Department of

Justice. There are data available from 1972 through 2018 at this time. Data are collected about all types of criminal events. Some of these involve assault or other forms of violence, but others such as theft, forgery or burglary do not. When someone reported on the survey that they were victimized by some type of crime, either violent or nonviolent, they were then asked detailed questions about that crime. Questions included who the perpetrator was, and whether or not the crime was reported to the police.

Box 1.1: Use of Language. Survivor vs. Victim of Violence

The language we use to describe people, places, and events is meaningful. Language is an important part of culture and as our society changes, the terms we use often do as well. Among practitioners, scholars, and advocates who work in the field of intimate partner violence, there is debate about whether to use the word *victim* or *survivor* to refer to people who have experienced violence (Hockett & Saucier, 2015). While some believe the term *survivor* emphasizes individual agency and acknowledges the way people triumph over difficult circumstances, others believe that the word *victim* more accurately captures the challenges individuals face not only in a violent relationship, but in the systems that are charged with helping (Gondolf & Fisher, 1988). It is important to note that government reports use 'victim' to describe those who have experienced violence (e.g., National Institute of Justice, 2017). In this book we use both terms depending on the context of the violence. The authors want to make it clear that neither term is used with any negative judgment as we all respect the experiences of men, women, and children who suffer from violence at the hands of a loved one.

Ideas about appropriate terminology also varies for sexual minorities. The terms "gay" and "lesbian" are used by many researchers. We use these terms if they were what was reported, since they reflect what the study participants used to label themselves in the data. Other terms such as "transgender" or "trans" are also used in the book to reflect how the researcher defined these variables.

Looking at the most recent information available, data from the 2018 NCVS indicated that rates of violent crimes in 2018 showed small increases over the rates in 2015 (Morgan & Ouderkerk, 2019). Violent crimes included rape and sexual assault, robbery assault (the most common violent crime), domestic violence (including intimate partner violence), stranger violence, and violent crime including injury or using a weapon. Since these data come from victim reports, homicide data were not included. The small increases in rates were seen across all types of violent crimes, except those involving firearms. In 76% of all nonfatal violent crimes, including partner abuse, the offender was perceived to be male (Morgan & Truman, 2018). Thus, women are far *less likely* to commit crimes of violence than men, especially with strangers.

Since the NCVS survey is a household survey and not dependent on police records, it is possible to ask about whether those victimized reported the crime to the police. Data from the NCVS indicated that overall 45% of violent victimizations were reported to the police in 2017. These rates have varied since data were first reported in 1993 but generally indicate higher levels of reporting to the police in more recent years (Morgan & Truman, 2018). However, others have critiqued the NCVS, as well as other victimization surveys, and suggest that better reporting data are needed (Xie & Baumer, 2019).

In general, people are more likely to be injured by someone they know than by a stranger (see Box 1.2). Looking specifically at intimate partner violence (IPV) experiences, percentages of victimization in 2015, 2016 and 2017 were 1.2, 1.0 and 1.0 per 1000 for "serious" IPV and 3.0, 2.2, and 2.4 per 1000 for any type of IPV (Morgan & Truman, 2018, p. 3). No data were provided for women and men separately on IPV victimization or perpetrator in these reports from the NCVS. More information on this issue of men and women as victims or perpetrators can be found in Chap. 5.

Box 1.2: Violent Criminal Offenses by Strangers

Sociological theory would suggest that those more injured in physical assaults would be less well known to the violent individuals who assaulted them, and that they would share fewer characteristics in common. This is believed to result from a general tendency for people to be more protective and caring for those seen as similar or part of the same group as they are, while strangers, or those who are not part of the group are seen as appropriate targets of aggression. However, data from the National Crime Victimization Survey from 1993 to 2011 finds no support for this idea (Rennison, Jacques, & Allen, 2016). Instead, people are more likely to assault others they are acquainted with, or know very well.

These patterns can be seen looking at whether or not people are more likely to assault someone of the same or of a different race. National data indicated that it was more likely that an assault and the resulting injury occurred *within* racial groups than *across* racial groups. A related prediction was that assaults and injuries would be greater for victims who were strangers to the perpetrator than those who were known to the perpetrator. Instead, acquaintances are *more* likely to be injured than strangers (Rennison et al., 2016). Similar patterns can be seen for more extreme violence. According to homicide data from the Centers for Disease Control, while 26% of homicide victims in 2014 were killed by a current for former spouse or partner, only 14% of homicide victims were killed by a stranger (Fowler, Jack, Lyons, Betz, & Petrosky, 2018). These general findings are consistent with data discussed throughout this book showing that many people are injured by those they live with and love—by lovers, or parents, or other family members.

Other national U.S. data is available on homicides. Data from the Centers for Disease Control for 2014 indicated that 9% of men experiencing homicide had been killed by a current or former spouse or intimate partner. For women, the numbers were much higher, with 48% of female homicide victims killed by a partner (Fowler et al., 2018). Thus, men are more likely to be killed by someone other than a spouse (typically by another man), but for women, a partner is the most likely to be the one who kills her.

As noted above, NCVS data indicated that the most crimes of violence are committed by men. Similar data can be found elsewhere. Smith (2014) reviewed the literature on long-term crime rates for women and men, noting "the striking persistence of the gender gap [in rates of crimes committed] over long periods of time…" (p. 139). This was found in homicide data going back to medieval times in Europe as well as in data on other types of violent crime. As McCarthy and Gartner (2014) noted, this gender gap is less evident in recent years, but this may be the result of criminologists now including IPV and child abuse as forms of violent crime. Formerly, these forms of violence within the home were not included in national crime data. As discussed in various chapters in this book, these forms of violence within the family are done by women as well as men. Women are more likely to use violence within a family setting than outside the home with strangers.

1.1.2 Changing Crime Rates

Like other forms of violent victimization, violent crime rates have changed over time. The rates peaked in the early 1990's and showed a rapid decline until early in the twenty-first century. Reports from all of the most recent years for the NCVS indicated that far fewer people reported experiencing a crime as compared to the 1990's. Since 2001, there have been small annual increases or drops of 1 or 2% for crime rates but the overall pattern has been relatively stable. Since 2010, the average rate of victimization from a violent crime was about 2 per 100 people. Since then, the rates have ranged from 2 to 3/1000 for women and 1 to 2/1000 for men (Catalano, 2013).

Tcherni-Buzzeo (2019) attempted to explain why these drops have occurred in violent crime, noting that this decline in violent crimes has been happening throughout the developed world, and across different demographic categories within the United States. He further noted that physical and sexual abuse of children has been dropping in the United States since 1995, but no comparable drop can be found for child neglect (which is not a crime of violence). After discussing many possible explanations for the declines in interpersonal violence, he concludes that tentative evidence best supports factors such as increasing numbers of cell phones making people more secure, better reentry programs for convicted offenders, reductions in poverty, declining alcohol consumption, and better education.

Changing levels of reported victimization for crimes of violence generally, as well as for victimization within the home, should be placed within a broader context of a very long-term general decline in people's experiences with violence of all types. A number of researchers have pointed to a decline for interpersonal violence rates since the Middle Ages in Western European countries and in the U.S., although there have been some periods when interpersonal violence rates increased slightly. This can be seen in terms of homicide rates, as well as for other crimes (Tonry, 2014). Tonry also noted the same pattern for hospital emergency rooms dealing with fewer and fewer intentional injuries of others in the U.S. Both of these indicators are relatively objective violence indicators, less subject to the types of factors discussed in Box 1.3.

Box 1.3: Data about crime and violent behavior depends on many factors

As Tonry (2016), the editor of the journal *Crime and Justice*, discussed, data about crime rates is affected by a number of variables:

- **What gets reported to the police or other agencies**. This is dependent on what people define as unacceptable or criminal, and such perceptions change over time and cultures.
- **What the police (or agency staff) feel is a crime and should be reported**. Police reports reflect views of what police perceive as reportable acts. Police may not consider something reported to them as a true crime or may even discourage the person from reporting or trying to pursue legal action.
- **What people report in victim surveys**. Many of the incidents identified in surveys are never reported to the police or other authorities, and do not show up in formal reports from police or these agencies. However, even such survey data depends on what types of incidents the victim considers to be something to be noted in responding to the survey.
- **How complete the record keeping is for crime reports**. In the past, paper records may have been incomplete for a variety of reasons. As computers are increasingly used for record keeping, police reports that may have been lost are now more likely to be maintained.

Tonry further noted that in spite of this historical trend for lower levels of violent behavior, there was a *rise* in reported crime *rates* in the mid-twentieth century, followed by a later decline that has continued into the twenty-first century. This increase followed by a decline was especially evident for reports for child abuse as well as for intimate partner violence (IPV) and for sexual assault and rape. He attributes this to a number of factors that affect reported rates of violence (see Box 1.3), all of which reflect underlying attitudes about what is considered acceptable behavior.

Support for Tonry's (2014) arguments about the importance of attitudes and perceptions in the interpretation of crime rates can be found in studies investigating other possible explanations for the changes. Tseloni, Mailley, Farrell, and Tilley (2010) did a careful analysis of the large drops in crime rates in 26 countries between

1995 and 2004, looking at several specific crime types (assault, burglary, and several types of theft). The general trends identified were similar across all the countries they examined, and were seen in many types of crimes. They concluded that any valid explanations for these drops needed to be factors that operated across countries, since they could not be explained by increased incarceration rates, or lead exposure or other variables that have been found to correlate with dropping crime rates in one region. In another even more comprehensive test of 15 different possible explanations for higher or lower rates of crime victimization in many different countries, Farrell (2013) found that the only general factor that had any predictive power across different locations was the level of security in the country. In countries and times when there was greater police presence or other forms of high security leading to reduced opportunities for crime, reported victimization rates were lower.

Others have also pointed to changes in attitudes that appear to be reflected in reported crime rates. Based on international survey data, Inglehart (2018) argued the as people feel more economically secure, they develop a different perspective on other people and how society should operate. Greater feelings of economic security were found to be associated with wanting people to have more say about government decisions, greater freedom speech for individuals, and more independence in the workplace. Other associated attitudes were support for equality of women with men, and a greater emphasis on self expression. With less feelings of economic security, there was a greater emphasis on policies that encouraged economic growth, maintaining order, and fighting crime.

These value and attitude changes have been linked to many forms of violence (Inglehart, 2018). In societies with greater economic security, and in individual countries as the economic situation improved, there were declines in rates of war with other countries, as well as lowered rates of murder and other violent crimes (Inglehart, 2018; Tonry, 2014). Attitudes supporting violent interactions such as crime, witch burning, slavery and torture are also correlated with lower levels of economic prosperity based on international survey data (Inglehart, 2018).

In a related argument, Kivivuori (2014) suggested that people in the U.S. and other affluent Western societies have become more "sensitive toward violence" (p. 289). This sensitivity is seen as leading to greater reporting of actions defined as criminal. Crime rates rise when there is a *higher likelihood of reporting* something as criminal. Such reports may reflect views of what people *should* do as much as measuring actual crime levels since the definitions of criminal behavior have changed over time. Supporting evidence is found in data from Finland where upward trends in *reports* of general violence, as well as reports of violence by school principals, and police detection of shoplifting by youths have all risen over the last 20 years, although there is no clear evidence of actual increases in any of the behaviors being reported (Kivivuori, 2014).

1.1.3 Fear of Crime

Although objective data indicate there has been a long-term decline in interpersonal violence and violent crimes in general, this is not the common perception. Instead, many people appear to believe that crime is at an all time high and that protective actions are needed to avoid being victimized (see Chap. 3 on these coping behaviors). Based on data from the national Pew Research Center, national perceptions of rising crime rates are simply wrong. Although as discussed earlier, crime rates have dropped substantially since the 1990s, most people think that crime rates have been rising in recent years (Gramlich, 2016, 2019).

These crime fears are believed to result from the high level of media attention given to portraying violent criminal acts. In one of the early papers on this issue, Heath and Gilbert (1996) noted that effects of media on crime fears could be seen in those watching popular crime reenactment television programs as well as in movies and television news. More recent studies have continued to replicate these findings. For example, Kort-Butler and Habecker (2018) reported on a 2014 survey of Nebraska adults who were asked about media use and crime fears. viewing violence on television was especially related to worry and anger over crime, as was having been personally victimized. Dolliver, Kenney, Reid, and Prohaska (2018) argue that it is because of fears generated by the media that there is a high level of support for "defensive" (p. 400) behaviors such as allowing people to openly carry guns and passing laws requiring longer prison sentences for those convicted of crimes. In a direct test of these effects in a national sample in 2012, Dolliver and his colleagues found that all types of media consumption correlate with increased fears of crime. These fears strongly predicted support for defensive and punitive criminal justice policies.

1.2 Views About the Acceptability of Family Violence

Researchers have often argued that those who consider a behavior to be wrong are less likely to do that behavior (Dibble & Straus, 1980). However, as Dibble and Straus pointed out in an early paper, even if one is not supportive of family violence, circumstances may lead to one being violent in spite of these negative attitudes. A specific example of this was that if one's intimate partner is violent to you, it is quite likely that you would return that violence, perhaps in self defense, even if you are not personally supportive of IPV. As noted in Chap. 5, *mutual* IPV is the most common pattern for IPV, so this situation may be operating in many couples.

Although attitudes do not necessarily predict behavior, they are one of the important factors that do relate to how we act. Our attitudes affect our own behavior as well as our judgments about the acceptability of what others do. In this section, we review some of the research on attitudes relating to IPV and to child maltreatment or spanking. As outlined below, consistent with changes in crime statistics and views about the acceptability of various forms of criminal behavior, there has also been increasing disapproval of both IPV and spanking in the U. S. population, and in professionals who work with victims and perpetrators of family violence. For more detailed discussion of these issues, see Chaps. 4–6.

1.2.1 Attitudes About Intimate Partner Violence

Although the acceptability of intimate partner violence and wife beating varies greatly across countries, it is clear that there is a growing consensus around the world that such behavior is not acceptable (Pierotti, 2013). These views can be seen especially among those who are more educated (Wang, 2016). As Pierotti discussed, this international trend is especially noticeable among women. In another study based on international data from many studies, Hayes and Boyd (2017) found that approval of IPV was associated with higher levels of gender inequality within the country.

As discussed in Chaps. 4 and 5, the high level of disapproval of IPV can also be found in U.S. data. In a large survey of adults in California identified through a random procedure, Sorenson and Taylor (2005) asked people to answer questions about a hypothetical scenario involving an example of IPV in 2000 and 2001. Overall, 96% of the sample identified a man using violence against his female partner as wrong, while 93% viewed a woman using violence against her male partner as wrong. Greater disapproval for male violence was specifically seen for slapping, forced sex, and punching.

Arguing that there was possibly more acceptance of IPV among rural than urban U.S. populations, Schwab-Reese and Renner (2017) surveyed residents living in a county in Iowa which consisted mostly of small towns and a largely white population between 1999 and 2004. More than half the sample had some college education, so it was a highly educated sample, and may not be representative of many rural areas. Overall, 96% of men and women indicated that it was never acceptable for a male to use violence against his female partner. However, 80% or men and 88% of women reported it was never acceptable for a woman to be violent toward her male partner. Thus, there was more acceptance of female perpetrated IPV than male perpetration for both women and men in the sample. Also, for both sexes, the highest level of acceptance was for IPV in response to being hit by their partner. Note, though, that overall, there was strong disapproval of IPV in these samples.

Studies of U.S. college students have indicated similar findings of overall disapproval of IPV in dating couples. But levels of disapproval for male and female perpetrated IPV differ. For example, Hammock, Richardson, Lamm, Taylor, and Verlaque (2017) again used scenarios to describe different forms of IPV and asked their sample of students at a south Eastern university to evaluate each member of a violent couple. Ratings were more positive about female victims than male victims, and female perpetrators than male perpetrators. Physical violence was rated more negatively than psychological violence. Data were collected for same-sex couples, but no significant effects were reported for differences across gay and heterosexual couples. In a similar study where college students from psychology classes in the Midwest university were asked to evaluate scenarios involving verbal abuse in a heterosexual couple, Capezza, D'Intino, Flynn, and Arriaga (2017) reported that psychological abuse was rated more negatively than a comparison scenario with no verbal abuse. Male perpetrators were rated more negatively than female perpetrators.

A number of studies have argued that various forms of media portray IPV and these portrayals shape attitudes and acceptability of male to female and female to male partner violence (e.g., Scarduzio, Carlyle, Harrius, & Savage 2017). Attitudes and societal disapproval of IPV can be seen in an examination of how the media treats cases in which an athlete has been accused of IPV. Spencer and Limperos (2018) analyzed the coverage of ESPN relating to IPV among National Football League (NFL) players before and after the airing of Ray Rice's assault of his partner, knocking her unconscious, in an elevator. Afterwards, there was far more coverage of player IPV. There was also a strong public response arguing that the NLF needed to respond more actively to this type of player behavior. As Brown, Murphy, and Maxwell (2018) report, there is greater disapproval of athletes using violence against their partners than for accusations of assault of another patron outside a bar or drug possession. Although the large majority of media reports of IPV involve male athletes, there have been a few reports of female athletes perpetrating violence against their partners (Brown et al. 2018). The fact that such accounts are newsworthy, and the high degree of disapproval both indicate societal disapproval of IPV behavior.

1.2.2 Attitudes About Physical Punishment of Children

As discussed in Chap. 6, parents using physical forms of punishment against children for what they describe as *discipline* has been found to be a predictor of physical child abuse (Taylor, Fleckman, & Lee 2017). In an article titled "Ending the Spanking Debate," Afifi and Romano (2017) argue that the evidence at this point is quite clear that spanking (hitting the child on the buttocks with an open hand) may have negative effects on the child. They further note that spanking has not been found to have any beneficial effects and has been banned in many countries. However, spanking remains a common practice in many parts of the world, and many people continue to argue that spanking is safe and necessary to discipline children. This can be seen in a 2013 survey of Canadian parents. Using a volunteer sample recruited through posters and at community organizations, Afifi and Romano reported that over 1/3 endorsed the idea of using corporal punishment to discipline children. Another study found that supportive beliefs about spanking were correlated with self reports of using corporal punishment with their own children (Fréchette & Romano, 2017), indicating a link between attitudes and behavior.

There is also evidence that many people in the United States agree with the idea of spanking children. Using data from the General Social Survey, a repeated nationally representative U.S. sample, Hoffman, Ellison, and Bartkowski (2017) found that there has been a general trend toward less support for parents using spanking as a means of disciplining their children during the period from 1986 to 2014. However, attitudes differ across groups, with greater support among conservative Protestant Christians. The survey question used was agreement with the idea that "it is sometimes necessary to discipline a child with a good, hard spanking" (p. 86). Over the years of the survey, agreement with this item ranged from slightly less than 80% to about 65% in 2014 for those who were not Conservative Protestants and from over 90% to a little over 80% for those who were. These numbers do indicate a high level of support for at least occasional use of spanking.

Negative views of spanking and other forms of physical punishment are clearly evident among professionals. Members of the American Professional Society on the Abuse of Children consist of mental health professionals, physicians, child welfare professionals and other professionals working on issues related to child abuse. This group was surveyed in 2015 about their attitudes about corporal punishment of children by Taylor et al. (2017). Questions included "Spanking is a normal part of parenting" (Negatively scored) and "Overall, spanking is a bad disciplinary technique." Overall, the reported attitudes of the professionals surveyed were in opposition to spanking. For example, 74% disagreed that spanking was a normal part of parenting and 82% agreed that spanking is a bad disciplinary technique. These attitudes were much more negative than reported in earlier studies. However, given the widespread use of spanking, some continue to argue that it should not be categorically opposed (e.g., Larzelere, Gunnoe, Ferguson, & Roberts, 2019).

1.3 Measuring Violent Behavior and Attitudes

In understanding research on IPV or child abuse, it is important to note what group the data come from. Findings are quite dependent on the sample used. In general, there are three basic types of samples used in the research discussed in this book: representative, convenience, and volunteer. Representative samples attempt to represent an entire population, allowing us to make generalizations about issues such as how common IPV is in the U.S. population at the time the survey was done. The date of publication of data may be quite different from the time of data collection, so both types of information are provided when this information is available. Typically, these representative samples are initially obtained through a random procedure of some type (see Babbie, 2016), but are adjusted if the researchers find that some groups that are important to the study are not well represented in the final data. Such samples yield good information about an entire group. However, if the group is defined as all students attending public high school in a particular location, their results may not be generalizable to other high school students in private schools in the same area or to high school students in other areas.

It is even more problematic to attempt to generalize the findings of a particular data collection if other types of samples are used. Convenience samples are samples chosen by the researcher. This type of sample is seen in many studies of college students when entire classes are sampled. They are also typical of clinical samples where people seeking some type of treatment are interviewed or surveyed. Samples of those identified as being abusive parents by a specific locality would be convenience samples. With such samples, it is never clear if the data obtained can be generalized to other groups. Finally, volunteer samples are found when some type of notice is used to advertise a study, and people are requested to let the researcher know if they are interested. Such samples have all the generalization issues of convenience samples, but they are further biased by the fact that study participants have volunteered.

As already suggested, measurement of violent behavior of any type is not always direct or easy to do. Sampling is not the only concern. Different forms of measurement often provide different data, an issue that we return to in the chapters to follow. Most studies use a series of questions about IPV or child abuse, and label people in the sample based on their answers to these questions. If the questions of one study are different from those in another study, it is never clear how to explain the variations in findings.

Any time people are asked about their behavior or experiences, even if they attempt to answer honestly, they may not be accurate in remembering things they have done or had done to them in the past, especially if asked to summarize over a long time period. For this reason, many scales ask only about things that have happened in the last year or even the last 6 months. Another issue is that they may not want to answer honestly for any of a number of possible reasons. For example, they may be embarrassed to admit being hit by their intimate partner or by a parent. If asked about their own violence, they may want to minimize their own aggressive behavior or may even deny it completely. As discussed in Chap. 5, when both members of a couple answer questions about what violent actions they did to a partner and what the partner did to them, their answers often differ from what the partner reports in response to the same questions. Readers of this book are urged to consider these types of issues in interpreting the data reported in various chapters.

1.4 Organization of the Book

This chapter provided a general introductory overview of the status of violence in the United States. Next, in Chap. 2, the focus is theories about where violence comes from. Why are some individuals more violent than others? Of course, aggression can be expressed in nonviolent ways, so general theories about aggression are also discussed. As can be seen, there is evidence for learning as a predictor of aggression, as well as a number of biological factors.

Chapter 3 is again a theoretical or basic chapter. In this chapter, the concern is *how* victims (or survivors) react and *why* they react in the ways they do. Theories about general reactions to any type of victimization, such as natural disasters or accidents are discussed, as well as specific data about how people react when victimized by someone in the family or other close relationship. Coping strategies and posttraumatic growth are also discussed.

Chapter 4 examines the situation for battered women. As will be explained, societal views about battered women have changed through the last 70 years. Now, there are shelters where battered women can seek emergency protection or other assistance, which has led to a large body of work about the women who seek this assistance, the group known as battered women. Findings of this research are described.

Chapter 5 is also concerned with intimate partner violence, but the focus is quite different. A good deal of IPV exists that does not fit the common conceptualization of battered women and their male batterers. Much of these data come from general population surveys. These are supplemented by studies based on college student samples. A major concern of this research is evidence for female violence toward partners and whether women are just as violent as men. As research continues to explore this issue, the more recent studies suggest that even though there is clear evidence for female violence, men tend to be the ones using the most violent forms of aggression. There is also clear evidence that those in other types of partnerships, such as gays and lesbians, and transgendered individuals also may have violence as part of their partnership.

Other types of violence beyond intimate partner violence are the focus of the next chapters. In Chap. 6, we discuss the research on parental abuse and neglect of children. We examine the characteristics of abusive parents and then turn to the question of the consequences of this type of violence on the child victims. Physical violence, as well as psychological abuse and incest and sexual abuse are also discussed. Effects on children of witnessing parental IPV is also considered as a form of child maltreatment. Other types of abuse within the family are the focus of Chap. 7. Included are elder abuse, sibling violence and abuse of family pets. These important issues are much less commonly the topic of published research, but we attempt to summarize what we do know about these other forms of family violence.

The last three chapters address treatment issues. In Chap. 8, the focus is treatment programs for victims of IPV and child maltreatment. These programs, administered by shelters or by counselors may also address needs of the children of abusive parents as well as survivors or victims of IPV. Chapter 9 turns to the question of how society addresses those who perpetrate violence against family members or those they are in close relationships with. Identification of these perpetrators is often one of the difficulties in those working to end these types of violence. Unfortunately, many perpetrators are never identified. If they are identified, are there effective treatment programs for them? Unfortunately, as discussed, often the answer is *no*. In Chap. 10, we examine the helpgivers, noting their initially high levels of motivation. Over time, as some become frustrated, they may experience burnout or other negative reactions to their work. Suggestions about self care are offered for these helpgivers.

The last section of the book contains a number of actual case studies from the clinical files of co-authors Christina Newhill and Rachel Fusco, as well as some additional cases from one of their students and another colleague. These cases have been cited throughout the book to demonstrate some of the more theoretical issues being discussed in the text of the book.

References

Afifi, T. O., & Romano, E. (2017). Ending the spanking debate. *Child Abuse & Neglect, 71*, 3–4. https://doi.org/10.1016/j.chiabu.2017.08.020

Babbie, E. R. (2016). *The practice of social research* (14th ed.). Belmont, CA: Cengage Wadsworth Publishers.

Brown, K. A., Murphy, B., & Maxwell, L. C. (2018). Tried in the court of public opinion: Effects of involvement in criminal transgressions on athlete image. *Communication & Sport, 6*, 283–307. https://doi.org/10.1177/2167479517697426

Capezza, N. M., D'Intino, L. A., Flynn, M. A., & Arriaga, X. B. (2017). Perceptions of psychological abuse: The role of the perpetrator gender, victim's response, and sexism. *Journal of Interpersonal Violence*, 1–23. https://doi.org/10.1177/0886260517741215

Catalano, S. (2013). *Intimate partner violence: Attributes of victimization, 1993–2011*. Washington, DC: U.S. Department of Justice, Office of Justice Programs.

Dibble, U., & Straus, M. A. (1980). Some social structural determinants of inconsistency between attitudes and behavior: The case of family violence. *Journal of Marriage and the Family, 42*, 71–80. https://doi.org/10.2307/351935

Dolliver, M. J., Kenney, J. L., Reid, L. W., & Prohaska, A. (2018). Examining the relationship between media consumption, fear of crime, and support for controversial criminal justice policies using a nationally representative sample. *Journal of Contemporary Criminal Justice, 34*(4), 399–420. https://doi.org/10.1177/1043986218787734J

Farrell, G. (2013). Five tests for a theory of the crime drop. *Crime Science: An Interdisciplinary Journal, 2*, 5. https://doi.org/10.1186/2193-7680-2-5

Fowler, K. A., Jack, S. P., Lyons, B. H., Betz, C. J., & Petrosky, E. (2018). Surveillance for violent deaths — national violent death reporting system, 18 states, 2014. *MMWR Surveillance Summary, 67*(SS-2), 1–36. https://doi.org/10.15585/mmwr.ss6702a1

Fréchette, S., & Romano, E. (2017). How do parents label their physical disciplinary practices? A focus on the definition of corporal punishment. *Child Abuse & Neglect, 71*, 92–103. https://doi.org/10.1016/j.chiabu.2017.02.003

Gondolf, E. W., & Fisher, E. R. (1988). *Battered women as survivors: An alternative to treating learned helplessness*. Washington, DC: Lexington Books.

Gramlich, J. (2016). *Voters' perceptions of crime continue to conflict with reality.* PEW Research Center. Retrieved from https://www.pewresearch.org/fact-tank/2016/11/16/voters-perceptions-of-crime-continue-to-conflict-with-reality/

Gramlich, J. (2019). *5 facts about crime in the U.S.* PEW Reserch Center. Retrieved from https://www.pewresearch.org/fact-tank/2019/10/17/facts-about-crime-in-the-u-s/

Hammock, G. S., Richardson, D. S., Lamm, K. B., Taylor, E., & Verlaque, L. (2017). The effect of gender of perpetrator and victim on perceptions of psychological and physical intimate partner aggression. *Journal of Family Violence, 32*, 357–365. https://doi.org/10.1007/s10896-016-9850-y

Hayes, B. E., & Boyd, K. A. (2017). Influence of individual- and national-level factors on attitudes toward intimate partner violence. *Sociological Perspectives, 60*, 685–701. https://doi.org/10.1177/0731121416662028

Heath, L., & Gilbert, K. (1996). Mass media and fear of crime. *American Behavioral Scientist, 39*(4), 379–386. https://doi.org/10.1177/0002764296039004003

Hockett, J. M., & Saucier, D. A. (2015). A systematic literature review of "rape victims" versus "rape survivors": Implications for theory, research, and practice. *Aggression and Violent Behavior, 25*, 1–14. https://doi.org/10.1016/j.avb.2015.07.003

Hoffman, J. P., Ellison, C. G., & Bartkowski, J. P. (2017). Conservative Protestantism and attitudes toward corporal punishment, 1986–2014. *Social Science Research, 63*, 81–94. https://doi.org/10.1016/j.ssresearch.2016.09.010

Inglehart, R. F. (2018). *Cultural evolution: People's motivations are changing, and reshaping the world*. New York: Cambridge University Press.

Kivivuori, J. (2014). Understanding trends in personal violence: Does cultural sensitivity matter? *Crime and Justice, 43*, 289–340. https://doi.org/10.1086/677664

Kort-Butler, L. A., & Habecker, P. (2018). Framing and cultivating the story of crime: The effects of media use, victimization, and social networks on attitudes about crime. *Criminal Justice Review, 43*(2), 127–146. https://doi.org/10.1177/0734016817710696

Larzelere, R. E., Gunnoe, M. L., Ferguson, C. J., & Roberts, M. W. (2019). The insufficiency of the evidence used to categorically oppose spanking and its implications for families and psychological science: Comment on Gershoff et al. (2018). *American Psychologist, 74*(4), 497–499. https://doi.org/10.1037/amp0000461

McCarthy, B., & Gartner, R. (2014). Introduction. In R. Gartner & B. McCarthy (Eds.), *The Oxford handbook of gender, sex, and crime* (pp. 1–16). New York: Oxford University Press.

Morgan, R. E., & Ouderkerk, B. A. (2019). *Criminal victimization, 2018*. Washington, DC: U.S. Department of Justice, Office of Justice Programs. NCJ 252472.

Morgan, R. E., & Truman, J. L. (2018). *Criminal victimization, 2018*. Washington, DC: U.S. Department of Justice, Office of Justice Programs. NCJ 253043.

National Institute of Justice. (2017). Victims and victimization. Retrieved from https://www.nij.gov/topics/victims-victimization/pages/welcome.aspx

Pierotti, R. S. (2013). Increasing rejection of intimate partner violence: Evidence of global cultural diffusion. *American Sociological Review, 78*, 240–265. https://doi.org/10.1177/0003122413480363

Rennison, C. M., Jacques, S., & Allen, A. (2016). Victim injury and social distance: A national test of a general principle of conflict. *Violence and Victims, 31*, 726–750. https://doi.org/10.1891/0886-6708.VV-D-15-00023

Scarduzio, J. A., Carlyle, K. E., Harrius, K. L., & Savage, M. W. (2017). "Maybe she was provoked": Exploring gender stereotypes about male and female perpetrators of intimate partner violence. *Violence Against Women, 23*, 89–113. https://doi.org/10.1177/1077801216636240

Schwab-Reese, L. M., & Renner, L. M. (2017). Attitudinal acceptance of and experiences with intimate partner violence among rural adults. *Journal of Family Violence, 32*, 115–123. https://doi.org/10.1007/s10896-016-9895-y

Smith, G. T. (2014). Long-term trends in female and male involvement in crime. In R. Gartner & B. McCarthy (Eds.), *The Oxford handbook of gender, sex, and crime* (pp. 139–157). New York: Oxford University Press.

Sorenson, S. B., & Taylor, C. A. (2005). Female aggression toward male intimate partners: An examination of social norms in a community-based sample. *Psychology of Women Quarterly, 29*, 78–96. https://doi.org/10.1111/j.1471-6402.2005.00170.x

Spencer, E. A., & Limperos, A. M. (2018). ESPN's coverage of intimate partner violence in the National Football League. *Communication and Sport*, 1–23. https://doi.org/10.1177/2167479518817759

Taylor, C. A., Fleckman, J. M., & Lee, S. J. (2017). Attitudes, beliefs, and perceived norms about corporal punishment and related training needs among members of the "American Professional Society on the Abuse of Children.". *Child Abuse & Neglect, 71*, 56–68. https://doi.org/10.1016/j.chiabu.2017.04.009

Tcherni-Buzzeo, M. (2019). The "Great American crime decline": Possible EXPLANATIONS. In M. D. Krohn et al. (Eds.), *Handbook on crime and deviance* (2nd ed., pp. 1–35). New York, NY: Springer.

Tonry, M. (2014). Why crime rates are falling throughout the Western world. *Crime and Justice, 43*, 1–63. https://doi.org/10.1086/678181

Tonry, M. (2016). What should we expect from police data: Can they tell us whether crime rates Rise or fall? Cahiers—*Police Studies* (Forthcoming); Minnesota Legal Studies Research Paper No. 16–36. Available at SSRN. Retrieved from https://ssrn.com/abstract=2853699

Tseloni, A., Mailley, J., Farrell, G., & Tilley, N. (2010). Exploring the international decline in crime rates. *European Journal of Criminology, 7*, 375–394. https://doi.org/10.1177/1477370810367014

Wang, L. (2016). Factors influencing attitude toward intimate partner violence. *Aggression and Violent Behavior, 29*, 72–78. https://doi.org/10.1016/j.avb.2016.06.005

Xie, M., & Baumer, E. P. (2019). Crime victims' decisions to call the police: Past research and new directions. *Annual Review of Criminology, 2*, 217–240. https://doi.org/10.1146/annurev-criminol-011518-024748

Chapter 2
Causal Factors in Aggression and Violence: Examining Social and Biological Theories

In this chapter, we examine the research on various factors that are associated with aggressive behavior, with a focus on physical violence. Psychologists have spent many years trying to better understand the conditions that explain why some people are more aggressive than others. As these studies have been done, it becomes increasingly clear that the causal explanations for aggressive behavior are complex and any act of aggression has multiple determinants. These include the particular circumstances one is in at the time as well as lifelong patterns of learning and socialization. There are also a number of important biological factors that are correlated with higher or lower levels of aggressiveness. Each of these major correlates of aggression is briefly examined in this chapter.

In addition to the extensive scientific literature on aggression, there are also many other types of resources now available for people to better understand individual acts of aggression and ways to limit or stop acts of violence and aggression. Groups such as the American Psychological Association have instituted offices devoted to helping people control their own violence as well as discussing how people learn to be violent. Their website provides many resources for this. See http://www.apa.org/pi/prevent-violence/resources/index.aspx.

Aggression can be defined as behavior that is more violent or hostile than seems appropriate for the situation (Bushman, Bonacci, Pedersen, Vasquez, & Miller, 2005). As we examine the studies of causal factors in aggression, it is important to keep in mind that there are many types of aggression (Paulhus, Curtis, & Jones, 2018). Often the literature fails to distinguish among these different types and may group them all together or assume that one type of aggression can be generalized to other types. Different types of aggression may have different causal factors (Rhee & Waldman, 2011). In a comprehensive review of the literature, Hamby (2017) argued that there are four essential characteristics of aggression. It should be intentional, it should be seen as unwanted by the recipient, it should not be essential for the wellbeing of the potentially aggressive actor, and it should be harmful to the recipient. Aggressive acts that would not be considered as violence using this definition would include violations of social norms or feelings of anger that are not expressed in negative ways to others (Hamby, 2017).

I. H. Frieze et al., *Dynamics of Family and Intimate Partner Violence*,
https://doi.org/10.1007/978-3-030-42608-8_2

As will be discussed throughout this book, aggression can be one of the many forms of physical violence or directly hostile language or some other form of indirectly hostile speech. The later is generally labeled as psychological or emotional aggression. Sexual aggression is also considered as a form of aggression in this book. Aggression can be a reaction to provocation (reactive aggression) or unprovoked and initiated for no apparent reason. Although not technically *aggression*, using Hamby's definition, we also consider cases of physical and emotional neglect as we examine issues relating to aggression and maltreatment in the family.

The following case example illustrates aggression as a theme in a couple's career success. In this case, violence plays a regular role in their marriage with sexual pleasure serving as a reinforcer for continued episodes of fighting. The case also shows how such ongoing aggression in a relationship can lead to serious injury requiring medical care, but even such injury does not serve as an incentive for changing the behavior pattern in the couple's relationship.

Case Example

Harry and Jane both work as criminal defense attorneys and have been married for 10 years with no children. They both relish taking on cases involving clients accused of heinous sex crimes and are quite talented at aggressively and successfully defending such clients. Their home life in some ways reflects their work in that they frequently fight with each other verbally or physically, often following an accusation of infidelity. These physical fights usually culminate with passionate sex, which appears to serve as reward and an incentive for future fighting. One night, however, the fight escalated to the point where Harry broke Jane's arm, and she had to go to the emergency room. The emergency room doctor was suspicious about the cause of the broken arm, and asked the ER social worker to evaluate the couple. They freely admitted that Harry had broken Jane's arm, but she did not want to press charges, and neither had any interest in getting counseling. The social worker gave them a referral for counseling anyway but doubted they would follow up (Newhill, 1995).

2.1 Learning of Aggression

In order to understand people's behavior, psychologists often look to patterns of learning and reinforcement that have occurred over a person's lifetime, starting in early infancy (Rathus, 2005). Learning can occur as a reaction to direct or indirect rewards. We also learn by modeling or imitating what other people do around us. As the examples below demonstrate, we are most likely to imitate others who have received rewards for the behavior being modeled. Thus, the first step in looking at how aggression or violence is learned is to analyze ways in which this behavior is rewarded.

2.1.1 Rewards for Violence or Other Aggression

It is not uncommon in daily life to find situations in which violence is rewarded. In order to survive, any animal needs to be aggressive in gathering food. Carnivores kill other animals to eat, and even plant-eating animals may have to fight other animals for access to food. Sexual access requires fighting other animals in many species, especially for males. This type of aggression related to survival is one of our basic motives, and it occurs in all animals including humans (De Boer, 2018).

Although in modern society, humans generally do not have to kill animals or fight with others for food, it is common for young children to physically fight another child to take a toy away or prevent it from being taken from them by another. If the child is successful in having the desired toy to play with, this provides pleasure and reinforcement for the aggressive child. This reinforcement increases the likelihood that the successful aggressive behavior will be repeated in the future. The same type of reinforcement can happen with adults and with non-human animals (De Boer, 2018). For adults, if we yell at or hit our partner, and our partner responds by doing what we wanted them to do, we have been rewarded for our aggressiveness. It is quite likely we will do this again. As described in Chap. 4, a chapter on battered women, this type of pattern is believed to occur for men who are extremely violent toward a spouse or partner. Not only may the violent man get what he asked for (a reward for his violence), but the partner may also be willing to engage in sexual activity as a way of making up after a fight involving some type of violence. Sexual satisfaction may then add an additional layer of reward for the initial violence. Once this reinforcement has occurred, the individual who has learned to expect positive results from his violence would be expected to escalate his level of violence and become more aggressive. If the expected positive outcome does not occur, the previously reinforced person may become frustrated. Frustration is also linked to aggression, so the noncompliance may result in additional violence (Groves & Anderson, 2017). All of this can and often does happen without either party being consciously aware of these underlying dynamics.

Since the use of aggression to get something we want is so common, the question psychologists generally consider is not why people are aggressive, but how we train children *not* to use aggression (Russell, Robins, & Odgers, 2014). We may use some type of punishment to discourage children from using violence. As children age, they show a continuing decrease in aggressive behavior (Lansford, 2018), perhaps showing the effects of societal punishments for such behavior. Punishments become more severe for adults than for children. When adults use violence to assault others or to enable them to take things from others, we label this as criminal behavior and put people in jail to punish them and to keep them from being able to continue this behavior (see Chap. 1).

In spite of the laws and ideas about what behaviors are considered to be appropriate in adults, it appears that people may be encouraging aggression in others in non-conscious ways and may be giving unintended reinforcement for such behavior. Like other forms of reinforcement, the positive reinforcement from others who observe or are aware of violent interactions can increase the likelihood of future aggression in those performing these behaviors. If others observe us using violence or some other form of aggression and praise us for it, we have received social reinforcement for the behavior. Situations in which others have positive reactions to aggression are not uncommon. For example, aggressive teenage boys are likely to be admired and praised by their peers, especially if they are also athletes (Rodkin, Farmer, Pearl, & Van Acker, 2000). Perhaps because of this type of reinforcement, in a study of 16 high schools in Northern California, boys involved in playing football and basketball were more likely than their peers to have used violence against a dating partner and also held more stereotypic attitudes relating to gender roles (McCauley et al., 2014).

The following case from the media summarizes a case of a young man whose gender, class and athletic privilege both reinforced his entitlement to commit a violent rape but also led the judge in the case to issue an exceptionally lenient sentence suggesting an aim to support the perpetrator's privileged status. The victim of the rape articulated this idea clearly in a rebuttal to the court.

Media Case Example

Brock Turner, a 20 year old varsity swimmer and a student at Stanford University, was sentenced to only 6 months in jail after being convicted of raping a comatose young woman after a fraternity party. Turner's father, a Stanford alum, complained in a Twitter post that his son's life had been ruined for "20 min of action". The victim spoke out with strong criticism of how the legal system handles cases of sexual assault, arguing that legal inequities are often fostered by male and class privilege as demonstrated by the judge's concern that more severe punishment would disrupt Turner's studies and athletic career at Stanford. In the wake of the public outrage over the case, Stanford University withdrew Turner's athletic scholarship and Turner withdrew from school rather than face expulsion procedures (Stack, 2016).

Values supporting certain types of aggression have been associated with the southern part of the United States. Nisbett & Cohen's 1996 book on the *Culture of Honor* describes how Southern white men, especially those living in rural areas, were particularly accepting of violence when used for self-protection, or to defend one's honor. Statistical data indicating that the South led the country in homicides and in other forms of violence supported their analysis. This region also had higher subscriptions to magazines dealing with issues such as self-defense, weapons, and combat. However, it should be noted that these analyses are based on studies from the late twentieth century and may no longer reflect the modern South. However, a more recent study (Brown, Baughman, & Carvallo, 2018) suggests an honor culture may still exist in both the southern and western states of the U.S. Brown and his colleagues define honor culture as a situation where men seek to maintain their reputations for strength and bravery and won't tolerate disrespect. Within honor culture, women attempt to build a reputation for loyalty to their male partner and for sexual purity. When women act in ways that suggest they might be unfaithful, men are expected to feel jealous and to punish women for this. U.S. data from the early 2000s relating to male homicide of a female partner and rape were used to see if the honor states significantly differed as predicted on these measures. The predictions were supported. National data on adolescent behavior from the Youth Risk Behavior Survey administered by the CDC also indicated that there was more reported rape of young women in the honor states as predicted. However, no differences were found related to dating IPV. (Chap. 5 provides some data that might explain why dating IPV might be dependent on many other variables beyond an honor culture).

Attitudes supporting the use of physical violence can also be seen in those serving in the military and in their families. We might assume that military personnel and their families would be generally more accepting of aggression, since their jobs are so associated with this. Empirical data supports this assumption. In a survey of high school students who came from military-connected families in Southern California, rates of physical violence and non-physical aggression were relatively high among both boys and girls, although they were especially high for boys (De Pedro, Astor, Gilbreath, Benbenishty, & Berkowitz, 2016). The levels of violence were lower, though, for the students in schools where there was a warm school climate and a higher sense that staff were caring and wanted to be helpful to students. Perhaps in these schools with the warm social climate, other non-violent behaviors were more often reinforced?

Acceptance of partner violence and parental violence toward children differs across individuals within the United States (see Chaps. 1, 5 and 6), with some people showing more disapproval than others. Increasingly, though, violence directed against an intimate partner and against a child are not considered acceptable adult behavior by the majority of the population. International research on supportiveness of these types of violence also shows country differences. In a study comparing blame of a man who hit his dating or marital partner, Nguyen et al. (2013) found that college students in China and Japan were *more likely* than those in the U.S. to blame the violent male partner and less likely to blame the female victim. They also reported that women were more likely than men to blame the violent man in all three countries. Such data would suggest that it would be less likely that a man who was violent toward his wife or girlfriend would receive positive feedback for this in the U.S. than in either Japan or China, and that women would be less likely to offer reinforcement than men for this situation in all of these three countries. Related data can be found in a large survey of adults in California who were asked to respond to a vignette describing a situation of intimate partner violence (Taylor & Sorenson, 2005). Although most people felt the violent individual was at fault, there was a higher level of blame assigned to the victim in people born outside the United States as compared to those born in the U.S. These data would imply that some immigrants might be more likely to reinforce male partner violence than the native born U.S. population.

It should be noted that in both these studies just discussed, only a few people had a positive view of a man being violent toward his partner in the samples from all the countries examined. It appears that although partner violence may have been generally acceptable in earlier historical periods, and in some countries more than others, there is a general trend toward less approval of this behavior now, especially in the United States (Arriaga & Capezza, 2011; Frieze, 2005). However, as Arriaga and Capezza note in their review of this literature, although there are clear norms now in the U.S. about actual violence against one's partner, there is no comparable disapproval of psychological aggression. Psychological aggression might involve labeling the partner in an unacceptable way or humiliating him or her. This lack is a clear limitation since other studies have suggested that such psychological abuse may be more upsetting than physical aggression (see Chaps. 4 and 5).

There may be some unintended effects of people's understanding that some forms of violence, such as aggression against one's partner, are not generally acceptable. Perhaps because of these widely held norms about physical violence being unacceptable within a couple, the partner herself [or himself] may downplay the violence or psychological aggression used against them, possibly as a way of preserving the relationship. Evidence of this was seen in a study of college students cited earlier (Arriaga & Capezza, 2011). Of course, this creates a barrier that may keep the victimized person from seeking help.

The following case illustrates a common pattern of gradual escalation of aggression and control common to abusive relationships (see Chap. 4). It also illustrates how the victim, Becky, downplays the psychological aggression from her boyfriend, Bobby, and distorts what is happening by perceiving his behavior as evidence of love, rebuffing her mother's concern for her wellbeing.

Case Example

Becky, 16 years old, has been dating Bobby, 18 years old, for 6 months. At first, Bobby was attentive and caring toward Becky but as time went on, he became possessive and jealous, insisting that Becky check in with him via telephone several times a day and demanded that she stop hanging out with her girlfriends "because they'll introduce you to other guys". If Becky wasn't home when Bobby called her, he would accuse her of cheating on him and would call her a whore and a slut. When Becky's mother began to see what was going on and confronted Becky, Becky denied there was a problem, arguing that Bobby does these things "because he loves me so much." (Newhill, 1995).

2.1.2 *Learning by Observing Others*

Although it is clear that direct reinforcement and indirect reinforcement expressed through social approval may encourage aggressive behavior or any other reinforced behavior, these mechanisms are not the only ways in which learning affects us. We also learn by observing the behaviors of other people as well as the results of these behaviors (Huesmann, 2018). This is labeled as *modeling* or *observational learning*.

Observational learning occurs in many different ways. Young children learn basic patterns of interaction with other people by observing their parents and siblings. As we grow older, we begin to observe many different types of models. We may model things our friends do. We also model other adults in our environment.

Although we may not be consciously aware of this happening, if we see someone else being rewarded for doing something, we are more likely to do this same thing ourselves (perhaps nonconsciously expecting that we, too, will be rewarded). This is known as *vicarious reinforcement*. If a son observes that his father gets what he wants from her after being physically abusive toward his mother, he may feel that this is a good way to get things from his wife when he marries many years later (see Chap. 6 for more discussion of this process). There is evidence that children of parents who reward *non*violence are less aggressive, while children who are spanked tend to be more aggressive (Ma, Grogan-Kaylor, & Lee, 2018). The act of spanking by the parent can serve as a model of violent behavior for the child who is spanked as well as for other children in the family who observe this behavior. There is also evidence that children who are physically abused by their parents may then model this behavior with their own children (Alink, Cyr, & Madigan, 2019; Chap. 6).

Children may not model each parent equally. Modeling of the father would be more expected in a son than a daughter since modeling is especially likely when we can personally identify with the person doing the actions being rewarded. A daughter might be more likely to model her mother's behavior for the same reason. Parents are only one of many models who influence us. We model what we observe in the media and in our peers as well as others in the world around us.

Modeling can lead us to learn to be violent but it might also teach us non-violent strategies to get what we want (Coyne, Padilla-Walker, Holmgren, Davis, & Collier, 2018). Parents who are aware of the importance of observational learning in their children can choose to model the types of behavior they want their children to do. For example, parents can provide nonaggressive models for their children to imitate rather than modeling aggressive or violent behavior. However, such modeling needs to be consistent, and consciously monitoring one's behavior in this way is likely to be difficult if it is not what the parent would normally do.

The following case vignette illustrates the role of culture in shaping expectations of gender roles and how a young boy's behavior reflects what he learns about appropriate male behavior from his parents, including the expression of aggression that generalizes from the dynamics of the home environment to how the boy behaves at school.

Case Example #3

The Rashid family migrated from Iran to U.S. for economic reasons shortly after Basim was born. Ali is an I.T. (Information Technology) specialist and felt that the U.S. would allow him greater opportunity to advance in his field. Nur left university to marry Ali and is a full-time stay at home mom. The family speak Persian at home, though the parents and Basim speak English well enough to understand professionals. Adila has some language delays. Basim's school called with concern that his behavior is increasingly violent, and seems to be particularly directed toward his mother. Most recently Basim had asked his mother to take him to McDonalds after school for dinner because he prefers American food and didn't want to eat his mom's more traditional cooking. When Nur refused, Basim began hitting and kicking her. The principal and guidance counselor both spoke with Nur and found that she has been experiencing this quite a lot, and is concerned that Basim is copying his father's behavior. Nur states that he often shoves and slaps her, though she has never been bruised by him. Basim has told female teachers and staff that he doesn't have to listen to them because he is going to be a man, and they are only women. Social services began an investigation into the family. Ali reluctantly agreed to leave the home and stay with friends. Nur and her children hold American citizenship, so the social worker assisted Nur in applying for benefits. Nur was concerned because, even if Ali maintains support for the family, and they are able to obtain benefits, their standard of living would drop. In particular, Nur was concerned that they would lose their apartment and that she and the children may have to stay in a shelter until they could obtain Section 8 housing benefit… When Basim was interviewed by the SW, he said his dad yells at his mom and tells her and everyone else what to do. When asked if anything else happens, Basim said his mom gets a smack, and mimicked a slapping motion. The family were found to be in need of services and transferred to long-term in-home services.

As is true of many of the generalizations about learning of aggression, the influence of models is not always direct. Although generally, we think of observational learning as leading to us displaying the behavior we see in others, it is also possible that we may actively resist acting in ways we observe in others if we do not personally accept this behavior. Positive role models are people who inspire us and make us want to be like them. But, a negative role model is someone we don't want to copy (Lockwood, Jordan, & Kunda, 2002). Such a person may represent something that we do not like and consciously choose not to copy. If we have a violent parent, we may not want to be like this person, and this parent will serve as one of these negative role models for us.

The following case example depicts a young boy with an abusive father who, after positive exposure to a non-violent male role model, explicitly decides for himself that he will not act like his father and, instead, copies the positive non-aggressive modeling of an admired teacher.

Case Example

As a young boy living in Italy, Antonio frequently witnessed his alcoholic father brutally beat his mother for often the most minor of infractions. He would beat her if his meal was cold, he would beat her if the cat got out of the house and, sometimes, he would beat her just because he came home in a bad mood. Antonio and his mother immigrated to the United States when Antonio was 16, leaving his father behind with the idea that once his mother found a good job, his father would sell their house in Italy and then join them. During his time as a student in a New York City high school, Antonio was "taken under the wing" of his kindly history teacher who had sympathy for the young man's struggle to adjust as a new immigrant, and provided him with social support, serving as a father figure to the young man. Antonio was amazed at how kind his teacher was and how he handled student classroom misbehavior in a firm but fair and non-violent way. At the end of his junior year, Antonio decided for himself that he would never behave like his father, and, instead, wanted to emulate his strong but kind teacher, with plans to go to college and eventually become a teacher himself (Newhill, 1995).

2.1.3 Learning About Violence From the Media

The media of all types can serve as a place where people observe violence (and non-violent or prosocial forms of interaction) and may model what they see or learn about. Media may be a source of observational learning about violence and aggression, as well as having many other indirect effects that might also lead to higher levels of aggression. Rideout, Foehr, and Roberts (2010) sampled a nationally representative sample of more than 2000 children in the U.S, aged from 8 to 18. They suggested that overall, U.S. children spend more time with media than any other activity, averaging 7.4 h a day of exposure, often to more than one type of media at once. Data collected in 2009 were compared to data from similar studies in 2004 and 1999. Overall, television occupied the most time at 3.5 h a day, but TV viewing did decrease over the years of their research. Next most common was listening to music or audio recordings. Other media were the computer, video games, print media and movies. Exposure to all these media sources increased since 1999 except for movies and print media. Media exposure was highest for 11–14 year olds and for Blacks and Hispanics in the Rideout et al. survey. Other research has suggested that exposure to internet games and other forms of media is also quite common for adults (Weinstein, Przybylski, & Murayama, 2017). As Anderson et al. (2018) have pointed out, violent images are quite common in the media.

Studies drawing on a wide variety of methodologies have indicated that those more exposed to violent media also show several correlated effects (Bender, Plante, & Gentile, 2018). These include having more aggressive thoughts, experiencing more aggressive emotions, viewing the world as a more hostile place, and acting in more aggressive ways. In another review of the literature, data has shown that those more exposed to media in their regular lives outside of the laboratory have higher levels of aggressive thoughts and feelings (Anderson, Bushman, Donnerstein, Hummer, & Warburton, 2015). As Bushman (2016) found in a review of 37 different research studies, those who have had more exposure to violent media of all types tend to believe that the world is a more hostile place than those with less of this type of media exposure. This type of world view is also associated with having a more hostile personality. As Bender et al. (2018) discussed, recent studies have begun to examine changes in the brain resulting from such exposure to try to better understand the mechanisms by which media have these effects.

The most obvious way in which viewing or interacting with media in other ways affects behavior is by providing models of behavior (Anderson et al., 2015). This may be especially important for children. Wiedeman, Dolle, Finney, and Coker (2015) note that children and adolescents use media to learn about how to act in different situations. Such learned scripts may teach them how to use weapons, or, more generally, how people might act in various situations. As discussed earlier, people of all ages tend to copy behavior they see others engaging in. This can relate directly to partner violence, in our experience. We have heard reports from our clients of situation in which an abusive husband enjoys watching violent pornography and then demanding he and his wife model the same violent behaviors themselves, even if the wife does not wish to participate.

It has been suggested in reviews of research studies that the effects of modeling aggression can be even stronger when we go beyond watching others, and actually engage in simulated or actual aggressive behavior ourselves. Children and adolescents who play violent video games show higher levels of aggression as well as being *less* likely to engage in helpful or friendly behavior towards others (Ferguson, 2013, 2015). Consistent with this generalization, investigations of cases of very violent behavior in young men, such as in the Columbine High School shootings, have found that the perpetrators enjoyed playing violent video games on their computers. There is also a reported association between more playing of violent video games and delinquency (Anderson & Dill, 2000).

The following case addresses the controversy surrounding one of the ultraviolent first-person shooter games, *Grand Theft Auto*, which has been examined as a possible factor in actual violent incidents committed by young men who played the game obsessively.

Case Example

Grand Theft Auto, a controversial first-shooter video game series introduced in 2001 was immediately condemned by several European countries due to its extreme violence and misogyny. As the game's successive versions were released, 3D graphics enabled the violence to become more realistic and more sexual content was included, e.g. players could pay for prostitutes and then kill them to get their money back. Furthermore, the so-called "heroes" in the game commit a variety of extremely antisocial acts (including killing police officers and military personnel) without remorse and without suffering significant consequences. Interactive sex scenes, dubbed "Hot Coffee", were also embedded in later versions of the game which enabled players to have virtual sex with their in-game girlfriends (Associated Press, 2005).

In February 2005, a lawsuit was filed against the game's makers and distributors which argued that 17-year-old Devin Moore shot and killed three police officers in Alabama because he was inspired by the games to commit the murders. In another lawsuit, the attorney for teenager Cody Posey argued that Posey played the game obsessively before murdering three family members in New Mexico. The lawsuit was eventually dismissed when it was revealed that other factors, such as child abuse and psychotropic medication use, may have played a role in the murders. (Associated Press, 2005; Bernstein, 2013; Chalk, 2008).

One of the reported effects of viewing violent images has been labeled as *habituation* or *desensitization* (Bender et al., 2018; Rankin et al., 2009). In general, when someone is repeatedly exposed to a certain type of situation either in the media or in daily life, there is evidence that they notice this situation less over time and see it as less extreme than they might have on initial exposure. The more exposure, the higher the level of habituation. Habituation effects are believed to generalize to other related stimuli as well (Rathus, 2005). An example of this can be seen when someone drives a very familiar route. Often, they fail to notice their surroundings as they travel along this often traveled route.

It is often assumed that desensitization can result from exposure to violent media or videogame images (e.g., Anderson & Bushman, 2018). Thus, if we have seen someone in a bar fight on television many times, we begin to think of this as a common event, and perhaps as one that is not so very violent. Habituation to the violent images might generalize so that other types of violence might also been seen as less serious or extreme. However, very few laboratory studies demonstrating this have been published. Some report none of the predicted physiological effects that would indicate desensitization as a result of playing a violent video game. Others have suggested that habituation effects may require repeated exposure since it may not be evident with only a brief exposure (e.g., Gramlich, 2016: Read, Ballard, Emery, & Bazzini, 2016). But, the lack of supporting research does raise questions about whether or how the general concept of habituation might apply to violence portrayed in the media.

Media portrayals of crimes, rather than leading to habituation, instead may *increase* fears of crimes among those exposed to these images of violent crimes or terrorist activity (Hollis, Downey, del Carmen, & Dobbs, 2017). Such programming occurs not only in movies or videos and television dramas, but also in the news programs. After seeing such images over and over again, people may become fearful about leaving their homes, and they may buy locks and other forms of protection against intruders as protection against what they perceive is a very hostile world. In is interesting to note that the effect of repeated exposure here is not to lower the emotional reaction, but to raise it because of the belief that one might be personally victimized by the (perceived) *common* violence in the world. Other research has also raised questions about when and how desensitization might occur when playing violent video games (Read et al., 2016).

In spite of the many effects found in laboratory studies of the effects of violent media, studies of the media's effects on increasing aggressiveness do have to be looked at cautiously. In a very detailed review of the literature on the effects of playing a violent video game, Ferguson (2013) noted that such game playing in the laboratory does consistently demonstrate effects such as more hostile moods after playing the game. However, as Ferguson discussed in some detail, there was little evidence that this type of laboratory exposure was associated with a greater likelihood of actually committing a violent crime. In a direct analysis of this often suggested effect, Markey, Markey, and French (2015) found no evidence that those with more violent media game exposure were also more likely to commit more crimes. Consistent with the idea that playing violent video games does not necessarily lead to greater aggressiveness, Kühn et al. (2018) asked a German sample of students and community members to play the violent game Grand Theft Auto-V or the nonviolent Sims-3 game. The researchers compared the aggressiveness levels of the exposed sample before playing the assigned game to the same behaviors and attitudes measured after 2 months of game playing. No differences between the groups or between pre- and post-measures were found. A similar failure to replicate the effects of violent video games causing increased aggressive behavior was reported by Hilgard, Engelhardt, Rouder, Segert, and Bartholow (2019) using a sample of U.S. male undergraduate students in a controlled exposure study.

Much of the recent research on media and aggression has focused on violent games on video or the internet. In a detailed analysis of those who play such games, Przybylski, Deci, Rigby, and Ryan (2014) tested the hypothesis that one of the major reasons that people may experience hostile or aggressive reactions to playing video games is that they are not skilled at the games and feel frustrated they can't get better scores. They suggested that in many of the laboratory studies, students are exposed to games they are not familiar with, and don't know how to play them well. When they varied game skill requirements, they found that more difficult games did produce more aggressive thoughts and aggressive behavior than games that were not as difficult. Other studies have indicated that exposure to games that involve cooperative behavior may increase prosocial behavior among those who play such games (Coyne et al., 2018). So, the effects of playing computer games are complex.

In the real world, it appears that *more violent individuals* are most likely to seek out aggressive television, video games, and other media (Ferguson, 2002; Wiedeman et al., 2015). Thus, it may not be that the media is causing violence, so much as enhancing violent tendencies that already exist in certain individuals, and providing models for them of how to engage in violent actions.

2.1.4 Gender Differences in Aggression and Socialization of Girls and Boys

One of the most consistently reported gender differences in personality reported in studies in the U.S. and in other countries is for aggression, with males of all ages showing higher levels of aggression than females on average, although the overall difference is not always large (Hyde, 2014). These differences have been attributed to differing patterns of socialization, as well as to biological differences. Here we focus on socialization and the effects of cultural beliefs and learning. Biological factors are discussed later in the chapter.

2.1.4.1 Beliefs About Gender and Aggression

Gender stereotypes include ideas about the traits or personality of women and men, as well as ideas about what types of roles are appropriate for each gender and what the physical characteristics are for women and men. One of the most common stereotypes relating to traits is that men are more aggressive (Bosson, Vandello, & Buckner, 2019). Such judgments can be seen when people are asked to rate the characteristics of the typical man or the typical woman. Once one considers different groups of men or of women, though, these views become more complex (see Box 2.1). There is a large body of research showing how these basic gender beliefs affect behavior, as discussed below.

Box 2.1: Intersectionality and Gender Beliefs

Although people are quite willing to identify the characteristics of the typical woman or the typical man, and there is high consensus about these judgments, when asked about specific types of men or women, these judgments change (Bosson et al., 2019). Thus, a male intellectual might be seen much differently than a male blue-collar worker. A female athlete would not be rated in the same way as a housewife. African American women are viewed differently than Asian American women. Stereotypes for such intersectional identities tend to differ than the stereotypes associated with any of the individual demographic variables such as gender, occupation or race. When even more complex intersectionalities (such as middle-aged married female professors or elderly retired male locksmiths) are considered, stereotypes become even more complex and unique to that particular group.

There is evidence that although gender stereotypes are changing in some ways in the U.S., these changes are not large. In a study comparing ratings of U.S. college students in 1983 to those in 2014, Haines, Deaux, and Lofaro (2016) found very similar ratings for what those in their student sample believed were the typical characteristics of men as compared to women over this more than 30-year period. (There was a small, but statistically significant change overall in judgments of female role behavior, such that these were somewhat less stereotypical in 2014 than in 1983, but there was strong overall evidence for the persistence of gender stereotypes).

Gender rules relate to many different behaviors, including ideas about the expressions of aggression. In the United States, as in many other countries, there is not only an expectation that boys will be more aggressive than girls, but we also tend to approve of boys being more aggressive and may encourage them to fight back if provoked more than we would encourage this behavior in girls (Brannon, 2017). In an indirect demonstration of the power of these gender-related behavioral guidelines, Yang, Huesmann, and Bushman (2014) found that students asked to assume the role of a male avatar in a violent video game were more violent after the game than those asked to assume the role of a female avatar. Gender-role expectations can also be seen in evidence from a German study indicating that both women and men who engaged in more aggressive driving rated themselves as higher in masculinity than less aggressive drivers (Krahé, 2018).

2.1.4.2 Socialization of Aggression in Girls and Boys

Gender socialization begins very early in the life of the child and continues through childhood and into adulthood (Bosson et al., 2019). For very young children, parents are especially important models for how males and how females behave. Later, other models are often found by the child in the media and in observations of people in the life of the child. Thus, parents are not only models, but they serve an important role in reinforcing or rewarding behavior associated with gender role-expectations. Knowing the sex of their unborn child, parents may already begin to plan in various ways to welcome their new girl or their new boy and to envision how they will interact with the new child.

Gender expectations for very young children show up in other ways, as well. Studies done with infants dressed like girls have found that adults treat them differently than the same infants dressed as boys are treated. (It is quite difficult to identify whether a very young child is a boy or girl, so we tend to make this judgment by looking at what the child is wearing. This allows us to study reactions to the same child dressed as a girl as compared to being dressed as a boy). People tend to be more active with boys and use rougher play with them than they do with girls. Such behavior is probably based on stereotypes or beliefs that boys are more aggressive than girls, but by engaging in such behavior, people are also reinforcing the use of aggression in boys more than in girls. People also make other assumptions about girls and boys. Boys are seen as more athletic, while girls are seen as more nurturing.

Boys are believed to be less emotional than girls. All of these stereotypes affect the ways in which girls and boys are treated by other adults as well as by other children (Bosson et al., 2019).

In our interactions with children, we not only reward them for acting in ways we feel are appropriate for their gender, but we may also discourage them from doing things that are associated with the other gender. This applies to aggressiveness as well as to many other forms of behavior. Based on their experiences with adults or older children, children begin to learn at a young age about what types of things boys are expected to do and what girls are expected to do (Zosuls, Ruble, & Tamis-LeMonda, 2014). Once children learn about these expectations, they look for other ways in which they can demonstrate their *girlness* or *boyness*, generalizing the gender rules they have learned beyond the specific behaviors they have been rewarded or punished for doing. Children apply these gender expectations to their own behaviors as well as using them in evaluating other children. They may become upset with a child that is not *acting appropriately*, based on their gender expectations.

Looking in more detail at the process of gender socialization, there is evidence that the reinforcements provided by fathers to their children may be more important than those of mothers in terms of helping them learn about gender (Brannon, 2017). This is seen in U.S. studies, as well as in at least some other countries. In a study of 2-parent families with 3-year-old children in the Netherlands, Endendijk et al. (2017) examined the specific effects of fathers and mothers on aggressive behavior in their children. Overall, boys were found to be more aggressive than girls. They also reported that fathers who used physical control methods of discipline rather that verbal control had children who were more aggressive at a later time, based on reports of the parents. Mothers' form of discipline was not significantly related to later child aggressiveness. These data are consistent with U.S. studies also reporting that fathers are more important in terms of socializing aggression than mothers (Chaplin, Cole, & Zahn-Waxler, 2005).

This analysis of gender socialization encouraging aggressiveness in boys more than girls leads to the conclusion that men are likely to be more aggressive than women, and that boys are more aggressive than girls. Much data supports this conclusion. For example, one of the classic studies documenting these effects was a longitudinal study of 1000 boys and girls in New Zealand who were observed beginning in early childhood and continuing into their early adult years (Moffitt, Caspi, Rutter, & Silva, 2001). Boys and men were found to have higher rates of fighting, delinquent offending, problems controlling anger, and being arrested for violent crimes as compared to girls and women. This gender difference appears in quite young children. Much other data can be cited demonstrating this overall gender difference in the U.S. As discussed in Chap. 1, U.S. data shows a similar pattern of much higher rates of reports of men committing violent crimes than women.

There is also evidence that girls may express their aggressive feelings in very different ways than boys do (Bjorkqvist, 2018). Analyzing data from many countries, Bjorkqvist concluded that although boys and men are more likely than girls and women to use physical aggression or overt violence, there was no difference by gender in the use of verbal aggression or what she referred to as "indirect" aggression (p. 39). Females used more indirect aggression than physical aggression, while the reverse was true for males. Although the causal factors underlying this gender difference are not definitively known, it is generally assumed that girls and women use more verbal or indirect aggression because of prior experiences relating to gender socialization.

2.1.4.3 Reactions to Aggressive Behavior

Aggressiveness is one of the stereotypes associated with male roles, so it is not surprising that people evaluate such behavior in boys and men differently than they do the same behaviors in girls and women. Across societies and across different social groups within the same society, the rewards provided for aggression, or the punishments given for what people consider to be *inappropriate* aggression are not the same for everyone. These social expectations depend on gender. (They also differ across ethnic or SES groups or other social groups.) Girls are not expected to behave in the same way that boys do, especially in terms of expressing anger and aggression (Brannon, 2017; Ruble, Martin, & Berenbaum, 2006). When gender expectations are violated, others may express strong disapproval and may dislike the violator (Bosson et al., 2019).

Such patterns are especially evident in terms of aggression-related behavior. Traditionally, boys were observed to be concerned about appearing *weak*, since this is associated with *being a girl* (see Box 2.2). Boys were sometimes criticized for *not* fighting back if attacked by another boy (Maccoby, 1998). Children were also found to differentially reward boys and girls for fighting other children (Huesmann & Guerra, 1997). In more recent studies, there is less overt reward for boys than for girls for being physically aggressive, although there continues to be more acceptance of boys' violence with other children (Brannon, 2017). As children learn these rules, they not only apply them in viewing their own behavior as well as evaluating what other children are doing.

Box 2.2: IPV and Masculine Gender Role Stress

Aggression in boys and men may relate to their wanting to appear more *masculine*. Baugher and Gazmararian (2015) defined the concept of MGRS (masculine gender role stress) as the "experience of distress in the context of situations that an individual appraises as a threat to his masculine identity" (p. 108) and reviewed 20 research papers using this concept. In explaining how MGRS functioned, they pointed to gender expectations held by some men that they be dominant and not appear weak, since submissiveness and powerlessness were associated with women. According to these those experiencing MGRS, it is important that others respect them and they are seen as tough. If they feel that they are not meeting these expectations, they experience stress and react to this role-related stress by engaging in violence. They identify studies supporting this view and indicating that men high in MGRS have been found to demonstrate more anger and aggressive behavior toward others.

A scale developed by Eisler and Skidmore (1987) was used to measure MGRS. Men were asked to assess the degree to which a number of situations were stressful. Sample items included "comforting a male friend who is upset," "admitting to friends that you do housework," and "with a women who is more successful than you." Other items referred to being skilled sexually and being physically fit.

A consistent finding across studies was that higher scores of MGRS were associated with more acceptance of male IPV against women in hypothetical scenarios as well as higher sell-reported IPV in some studies. Although Baugher and Gazmararian had hypothesized that MGRS would also be associated with higher levels of violence directed toward gay men, the data were not strongly supportive of this prediction.

Of course, some people are more generally supportive of aggressiveness than others. As illustrated in Case #3 described earlier, some cultures teach boys that they are superior to girls and to adult women. In these cultures, boys and men may believe that what girls and women have to say can be ignored and that aggression is acceptable toward them.

Another domain in which aggressiveness is viewed positively (especially for adolescent boys and men) can be seen in reactions to athletes. For example, a older study looking at teenage boys participating on hockey teams indicated that members of the team who endorsed the idea that men should be admired and respected by others and saw masculinity as being demonstrated by toughness were more likely to get into fistfights while playing hockey with their teams. This study further reported that the more violent boys were rated as more competent by their coaches as well as by other members of the hockey teams (Weinstein, Smith, & Wiesenthal, 1995). Thus, those who were more aggressive were receiving reinforcement for this behavior from peers as well as adults.

This association of sports with violence in boys and young men may be becoming more complex. Based on national data collected in 2000 and 2001, Finkelday (2018) found that the association of violent behavior as young adults was associated with playing football, but not with other sports. In this study, violence was defined as participation in physical fights leading to injuries or threats or actual use of a weapon against someone else. Further analysis suggested that this association was strongest for men who may have compensated for their non-masculine behavior in other contexts. In a review of broad range of literature published on sports participation and aggression, Kimble, Russo, Bergman, and Galindo (2010) concluded that there was evidence of an association of aggressiveness and sports' participation, but the relationships were dependent upon the particular sport, and that the causal direction for sports and aggressiveness was not clear. Some studies suggested that general aggression might be lessened through playing sports. It was noted that some sports tended to be associated with higher levels of verbal aggression, while others were more associated with physical aggression.

2.1.4.4 Exceptions to Traditional Gender-Rules

As discussed, there is strong evidence that, on average, males of all ages are more aggressive than females. But, it is not the case that women and girls are never aggressive and don't use violence. Although these gender expectations are strong in children, they may be more evident in young children than in adults (Zosuls et al., 2014). As adults, both women and men associate some behaviors more with men and other behaviors more with women, but they also see themselves as acting in ways they associate with the other gender. An example of this is seen in an early study by Signorella and Frieze (1989). When college students were asked to describe a time they acted in a feminine manner, as well as a time when they acted in a masculine manner, nearly everyone was able to provide an example of doing this. The most common type of behavior associated with being masculine for both women and men was acting aggressively. Examples of feminine behavior were more varied. For the men, when acting in a way they defined as feminine, the most frequent answers related to being interpersonally warm or being fearful (Signorella & Frieze, 1989). Thus, although people learn the gender-based rules of behavior, they do not always follow these rules, especially in adulthood. Extending this idea that both men and women act in ways that are feminine in some situations and that are masculine in other situations, Mehta and Dementieva (2017) asked a sample of college students to record their behavior at the time they were prompted on their phones over a 2 week period. Prods were given by the researchers at different times of day, up to 5 times a day. When reporting on their own masculinity or femininity at the time, it was noted that men were more likely to rate themselves as acting in a feminine way when with women than when with other men. Both men and women reported acting in a more masculine way when with men than with women.

There is a growing literature now of aggression in girls, often focusing on negative effects of female aggression and how it can be lessened (e.g., Pepler, Madsen, Webster, & Levine, 2014). As with any type of human behavior, the gender differences reported are averages, with wide variations in the behavior across both women and men. Some women and girls are quite aggressive or even habitually violent, while some men and boys are not at all violent or aggressive.

Moffitt and her colleagues devote an entire chapter of their book to the one situation where this gender difference is reversed. In their study, women reported higher levels than men of engaging in physical aggression against an intimate partner. To test to see if this result relating to IPV was a self-report bias, they also asked about violence received from an intimate partner. Again, males reported higher rates of victimization than females. This issue is discussed in more detail in Chap. 5. It has been a topic of much discussion in the literature. The finding of which gender is more likely to engage in IPV is related to how this is measured, with recent studies focusing on acts of serious aggression showing men doing this more than women.

2.1.4.5 Directing Aggression Toward Males and Females

Another aspect of gender socialization is learning what types of people are labeled as being appropriate targets for aggression or violence from others. Probably few people would feel it would be appropriate to be violent to a frail older man, and there is little societal support in the U.S. today for adults being violent to children (see Chap. 6). Societal attitudes about violence toward other groups have also shown evidence of change, with some violence appearing to decrease, but other forms increasing. One example of this can be seen in data from the National Crime Victimization Survey conducted by the U.S. Department of Justice (Wilson, 2014). These data indicate that since the study began in 2004, until the most recent data from 2012, the number of all types of hate crimes has risen, and they are a larger percentage of all crimes. The percentage of *violent* hate crimes has also risen. Fewer than half of these crimes were reported to the police by the victims. Men are more likely to be victimized by these crimes, although the ratio of men to women was smaller over the time period of the study. Over 60% of these crimes were committed by men.

People do have gender-related social expectations about who are the reasonable targets of our aggression. Well-known criminologist, Felson (2014), pointing to the commonly taught idea that boys should not hit girls, as well as to research on criminal violence, argued that "Violence against women is different in some ways from violence against men. For example, it is more likely to involve sexual assault and less likely to involve strangers…" (Felson, 2014, p. 77). He went on to state that "Society treats offenders who commit violence against women much more harshly than offenders who target men." (p. 83), noting that when men do assault women, they tend to do it privately when others can't observe this. National data was cited indicating that victims and bystanders are more likely to report crimes to the police if a woman is the victim than if a man is victimized, and that when women are violent, their aggression is treated more leniently than similar aggression by a man (Felson, 2014). This prohibition against violence toward women is labeled as *chivalry* and is part of a larger belief that women and children should be protected, especially by men (Felson, 2002). There is clearly some evidence to support these claims, as discussed in Chaps. 5 and 9.

Although some might argue that beliefs about chivalry are not common in modern U.S. society, there is recent evidence supporting the continuing existence of these beliefs. Specific ideas associated with the idea of chivalry include the idea that women need to be protected by men, that in a disaster, women need to be rescued first, and that men should hold doors open for women (Farkas & Leaper, 2016). Farkas and Leaper created a scale with these and other items and administered it to teenagers in two public high schools in California. Although the boys and girls varied in how strongly they held these beliefs, the beliefs were not uncommon, and they were held more strongly by boys than girls. There were no differences across the sample in holding these beliefs among the White/European Americans, Asian Americans, and Latinas within the sample. Farkas and Leaper argued that these beliefs were related to a type of sexism called benevolent sexism (Glick & Fiske, 2001) that includes the idea that women need protection and that such protection should be provided by men.

Discussion of chivalry and the idea that women should not be targets of violence, especially from men, raises questions about battered women who are targets of high levels of violence from their partners. In attempting to understand this inconsistency, Mikulincer and Shaver (2011) suggest that men who batter wives or romantic partners may have insecure attachment to their partners and suggest that "domestic violence is an exaggerated form of protesting a partner's hurtful behavior…to discourage or prevent a partner from violating or breaking off the relationship…" (p. 247). They cite a number of studies supporting this idea in their review chapter. Building on these arguments, Dutton (2011) suggests that the same types of anxieties may help explain why some women are violent toward their romantic partners. This type of analysis implies that those who violate chivalry norms against violence may do so because of mental health problems.

Other data might support other conclusions, especially in regards to nonviolent aggression. For example, national data on adolescents collected by the CDC (Kahn, Kinchen, Shanklin, et al., 2014) indicated that in 2013, the median percentage of girls who were in a physical fight was 16.3%, while the comparable percentage for boys was 29.2%. However, girls were more likely than boys to be the targets of nonviolent bullying on school property and more often experienced cyberbullying. Comparable percentages were 24% for girls and 16% for boys for being bullied at school and for cyberbullying were 21% and 9%. This same survey further reported that 13% of these high school girls experienced dating violence, as did 7% of boys. Other recent studies have also indicated that girls are more often targets of cyberbullying than boys (Peterson & Densley, 2017).

2.2 The Role of Environmental Factors in Aggression

Along with learning to be aggressive, aggressive or violent behavior can also occur when people are frustrated. Such frustration can arise from many types of events in the environment. It can be caused by someone refusing to do something that one wants or trying to take something away, as mentioned earlier in the example of children taking toys from one another. Frustration can also relate to various types of unpleasant physical environments, as discussed below. Another type of environmental predictor of aggression relates to having cues or reminders of aggression. Box 2.3 describes how this can occur when there are visible guns.

Box 2.3: Guns as Cues for Violence
A number of studies have reported that the presence of visible weapons in a variety of settings can increase aggressive behavior. Benjamin Jr. and Bushman (2018) review this literature, and provide theory about how this occurs. The classic study showing this effect was published in 1967 (Berkowitz & LePage, 1967). In this laboratory study, male college students were asked to evaluate another student's performance on a task by administering one or more electrical shocks. In some conditions, they sat at a table with a rifle and a handgun, while in other conditions, there was a badminton racquet on the table, or nothing on the table. Study participants in the provocation condition were given several shocks by the other student (actually a confederate). When there was a weapon present, the study participants gave more shocks to the confederate than when the badminton racquet was present, or nothing was present. Other studies have demonstrated a similar *weapons effect.* As Benjamin Jr. and Bushman (2018) argued, the presence of a weapon arouses aggressive thoughts. These thoughts can lead to aggressive behavior, when something in the environment provokes angry feelings.

2.2.1 Frustration in the Environment

Some of the very early studies in psychology demonstrated that frustration was an important predictor of aggression (Dollard, Doob, Miller, Mowrer, & Sears, 1939). Such frustration often comes from some type of difficultly in the environment. Laboratory studies have demonstrated environmental frustrations such as pain (Berkowitz, 1993), being uncomfortably warm (Anderson, 1989), loud noises (Geen & O'Neal, 1969) or overcrowding (Renfrew, 1997) that are associated with higher rates of aggression. Often this type of aversive environment leads to attacks on the source of the negative stimulus, but it can also result in displaced violence or other lashing out toward people not directly involved in creating the frustration.

Laboratory or controlled studies of environmental frustrations on aggression continue to be published. One recent example indicated that people in what the researchers (Ng & Chow, 2016) defined as *secure* conditions tended to be less hostile toward undefined others than those in *insecure* conditions. In this series of three studies, Ng and Chow first exposed college students from Hong Kong to pictures involving either indoor [secure] or outdoor [insecure] scenes, then asked them to play a computer game. If they lost, they were given the opportunity to expose their opponent to loud noise [defined as aggressive behavior]. In the second study, using an MTurk sample from the United States, the *aggressive* behavior was choosing to expose people in a later study to unpleasant pictures as compared to pleasant pictures. Again, exposure to secure indoor pictures was associated with choosing to expose the later study participants to fewer negative pictures. Finally, in the third study, Hong Kong students were asked to play the game Minecraft in an indoor or an outdoor setting.

Afterwards they were again asked whether they would choose to expose future study participants to pleasant or unpleasant pictures. Earlier results were replicated. Such laboratory studies allow the researcher a high degree of control, but such studies may lack *external validity*. Thus, defining the indoor pictures as making people feel more secure was assumed by the researchers, but not directly tested. One might also question whether the *aggressive* behaviors in these studies were similar to engaging in actual violence.

Because of these possible validity concerns, much of the research on violence outside the laboratory as a result of environmental frustrations is now being done by analyzing actual behavior of people in their daily lives. For example, studies examining the role of temperature can take advantage of outside temperatures to see how they affect behavior. Krenzer and Splan (2017) looked at data on Major League Baseball to see how often batters were hit by a ball aimed at them by the pitcher during the season. A very small, but statistically significant, correlation of 0.022 was found, technically supporting the heat and aggression association. However, as the authors noted, this indicated a very small effect in practical terms. Other analyses indicated that a variety of other variables, such as the number of wild pitches, were better predictors of the batter being hit. In a review of the research on the effects of actual temperature on aggressive behavior outside the laboratory, Rinderu, Bushman, and Van Lange (2018) argued that general levels of heat or cold in an environment were not as important in predicting violence as other factors. Levels of poverty and degree of income inequality within the region were more strongly correlated with violence levels than temperature. Thus, the relationship between temperature and aggression appears to be much more complicated than initially believed.

Other studies have investigated the effects of environmental frustration on violence within partnerships and within the family. Schneider, Harknett, and McLanahan (2016) analyzed longitudinal data from mothers in 20 U.S. cities to see how IPV was related to economic conditions. Data came from the national Fragile Families and Child Wellbeing study, using data from the period from 2001 to 2010. Control variables for the analysis included the education level, race/ethnicity of the mother and number of small children in the home. Results indicated that consistent with the many laboratory studies documenting the association between frustration and aggression, economic hardship did predict these mothers experiencing more violent behavior as well as more controlling behavior (forms of IPV) from their partners As discussed in Chap. 4, attempts to exert psychological control over one's partner are often associated with partner battering. Overall, 15% of the mothers experiencing economic hardship in this study were in a violent relationship as compared to only 7% of the mothers not experiencing such hardship. Data for unemployment showed similar patterns. This was especially seen when the male partner was unemployed, although there was some effect for the mother's unemployment as well. The authors noted that their data suggested that anxiety associated with economic downturns appeared to be predictive of partner violence beyond the effects of possible financial problems in the relationship and the frustrations these might generate.

The possible effects of stress or frustration on aggressive behavior in the natural environment can also be seen in a study by Holmes, Yoon, and Berg (2017). Again using a large national U. S. sample from the National Survey of Child and Adolescent Well-Being, these researchers looked at the effects of maternal depression on young children. Having a depressed mother was predictive of higher levels of violent behavior in toddlers (aged 2–3 years). These findings could be related to modeling of partner violence in their parents, it may also relate to these young children experiencing more difficult homes generally with a less attentive mother who is depressed.

In yet another example, Card and Dahl (2011) analyzed national data on police calls for partner violence and compared this to game wins and losses for 17 Sunday NFL games. They suggested that frustration would be greatest in situations in which the home team unexpectedly lost, when the predictions had been for a win of 4 points or more. As predicted, in these situations, there was a greater level of police calls for partner violence. The unexpected loss was much more predictive of IPV than expected losses or losses when the outcome was unpredictable.

Other environmental frustrations can relate to problematic social relationships. In a study of 4000 adolescents from low income rural areas in North Carolina, Smokowski, Goo, Cotter, Evans, and Rose (2016) found that some of the most powerful predictors of aggression in their sample were parent-adolescent conflict, rejection by friends, and bullying at school. The specific neighborhoods the adolescents lived in and the type of school were much less significant in predicting levels of aggressiveness. Both boys and girls were found to be aggressive in this study. Aggressiveness was measured with items such as getting into fights and breaking rules.

2.2.2 *Environmental Influences that Lower Aggression*

Another consideration in analyzing the effects of the environment on aggressive behavior is that some factors may inhibit aggression. As discussed earlier, reinforcement or encouraging aggression by others generates more aggression. At the same time, expectations of disapproval or retaliation may keep people from being verbally or physically aggressive. Slotter and Finkel (2011) describe a long list of other inhibiting factors including self-control, empathy for others, and feelings about the potential target of the aggression. Other people do respond to the aggressiveness they witness and may act to physically restrain someone who is beginning to display violence. This type of bystander intervention is the focus of much research. Before people respond as observers to bullying, for example, they need to identify that this bullying is occurring and believe they have the ability to intervene (Jenkins & Nickerson, 2016).

The following case example illustrates the important role of bystanders, in this case neighbors, in mobilizing a critical intervention and how multiple systems of care can become involved with a family in which there is intimate partner violence. It also demonstrates the possible effects of economic frustration on partner violence.

Case Example #6

John is a 36 year-old married white male with five children who was brought to the crisis clinic for evaluation by Sheriff's deputies and a Department of Public Assistance (DPA) worker. ..John has abused Karen off and on throughout the 8 years of their marriage, but last Saturday he almost killed her…John reports that he injured his back in an auto accident 4 years ago and, because his back is still bad, John says nobody will hire him so he must work privately in a body shop he constructed in his garage. The shop, however, has been losing business and the family's finances are in a squeeze. This past Saturday, John and Karen were having a yard sale. John was working in his body shop and told Karen to keep the people at the yard sale out of his way; she started to argue with him so he attacked and beat her; he broke a broom over her head and was about to ram the broken end through her but stopped in time. Karen immediately left, went to the hospital for treatment of her injuries, and then went to the local battered women's shelter. …According to the neighbors, they called the sheriff after they observed the abuse going on in the yard, and when John admitted to the deputies that he had beaten his wife, they threw him in the squad car and brought him to the crisis clinic. The DPA worker then met them there. Upon evaluation, John initially threatened suicide (said he wanted to blow his brains out), but as the interview progressed, he said that if he could get some help, he would promise to get rid of his gun at home and could postpone any harm to himself.

2.3 Factors in the Person: Some People are More Aggressive than Others

As one considers the variables described here that are associated with higher and lower levels of violence or aggression, it is important to keep in mind that these variables are only one of many predictors of how aggressive an individual is likely to be. Some people appear to be more likely to respond aggressively than others no matter what the situation or how much they are provoked. Other people only rarely show any form of aggressiveness. General aggressiveness has often been considered as a basic personality characteristic (Berkowitz, 1989). More recently, researchers have been arguing that there are several underlying personality factors which may all contribute to aggressive behavior. For example, Paulhus et al. (2018) argued that aggression was a result of narcissism, Machiavelianism, psychopathology, and/or sadism.

Like other personality characteristics, the tendency to behave in an aggressive manner does appear to be relatively stable throughout life (Lansford, 2018). In a review of the literature, Lansford noted that aggressiveness can appear in children as young as 6 months of age. One of the studies examining how aggressive childhood behavior develops over time was done in the UK. Farrington (2019) provides an update of a longitudinal study following a sample of 411 delinquent boys in

London, beginning at age 10 and now aged 61. Interviews and studies of criminal records were used as data. These initially aggressive boys became aggressive men, often having criminal records. Their aggressiveness continued into middle age and older. A common pattern for all of them was having low verbal IQ, experiencing harsh parental discipline, and being high risk takers as children.

There is evidence that those who tend to be the most violent in interactions with an intimate partner have certain personality characteristics. In a meta-analysis of 61studies of intimate partner violence using North American samples, examining anger, hostility or other negative emotions, Birkley and Eckhardt (2015) found that, as expected, these negative emotions were higher for those engaging in IPV. This was true for both male and female perpetrators. Although these data suggest the presence of an aggressive personality, the authors did point out that the IPV perpetrators were not necessarily violent with other people in addition to their spouse or dating partner. Birkley and Eckhardt further stressed that the association they found was only a moderate one and that it was clear that IPV is not solely a function of the personality traits they examined.

Having an aggressive personality may be related to some of the biological factors discussed below. Other personality variables have also been associated with a generalized tendency to act in an aggressive or in a non-aggressive way. In a large longitudinal study of young adolescents in Australia, Zimmer-Gembeck, Nesdale, Webb, Khatibi, and Downey (2016) identified rejection sensitivity as an important predictor that interacted with attributions made about other children. Both boys and girls who were highly sensitive to social rejection and blamed their peers for this rejection were more likely to report being aggressive toward them. Other children who blamed themselves for being rejected rather than blaming their peers were more likely to socially withdraw than react with aggression.

2.3.1 Genetic Influences on Aggressiveness

As has been discussed, there are many learning and environmental factors that have been associated with higher levels of aggression. Studies using a variety of methodologies have indicated that general levels of aggressiveness also have some genetic basis (DiLalla & Gottesman, 1991; Gorelik, Shackelford, & Weeks-Shackelford, 2012). For example, observations of dominance in chimpanzees in zoo settings and analysis of genetic records showed evidence of inheritance of these traits (Weiss, King, & Enns, 2002). Those who breed animals have noted this effect of a genetic basis of aggressiveness over many centuries and are able to breed a variety of different animals to be more or less aggressive over successive generations (De Boer, 2018).

Studies of humans using similar types of analyses over more than one generation support the idea that there is some genetic basis of aggressiveness (Huesmann, Dubow, & Boxer, 2011). Early evidence of this was a study of those with criminal records or a pattern of delinquency who were found to be more likely to come from families where others show similar patterns of behavior (Miles & Carey, 1997).

More recently, Huesmann et al. (2011) reported on a study following families over 3 generations. Levels of aggressiveness in adults were predicted by the level of aggressiveness in their parents, suggesting some genetic basis. (Both males and females were included in this study, but gender differences were not examined.) However, closer examination of these data did suggest that the effects were not simply genetic transmission. Learning may have also explained much of the data, since parental aggression to the children as they were growing up was the most important predictor of adult aggression. Both learning and genetic predictors contribute to aggressiveness in this study and others. The following case example explicitly demonstrates these dynamics:

Case Example

John, 26 years old, came to the local walk-in crisis clinic asking for counseling to help him control his fantasies of hurting and humiliating women. John is a registered mentally disordered sex offender on parole and has a long history of sadistic assaultive behavior toward women. He is now married and, in spite of his prior behavior, says he loves his wife and is afraid he will seriously harm her and does not want that to happen. He tells the crisis worker that the previous night he tied up his wife and smothered her, almost killing her. John admits to having suffered severe physical abuse as a child at the hands of his father, and his father is currently serving a life sentence in prison for murdering a prostitute (Newhill, 1995).

Wertz et al. (2018) report on a study of possible genetic influences on antisocial and criminal behavior. Using longitudinal data, they were able to examine changes over up to 38 years of life for two large samples from New Zealand and from England and Wales. Criminal offending data were available from police records. Analyses of these data indicated some genetic influence on criminal offending as well as on lower educational achievement for both boys and girls. (An association of low educational attainment and criminal offending was also found, which replicates the data reported by Farrington, 2019, who noted the low verbal IQ was associated with aggressiveness). The genetic effects were seen by Wertz et al. even when family factors were controlled. However, the authors explicitly noted that the majority of their sample, including those with these genetic indicators, did not have a record of criminal offending, suggesting that environmental factors may override any genetic predispositions, at least in terms of criminal behaivor.

2.3.2 *Using Twin Studies to Understand Possible Genetic Influences*

Another methodology for finding evidence of biological factors is to compare the behavior of identical and fraternal twins. Such studies were a major method used by researchers to look for genetic influences on behavior before they were able to directly measure genes. Since identical twins share the same genes, one would expect them to be more similar than fraternal twins if genetics are a predictive factor in the behavior. Analyses of twins as a way of finding genetic influences has shown that antisocial behavior, including aggression, is more associated with identical than with fraternal twins (Rhee & Waldman, 2002). This comparison controls for environment, since either identical or fraternal twins are growing up in the same household, but the identical twins have a closer genetic similarity. Since twin studies control for family influences, they allow more confidence in a conclusion of a genetic basis of aggression than simply showing continuing patterns of behavior within generations of one family (Rhee & Waldman, 2011). In their 2011 meta-analysis of twin studies of aggression, they found clear evidence over the 14 studies they analyzed that there was a genetic as well as a learning component related to level of aggressiveness. These studies look at both boys and girls. As they noted, though, more research is needed to examine different types of aggression since some types may have a stronger genetic component than other types.

The research on inheritance of aggressiveness has generally not differentiated genetic effects in females as compared to males, although more such work is now being done. Several different issues are being examined. First, there may be a general association of genes predicting aggressiveness being more likely to occur in males than females. The commonly reported gender difference of girls and women being lower in aggression than boys and men is believed to have a genetic basis, although, as discussed earlier, we also tend to socialize boys differently than girls in regards to acceptability of aggressive behavior. Building on this body of work, Martel (2013) outlines arguments about how these sex differences might also relate to differing patterns of psychopathology in women and men, focusing on the greater externalizing (aggression-related) disorders found in males and the internalizing patterns in females.

Other arguments are more complex and suggest that genes may interact with environment factors, even before birth, in differing ways for females and males. There is evidence that basic sex differences in development prenatally may relate to the greater aggressiveness in males of all ages. Evidence of this can be seen in observations of very young children. Starting in early infancy, boys have been found to have higher levels of active, aggressive behavior than girls (Hudziak et al., 2003). However, based on their analysis of twin data, it appeared that the level that genetic factors appeared to predict aggressiveness was stronger for girls than boys. Perhaps the early environmental influences are more important for boys than girls?

Other genetic factors than those directly associated with aggressiveness may act indirectly to raise (or lower) levels of aggressiveness. These include the tendency to externalize blame (seeing others as responsible to one's misfortunes), difficulty in controlling one's impulses, and lack of empathy (Tackett & Krueger, 2011). Each of these variables has itself been linked to genetic factors. For example, empathy has been found to have a genetic component (Malik, Zai, Abu, Nowrouzi, & Beitchman, 2012), but, like aggressiveness, it can also be affected by how one is raised. A number of studies have reported that empathy or concern for and understanding of the suffering of others tends to make people less aggressive. If one is more aware of and affected by the suffering of others, it would be expected that he or she would be more reluctant to cause such suffering. But, empathy is not always linked to lower levels of aggression. In a major meta-analysis of the relationship between these two variables as reported in 86 different studies, Vachon, Lynam, and Johnson (2014) found the expected negative relationship, but it was quite small. They were surprised by this outcome and outlined a number of methodological issues that might contribute to this small relationship. They did note that empathy was most associated with verbal aggression and less with physical and sexual aggression. Other studies have suggested that the general relationship may be a complex one that depends on the situation and how it is interpreted by those acting in that setting. For example, one study indicated that those with higher empathy might act *more* aggressively to protect someone else who they care about. Thus, the effects of empathy levels are not always to lower aggressiveness (Buffone & Poulin, 2014) and may depend on the situation.

To summarize the conclusions of the research on the genetic basis of aggression, there is strong consensus that there is a genetic component to aggressiveness. However, this effect is generally small. This is consistent with other research attempting to link personality with genetic factors. It is estimated that the degree of heritability of any aspect of personality is less than 40% and may be much lower, although some dimensions may have a greater genetic component than others (Plomin, DeFries, Knopik, & Neiderhiser, 2016). A good deal of research activity now is attempting to find specific genes that relate to aggression and to other psychological characteristics, but the answers are not yet available. It is likely that future research will identify many genes that contribute in different ways. Plomin and his colleagues note that separating the effects of the environmental from genetic contributions to personality is complicated by the fact that parents and children share some genetic traits that may lead to complex interactions relating to parenting behavior and its effects on children. Turkheimer (2016), a behavior geneticist who has worked on identifying the relationships between genes and behavior for many years, takes these arguments even further in suggesting that we will probably never find clear and direct associations between specific genes and complex patterns of behavior, independent of the environment.

2.3.3 Brain Anatomy and Aggression

One way in which genes are believed to operate is in guiding the formation of the brain. An ever-increasing body of work has found that certain structures in the brain are associated with higher levels of aggressiveness (Bartholow, 2018; Yang, Joshi, Jahanshad, Thompson, & Baker, 2016). For example, higher levels of amygdala activation in the brain are associated with stronger reactions to threat or frustration in the environment, which in turn appear to be a predictor of reactive aggressiveness and other forms of antisocial personality (Baskin-Sommers, 2016). However, as this study noted, those who initiate aggression more and tend to be less empathetic have *lower* levels of amygdala activation, suggesting that different types of aggression may have different underlying biological causes or correlates. As Denson (2011) notes in his review of the neurological data, there appears to be a network of regions in the brain that underlie anger, aggression and angry thoughts. There is also evidence that high levels of exposure to violent media may affect the functioning of this neural network. Much research is being done in this area, so any conclusions now are very preliminary. One topic of study is whether these brain structures are determined by genetic factors, by the environment one has previously experienced, or, as is more likely, a combination of both. There is clear evidence that not only do the genetic factors and patterns of learning through childhood interact in predicting childhood and adult behavior (Van Goozen, Fairchild, Snoek, & Harold, 2007), but also that some people are more affected by environmental influences than others (Belsky, Bakermans-Kranenburg, & van IJzendoorn, 2007).

Evidence of interactions in these factors is being demonstrated in a number of studies. For example, one of the personality factors found to affect aggressiveness is having a tendency to be callous and unemotional. Using a sample of adolescent twins who had been found to demonstrate aggressive behavior, Mann, Tackett, Tucker-Drob, and Harden (2018) found that those with high levels of the callous-unemotional traits showed the strongest evidence of genetic influences on aggressive behavior.

2.3.4 Interactions in Biological and Environmental Factors in Explaining Aggression

As noted more than once already in this chapter, it is clear that there is no one cause of aggression or violence. Many variables contribute, including socialization, learned values in the community, and a variety of biological factors. The interaction of biological and environmental factors is the focus of a newly developed discipline of social neuroscience (e.g., Harmon-Jones & Inzlicht, 2016) as well as of the field of epigenetics (Moore, 2015). These interactions occur in many different ways. Genetic influences are not always direct. Early life experiences can change the way genes are expressed, especially in environments that are negative. Complicating this even further is evidence that a person's genotype can relate to the probability of being exposed to different risks in the environment (Moffitt, Caspi, & Rutter, 2006). Moffitt and her colleagues provided a detailed discussion of how these interactions could lead to psychopathology. Other work indicated that negative environmental influences affected how genes were expressed, and that the specific effects varyed across the life span (Karmiloff-Smith, Casey, Massand, Tomalski, & Thomas, 2014).

Research continues to find complex interactions between genetic predictors of aggressiveness, family influences during childhood, and the effects of the immediate environment. For example, Wertz et al. (2016) analyzed data from more than 2000 twins to examine how these variables interacted in explaining anti-social behavior in girls and boys at ages 5 and 12. Girls displayed less of this aggressive behavior than boys. Genetic factors in this study did appear to be more important for boys than girls. Girls were more affected by the family environment. However, a longitudinal study of over 2000 girls indicated that a small group of these girls showed a continuing pattern through childhood of high levels of disruptive and antisocial behavior that was already evident by the time they were 5 years old (Hipwell et al., 2002). Although genetic data were not obtained, these early patterns do suggest a possible biological underpinning of the behavior in these girls.

Consistent with these studies, Walters, Chiocchetti, and Freitag (2016) conducted a major review of literature on the development of aggression, considering both genetic and epigenetic mechanisms. They differentiated what they labeled as reactive aggression with pre-mediated aggression. Reactive aggression occurs as a response to an environmental threat or provocation. Pre-mediated aggression was associated with callous-unemotional traits. Both types of aggressiveness showed evidence for genetic and epigenetic influences, with early maltreatment being associated with modifications of the person's responses to stress as well as the immune system. Impulsive aggression was especially related to hormone levels.

One of the important ways in which these interactions between the current biological state and the environment occur is in terms of levels of testosterone, and other hormones such as cortisol or oxytocin. These hormone levels have biological causes as well as being affected by what is happening in the environment, with learning and other social variables also playing a role in how the hormones function (Christiansen, 2001). Although most researchers are interested in how levels of hormones such as testosterone might affect behavior, there is also evidence that the behavior can affect the levels of hormones. Thus, engaging in violent or aggressive behavior may in turn lead to rises in levels of testosterone (Eriksson, 2008).

2.3.5 *Testosterone*

In humans and other animals, prenatal levels of testosterone affect the development of the male genitals as well as the structure of the brain (Grotzinger et al., 2018). After birth, overall testosterone levels are low, but they rise again at puberty, especially for adolescent boys, who have much higher levels on average than girls through adolescence and into middle age (Christiansen, 2001). Much research has indicated that the hormone, testosterone, is associated with aggression in animals, including humans (e.g., Harmon-Jones & Inzlicht, 2016). Along with aggressiveness is dominance behavior, which is also affected by testosterone (Van Honk, Bos, & Terburg, 2014). Thus, the general pattern of men being more aggressive is also consistent with the fact that testosterone levels are higher in men than women. Testosterone is also related to sexual interest, and rises in testosterone appear to relate to increased sexual arousal in the presence of an attractive partner, especially for male animals and human men (Carre & Olmstead, 2015). There may be other effects of testosterone as well. A recent study indicated that providing a sample of mostly young men with a single dose of testosterone was related to a decline in thoughtful behavior in this sample (Nave, Nadler, Zava, & Camerer, 2017).

Evidence of the effects of base levels of testosterone on aggression in men are especially seen in studies of large samples of adult men. Using a sample of over 4000 male army veterans aged 33–42, Mazur and Booth (2014) measured base testosterone levels in their blood and related these levels to a number of behaviors related to aggression. Analyses indicated statistically significant, but low correlations of testosterone with earlier experiences with juvenile delinquency, having had trouble with alcohol use, and engaging in physical violence as adults with other men or with women in intimate partnerships.

Another approach to examining the effects of testosterone is to closely observe how changes in the environment relate to changing testosterone levels. One type of situation that can be studied in the laboratory is to examine testosterone levels in those who have had a success experience in a competitive situation. This group is compared to another group that does the same task, but loses in this task. The general finding is that men, but not women, tend have rises in testosterone after winning a competition, while they have decreases after losing (Carre & Olmstead, 2015). These testosterone changes are then associated with higher aggressiveness in the winners and reduced aggressiveness in the losers. There is high variability, though, such that these increases or decreases are much higher in some men than in others.

Other studies indicate that even watching a team one identifies with that wins a competition can lead to rises in testosterone levels (Gray, McHale, & Carre´, 2016). In their detailed review of the literature, Gray and his colleagues also discussed field research showing rises in testosterone before competition even begins. This is believed to result in more aggressive activity in the competition, and appears to be especially associated with competitions in the home field or court. Supporting these studies, Eisnegger, Haushofer, and Fehr (2011) argued that testosterone rises are best interpreted as related to the search for and maintenance of social status. Winning a sports competition is often associated with higher status, especially for men.

Although this association of winning and testosterone is generally assumed to apply only to men, it has also been reported for some women. To study this, Edwards and Casto (2013) used a sample of women involved in high-level athletic competition (women on teams participating in highly competitive intercollegiate sports). Looking at testosterone levels in their saliva, Edwards and Casto (2013) found that these women showed the same pattern as male athletes of having rises in testosterone levels when involved in competition.

Thus, a large body of research such as the studies described above as well as recent studies such as Kaldewaij et al. (2019) or Probst, Golle, Lory, and Lobmaier (2018) links human aggression to testosterone levels. Some recent research suggests, though, that the relationships are not always straightforward, and further indicates that effect sizes may be low. These low effect sizes indicate that testosterone levels only have a small effect in predicting aggression levels. As discussed below, one reason for this is that testosterone effects tend to interact with levels of the hormone, cortisol (Grotzinger et al., 2018). Another factor is that in addition to baseline levels of testosterone resulting from brain and other biological processes, there is also another type of testosterone that is created in direct response to current events in the situation (Eisnegger et al., 2011). The *free* or fluctuating levels of testosterone that are in response to the surrounding environment do not always function in the same way as the base-level testosterone (Carre & Olmstead, 2015).

As Carre and Olmstead (2015) explain in their summary of the literature on the effects of testosterone in humans, another reason for weak findings in many studies may relate to the fact that clearer specification is needed about what type of aggression is being considered, along with assessment of fluctuating as compared to baseline levels of this hormone. Fluctuating levels of testosterone appear to be more highly related to *reactive* aggression, which is not premediated and involves anger and responding to frustration. *Proactive* aggression, which is instrumental and based on thoughts about how to best achieve a particular goal (Angus, Schutter, Terburg, van Honk, & Harmon-Jones, 2016), may be less affected by testosterone. Adding complexity, there is evidence that there are complex interactions of testosterone levels with levels of cortisol. These data are discussed in more detail below. To add to the complexity, the effects of these two hormones may be different for women and men. For example, Cote, McCormick, Geniole, Renn, and MacAulay (2013) found that sleep deprivation lowered the levels of fluctuating testosterone as well as being associated with less aggressive behavior for college men in a laboratory study as compared to a non-sleep derived control group. These data support the association of testosterone and aggressiveness in men. However, the effects of sleep deprivation and testosterone were not found in women.

2.3.6 Testosterone and Other Hormones

As already mentioned, a number of studies have indicated that testosterone effects are moderated by cortisol levels. For more information on the interactions of these two hormones, see the review by Montoya, Terburg, Bos, and van Honk (2012). The major effect of cortisol is to increase fear or anxiety, which leads to withdrawal from the situation. Thus, it is not surprising that these two hormones may have contradictory effects. This can be seen in a number of laboratory studies. For example, Platje et al. (2015) find that in a sample of male and female adolescents, aggressive behavior was predicted by an interaction of testosterone levels *and* cortisol levels. Grotzinger et al. (2018) report similar findings with male and female adolescents. When cortisol levels were high, levels of aggression tended to be low. In another study, baseline levels of testosterone were correlated with antisocial behavior for both men and women in a study of undergraduate women and men. However, this effect was found to interact with cortisol levels for men in this study. (Unfortunately, the testosterone-cortisol interactions were not tested for women in this study) (Welker, Lozoya, Campbell, Neumann, & Carre, 2014). Looking at these effects in a real world situation, Sherman, Lerner, Josephs, and Renshon (2016) found that in a sample of male executives, among those low in cortisol, the level of testosterone in the executive predicted the number of subordinates reporting to him. Testosterone effects were not seen in those with high cortisol levels in this study, consistent with Grotzinger et al. (2018).

A number of studies have studied testosterone-cortisol interactions in both men and women by observing how people react to images of angry faces (Montoya et al., 2012). Researchers in these studies make the assumption that seeing someone else with an angry face signals threat from that individual. Some of these studies involve administration of the relevant hormones. Generally, higher levels of free testosterone are associated with more attentiveness to the angry faces, but this effect decreases if cortisol levels are high. A German study of undergraduate men found that the relationships among testosterone, cortisol and dominance depend on the underlying personality of the young man being analyzed (Pfattheicher, 2017). Thus, more research is clearly needed to clarify these effects. Other hormones such as serotonin may also interact with testosterone levels, although data on this issue is limited (Montoya et al., 2012).

Another hormonal factor that has been related to aggressive behavior is oxytocin. However, this hormone has only recently been studied in depth, and results are often inconsistent (see Bartz, Zaki, Bolger, & Oshsner, 2011). As Bartz and her colleagues explained, the hypothesized effects of oxytocin are reduction of social anxiety and raising the importance of social cues in the environment. Given these effects, it is not hard to further hypothesize that oxytocin might reduce aggression, although this was not discussed in the Bartz et al. review. Since that time, these ideas have been investigated in a number of studies. Demirci, Ozmen, Kilic, and Oztop (2016) studied a sample of 40 boys ranging in age from 7 to 18 diagnosed as having ADHD. Blood levels of oxytocin were measured. Levels were found to be negatively correlated with self-ratings of general aggressiveness, and positively correlated with self-rated empathy scores, supporting the basic predictions of the Bartz et al. review.

In another study done in the Netherlands, Berends et al. (2019) used a computer game to examine aggressive behavior in a sample of 57 men recruited from the community. The game involved the study participant and a second player (who was actually fictional and displayed a controlled series of behaviors in the game). An aggressive response in the game was defined as taking away points from the other player. This was defined as aggressive since it did not add to the person's score and did not affect the study participant's final outcome. At some points in the game, the other player subtracted points from the study participant. Half the sample received a nasal dose of oxytocin, while the other half had a placebo. As predicted, those receiving oxytocin were less likely to make the aggressive responses.

This same game was used in an Israeli study (Ne'eman, Perach-Barzilay, Fischer-Shofty, & Shamay-Tsoory, 2016), using 48 male and female study participants ranging in age from 19 to 46. Results were quite different from those reported by Berends et al. Oxytocin levels were found to be positively associated with aggressive responses. This was interpreted as resulting from oxytocin administration leading to more attention to social cues. Since the other player in the game was perceived as acting in a hostile way, the study participant behavior in the oxytocin condition was explained as a response to this provocation. The provocation prediction was replicated in a U.S. college student study, again using both male and female study participants (Romney, Hahn-Holbrook, Norman, Moore, & Holt-Lunstad, 2019). The aggressive response in this study was giving an unpleasant burst of sound to the fictional opponent in a competition to see who could display the fastest reaction time. No effect of gender was found for administering the unpleasant sound. There was a small, but statistically significant effect, for oxytocin administration to be associated with higher levels of aggressiveness. Clearly, more research is needed to clarify the effects of oxytocin and to better determine how this hormone interacts with testosterone.

2.3.7 Alcohol and Aggression

An environmental factor often associated with violent and aggressive behavior is alcohol. The alcohol-aggression link is seen in humans (Parrott & Eckhardt, 2018) as well as other animals (De Boer, 2018). This association is complex and not always direct. Alcohol does lessen cognitive processing and reasoning ability, so people who are drinking may be less able to interpret the situation they are in and less able to control their own behaviors. They may perceive others as challenging or threatening them in some way and respond aggressively because of this in situations where others might perceive something quite different. Another effect is that we may not be as likely to consider reasons we should *not* be aggressive or behave in ways we might act when not drinking. This explanation can be used to explain why we may do other types of *bad* behaviors such as gambling or eating less unhealthy foods after having an alcoholic drink (Steele & Southwick, 1985). This lack of attention given to negative future consequences can also been seen in a controlled laboratory study where reduced fears of being shocked were found in study participants who had drunk alcohol (Curtin, Patrick, Lang, Cacioppo, & Birbaumer, 2001). As Parrott and Eckhardt (2018) described it, there is narrower focus of attention when one has consumed a large quantity of alcohol making it difficult to consider consequences of one's actions, or even outside factors that might be causing someone to act in a way that can provoke an aggressive response. This may also explain why having a drink with a romantic partner may be more likely to lead to a sexual encounter than if the couple had not been drinking.

Drinking alcohol has often been cited as a factor in criminal behavior (Sheehan & Lau-Barraco, 2016). Alcohol is also associated with partner violence (Eckhardt, Parrott, & Sprunger, 2015) as well as engaging in dating violence and being victimized by violence from a dating partner (Reyes, Foshee, Bauer, & Ennett, 2014). However, the relationship between alcohol and violent or criminal behavior is not always straightforward. To better understand this, Sheehan and his colleagues argued that one must also consider various forms of self-regulation, since these may inhibit aggressive responses to alcohol. Although other studies have indicated possible effects of other drugs, most researchers argue that alcohol is the substance most directly related to aggression (Tomlinson, Brown, & Hoaken, 2016). One reason for this may be that there is a hormonal response of raised testosterone levels as one begins to consume alcohol, creating a feeling of physiological arousal. This rise occurs in both women and men (Eriksson, 2008).

The following case example illustrates how heavy alcohol abuse is often associated with intimate partner violence. In this case, the victim reports that her husband usually apologizes after an episode of abuse, promising to change but, inevitably, the next time he is drinking heavily, the abuse occurs again, which is a common pattern in ongoing intimate partner violence.

Case Example #7

Julie is a 25 year old married white female with one child who was brought to the crisis clinic by her sister-in-law. Julie states that her husband kicked her out of the house 2 days ago and she has no place to go and is, essentially, homeless. Her sister-in-law took her in to stay with her family but her husband (Julie's brother-in-law) says he wants Julie to leave because his brother will get too upset. Julie's husband drinks heavily on a daily basis, beats her up regularly and she doesn't know what to do. Julie presents as an attractive young woman who is upset and desperate. Her speech is pressured, affect is somewhat labile in presentation, there is no evidence thought disorder, and she denies suicidal or homicidal ideation. Julie has stayed at the battered women's shelter before but has never been willing to stay longer than overnight. When I inquired as to why she doesn't stay longer at the shelter, she says that she has always contacted her husband, he apologizes and promises never to hit her again and so she returns home. Things are good for a couple weeks or so but then his drinking escalates and inevitably he abuses her again. Julie realizes she needs to do more than what she has done so far to change her situation, including staying at the shelter and getting counseling, so I called the shelter and she talked with them on the phone and agreed to go there and commit to staying for a few days. Her sister-in-law agreed to drive her over.

Others have tried to better understand the relationship of couple violence and alcohol. An interesting study reported by Testa and Derrick (2014) used a daily dairy methodology where both partners in a couple reported on their own and partner's drinking and verbal and physical aggressiveness to each other each day. The sample used for this study consisted of 200 married and cohabitating couples who had been recruited for an alcohol study. Thus, potential study participants did not know that the study would include questions about partner violence. Daily reports were collected over a 56 day period, although some of the reports were not submitted and treated as missing data. As predicted, drinking alcohol was associated with both perpetrating as well as being the recipient of verbal and physical aggression from the partner. The same types of relationships were found for both women and men. Findings were statistically significant, although the actual relationships found were quite small, indicating that many other factors were also affecting the relationships among these variables.

Devries et al. (2013) documented another type of relationship between alcohol and partner abuse. In a review of over 50 published studies in the literature, they found that women victimized by physical or sexual abuse tended to consume more alcohol. Longitudinal studies in their database did indicate that it was being victimized by partner violence that predicted higher levels of drinking, indicating this may have been a coping response in these violence survivors (see Chap. 3). Such data may also indicate why other studies have reported higher levels of alcohol use was correlated with being a victim of violence.

2.3.8 Cognitive Factors and Aggression

Higher level cognitive processes also contribute to acts of aggression. As Dodge (2011) discusses, when people perceive that another person is acting in a hostile manner, it is likely they will respond to this with their own aggression. But, the same action may be perceived very differently by some people, and this non-hostile cognition may lead to a non-hostile response to the same action. For example, in a laboratory study, Bartlett, Witkower, Mancini, and Saleem (2016) demonstrated that the hostile act of blasting another person with a loud noise generally led to the study participant sending back another loud noise. But, if the initially hostile person apologized or explained that the equipment was not working properly, the study participant was less likely to respond back with the loud noise.

Perceptions of others depend on one's past history as well as on biological factors in the brain (Dodge, 2011). These perceptions occur very quickly, and we are generally not conscious of this process. General patterns of social information processing relating to coding behavior of others as provocation appear to develop at quite a young age. Other biological variables such level of autonomic reactivity also relate to violent behavior. As Dodge elaborates in his chapter, all of these factors interact and build increasing patterns of aggressive behavior. Early experiences of victimization from family members in young children may initiate some of these patterns. Other forms of early life stress may also affect the brain in ways that increase the likelihood of an aggressive response.

2.4 Summary

As this chapter has demonstrated, aggression and violence are complex behaviors with many possible contributing factors. For a detailed discussion of how these contributing factors interact, see Anderson and Bushman's (2018) discussion of their General Aggression Model. Learning contributes to making people either more or less violent or aggressive in many ways. Reinforcement and modeling of others' behaviors are both major mechanisms creating learning. Girls and boys may receive very different patterns of learning about aggression. A variety of environmental factors affect our immediate responses. Genetic factors also contribute to levels of aggressiveness, often in complex ways. Other biological variables such as the hormone testosterone as well as other hormones such as cortisol and oxytocin are important. Alcohol levels contribute to aggression. Cognitive interpretations of the actions of others add yet another layer of complexity.

References

Alink, L. R. A., Cyr, C., & Madigan, S. (2019). The effect of maltreatment experiences on maltreating and dysfunctional parenting: A search for mechanisms. *Development and Psychopathology, 31*, 1–7. https://doi.org/10.1017/S0954579418001517

Anderson, C. A. (1989). Temperature and aggression: Ubiquitous effects of heat on occurrence of human violence. *Psychological Bulletin, 106*, 74–96. https://doi.org/10.1037/0033-2909.106.1.74

Anderson, C. A., & Bushman, B. J. (2018). Media violence and the general aggression model. *Journal of Social Issues, 74*, 386–413. https://doi.org/10.1111/josi.12275

Anderson, C. A., Bushman, B. J., Bartholow, B. D., Cantor, J., Christakis, D., Coyne, S. M., et al. (2018). Screen violence and youth behavior. *Pediatrics, 140*(s2), e20161758.

Anderson, C. A., Bushman, B. J., Donnerstein, E., Hummer, T. A., & Warburton, W. (2015). SPSSI research summary on media violence. *Analysis of Social Issues and Public Policy, 15*, 4–19. https://doi.org/10.1111/asap.12093

Anderson, C. A., & Dill, K. E. (2000). Video games and aggressive thoughts, feelings, and behavior in the laboratory and life. *Journal of Personality and Social Psychology, 78*, 772–790. https://doi.org/10.1037/0022-3514.78.4.772

Angus, D. J., Schutter, D. J. L. G., Terburg, D., van Honk, J., & Harmon-Jones, E. (2016). A review of social neuroscience research on anger and aggression. In E. Harmon-Jones & M. Inzlicht (Eds.), *Social neuroscience: Biological approaches to social psychology*. New York: Psychology Press.

Arriaga, X. B., & Capezza, N. M. (2011). The paradox of partner aggression: Being committed to an aggressive partner. In P. R. Shaver & M. Mikulincer (Eds.), *Human aggression and violence: Causes, manifestations, and consequences* (pp. 367–383). Washington, DC: American Psychological Association.

Associated Press. (2005). Suit: Video games sparked police shootings. *ABC News,* February 15. Retrieved from: http://abcnews.go.com/US/wireStory?id=502424

Bartholow, B. D. (2018). The aggressive brain: Insights from neuroscience. *Current Opinion in Psychology, 19*, 60–64. https://doi.org/10.1016/j.copsyc.2017.04.002

Bartlett, C., Witkower, Z., Mancini, C., & Saleem, M. (2016). Breaking the link between provocation and aggression: The role of mitigating information. *Aggressive Behavior, 999*, 1–8. https://doi.org/10.1002/ab.21650

Bartz, J. A., Zaki, J., Bolger, N., & Oshsner, K. N. (2011). Social effects of oxytocin in humans: Context and person matter. *Trends in Cognitive Science, 15*, 301–309. https://doi.org/10.1016/j.tics.2011.05.002

Baskin-Sommers, A. R. (2016). Dissecting antisocial behavior: The impact of neural, genetic, and environmental factors. *Clinical Psychological Science, 4*, 500–510. https://doi.org/10.1177/216702615626904

Baugher, A. R., & Gazmararian, J. A. (2015). Masculine gender role stress and violence: A literature review and future directions. *Aggression and Violent Behavior, 24*, 107–112. https://doi.org/10.1016/j.avb.2015.04.002

Belsky, J., Bakermans-Kranenburg, M. J., & van IJzendoorn, M. H. (2007). For better and for worse: Differential susceptibility to environmental influences. *Current Directions in Psychological Science, 16*, 300–304. https://doi.org/10.1111/j.1467-8721.2007.00525.x

Bender, P. K., Plante, C., & Gentile, D. A. (2018). The effects of violent media content on aggression. *Current Opinion in Psychology, 19*, 104–108. https://doi.org/10.1016/j.copsyc.2017.04.003

Benjamin Jr., A. J., & Bushman, B. J. (2018). The weapons effect. *Current Opinion in Psychology, 19*, 93–97. https://doi.org/10.1016/j.copsyc.2017.04.011

Berends, Y. R., Tulen, J. H. M., Wierdsma, A. I., van Pelt, J., Feldman, R., Zagoory-Sharon, O., et al. (2019). Intranasal administration of oxytocin decreases task-related aggressive responses in healthy young males. *Psychoneuroendocrinology, 106*, 147–154. https://doi.org/10.1016/j.psyneuen.2019.03.027

Berkowitz, L. (1989). Frustration-aggression hypothesis: Examination and reformulation. *Psychological Bulletin, 106*, 59–73. https://doi.org/10.1037/0033-2909.106.1.59

Berkowitz, L. (1993). Pain and aggression: Some findings and implications. *Motivation and Emotion, 17*, 277–293. https://doi.org/10.1007/BF00992223

Berkowitz, L., & LePage, A. (1967). Weapons as aggression-eliciting stimuli. *Journal of Personality and Social Psychology, 7*, 202–207. https://doi.org/10.1037/h0025008

Bernstein, J. (2013). Way beyond anything we've done before: Building the world of Grand Theft Auto V. *Buzzfeed News,* August 13. Retrieved from: https://www.buzzfeed.com/josephbernstein/way-beyond-anything-weve-done-before-building-the-world-of-g?utm_term=.oqDjNN3g5#.snxZNNVGr

Birkley, E. L., & Eckhardt, C. I. (2015). Anger, hostility, internalizing negative emotions, and intimate partner violence perpetration: A meta-analytic review. *Clinical Psychology Review, 37*, 40–56. https://doi.org/10.1016/j.cpr.2015.01.002

Bjorkqvist, K. (2018). Gender differences in aggression. *Current Opinion in Psychology, 19*, 39–42. https://doi.org/10.1016/j.copsyc.2017.03.030

Bosson, J. K., Vandello, J. A., & Buckner, C. E. (2019). *The psychology of sex and gender*. Los Angeles, CA: Sage.

Brannon, L. (2017). *Gender: Psychological perspectives* (7th ed.). New York: Routledge.

Brown, R. P., Baughman, K., & Carvallo, M. (2018). Culture, masculine honor, and violence toward women. *Personality and Social Psychology Bulletin, 44*(4), 538–549. https://doi.org/10.1177/0146167217744195

Buffone, A. E. K., & Poulin, M. J. (2014). Empathy, target distress, and neurohormone genes interact to predict aggression for others- Even without provocation. *Personality and Social Psychology Bulletin, 40*, 1406–1422. https://doi.org/10.1177/0146167214549320

Bushman, B. J. (2016). Violent media and hostile appraisals: A meta-analytic review. *Aggressive Behavior*. https://doi.org/10.1002/ab.21655

Bushman, B. J., Bonacci, A. M., Pedersen, W. C., Vasquez, E. A., & Miller, N. (2005). Chewing it can chew you up: Effects of rumination on triggered displaced aggression. *Journal of Personality and Social Psychology, 88*, 969–983. https://doi.org/10.1037/0022-3514.88.6.969

Card, D., & Dahl, G. B. (2011). Family violence and football: The effect of unexpected emotional cues on violent behavior. *The Quarterly Journal of Economics, 126*, 103–143. https://doi.org/10.1093/qje/qjr001

Carre, J. M., & Olmstead, N. A. (2015). Social neuroendocrinology of human aggression: Explaining the role of competition-induced testosterone dynamics. *Neuroscience, 286*, 171–186. https://doi.org/10.1016/j.neuroscience.2014.11.029

Chalk, A. (2008). Vice City wrongful death suit dismissed. Escapist Magazine. Retrieved from: http://www.escapistmagazine.com/news/view/83973-Vice-City-Wrongful-Death-Suit-Dismissed

Chaplin, T. M., Cole, P. M., & Zahn-Waxler, C. (2005). Parental socialization of emotion expression: Gender differences and relations to child adjustment. *Emotion, 5*, 80–88. https://doi.org/10.1037/1528-3542.5.1.80

Christiansen, K. (2001). Hormones and sport: Behavioural effects of androgen in men and women. *Journal of Endocrinology, 170*, 39–48. 0022-0793/01/0170-039.

Cote, K. A., McCormick, C. M., Geniole, S. N., Renn, R. P., & MacAulay, S. D. (2013). Sleep deprivation lowers reactive aggression and testosterone. *Biological Psychology, 92*, 249–256. https://doi.org/10.1016/j.biopsycho.2012.09.011

Coyne, S. M., Padilla-Walker, L. M., Holmgren, H. G., Davis, E. J., & Collier, K. M. (2018). A meta-analysis of prosocial media on prosocial behavior, aggression, and empathic concern: A multidimensional approach. *Developmental Psychology, 54*, 331–347. https://doi.org/10.1037/dev0000412

Curtin, J. J., Patrick, C. J., Lang, A. R., Cacioppo, J. T., & Birbaumer, N. (2001). Alcohol affects emotion through cognition. *Psychological Science, 12*, 527–531. https://doi.org/10.1111/1467-9280.00397

De Boer, S. F. (2018). Animal models of excessive aggression: Implications for human aggression and violence. *Current Opinion in Psychology, 19*, 81–87. https://doi.org/10.1016/j.copsyc.2017.04.006

De Pedro, K. T., Astor, R. A., Gilbreath, T., Benbenishty, R., & Berkowitz, R. (2016). Examining the relationship between school climate and peer victimization among students in military-connected public schools. *Violence and Victims, 31*, 751–766. https://doi.org/10.1891/0886-6708.VV-D-15-00009

Demirci, E., Ozmen, S., Kilic, E., & Oztop, D. B. (2016). The relationship between aggression, empathy skills and serum oxytocin levels in male children and adolescents with attention deficit and hyperactivity disorder. *Behavioural Pharmacology, 27*, 681–688. https://doi.org/10.1097/FBP.0000000000000234

Denson, T. F. (2011). A social neuroscience perspective on the neurolbiological bases of aggression. In P. R. Shaver & M. Mikulincer (Eds.), *Human aggression and violence: Causes, manifestations, and consequences* (pp. 105–120). Washington, DC: American Psychological Association.

Devries, K. M., Child, J. C., Bacchus, L. J., Mak, J., Falder, G., Graham, K., et al. (2013). Intimate partner violence victimization and alcohol consumption in women: A systematic review and meta-analysis. *Addiction, 109*, 379–391. https://doi.org/10.1111/add.12393

DiLalla, L. F., & Gottesman, I. I. (1991). Biological and genetic contributions to violence—Widom's untold tale. *Psychological Bulletin, 109*, 125–129. https://doi.org/10.1037/0033-2909.109.1.125

Dodge, K. A. (2011). Social information processing patterns as mediators of the interaction between genetic factors and life experiences in the development of aggressive behavior. In P. R. Shaver & M. Mikulincer (Eds.), *Human aggression and violence: Causes, manifestations, and consequences* (pp. 165–185). Washington, DC: American Psychological Association.

Dollard, J., Doob, L. W., Miller, N. E., Mowrer, O. H., & Sears, R. R. (1939). *Frustration and aggression*. New Haven, CT: Yale University Press.

Dutton, D. G. (2011). Attachment and violence: An anger born of fear. In P. R. Shaver & M. Mikulincer (Eds.), *Human aggression and violence: Causes, manifestations, and consequences* (pp. 259–275). Washington, DC: American Psychological Association.

Eckhardt, C. I., Parrott, D. J., & Sprunger, J. G. (2015). Mechanisms of alcohol-facilitated intimate partner violence. *Violence Against Women, 21*, 939–957. https://doi.org/10.1177/1077801215589376

Edwards, D. A., & Casto, K. V. (2013). Women's intercollegiate athletic competition: Cortisol, testosterone, and the dual-hormone hypothesis as it relates to status among teammates. *Hormones and Behavior, 64*, 153–160. https://doi.org/10.1016/j.yhbeh.2013.03.003

Eisler, R. M., & Skidmore, J. R. (1987). Masculine gender role stress: Scale development and component factors in the appraisal of stressful situations. *Behavior Modification, 11*(2), 123–136. https://doi.org/10.1177/01454455870112001

Eisnegger, C., Haushofer, J., & Fehr, E. (2011). The role of testosterone in social interaction. *Trends in Cognitive Science, 15*, 264–271. https://doi.org/10.1016/j.tics.2011.04.008

Endendijk, J. J., Groeneveld, M. G., van der Pol, L. D., van Berkel, S. R., Hallers-Haalboom, E. T., Bakermans-Kranenburg, M. J., et al. (2017). Gender differences in child aggression: Relations with gender-differentiated parenting and parents' gender-role stereotypes. *Child Development, 88*, 299–316. https://doi.org/10.1111/cdev.12589

Eriksson, C. J. P. (2008). Role of alcohol and sex hormones on human aggressive behavior. In D. Pfaff, C. Kordon, P. Chanson, & Y. Christen (Eds.), *Hormones and social behavior* (pp. 177–186). Berlin, Germany: Springer.

Farkas, T., & Leaper, C. (2016). Chivalry's double-edged sword: How girls' and boys' paternalistic attitudes relate to their possible family and work selves. *Sex Roles, 77*, 220–230. https://doi.org/10.1007/s11199-015-0556-z

Farrington, D. P. (2019). The development of violence from age 8 to 61. *Aggressive Behavior, 45*, 365–376. https://doi.org/10.1002/ab.21831

Felson, R. B. (2002). *Violence and gender reexamined*. Washington, DC: American Psychological Association.

Felson, R. B. (2014). Back to basics: Gender and the social psychology of aggression. In R. Gartner & B. McCarthy (Eds.), *The Oxford handbook of gender, sex, and crime* (pp. 77–98). NY: Oxford University Press.

Ferguson, C. J. (2002). Media violence: Miscast causality. *American Psychologist, 57*, 446–447. https://doi.org/10.1037/0003-066X.57.6-7.446b

Ferguson, C. J. (2013). Violent video games and the Supreme Court: Lessons for the scientific community in the wake of Brown v. Entertainment Merchants Association. *American Psychologist, 68*, 57–74. https://doi.org/10.1037/a0030597

Ferguson, C. J. (2015). Do angry birds make for angry children? A meta-analysis of video game influences on children's and adolescents' aggression, mental health, prosocial behavior, and academic performance. *Perspectives on Psychological Science, 10*, 646–666. https://doi.org/10.1177/1745691615592234

Finkelday, J. G. (2018). Adolescent male sports participation and emerging adulthood: Examining variation by gender-typed behavior. *Deviant Behavior*. https://doi.org/10.1080/01639625.2018.1512259

Frieze, I. H. (2005). *Hurting the one you love: Violence in relationships*. Belmont, CA: Thompson Wadsworth.

Geen, R. G., & O'Neal, E. C. (1969). Activation of cue-elicited aggression by general arousal. *Journal of Personality and Social Psychology, 11*, 289–292. https://doi.org/10.1037/h0026885

Glick, P., & Fiske, S. T. (2001). An ambivalent alliance: Hostile and benevolent sexism as complementary justifications for gender inequality. *American Psychologist, 56*, 109–118. https://doi.org/10.1037/0003-066X.56.2.109

Gorelik, G., Shackelford, T. K., & Weeks-Shackelford, V. A. (2012). Human violence and evolutionary consciousness. *Review of General Psychology, 16*, 343–356. https://doi.org/10.1037/a0027991

Gramlich, J. (2016). *Voters' perceptions of crime continue to conflict with reality*. PEW Research Center. https://www.pewresearch.org/fact-tank/2016/11/16/voters-perceptions-of-crime-continue-to-conflict-with-reality/

Gray, P. B., McHale, T. S., & Carre´, J. M. (2016). A review of male field studies of hormones and behavioral reproductive effort. *Hormones and Behavior*. https://doi.org/10.1016/j.yhbeh.2016.07.004

Grotzinger, A. D., Mann, F. D., Patterson, M. W., Tackett, J. L., Tucker-Drob, E. M., & Harden, K. P. (2018). Hair and salivary testosterone, hair cortisol, and externalizing behaviors in adolescents. *Psychological Science, 29*, 688–699. https://doi.org/10.1177/0956797617742981

Groves, C. L., & Anderson, C. A. (2017). Adversive events and aggression. *Current Opinion in Psychology, 19*, 144–148. https://doi.org/10.1016/j.copsyc.2017.03.027

Haines, E. L., Deaux, K., & Lofaro, N. (2016). The times they are a-changing…or are they not? A comparison of gender stereotypes, 1983–2014. *Psychology of Women Quarterly, 40*, 353–363. https://doi.org/10.1177/0361684316634081

Hamby, S. (2017). On defining violence, and why it matters. *Psychology of Violence, 7*, 167–180. https://doi.org/10.1037/vio0000117

Harmon-Jones, E., & Inzlicht, M. (Eds.). (2016). *Social neuroscience: Biological approaches to social psychology*. New York: Psychology Press.

Hilgard, J., Engelhardt, C. R., Rouder, J. N., Segert, I. L., & bartholow, B. D. (2019). Null effects of game violence, game difficulty, and 2D:4D digit ratio on aggressive behavior. *Psychological Science, 30*(4), 606–616. https://doi.org/10.1177/0956797619829688

Hipwell, A. E., Loeber, R., Stoutamer-Loeber, M., Keenan, K., White, H. R., & Kroneman, L. (2002). Characteristics of girls with early onset disruptive and antisocial behavior. *Criminal Behaviour and Mental Health, 12*, 99–118. https://doi.org/10.1002/cbm.489

Hollis, M. E., Downey, S., del Carmen, A., & Dobbs, R. R. (2017). The relationship between media portrayals and crime: Perceptions of fear of crime among citizens. *Crime Prevention and Community Safety, 19*(1), 46–60. https://doi.org/10.1057/s41300-017-0015-6

Holmes, M. R., Yoon, S., & Berg, K. A. (2017). Maternal depression and intimate partner violence exposure: Longitudinal analyses of the development of aggressive behavior in an at-risk sample. *Aggressive Behavior, 9999*, 1–11. https://doi.org/10.1002/ab.21696

Hudziak, J. J., van Beijsterveldt, C. E. M., Bartels, M., Rietveld, M. J. H., Rettew, D. C., Derks, E. M., et al. (2003). Individual differences in aggression: Genetic analyses by age, gender, and informant in 3-,7-, and 10-year-old Dutch twins. *Behavior Genetics, 33*, 575–589. https://doi.org/10.1023/A:1025782918793

Huesmann, L. R. (2018). An integrative theoretical understanding of aggression: A brief exposition. *Current Opinion in Psychology, 19*, 119–124. https://doi.org/10.1016/j.copsyc.2017.04.015

Huesmann, L. R., Dubow, E. F., & Boxer, P. (2011). The transmission of aggressiveness across generations: Biological, contextual, and social learning processes. In P. R. Shaver & M. Mikulincer (Eds.), *Human aggression and violence: Causes, manifestations, and consequences* (pp. 123–142). Washington, DC: American Psychological Association.

Huesmann, L. R., & Guerra, N. G. (1997). Children's normative beliefs about aggression and aggressive behavior. *Journal of Personality and Social Psychology, 72*, 408–419. https://doi.org/10.1037/0022-3514.72.2.408

Hyde, J. S. (2014). Gender similarities and differences. *Annual Review of Psychology, 65*, 373–398. https://doi.org/10.1146/annurev-psych-010213-115057

Jenkins, L. N., & Nickerson, A. B. (2016). Bullying participant roles and gender as predictors of bystander intervention. *Aggressive Behavior, 9999*, 1–10. https://doi.org/10.1002/ab.21688

Kahn, L., Kinchen, S., Shanklin, S. L., et al. (2014). *Youth risk behavior surveillance-United States* (p. 2013). Atlanta, GA: Centers for Disease Control and Prevention, U.S. Department of Health and Human Services.

Kaldewaij, R., Koch, S. B. J., Zhang, W., Hashemi, M. M., Klumpers, F., & Roelofs, K. (2019). High endogenous testosterone levels are associated with dimished neural emotional control in aggressive police recruits. *Psychological Science*, 1–13. https://doi.org/10.1177/0956797619851753

Karmiloff-Smith, A., Casey, B. J., Massand, E., Tomalski, P., & Thomas, M. S. C. (2014). Environmental and genetic influences on neurocognitive development: The importance of multiple methodologies and time-dependent intervention. *Clinical Psychological Science, 2*, 628–637. https://doi.org/10.1177/2167702614521188

Kimble, N. B., Russo, S. A., Bergman, B. G., & Galindo, V. H. (2010). Revealing an empirical understanding of aggression and violent behavior in athletics. *Aggression and Violent Behavior, 15*, 446–462. https://doi.org/10.1016/j.avb.2010.08.001

Krahé, B. (2018). Genderer self-concept and the aggressive expression of driving anger: Positive femininity buffers negative masculinity. *Sex Roles, 79*, 98–108. https://doi.org/10.1007/s11199-017-0853-9

Krenzer, W. L. D., & Splan, E. D. (2017). Evaluating the heat-aggression hypothesis: The role of temporal and social factors in predicting baseball related aggression. *Aggressive Behavior*, 1–6. https://doi.org/10.1002/ab.21726

Kühn, S., Kugler, D. T., Schmalen, K., Weichenberger, M., Witt, C., & Gallinat, J. (2018). Does playing violent video games cause aggression? A longitudinal intervention study. *Molecular Psychiatry*. https://doi.org/10.1038/s41380-018-0031-7

Lansford, J. E. (2018). Development of aggression. *Current Opinion in Psychology, 19*, 17–21. https://doi.org/10.1016/j.copsyc.2017.03.015

Lockwood, P., Jordan, C. H., & Kunda, Z. (2002). Motivation by positive or negative role models: Regulatory focus determines who will best inspire us. *Journal of Personality and Social Psychology, 83*, 854–864. https://doi.org/10.1037/0022-3514.83.4.854

Ma, J., Grogan-Kaylor, A., & Lee, S. J. (2018). Associations of neighborhood disorganization and maternal spanking with children's aggression: A fixed-effects regression analysis. *Child Abuse & Neglect, 76*, 106–116. https://doi.org/10.1016/j.chiabu.2017.10.013

Maccoby, E. E. (1998). *The two sexes: Growing up apart, coming together.* Cambridge, MA: Harvard University Press.

Malik, A. I., Zai, C. C., Abu, Z., Nowrouzi, A., & Beitchman, J. H. (2012). The role of oxytocin and oxytocin receptor genes in childhood-onset aggression. *Genes, Brain and Behavior, 11*, 545–551. https://doi.org/10.1111/j.1601-183X.2012.00776.x

Mann, F. D., Tackett, J. L., Tucker-Drob, E. M., & Harden, K. P. (2018). Callous-unemotional traits moderate genetic and environmental influences on rule-breaking and aggression: Evidence for gene x trait interaction. *Clinical Psychological Science, 6*, 123–133. https://doi.org/10.1177/2167702617730889

Markey, P. M., Markey, C. N., & French, J. E. (2015). Violent video games and real-world violence: Rhetoric versus data. *Psychology of Popular Media Culture, 4*(4), 277–295. https://doi.org/10.1037/ppm0000030

Martel, M. M. (2013). Sexual selection and sex differences in the prevalence of childhood externalizing and adolescent internalizing disorders. *Psychological Bulletin, 139*, 1121–1259. https://doi.org/10.1037/a0032247

Mazur, A., & Booth, A. (2014). Testosterone is related to deviance in male army veterans, but relationships are not moderated by cortisol. *Biological Psychology, 96*, 72–76. https://doi.org/10.1016/j.biopsycho.2013.11.015

McCauley, H. L., Jaime, M. C. D., Tancredi, D. J., Sliverman, J. G., Decker, M. R., Austin, S. B., et al. (2014). Differences in adolescent relationship abuse perpetration and gender-inequitable attitudes by sport among male high school athletes. *Journal of Adolescent Health, 54*, 742–744. https://doi.org/10.1016/j.jadohealth.2014.01.001

Mehta, C. M., & Dementieva, Y. (2017). The contextual specificity of gender: Femininity and masculinity in college students' same- and other-gender peer contexts. *Sex Roles, 76*, 604–614. https://doi.org/10.1007/s11199-016-0632-z

Mikulincer, M., & Shaver, P. R. (2011). Attachment, anger, and aggression. In P. R. Shaver & M. Mikulincer (Eds.), *Human aggression and violence: Causes, manifestations, and consequences* (pp. 241–257). Washington, DC: American Psychological Association.

Miles, D. R., & Carey, G. (1997). Genetic and environmental architecture of human aggression. *Journal of Personality and Social Psychology, 72*, 207–217. https://doi.org/10.1037/0022-3514.72.1.207

Moffitt, T. E., Caspi, A., & Rutter, M. (2006). Measured gene-environment interactions in psychopathology. *Perspectives in Psychological Science, 1*, 5–27. https://doi.org/10.1111/j.1745-6916.2006.00002.x

Moffitt, T. E., Caspi, A., Rutter, M., & Silva, P. A. (2001). *Sex differences in antisocial behavior: Conduct disorder, delinquency, and violence in the Dunedin Longitudinal study*. Cambridge: Cambridge University Press.

Montoya, E. R., Terburg, D., Bos, P. A., & van Honk, J. (2012). Testosterone, cortisol, and serotonin as key regulators of social aggression: A review and theoretical perspective. *Motivation and Emotion, 36*, 65–73. https://doi.org/10.1007/s11031-011-9264-3

Moore, D. S. (2015). *The developing genome: An introduction to behavioral epigenetics*. New York, NY: Oxford University Press.

Nave, G., Nadler, A., Zava, D., & Camerer, C. (2017). Single-dose testosterone administration impairs cognitive reflection in men. *Psychological Science, 28*, 1398–1407. https://doi.org/10.1177/0956797617709592

Ne'eman, R., Perach-Barzilay, N., Fischer-Shofty, M., & Shamay-Tsoory, A. A. S. G. (2016). Intranasal administration of oxytocin increases human aggressive behavior. *Hormones and Behavior, 80*, 125–131. https://doi.org/10.1016/j.yhbeh.2016.01.015

Newhill, C. E. (1995). A crisis casebook. Unpublished manuscript.

Ng, H. K. S., & Chow, T. S. (2016). The effects of environmental resource and security on aggressive behavior. *Aggressive Behavior, 9999*, 1–11. https://doi.org/10.1002/ab.21690

Nguyen, T. T., Morinaga, Y., Frieze, I. H., Cheng, J., Li, M., Doi, A., et al. (2013). College students' perceptions of intimate partner violence: A comparative study of Japan, China, and the United States. *International Journal of Conflict and Violence, 7*, 261–273. https://doi.org/10.4119/UNIBI/ijcv.303

Nisbett, R. E., & Cohen, D. (1996). *Culture of honor*. Boulder, CO: Westview.

Parrott, D. J., & Eckhardt, C. I. (2018). Effects of alcohol on human aggression. *Current Opinion in Psychology, 19*, 1–5. https://doi.org/10.1016/j.copsyc.2017.03.023

Paulhus, D. L., Curtis, S. R., & Jones, D. N. (2018). Aggression as a trait: The Dark Tetrad alternative. *Current Opinion in Psychology, 19*, 88–92. https://doi.org/10.1016/j.copsyc.2017.04.007

Pepler, D. J., Madsen, K. C., Webster, C. D., & Levine, K. S. (Eds.). (2014). *The development and treatment of girlhood aggression*. New York, NY: Psychology Press.

Peterson, J., & Densley, J. (2017). Cyber violence: What do we know and where do we go from here? *Aggression and Violent Behavior, 34*, 193–200. https://doi.org/10.1016/j.avb.2017.01.012

Pfattheicher, S. (2017). Illuminating the dual-hormone hypothesis: About chronic dominance and the interaction of cortisol and testosterone. *Aggressive Behavior, 43*, 85–92. https://doi.org/10.1002/ab.21665

Platje, E., Popma, A., Vermeiren, R. R. J. M., Doreleijers, T. A. H., Meeus, W. H. J., van Lier, P. A. C., et al. (2015). Testosterone and cortisol in relation to aggression in a non-clinical sample of boys and girls. *Aggressive Behavior, 41*, 478–487. https://doi.org/10.1002/ab.21585

Plomin, R., DeFries, J. C., Knopik, V. S., & Neiderhiser, J. M. (2016). Top 10 replicated findings from behavioral genetics. *Perspectives on Psychological Science, 11*, 3–23. https://doi.org/10.1177/1745691615617439

Probst, F., Golle, J., Lory, V., & Lobmaier, J. S. (2018). Reactive aggression tracks within-participant changes in women's salivary testosterone. *Aggressive Behavior*, 1–10. https://doi.org/10.1002/ab.21757

Przybylski, A. K., Deci, E. L., Rigby, C. S., & Ryan, R. M. (2014). Competence-impeding electronic games and players' aggressive feelings, thoughts, and behaviors. *Journal of Personality and Social Psychology, 106*(3), 441–457. https://doi.org/10.1037/a0034820

Rankin, C. H., Abrams, T., Barry, R. J., Bhatnagar, S., Clayton, D. F., Colombo, J., et al. (2009). Habituation revisited: an updated and revised description of the behavioral characteristics of habituation. *Neurobiology of Learning and Memory, 92*, 135–138. https://doi.org/10.1016/j.nlm.2008.09.012

Rathus, S. A. (2005). *Psychology: Concepts & connections* (9th ed.). Belmont, CA: Wadsworth.

Read, G. L., Ballard, M., Emery, L. J., & Bazzini, D. G. (2016). Examining desensitization using facial electromyography: Violent videogames, gender, and affective responding. *Computers in Human Behavior, 62*, 201–211. https://doi.org/10.1016/j.chb.2016.03.074

Renfrew, J. W. (1997). *Aggression and its causes*. New York, NY: Oxford University Press.

Reyes, H. L. M., Foshee, V. A., Bauer, D. J., & Ennett, S. T. (2014). Proximal and time-varying effects of cigarette, alcohol, marijuana and other hard drug use on adolescent dating aggression. *Journal of Adolescence, 37*, 281–289. https://doi.org/10.1016/j.adolescence.2014.02.002

Rhee, S. H., & Waldman, I. D. (2002). Genetic and environmental influences on antisocial behavior: A meta-analysis of twin and adoption studies. *Psychological Bulletin, 128*, 490–529. https://doi.org/10.1037/00ss-2909.128.490

Rhee, S. H., & Waldman, I. D. (2011). Genetic and environmental influences on aggression. In P. R. Shaver & M. Mikulincer (Eds.), *Human aggression and violence: Causes, manifestations, and consequences* (pp. 143–164). Washington, DC: American Psychological Association.

Rideout, V. J., Foehr, U. G., & Roberts, D. F. (2010). *Generation M^2: Media in the lives of 8- to 18-year olds*. Menlo Park, CA: Kaiser Family Foundation.

Rinderu, M. I., Bushman, B. J., & Van Lange, P. A. M. (2018). Climate, aggression, and violence (CLASH): a cultural-evolutionary approach. *Current Opinion in Psychology, 19*, 113–118. https://doi.org/10.1016/j.copsyc.2017.04.010

Rodkin, P. C., Farmer, T. W., Pearl, R., & Van Acker, R. (2000). Heterogeneity of popular boys: Antisocial and prosocial configurations. *Developmental Psychology, 36*, 14–24. https://doi.org/10.1037/0012-1649.36.1.14

Romney, C., Hahn-Holbrook, J., Norman, G. J., Moore, A., & Holt-Lunstad, J. (2019). Where is the love? A double-blind, randomized study of the effects of intranasal oxytocin on stress regulation and aggression. *International Journal of Psychophysiology, 136*, 15–21. https://doi.org/10.1016/j.ijpsycho.2018.08.010

Ruble, D. N., Martin, C. L., & Berenbaum, S. A. (2006). Gender development. In N. Eisenberg, W. Damon, & R. M. Lerner (Eds.), *Handbook of child psychology* (Social, emotional, and personality development) (Vol. 3, 6th ed., pp. 858–932). Hoboken, NJ: Wiley. https://doi.org/10.1002/9780470147658.chpsy0314

Russell, A. A., Robins, S. J., & Odgers, C. L. (2014). Developmental perspectives: Sex differences in antisocial behavior from childhood to adulthood. In R. Gartner & B. McCarthy (Eds.), *The Oxford handbook of gender, sex, and crime* (pp. 286–315). New York, NY: Oxford University Press.

Schneider, D., Harknett, K., & McLanahan, S. (2016). Intimate partner violence in the great recession. *Demography, 53*, 471–505. https://doi.org/10.1007/s13524-016-0462-1

Sheehan, B. E., & Lau-Barraco, C. (2016). A conceptual model of ego depletion and alcohol-related aggression. *Agression and Violent Behavior.* https://doi.org/10.1016/j.avb.2016.08.002

Sherman, G. D., Lerner, J. S., Josephs, R. A., & Renshon, J. (2016). The interaction of testosterone and cortisol is associated with attained status in male executives. *Journal of Personality and Social Psychology, 1110*, 921–929. https://doi.org/10.1037/pspp0000063

Signorella, M. L., & Frieze, I. H. (1989). Gender schemas in college students. *Psychology-A Journal of Human Behavior, 26*(4), 16–23.

Slotter, E. B., & Finkel, E. J. (2011). I^3 theory: Instigating, impelling, and inhibiting factors in aggression. In P. R. Shaver & M. Mikulincer (Eds.), *Human aggression and violence: Causes, manifestations, and consequences* (pp. 35–52). Washington, DC: American Psychological Association.

Smokowski, P. R., Goo, S., Cotter, K. L., Evans, C. B. R., & Rose, R. A. (2016). Multi-level risk factors and developmental assets associated with aggressive behavior in disadvantaged adolescents. *Aggressive Behavior, 42*, 222–238. https://doi.org/10.1002/ab.21612

Stack, L. (2016). Light sentence for Brock Turner in Stanford rape case draws outrage. The New York Times, June 6. Retrieved from: https://www.nytimes.com/2016/06/07/us/outrage-in-stanford-rape-case-over-dueling-statements-of-victim-and-attackers-father.html?_r=0

Steele, C. M., & Southwick, L. (1985). Alcohol and social behavior I: The psychology of drunken excess. *Journal of Personality and Social Psychology, 48*, 18–34. https://doi.org/10.1037/0022-3514.48.1.18

Tackett, J. L., & Krueger, R. F. (2011). Dispositional influences on human aggression. In P. R. Shaver & M. Mikulincer (Eds.), *Human aggression and violence: Causes, manifestations, and consequences* (pp. 89–104). Washington, DC: American Psychological Association.

Taylor, C. A., & Sorenson, S. B. (2005). Community-based norms about intimate partner violence: Putting attributions of fault and responsibility into context. *Sex Roles, 53*, 573–589. https://doi.org/10.1007/s11199-005-7143-7

Testa, M., & Derrick, J. L. (2014). A daily process examination of the temporal association between alcohol use and verbal and physical aggression in community couples. *Psychology of Addictive Behaviors, 28*, 127–138. https://doi.org/10.1037/a0032988

Tomlinson, M. F., Brown, M., & Hoaken, P. N. S. (2016). Recreational drug use and human aggressive behavior: A comprehensive review since 2003. *Aggression and Violent Behavior, 27*, 9–29. https://doi.org/10.1016/j.avb.2016.02.004

Turkheimer, E. (2016). Weak genetic explanation 20 years later: Reply to Plomin et al (2016). *Perspectives on Psychological Science, 11*, 24–28. https://doi.org/10.1177/1745691615617442

Vachon, D. D., Lynam, D. R., & Johnson, J. A. (2014). The (non)relation between empathy and aggression: Some surprising results from a meta-analysis. *Psychological Bulletin, 140*, 751–773. https://doi.org/10.1037/a0035236

Van Goozen, S. H. M., Fairchild, G., Snoek, H., & Harold, G. T. (2007). The evidence for a neurobiological model of childhood antisocial behavior. *Psychological Bulletin, 133*, 149–182. https://doi.org/10.1037/0033-2909.133.1.149

Van Honk, J., Bos, P. A., & Terburg, D. (2014). Testosterone and dominance in humans: Behavioral and brain mechanisms. In J. Decety & Y. Christen (Eds.), *New frontiers in social neuroscience, research and perspectives in neurosciences* (Vol. 21, pp. 201–214). New York, NY: Springer. https://doi.org/10.1007/978-3-319-02904-7_12

Walters, R., Chiocchetti, A. G., & Freitag, C. M. (2016). The neurobiological basis of human aggression: A review on genetic and epigenetic mechanisms. *American Journal of Medical Genetics, 171B*, 650–675. https://doi.org/10.1002/ajmg.b.3238

Weinstein, M. D., Smith, M. D., & Wiesenthal, D. L. (1995). Masculinity and hockey violence. *Sex Roles, 33*, 831–847. https://doi.org/10.1007/BF01544782

Weinstein, N., Przybylski, A. K., & Murayama, K. (2017). A prospective study of the motivational and health dynamics of Internet Gaming Disorder. *PeerJ, 5, e3838*. https://doi.org/10.7717/peerj.3838

Weiss, A., King, J. E., & Enns, R. M. (2002). Subjective well-being is heritable and genetically correlated with dominance in chimpanzees (Pan troglodytes). *Journal of Personality and Social Psychology, 83*, 1141–1149. https://doi.org/10.1037/0022-3514.83.5.1141

Welker, K. W., Lozoya, E., Campbell, J. A., Neumann, C. S., & Carre, J. M. (2014). Testosterone, cortisol and psychopathic traits in men and women. *Physiology & Behavior, 129*, 230–236. https://doi.org/10.1016/j.physbeh.2014.02.057

Wertz, J., Caspi, A., Belsky, D. W., Beckley, A. L., Arseneault, L., Barnes, J. C., et al. (2018). Genetics and crime: Integrating new genomic discoveries into psychological research about antisocial behavior. *Psychological Science, 29*, 791–803. https://doi.org/10.1177/0956797617744542

Wertz, J., Zavos, H. M. S., Matthews, T., Gray, R., Best-Lane, J., Pariante, C. M., et al. (2016). Etiology of pervasive versus situational antisocial behaviors: A multi-informant longitudinal cohort study. *Child Development, 87*, 312–325. https://doi.org/10.1111/cdev.12456

Wiedeman, J. A. B., Dolle, A. L., Finney, E. J., & Coker, K. L. (2015). Factors influencing the impact of aggressive and violent media on children and adolescents. *Aggression and Violent Behavior, 25*, 191–198. https://doi.org/10.1016/j.avb.2015.04.008

Wilson, M. M. (2014). *Hate crime victimization, 2004–2012-Statistical tables*. Washington, DC: Bureau of Justice Statistics, U.S. Department of Justice.

Yang, S., Huesmann, L. R., & Bushman, B. J. (2014). Effects of playing a violent video game as a male versus female avatar on subsequent aggression in male and female players. *Aggressive Behavior*, 1–5. https://doi.org/10.1002/ab.21551

Yang, Y., Joshi, S. H., Jahanshad, N., Thompson, P. M., & Baker, L. A. (2016). Neural correlates of proactive and reactive aggression in adolescent twins. *Aggressive Behavior*, 1–11. https://doi.org/10.1002/ab.21683

Zimmer-Gembeck, M. J., Nesdale, D., Webb, H. J., Khatibi, M., & Downey, G. (2016). A longitudinal rejection sensitivity model of depression and aggression: Unique roles of anxiety, anger, blame, withdrawal and retribution. *Journal of Abnormal Child Psychology, 44*, 1291–1307. https://doi.org/10.1007/s10802-016-0127-y

Zosuls, K. M., Ruble, D. N., & Tamis-LeMonda, C. S. (2014). Self-socialization of gender in African American, Dominican immigrant, and Mexican immigrant toddlers. *Child Development, 85*, 2202–2207. https://doi.org/10.1111/cdev.12261

Chapter 3
Survivor Coping: Theories and Research About Reactions to All Types of Victimization

In this chapter, we turn to a discussion of the psychological impact of violence and abuse on those who experience this abuse. We review some of the theoretical, empirical and clinical work on general reactions to victimization, focusing on posttraumatic stress disorder (PTSD). In later chapters, we will look more specifically at the reactions of those victimized by particular types of relationship or family violence or abuse. We first review the theory and data relating to PTSD and experiences of trauma. Many of these theories refer to any type of traumatic experience, and extend beyond the types of family and partner aggression that are the focus of this book. Other types of trauma considered here would include that experienced in war, as well as accidents, or natural disasters. We then look more at posttraumatic symptoms, and at criticisms of how stress reactions are measured. Research on coping reactions and treatment for traumatic symptoms are also discussed along with the concept of resilience.

Here and elsewhere in the book, we use the term *victims* to refer to those who have experienced some form of trauma. This term is considered controversial (Hockett & Saucier, 2015). Many who have worked with women who have been raped, battered or suffered from incest or other forms of child maltreatment want to use the label of *victim* and prefer call these women *survivors* (Gondolf & Fisher, 1988). It is argued that because these women have had to overcome significant trauma, the survivor term better reflects their strengths and resilience. But, we must not forget that the victims of these crimes and other trauma have suffered from a destructive or injurious action and, as a result, may not always or primarily react in positive ways (Davis, 2014), nor should we expect that they possess superhuman strength simply because they survived trauma (Sehgal, 2016). Thus, the term *survivor* may not be a good descriptor for many who have experienced a traumatic event. Hockett and Saucier (2015) discuss the implications of these terms in more detail. We will typically use the term *victim* in this chapter to be consistent with much of the current research literature as well as government statistics relating to interpersonal violence and trauma (National Institute of Justice, 2017). However, when the empirical work refers to *survivors,* we do use this term as well.

I. H. Frieze et al., *Dynamics of Family and Intimate Partner Violence*,
https://doi.org/10.1007/978-3-030-42608-8_3

Trauma can come from many types of events, including violence in relationships. The clinical label for the psychological and physical reaction to trauma is posttraumatic stress disorder (PTSD). Other types of traumatic stress are associated with experiencing natural disasters, being in a severe automobile or other accident, military combat, being tortured and kept as a hostage, or even having a life-threatening illness (APA, 2013). Being a crime victim is also associated with PTSD (Frieze et al., 1987). Rape trauma syndrome, a reaction experienced by rape victims which closely resembles PTSD, was identified many years ago and is now included within the PTSD diagnosis (Tannura, 2014).

Witnessing others involved in traumatic events can also produce PTSD-like reactions. Perhaps for this reason, people providing care for those experiencing traumatic experiences or injuries also experience high rates of PTSD-like symptoms (Kanno & Newhill, 2009, or see Chap. 10). Some of these reactions can be seen in this example from Newhill (1995):

> "I worked as the night counselor in a battered women's shelter and because of my work hours, I saw some of the worst cases – women beaten by drunk boyfriends and husbands – at night people drink more, are more likely to be around their families and get into fights. It was very stressful and in response, I began isolating myself, not wanting to go out with friends, feeling depressed and just having general hopeless feelings about the state of the world, like feeling that the world is full of awful people and you can't trust anyone. I realized I had to get out and so I quit my job. I was good at my job but it was just too much for me over time." (Domestic violence counselor quoted in: Newhill, 1995)

3.1 Posttraumatic Stress Disorder or PTSD

The American Psychiatric Association has developed a manual listing a large variety of psychiatric diagnoses. These diagnoses are collected and published in the Diagnostic and Statistical Manual of Mental Disorders or DSM (APA, 2013). Over time, this manual has evolved as psychiatrists and other clinicians and researchers identify new disorders or change their ideas about how existing disorders should be classified. Several versions of the DSM have been published since 1952, with the latest revision, the DSM-5, published in 2013.

One of the disorders now officially recognized in the DSM is *posttraumatic stress disorder* or PTSD, which was first included in the DSM-III in 1980. The DSM-5, states that the essential feature of posttraumatic stress disorder is the "development of characteristic symptoms following exposure to one or more traumatic events….In some individuals, fear-based re-experiencing, emotional, and behavioral symptoms may predominate. In others, anhedonic or dysphoric mood states and negative cognitions may be most distressing. In some other individuals, arousal and reactive-externalizing symptoms are prominent" (APA, 2013; p. 274). To clarify, *anhedonic symptoms* involve feelings of detachment from others, and an inability to feel interest and pleasure from things and activities that normally bring enjoyment. *Dysphoria* is a mood state in which a person feels intense feelings of depression, discontent and indifference to the world around them (APA, 2013, p. 821). For example, a client said to one of the authors:

> After multiple times in which my boyfriend hit me and told me I was just a whore, I began to believe it myself. I felt worthless and horribly depressed about my life and the world. I love to read and I couldn't enjoy reading anymore – I couldn't remember what I had read when I tried to read. Food tasted like sawdust and everything around me just seemed gray.

In this example, the client describes how the abuse she endured resulted in not being able to enjoy an activity she used to love. Even enjoyment of food—something most of us derive pleasure from - had disappeared.

3.1.1 Diagnostic Criteria for PTSD

There are eight diagnostic criteria for Posttraumatic Stress Disorder in the DSM-5. These are used for adults, adolescents and children older than 6 years (see Box 3.1 or www.dsm5.org/Documents/PTSD%20Fact%20Sheet.pdf) since many cannot be measured in very young children. The first criterion (Criterion A) for PTSD is that the person was "exposed to actual or threatened death, serious injury, or sexual violence in one (or more) of the following ways: directly experiencing the traumatic event(s), witnessing in person the event(s) as it occurred to others, learning that the traumatic event(s) occurred to a close family member or close friend (in cases of actual or threatened death of a family member or friend, the event(s) must have been violent or accidental), experiencing repeated or extreme exposure to aversive details of the traumatic event(s) (e.g., first responders collecting human remains, police officers repeatedly exposed to details of child abuse)." (APA, 2013, p. 271; Newhill & Sites, 2000). An important note is that the Criterion A "does not apply to exposure through electronic media, television, movies, or pictures, unless this exposure is work related" (APA, 2013, p. 271). Some people have claimed that watching televised coverage of the 2013 Boston Marathon bombing or the aftermath of the 9/11 terrorist attack caused them to develop PTSD. However, the DSM-5 explicitly rejects this type of indirect traumatic exposure as meeting the criteria for PTSD. Other criteria for a PTSD diagnosis relate to the reactions of the person to this traumatic event.

Box 3.1: Symptoms of Post-Traumatic Stress Disorder

- Exposure to actual or threatened death, serious injury or sexual violation. The exposure must result from one or more of the following scenarios, in which the individual:
  - directly experiences the traumatic event;
  - witnesses the traumatic event in person;

  - learns that the traumatic event occurred to a close family member or close friend (with the actual or threatened death being either violent or accidental; or

- Experiences first-hand repeated or extreme exposure to aversive details of the traumatic event (not through media, pictures, television or movies unless work-related).The disturbance, regardless of its trigger, causes clinically significant distress or impairment in the individual's social interactions, capacity to work or other important areas of functioning;
- The disturbance is not the physiological result of another medical condition, medication, drugs or alcohol
- Behavioral symptoms that accompany PTSD may be categorized into four distinct diagnostic clusters. These clusters are described as:

  - Re-experiencing: covers spontaneous memories of the traumatic event, recurrent dreams related to it, flashbacks, or other intense or prolonged psychological distress;
  - Avoidance: refers to distressing memories, thoughts, feelings, or external reminders of the event that one wishes to avoid;
  - Negative cognitions and mood: represents myriad feelings, from a persistent and distorted sense of blame of self or others, to estrangement from others or markedly diminished interest in activities, to an inability to remember key aspects of the event;
  - Arousal: is marked by aggressive, reckless or self-destructive behavior, sleep disturbances, hyper-vigilance or related problems.
  - The number of symptoms that must be identified depends on the cluster. DSM-5 would only require that a disturbance continue for more than a month and would eliminate the distinction between acute and chronic phases of PTSD

From the DSM-5 (APA, 2013).

3.1.2 PTSD Reactions to Trauma

The American Psychiatric Association (2013) estimates that in the United States, the lifetime risk for developing PTSD by the time an individual reaches 75 years of age is approximately 8.7%. Rates in other parts of the world, including most Asian, African and Latin American countries, are significantly lower, around 0.5–1.0%. Different groups, by virtue of occupation and life experiences, have different rates of PTSD, and not everyone exposed to the same stressor has the same reaction. The highest rates of PTSD have been found among war combat veterans and others whose occupations have a high risk of exposure to traumatic situations, such as police officers, firefighters, emergency medical personnel and other first responders to disaster (Richardson, Frueh, & Acierno, 2010). [Even so, most individuals in such high-risk occupations, even when exposed repeatedly to traumatic stressors, do not go on to develop full-threshold PTSD, although many may evidence subthreshold symptoms, meaning that they don't meet full criteria for the disorder but do suffer some of the symptoms (APA, 2013).]

As outlined in the DSM-5, people react to trauma experiences in a variety of ways. Many report heightened levels of anxiety. This anxiety can be expressed as outbursts of anger, irritability, or sleep disorders (including nightmare relating to the traumatic event). Some people may handle their anxiety by withdrawing and isolating themselves from others. People experiencing PTSD may have difficulty concentrating and doing the tasks of everyday life. They might also appear to be less emotional than previously and may not enjoy things they had done previously. For example, in the quote from the client above, she stated that she always loved to read but, following the trauma of being physically and emotionally abused by her boyfriend, she couldn't enjoy reading and couldn't concentrate when she tried to read. Problems with sexual responding are also common for those with PTSD, particularly for those who have suffered sexual forms of trauma, such as sexual abuse or rape (Meston & Lorenz, 2013). Any of these reactions generally occur soon after the precipitating event, but can be delayed several weeks. Effects of traumatic exposure to an avalanche in Iceland were found 16 years later (Thordardottir et al., 2015), so the effects of exposure can last for many years.

3.1.2.1 Intrusive Cognitions

In a review of the literature, Iyadural and her colleagues in Europe (Iyadural et al., 2019) argued that intrusive memories of a traumatic event were a core feature of PTSD. Such memories are quite distressing and intrude involuntarily into daily life for someone exposed to earlier trauma. They discussed why such memories occurred and outlined treatments that might be effective in lessening such memories. Such intrusive thoughts were often reported by a sample of adults at a Danish treatment providing psychological treatment for victims of child sex abuse (McBride, Hyland, Murphy, & Elklit, 2019). Others in this sample reported doing things to avoid these memories, while some said they were not able to remember parts of the trauma. It is interesting to contrast such findings with other research suggesting that people may repress memories of early trauma, especially child sexual abuse (see Chap. 6). Englehard, McNally, and van Schie (2019) suggested that one explanation that might explain why young children would not remember early sexual abuse was that they did not understand what was happening at the time, and thus did not clearly remember the abuse, but later, might recall this when they more fully understood the meaning of this abuse.

The findings on intrusive memories have been expanded to include a more general concept of intrusive cognitions (Oulton, Strange, Nixon, & Takarangi, 2018). As Oulton and her colleagues have discussed, the spontaneous thoughts arising after experiencing a trauma are not always memories. Some are images of what might have happened, or what could happen in the future. Such images can be quite vivid.

They may also function to maintain negative reactions to earlier trauma by creating expectations for new trauma experiences. Berntsen and Rubin (2015) labeled these types of images as "Pretraumatic stress reactions" (p. 663). As they noted, people who have not experienced previous trauma, as well as those who have, may experience thoughts about possible future events. In a study of Danish soldiers before deployment, ratings of how stressful they felt future events might be predicted levels of PTSD after deployment. Although not directly tested, Berntsen and Rubin hypothesized that those already experiencing PTSD-related symptoms might be especially likely to have concerns about future traumatic events.

Similar ideas can be seen in a Turkish study of domestic violence survivors (Salcioglu, Urhan, Pirinccioglu, & Aydin, 2017). In this study, Salcioglu et al. surveyed women from domestic violence shelters in Turkey. Although the mean number of months since last assaulted was nearly 10 months, many of the women reported being fearful about being subjected to future violence. Concerns about feeling helpless and not having control over their lives in the future were also common responses. These reports appeared to fit the framework of being pre-traumatic stress reactions since they were associated more with fears about the future than with reactions to past trauma.

3.1.2.2 Other Types of Reactions to Trauma

Another type of reaction to trauma associated especially with veterans is increased levels of violence and aggression in everyday life. A sample of 175 returning U.S. veterans from Iraq found that PTSD was associated with depression and generalized anger and aggression (Bhardwaj, Angkaw, Franceschetti, Rao, & Baker, 2019). Depression was a mediator that led to higher levels of hostility and aggression toward the self. PTSD was also directly related to anger. This association between PTSD and aggression has been used successfully as a defense for veterans in homicide trials, citing PTSD-related insanity as a causal factor (Miller, 2012).

Responses of the victim are not only emotional, but can also be manifested in physical ways. PTSD may result in physical illness, resulting from a less effective immune system (Pietrzak et al., 2013). Heightened norepinephrine levels were found to be associated with PTSD in a systematic review and meta-analysis by Pan, Kaminga, Wen, and Liu (2018). Norepinephrine is considered as a biological indicator of stress and may relate to some of the reported symptoms associated with PTSD. Cortisol, another stress indictor in the blood (see Chap. 2), was found in an empirical study of people exposed to workplace violence in a Canadian psychiatric hospital (Marin et al., 2019).

3.1.3 Clinical Example

The clinical cases in the Appendix illustrate the traumatic circumstances that can lead to PTSD as well as the common symptoms associated with such trauma reactions. Here is one example.

Case Example #2

"Joyce" is a 22-year-old single African-American woman who, under extreme stress, came to the crisis clinic with her 4 year old daughter for help because of trauma flashbacks and periods of dissociation. Joyce tells the crisis worker that a little over 2 years ago, she started going out with a man named "George". Their relationship went well at first, and so she allowed him to move with her (her other child, a 2-year-old boy, is his biological child). Soon, however, George started beating Joyce frequently and severely. Once he beat her breasts so badly they got infected and she had to have surgery. Joyce finally kicked George out of the house, but he continued to come around and abuse her—he would follow her in parks and on the street, and then would attack her. Sometimes she was successful in pressing charges and having him put in jail, but recently the police had been unwilling to act on her complaints.

Joyce tried to get help from every resource she could think of including the police (repeatedly), the local district attorney, and Haven House* (the local domestic violence shelter), but got nowhere. The situation had progressed to the point that George was calling her constantly and threatening that he was going to kill her. Joyce developed ulcers, couldn't sleep, had problems concentrating and lost weight. When she was able to fall asleep, Joyce reported having nightmares related to the abuse. George had also beaten Joyce's two children, and the children began having nightmares, flashbacks of the abuse, angry outbursts and showed fear toward adult men in general. Finally, in desperation, Joyce borrowed a gun from her sister, and after a particularly brutal beating in which George poked Joyce's eye in with a stick (she required many stitches), she finally went out, found George sitting on a park bench, and after much deliberation, walked up and shot him. She then went to a pay phone and turned herself in to the police. Joyce states that for the first time—sitting in jail - she felt safe.

George did not die from the gunshot wound and was still recovering in the county hospital when Joyce came to the crisis clinic for help. The crisis worker called Haven House and they said they now had room for Joyce and her children (they didn't before, which is why they couldn't help her previously) and staff agreed to come down to the clinic immediately to pick them up. Joyce's sister had posted her bail. Joyce states that her nerves are so bad, she has had no sleep in days, and is at the end of her rope. The crisis worker referred her to the crisis psychiatrist for temporary medication (Joyce does not drink or use illicit drugs) and the doctor prescribed valium, 10 mg. twice a day.

In this case scenario, the client Joyce met full criteria for a diagnosis of post-traumatic stress disorder, as did her young children. Joyce was repeatedly exposed to threatened death and actual serious injury via directly experiencing George's brutal abuse. In addition, she witnessed the physical abuse of her children. Joyce experienced symptoms across all of the criteria for the PTSD disorder, causing significant physical and emotional distress and interference with her daily life because of this.

Looking at her symptoms in more detail, one can see how PTSD reactions function. First, Joyce experienced intrusive *re-experiencing symptoms*, i.e. recurrent, involuntary and intrusive memories and traumatic nightmares (as did her children). She also reported *avoidance*, i.e. repeated efforts to avoid encountering George. Joyce's children, in fact, were fearful and avoidant toward all adult men. Third, Joyce reported *negative alterations in cognitions and mood*, i.e. as a result of the abuse, she came to perceive the world as a dangerous place and viewed men in general as potentially dangerous. At times, Joyce blamed herself for the abuse, particularly for not being able to protect her children, and thus felt persistent feelings of fear, guilt, anger and shame. Self-blame is a common reaction by victims (see Box 3.2). Finally, both Joyce and her children showed *alterations in arousal and reactivity*, i.e. Joyce became hypervigilant, had problems concentrating, and had severe problems sleeping. Her children also had problems sleeping and were irritable and exhibited angry outbursts. Joyce did not use drugs or alcohol so that was ruled out as a cause of her symptoms and she did not report any medical conditions that could be potential causes. Finally, she reported periods of dissociation, particularly during and after incidents of abuse in which she experienced feeling as if she were an outside observer of or detached from herself, e.g. feeling like "this is not happening to me" or as if she were in a dream or a movie.

Box 3.2: Forms of self blame

People often blame themselves for being victimized by a traumatic event and some forms of self blame focus on the self as bad while others focus on blaming a person's choices or decisions. Each form of self blame has different psychological correlates and future consequences:

1. **Blaming oneself for being a bad person**. *I deserved this because of the type of person I am.* any negative implications for believing that one can easily be a victim again.
2. **Blaming oneself for being an unlucky person**. *I am a loser and these things always seem to happen and they will probably happen again.* Such a belief would be associated with low feelings of control and high anxiety for the future.

3. **Blaming one's past choices and behavior**. *I should have known better and not done that.* If the individual believes he or she can change their behavior, then there are relatively few negative implications regarding beliefs about future victimization.
4. **Blaming oneself for making poor choices in relationships.** *I should have known he was abusive and never married him. I deserve what has happened.* Such beliefs would not have positive future implications.
5. **Blaming one's "former self".** *I did stupid things before, but I have changed and would no longer do the same things.* Such beliefs provide optimism for the future.
6. **Feeling responsible for changing the future**. *If I make sure to make my home safer, no one can break in again.* If the necessary actions are feasible, the person may feel very secure about the future.
7. **Feeling responsible for minimizing ones stress reactions**. *I am feeling very upset now about being victimized, but I can do things to make myself feel better.* This type of self responsibility is oriented toward the present and may or may not have long term implications.

Joyce's experiences of abuse were extreme, and the trauma experienced was severe. It is not necessary to experience trauma as severe as what Joyce and her children went through to develop PTSD, but Joyce's experience provides a clinical illustration of how the various symptoms can co-exist in one individual and one family. This case also illustrates how even when an abused victim takes all the right steps, including evicting the abuser from the home and contacting the police for help, she may not get the help she needs and, with escalation of the abuse via threats and stalking, may resort to using a violent action to fight back.

3.1.4 Research Relating to the Diagnosis of PTSD

Although the PTSD diagnosis was developed by the American Psychiatric Association, this classification is used widely in other countries as well as in the U.S.. In 2018 Fried et al. published results of a multi-site study to examine the question of whether the set of PTSD symptoms identified in the DSM were generally found together in samples from the Netherlands, Denmark, and military veterans from the Middle East. Everyone in the samples from this research project had been formally diagnosed with PTSD, using standard procedures. Across all four groups, the most common symptoms were similar to those of Joyce, the case we described earlier. Within the Fried et al. samples, the most common reactions were memory intrusions, sleep problems and hypervigilance. Overall, the veteran group had the highest levels of symptoms. Along with the other generally high symptoms, many of them also suffered from problems concentrating, feeling a need to avoid places or things, and heightened physiological reactivity. A detailed analysis of how symptoms inter-related indicated that similar patterns of symptoms were found across the four groups.

In a Swedish study of people who directly experienced a tsunami while on vacation in Asia, Bondjers, Willebrand, and Arnberg (2018) found the about 25% reported no posttraumatic stress symptoms. Among the rest of the sample, there were four levels of symptom severity reported in response to a mailed survey. Severity ranged from minimal, to low, moderate and severe. A follow-up survey indicated that the initial severity of reactions was highly predictive of experiences reported 3 years later. Those survivors who lost a friend or relative or who personally felt their live was threatened were least likely to be in the low symptom group, but their symptoms ranged from low to severe.

These studies suggest that the PTSD diagnosis may not indicate that someone has all the symptoms associated with this psychiatric diagnosis. It also demonstrates that many people who do experience events that would appear to be highly traumacized do not necessarily develop PTSD, although they may have some of the symptoms. These findings and others raise questions about the DSM-5 PTSD diagnosis, as we explore in more detail in the next section of the chapter.

3.1.5 *Criticisms of DSM-5 and the ICD-11, an International Classification System for Reactions to Trauma*

There have been many criticisms of the DSM approach of the American Psychiatric Association. One of the earliest concerns related to whether or not this was an appropriate label for battered women or rape survivors who had been traumatized by the assault(s) (see Box 3.3). This basic concern related to the diagnosis itself. With its inclusion as a formal psychiatric diagnosis, by definition, PTSD became one of many psychiatric illnesses. It was argued that this resulted in blaming the woman who had been raped or survived physical violence from her husband, since she was now defined as having a mental illness.

Box 3.3: Should we use the DSM to label female victims?
Many feminist scholars have critiqued the psychiatric/medical model approach of the DSM, particularly when assessing the impact and consequences of male violence toward female victims (Dodd, 2015; Koss, Bailey, Yuan, Herrera, & Lichter, 2003). These writers argue that labeling a woman who has survived trauma as having a psychiatric illness situates the problem with the woman rather than as a problem related to male socialization around power and control which would lead to different approaches toward prevention. Psychiatrist Allen Frances, who was chair of the DSM-IV Task Force, has been one of the outspoken critics of the current DSM-5, arguing that the most recent version, in particular, has cast too wide a net and has gone so far as to label normal human experiences as mental disorders (Frances, 2013). Haslam (2016) refers to this as "concept creep" which refers to the boundaries of a concept, such as PTSD, stretching to the point that its meaning becomes diluted and overextended. To experience significant distress after being beaten by an intimate partner is a normal reaction, not a mental disorder or "psychological problem". However, on the other side of the argument, individuals suffering from symptoms consistent with how PTSD is described, are suffering psychological and emotional distress that may impair their ability to function, e.g. to go to work or take care of their children. Although they have been victimized by violence, such individuals may still benefit from getting treatment for their symptoms and withholding treatment based on ideological convictions is not justified nor does providing treatment preclude simultaneously working on methods for preventing such violence and ensuring perpetrators are held responsible for their actions. Providing an appropriate diagnosis serves to guide treatment and make sure that an individual receives appropriate treatment that will help and not harm.

Many other types of criticisms have been raised specifically about the DSM-5. Galatzer-Levy and Bryant (2013) argued that the DSM-5 was a "broad and error-prone diagnostic scheme…" (p. 660). Many scholars have questioned the growing number of events considered traumatic (e.g., Carvajal, 2018; Haslam, 2016). Over time, the types of events included within the PTSD definition of trauma have continued to expand, meaning more and more people are diagnosed with PTSD (McNally, 2016). At the same time, as seen in the Bondjers et al. (2018) study of Swedish tourists discussed above, many people do not show evidence of the many PTSD symptoms in spite of experiencing events most would consider to be highly traumatic. Carvajal (2018) argued that only about 20% of people exposed to one of the many events considered to be potentially traumatic showed evidence of PTSD. Additionally, few had all the symptoms associated with the DSM-5 diagnosis. He noted that the new International Classification of Disease (ICD-11) developed by the United Nations World Health Organization (2018) (see https://www.who.int/classifications/icd/en/) might be a more accurate reflection of the empirical data on reactions to trauma. The World Health Organization released the ICD-11 in June 2018. Like the DSM, this is a diagnostic system that includes mental illness classifications. It also includes a wide variety of diseases and health conditions and is used widely around the world. For more information on the ICD-11 as it relates to traumatic stress, see Cloitre et al. (2018) who reported on the scale being developed to formally measure reactions to trauma using this diagnostic system.

It does appear that the DSM-5 and the ICD-11 diagnoses do yield somewhat different information. A formal comparison of a group of patients in Australia diagnosed with PTSD after receiving a severe injury indicated that fewer were diagnosed with PTSD, using the ICD-11 (O'Donnell et al., 2014). However, within this group of patients, each of the two systems identified somewhat different groups who would meet the traumatic stress requirement. In another comparison of these systems, Hansen et al. (2017) analyzed data from the sample reported in the Fried et al. (2018) sample to compare the two classification systems. Results indicated that the two systems were similar in making diagnoses for the pain patient sample and for the military personnel who had been deployed in the Middle East. However, a student sample yielded far fewer PTSD diagnoses for the ICD-11 system than the DSM-5. The authors noted that mental illness rates were much lower overall in the student sample, and many of these students did not meet criteria using the ICD-11 system.

A third major classification system for mental disorders is now being developed by the U.S. National Institute of Mental Health (NIMH) (Clark, Cuthbert, Lewis-Fernández, Narrow, & Reed, 2017). This system is intended to aid in understanding how mental disorders develop, rather than being used primarily for diagnosis, as the DSM and ICD are typically utilized. This new Research Domain Criteria (RDoC) project will draw on advances in behavioral and neuroscience research. An ultimate goal of this project is to better understand how the brain and behavior relate to one another as this relates to psychopathology. As Clark and her colleagues explained this initiative in detail, they also provided an excellent review of the history of and a comparison of the DSM and ICD approaches.

3.1.6 A Closer Look at PTSD and Determining the Severity of "Traumatic" Events

A large body of work has attempted to measure the severity of traumatic events, based on the assumption that overall PTSD rates and levels of PTRS-related symptoms should be higher for more serious types of traumas (e.g., Rubin & Feeling, 2013). In contrast to this work that shows some events to be more traumatic than other events, other research has indicated that even when exposed to events that some would consider to be quite serious, such as a life-threatening natural disaster, not everyone experiences PTSD. At the same time, other types of events, such as microaggressions, that are unintended and not considered serious by many people, have been shown to correlate with PTSD symptoms . Such findings raise questions about what types of events should be considered traumatic. In this section we review some of the research relating to severity levels of different potentially traumatic events.

3.1.6.1 Defining Severity Levels for Trauma

Research has suggested that PTSD rates may be higher after certain types of trauma. For example, trauma caused by acts of humans, rather than so-called acts of God or nature, may produce more severe trauma reactions. Thus, rates of PTSD tend to be high for survivors of child maltreatment (Cicchetti, 2016) and for battered women (Walker, 2016). Childhood trauma, IPV and sexual assault were most associated with PTSD in a national sample of U.S. women (Lipsky, Kernic, Qiu, & Hasin, 2016). Lipsky and her colleagues also reported that this pattern could be seen for non-Hispanic White, non-Hispanic Black and Hispanic women in the sample.

The effect of the trauma being attributed to an event caused by specific people can also be seen in the interviews of survivors of the Buffalo Creek, West Virginia, dam collapse and flood in 1972, 14 years after the disaster occurred. This was one of the worst coal industry disasters in West Virginia history. Over 100 people were killed and another 1100 were injured. The flooding left about 4000 homeless. Data indicated that 65% of the sample had experienced some form of PTSD or other traumatic reaction to the events (Green et al., 1990; Green et al., 1990). In 2012, West Virginia marked the 40th anniversary in Man, the town near where the flood occurred in Buffalo Creek, by showing slides of the disaster as well as holding a reading of the names of those who died in the flood. Survivor Bill Owens, 54, remembered the day when a wall of water and debris swept away his town, killing five of his family members. The memories remain highly painful, Owens told the Charleston Gazette in an interview: "This is the first (memorial) that I've been to," he said. "That's how hard it is for me." (Associated Press, 2012).

In the case of the Buffalo Creek disaster, as the causes of the flooding were investigated, evidence mounted that the Pittston Coal Company officials knew that dumping coal refuse into the dam might result in stressing the dam's ability to hold the water and debris, leading to a flood. This revelation heightened survivors' feelings of shock and trauma (Governor's Ad Hoc Commission of Inquiry, 1973) because it appeared that the flood could have been prevented if the coal company officials had taken proper action. Thus, the trauma was caused more by acts of humans, rather than an unavoidable accident or act of nature, as some initially thought.

When one is victimized through the actions of another person, this may cause changes in our beliefs about other people. Most of us generally trust other people (Dunning, Fetchenhauer, & Schlosser, 2019), especially those we are close to. When we are assaulted by someone, especially someone close to us, we may change these beliefs about the world. This type of reaction is identified in the DSM-5 as one of the reactions associated with Criterion D: "Persistent and exaggerated negative beliefs or expectations about oneself, others, or the world" (American Psychiatric Association, 2013, p. 272). One of the examples given for this is the belief that others cannot be trusted. Another is the idea that the world is completely dangerous. Such changes in one's world view are especially difficult for the victimized child, since he or she may never develop the basic feelings of safety and trust that are associated with daily life for most adults (Macmillan, 2001).

Other research has concluded that exposure to trauma has more negative consequences when this occurs early in life than later traumas do. This was demonstrated in a study by Ogle, Rubin, and Siegler (2013). A sample of alumni from the University of North Carolina and their spouses was used to determine how people reacted to traumas experienced at different times in their lives. Members of this 60–70 year old sample were asked if they had experienced any of a set of events determined to be traumatic at various points in their lives and what reactions they now had to these events. The most commonly mentioned childhood event was witnessing family violence, followed by sexual assault. For older groups, the most traumatic event was the unexpected death of a loved one. The self-reported PTSD symptoms associated with the childhood events were more severe than those associated with events at older ages. Those experiencing early trauma also reported higher levels of current PTSD symptoms.

3.1.6.2 Microaggressions

The example of microaggressions provides evidence that incidents that some would argue are not important (Lilienfeld, 2017) can rise to the level of trauma for the recipient. Although the term *microaggression* has been in the literature since the late twentieth century, it has received little attention until this century (Lilienfeld, 2017). College campuses are now increasingly attempting to educate people about this type of aggression and acting to diminish this behavior. Lilienfeld argued that the term is not well defined but is generally associated with subtle insults or slights directed at women and minorities. Research has demonstrated the existence of microaggressions directed toward people of color, women, those involved in the LGBTQ community, and older adults (Lui & Quezada, 2019) as well as those in blue collar groups (Cook & O'Hara, 2019) and those belonging to religious minorities such as Jews and Muslims (Hodge, 2019).

Microaggressive behavior is believed to be based on (sometimes nonconscious) negative stereotypes of various groups (Lui & Quezada, 2019). This might include ignoring someone in a group conversation (something men are accused of doing to women) or using derogative terms to refer to some group membership. It could be expressing surprise when a member of a group not believed to be intelligent demonstrates a high level of performance.

Lui and Quezada presented a formal meta-analysis of published and unpublished studies and dissertations investigating microaggressions through February 2018. A total of 72 studies were identified. Across all types of samples, there was clear evidence of negative effects for the targets of microaggressions. Other analyses indicated a correlation between those experiencing microaggressions and more overt forms of discrimination. Supplementing these findings, Moody and Lewis (2019) found that Black women who had experienced higher levels of microaggression against them also had higher levels of posttraumatic stress symptoms.

3.1.6.3 PTSD and Trauma Severity

Although there is clear evidence that some types of events are more likely to result in PTSD than others, there is also data indicating that objective ratings of the severity of trauma are not necessarily reflected in symptom severity. For example, one type of potentially traumatic event is having a life-threatening injury. Boals, Trost, Rainey, Foreman, and Warren (2017) were able to draw on medical data from injured patients at a Level 1 Trauma Center. Medical assessments were made for a sample of 460 patients. Screening data from the hospital and self reports of PTSD symptoms were also collected for these patients at the time of admission, as well as 3 and 6 months later. Analyses indicated that there was no significant relationship between the severity of the injury and the PTSD measures. However, the injury severity measures were found to predict depression, pain and physical health 6 months after the injury. Boals et al. argued that psychological distress is determined by many factors such as personality, prior trauma history, levels of social support and other variables unrelated to the traumatic event.

Others have made similar arguments. Rubin and Feeling (2013) used four different samples to investigate the relationship between objectively measured severity levels of potentially traumatic events to symptom severity experienced after one experienced an event that was seen as the "most troubling and stressful to you now" (p. 378, Rubin & Feeling, 2013). There was not a significant correlation between the objective severity of the event and the severity of PTSD symptoms. Bolvin and Marx (2011) in a major review of the DSM-5 and symptom severity research also noted that symptoms vary widely across individuals in reactions to the same type of event. Building and extending these ideas, McNally (2016) noted that people vary in assessing severity levels of events based on their own past history, as well as their knowledge of what types of events people are being exposed to around the world.

3.1.7 Trauma Reactions and Victims' Fears about Further Victimization

As was demonstrated with reactions to microaggressions, trauma victims' initial emotional reactions are sometimes greater than might be predicted solely on the basis of the actual harm or injury sustained as a result of the traumatic event. One reason for this is that just the experience of being confronted with a traumatic event can raise fears for the future and possibly something even worse occurring. Archer's (2019) study of a large sample of U.S. college students provided empirical data supporting this idea. He found that those who personally experienced a sexual assault [as well as those who knew someone who had this experience] had a greater level of fear about being victimized again than they had had previously. Archer also noted that these new fears led to self-protective behaviors such as carrying mace or a weapon or something that could be used as a weapon or asking someone to accompany you when walking at night. Although women overall had higher levels of sexual assault fears than men, both men and women developed higher levels of fear after being personally victimized or knowing someone else who was.

It does appear that when we are concerned about potentially being confronted with a traumatic or difficult event, we tend to take protective actions if we can. Such actions can be thought of as personal safety rules (see Box 3.4). Once these protective actions or guidelines have been developed, we believe that following them will keep us safe and free from future harm (Ruhs, Greve, & Kappes, 2017). In a qualitative study of Australian adolescents, Fileborn (2016) asked both men and women to describe things that contributed to their feeling safe when they went out for the evening. The large majority of both women and men reported usually or always feeling safe in these situations in the past, but perhaps this was because of their having strategies for being safe. Some strategies identified included making sure there were friends nearby or not getting too drunk. Both men and women described initial concerns about assault from men, but typically had strategies they used to make sure this did not happen.

Box 3.4: Personal Safety Rules

Many people follow personal safety rules that can help keep them safe in their daily lives. Police departments and other safety organizations offer lists of safety rules shown to be effective in enhancing personal safety. Below is a list of some of these personal safety rules (Griffin, Montsinger & Carter, 1995; Montclair Safety & Improvement Council, 2016)

- Avoid high crime areas, especially at night. If you must venture into such an area, go with a friend or family member, and let others know where you are going and when you will return.
- Be aware of your surroundings at all times, walk with a strong stride and posture so you do not appear as someone who could be easily victimized.
- Keep mace or pepper spray in your pocket or purse and carry it when out, particularly at night.
- Always leave your headlights on when arriving home after dark until you have unlocked the garage door, or unlocked the front door.
- When driving, keep car doors and windows locked.
- When arriving home by private auto or taxi, ask the driver to wait unto you are safely inside.
- Have the door key in your hand so you can open the door immediately when you return home.

- If you are a woman alone, list only your first initial and last name on the mailbox, or in the telephone directory.
- When moving into a new apartment or residence, always have the locks re-keyed, or changed.
- Know who is at your door before opening it. Wide angle door viewers (180° or 190°) enable you to identify the visitor. You can see the person, that person can't see you.
- Never rely on chain locks. They are a privacy lock, but not a security lock.
- Never dress in front of windows, always close your drapes and keep doors and windows locked.
- Never let anyone into your home without proper identification. Don't be afraid to ask for identification.
- Never let strangers into your home to use the telephone. Make the call for them while they wait outside.
- Always leave outside lights on after dark, or use motion lights.
- If you receive a wrong number phone call, don't give out your name or phone number.
- If you receive an obscene phone call, hang up and call police.
- In an apartment building, never ever be alone in the laundry room.
- If you suspect anyone is in your house, do not go in. Go to a neighbor and call the police.
- If you see or hear anything suspicious, call the police.

(for more information see the Montclair Safety & Improvement Council website: http://www.montclairsic.org/index.htm

This list shows that personal safety rules are often primarily focused on keeping one safe from criminal behavior of strangers or casual acquaintances, and avoiding potentially harmful accidents such as fires or flood damage. This is all important. What is often missing is rules that can help us avoid being victimized by abuse from individuals we know and may care about and trust. It can be devastating when such trust appears to be misplaced.

We may believe that we are particularly skillful in protecting ourselves from harm because of our own personal safety behaviors. For example, people often assume they are able to safely use a cell phone while driving, although they fear that others won't be able to do this as well as we can (Sanbonmatsu, Strayer, Behrends, Ward, & Watson, 2016). In another demonstration of this bias, Horswill and his Australian colleagues (Horswill, Garth, Hill, & Watson, 2017) have found that people generally overestimate how skilled they are at driving, rating themselves as more skillful than the typical driver.

Fears about future trauma can also be created by the media (Furedi, 2018). As Fuerdi discussed in his 2018 book, the twenty-first century appears to be one in which there is a higher overall level of fear about crime and other negative things happening than was true in the twentieth century. He argued that the media has been a major reason for this. If, indeed, people are more fearful now than in earlier years, perhaps this relates to a perceived inability to counter the feared event?

In general, experiencing a traumatic event is not something we generally expect. Research largely conducted in the twentieth century indicated that many of us go through life assuming that we are basically safe from harm and that negative events are more likely to happen to others than to us. This is labeled as a *perception of personal invulnerability* or *unrealistic optimism* (Sharot, Korn, & Dolan, 2011). People were found to generally want to believe that the world is rational and that things happen for a reason. Furthermore, we may assume that the reasons that the bad things that happen to others don't apply to us (Janoff-Bulman, 1992). We may assume that other people are victimized because they made bad or foolish decisions and, thus, deserve what happens to them (Janoff-Bulman, 1992; Niemi & Young, 2016). For example, we may assume that if a woman wears scanty clothing and suffers a sexual assault, then all a woman needs to do to be safe is to dress modestly. This can extend to thinking that a scantily dressed woman is "asking" to be assaulted or is "bringing it on herself" and, thus, the assault is her fault. When we apply these assumptions to ourselves after being personally victimized, then we may experience self-blame (see Box 3.2 earlier in the chapter).

3.2 Coping with Traumatic or Stressful Experiences

Researchers and clinicians have identified a wide range of coping responses that people use in response to stress, including the stress associated with traumatic events and the experience of victimization. Probably the most widely-cited typology differentiates between problem-focused coping and emotion-focused ways of coping (Folkman & Lazarus, 1985, 1988). Folkman and Lazarus identified a two-stage process for dealing with stress. First is the appraisal where one judges whether a situation is irrelevant, positive or stressful. Next, a stressful situation is determined to be a threat, a challenge or a harm or loss. This second part of the appraisal depends on how well the persons believes she or he can cope with the situation. This coping can either address the emotions arising from the situation or try to solve the problems that created the situation. Emotion-focused forms of coping include distancing oneself from the situation emotionally, exerting self control, seeking social support, employing ways to escape or avoid the situation, which may be constructive (e.g. changing one's phone number so an abusive boyfriend cannot get in contact) or destructive behavior (e.g. drug or alcohol use), accepting responsibility, and positive reappraisal, which therapists call *reframing*. Problem-focused forms of coping can include aggressive interpersonal efforts to alter the situation, as well as cool, rational, deliberate efforts to problem solve. Over time, researchers have identified many examples of both types of coping. In the discussion here, the focus is on forms of coping that have been found to be especially important for trauma victims because how one copes with a traumatic experience can have a long term impact on mental and physical health (Hager & Runtz, 2012). In general, problem-focused coping tends to have a more positive impact on the reduction of stress than emotion-focused coping, but not always.

Although the basic Folkman and Lazarus model is still used in many research studies, a major expansion and elaboration of the model has been increasingly cited (Carver & Connor-Smith, 2010). As Carver and Connor-Smith explain, if the initial assessment of a situation suggests a negative outcome, stress is created. If that assessment, instead, is that the situation provides a challenge or opportunity for gain if one applies effort, there is little stress, assuming one has a high expectation for success. If stress is created, emotion-focused coping attempts to minimize distress. However, such attempts can include disengagement-related behaviors such as avoidance, denial, wishful thinking, or substance which do little, if anything, to change the situation creating the stress and may make it worse. Emotion-focused coping can also include behaviors such as seeking emotional support from others, or redefining or restructuring how the stressor is perceived, which can be highly effective in reducing stress. They might also involve relaxing that would allow one to more clearly consider the problem, and perhaps move to problem-focused coping attempts.

Carver and Connor-Smith discuss ways in which problem-focused strategies can be successful in removing the stress if they involve directing engaging with the potentially stressful situation. However, problem-focused coping might involve distracting the self through doing something else, or through accepting the situation, and, thus, not lead to removing the stress. They also note that one might be able to anticipate a difficult event in the future and take proactive steps in advance to prevent the event a topic discussed earlier. In the following more detailed discussion, we report on studies using both of these models, as well as other elaborations of the original Folkman and Lazarus model.

3.3 Problem-Focused Coping Strategies

As this chapter has shown, the experience of a traumatic event creates a variety of effects in the victim of that event. Not only are there physical or other direct effects, but there are also psychological effects that may create stress or anxiety. In additional to coping with the immediate effects of the trauma, the victim may have fears that the same thing, or something even worse could happen in the future. People think about what happened and try to understand what happened and why it happened. They want to make sure it won't happen again.

3.3.1 Blaming Oneself After Being Victimized

A common response in thinking about what happened is to think about what one might have done differently, a process associated with self blame (see Box 3.2). In a classic paper, Janoff-Bulman (1979) outlined two different ways in which this self blame might function. It can be characterological or behavioral self-blame Characterological blame involves seeing the cause as something basic to one's personality, and not easily changeable. Behavioral blame looks to specific behaviors that might have made the negative event more likely. These can be changed in the future.

Although one might assume that self blame would have negative consequences for the victim, researchers have speculated that it can be beneficial, especially for events that are unlikely to reoccur or where there is a clear way in which one might have acted differently. If the victim can identify things she might have done differently, she can then decide that doing these things in the future will lead to her being safe and, thus, restore her sense of personal invulnerability. Of course, such self-blaming is probably not beneficial when the victimizer is an intimate partner or a parent or caregiver. In such cases, it would be unlikely that the victim could completely avoid future victimization by acting differently if she (or he) remains with the violent intimate partner or family member.

One form of self blame that appears to be helpful is sometimes seen in battered women who have successfully left their abusers. These women might blame their "former self" for staying, and feel that they have now changed (Meerholz et al., 2019). Such blame of a former self and seeing oneself as now being a better person may also be related to finding meaning in the victimizing event (McFarland & Alvaro, 2000). Self blame can also take a very destructive form including inducing guilt, shame and elevated risk for PTSD. For example, these thoughts about what might have been done differently can lead to feeling guilty for not doing these things (Kahn & Mathie, 2000). Even more distressing, if one blames one's basic personality for the victimization, this can't be readily changed, and there is no reassurance that the future can be better which can induce feelings of hopelessness and helplessness (Janoff-Bulman & Frieze, 1983).

A study of sixty-three women who had experienced IPV reported that shame, guilt-related distress, and guilt-related cognitions showed significant associations with symptoms of PTSD (Beck et al., 2011). In an earlier study, Silver, Boon and Stones (1983) found that victims of incest who continued to ask "why me" and to blame themselves for being victimized were more distressed than those who did not continue to ponder these issues. These data would suggest that beneficial self blame is likely to be an early response to being victimized. A continuing pattern of self blaming, however, may be indicative of non-recovery. Self blaming and guilt may become a general pattern of reacting to other negative events. Individuals who suffered abuse perpetrated by a close other such as a parent, are at particular risk of self-blame for incidents of abuse suffered as an adults (Babcock & DePrince, 2012).

3.3.2 *Taking Action to Make Sure It Won't Happen Again*

Another category of coping responses involves some form of problem solving or taking action to solve the problem. The actions involved might have been determined by earlier thinking about what happened and why. For example, a person can take a class to learn self-defense skills in order to learn how to fight back as a way to avoid being victimized again (Hollander, 2014). Or, one can become more cautious and careful in daily life, as noted in the earlier discussion of personal safety rules.

There has been extensive research about how people respond to having experienced a home break in or who fear this happening. People who have experienced a burglary or break in of their home may take a number of precautions to prevent another break in including purchasing locks, installing window bars or getting a guard dog (Wollinger, 2017). Others may buy a gun and obtain training for using it (Schreck, Berg, Fisher, & Wilcox, 2018). Such strategies, however, would not be effective in protecting against assault from someone in a close relationship, particularly if the abuser lives with the victim.

Safety planning in case of a future potential assault is a major concern for battered women (Logan, 2018 or see Chap. 8). This is often a focus of assistance provided at battered women's centers or other domestic violence agencies. One form of safety seeking is leaving the abusive partner. Renner and Hartley (2018) sampled a group of abused women seeking legal services such as divorce proceedings or protection from abuse orders. Receiving this type of help was generally beneficial for the women in lowering PTSD symptoms.

Some survivors of IPV attempt to develop strategies for being more cautious or careful as a reaction to battering by an intimate partner (see Box 3.5). For example, women who are physically assaulted by their husbands often attempt to determine what the circumstances were that led to the beating and try to avoid replicating the same situation in the future in hopes that will forestall violence, e.g. "if I just make sure his supper is hot and hasn't gotten cold, I'll be safe". They are typically optimistic that this will work and that the violence will stop (Frieze, 1979). Unfortunately, in reality, such efforts are rarely successful and the violence is likely to occur again.

Box 3.5: Coping Strategies of Battered Women

Women experiencing physical or psychological aggression from their intimate partners have found many ways to cope with this situation. As Anderson, Renner, and Bloom (2017) discussed, abused women are concerned about safety and make decisions about how they can best be safe based on their assessments of how dangerous their batterer is to them or their children. They also consider their own social, economic, and geographic situations and what resources are available to them. [For example, rural women may find that their situations are much more isolated, and fewer resources are available to them than would be the case for urban or suburban women.] Anderson and her colleagues found that simply asking abused women how they protected themselves yielded responses such as "I didn't do anything" or "I did whatever he [the abuser] told me to do" (p. 611–612). A small sample of 22 physically and psychologically abused women were asked more detailed questions about specific actions taken. In responding to the researchers, it was clear to them that rather than being helpless, all of the women in the study were active in responding to the on-going violence in their lives and taking protective actions.

In a systematic review of 48 studies, Rizo, Givens, and Lombardi (2017) concluded that abused women employed both problem-focused and emotion-focused types of coping. The strategies found to be the most helpful were safety planning and other problem-focused strategies, reappraisal of their situation, doing things to make them feel better, and seeking various types of help from others. Least helpful were self-criticism, considering suicide or homicide of the abuser, minimizing what was happening and substance abuse. A variety of emotion-focused and problem-focused can be seen within these groupings of most and least effective coping strategies. The authors concluded that active or engaged coping was more typical for those who had not also experienced childhood physical or sexual abuse while more avoidant or disengaged coping was associated with earlier childhood abuse. These less effective strategies were also seen for those abused women who were experiencing higher levels of violence, had fewer sources of social support or lacked other resources.

None of the reviewed studies were longitudinal, so it was impossible to determine causal directions. As Rizo and her colleagues noted, simply advising women experiencing IPV to take positive steps to resolve their situation might not be effective if the women lack resources to leave their partners or effectively cope on their own.

3.3.3 Reaching Out to Others for Help

When one is victimized, one may turn to others for help in dealing with the situation rather than attempting to cope by oneself. Sources of help in the face of trauma can be informal resources or formal sources of assistance. Informal help includes counseling from a minister or rabbi, or assistance from family, friends or neighbors. Formal sources of help include turning to a doctor or hospital for medical assistance, requesting assistance from law enforcement officials, or seeking help from professionals in dealing with paperwork or other forms of practical assistance. (see Box 3.6 for information on PTSD treatment). A large majority of people of all ages turn to others to share highly emotional experiences—both positive and negative. Such sharing and the social support that accompanies it may be very important but, unfortunately, may not always work out as hoped for by the victim (see Box 3.7).

Box 3.6: Treatment for PTSD

Several types of treatment have been developed by the social workers, psychologists and others who help people with symptoms of PTSD. [For more discussion of treatment of family violence survivors, see Chap. 8].

In a major review of the literature, Gutermann et al. (2016) reviewed 135 published studies writing about PTSD treatment for children and young adults up to the age of 25. Many different types of trauma were included in these studies, although the most common was child sex abuse or child physical abuse. Cognitive Behavioral Therapy or CBT was found to be the most effective type of treatment, especially when individual sessions rather than group sessions were held. As they noted, similar findings have been seen for adults experiencing PTSD (see Chap. 8). Trauma-focused CBT was identified as the best type of treatment for PTSD.

Another therapy specifically developed for PTSD treatment is exposure therapy (Foa & Rauch, 2004). This treatment is based on data indicating that after experiencing trauma, survivors are often concerned that the world is too dangerous and that they need to find better ways to cope. Traumatic memories make these feelings worse. Exposure therapy provides the survivor with images of what happened, and helps them to think in more positive ways about how they might effectively cope in the future. This type of treatment has been widely used. A systematic review and meta-analysis published in 2016 (Cusak et al., 2016) supported the effectiveness of this method. More recently, virtual-reality has been used to make the therapeutic exposure more realistic. This has been found to be effective in treating PTSD in returning veterans experiencing PTSD (Beidel et al., 2019). Both CBT and exposure therapy are recommended as valid treatments by the American Psychological Association (2019) along with several other types of treatments.

In other research on adults, it was noted that alcohol or other substance abuse behavior was so common for those asking for PTSD treatment that clinicians should treat for both problems (Roberts, Roberts, Jones, & Bisson, 2015; Zang et al., 2017). Roberts and his colleagues reviewed 14 studies in detail that included PTSD and substance abuse treatment, noting that this combination was quite difficult to treat and it was not uncommon to find substance abuse reoccurring several months after treatment had ended.

Box 3.7: When Help from Others is Denied or Not Available

When natural disasters occur around the world, large communities are traumatized with people needing many types of assistance over a long period of time. Often there is assistance provided by formal and informal helpgivers, but not always and not for everyone who may need it. People may not receive the help they had been expecting, or may not receive help as long as it is needed (Kaniasty, de Terte, Gullaran, & Bennett, 2019).

Seeking, but not receiving help can be quite traumatic and add to victim distress (Dworkin, Brill, & Ullman, 2019). An example of this can be seen in Case #2 discussed earlier in the chapter, and Joyce's futile efforts to get help for her abuse. When help is provided, the victim has reassurance that help will also be available in the future, as well as having direct positive benefits from that help. But, this is not always realistic. Ferrell, Russin, and Hardy (2019) analyzed responses of helpgivers in an on-line forum for trauma survivors. Some of these helpgivers explained that helping others with PTSD symptoms was emotionally draining and sometimes interfered with their own daily needs.

Even when we know the person asking for help, we may not respond positively to requests for assistance. As Amar, Tuccinardi, Heislein, and Simpson (2015) noted, those called on for help by someone experiencing partner violence may not feel they know how to help. They may also feel emotionally drained over time and unable to continue providing assistance in a situation of continuing abuse. In some cases, those offering help were assaulted themselves by the abuser (Gregory, Williamson, & Feder, 2017).

Others may feel that the person is at least somewhat responsible for what has happened and may not feel sympathetic (Meyer, 2016). Thus, a friend or family member of a victim of IPV might blame her staying with him after he was violent, and may not be willing to provide assistance or emotional support after the latest beating.

We are particularly reluctant to help those we do not know, even in situations when we might be able to do something to stop someone from being victimized. One of the most notorious examples of bystander indifference to a situation of violent trauma was the case of Catherine ("Kitty") Genovese, who was murdered on her Queens, New York, doorstep in full view of acquaintances, neighbors, and strangers on the street. All of these direct witnesses did nothing to help Kitty or call the police for help even though she was stabbed repeatedly, called for help and was stalked by her killer for more than an hour (Rosenthal, 2015). There may be reasons that bystanders fail to help. Research has indicated that those who attempt to intervene when someone appears to be in a situation where partner violence is occurring or in a situation that could lead to a sexual assault may report that the (potential) victim got angry or did not appreciate their assistance (Banyard, Moschella, Grych, & Jouriles, 2019).

Research shows that positive social support is tied to positive effects on the immune system and on the cardiovascular system (Uchino et al., 2018). There are a number of ways in which social support can be given (Feeney & Collins, 2015). Just by being there and letting the person talk, others may enable the stressed individual to work through feelings of depression or loss or fear. Their presence may be comforting. They can convey understanding and acceptance. Social support can also allow one to develop strengths and cope with a traumatizing event and respond in positive ways.

Now, let's look at a real-life case example in which positive forms of help were provided by a range of other people. This case illustrates how multiple systems of care can become involved positively with a family in which there is intimate partner violence and demonstrates the important role of bystanders taking action in mobilizing a critical component of help—in this case, calling the police. It also shows how both the batterer and victim move through certain pathways in the process of getting help and how follow-up care is important following a crisis situation.

Case Example 6

John is a 36 year-old married white male with five children who was brought to the crisis clinic for evaluation by Sheriff's deputies and a Department of Public Assistance (DPA) worker. John's wife, Karen, was seen 4 days prior by one of the clinic social workers for evaluation of depression. John has abused Karen off and on throughout the 8 years of their marriage, but last Saturday he almost killed her. Because of the violence in the home, the five children were removed last year and placed in the Dependent Children's Home by Child Protective Services and are currently in foster care...Karen is now staying with a friend. This morning the DPA worker tried to reach Karen in order to discuss the situation with the children, but found out she was gone because of the recent incident of abuse. The DPA worker then attempted to make a home visit to talk to John, but neighbors said he was being held at the sheriff's department. According to the neighbors, they called the sheriff after they observed the abuse going on in the yard, and when John admitted to the deputies that he had beaten his wife, they threw him in the squad car and brought him to the crisis clinic. The DPA worker then met them there. Upon evaluation, John initially threatened suicide (said he wanted to blow his brains out), but as the interview progressed, he said that if he could get some help, he would promise to get rid of his gun at home and could postpone any harm to himself.

3.4 Emotion-Focused Coping Strategies That Are Often Ineffective

3.4.1 Coping via Withdrawal or Escape

As discussed, there are a number of negative emotions associated with PTSD. Withdrawing or escaping from these negative feelings is a common reaction of victims of trauma. This is typically categorized as a form of emotion-focused copingIt may be necessary to engage in some form of emotion-focused coping before one can engage in more effective problem-focused coping. As Logan noted in her 2018 report on safety planning, those who are not able to manage the negative emotions associated with being a domestic assault survivor find it very difficult to do safety planning.

There are many forms of emotional withdrawal. Withdrawal can involve denial that the event happened or minimizing what happened. Sleeping long hours is a form of withdrawal while suicide attempts may represent an extreme form of withdrawal. In a study of men and women exposed to the Deepwater Horizon Oil Spill, Bell et al. (2018) found that those with clinical levels of PTSS (posttraumatic stress symptoms) displayed a variety of avoidant emotional-focused coping. These included denial, self-distraction, and substance abuse. Another study (Allen, Mercer, & Lilly, 2016) of people responding to 911 emergency calls (a highly stressful job) found that reported PTSS symptoms were especially high in those who had reported being a survivor of earlier child maltreatment. There was also an association of avoidant coping for this group in attempting to address their PTSS symptoms. Allen and her colleagues suggested that those exposed to early childhood trauma may have learned maladaptive coping strategies as a result of those experiences.

3.4.2 Coping through Alcohol or Other Drugs

Another way to avoid thinking about a highly stressful event is to use drugs or alcohol to numb painful feelings. As discussed in Chaps. 4 and 6, use of alcohol and other drugs has been reported found to be high for battered women as well as for victims of child maltreatment. This coping strategy has been found for others experiencing traumatic such as those in the military (Smith & Cottler, 2018). In one of the author's own research studies, we found that for men who had graduated from an Ivy League university in 1966, surveyed 25 years after graduation, there was more current alcohol use in those who were military veterans as compared to their classmates who had not served in the military (Bookwala, Frieze, & Grote, 1994). We were somewhat surprised about this finding since this alumni group had very high income levels and may have been somewhat protected from the adversities of the Vietnam military experience. The veteran group also reported higher levels of depression and were more likely to have questioned their values in the years after the war. All of these reactions are consistent with those seen in other studies of trauma victims. More recent research has continued to show a strong relationship between alcohol use and PTSD in veterans (Erwin et al., 2017). Erwin and her colleagues further noted that it was not clear that the alcohol was effective in reducing PTSD symptoms, but rather appeared to be a method of coping with PTSD symptoms.

Alcohol use has been shown to be a coping strategy for other types of trauma, as well. The Obama White House released a report on sexual assaults on college campuses (Not alone, 2014), revealing that alcohol use by both perpetrators and victims played a significant role in heightening risk for sexual and other forms of assault amongst college students, with most victims being young female students (Krebs, Lindquist, Warner, Fisher, & Martin, 2007, 2009). Thus, alcohol played a role in elevating the risk of experiencing trauma as well as serving as a coping tool for dealing with trauma. Use of alcohol as a form of self-medication to feel better when experiencing PTSD symptoms was directly examined in a representative U.S. community sample (Leeies, Pagura, Sareen, & Bolton, 2010). In this study, 14% of those with PTSD reported self-medication with alcohol and an additional 7% reported using other drugs, often combined with alcohol, for this purpose. Men were more likely to cope in this way than women. Thege et al. (2017) concluded after a systematic review of over 3000 studies that addiction to alcohol or drugs was more associated with those exposed to childhood trauma than to adult trauma.

Although the exact mechanism involved is not clear, it does appear that alcohol use may initially make it easier to handle stress and forget the trauma, but over time, continuing to drink may heighten anxiety and make the trauma symptoms worse. Cross, Crow, Powers, and Bradley (2015) replicated the association of early childhood trauma and problematic alcohol and substance abuse in a low income African American sample. They strongly argued that clinicians dealing with clients who abuse alcohol should explore the possibility that the alcohol abuse was triggered by an earlier trauma, because of this common association of alcohol abuse as a reaction to trauma. The following is an example from one of the author's clinical practice:

> Christine, age 19, was admitted to a private alcohol rehabilitation clinic following her second DWI (Driving While Intoxicated) conviction. Initially Christine denied any other problems other than "liking to get drunk and party". However, it soon became clear that Christine was depressed and used alcohol to buffer painful feelings. Christine's therapist, however, was unable to identify what was underlying the depression, although she suspected some kind of early trauma had occurred. During therapy, Christine revealed that she had been sexually and physically abused by an uncle when she was a young child. Christine's therapist, then, addressed this with Christine in treatment. Christine was eventually able to talk about these early traumatic experiences and how her use of alcohol was a way of dealing with and pushing away the painful feelings (Newhill, 1995).

3.4.3 Learned Helplessness

When people feel that they have no way of dealing with a negative situation, they may display what is called *learned helplessness* (Maier & Seligman, 2016). Once this happens, they may give up, and may fail to see a solution to their difficulties when one does become available. Those who adopt or fall into a pattern of learned helplessness become unable to take any steps to make their lives better. Here is a short case example illustrating learned helplessness:

> Rose, a 45 year old married white woman, was brought to the county hospital emergency room by her husband. The husband told the ER doctor that Rose had taken pills in a suicide attempt. Rose denied this and stated her husband "lies all the time". Alone with the doctor, Rose stated that her husband has abused her continually over the course of the past 15 years. He has broken her ribs and both arms, blackened her eyes repeatedly and caused a miscarriage once by kicking her in the stomach. When the ER doctor asked Rose why she hasn't left her husband or gone to a battered women's shelter, Rose tells the doctor that there is nothing she can do: "He'll find me and just drag me back home again. Besides I know that if I just learned to be a better wife and not make him angry, he'd stop. Everything I do is the wrong thing." The ER doctor eventually felt so frustrated with his inability to mobilize Rose to do something about her situation that he discharged her with a referral for counseling, telling the charge nurse "I hope she doesn't come back. All we can do is patch her up"(Newhill, 1995).

A study of women in Turkey who had been interviewed at a shelter for women were asked about experiences of trauma, and reactions to this trauma (Salcioglu et al., 2017). Nearly 90% of the women reported experiencing abuse in their homes from partners or other family members. Their responses indicated that many were fearful about being once again abused if they returned to their family and felt they had little if any control of stopping this. PTSD was diagnosed in 48% of the women and nearly a third were depressed. Levels of fear and helplessness were more predictive of PTSD and depression than the actual degree of abuse received.

Logan (2018) referred to these helpless and fearful feelings as having low *safety efficacy*. In an analysis of the responses of 821 U.S. women about personal safety concerns, Logan found that low safety efficacy was not associated with a past victimization experience. However, it was related to feeling scared, or feeling frozen or humiliated in a past conflict situation. Logan interpreted these data as supporting a mind-set that either lead to taking action to make sure one was safe, or a mind-set that was associated with feelings of helplessness that were then associated with depression about the future.

3.5 Emotion-Focused Coping Strategies That Can be Effective

3.5.1 Coping Through Distraction

As researchers have expanded their ideas about coping, it is clear that some coping strategies that focus on changing the stress and upset associated with the traumatic event can be effective. Finding activities that distract one from thinking about the trauma often appears to be helpful, especially for trauma that cannot be avoided. For example, Beecham (2014) recruited a sample of employed women in the UK who had experienced abuse from an intimate partner, using snowball sampling. The women were asked how they had or were coping with the abuse through their work. One respondent described her job as a refuge (p. 600) and allowed her to be in control, unlike her situation at home. Work also allowed the women to disengage from their upset about home, and give them other issues to think about. Their identities at work also served as a buffer against the psychological abuse and belittling they received from their partner, showing them they were capable and in control. The women felt more confident at work, as well as it being a place of safety.

In another example of using distraction as a method of coping, Lee et al. (2017) surveyed adolescents in the Republic of Korea who had involved with a ferry that sank and killed 250 high school students. The adolescents in the sample reported on their internet use before and after the disaster. Those with low levels of PTSD increased internet use a small amount, but those with high levels of PTSD increased substantially, to a level the researchers described as problematic internet use. Thus, in this case, distraction did not appear to be an effective coping strategy. The internet use may have been a method of withdrawal.

It may be beneficial in managing emotions to focus on something positive, no matter how difficult the situation (Folkman & Moskowitz, 2000). This may take the form of stopping and taking time out from an otherwise stressful situation to enjoy a beautiful sunset, or by finding small goals that can be easily achieved, or using mindfulness as a coping strategy while dealing with ongoing trauma (Bowen, De Boer, & Bergman, 2017). Finding humor in a difficult situation can also reduce tension and assist in dealing with otherwise traumatic events. Such efforts may be especially important for coping with chronic stress, in contrast to dealing with a specific and time-limited traumatic event. Folkman (2001) has found that those who react to trauma with more positive affect are more able to use a variety of other coping strategies.

Another form of effective distraction may be physical exercise (Pebole & Hall, 2019). As Pebole and Hall outline, exercise does have positive health benefits. It has also been associated with decreased depression. Research on male veterans in the U.S. has demonstrated a positive effect on PTSD, but little work has been done with women or with those experiencing PTSD for other types of trauma. The researchers urge that this type of distraction be systematically examined as a form of PTSD treatment.

3.5.2 Redefining the Meaning of the Traumatic Event

It has long been known that when a traumatic event happens, many victims try to understand and find some meaning in the event by putting it into a larger context (e.g., Janoff-Bulman & Frieze, 1983). In a widely cited review and theory paper, Park (2010) discussed the issue of "meaning-making efforts" (p. 258) after one is traumatized. As she explained, people have general beliefs about how the world functions. If an expected traumatic event happens, these world views are threatened, creating stress. People then might engage in one of several possible actions to reduce the discrepancy between what one expected to happen and what actually happened. Park argued that this process is often nonconscious, but not necessarily. [Although not specifically discussed, it is likely that when one is victimized in spite of following the personal safety rules believed to keep one safe, this would create this type of discrepancy. See Box 3.4 for more discussion of personal-safety rules].

3.5.2.1 Downward Comparison

One way of reframing or finding meaning is to compare one's own experiences to others who were victimized in much the same way. By comparing oneself to another person who may have had even worse things happen, one might feel that his or her own situation is not as bad (Taylor, Buunk & Aspinwall, 1990). An early example of this was described by Scheppele and Bart (1983) who interviewed rape victims. Although all of the women in the study were legally classified as rape victims, many of the women who were forced to perform sexual acts other than sexual intercourse defined themselves as having "escaped" being raped. Perhaps this is one way they attempted to cope with their trauma from forced sexual activity, i.e. by defining what happened to them as not as bad as "true rape"?

3.5.2.2 Framing the Event in a Wider Spiritual Context

Ideas about spirituality or religious meaning are other forms of redefining what has happened and giving it a larger meaning. As de la Rosa, Barnett-Queen, Messick, and Gurrola (2016) pointed out, religious beliefs serve as a global belief system that provide an explanation for suffering and loss. Religious beliefs can give people a sense of optimism about the future, and a sense of control over the events in their lives. A belief in God is often associated with the idea that things happen for a reason. Thus, someone might feel that they were victimized purposely, as a message from God, that they needed to lead a more spiritual or moral life. Religious or spiritual beliefs were found to be strongly predictive of coping with IPV in a sample of Mexican American women interviewed in a shelter for domestic violence (de la Rosa et al., 2016). However, no data were collected on how spirituality or religion had this effect. Using a sample of largely Black women recruited from the community who had experienced IPV within the last 6 months, Howell, Thurston, Schwartz, Jamison, and Hasselle (2018) found a similar pattern of spirituality being one of the most important predictors of resilience. These researchers argued that their spirituality provided comfort for these women and helped them find a deeper meaning in their lives.

Other studies offer more information about the mechanisms. African American women in the United States have been found to be especially likely to use their spiritual or religious faith as a primary form of coping with stress or trauma (Mattis, 2002). In a qualitative study of 23 African American women from Michigan and New York, Mattis (2002) found that about half of the women specifically mentioned that their religion helped them see a larger meaning in both the positive and negative events in their lives. Many of the women also felt that their religion aided them in accepting the realities of their sometimes difficult and chronically stressful everyday lives. As potential helpers, clergy in organized religions have frequently been asked for religious help from abused women (Johnson, 2015).

3.5.2.3 Changing Personal Goals

As one considers the traumatic event and redefines this within a broader context, one may develop new behaviors and goals consistent with this redefinition. For example, one might decide to lead a more religious life. Perhaps related to finding meaning by redefining why one was victimized is the reaction of responding to a situation of being battered by a partner by changing one's life to work in a shelter for battered women and help other women who have experienced the same type of trauma. Chapter 8 outlines how it is quite common to find staff in battered women's shelters who describe themselves as previously battered and wanting to help other women in this situation. Other research has indicated a general association between help others and satisfaction, as indicated by positive responses such as feeling good about oneself, and energized in other relationships (Grayman-Simpson & Mattis, 2012).

A more general association between having experienced personal trauma and being willing to help others has also been reported (Frazier et al., 2013). In a longitudinal study of undergraduates, Frazier and her colleagues were able to study the predictors of daily helping in the last 2 weeks. The number of lifetime traumas the person had experienced were the strongest predictor, even after controlling for religious commitment and other personality variables. Volunteer activities generally were also higher for those with personal trauma experiences. As Frazier and her colleagues pointed out, these data were consistent with many other studies showing similar relationships, especially the pattern of helping other survivors after experiencing the same type of trauma. But, as they noted, their data indicated a more general willingness to help others beyond the specific victimization experience they had had.

3.5.2.4 Finding Meaning Through Writing About What Happened

It has been argued that one way people may find meaning in experiencing a traumatic event is in writing about it (Park, 2010). Pennebaker and Beall (1986) proposed what has now become a popular technique of treating symptoms of PTSD through expressive writing. Noting that many experiencing PTSD have not disclosed their feelings about this to others, Pennebaker and Beall argued that writing about these feelings could be quite beneficial. Pavlacic, Buchanan, Maxwell, Hopke, and Schulenberg (2019) published a meta-analysis of 264 published studies using this technique. Formal analyses indicated that writing had generally been found to have some effectiveness in lowering stress associated with PTSD across this body of published research. However, not all studies found effects. Pennebaker (2018) himself has no real theory about why these effects occur and what the necessary conditions are. Park's suggestion that it relates to reframing or finding meaning in the traumatic event may provide one explanation. Sloan and Marx (2017) offer other suggestions for enhancing the effectiveness of this intervention.

3.5.2.5 Obsessing About Meaning and Rumination

As Park (2010) noted, if one is not able to redefine or reframe unexpected trauma, this can lead to rumination. Rumination after a traumatic event occurs can also create PTSD and increase negative reactions some time after the event has occurred (Spinhoven, Penninx, Krempeniou, van Hemert, & Elzinga, 2015). Rumination involves repeatedly thinking about the meaning and causes of negative feelings such as depression (Lyubomirsky, Layous, Chancellor, & Nelson, 2015). It may be triggered by a traumatic event and additional traumatic exposure and make it worse. Rumination is associated with hopelessness and self-criticism. It can lead to self-injury and engaging in dangerous activities. It tends to be focused on the past, unlike worry which is future oriented and may be associated with problem-focused coping. Instead, ruminators have an impaired ability to generate solutions to problems and little motivation even if they think of something that might potentially resolve an issue causing stress. There is also evidence that those who often ruminate may be rejected by other people, and even when they do seek social support, they may not receive it (Lyubomirsky et al., 2015).

Evidence of rumination was found in a study of 65 women who had experienced physical or sexual assault, child sexual abuse, or intimate partner violence and had been diagnosed with PTSD (Brown, Hetzel-Riggin, Mitchell, & Bruce, 2018). Data relating to negative affect, rumination and PTSD symptoms were collected. A path analysis of the data indicated that rumination appeared to be a major mechanism that related negative affect to other PTSD symptoms. The authors suggested that these data were consistent with high levels of guilt and shame associated with female survivors of abuse. Treatment for these survivors might have enhanced effectiveness if the pattern of high levels of rumination was directly addressed in these survivors.

3.6 PTSD, Coping, and Posttraumatic Growth

As this chapter has discussed, there are many ways in which people attempt to cope with traumatic experiences in their lives. Those who are able to overcome PTSD or other stress reactions tend to be more mentally and physically healthy (Goldstein & Brooks, 2013). Specific coping responses depend on the particular situation and on the personality of the victim. As discussed earlier, there are a number of different forms of coping. It is difficult to determine which of these strategies is more effective, and this may well vary across individuals. One of the difficulties of doing controlled studies of coping effectiveness is that it is very difficult to know if those who appear to have fewer symptoms after experiencing a traumatic event were initially experiencing a relatively low level of trauma, or if it was the coping style employed that led to better outcomes. Timing may also matter, since symptoms change over time and can sometimes get worse for some period before getting better (Galatzer-Levy, Huang, & Bonanno, 2018).

One positive effect of trauma is a reaction labeled as posttraumatic growth (PTG). Tedeschi and Calhoun (Calhoun & Tedeschi, 2014; Tedeschi & Calhoun, 2004) introduced this concept to the literature as a way of describing some of the positive reports seen in clinical practice as people recovered from trauma. As Infurna and Jayawickreme (2019) discussed in their review of research on PTG, there is a standard scale measuring this. It is a self-report scale where people are asked if they have experienced any of a number of positive outcomes after experiencing trauma. Items assess changes such as developing new interests, having better relations with others, feeling increased spirituality, wanting to help others, and having a greater appreciation of life (Xiaoli et al., 2019). In a systematic review of the literature based on 26 studies meeting their criteria, Xialoi and colleagues noted that about half of those who participated in the various published studies reported moderate to high levels of PTG. Younger adults were more likely than those over 60 to report PTG, and women reported this more than men.

Brooks, Graham-Kevan, Robinson, and Lowe (2019) sampled 268 community volunteers in the New England area of the U.S. who had experienced a trauma of some type. The largest categories of traumatic events were the death of someone close, accidents, and an assault by a partner or someone else. Their scale of PTG included items such as discovering one was stronger than believed earlier and now knowing one can handle difficulties in life. They were also asked about use of various coping strategies such as using active coping, emotional coping, becoming more spiritual or using avoidant coping. All of the coping strategies were correlated with PTG except avoidant coping. An unexpected finding was that having had intrusive thoughts was *positively* correlated with PTG. In trying to explain this, Brooks et al. speculated that such thoughts might have led to a reassessment of the event, leading eventually to successful coping and PTG.

In a review of studies addressing the issue of PTG in battered women, Ulloa, Hammett, Guzman, and Hokoda (2015) found 17 studies that reported on this. They noted that the general pattern was that PTG was reported in formerly battered women after they had decided to leave their abusive partner. Three commonly reported forms of PTG were feeling better about oneself, having greater spiritual awareness and becoming more active in helping others.

Although there is clearly much research examining PTG, Infurna and Jayawickreme (2019) raised questions about whether these findings reflected actual reality or were instead an illusion of growth. As they pointed out, people might report feeling better either to look better to others or to themselves. They may believe they have made positive changes, but this might not reflect objective reality. They further pointed out that the PTG scales ask only about positive changes and don't assess negative changes or other continuing PTSD symptoms. Infurna and Luthar (2018) noted in an earlier paper that PTSD has several important dimensions. These include low levels of life satisfaction, strong negative affect, low positive affect, problems with general health, and concerns with physical functioning. It is very possible that someone could show increased positive affect, but still suffer in these other dimensions. Full recovery from PTSD would imply changes in all of these dimensions.

3.7 Differences in How Individuals React to Traumatic Events

People who have experienced a traumatic event can react to the experience in a variety of ways. Some individuals appear to sustain no negative effects, while others may have quite extreme reactions. Certain demographic groups within our society appear to be more likely to experience PTSD than others. Racial and ethnic differences have been found in the incidence and prevalence of serious trauma reactions including PTSD (Roberts, Gilman, Breslau, Breslau, & Koenen, 2011). In a large U.S. sample, overall, about 9% of Blacks, 7% of Whites and 4% of Asians reported experiencing PTSD. Blacks were more likely to develop PTSD after exposure to a traumatic event, though. Types of trauma experiences also varied by race. Blacks and Hispanics had higher risk of child maltreatment, especially witnessing parental IPV. Similar findings can be seen in a study by Alegría et al. (2013) who assessed whether PTSD varied in prevalence, diagnostic criteria, endorsement, and type and frequency of potentially traumatic events by analyzing data from a large representative U.S. sample of white, Latino, Asian, African-American and Afro-Caribbean adults. The researchers found marked differences across groups with Asians having the lowest prevalence rates of PTSD, while African-Americans reported higher rates as compared to non-Latino whites, even after controlling for type and frequency of traumatic events and various sociodemographic, clinical and social support factors. These differences may be explained by differences in risk factors in the environment. For example, poor housing quality associated with low-income communities is related to lower levels of well-being generally (Coley, Leventhal, Lynch, & Kull, 2013). There is more environmental pollution and other hazardous risk in low-income and black areas (e.g., Banzhaf, Ma, & Timmins, 2019) and less spending generally on parks, transportation and schools in these areas (Zuk et al., 2015).

There are also gender differences in reporting reactions to trauma. Women are more likely than men to report traumatic reactions and to be diagnosed with PTSD. In a widely cited review of the literature, Tolin and Foa (2006) compared levels of PTSD in women and men. In order to control for the type of trauma experienced, this was held constant in the analysis. Results showed a consistent effect for women to be higher in PTSD after all types of trauma except child sex abuse. Similar results were reported by Lehavot, Katon, Chen, Fortney, and Simpson (2018) in an analysis based on over 36,000 U.S. adults. Within the Levavot et al. study, women veterans had the highest rates of PTSD, followed by women civilians.

Rates for veterans were higher than for civilians for men, but both groups were lower than either of the female groups. It is not clear if this means women actually react more to negative events, if they are merely more willing to admit that they are experiencing negative reactions, or this consistent gender difference is related to the types of trauma that women are more likely to experience (interpersonal assaults such as IPV and sexual abuse) (APA, 2013). One explanation for women being more likely to report having PTSD symptoms is that women are socialized to be more open than men about their emotions, especially admitting fears and anxieties (Yoder, 2013). Men, on the other hand, may be socialized to be *tough* and not to react emotionally to trauma or to seek help after experiencing a traumatic event. Since we can never truly know how strongly someone is reacting, independently of what they say, it is impossible to know if women are really experiencing higher rates of PTSD or other psychological symptoms, or if they are simply more willing and able to reveal their symptoms and feelings to others.

Personality factors that have been found to relate to experiencing PTSD. Having negative appraisals of life events, a pessimistic outlook, and inappropriate coping strategies can elevate risk for developing an acute stress disorder in the face of experiencing trauma (APA, 2013; Araujo et al., 2014). In a classic paper published in 1987 on resilience, Rutter described a general tendency of some individuals to be resilient to all types of stresses in their lives. Since that time, thousands of papers have refined this concept. In more recent papers, resilience is defined as "the capacity to overcome significant life adversity" (Infurna & Luthar, 2018, p. 43). Resilience was found to be associated with emotional-regulation, interpersonal strengths, optimism, and meaning making in a study of adolescents and adults in a low-income community in Appalachia (Hamby, Grych, & Banyard, 2018).

One debate in the literature relates to posttraumatic growth and to the prevalence of resilience. In a review of 54 studies, Galatzer-Levy et al. (2018) found evidence that most people display resilience in response to major life stressors. As they explained, there is evidence that the majority of people have been exposed to at least one potentially traumatic event, and often to many such events, and only a minority develop PTSD. Of those who do develop PTSD, the largest group of people have recovered from this. Other patterns are experiencing chronic stress in response to trauma, and have delayed PTSD symptoms some time after the event occurred. They also noted that there was no evidence that these patterns were related in any meaningful way to the severity of the event. These data would imply that most people are resilient.

These conclusions, based on an analysis of other studies indicating high levels of resilience, were critiqued by Infurna and Luthar (2018). As they outlined, PTSD responses to trauma involve a variety of different reactions including lack of positive affect, higher levels of negative affect, worsened physical health and other symptoms. Most studies focus on only a small subset of all the possible reactions. Of those studies looking at more than one of these types of reactions, a much smaller percentage of people would be classified as resilient. They argue that a better summary of reactions to traumatic events is that most people do recover, although they do have some PTSD symptoms after the event.

Consistent with the view that only a minority of people are truly resilient is work by well-known researchers such as Caspi and Morritt (2018) that there is a general human tendency that predicts a person's likelihood of developing any type of mental disorder. They name this the *p dimension* and argue it is somewhat analogous to the *g factor* of general intelligence. People vary in terms of how much of this tendency exists in their personality, and it shows up quite early in childhood. They suggest this is probably genetically based and may be evident in the structure of the brain. The paper presenting this theory has already been widely cited, but the ideas are acknowledged to need further research.

3.8 Summary

This chapter has reviewed the research on general reactions of individuals who are victimized by a range of types of assaults, accidents, natural disasters and other stressful and traumatic events. We discussed in detail one reaction syndrome that has been identified by the American Psychiatric Association as posttraumatic stress disorder or PTSD. PTSD involves a number of symptoms including anxiety, sleep and eating disorders, anger, and other reactions that may last for months, or even years. Repeated trauma and victimization caused by another person, the situation of many people victimized by family violence, are especially stressful. A new classification system, the ICD-11 is also briefly discussed.

Once one has been exposed to a traumatic event, the person may no longer feel safe in his or her daily life, which adds to stress levels, and elevates risk for trauma reactions from future stressful events. There are many forms of coping with victimization. One basic type of coping involves trying to lower stress levels through trying to ignore what happened or diverting attention to other things. Other coping occurs when the victim does something concrete to try to change the situation that led to the victimization or to ensure it will not happen again. Determining what might create safety for the future may include self blame, a relatively controversial form of coping. Redefining the traumatic event as some type of personal challenge or as not as bad as initially believed or finding some other form of meaning in the trauma may be an effective form of coping.

The majority of people do not develop PTSD symptoms after exposure to a potentially traumatic event. This suggests that many people are resilient. Others may show posttraumatic growth and feel stronger after recovering from trauma. Possible biological factors in resilience are briefly discussed.

References

Abernathy, B. E. (2008). Who am I now? Helping trauma clients find meaning, wisdom, and a renewed sense of self. In G. R. Walz, J. C. Bleuer, & R. K. Yep (Eds.), *Compelling counseling interventions: Celebrating VISTAS' fifth anniversary* (pp. 199–208). Ann Arbor, MI: Counseling Outfitters.

Alegría, M., Fortuna, L. R., Lin, J. Y., Norris, F. H., Gao, S., Takeuchi, D. T., et al. (2013). Prevalence, risk, and correlates of posttraumatic stress disorder across ethnic and racial minority groups in the United States. *Medical Care, 51*(12), 1114–1123.

Allen, C. E., Mercer, M. C., & Lilly, M. M. (2016). Duty-related posttraumatic stress symptoms in 911 telecommunicators: The roles of childhood trauma exposure and emotion-focused coping. *Journal of Aggression, Maltreatment & Trauma, 25*, 686–701. https://doi.org/10.1080/10926771.2016.1175534

Amar, A. F., Tuccinardi, N., Heislein, J., & Simpson, S. (2015). Friends helping friends: A non-randomized control trial of a peer-based response to dating violence. *Nursing Outlook, 63*, 496–503. https://doi.org/10.1016/j.outlook.2015.01.004

American Psychiatric Association. (2013). *Diagnostic and statistical manual of mental disorders, fifth edition (DSM-5)*. Washington, DC: Author.

American Psychological Association. (2019). Summary of the clinical practice guideline for the treatment of posttraumatic stress disorder (PTSD) in adults. *American Psychologist, 74*, 596–607. https://doi.org/10.1037/amp0000473

Anderson, L. M., Renner, L. M., & Bloom, T. L. (2017). Exploring protective strategies among rural women in an abusive relationship. *Issues in Mental Health Nursing, 38*, 610–618. https://doi.org/10.1080/1612840.2017.1322159

Araujo, A. X., Berger, W., Coutinho, E. S. F., Marques-Portella, C., Luz, M. P., Cabizuca, M., et al. (2014). Comorbid depressive symptoms in treatment seeking PTSD outpatients affect multiple domains of quality of life. *Comprehensive Psychiatry, 55*(1), 56–63.

Archer, R. J. (2019). Sexual assault victimization, fear of sexual assault, and self-protective behaviors: A test of general strain theory. *Victims & Offenders*. https://doi.org/10.1080/15564886.2019.1608882

Associated Press. (February 27, 2012). Buffalo Creek disaster remembered 40 years later. Herald-dispatch.com, Huntington West Virginia. https://www.herald-dispatch.com/news/buffalo-creek-disaster-remembered-years-later/article_8e5c4ffa-ff22-5f6d-a316-1677f0c2f81b.html

Babcock, R. L., & DePrince, A. P. (2012). Childhood betrayal trauma and self-blame appraisals among survivors of intimate partner abuse. *Journal of Trauma & Dissociation, 13*(5), 526–538. https://doi.org/10.1080/15299732.2012.694842

Banyard, V., Moschella, E., Grych, J., & Jouriles, E. (2019). What happened next? New measures of consequences of bystander actions to prevent interpersonal violence. *Psychology of Violence*. https://doi.org/10.1037/vio0000229. Advance online publication.

Banzhaf, S., Ma, L., & Timmins, C. (2019). Environmental justice: The economics of race, place, and pollution. *Journal of Economic Perspectives, 33*(1), 185–208. https://doi.org/10.1257/jep.33.1.185

Beck, J. G., McNiff, J., Clapp, J. D., Olsen, S. A., Avery, M. L., & Hagewood, J. H. (2011). Exploring negative emotion in women experiencing intimate partner violence: Shame, guilt and PTSD. *Behavior Therapy, 42*(4), 740–750.

Beecham, D. (2014). An exploration of the role of employment as a coping resource for women experiencing intimate partner abuse. *Violence and Victims, 29*, 594–606. https://doi.org/10.1891/0886-6708.VV-D-12-00086

Beidel, D. C., Frueh, B. C., Neer, S. M., Bowers, C. A., Trachik, B., Uhde, T. W., et al. (2019). Trauma management therapy with virtual-reality augmented exposure therapy for combat-related PTSD: A randomized controlled trial. *Journal of Anxiety Disorders, 61*, 64–74. https://doi.org/10.1016/j.janxdis.2017.08.005

Bell, T. R., Langhinrichsen-Rohling, J., & Varner, S. J. (2018). Posttraumatic adaptation after the Deepwater Horizon oil spill: The unique role of coping and oil contact on community members' stress. *Current Psychology, 37*, 301–312. https://doi.org/10.1007/s12144-016-9513-4

Berntsen, D., & Rubin, D. C. (2015). Pretraumatic stress reactions in soldiers deployed to Afghanistan. *Clinical Psychological Science, 3*, 663–674. https://doi.org/10.1177/2167702614551766

Bhardwaj, V., Angkaw, A. C., Franceschetti, M., Rao, R., & Baker, D. G. (2019). Direct and indirect relationships among posttraumatic stress disorder, depression, hostility, anger, and verbal and physical aggression in returning veterans. *Aggressive Behavior, 45*, 417–426. https://doi.org/10.1002/ab.21827

Boals, A., Trost, Z., Rainey, E., Foreman, M. L., & Warren, A. M. (2017). Severity of traumatic injuries predicting psychological outcomes: A surprising lack of empirical evidence. *Journal of Anxiety Disorders, 50*, 1–6. https://doi.org/10.1016/j.janxdis.2017.04.004

Bolvin, M. J., & Marx, B. P. (2011). The importance of the peritraumatic experience in defining traumatic stress. *Psychological Bulletin, 137*, 47–67. https://doi.org/10.1037/a0021353

Bondjers, K., Willebrand, M., & Arnberg, F. K. (2018). Similarity in symptom patterns of posttraumatic stress among disaster-survivors: A three-step latent profile analysis. *European Journal of Psychotraumatology, 9*, 1546083. https://doi.org/10.1080/20008198.2018.1546083

Bookwala, J., Frieze, I., & Grote, N. (1994). The long-term effects of military service on quality of life: The Vietnam experience. *Journal of Applied Social Psychology, 24*, 529–545. https://doi.org/10.1111/j.1559-1816.1994.tb00597.x

Bowen, S., De Boer, D., & Bergman, A. L. (2017). The role of mindfulness as approach-based coping in the PTSD-substance abuse cycle. *Addictive Behaviors, 64*, 212–216.

Brooks, M., Graham-Kevan, N., Robinson, S., & Lowe, M. (2019). Trauma characteristics and posttraumatic growth: The mediating role of avoidance coping, intrusive thoughts, and social support. *Psychological Trauma: Theory, Research, Practice, and Policy, 11*(2), 232–238. https://doi.org/10.1037/tra0000372

Brown, W. J., Hetzel-Riggin, M. D., Mitchell, M. A., & Bruce, S. E. (2018). Rumination mediates the relationship between negative affect and posttraumatic stress disorder symptoms in female interpersonal trauma survivors. *Journal of Interpersonal Violence*, 1–22. https://doi.org/10.1177/0886260518818434

Calhoun, L. G., & Tedeschi, R. G. (Eds.). (2014). *Handbook of posttraumatic growth: Resesarch and Practice*. Milton Park, Abingdon: Routledge.

Carvajal, C. (2018). Posttraumatic stress disorder as a diagnostic entity—Clinical perspectives. *Dialogues in Clinical Neuroscience, 20*(3), 161–168.

Carver, C. S., & Connor-Smith, J. (2010). Personality and coping. *Annual Review of Psychology, 61*, 679–704.

Caspi, A., & Morritt, T. E. (2018). All for one and one for all: Mental disorders in one dimension. *The American Journal of Psychiatry, 175*(9), 831–844. https://doi.org/10.1176/appi.ajp.2018.17121383

Cicchetti, D. (2016). Socioemotional, personality and biological development: Illustrations from a multilevel developmental psychopathology perspective on child maltreatment. *Annual Review of Psychology, 67*, 187–211. https://doi.org/10.1146/annurev-psych-122414-033259

Clark, A. A., Cuthbert, B., Lewis-Fernández, R., Narrow, W. E., & Reed, G. M. (2017). Three approaches to understanding and classifying mental disorder: ICD-11, DSM-5, and the National Institute of Mental Health's Research Domain Criteria (RDocC). *Psychological Science in the Public Interest, 18*(2), 72–145. https://doi.org/10.1177/1529100617727266

Cloitre, M., Shevlin, M., Brewin, C. R., Bisson, J. I., Roberts, N. P., Maercker, A., et al. (2018). The International Trauma Questionnaire: Development of a self-report measure of ICD-11 PTSD and complex PTSD. *Acta Psychiatric Scandinavica, 138*, 536–546. https://doi.org/10.1111/acps.12956

Coley, R. L., Leventhal, T., Lynch, A. D., & Kull, M. (2013). Relations between housing characteristics and the well-being of low-income children and adolescents. *Developmental Psychology, 49*, 1775–1789. https://doi.org/10.1037/a0031033

Cook, J. M., & O'Hara, C. C. (2019). An emerging theory of the persistence of social class microaggressions: an interpretative phenomenological study. *Counselling Psychology Quarterly.* https://doi.org/10.1080/09515070.2019.1596880

Cross, D., Crow, T., Powers, A., & Bradley, B. (2015). Childhood trauma, PTSD, and problematic alcohol and substance use in low-income, African-American men and women. *Child Abuse & Neglect, 44*, 26–35. https://doi.org/10.1016/j.chiabu.2015.01.007

Cusak, K., Jonas, D. E., Forneris, C. A., Wines, C., Sonis, J., Middleton, J. C., et al. (2016). Psychological treatments for adults with posttraumatic stress disorder: A systematic review and meta-analysis. *Clinical Psychology Review, 43*, 128–141. https://doi.org/10.1016/j.cpr.2015.10.003

Davis, L. E. (2014). Have we gone too far with resiliency? *Social Work Research, 18*(1), 5–6.

de la Rosa, I. A., Barnett-Queen, T., Messick, M., & Gurrola, M. (2016). Spirituality and resilience among Mexican American IPV survivors. *Journal of Interpersonal Violence, 31*, 3332–3351. https://doi.org/10.1177/0886260515584351

Dodd, J. (2015). "The name game": Feminist protests of the *DSM* and diagnostic labels in the 1980s. *History of Psychology, 18*(3), 312–323.

Dunning, D., Fetchenhauer, D., & Schlosser, T. (2019). Why people trust: Solved puzzles and open mysteries. *Current Directions in Psychological Science, 28*, 366–371. https://doi.org/10.1177/0963721419838255

Dworkin, E. R., Brill, C. D., & Ullman, S. E. (2019). Social reactions to disclosure of interpersonal violence and psychopathology: A systematic review and meta-analysis. *Clinical Psychology Review, 72*. https://doi.org/10.1016/j.cpr.2019.101750

Englehard, I. M., McNally, R. J., & van Schie, K. (2019). Retrieving and modifying traumatic memories: Recent research relevant to three controversies. *Current Directions in Psychological Science, 28*, 91–96. https://doi.org/10.1177/0963721418807728

Erwin, M. C., Charak, R., Durham, T. A., Armour, C., Lv, X., Southwick, S. M., et al. (2017). The 7-factor hybrid model of DSM-5 PTSD symptoms and alcohol consumption and consequences in a national sample of trauma-exposed veterans. *Journal of Anxiety Disorders, 51*, 14–21. https://doi.org/10.1016/j.janxdis.2017.08.001

Feeney, B. C. & Collins, N. L. (2015). A new look at social support: A theoretical perspective on thriving through relationships. *Social Psychology Review, 19*(2), 113–147. https://doi.org/10.1177/1088868314544222

Ferrell, E. L., Russin, S. E., & Hardy, R. M. (2019). Informal caregiving experiences in post-traumatic stress disorder: A content analysis of an online community. *Journal of Community Psychology, 47*, 757–771. https://doi.org/10.1002/jcop.22151

Fileborn, B. (2016). Doing gender, doing safety? Young adults'production of safety on a night out. *Gender, Place & Culture, 23*(8), 1107–1120. https://doi.org/10.1080/0966369X.2015.1090413

Fisher, N. L., Lamis, D. A., Petersen-Coleman, M. N., Moore, C. S., Zhang, H., & Kaslow, N. J. (2016). Mediating effects of existential and religious well-being among abused, suicidal African American women. *Journal of Family Violence, 31*, 315–323. https://doi.org/10.1007/s10896-015-9771-1

Foa, E. B., & Rauch, S. A. M. (2004). Cognitive changes during Prolonged Exposure versus Prolonged Exposure Pplus Cognitive Restructuring in female assault survivors with posttraumatic stress disorder. *Journal of Consulting and Clinical Psychology, 72*(5), 879–884. https://doi.org/10.1037/0022-006X.72.5.87

Folkman, S. (2001). Revised coping theory and the process of bereavement. In M. S. Stroebe, R. O. Hansson, W. Stroebe, & H. Schut (Eds.), *Handbook of bereavement research: Consequences, coping, and care* (p. 563–584). American Psychological Association. https://doi.org/10.1037/10436-024

Folkman, S., & Lazarus, R. S. (1985). If it changes, it must be process: Study of emotion and coping during three stages of a college examination. *Journal of Personality and Social Psychology, 48*(1), 150–170. https://doi.org/10.1037/0022-3514.48.1.150

Folkman, S., & Lazarus, R. S. (1988). Coping as a mediator of emotion. *Journal of Personality and Social Psychology, 54*(3), 466–475. https://doi.org/10.1037/0022-3514.54.3.466

Folkman, S., & Moskowitz, J. T. (2000). Positive affect and the other side of coping. *American Psychologist, 55*(6), 647–654. https://doi.org/10.1037/0003-066X.55.6.647

Frances, A. (2013). *Saving normal: An insider's revolt against out-of-control psychiatric diagnosis, DSM-5, Big Pharma, and the medicalization of ordinary life*. New York, NY: HarperCollins.

Frazier, P., Greer, C., Gabrielsen, S., Tennen, H., Park, C., & Tomich, P. (2013). The relation between trauma exposure and prosocial behavior. *Psychological Trauma: Theory, Research, Practice, and Policy, 5*, 286–294. https://doi.org/10.1037/a0027255

Fried, E. I., Eidhof, M. B., Palic, S., Constantini, G., Huisman-van Dijk, H. M., Bockting, C. L. H., et al. (2018). Replicability and generalizability of Posttraumatic Stress Disorder (PTSD) networks: A cross-cultural multisite study of PTSD symptoms in four trauma patient samples. *Clinical Psychological Science, 6*, 335–351. https://doi.org/10.1177/2167702617745092

Frieze, I. H. (1979). Perceptions of battered wives. In I. H. Frieze, D. Bar-Tal, & J. S. Carroll (Eds.), *New approaches to social problems: Applications of attribution theory*. (pp. 79–108). San Francisco, CA: Jossey-Bass.

Frieze, I. H., Hymer, S., & Greenberg, M. S. (1987). Describing the crime victim: Psychological reactions to victimization. *Professional Psychology, 18*, 299–315.

Furedi, F. (2018). *How fear works: Culture of fear in the twenty-first century*. New York, NY: Bloomsbury Continuum.

Galatzer-Levy, I. R., & Bryant, R. A. (2013). 636,120 ways to have posttraumatic stress disorder. *Perspectives on Psychological Science, 8*(6), 651–662. https://doi.org/10.1177/1745691613504115

Galatzer-Levy, I. R., Huang, S. H., & Bonanno, G. A. (2018). Trajectories of resilience and dysfunction following potential trauma: A review and statistical evaluation. *Clinical Psychology Review, 63*, 41–55. https://doi.org/10.1016/j.cpr.2018.05.008

Goldstein, S., & Brooks, R. B. (Eds.). (2013). *Handbook of resilience in children*. New York, NY: Springer.

Gondolf, E. W., & Fisher, E. R. (1988). *Battered women as survivors: An alternative to treating learned helplessness*. Washington, DC: Lexington Books.

Governor's Ad Hoc Commission of Inquiry (1973). *The Buffalo Creek flood and disaster: Official report*. Retrieved May 2, 2014 from: http://www.wvculture.org/history/disasters/buffcreekgov-report.html

Grayman-Simpson, N., & Mattis, J. S. (2012). Doing good and feeling good among African Americans: Subjective religiosity, helping, and satisfaction. *Journal of Black Psychology, 39*(4), 411–427. https://doi.org/10.1177/0095798412461809

Green, B. L., Grace, M. C., Lindy, J. D., Gleser, G. C., Leonard, A. C., & Kramer, T. L. (1990). Buffalo Creek survivors in the second decade: Comparison with unexposed and nonlitigant groups. *Journal of Applied Social Psychology, 20*(3), 1033–1050. https://doi.org/10.1111/j.1559-1816.1990.tb00388.x

Green, B. L., Lindy, J. D., Grace, M. C., Gleser, G. C., Leonard, A. C., Korol, M., et al. (1990). Buffalo Creek survivors in the second decade: Stability of stress symptoms. *American Journal of Orthopsychiatry, 60*, 43–54. https://doi.org/10.1037/h0079168

Gregory, A. C., Williamson, E., & Feder, G. (2017). The impact of informal supporters of domestic violence survivors: A systematic literature review. *Trauma, Violence & Abuse, 18*(5), 562–580. https://doi.org/10.1177/1524838016641919

Griffin, W., Montsinger, J. & Carter, N. (1995). *Personal safety handbook: Targeting safety in human services*. Durham, N.C.: Brendan Associates.

Gutermann, J., Schreiber, F., Matulis, S., Schwartzkopff, L., Deppe, J., & Steil, R. (2016). Psychological treatments for symptoms of posttraumatic stress disorder in children, aloles-cents, and young adults: A meta-analysis. *Clinical Child Family Psychological Review, 19*, 77–93. https://doi.org/10.1007/s10567-016-0202-5

Hager, A. D., & Runtz, M. G. (2012). Physical and psychological maltreatment in childhood and later health problems in women: An exploratory investigation of the roles of perceived stress and coping strategies. *Child Abuse and Neglect, 36*(5), 393–403.

Hamby, S., Grych, J., & Banyard, V. (2018). Resilience portfolios and poly-strengths: Identifying protective factors associated with thriving after adversity. *Psychology of Violence, 8*(2), 172–183. https://doi.org/10.1037/vio0000135

Hansen, M., Hyland, P., Karstoft, K., Vaegter, H. B., Bramsen, R. H., Nielsen, A. B. S., et al. (2017). Does size really matter? A multisite study assessing the latent structure of the proposed ICD-11 and DSM-5 diagnostic criteria for PTSD. *European Journal of Psychotraumatology, 8*(sup7), 1398002. https://doi.org/10.1080/20008198.2017.1398002

Haslam, N. (2016). Concept creep: Psychology's expanding concepts of harm and pathology. *Psychological Inquiry, 27*, 1–17. https://doi.org/10.1080/1047840X.2016.1082418

Hockett, J. M., & Saucier, D. A. (2015). A systematic literature review of "rape victims" versus "rape survivors": Implications for theory, research, and practice. *Aggression and Violent Behavior, 25*, 1–14. https://doi.org/10.1016/j.avb.2015.07.003

Hodge, D. R. (2019). Spiritual microaggressions: Understanding the subtle messages that foster religious discrimination. *Journal of Ethnic & Cultural Diversity in Social Work.* https://doi.org/10.1080/15313204.2018.1555501

Hollander, J. A. (2014). Does self-defense training prevent sexual violence against women? *Violence Against Women, 20*(3), 252–269.

Horswill, M. S., Garth, M., Hill, A., & Watson, M. O. (2017). The effect of performance feedback on drivers' hazard perception ability and self-ratings. *Accident Analysis and Prevention, 101*, 135–142. https://doi.org/10.1016/j.aap.2017.02.009

Howell, K. H., Thurston, I. B., Schwartz, L. E., Jamison, L. E., & Hasselle, A. J. (2018). Protective factors associated with resilience in women exposed to intimate partner violence. *Psychology of Violence, 8*, 438–447. https://doi.org/10.1037/vio0000147

Infurna, F. J., & Jayawickreme, E. (2019). Fixing the growth illusion: New directions for research in resilience and posttraumatic growth. *Current Directions in Psychological Science, 28*(2), 152–158. https://doi.org/10.1177/0963721419827017

Infurna, F. J., & Luthar, S. S. (2018). Re-evaluating the notion that resilience is commonplace: A review and distillation of directions for future research, practice, and policy. *Clinical Psychology Review, 65*, 43–56. https://doi.org/10.1016/j.cpr.2018.07.003

Iyadural, L., Visser, R. M., Lau-Zhu, A., Porcheret, K., Horsch, A., Holmes, E. A., et al. (2019). Intrusive memories of trauma: A target for research bridging cognitive science and its clinical application. *Clinical Psychology Review, 69*, 67–82. https://doi.org/10.1016/j.cpr.2018.08.005

Janoff-Bulman, R. (1979). Characterological versus behavioral self-blame: Inquiries into depression and rape. *Journal of Personality and Social Psychology, 37*, 1798–1809. https://doi.org/10.1037/0022-3514.37.10.1798

Janoff-Bulman, R. (1992). *Shattered assumptions: Towards a new psychology of victimization.* New York, NY: Free Press.

Janoff-Bulman, R., & Frieze, I. H. (1983). A theoretical perspective for understanding reactions to victimization. *Journal of Social Issues, 39*(2), 1–17.

Johnson, A. J. (Ed.). (2015). *Religion and men's violence against women*. New York: Springer.

Kahn, A. S., & Mathie, V. A. (2000). Understanding the unacknowledged rape victim. In C. B. Travis & J. W. White (Eds.), *Psychology of women; 4. Sexuality, society, and feminism* (p. 377–403). American Psychological Association. https://doi.org/10.1037/10345-015

Kaniasty, K., de Terte, I., Gullaran, J., & Bennett, S. (2019). A scoping review of postdisaster social support investigations conducted after disasters that struck the Australia and Oceania continent. *Diasters*. https://doi.org/10.1111/disa.12390

Kanno, H., & Newhill, C. E. (2009). Social workers and battered women: The need to study client violence in the domestic violence field. *Journal of Aggression, Maltreatment and Trauma, 18*, 46–63.

Koss, M. P., Bailey, J. A., Yuan, N. P., Herrera, V. M., & Lichter, E. L. (2003). Depression and PTSD in survivors of male violence: Research and training initiatives to facilitate recovery. *Psychology of Women Quarterly, 27*, 130–142. https://doi.org/10.1111/1471-6402.00093

Krebs, C. P., Lindquist, C. H., Warner, T. D., Fisher, B. S., & Martin, S. L. (2007). *The campus sexual assault (CSA) study*. Washington, DC: National Institute of Justice, U.S. Department of Justice.

Krebs, C. P., Lindquist, C. H., Warner, T. D., Fisher, B. S., & Martin, S. L. (2009). College women's experiences with physically forced, alcohol- or other drug-enabled, and drug-facilitated sexual assault before and since entering college. *Journal of American College Health, 57*(6), 639–647.

Lee, J., Kim, S., Kang, H., Kim, S., Bae, K., Kim, J., et al. (2017). Relationship between problematic internet use and post-traumatic stress disorder symptoms among students following the Sewol Ferry disaster in South Korea. *Psychiatry Investigation, 14*, 871–875. https://doi.org/10.4306/pi.2017.14.6.871

Leeies, M., Pagura, J., Sareen, J., & Bolton, J. M. (2010). The use of alcohol and drugs to self-medicate symptoms of posttraumtic stress disorder. *Depression and Anxiety, 27*, 731–736. https://doi.org/10.1002/da.20677

Lehavot, K., Katon, J. G., Chen, J. A., Fortney, J. C., & Simpson, T. L. (2018). Post-traumatic stress disorder by gender and veteran status. *American Journal of Preventive Medicine, 54*(1), x1–e9.

Lilienfeld, S. O. (2017). Microaggressions: Strong claims, inadequate evidence. *Perspectives on Psychological Science, 12*(1), 138–169. https://doi.org/10.1177/1745691616659391

Lipsky, S., Kernic, M. A., Qiu, Q., & Hasin, D. S. (2016). Traumatic events associated with post-traumatic stress disorder: The role of race/ethnicity and depression. *Violence Against Women, 22*, 1055–1074. https://doi.org/10.1177/1077801215617553

Logan, T. K. (2018). Factors influencing safety efficacy: Examining past experience, mind-set, and emotional management. *Journal of Interpersonal Violence*, 1–25. https://doi.org/10.1177/0886260518802849

Lui, P. P., & Quezada, L. (2019). Associations between microaggression and adjustment: A meta-analytic and narrative review. *Psychological Bulletin, 145*, 45–78. https://doi.org/10.1037/bul0000172

Lyubomirsky, S., Layous, K., Chancellor, J., & Nelson, S. K. (2015). Thinking about rumination: The scholarly contnributions and intellectual legacy of Susan Nolen-Hoeksema. *Annual Review of Clinical Psychology, 11*, 1–22. https://doi.org/10.1146/annurev-clinpsy-032814-112733

Macmillan, R. (2001). Violence and the life course: The consequences of victimization for personal and social development. *Annual Review of Sociology, 27*, 1–22. https://doi.org/10.1146/annurev.soc.27.1.1

Maier, S. F., & Seligman, M. E. P. (2016). Learned helplessness at fifty: Insights from neuroscience. *Psychological Review, 123*(4), 349–367. https://doi.org/10.1037/rev0000033

Marin, M., Geoffrion, S., Juster, R., Giguère, C., Marchand, A., Lupien, S. J., et al. (2019). High cortisol awakening response in the aftermath of workplace violence exposure moderates the association between acute stress disorder symptoms and PTSD symptoms. *Psychoneuroendocrinology, 104*, 238–242. https://doi.org/10.1016/j.psyneuen.2019.03.006

Mattis, J. S. (2002). Religion and spirituality in the meaning-making and coping experiences of African American women: A qualitative analysis. *Psychology of Women Quarterly, 26*, 309–321.

McBride, O., Hyland, P., Murphy, J., & Elklit, A. (2019). Network analysis of posttraumatic stress experiences of adults seeking psychological treatment for childhood sexual abuse. *Journal of Traumatic Stress*, 1–10. https://doi.org/10.1002/jts.22381

McFarland, C., & Alvaro, C. (2000). The impact of motivation on temporal comparisons: Coping with traumatic events by perceiving personal growth. *Journal of Personality and Social Psychology, 79*(3), 327–343. https://doi.org/10.1037/0022-3514.79.3.327

McNally, R. J. (2016) The expanding empire of psychopathology: The case of PTSD. *Psychological Inquiry, 27*, 46-49. https://doi.org/10.1080/1047840X.2016.1108168

Meerholz, E. W., Spears, R., Epstude, K. (2019). Having pity on our victims to save ourselves: Compassion reduces self-critical emotions and self-blame about past harmful behavior among those who highly identify with their past self. *PLoS ONE 14*(12): e0223945. https://doi.org/10.1371/journal.pone.0223945

Meston, C. M., & Lorenz, T. A. (2013). Physiological stress responses predict sexual functioning and satisfaction differently in women who have and have not been sexually abused in childhood. *Psychological Trauma: Theory, research, practice and policy, 5*(4), 350–358.

Meyer, S. (2016). Still blaming the victim of intimate partner violence? Women's narratives of victim desistance and redemption when seeking support. *Theoretical Criminology, 20*(1), 75–90. https://doi.org/10.1177/1362480615585399

Miller, L. (2012). Posttraumatic stress disorder and criminal violence: Basic concepts and clinical-forensic applications. *Aggression and Violent Behavior, 17*, 354–364. https://doi.org/10.1016/j.avb.2012.03.007

Montclair Safety & Improvement Council (2016). *Personal Safety Tips*. Downloaded September 5, 2016 from: http://www.montclairsic.org/personalsafety.htm

Moody, A. T., & Lewis, J. A. (2019). Gendered racial microaggressions and traumatic stress symptoms among black women. *Psychology of Women Quarterly, 43*(2), 201–214. https://doi.org/10.1177/0361684319828288

Muscanell, N. L., & Guadagno, R. E. (2012). Make new friends or keep the old: Gender and personality differences in social networking use. *Computers in Human Behavior, 28*(1), 107–112.

National Institute of Justice. (2017). Victims and victimization. Retrieved from https://www.nij.gov/topics/victims-victimization/pages/welcome.aspx

Newhill, C. E. (1995). *A crisis casebook.* Unpublished manuscript. School of Social Work. University of Pittsburgh.

Newhill, C. E., & Sites, E. W. (2000). Identifying human remains following an air disaster: The role of social work. *Social Work in Health Care, 31*, 85–105.

Niemi, L., & Young, L. (2016). Who blames the victim? *The New York Times,* June 24.

Not alone: The first report of the White House Task Force to Protect Students from Sexual Assault. (2014). Retrieved June 10, 2014 from: http://www.whitehouse.gov/sites/default/files/docs/report_0.pdf

O'Donnell, M. L., Alkemade, N., Nickerson, A., Creamer, M., McFarlane, A. C., Silove, D., et al. (2014). Impact of the diagnostic changes to post-traumatic stress disorder for DSM-5 and the proposed changes to ICD-11. *The British Journal of Psychiatry, 205*, 230–235. https://doi.org/10.1192/bjp.bp.113.135285

Ogle, C. M., Rubin, D. C., & Siegler, I. C. (2013). The impact of developmental timing of trauma exposure on PTSD symptoms and psychosocial functioning among older adults. *Developmental Psychology, 49*, 2191–2200. https://doi.org/10.1037/a0031985

Oulton, J. M., Strange, D., Nixon, R. D. V., & Takarangi, M. K. T. (2018). PTSD and the role of spontaneous elaborative "nonmemories". *Psychology of Consciousness: Theory, Research, and Practice, 5*(4), 398–413. https://doi.org/10.1037/cns0000158

Pan, X., Kaminga, A. C., Wen, S. W., & Liu, A. (2018). Catecholamines in post-traumatic stress disorder: A systematic review and meta-analysis. *Frontiers in Molecular Neuroscience, 11*, 450. https://doi.org/10.3389/fnmol.2018.00450

Park, C. L. (2010). Making sense of the meaning literature: An integrative review of meaning making and its effects on adjustments to stressful life events. *Psychological Bulletin, 136*, 257–301. https://doi.org/10.1037/a0018301

Pavlacic, J. M., Buchanan, E. M., Maxwell, N. P., Hopke, T. G., & Schulenberg, S. E. (2019). A meta-analysis of expressive writing on posttraumatic stress, posttraumatic growth, and quality of life. *Review of General Psychology, 23*, 230–250. https://doi.org/10.1177/1089268019831645

Pebole, M. M., & Hall, K. S. (2019). Physical activity promotion in women with PTSD: What we need for progress. *Psychology of Sport & Exercise, 41*, 127–129. https://doi.org/10.1016/j.psychsport.2018.12.013

Pennebaker, J. W. (2018). Expressive writing in psychological science. *Perspectives on Psychological Science, 13*(2), 226–229. https://doi.org/10.1177/1745691617707315

Pennebaker, J. W., & Beall, S. K. (1986). Confronting a traumatic event: Toward an understanding of inhibition and disease. *Journal of Abnormal Psychology, 95*, 274–281. https://doi.org/10.1037/0021-843X.95.3.274

Pietrzak, R. H., Feder, A., Singh, R., Schechter, C. B., Bromet, E. J., Katz, C. L., et al. (2013). Trajectories of PTSD risk and resilience in World Trade Center responders: an 8-year prospective cohort study. *Psychological Medicine, 44*(1), 205–219.

Renner, L. M., & Hartley, C. C. (2018). Psychological well-being among women who experienced intimate partner violence and received civil legal services. *Journal of Interpersonal Violence*, 1–22. https://doi.org/10.1177/0886260518777552

Richardson, L. K., Frueh, B. C., & Acierno, R. (2010). Prevalence estimates of combat-related PTSD: A critical review. *Australian and New Zealand Journal of Psychiatry, 44*(1), 4–19.

Rizo, C. F., Givens, A., & Lombardi, B. (2017). A systematic review of coping among heterosexual female IPV survivors in the United States with a focus on the conceptualization and measurement of coping. *Aggression and Violent Behavior, 34*, 35–50. https://doi.org/10.1016/j.avb.2017.03.006

Roberts, A. L., Gilman, S. E., Breslau, J., Breslau, N., & Koenen, K. C. (2011). Race/ethnic differences in exposure to traumatic events, development of post-traumatic stress disorder, and treatment-seeking for post-traumatic stress disorder in the United States. *Psychological Medicine, 41*, 71–83. https://doi.org/10.1017/S0033291710000401

Roberts, N. P., Roberts, P. A., Jones, N., & Bisson, J. I. (2015). Psychological interventions for post-traumatic stress disorder and comorbid substance use disorder: A systematic review and meta-analysis. *Clinical Psychology Review, 38*, 25–38. https://doi.org/10.1016/j.cpr.2015.02.007

Rosenthal, A. M. (2015). Thirty-eight witnesses: The Kitty Genovese case. Hoopla digital.

Rubin, D. C., & Feeling, N. (2013). Measuring the severity of negative and traumatic events. *Clinical Psychological Science, 1*, 375–389. https://doi.org/10.1177/2167702613483112

Ruhs, F., Greve, W., & Kappes, C. (2017). Coping with criminal victimization and fear of crime: The protective role of accommodative self-regulation. *The British Psychological Society, 22*, 359–377. https://doi.org/10.1111/lcrp.12106

Rutter, M. (1987). Psychosocial resilience and protective mechanisms. *American Journal of Orthopsychiatry, 57*(3), 316–331. https://doi.org/10.1111/j.1939-0025.1987.tb03541.x

Salcioglu, E., Urhan, S., Pirinccioglu, T., & Aydin, S. (2017). Anticipatory fear and helplessness predict PTSD and depression in domestic violence survivors. *Psychological Trauma: Theory, Research, and Policy, 9*, 117–125. https://doi.org/10.1037/tra0000200

Sanbonmatsu, D. M., Strayer, D. L., Behrends, A. A., Ward, N., & Watson, J. M. (2016). Why drivers use cell phones and support legislation to restrict this practice. *Accident Analysis and Prevention, 92*, 22–33. https://doi.org/10.1016/j.aap.2016.03.010

Schepple, K. L., & Bart, P. B. (1983). Through women's eyes: Defining danger in the wake of sexual assault. *Journal of Social Issues, 39*(2), 63–81. https://doi.org/10.1111/j.1540-4560.1983.tb00141.x

Schreck, C. J., Berg, M. T., Fisher, B. S., & Wilcox, P. (2018). That door that you just kicked in was locked for *your* protection, not mine: Developing and testing competing theoretical models of crime prevention behavior. *Journal of Research in Crime and Delinquency, 55*(2), 316–345. https://doi.org/10.1177/0022427817751570

Sehgal, P. (2016). The forced heroism of the 'survivor'. *The New York Times,* May 3.

Sharot, T., Korn, C. W., & Dolan, R. J. (2011). How unrealistic optimism is maintained in the face of reality. *Nature Neuroscience, 14*(11), 1475–1479. https://doi.org/10.1038/nn.2949

Silver, R. L., Boon, C., & Stones, M. H. (1983). Searching for meaning in misfortune: Making sense of incest. *Journal of Social Issues, 39*(2), 81–101. https://doi.org/10.1111/j.1540-4560.1983.tb00142.x

Sloan, D. M., & Marx, B. P. (2017). Maximizing outcomes associated with expressive writing. *Clinical Psychology: Science and Practice, 25*, e12231. https://doi.org/10.1111/cpsp.12231

Smith, N. D. L., & Cottler, L. B. (2018). The epidemiology of post-traumatic stress disorder and alcohol disorder. *Alcohol Reearch: Current Reviews, 39*(2), 113–120.

Smith, P. H., Murray, C. E., & Coker, A. L. (2010). The coping window: A contextual understanding of the methods women use to cope with battering. *Violence and Victims, 25*, 18–28. https://doi.org/10.1891/0886-6708.25.1.18

Smith, T. C., Ryan, M. A. K., Wingard, D. L., Slymen, D. J., Sallis, J. F., & Kritz-Silverstein, D. (2008). New onset and persistent symptoms of posttraumatic stress disorder self-reported after deployment and combat exposures: Prospective population based U.S. military cohort study. *British Medical Journal, 336*, 366–371.

Spinhoven, P., Penninx, B. W., Krempeniou, A., van Hemert, A. M., & Elzinga, B. (2015). Trait rumination predicts onset of Post-Traumatic Stress Disorder through trauma-related cognitive appraisals: A 4-year longitudinal study. *Behaviour Research and Therapy, 71*, 101–109. https://doi.org/10.1016/j.brat.2015.06.004

Tannura, T. A. (2014). Rape trauma syndrome. *American Journal of Sexuality Education, 9*(2), 247–256.

Taylor, S. E., Buunk, B. P., & Aspinwall, L. G. (1990). Social comparison, stress, and coping. *Personality and Social Psychology Bulletin, 16*, 74-89. https://doi.org/10.1177/0146167290161006

Tedeschi, R. G., & Calhoun, L. G. (2004). Posttraumatic growth: Conceptual foundations and empirical evidence. *Psychological Inquiry, 15*, 1–18.

Thege, B. K., Horwood, L., Slater, L., Tan, M. C., Hodgins, D. C., & Wild, T. C. (2017). Relationship between interpersonal trauma exposure and addictive behaviors: A systematic review. *BMC Psychiatry, 17*, 164. https://doi.org/10.1186/s12888-017-1323-1

Thoits, P. A. (2010). Stress and health: Major findings and policy implications. *Journal of Health and Social Behavior, 51*(1 suppl), S41–S53.

Thordardottir, E. B., Valdimarsdottir, U. A., Hansdottir, I., Resnick, H., Shipherd, J. C., & Gudmundsdottir, B. (2015). Posttraumatic stress and other health consequences of catastrophic avalanches: A 16-year follow-up of survivors. *Journal of Anxiety Disorders, 32*, 103–111. https://doi.org/10.1016/j.janxdis.2015.03.005

Tolin, D. F., & Foa, E. B. (2006). Sex differences in trauma and posttraumatic stress disorder: A quantitative review of 25 years of research. *Psychological Bulletin, 132*(6), 959–992. https://doi.org/10.1037/0033-2909.132.6.959

Uchino, B. N., Bowen, K., de Grey, R. K., Mikel, J., & Fisher, E. B. (2018). Social support and physical health: Models, mechanisms and opportunities. In E. B. Fisher, L. D. Cameron, A. J. Christensen, E. Ehlert, Y. Gao, B. Oldenburg, & F. J. Snoek (Eds.), *Principles and concepts of behavioral medicine: A global handbook.* (pp. 341–372). New York: Springer.

Ulloa, E. C., Hammett, J. F., Guzman, M. L., & Hokoda, A. (2015). Psychological growth in relation to intimate partner violence: A review. *Aggression and Violent Behavior, 25*, 88–94. https://doi.org/10.1016/j.avb.2015.07.007

Walker, L. E. (2016). *The battered woman syndrome* (4th ed.). New York, NY: Springer.

Wollinger, G. R. (2017). Choice behavior after burglary victimization: Moving, safety precautions, and passivity. *European Journal of Criminology, 14*(3), 329–343. https://doi.org/10.1177/1477370816661738

United Nations World Health Organization. (2018). The ICD-11 is here. https://www.who.int/classifications/icd/en/

Xiaoli, W., Kaminga, A. C., Wenjie, D., Jing, D., Zhipeng, W., & Xionfeng, P. (2019). The prevalence of moderate-to-high posttraumatic growth: A systematic review and meta-analysis. *Journal of Affective Disorders, 243*, 408–415. https://doi.org/10.1016/j.jad.2018.09.023

Yoder, J. D. (2013). *Women and gender: Making a difference* (4th ed.). Cornwall-on-Hudson, NY: Sloan Publishing.

Zang, Y., Yu, J., Chazin, D., Asnaani, A., Zandberg, L. J., & Foa, E. B. (2017). Changes in coping behavior in a randomized controlled trial of concurrent treatment for PTSD and alcohol dependence. *Behaviour Research and Therapy, 90*, 9–15. https://doi.org/10.1016/j.brat.2016.11.013

Zuk, M., Bierbaum, A. H., Gorska, K., Loukaitou-Sideris, A., Ong, P., & Thomas, T. (2015). Gentrification, displacement and the role of public investment: A literature review. *Community Development Investment Center Working Paper* 2015-5, Federal Reserve Bank of San Francisco.

Chapter 4
Violence and Abuse in Intimate Partner Relationships: Battered Women and Their Batterers

Published Case Example

The night of August 30, 2016, Pennsylvania state police closed in on the barn where Kevin Ewing had been holding his wife Tierne hostage, just a few miles from where the couple had lived and raised their two children. Mr. Ewing saw the troopers moving across the field and ordered them to get back. A few moments later, the police heard three shots. Entering the barn, state trooper Sarah Teagarden saw Mrs. Ewing dead on the floor from two gunshot wounds and Mr. Ewing lying on the floor next to her with a self-inflicted gunshot wound to the head. He was taken to the hospital where he died the next morning. This murder-suicide was the culmination of decades of escalating physical and psychological abuse of Mrs. Ewing at the hands of her husband. Only a month earlier, Mr. Ewing kidnapped and held his estranged wife hostage, torturing her for 12 days. Following her escape, Mr. Ewing was charged with kidnapping and assault "for branding her with a metal rod, binding her with wire and locking her in a closet, covering her mouth with duct tape, pistol-whipping her, and threatening repeatedly that he would shoot her in the head then shoot himself, too" (Kane, 2016, p. A-6).

Kevin and Tierne Ewing were a couple from the time they were in the 8th grade, but their relationship was characterized from the beginning by verbal and physical abuse according to police, family members and neighbors. Fifteen years prior to her murder, Mrs. Ewing had finally obtained a protection-from-abuse (PFA) order, which was soon violated by her estranged husband resulting in Mr. Ewing spending 7 months in jail. The couple reunited after Mr. Ewing was released from jail but it wasn't long before the abuse started again. A cycle comprised of abuse, obtaining a PFA order, violating the PFA order, criminal charges, subsequent brief jail terms related to the abuse, and then reuniting as a couple repeated itself over the years. Washington County Assistant District Attorney Kristen Clingerman, a special victims prosecutor,

I. H. Frieze et al., *Dynamics of Family and Intimate Partner Violence*,
https://doi.org/10.1007/978-3-030-42608-8_4

tried her best to protect Mrs. Ewing by legal means but to no avail. Trooper Teagarden said she had seen similar behavior from abused women, stating: "Anybody you would talk to would ask 'Why did she go back?' But, mental health professionals will tell you, and I've seen it again and again, battered women, this is what they do. They go back. Mrs. Ewing is the classic, quintessential example of battered women's syndrome. The question is, how do you teach these girls, these women not to go back?" Mrs. Ewing's death was senseless, but it was not unexpected. (Kane, 2016).

The focus of this chapter is on couples where men perpetrate severe violence, often labeled as *battering*, against their female partners in committed relationships. Like the case of Kevin and Tierne Ewing, such couples generally live together and are often married, although, as explained in this chapter, the pattern of the battering relationship often starts earlier before the couple is in a committed relationship. For the Ewings, it began soon after eighth grade.

Intimate partner violence (IPV) does not necessarily take the form of severe violence or battering where one partner dominates the other. Chapter 5 looks more closely at relationships with what may be relatively low violence levels, often perpetrated by both the male and female partner. Other patterns described in Chap. 5 are joint couple violence or relationships where the woman is the more violent partner. Violence in an earlier stage of a heterosexual relationship, often labeled as *dating violence*, is another form of intimate couple violence or aggression, but in a less committed stage of the relationship that is also examined in Chap. 5. Violence within gay male and lesbian couples has similar patterns to the patterns of heterosexual IPV, is also discussed in Chap. 5. Leaving aside these other forms of IPV, this chapter looks at what are traditionally known as battered women and their male batterers.

4.1 History of Research on Battered Women

In the 1970s, feminist activists and researchers began to write about and publicize the situation of the battered woman who was physically and emotionally abused by the man she lived with (see Martin, 1976; Pagelow, 1981; Walker, 1979). Until this time, there was very little attention given to partner violence within psychological and social science research. After these early books, this began to change. Along with increased attention among researchers and the public, battered women's shelters were set up to provide emergency housing for women attempting to escape from an attack by their partner in the United States as well as in other countries such as England (Walker, 2001; see Chap. 8). Although these shelters were initially established by small groups of women relying on donations, they eventually became institutionalized. Once shelters were established, many quickly found that the need for emergency shelter was far greater than they were able to provide, and women had to be turned away (Koss, White, & Lopez, 2017).

Along with rape, the problem of battered women was seen as one of the major issues confronting women by feminist activists in the 1970s and 1980s (Frieze, 2005). In addition to helping individual women through providing emergency housing, there was also lobbying to change our legal codes beginning in those years. Feminists were quite active in the 1970s and 1980s in identifying wife battering as a crime and arguing that more legal action was needed to make men stop battering their partners (Murray, 1988; United States Commission on Civil Rights, 1978; Van Hasselt, Morrison, Bellack, & Hersen, 1988). Laws had previously addressed male violence toward his wife or partner to some level, but there was a general tolerance of violence within marriage. Only very serious violence or murder was taken seriously (Pleck, 1989). Walker (2001) and Barner and Carney (2011) outline some of the changes in laws through the twentieth century.

One of the early theories explaining the reactions of battered women was developed by Walker (1979), who outlined a pattern of reactions which she labeled as the *Battered Woman Syndrome* in her book, *The Battered Woman*. A similar theory was proposed by Graham, Rawlings and Rimini (1988) as they related the experiences of battered women to those of a group of hostages held during a bank robbery. The robbery victims experienced what came to be known as the *Stockholm Syndrome*. A number of other theorists have also discussed the dynamics of battering relationships. Some of the newer theories focus on the motivations of the violent man. Partner battering has been labeled as *patriarchal terrorism* (Johnson, 1995), and later was renamed *intimate terrorism* (Johnson & Ferraro, 2000). Stark (2007) presented another analysis of both the abusive man and his female partner in his book *Coercive Control: How Men Entrap Women in Personal Life*.

4.2 Dynamics of Violent Relationships

Many authors have provided vivid examples to explain the life of the battered woman and how this type of relationship develops over time. It appears that battering relationships often follow a general pattern. The description below of this type of violence is based on the first author's own interviews with battered women and on clinical work and research by Johnson (1995), by Pagelow (1981), by Stark (2007), by Tjaden and Thoennes (1998), and by Walker (1979). After describing the general pattern of wife battering, specific research findings are reviewed as they relate to different aspects of this type of relationship.

4.2.1 How Does the Battering Relationship Develop?

The beginnings of what will become wife battering can often be seen very early in a relationship, often when the couple begins to be in a serious dating relationship. These relationships often appear to be very romantic, with the male partner very involved in the life of the woman. He frequently communicates and is generous with gifts. He likes to know what his partner is doing and may call or check with her frequently in other ways. He wants to be with her any time he can, and may become jealous when she is not with him or shows interest in any other man. At this early stage of the relationship, this desire for a high level of intimacy and involvement in her life is seen by her and others as indicating his strong love for her.

Although the intensity and superficially romantic behavior continues, at some point, perhaps when he is feeling upset about something, the man slaps or hits his female partner. He does no real physical harm to her. He apologies and begs her to forgive him. He says he does not know what came over him, and proclaims and he will never do anything like this again. Since she cares about him, she is quick to forgive him. They may reaffirm their caring for one another through passionate sex. Note that although neither is likely to be consciously aware of this, the passionate sex and expression of caring from her is reinforcing his earlier violence. As discussed in Chap. 2, behaviors that are reinforced are likely to occur again.

After this first incident of violence, the relationship goes back to its earlier patterns. He continues to care about what she is doing, and she welcomes this display of his caring. But, eventually something happens, and he is violent again. The violence may be somewhat more severe this second time. He again apologizes, saying he can't understand how this happened. He assures her that he won't use violence against her again. She sees his distress and is again willing to accept his apology. He notes how much he loves her and seems to want reassurance from her that she still loves him. They reaffirm their caring, perhaps again with passionate sex. As in the original incident, the violence has again been reinforced.

Over time, his use of violence occurs again and again, perhaps getting a bit more severe every time. His apologies become shorter and shorter, and eventually stop completely. Along with his physical violence, he also becomes psychologically abusive. He blames her for his violence, saying that if she would only do the things he asks, he would not have to use force against her. She may accept this accusation, and blame herself for the violence. He begins to tell her that she has so many faults, no one else would ever want to be with her. He may force her to have sex, a situation now labeled as marital rape (see Box 4.1).

Box 4.1: Types of Intimate Partner Violence

According to the U.S. Centers for Disease Control and Prevention [there are four main types of intimate partner violence as proposed by Saltzman, Fanslow, McMahon, & Shelley, 2002]:

- **Physical violence** is the intentional use of physical force with the potential for causing death, disability, injury, or harm. Physical violence includes, but is not limited to, scratching; pushing; shoving; throwing; grabbing; biting; choking; shaking; slapping; punching; burning; use of a weapon; and use of restraints or one's body, size, or strength against another person.
- **Sexual violence** is divided into three categories: (1) use of physical force to compel a person to engage in a sexual act against his or her will, whether or not the act is completed; (2) attempted or completed sex act involving a person who is unable to understand the nature or condition of the act, to decline participation, or to communicate unwillingness to engage in the sexual act, e.g., because of illness, disability, or the influence of alcohol or other drugs, or because of intimidation or pressure; and (3) abusive sexual contact.
- **Threats of physical or sexual violence** use words, gestures, or weapons to communicate the intent to cause death, disability, injury, or physical harm.
- **Psychological/emotional violence** involves trauma to the victim caused by acts, threats of acts, or coercive tactics. Psychological/emotional abuse can include, but is not limited to, humiliating the victim, controlling what the victim can and cannot do, withholding information from the victim, deliberately doing something to make the victim feel diminished or embarrassed, isolating the victim from friends and family, and denying the victim access to money or other basic resources. It is considered psychological/emotional violence when there has been prior physical or sexual violence or prior threat of physical or sexual violence. In addition, stalking is often included among the types of IPV. Stalking generally refers to "harassing or threatening behavior that an individual engages in repeatedly, such as following a person, appearing at a person's home or place of business, making harassing phone calls, leaving written messages or objects, or vandalizing a person's property" (Tjaden & Thoennes, 1998).

This information comes from the CDC. See the website for further information at http://www.cdc.gov/violenceprevention/intimatepartnerviolence/definitions.html

As this pattern develops, it has happened gradually, and neither party may be truly aware that his violence now defines their relationship. Both partners may continue to believe that the most recent violence was caused by particular events occurring at that time and don't expect the violence to reoccur. She hides the violence from others, because of feeling guilty, either for causing him to beat her or because of deciding to stay with or even marry a violent man. Her need to hide the violence she is experiencing from her partner may lead to a sense of social isolation, since she feels she cannot talk to others about her situation. She may find that her partner gets angry when she spends time with friends or family, and may also limit her social contacts because of fears of his violence. As discussed in more detail below, she begins to suffer from a variety of emotional and physical health problems.

The following case illustrates this common pattern of an episode of abuse occurring, the perpetrator apologizing and being contrite. It also demonstrates his promising to change but, without intervention, the abuse often occurs again and, in this case, heavy alcohol abuse was (as it often is, Testa & Derrick, 2013) associated with intimate partner violence. The case also shows how the female victim of abuse may try to leave multiple times before she makes a commitment to really leave and/or get assistance.

Case Example #7
Julie is a 25-year old married white female with one child who was brought to the crisis clinic by her sister-in-law. Julie states that her husband kicked her out of the house 2 days ago and she has no place to go and is, essentially, homeless. Her sister-in-law took her in to stay with her family but her husband (Julie's brother-in-law) says he wants Julie to leave because his brother will get too upset. Julie's husband drinks heavily on a daily basis, beats her up regularly and she doesn't know what to do. Julie presents as an attractive young woman who is upset and desperate. Her speech is pressured, affect is somewhat labile in presentation, there is no evidence thought disorder, and she denies suicidal or homicidal ideation. Julie has stayed at the battered women's shelter before but has never been willing to stay longer than overnight. When I inquired as to why she doesn't stay longer at the shelter, she says that she has always contacted her husband, he apologizes and promises never to hit her again and so she returns home. Things are good for a couple weeks or so but then his drinking escalates and inevitably he abuses her again. Julie realizes she needs to do more than what she has done so far to change her situation, including staying at the shelter and getting counseling, so I called the shelter and she talked with them on the phone and agreed to go there and commit to staying for a few days. Her sister-in-law agreed to drive her over.

As this point, the relationship can now be labeled as the type of battering relationship described in the many writings on battered women. Violence may be quite common in these relationships, but there may also be long periods of no violence. The male partner is violent to the children as well as to her. He destroys her possessions and may kill or injure any pets (see Chap. 7). She may experience severe injuries. The battered woman lives in constant fear that something she might do will initiate another incident of violence. Her self esteem lowers as she hears repeated comments from him about things she does wrong and about negative aspects of her personality. He may make nasty comments about her in front of other people. He also discourages her from seeing friends or family, saying that she gets upset when she does this.

She may react to this continuing pattern of abuse in various ways, as discussed later in this chapter in more detail. She is likely to try to fight back, but often this results in him being even more violent. She may try to get help from any family or friends she still has contact with. Calling the police is another way she might try to get the violence to stop, but if he is arrested, he is often even more violent when he comes home. If she does fight back, she might even be arrested, too (see Chap. 5). She may seek refuge in a battered women's shelter, where she can be safe for a little while. But, she will typically return to her abuser after she feels he has calmed down. He may have sent her a message that he loves her and wants her to return, or he may threaten her and tell her he will harm someone she cares about or do damage to some possession or a loved pet if she does not return. She may realize she cannot escape him if she tries to return to work. And, she has nowhere else she can go to live where he cannot find her.

The following case illustrates how even when an abused victim takes action and evicts the abuser from the home, the abuser may stalk and continue to assault the victim. (More information is available about this case in the case appendix). Case #2 shows how victims may seek help through all the appropriate channels, e.g. calling the police or seeking refuge at a shelter, but not receive the help needed. It also shows how a woman who has been repeatedly abused and hasn't been able to get help, resorts to a violent action to protect herself and her children.

Case Example #2

"Joyce" is a 22-year-old single African-American woman who, under extreme stress, came to the crisis clinic with her 4 year old daughter for help. Joyce tells the crisis worker that a little over 2 years ago, she started going out with a man named "George". Their relationship went well at first, and so she allowed him to move with her (her other child, a 2-year-old boy, is his biological child). Soon, however, George started beating Joyce frequently and severely. Once he beat her breasts so badly they got infected and she had to have surgery. Joyce finally kicked George out of the house, but he continued to come around and abuse her—he would follow her in parks and on the street, and then would attack her. Sometimes she was successful in pressing charges and having him put in jail, but recently the police had been unwilling to act on her complaints.

Joyce tried to get help from every resource she could think of including the police (repeatedly), the local district attorney, and Haven House* (the local domestic violence shelter), but got nowhere. The situation had progressed to the point that George was calling her constantly and threatening that he was going to kill her. Joyce developed ulcers, couldn't sleep and lost weight. George had also beaten Joyce's two children, and the children began having nightmares, angry outbursts and showing fear toward adult men in general. Finally, in desperation, Joyce borrowed a gun from her sister, and after a particularly brutal beating in which George poked Joyce's eye in with a stick (she required many stitches), she finally went out, found George sitting on a park bench, and after much deliberation, walked up and shot him. She then went to a pay phone and turned herself in to the police. Joyce states that for the first time – sitting in jail - she felt safe.

4.3 Types of Abuse

As the overview above suggests, a battering relationship often includes many different types of abuse (Carney & Barner, 2012). Although the types of abuse can be defined in many ways, we present the official U.S. government definitions in Box 4.1. As can be seen, IPV can be physical violence, sexual violence, threats of violence, or psychology or emotional aggression. Other types of violence or aggression have also been associated with IPV as outlined in Box 4.2.

Box 4.2: Other Types of Partner Abuse

In addition to the types of abuse outlined in the text, partner abuse can take a number of other forms:

- **Kidnapping**. A recent study was published exploring cases of intimate partner kidnapping reported in FBI statistics (Blumenstein, 2015). This tends to be something that young men do, kidnapping a young woman. People under the age of 18 were not included in this study. Blumenstein argued that this type of intimate partner kidnapping was more common than non-intimate kidnapping among adults.
- **Stalking**. A desire to know what the partner is doing is often seen early in the relationship which develop into battering relationships (Williams & Frieze, 2005) as well as during the relationship. It may be especially common during the breakup period (Norris, Huss, & Palarea, 2011).
- **Economic Abuse**. Controlling the partner's ability to acquire or use money and other economic resources. It may include interfering with the woman's job, stealing money from her, or generating debt in her name. Adams, Beeble, and Gregory (2015) argue that this is a form of coercive control and can prevent a woman from becoming self-sufficient.
- **Homicide**. Both male and female partners do kill their partners. In a review of the literature, Australian researchers Erikkson and Mazerolle (2013) argue that the motives for intimate partner homicide tend to differ for men and women. Men are more likely kill their female partner when jealous, when they feel a loss of control, or when she threatens to leave him. Women are more likely to kill their male partners out of desperation, resulting from previous violence from the partner, or out of feelings of social isolation.

Psychological or emotional abuse is generally found to be common and occurs in most battering as well as other types of violent intimate partnerships (Carney & Barner 2012). All these types of abuse tend to be highly correlated (Nathanson, Shorey, Tirone, & Rhatigan, 2012; Stark, 2007). However, some types of violence may be evident early in the relationship, and others are added later. Whether physical violence or psychological abuse comes first varies across individual couples.

Salis, Salwen, and O'Leary (2014) noted in a sample of couples drawn from the community, who were not preselected as physically aggressive, that high levels of psychological aggression were predictive of physical violence a year later.

Emotional or psychological abuse is an important aspect of coercive control (Stark, 2007). As Hamberger, Larsen, and Lehner (2017) discussed in their review of the literature on this aspect of IPV, the idea of wanting to control the partner has been mentioned for many years in the literature on motivations of batterers. Coercive control involves three major elements: (1) the desire to control what the partner does; (2) the partner's view of this control as negative; and (3) the ability of the abuser to control the partner through credible threats of violence.

Every relationship is different, but it is not uncommon for several types of violence or abuse to occur in the same relationship. However, a relationship may have only one of these elements. In a qualitative study of divorcing mothers, Crossman, Hardesty, and Raffaelli (2016) found that even without any type of physical violence, women experiencing the emotional abuse associated with coercive control reported feeling high levels of threat and fear. Their concerns were similar to those women reporting coercive control and physical violence from their partners.

Although many studies tend to focus on the physical abuse, Nathanson et al. (2012) found that it was psychological abuse even more than physical abuse that predicted PTSD symptoms in women and intentions to leave their abuser. More specifically, Lacey and his colleagues noted that psychological abuse such as being called names in front of family members was especially predictive of trying to leave the abusive partner (Lacey, Saunders, & Zhang, 2011). Early research has noted that sexual abuse may be especially traumatic (Frieze, 1983). In a study of women recruited from family practice clinics, about 41% reported having been victims of interpersonal violence from an intimate partner, and of those women, 58% said they had also experienced sexual abuse (Coker, Smith, Bethea, King, & McKeown, 2000). Thus, some type of forced sex often accompanies other forms of physical violence.

In a more recent empirical study of coercive control, Dichter, Thomas, Crits-Christoph, Odgen, and Rhodes (2018) used a sample drawn from women patients in two hospital emergency departments who reported recent IPV victimization. In their sample of 553 women, they found that those experiencing coercive control from their partner also were subjected to higher levels of physical and sexual violence as well as higher levels of other forms of psychological aggression. Many of the women did fight back. There were higher reports of the women in the coercive control victimization group using physical violence than in the non-coercive control group. Coercive control was assessed with a scale that included items such as "He makes me feel unsafe, even in my own home" or "He can scare me without laying a hand on me" (p. 598).

Homicide is another very unfortunate form of IPV. The CDC reported that between 2003 and 2014, 4442 women died as a result of IPV (Petrosky et al., 2017). These data come from the CDC National Death Reporting System, and do not include all states, so the national totals would be much higher. These reported cases typically occurred during an argument, typically with the current intimate partner, but sometimes with a former partner. Young women, especially racial minority women, were more likely than older women or white women to be killed by an intimate partner.

Another type of abuse involves the batterer interfering with a job held by the abused woman. Showalter (2016) reviewed 20 studies addressing this issue. She found that many battered women reported receiving harassment from the abuser at work. This included numerous unwanted calls from the abuser as well as him showing up unexpectedly at their place of employment. The women complained that this led to an inability to concentrate and poorer work performance because of this. Harassment at home also resulted in not being able to get to work for these women. Not surprisingly, the women were sometimes fired because of these difficulties. Showalter concluded that such workplace concerns made the women less able to feel financially secure enough to leave their abusers.

4.3.1 Measurement of IPV

When formal research is done on IPV or violence against an intimate partner, researchers have to rely on formal scales to provide quantitative data. Most research on violence in relationships relies on these self-reports of different violent acts reported either by the person committing the violence, or the recipient or both. Such behavior often occurs in private settings and would be unlikely to occur in the presence of a scientific observer. Thus, there are few alternatives to the reliance on these self-reports for the researcher.

Measurement of IPV is quite complicated (e.g., Follingstad & Ryan, 2013). The most commonly used scale for measuring partner violence is the Conflict Tactics Scale or CTS (Straus, 1979). This scale focuses on physical violence, although a few items refer to other types of violence. The CTS has been criticized by many researchers (Follingstad & Ryan, 2013; Woodin, Sotskova, & O'Leary, 2013). A revised version of the original scale (the CTS2) was published in 1996 (Straus, Hamby, Boney-McCoy, & Sugarman, 1996), but the newer version of the CTS scale has not been well accepted. Most of the studies cited in this book use the Conflict Tactics Scale (CTS) to assess levels of violence, even though this does not measure the many types of partner violence mentioned earlier, and instead measures primarily acts of physical violence. Chapter 5 describes the IPV measurement process in more detail.

4.4 Why Do Some Men Become Batterers?

There has been far more research on battered women than on their abusers, but this is beginning to change. One reason for this lack of research has been that these men may not feel that they have a problem and do not present themselves for psychological treatment. They are also difficult to locate because they don't respond to recruitments for participants in a study of violence in marriage or even in a study described as addressing something like *marriage dynamics*. However, in the past decade, more and more states have adopted mandatory arrest policies or other procedures to make sure that reports of severe partner violence are not ignored. This led to violent men being arrested and often being forced to participate in a treatment program (see Maxwell, 2012 for a review of these programs or Chap. 9). So, now batterers are more available for research. Before this, much of our knowledge about the men came from the women they abused rather than directly from interviews of the batterers themselves. Now, the men arrested for partner violence can be questioned directly. However, there may still be concerns about reports of these men in non-voluntary treatment programs who are motivated to say they have stopped their violence or other abuse. Keeping such limitations in mind, we briefly review some theories about motivations for battering, as well as empirical studies of battering men.

When men arrested for partner violence were asked why they were violent, the most typical answers are that it was done because they were provoked by their partner (33% of violent incidents on average), in self defense (29%) and feelings of stress (29%) (Elmquist et al., 2014). Thus, two of the most common explanations were essentially blaming the partner. These responses were based on checking how often each of a list of possible reasons was a cause for a violent episode, with the men being allowed to check more than one reason. In addition, the men reported that in about 25% of the episodes, wanting to prove their love for their partner was also a factor motivating their violence.

Researchers generally assume that people may not be aware of the factors that may be actually guiding their behavior, so the reports of batterers may not be the only explanation for their violence. As discussed in Chap. 2, acts of violence or aggression can have many underlying causes. Some of these relate to general patterns of learned behavior. Starting in childhood, people may learn that they can get things they want from others through physical aggression. Stark (2007) argued that the desire for control over their partner was one of the major motivating factors in batterers. Batterers may have also learned through observation of their own violent parents that partner violence is effective in getting what one wants (see Chap. 6). Once a pattern of behavior is learned, when the behavior is reinforced, it becomes even more likely to be repeated. Thus, if the initial violence is followed by exciting sex or by caring behavior, the initiator may perhaps (nonconsciously) repeat the behavior to have these same positive outcomes again. Some perpetrators of partner violence do say that the violence itself is sexually arousing (Langhinrichsen-Rohling, McCullars, & Misra, 2012). If the violence of the male partner also results in the woman being a little nicer to him, it is also further reinforced.

Another learning variable discussed in Chap. 2 is attitudes supportive of violence. When others are also engaged in aggressive behavior toward a partner, there is implied social acceptance of this behavior. In a recent demonstration that appears to support this type of indirect social reinforcement, DePrince and Belknap (2014) reported that patterns of psychological abuse appeared to be similar within neighborhoods. Another study of men arrested for partner violence found that those reporting higher levels of violence were more likely to overestimate how common such behavior was in other men (Neighbors et al., 2010). As discussed in Chaps. 1 and 5, the U.S. population has become less accepting of partner battering over the latter part of the twentieth century.

4.4.1 Personality and Battering

Batterers may show a more general behavior of being violent in many situations outside the home. This type of generalized behavior might be attributed to learning, but high levels of aggression generally are associated with a violent personality and often attributed to biological factors (see Chap. 2). In a meta-analysis of 61 published studies, Birkley and Eckhardt (2015) found that general levels of anger and hostility were significantly related to the likelihood of engaging in violence against one's partner. They further suggested that teaching anger regulation should be a part of any treatment for batterers.

Other studies have also found evidence for personality being a factor in battering. Using data from the U.S. National Longitudinal Study of Adolescent Health, collected in 2001 and 2002, Ulloa and Hammett (2016) found evidence that low levels of empathy were associated with perpetration of intimate partner violence for male batterers. Low empathy was also found to be associated with a higher likelihood of engaging in partner violence again after treatment in a sample of men in treatment for partner violence in Spain (Romero-Martinez, Lila, & Moya-Albiol, 2016). This study also noted very high levels of antisocial traits in the men in the sample. In another paper from this same group of researchers in Spain, Romero-Martinez, Lila, Sarinana-Gonzalez, Gonzalez-Bono, and Moya-Albiol (2013) analyzed testosterone levels and cognitive functioning in a small sample of Spanish men from a battering treatment program and a control group. Although they did find some effects of testosterone, it appeared that deficits in cognitive functioning were more predictive of battering than testosterone. Men who had trouble understanding their wives because of these deficits may have been violent because of the frustration this generated.

In a newer analysis of personality factors Wagers, Wareham, and Sellers (2019) proposed another way of looking at a desire for control as a motive for battering. A sample of college students was used to examine the relationship between a general feeling of low self-esteem and a feeling one cannot control events in one's life with engaging in IPV. Those with what was labeled a strong sense of internal power were found to be less likely to engage in partner abuse.

4.4.2 Battering in Response to Stress

As described earlier, the initial violence in the battering relationship often occurs when the man is under stress or frustrated for some reason. One form of stress may be economic problems. A study of those going to an emergency room for treatment of trauma indicated that partner violence was more common among those with low income levels than those with higher incomes (Caetano, Cunradi, Alter, Mair, & Yau, 2019). Supporting the role of frustration is research showing that partner violence is more common in groups known to have higher levels of stress, such as being a member of a disadvantaged minority group or being lower in SES. A meta-analysis of over 200 studies examining risk factors in partner violence (Capaldi, Knoble, Shortt, & Kim, 2011) found these were both significant predictors of partner violence. Other analyses in this same review found that when stress levels were measured directly, they were associated with a greater likelihood of partner violence. However, the review was not restricted to battering relationships and included research on partnerships with lower levels of violence. Since these relationships with less severe or one-sided violence are far more common than battering relationships (see Chap. 5), these data may not apply directly to predicting batterer's violence.

Another group that may experience higher levels of stress is legal and illegal immigrants who also appear to have relatively high rates of family violence (Prakash, Prevot, Kola, & Wood, 2019). Stress was specifically cited as an explanation for why immigrant Mexican men who had recently come to the United States were more violent (Grzywacz, Rao, Gentry, Marin, & Arcury, 2009) Based on interviews with men and women (all in violent partnerships, but not interviewed if partnered to each other), the researchers concluded that conflict within the couple over changes in the family resulting from employment of wives contributed to stress and violence in the men. Because women were employed, they were no longer able to do as many things in the home, and men had to help with cooking and cleaning, which they resented. They may have felt that they were having to do what they labeled as women's work. Women also became more independent and were not willing to leave financial decisions up to their husbands.

The Case #12 involves an immigrant family from Guatemala and shows how lack of English fluency can leave the abused woman particularly stressed, isolated and vulnerable to ongoing abuse. Emotional coercion and threats by the abusive husband, with or without physical violence, may be used to force the abused wife into sex. It also shows how an initial disclosure may occur shortly after the most recent episode of violence, when the victim is afraid and angry, however, the victim may retract because of coercion by the abuser and/or their extended family, fear of losing the abuser's financial and emotional support, or fear of child welfare involvement.

Case Example #12
Itzel and Felipe migrated to the U.S. for work 3 years ago. Itzel did office cleaning before she was pregnant with Francisco. Felipe used to do itinerant agricultural work, but took full-time employment in a restaurant kitchen when Itzel became pregnant. Felipe speaks English well enough to communicate and take care of day to day needs, whereas Itzel cannot speak, write, or understand English at all. Because of this, Felipe has full control of the family's shared checking account and makes all of the family's business decisions. The family became known to social services when a downstairs neighbor called to say that there is often shouting and banging around upstairs, often accompanied by Francisco crying. When the family were interviewed, Itzel had a visible bruise on her neck and cheek. Felipe denied that he has ever been physically violent, and stated Itzel's injury was from a fall in which she hit her face on the coffee table. Felipe also states that Itzel doesn't want to take care of the finances and isn't interested in taking English classes. Itzel claimed in her interview that Felipe has become increasingly angry due to a combination of financial stress and changes in their relationship since Francisco was born. Itzel states Felipe has always had a temper, but he didn't start hitting her until after Francisco was born. He has also told Itzel that, despite their small income, she cannot work. This is even despite the fact that Itzel has a Spanish-speaking friend who would keep Francisco for her in exchange for errands around the house. Itzel states also that she knows Felipe has been seeing other women, he often stays out late and either comes home drunk, or not at all. Felipe has become upset about their decreasing sex life, and says that he takes care of Itzel and Francisco so she owes him. Itzel denies she has ever been physically forced to have sex, but states that Felipe will get very angry and threaten to withhold money. Itzel also states that Felipe will not allow her to take free English classes, because he says she will start meeting men behind his back. Felipe is a doting father to Francisco and has not done anything to hurt him, though he will yell at Itzel and hit her even if she is holding Francisco. Felipe was soon asked to leave the home for the duration of the investigation. When Itzel found out, she immediately recanted everything she had said, stated she did get a bruise from a fall, and that she was just so angry at Felipe for infidelity that she wanted to scare him. Itzel was advised that if she allows Felipe to move back in before services can be secured, that Francisco will be removed. The family were referred to intensive in-home services provided by a Spanish language family support agency.

Another stress factor possibly relating to partner violence is pregnancy. As James, Brody, and Hamilton (2013) found in a meta-analysis of 92 studies, higher rates of violence and emotional abuse were sometimes reported when the female partner was pregnant, although this is not always the case. Abuse during pregnancy was higher when the partners were not married and the pregnancy was not intended.

It is likely that both of these situations might be associated with higher levels of stress. Perhaps the conflicting results relating to the effects of pregnancy are related to this sometimes being a stressful situation, but not always?

The following example was reported in the New York Times from testimony delivered in 1977 during a hearing before the New York Senate Democratic Task Force on Women and the Assembly Majority Panel on Women's Issues in 1977 (Klemesruda, 1977):

> During testimony at the hearing, Hortense Barber told the panel that her husband beat her for the first time after she told him she was pregnant with their first child: "He knocked out my two front teeth and split open my upper lip" and later, as her pregnancy continued, he blackened her eyes multiple times, threw a knife at her which cut her knee, and punched her in the throat after she came home from palate surgery, which ruptured the stitches. She finally left home and filed for divorce after he broke a plate over her head and a shard from the plate lodged in her arm. Her husband looked at the wound, told her it shouldn't keep her from doing the housework and ordered her to clean the house or he would kill her. After her husband left for work, Mrs. Barber packed a suitcase, took the $300 she had saved for furniture, grabbed her 9 month old baby and left.

The batterer's behavior might relate to the basic level of attachment to his partner. Although not directly applied to the situation of partner battering, Spitzberg and Cupach (2014) outline a very interesting theory about men who stalk their partners when they attempt to leave, arguing that they may have an insecure or anxious attachment style. Those with this pattern of attachment to a romantic partner are often quite distressed over a possible breakup of the relationship, and may exhibit anger and jealousy toward their partner. As noted above, these types of reactions are often seen in battering men. Spitzberg and Cupach report some empirical support for their association of stalking with attachment style. In a related study of stalking and surveillance behaviors, men who were highly attentive early in the relationship, always wanting to know where their partner was, were more likely to engage in these same types of behaviors after the breakup of the relationship (Williams & Frieze, 2005). Others have also noted the association of violent stalking and battering (Logan, Leukefeld, & Walker, 2000; Mechanic, Weaver, & Resick, 2000).

4.4.3 Violence as an Expression of Masculinity

Finally, although a good deal of research has looked at a possible relationship between ideals about masculinity and violence (see Chap. 2), and this has been looked at as a possible predictor of partner violence, results have been mixed. Reidy, Berke, Gentile, and Zeichner (2014) investigated this in an on-line study using volunteers on the MTurk website. The initial sample consisted of 600 men from the U.S. ranging in age from 18 to 50 who identified as heterosexual. As expected, those with higher scores on a measure of hyper-masculinity were more likely to engage in both physical and sexual violence as well as psychological aggression. Another predictor of all three types of aggression was what they labeled as the *Masculine*

Role Discrepancy Stress scale. This was based on items such as "I worry that people judge me because I'm not like the typical man" and "I worry that women find me less attractive because I 'm not as macho as other guys" (p. 161). Thus, both men rating themselves as more masculine and those who wished they were more masculine tended to be more likely to abuse their female partners.

As this brief survey suggests, there is no simple answer to the question about why some men are abusive. It is likely that there are different patterns of partner violence, and some predictors may be more associated with some types of abuse than others. This issue of different patterns of partner violence is explored in more detail in Chap. 5. As Karantzas, Simpson, and Miller (2019) have suggested, better understanding of battering may come with theory generated from relationship science.

4.5 Reactions to Being Battered

The following case vignette illustrates how victims of domestic violence are often seen in the emergency room when they sustain injuries so severe that they must access medical treatment. This opens an opportunity for emergency personnel to identify the presence of domestic violence and arrange for help. The vignette also shows how a woman who is severely battered by her male partner may make a suicide gesture or attempt either to force access to help or as an act of desperation. Emergency room contact is often a time when victims are most motivated to seek help as they are safe in that environment, the most recent violence may be severe, and transportation to a shelter is available.

Case Example #8

Rose is a 44 year old married white female who was brought to a rural community hospital emergency room by her husband, Tom. Tom told the ER doctor that his wife had taken pills in a suicide attempt. Rose denied this, stating that her husband lies all the time. Later, however, when talking with the crisis social worker, Rose admitted that she had taken the pills because she had felt hopeless about the situation with her husband. She didn't want to die, but just wanted to "go to sleep and escape" the physical and emotional pain she was experiencing.

Upon evaluation by the crisis social worker, Rose presented as alert, completely oriented, although she thought today is February fourth when it was actually December 14th. Rose states that her husband has abused her for 15 years of her 18 year marriage and that she wants help. She has a large hematoma on her forehead and is complaining of severe stomach pain - her husband had kicked her in the stomach. Rose states that Tom has, over the years, broken both of her wrists, broken both her legs, cracked her ribs and given her multiple black eyes, cuts, and abrasions. Up until now she hoped he would change and stop the violence if she were a "better wife" but realizes now that hope is futile and she is motivated to get help. Rose agreed to go to the Battered Women's Shelter and I contacted them and they agreed to accept her once she is completely medically stable and ready for discharge. Rose told the social worker that she felt better after talking.

4.5.1 Emotional Reactions and Health Effects of IPV

Post-traumatic stress disorder (PTSD), a complex disorder with many associated symptoms (see Chap. 3; Rizo, Givens, & Lombardi, 2017), has been identified by researchers for many years as a general response to battering (Walker, 2016). Probably the most commonly studied mental health problem associated with partner violence is depression, one aspect of PTSD (Devries et al., 2013; Scott-Tilley, Tilton, & Sandel, 2010). Other symptoms include emotional distress and suicidal thoughts (Pill, Day, & Mildred, 2017). As Pill and her colleagues concluded in their review of the research on women's responses to IPV victimization, the repeated nature of IPV can result in even more serious reactions now being referred to as *complex PTSD*. Data from a large national database of emergency department records indicated that those identified as experiencing physical violence from an intimate partner were more likely to report anxiety, mood disorders and self-harming behaviors than a comparison group of other emergency department cases (Beydoun, Williams, Beydoun, Eid, & Zonderman, 2017). About .06% of the women seeking assistance in the Emergency Department were classified as experiencing physical intimate partner violence.

The experience of partner violence has a negative impact not only on mental health, but also on physical health. This can be seen in a variety of different types of samples. For example, George et al. (2019) examined radiology reports of 185 patients identified in emergency department records. Compared to a comparison group, those identified in the IPV group were more likely to have experienced fractures, especially on the face, and gynecological difficulties. Facial injuries and higher levels of cardiovascular disease were seen in women who identified as having experienced intimate partner violence in an oral surgery clinic (Halpern et al., 2017). One study estimated that 75% of the injuries from partner violence are to the face (Halpern et al., 2016). Because of this, dental providers may be an important group for identifying women experiencing partner violence. Because of the many injuries to the head, battered women may also experience injury to the brain and associated cognition problems (Wong, Fong, Lai, & Tiwari, 2014).

Other health consequences can be seen in an analysis of electronic health records of over 14 million female patients between the ages of 18 and 65. Within this group, 5870 were identified as having experienced "domestic violence" (Karakurt, Patel, Whiting, & Koyuturk, 2017). Statistical comparisons indicated that the women who had reported domestic violence were more likely to have had injuries of all types, especially to the face. In addition, they had higher rates of a large number of health problems including cardiovascular and gastrointestinal problems, allergies, skin problems and respiratory disease.

A growing body of literature suggests that psychosocial stress, depression, and social isolation often associated with IPV contribute to risk of cardiovascular disease (Centers for Disease Control and Prevention, 2015). Stress related to intimate partner violence usually persists after a woman leaves an abusive relationship. This continued stress may leave her vulnerable to heart disease and other health problems, highlighting the importance of prevention and early intervention efforts (Scott-Storey, Wuest, & Ford-Gilboe, 2009).

4.5.2 Coping: Cognitive and Behavioral Reactions

Battered women react to the physical and psychological violence they are receiving in a variety of ways (see Hamby's 2014 book, *Battered women's protective strategies: Stronger than you know*, for a detailed discussion of coping strategies of battered women). Coping strategies may relate to trying to manage one's emotions or to attempting to change the situation (see Chap. 3). For example, the battered woman may cope by abusing alcohol or drugs (Weiss, Dixon-Gordon, Duke, & Sullivan, 2015). These are considered emotion-focused coping strategies. In their review of 48 published studies of battered women in the United States, Rizo et al. (2017) conclude that many of these types of emotion-focused strategies did not appear to have beneficial effects for battered women.

Other types of coping strategies, labeled as problem focused, relate to attempting to change the situation creating the stress. Such strategies can take many forms, some more effective than others. As mentioned earlier, when the violence first starts, many women respond by forgiveness (McNulty, 2011). Such a reaction may not have positive consequences for the woman who was the target of the violence. Although research on all types of couples generally indicates that forgiving the partner often has beneficial effects in maintaining the relationship, this generalization does not appear to apply to violent partnerships. McNulty's longitudinal study of 72 married couples indicated that forgiveness had beneficial effect for many couples, as expected. But, this was **not the case** for 37 couples with physical or psychological aggression. For these couples, forgiving the aggression meant it was *less* likely to decrease over time. Instead, women who *did not forgive* their partner for his violence were more likely have decreases in violence. This same pattern was noted in the interview studies of the first author of this book. Women who reacted very strongly and negatively to the first instance of violence were less likely to find themselves later in a battering relationship (Frieze, 2005). However, this negative reaction did sometimes result in an early breakup of the relationship.

Relating to this early forgiveness, another strategy that may tend to occur more often in more violent relationships is for the battered woman to try to placate her abuser (Parker, Gielen, Castillo, Webster, & Glass, 2016). For example, she might try hard to do the things he asks her to do. Or, she might try to keep things quiet in the home. This type of behavior was reported by them to have been quite common earlier in a group of battered women who had finally asked for legal protection from a violent partner.

Another common reaction of battered women is to take actions to protect themselves from future violence. Such safety planning has been found to be one of the more helpful coping strategies for a battered woman (Rizo et al., 2017). Safety strategies vary widely, depending on the needs and resources of the battered women (Logan & Walker, 2018). For example, packing a bag that would allow for a quick escape or hiding weapons might be strategies appropriate for some battered women (Messing et al., 2017). Messing and her colleagues surveyed over 1000 women who had sought some type of help for IPV victimization. Two of the most popular strategies reported were leaving a key with a friend and telling other people they might need help in the future. However, neither of these strategies were associated with decreases in violence from the partner in this study. One of the most effective strategies in terms of reducing future violence was going to a battered woman's shelter (see Chap. 8) (Messing et al., 2017).

As mentioned earlier, as the battering situation gets worse and worse, the battered woman may become desperate. Threats made by the batterer that he would kill her if she tried to leave may be taken quite seriously. When the woman feels totally trapped, and depressed, she may finally decide to attempt to kill herself (Devries et al., 2013). Suicidal thoughts or actual suicide attempts are found in higher levels in battered women and other female victims of violence at much higher levels than in non-abused women (Rizo et al., 2017). Feelings of desperation can also lead to attempts by the battered women to kill her partner (Stein & Miller, 2012). But these extreme behaviors are a last resort and are rare. It does appear that when a battered woman does kill her spouse, potential jurors are now more receptive to the idea of her being not guilty because of self defense than was likely the case many years ago (Mossière, Maeder, & Pica, 2018).

4.5.3 *Trying to Leave the Abusive Partner*

As this overview has suggested, the battering relationship develops over time and there are many reasons why battered women might remain with their abusive partners (DeKeseredy, Dragiewicz, & Schwartz, 2017; Torres et al., 2016). Torres and her colleagues developed a scale of reasons for feeling they could not leave, based on a review of previous work, and administered it to a sample of battered women in Spain. Reasons fell into six major groups, based on factor analysis of the individual items. Most commonly cited was fear of harm for herself or her children if she tried to leave, but items about feeling sorry for her partner and feeling embarrassed correlated with the fear items and were included in this factor. Feelings of attachment to the batterer and fear of loneliness was the second most cited factor for feeling trapped in the battering relationship. Feeling confused or having other emotional problems was next highest, followed by lack of income and other economic concerns, blaming oneself for the violence, and concerns about the impact of her leaving on the children. They did note that studies done in other countries have sometimes cited different factors. It is not clear if these data would be directly applicable to the situation of battered women in the U.S. although it seems likely.

Data on reasons of battered women for staying or leaving in the U.S. come from a creative content analysis of twitter accounts in response to the severe violence displayed by football player Ray Rice toward his partner in an elevator Cravans, Whiting, & Aamar, 2015). In a series of responses to the tag "whyIstayed," one set of responses included blaming themselves, making excuses for the violence and believing that emotional abuse was not *real* abuse. Another category related to feelings of worthlessness, often based on long-term criticism and other psychological abuse she had been receiving. A third category was fear of the batterer and what he might do to them if they tried to leave. Other themes included believing they could change their abuser or help him in some way; believing that children would be harmed if they tried to leave; religious beliefs that required them to stay; concerns over loss of income; and concerns over having to leave friends and family to actually get away or not having others who could help. A very different set of themes emerged in response to the tag "whyIleft." One set of themes related to finally being able to understand that they needed to leave. A second theme was having support from other people or from God. Other themes included feeling a need to protect children from abuse or from witnessing it; and fear of even more violence or even being killed if they did not leave.

Issues involved in trying to leave her batterer were further investigated in an interview study of 14 women either in a battered women's shelter or a non-residential program serving domestic violence survivors (Messing, Mohr, & Durfee, 2015). Initial denial that the abuse had gotten as bad as it did was a common response. Others mentioned vacillating between anger and wanting to leave and hopes that they would be able to reconcile with the batterer. Sadness over termination of the relationship to someone they loved was also mentioned by several of the women.

The following case illustrates how financial concerns can be paramount for a battered woman when faced with the loss of a primary earner, especially when the woman does not work or is unable to hold employment providing a living wage. In situations where the battered woman chooses to leave with children, it is vital for someone—a friend, neighbor or social worker - to support her in accessing any benefits that she may be entitled to. Food stamps, cash benefits, housing subsidies, Medicaid, and child care subsidies all require documentation and take time to process and sometimes a great deal of effort to maintain. If the woman can safely obtain passports, birth certificates, and other vital documents upon choosing to leave, they should be encouraged to do so in order to begin this process. As Cho, Shamrova, Han, and Levchenko (2017), discussed, immigrant women may have special issues that make it especially hard for them to leave. They may also have difficulties in seeking help for the abuse (Messing, Vega, & Durfee, 2017).

Case Example #3

The Rashid family migrated from Iran to U.S. for economic reasons shortly after Basim was born. Ali is an I.T. (Information Technology) specialist and felt that the U.S. would allow him greater opportunity to advance in his field. Nur left university to marry Ali and is a full time stay at home mom. The family speak Persian at home, though the parents and Basim speak English well enough to understand professionals. Adila has some language delays. Basim's school called with concern that his behavior is increasingly violent, and seems to be particularly directed toward his mother. Most recently Basim had asked his mother to take him to McDonalds after school for dinner because he prefers American food and didn't want to eat his mom's more traditional cooking. When Nur refused, Basim began hitting and kicking her. The principal and guidance counselor both spoke with Nur and found that she has been experiencing this quite a lot, and is concerned that Basim is copying his father's behavior. Nur states that he often shoves and slaps her, though she has never been bruised by him. Basim has told female teachers and staff that he doesn't have to listen to them because he is going to be a man, and they are only women. Social services began an investigation into the family. Ali reluctantly agreed to leave the home and stay with friends. Nur and her children hold American citizenship, so the social worker assisted Nur in applying for benefits. Nur was concerned because, even if Ali maintains support for the family and they are able to obtain benefits, their standard of living would drop. In particular, Nur was concerned that they would lose their apartment and that she and the children may have to stay in a shelter until they could obtain Section 8 housing benefit. Ali fully denied any violence, and stated that in fact Nur often yells at him and has slapped him in front of the children. Ali also denied that Basim is showing any behavior problems. Because of language delay, Adila could not be interviewed in English or with a Persian translator. When Basim was interviewed by the SW, he said his dad yells at his mom and tells her and everyone else what to do. When asked if anything else happens, Basim said his mom gets a smack, and mimicked a slapping motion. The family were found to be in need of services and transferred to long-term in-home services.

Many battered women do leave, but it is not uncommon for them to go back to the batterer after trying to leave, as the case of the Ewings at the beginning of this chapter illustrated. In a national U.S. sample, women were asked if they had ever left their current partner because he was violent toward you (Lacey et al., 2011). Because of the wording of the question, any women who had already left and were no longer with the batterer were not included in study. Thus, the sample of leavers was a group who had left and returned to the abuser at least once. This sample who had left at least once was then divided into a group of Non-Hispanic White women (n = 269) and women of color (n = 108). Data indicated that 41% of the White women and 14% of the women of color had tried to leave once. The rest had tried to leave 2 or more times (and returned). Many of the women returned after only a few days of being away. About 20% of the total sample had stayed away 76 or more days, so the majority of the women returned after a shorter time.

Case Example #3, described earlier, illustrates how battered women may exhibit a genuine wish to leave their situation, but then change their mind. This may be out of fear, loyalty to the abuser, loneliness, or the experience of manipulation or intimidation. When children are involved in abusive situations, social services may mandate that a parent leave with the child or children and may remove the child or children if the parent cannot or will not do so. As a result, mothers may hide the status of the relationship with the abuser from a CPS caseworker out of fear of losing their children.

4.6 Seeking Help From Others

4.6.1 Societal Attitudes About Battering in Intimate Relationships

Societal attitudes about partner violence and battered women have been changing for some time, gradually becoming less tolerant of the violence and more supportive of the battered women (Frieze, 2005). These changes in attitudes over time suggest that although a battered woman might have been very reluctant to seek help from others in the mid-twentieth century because of the negative reaction she might have expected to receive from others, she should be more willing to get assistance from others today. However, the reality of these changing attitudes is not always reflected in the perceptions of battered women today.

Overstreet and Quinn (2013) surveyed the now quite extensive literature to look for evidence of different types of stigma against battered women. They found evidence for three types of stigma. Many studies referred to what they labeled as *anticipated stigma*. This was coded when studies cited fears of disclosing their status as a battered woman because of expected disapproval or anticipations that others would not help if asked. Anticipated stigma was related to a reluctance to approach friends or family for help as well as preventing battered women from seeking assistance from health care providers. Another form of stigma was labeled as *stigma internalization*. This occurred when battered women did seek help and received negative reactions, leading to them accepting these judgments and blaming themselves or feeling embarrassed about the violence they received. Finally, *cultural stigma* related to negative societal views about battered women. One unanticipated effect of cultural stigma was that women whose personal situation differed from what the society defined as a *typical battered woman* may have had difficulty being believed or being offered services generally provided to battered women. For example, battered women living with a violent lesbian partner did not fit the stereotype that they had been victimized by a violent male partner.

As Murray, Crowe, and Overstreet (2018) summarize in a later paper, these beliefs result in several types of reactions in the battered women. These include blaming the victim for her abuse, treating her differently than other women, attributing her less social standing, isolating her from other people, and making her feel shame. Further analyses in this study provide more detailed information about the specific types of stigma that battered women report experiencing.

Evidence for the continuing existence of these types of stigma can be found in several relatively recent studies. For example, in a North Carolina convenience sample of mostly women who reported being abused in a former relationship with an intimate partner in North Carolina, Murray, Crowe, and Brinkley (2015) found that many of those in the sample felt that they had been blamed by others for the abuse. In another study (Crowe & Murray, 2015), these researchers reported that battered women also experience stigma from formal help givers such as mental health professionals and from people working in law enforcement or the courts. The most commonly mentioned responses from others were feelings of being blamed for the violence or being told that their experiences were not important. Murray and Crowe (2016) have written a book to try to help battered women overcome feelings of these types of stigma.

It appears that some religious groups may not always be helpful to battered women because of underlying religious views relating to gender and marriage. In a book edited by Johnson (2015), he states in the preface that the book "is concerned with empowering mental health professions to deliver culturally sensitive interventions when working with religious clients…" (p. vii). There is also evidence that some communities are more supportive and helpful than others. For example, DePrince and Belknap (2014) reported that Latino communities were more supportive of battered women's situation than other types of communities.

Schackner, Weiss, Edwards, and Sullivan (2017) surveyed a sample of women responding to flyers, and who reported being physically victimized by a current male partner in the last 6 months and having a monthly income under $4200. Over 80% of the final sample of 212 women reported disclosing the violence to at least one person. Both positive and negative reactions were reported, at about equal levels, with slightly more positive reactions. Those receiving higher levels of negative reactions also reported more severe PTSD symptoms. Woerner, Wyatt, and Sullivan (2018) replicated these findings, noting that when reactions of others to disclosure of IPV were highly negative, with few positive reactions, the women reported the highest levels of depression and PTSD.

4.6.2 Help from Friends and Family

Most battered women do seek some type of help from others (Cho et al., 2017; Parker et al., 2016). Studies have shown that women assaulted by their partners are most likely to first turn to family or friends in seeking outside help (Sylaska & Edwards, 2014). They may also seek or want help from neighbors (McDonnell, Burke, Gielen, O'Campo, & Weidl, 2011). Some women survivors may hesitate to talk to others for a variety of reasons beyond concern about negative stigma. A group of women who have special concerns with secrecy are affluent women who are concerned about their friends or neighbors learning about the violence they are experiencing (Haselschwerdt & Hardesty, 2017).

It does appear that friends are often more helpful than family when a battered woman seeks help, although advice from either friends or family can be positive or negative (Sylaska & Edwards, 2014). For example, unsolicited suggestions to leave the abusive partner were often perceived negatively. In a qualitative study of those turned to for advice, Latta and Goodman (2011) found that these potential helpers did try to be helpful in various ways, although they often found that they felt frustrated by their efforts. In another study of attitudes about helping others in a rural area, Banyard, Edwards, Moschella, and Seavey (2019) interviewed 74 young adults from 16 different rural communities. Although most of the sample argued that their communities were close-knit and people helped each other, it was also noted that people were reluctant to speak with others about personal issues, especially serious issues such as domestic violence. There was also a sense that victims of IPV brought the violence on themselves, and they needed to respect themselves more and not tolerate the violence. These data would suggest that even when these data were collected, IPV survivors might anticipate receiving negative reactions from others.

4.6.3 Other Sources of Help

At some point in the relationship, some victims of do seek formal help beyond family and friends. This can be from the police, from social agencies such as shelters or safe houses, from counselors, or from clergy. Help may also be available through filing of legal action to bar an abusive person from the home (see Chap. 9 for more information on services for the violent partner and Chap. 8 for services for the abused partner). This type of legal help is often labeled as a *Protection from Abuse Order* or simply a *Protection Order*. It does appear that often the women seeking these orders have previously attempted to deal with the violence themselves by placating their abusive partner or trying to leave the partner with the help of friends or family rather than turning to formal caregivers (Parker et al., 2016). Only 4% of Parker et al.'s sample of 197 women seeing these protection orders previously had stayed at a shelter for battered women. Other research indicated that protection orders can be effective. Logan and Walker (2010) surveyed 213 women who had obtained a protective order against a male intimate partner. The large majority of their sample were white women, with an average age of 33. Data indicated that 6 months after receiving a protective order, there was a lower level of reported violence against the women, even when the orders were violated. The women also reported being less fearful of future harm and felt that the protective order had been fairly or extremely effective. In a review of 43 scholarly articles on the effects of protective orders, Russell (2012) concluded that overall, 40–50% of these orders are violated at least once, but the women who obtain the orders tend to find them effective.

Other data suggest that many women seek more than one type of formal assistance. Messing and her colleagues (Messing, O'Sullivan, Cavanaugh, Webster, & Campbell, 2017; Messing, Vega, & Durfee, 2017) surveyed a group of women seeing domestic violence services of some type. Within this group, 71% had sought a protective order, 74% had called the police and 19% had gone to a shelter for battered women. Longitudinal data was also available in this study, allowing the researchers to see if there was a relationship between the type of assistance sought and the level of violence experienced afterwards. Those who went to a shelter and those calling the police reported the greatest reduction in severe violence afterwards. Some reduction in moderate violence, but not in severe violence was seen in those receiving protective orders. No effects were found for those receiving counseling. Trying to hide was associated with higher rates of stalking and severe violence. Those couples who did separate and had no contact were omitted from the sample. However, the outcomes associated with various forms of formal help do not always appear to be positive. Rancher, Jouriles, and McDonald's (2018) sample of women in a shelter indicated that police involvement sometimes added to the stress of the women who called for assistance. Chapter 9 provides more information about police assistance.

The last case in this chapter depicts the role of a shelter in helping a battered woman get help from other sources, such as mental health services and addiction treatment services. It also illustrates how although an abusive partner is violent in the couple relationship, he may be a good parent for the couple's child and even handle challenges, such as a child's disability, well. It also highlights the type of event that finally triggers a person to leave an abusive relationship and the challenges involved in learning how to be independent after one has left an abusive relationship and the strengths that emerge in someone who has been abused once they leave and are on their own.

Case Example #28

Barbara and her former husband have a long history of marital discord with her citing his insane jealousy as being the primary difficulty in that he monitored her every move and was very controlling, including deciding who she could and could not associate with in terms of friends and family. She had a baby 16 months ago that has cerebral palsy due to birth trauma caused by use of forceps in the delivery, and the child's problems put added stress on the marriage. Although her husband abused Barbara, he was very loving towards the baby and actually was able to cope better with the child's problems than Barbara was, according to her, and so he now has custody. The last straw for her, in terms of the marriage, occurred 3 months ago when the husband slammed her against the wall and almost choked her to death. He now lives in another town in the county with the baby, and Barbara has her own apartment, surviving on small alimony payments. She is having a very difficult time learning to be independent and living on her own. She went straight from living with her parents to getting married and living with her husband and, until now, has never lived alone. She has no job skills but on her own has applied for Project Step and a job training program through the JTPA (Job Training Partnership Act) program. Barbara has three different job ideas she is interested in: secretarial work, graphic design and drafting. She took a drafting course a couple years ago, but couldn't complete it because heavy use of LSD impaired her thinking and she was hospitalized for injuries caused by her husband's abuse and missed too many classes as a result. Barbara states that her husband opposed her efforts to learn a trade. Barbara says that her future goals include obtaining an apartment without cockroaches and a car that doesn't break down. Along with what she is already doing to help herself, Barbara would also benefit from ongoing counseling at our mental health outpatient clinic as well as alcohol/drug counseling.

4.7 Summary

In this chapter, we focus on women abused by a male partner. This is the situation of the battered woman, sometimes labeled as the IPV survivor. This abuse can take many forms including physical and sexual violence, as well as threats of violence and psychological or emotional abuse. .A brief history of the research in this area is followed by a summary of research findings about how these relationships develop and the typical patterns seen once the violence is well established. Battering men might have any of a number of motivations or factors that might predict their behavior such as stress or a general aggressiveness. The battered woman responds to the increasing levels of violence and abuse in many ways. She has physical injuries and illnesses as well as emotional trauma. She is likely to take action to protect herself or to try to prevent future violence. She may try to leave but often returns at least once before finally leaving for good. She seeks help from family and friends as well as more formal help givers. She may turn to the police or other legal assistance as well. A number of case histories from our files are included to demonstrate some of the findings from the research.

References

Adams, A. E., Beeble, M. L., & Gregory, K. A. (2015). Evidence of the construct valildity of the scale of economic abuse. *Violence and Victims, 30*, 363–376. https://doi.org/10.1891/0886-6708.VV-D-13-00133

Banyard, V. L., Edwards, K. M., Moschella, E. A., & Seavey, K. M. (2019). "Everybody's really close-knit": Disconnections between helping victims of intimate partner violence and more general helping in rural communities. *Violence Against Women, 25*, 337–358. https://doi.org/10.1177/1077801218768714

Barner, J. R., & Carney, M. M. (2011). Interventions for intimate partner violence: A historical review. *Journal of Family Violence, 1*, 16–28. https://doi.org/10.1007/s10896-011-9359-3

Beydoun, H. A., Williams, M., Beydoun, M. A., Eid, S. M., & Zonderman, A. B. (2017). Relationship of physical intimate partner violence with mental health diagnoses in the Nationwide Emergency Department sample. *Journal of Women's Health, 26*. https://doi.org/10.1089/jwh.2016.5840

Birkley, E. L., & Eckhardt, C. I. (2015). Anger, hostility, internalizing negative emotions, and intimate partner violence perpetration: A meta-analytic review. *Clinical Psychology Review, 37*, 40–56. https://doi.org/10.1016/j.cpr.2015.01.002

Blumenstein, L. (2015). Exploratory study on intimate partner kidnapping: Is this a prevailing issue in intimate partner relationships? *Partner Abuse, 6*, 403–424. https://doi.org/10.1891/1946-6560.6.4.403

Caetano, R., Cunradi, C. B., Alter, H. J., Mair, C., & Yau, R. K. (2019). Drinking and intimate partner violence severity levels among U.S. ethnic groups in an urban emergency department. *Academic Emergency Medicine*. https://doi.org/10.1111/acem.13706

Capaldi, D. M., Knoble, N. B., Shortt, J. W., & Kim, H. K. (2011). A systematic review of risk factors for intimate partner violence. *Partner Abuse, 3*, 231–280. https://doi.org/10.1891/1946-6560.3.2.231

Carney, M. M., & Barner, J. R. (2012). Prevalence of partner abuse: Rates of emotional abuse and control. *Partner Abuse, 3*, 286–335. https://doi.org/10.1891/1946-6560.3.3.286

Centers for Disease Control and Prevention. (2015). https://www.cdc.gov/violenceprevention/intimatepartnerviolence/consequences.html

Cho, H., Shamrova, D., Han, J., & Levchenko, P. (2017). Patterns of intimate partner violence victimization and survivors' help-seeking. *Journal of Interpersonal Violence*, 1–25. https://doi.org/10.1177/0886260517715027

Coker, A. L., Smith, P. H., Bethea, L., King, M. R., & McKeown, R. E. (2000). Physical health consequences of physical and psychological intimate partner violence. *Archives of Family Medicine, 9*, 451–457.

Cravans, J. D., Whiting, J. B., & Aamar, R. O. (2015). Why I stayed/left: An analysis of voices of intimate partner violence on social media. *Contemporary Family Therapy, 37*, 372–385. https://doi.org/10.1007/s10591-015-9360-8

Crossman, K. A., Hardesty, J. L., & Raffaelli, M. (2016). "He could scale me without laying a hand on me": Nonviolent coercive control during marriage and after separation. *Violence Against Women, 22*, 454–473. https://doi.org/10.1177/1077801215604744

Crowe, A., & Murray, C. E. (2015). Stigma from professional helpers toward survivors of intimate partner violence. *Partner Abuse, 6*, 157–179. https://doi.org/10.1891/1946-6560.6.2.157

DeKeseredy, W. S., Dragiewicz, M., & Schwartz, M. D. (2017). *Abusive endings: Separation and divorce violence against women*. Oakland, CA: University of California Press.

DePrince, S. E. B., & Belknap, J. (2014). Intimate partner abuse experiences and clinical responses. *Clinical Psychological Science, 2*, 258–271. https://doi.org/10.1177/2167702613507556

Devries, K. M., Mak, J., Bacchus, L. J., Child, J. C., Falder, G., Petzold, M., et al. (2013). Intimate partner violence and incident depressive symptoms and suicide attempts: A systematic review of longitudinal studies. *PLoS Medicine, 10*, e1001439. https://doi.org/10.1371/journal.pmed.1001439

Dichter, M. E., Thomas, K. A., Crits-Christoph, P., Odgen, S. N., & Rhodes, K. V. (2018). Coercive control in intimate partner violence: Relationship with women's experience of violence, use of violence, and danger. *Psychology of Violence, 8*, 596–604. https://doi.org/10.1037/vio0000158

Elmquist, J., Hamel, J., Shorey, R. C., Labrecque, L., Ninnemann, A., & Stuart, G. L. (2014). Motivations for intimate partner violence in men and women arrested for domestic violence and court referred to batterer intervention programs. *Partner Abuse, 5*, 359–374. https://doi.org/10.1891/1946-6560.5.4.359

Erikkson, L., & Mazerolle, P. (2013). A general strain theory of intimate partner homicide. *Aggression and Violent Behavior, 18*, 462–470. https://doi.org/10.1016/j.avb.2013.07.002

Follingstad, D. R., & Ryan, K. M. (2013). Contemporary issues in the measurement of partner violence. *Sex Roles, 69*, 115–119. https://doi.org/10.1007/s11199-013-0298-8

Frieze, I. H. (1983). Investigating the causes and consequences of marital rape. *Signs, 8*, 532–553.

Frieze, I. H. (2005). *Hurting the one you love: Violence in relationships*. Belmont, CA: Thomson Wadsworth.

George, E., Phillips, C. H., Shah, N., Lewis-O'Connor, A., Rosner, B., Stoklosa, H. M., et al. (2019). Radiologic findings in intimate partner violence. *Radiology*, 1–8. https://doi.org/10.1148/radiol.2019180801

Graham, D. L. R., Rawlings, E., & Rimini, N. (1988). Survivors of terror: Battered women, hostages, and the Stockholm Syndrome. In K. Yllo & M. Bograd (Eds.), *Feminist perspectives on wife abuse* (pp. 217–233). Thousand Oaks: Sage Publications, Inc..

Grzywacz, J. G., Rao, P., Gentry, A., Marin, A., & Arcury, T. A. (2009). Acculturation and conflict in Mexican immigrants' intimate partnerships: The role of women's labor force participation. *Violence Against Women, 15*, 1194–1212. https://doi.org/10.1177/1077801209345144

Halpern, L., Rian, C., Rogers, J., Padron, V., Isaza, S., Sotherland, J., et al. (2016). The impact of intimate partner violence exposure on orofacial and stress-related health consequences in female patients. *Violence and Gender, 3*, 181–188. https://doi.org/10.1089/vio.2016.0011

Halpern, L. R., Shealer, M. L., Cho, R., McMichael, E. B., Rogers, J., Ferguson-Young, D., et al. (2017). Influence of intimate partner violence (IPV) exposure on cardiovascular and salivary biosensors: Is there a relationship? *Journal of the National Medical Association, 109*, 252–260. https://doi.org/10.1016/j.jnma.2017.08.001

Hamberger, L. K., Larsen, S. E., & Lehner, A. (2017). Coercive control in intimate partner violence. *Aggression and Violent Behavior, 37*, 1–11. https://doi.org/10.1016/j.avb.2017.08.003

Hamby, S. (2014). *Battered women's protective strategies: Stronger than you know*. New York, NY: Oxford University Press.

Haselschwerdt, M. L., & Hardesty, J. L. (2017). Managing secrecy and disclosure of domestic violence in affluent communities. *Journal of Marriage and the Family, 79*, 556–570. https://doi.org/10.1111/jomf.12345

James, L., Brody, D., & Hamilton, Z. (2013). Risk factors for domestic violence during pregnancy: A meta-analytic review. *Violence and Victims, 28*(3), 359–380. https://doi.org/10.1891/0886-6708.VV-D-12-00034

Johnson, M. P. (1995). Patriarchal terrorism and common couple violence: Two forms of violence against women. *Journal of Marriage and the Family, 75*, 283–294. https://doi.org/10.2307/353683

Johnson, A. L. (2015). Preface. In A. J. Johnson (Ed.), *Religion and men's violence against women* (pp. vii–xiv). New York, NY: Springer.

Johnson, M. P., & Ferraro, K. J. (2000). Research on domestic violence in the 1990s: Making distinctions. *Journal of Marriage and the Family, 62*, 948–963. https://doi.org/10.1111/j.1741-3737.2000.00948.x

Kane, K. (2016), Longtime abusive relationship ends with couple's deaths. *The Pittsburgh Post-Gazette,* September 1, pp. A1, A6. Retrieved from: http://www.post-gazette.com/local/washington/2016/08/31/Man-who-abducted-killed-wife-in-Washington-County-dies-from-self-inflicted-wound/stories/201608310345

Karakurt, G., Patel, V., Whiting, K., & Koyuturk, M. (2017). Mining electronic health records data: Domestic violence and adverse health effects. *Journal of Family Violence, 32*, 79–87. https://doi.org/10.1007/s10896-016-9872-5

Karantzas, G. C., Simpson, J. A., & Miller, P. G. (2019). Insights into interpersonal violence, aggression, and maltreatment: Bridging relationship science with personality and social psychology. *Journal of Social and Personal Relationships*, 1–6. https://doi.org/10.1177/0265407519826750

Klemesruda, J. (1977). Wives recite litany of abuse by their husbands. *The New York Times*, April 30, 1977. Retrieved from http://www.nytimes.com/1977/04/30/archives/wives-recite-litany-of-abuse-by-their-husbands.html

Koss, M. P., White, J. W., & Lopez, E. C. (2017). Victim voice in reenvisioning responses to sexual and physical violence nationally and internationally. *American Psychologist, 72*, 1019–1030. https://doi.org/10.1037/amp0000233

Lacey, K. K., Saunders, D. G., & Zhang, L. (2011). A comparison of women of color and non-Hispanic white women on factors related to leaving a violent relationship. *Journal of Interpersonal Violence, 25*, 1036–1055. https://doi.org/10.1177/0886260510376496

Langhinrichsen-Rohling, J., McCullars, A., & Misra, T. A. (2012). Motivations for men and women's intimate partner violence perpetration: A comprehensive review. *Partner Abuse, 3*, 429–468. https://doi.org/10.1891/1946-6560.3.4.429

Latta, R. E., & Goodman, L. A. (2011). Intervening in partner violence against women: A grounded theory exploration of informal network members' experiences. *The Counseling Psychologist, 39*, 973–1023. https://doi.org/10.1177/0011000011398504

Logan, T. K., Leukefeld, C., & Walker, B. (2000). Stalking as a variant of intimate violence: Implications from a young adult sample. *Violence and Victims, 15*, 91–111.

Logan, T. K., & Walker, R. (2010). Civil protective order effectiveness: Justice or just a piece of paper? *Violence and Victims, 25*, 332–348. https://doi.org/10.1891/0886-6708.25.3.332

Logan, T. K., & Walker, R. (2018). Looking into the day-to-day process of victim safety planning. *Journal of Family Violence, 33*, 197–211. https://doi.org/10.1007/s10896-018-9951-x

Martin, D. (1976). *Battered wives*. San Francisco: Glide Publications.

Maxwell, C. D. (2012). The crime control effects of criminal sanctions for intimate partner violence. *Partner Abuse, 3*, 469–500. https://doi.org/10.1891/1946-6560.3.4.469

McDonnell, K. A., Burke, J. G., Gielen, A. C., O'Campo, P., & Weidl, M. (2011). Women's perceptions of their community's social norms towards assisting women who have experienced intimate partner violence. *Journal of Urban Health: Bulletin of the New York Academy of Medicine, 88*, 240–253. https://doi.org/10.1007/s11524-011-9546-9

McNulty, J. K. (2011). The dark side of forgiveness: The tendency to forgive predicts continued psychological and physical aggression in marriage. *Personality and Social Psychology Bulletin, 37*, 770–783. https://doi.org/10.1177/0146167211407077

Mechanic, M. B., Weaver, T. L., & Resick, P. A. (2000). Intimate partner violence and stalking behavior: Exploration of patterns and correlates in a sample of acutely battered women. *Violence and Victims, 15*, 55–72.

Messing, J. T., Mohr, R., & Durfee, A. (2015). Intimate partner violence and women's experiences of grief. *Child & Family Social Work, 20*, 30–39. https://doi.org/10.1111/cfs.12051

Messing, J. T., O'Sullivan, C. S., Cavanaugh, C. E., Webster, D. W., & Campbell, J. (2017). Are abused women's protective actions associated with reduced threats, stalking, and violence perpetrated by their male partners? *Violence Against Women, 23*, 263–286. https://doi.org/10.1177/1077801216640381

Messing, J. T., Vega, S., & Durfee, A. (2017). Protection order use among Latina survivors of intimate partner violence. *Feminist Criminology, 12*, 199–233. https://doi.org/10.1177/1557085116678924

Mossière, A., Maeder, E. M., & Pica, E. (2018). Racial composition of couples in battered spouse syndrome cases: A look at juror perceptions and decisions. *Journal of Interpersonal Violence, 33*, 2867–2890. https://doi.org/10.1177/0886260516632355

Murray, S. B. (1988). The unhappy marriage of theory and practice: An analysis of a battered women's shelter. *National Women's Studies Association Journal, 1*, 75–92.

Murray, C. E., & Crowe, A. (2016). *Overcoming the stigma of intimate partner violence*. New York, NY: Routledge. https://doi.org/10.4324/9781315651033

Murray, C. E., Crowe, A., & Brinkley, J. (2015). The stigma surrounding partner violence: A cluster analysis study. *Partner Violence, 6*, 320–336. https://doi.org/10.1891/1946-6560.6.3.320

Murray, C. E., Crowe, A., & Overstreet, N. M. (2018). Sources and components of stigma experienced by survivors of intimate partner violence. *Journal of Interpersonal Violence, 33*, 515–536. https://doi.org/10.1177/0886260515609565

Nathanson, A. M., Shorey, R. C., Tirone, V., & Rhatigan, D. L. (2012). The prevalence of mental health disorders in a community sample of female victims of intimate partner violence. *Partner Abuse, 3*, 59–75. https://doi.org/10.1891/1946-6560.3.1.59

Neighbors, C., Walker, D. D., Mbilinyi, L. F., O'Rourke, A., Edleson, J. L., Zegree, J., et al. (2010). Normative misperceptions of abuse among perpetrators of intimate partner violence. *Violence Against Women, 16*, 370–386. https://doi.org/10.1177/1077801210363608

Norris, S. M., Huss, M. T., & Palarea, R. E. (2011). A pattern of violence: Analyzing the relationship between intimate partner violence and stalking. *Violence and Victims, 26*, 103–115. https://doi.org/10.1891/0886-6708.26.1.103

Overstreet, N. M., & Quinn, D. M. (2013). The intimate partner violence stigmatization model and barriers to help seeking. *Basic and Applied Social Psychology, 35*, 109–122. https://doi.org/10.1080/01973533.2012.746599

Pagelow, M. D. (1981). *Women-battering: Victims and their experiences*. Beverly Hills, CA: Sage.

Parker, E. M., Gielen, A., Castillo, R., Webster, D. W., & Glass, N. (2016). Intimate partner violence and patterns of safety strategy use among women seeking temporary protective orders: A latent class analysis. *Violence Against Women, 22*, 1663–1681. https://doi.org/10.1177/1077801216631436

Petrosky, E., Blair, J. M., Betz, C. J., Fowler, K. A., Jack, S., & Lyons, B. H. (2017). Racial and ethinc differences in homicides of adult women and the role of intimate partner violence—United States, 2003-2014. *MMWR. Morbidity and Mortality Weekly Report, 66*, 741–746.

Pill, N., Day, A., & Mildred, H. (2017). Trauma responses to intimate partner violence: A review of current knowledge. *Aggression and Violent Behavior, 34*, 178–184. https://doi.org/10.1016/j.avb.2017.01.014

Pleck, E. (1989). Criminal approaches to family violence: 1640-1980. In L. Ohlin & M. Tonry (Eds.), *Family violence* (pp. 19–57). Chicago: University of Chicago Press.

Prakash, N., Prevot, J., Kola, B., & Wood, S. K. (2019). Improving health outcomes for immigrant families through IPV screening: Resources and recommendations for pediatric health care providers. *Current Problems in Pediatric Adolescent Health Care, 49*, 7–15. https://doi.org/10.1016/j.cppeds.2018.11.007

Rancher, C., Jouriles, E. N., & McDonald, R. (2018). Intimate partner violence, police involvement, and women's trauma symptoms. *Journal of Interpersonal Violence*, 1–14. https://doi.org/10.1177/0886260518780409

Reidy, D. E., Berke, D. S., Gentile, B., & Zeichner, A. (2014). Man enough? Masculine discrepancy stress and intimate partner violence. *Personality and Individual Differences, 68*, 160–164. https://doi.org/10.1016/j.paid.2014.04.021

Rizo, C. F., Givens, A., & Lombardi, B. (2017). A systematic review of coping among heterosexual female IPV survivors in the United States with a focus on the conceptualization and measurement of coping. *Aggression and Violent Behavior, 37*, 35–50. https://doi.org/10.1016/j.avb.2017.03.006. 1359–1789.

Romero-Martinez, A., Lila, M., & Moya-Albiol, L. (2016). Empathy impairments in intimate partner violence perpetrators with antisocial and borderline traits: A key factor in the risk of recidivism. *Violence and Victims, 31*, 347–360. https://doi.org/10.1891/0886-6708.VV-D-14-00149

Romero-Martinez, A., Lila, M., Sarinana-Gonzalez, P., Gonzalez-Bono, E., & Moya-Albiol, L. (2013). High testosterone levels and sensitivity to acute stress in perpetrators of domestic violence with low cognitive flexibility and impairments in their emotional decoding process: A preliminary study. *Aggressive Behavior, 39*, 355–369. https://doi.org/10.1002/ab.21490

Russell, B. (2012). Effectiveness, victim safety, characteristics, and enforcement of protective orders. *Partner Abuse, 3*, 531–552. https://doi.org/10.1891/1946-6560.3.4.531

Salis, K. L., Salwen, J., & O'Leary, K. D. (2014). The predictive utility of psychological aggression for intimate partner violence. *Partner Abuse, 5*, 83–97. https://doi.org/10.1891/1946-6560.5.1.83

Saltzman, L. E., Fanslow, J. L., McMahon, P. M., & Shelley, G. A. (2002). *Intimate partner violence surveillance: uniform definitions and recommended data elements, version 1.0*. Atlanta, GA: Centers for Disease Control and Prevention, National Center for Injury Prevention and Control.

Schackner, J. N., Weiss, N. H., Edwards, K. M., & Sullivan, T. P. (2017). Social reactions to IPV disclosure and PTSD symptom severity: Assessing avoidant coping as a mediator. *Journal of Interpersonal Violence*, 1–19. https://doi.org/10.1177/0886260517727493

Scott-Storey, K., Wuest, J., & Ford-Gilboe, M. (2009). Intimate partner violence and cardiovascular risk: Is there a link? *Journal of Advanced Nursing, 65*, 2186–2197. https://doi.org/10.1111/j.1365-2648.2009.05086.x

Scott-Tilley, D., Tilton, A., & Sandel, M. (2010). Biologic correlates to the development of post-traumatic stress disorder in female victims of intimate partner violence: Implications for practice. *Perspectives in Psychiatric Care, 46*, 26–36. https://doi.org/10.1111/j.1744-6163.2009.00235.x

Showalter, K. (2016). Women's employment and domestic violence: A review of the literature. *Aggression and Violent Behavior, 31*, 37–47. https://doi.org/10.1016/j.avb.2016.06.017

Spitzberg, B. H., & Cupach, W. R. (2014). *The dark side of relationship pursuit from attraction to obsession and stalking* (2nd ed.). New York: Routledge.

Stark, E. (2007). *Coercive control: How men entrap women in personal life*. New York, NY: Oxford University Press.

Stein, M. L., & Miller, A. K. (2012). Distress resulting from perceivers' own intimate partner violence experiences predicts culpability attributions toward a battered woman on trial for killer her abuser: A path model. *Journal of Interpersonal Violence, 27*, 2527–2544. https://doi.org/10.1177/0886260512436388

Straus, M. A. (1979). Measuring intrafamily conflict and violence: The Conflict Tactics Scale. *Journal of Marriage and the Family, 41*, 75–88. https://doi.org/10.1007/351733

Straus, M. A., Hamby, S. L., Boney-McCoy, S., & Sugarman, D. B. (1996). The revised Conflict Tactics Scales (CTS2): Development and preliminary psychometric data. *Journal of Family Issues, 17*, 283–316. https://doi.org/10.1177/019251396017003001

Sylaska, K. M., & Edwards, K. M. (2014). Disclosure of intimate partner violence in informal support network members: A review of the literature. *Trauma, Violence & Abuse, 15*, 3–21. https://doi.org/10.1177/1524838013496335

Testa, M. & Derrick, J. L. (2013). A daily process examination of the temporal association between alcohol use and verbal and physical aggression in community couples. *Psychology of Addictive Behaviors, 28*, 127–138. https://doi.org/10.1037/a0032988

Tjaden, P., & Thoennes, N. (1998). *Stalking in America: Findings from the national violence against women survey*. Washington, DC: National Institute of Justice.

Torres, A., Navarro, P., Gutierrez, F., Tarragona, M. J., Imaz, M. L., Ascaso, C., et al. (2016). Partner violence entrapment scale: Development and psychometric testing. *Journal of Family Violence, 31*, 137–145. https://doi.org/10.1007/s10896-015-9751-5

Ulloa, E., & Hammett, J. F. (2016). The role of empathy in violent intimate relationships. *Partner Abuse, 7*, 140–156. https://doi.org/10.1891/1946-6560.7.2.140

United States Commission on Civil Rights. (1978). *Battered women: Issues of public policy*. Washington, DC: United States Commission on Civil Rights.

Van Hasselt, V. B., Morrison, R. L., Bellack, A. S., & Hersen, M. (1988). Overview. In V. B. Van Hasselt, R. L. Mossison, A. S. Bellack, & M. Hersen (Eds.), *Handbook of family violence* (pp. 3–8). New York: Plenum.

Wagers, S. M., Wareham, J., & Sellers, C. S. (2019). Testing the validity of an internal power theory of interpersonal violence. *Journal of Interpersonal Violence*, 1–26. https://doi.org/10.1177/0886260519834092

Walker, L. E. (1979). *The battered woman*. New York, NY: Harper & Row.

Walker, L. E. A. (2001). Battering in adult relationships. In J. Worell (Ed.), *Encyclopedia of women and gender: Sex similarities and differences and the impact of society on gender* (pp. 169–188). New York, NY: Academic.

Walker, L. E. (2016). *The battered woman syndrome* (4th ed.). New York, NY: Springer.

Weiss, N. H., Dixon-Gordon, K. L., Duke, A. A., & Sullivan, T. P. (2015). The underlying role of posttraumatic stress disorder symptoms in the association between intimate partner violence and deliberate self-harm among African American women. *Comprehensive Psychiatry, 59*, 8–16. https://doi.org/10.1016/j.comppsych.2014.05.018

Williams, S. L., & Frieze, I. H. (2005). Courtship behaviors, relationship violence and breakup persistence in college men and women. *Psychology of Women Quarterly, 29*, 248–257. https://doi.org/10.1111/j.1471-6402.2005.00219.x

Woerner, J., Wyatt, J., & Sullivan, T. P. (2018). Analysis of social reactions to intimate partner violence disclosure and associations with mental health symptoms. *Violence Against Women*, 1–19. https://doi.org/10.1177/1077801218811681

Wong, J. Y., Fong, D. Y., Lai, V., & Tiwari, A. (2014). Bridging intimate partner violence and the human brain: A literature review. *Trauma, Violence & Abuse, 15*, 22–33. https://doi.org/10.1177/1524838013496333

Woodin, E. M., Sotskova, A., & O'Leary, K. D. (2013). Intimate partner violence assessment in an historical context: Divergent approaches and opportunities for progress. *Sex Roles, 69*, 120–130. https://doi.org/10.1007/s11199-013-0294-z

Chapter 5
Expanding Our Thinking About Intimate Partner Violence: Examinations of Partner Violence Using Non-Shelter Samples

As discussed in Chap. 4, social science researchers and U.S. society, more generally, became aware of issues relating to intimate partner violence (IPV) through a number of books and research reports relating to battered women published beginning in the early 1970s. Much of this work was based on interviews of women seeking help at battered women's shelters or other means of legal or other professional help for the extreme violence they were experiencing. These relationships were the focus of Chap. 4.

In this chapter, we examine other sources of research on partner violence, drawing from a number of types of samples in the community. As in Chap. 4, IPV in this chapter is defined in terms of physically aggressive behaviors (including rape and sexual assault) as well as emotional or psychological aggression, although much of the literature focuses on physical forms of aggression, ranging from mild to severely violent behaviors. This research discussed in this chapter is based on several types of samples. These include general population surveys of couples and convenience samples of adults as well as various samples of college students and younger dating couples. Other studies utilize samples designed to look at violence within LGBTQ or sexual minority couples. Many of these studies present a very different picture of partner violence than that traditionally associated with battered women, the focus of Chap. 4.

5.1 Descriptive Data: IPV in Couples Sampled in the General Population

We begin the chapter with an overview of the prevalence of IPV in samples that are not drawn from shelters. As will be seen in these studies, there is a good deal of evidence that both women and men engage in various forms of IPV with their partners. Some studies show women being more likely to engage in physical IPV than men.

I. H. Frieze et al., *Dynamics of Family and Intimate Partner Violence*,
https://doi.org/10.1007/978-3-030-42608-8_5

Men and women also have similar motives for their abusive behavior, and both men and women appear to be physically and emotionally affected by IPV. These findings have led to much debate about gender symmetry and whether IPV differs for women and men. This chapter concludes with a discussion of whether men or women are more likely to be the perpetrators of IPV.

5.1.1 Studies of Married and Cohabitating Couples

In a broad examination of violence within the family published in 1980, sociologist Murray Straus and his colleagues published data on marital violence as well as parental violence against children in a book called *Behind Closed Doors: Violence in the American Family* (Straus, Gelles, & Steinmetz, 1980). Based on a newly developed measure of family violence, called the Conflict Tactics Scale (CTS, see Box 5.1 for more information about this scale), their data suggested relatively high levels of violence within couples as well as for parents toward children. In examining the data, many were especially surprised to see reports of so many women using violence against their male partners. Clearly, this was a very different picture of IPV than the idea of a victimized woman battered by her husband or male partner, the type of IPV discussed in Chap. 4.

Box 5.1: The Conflict Tactics Scale for Measuring Intimate Partner Violence

When some of the very early research on intimate partner violence was conducted, researchers simply asked battered women about the violence they had experienced (Woodin, Sotskova, & O'Leary, 2013; Chap. 4). Such information might then simply be reported by providing examples or summarizing some of the most common responses in an open-ended way. Suggesting that greater clarity was needed about intrafamily violence, sociologist Murray Straus and his colleagues (Straus, 1979; Straus et al., 1980 published scales developed for a national interview study of violence in U.S. families that were called the Conflict Tactics Scale (CTS). As Straus (1979) wrote "The CTS consists of a list of actions which a family member might take in a conflict with another member" (p. 78). By presenting the questions in the context of disagreements and conflicts, Straus argued that people would be more willing to answer these questions "since almost everyone recognizes that families have conflicts and disagreements…" (p .79). He also ordered the questions to first ask about more socially acceptable behavior such as discussing the issue calmly, and then moved on to non-violent behaviors such as sulking or saying something to spite the other person, before moving on to actual violence such as throwing something or hitting the partner. People were asked how often they and their partner had done each of the listed behaviors in the past year or if the events had ever happened.

Traditionally, the CTS is scored by researchers so that if someone has slapped or pushed someone, this person is labeled as *violent*, and placed in the same group as someone using a weapon or chocking or doing other potentially fatal acts. Because of relatively small numbers of people in most samples who report ever having done a violent act against an intimate partner, it is often not possible to assess actual levels of violence by adding up the various items because of statistical problems with the distribution of the scores. Instead, the sample is divided into a nonviolent and a violent group. However, when looking at larger samples, researchers have begun to separate those using differentiate different levels of violence or to separate very serious violence with the potential for serious injury from less violent acts.

Soon, nearly all researchers looking at intimate partner violence began to use the actual CTS or some modification of this scale to assess IPV (Langhinrichsen-Rohling, 2005; Ryan, 2013). Many modifications in the CTS were made across different studies (e.g., see Rathus & Feindler, 2004, or Woodin et al.'s 2013, discussion of this process). The original CTS included 8 examples of overt acts of physical aggression. This list was necessarily limited, not including acts such as chocking, scratching, trying to suffocate, hitting with a car, or any of the many others ways in which violence could occur. Threats of violence are considered as part of violent behavior. There was no separate measure of psychological or emotional aggression (see Box 5.2).

Although widespread use of the CTS, and modifications of the basic scale, allowed researchers to more easily compare their findings across studies of married partners, as well as other types of relationships such as dating couples and same-sex partners, many criticized the scale in its original as well as revised forms (e.g., Jones, Browne, & Chou, 2017; Woodin et al., 2013). For example, the CTS was specifically written to invoke ideas about disagreements in couples. However, other types of aggression outside of conflicts are quite possible. As Ryan and Mohr (2005) reported, college students can easily generate a quite detailed list of actions associated with "playful force during sex" and "playful aggression at other times" (p. 591). None of these would be included in the CTS score. Thus, it is likely that the CTS scale misses a good deal of violence in couples. Although there are many potential issues with the CTS, it appears now that the biggest problem is the inability to separate severe violence from the more common types of less serious IPV.

Box 5.2: Psychological Aggression and Coercive Control

One form of intimate partner violence is psychological or emotional aggression. This appears to be one of the most common forms of IPV. One of the most comprehensive descriptions of this can be found in Stark's, 2007 book, *Coercive Control: How Men Entrap Women in Personal Life*. This book describes how battering men also use a variety of psychological forms of aggression against female partners. Although the focus in this book was on women as victims, there is evidence that it is possible for women to use coercive control against men (Hines & Douglas, 2018).

Behaviors classified as this type of IPV include being told by a partner that one is a loser or a failure, and being humiliated or made fun of, and being called names like ugly, fat, crazy or stupid. Verbal or nonverbal threats were also classified as a form of emotional aggression. The CDC has now developed a scale that includes many aspects of psychological aggression or coercive control (Black et al., 2011). These behaviors included keeping one from seeing or talking to family or friends, keeping track of where one is or demanding to know what one was doing, threatening to harm him or herself or commit suicide because of one's behavior, threatening to harm a pet, threatening to take one's children away, not letting one have access to money or destroying something important. Overall, 48% of the women and 49% of the men in the 2010 CDC sample indicated that they had experienced some form of psychological aggression from a partner (Black et al., 2011). Someone keeping track of what the person is doing or where they are was the most commonly reported form of psychological aggression, 62% of women and 63% of men who said they had experienced some form of psychological aggression reported that this was something their partner did to them.

Arriaga and Schkeryantz (2015) argued that victims may not be aware of the negative effects resulting from psychological aggression. In two laboratory studies of university students involved in a current romantic relationship who reported at least one instance of some form of IPV, these researchers found that psychological distress and upset about the relationship was higher for both perpetrators and victims of psychological aggression. Much of the psychological aggression was mutual. The association for psychological aggression was higher than an association of distress with physical IPV. A second longitudinal study replicated these findings and further asked about why study participants were experiencing distress. There appeared to be little evidence that the students associated their distress with the psychological IPV occurring in the relationship. The researchers concluded that these data suggested "a pattern of "invisible harm" in which individuals victimized by psychological aggression may not recognize the harm they are experiencing" (p. 1332).

In generating the data for their book, Straus and his team conducted interviews with a national U.S. random sample in 1976. After a household was selected, if there was a married couple or a man and woman living together in the household, either the man or the woman was asked to participate, yielding a final sample of over 2000 adults. The response rate was 65%, which is relatively high for this type of survey. Although the reports of the women were slightly different from those of the men, as is typically the case in these types of studies, data were averaged across both. In the last 12 months, 12% of men were found to be violent toward their female partner, 11.5% of women were violent toward their male partner, and in 15.6% of couples both partners used violence with each other. Much of this "violent" behavior involved actions that were not likely to cause serious injury such as slapping or pushing. Numbers were much lower for severe violence, with 3.8% of men, 4.6% of women, and 6.1% of couples where both used severe violence, such as using a knife or gun. Note that the reported use of severe violence was higher for women than men.

Since this initial survey of a general population sample, many subsequent studies have been done using survey and interview techniques to assess intimate partner violence. We review some of this research in this chapter. As will be seen, percentages of women and men using IPV in these studies depend on the particular sample, how questions are phrased, and the degree of rapport between study participants and researchers (Winstok, 2013; Woodin et al., 2013). Many researchers have continued to use the CTS developed by Straus and his colleagues to measure IPV, although various modification in the scale have been made by different researchers. This makes it difficult to directly compare levels of reported IPV across studies. There has also been an elaboration of the definition of intimate partner *violence* to include emotional or psychological abuse in some of the IPV research (see Box 5.2).

IPV became a popular research topic in the 1980s, with many wanting to further understand the earlier data published by Straus et al. and to better understand how these findings related to those generated by the research on battered women discussed in Chap. 4. In these later studies, general community samples using the CTS or similar measures have yielded similar or lower rates of violent actions of adults toward marital or intimate partners than those reported by the Straus group. The pattern of relatively equal rates of IPV perpetration for women and men has continued to replicate in much of the research, although the most recent work separating serious and less serious violence indicates differing patterns by gender.

Some of the early follow-up studies drew upon a nationally representative sample called the National Survey of Families and Households (NSFH) which was done in 1987 and 1988 (see Bumpass & Sweet, 1989, for methodological information). In this survey, modified questions based on the CTS asked about physical aggression within the couple in the last 12 months. In a reanalysis of one of these studies, Anderson (2002) reported there was mutual violence in 7% of the couples, in 2% of the sample, only the woman was violent, and in 1%, only the man was violent. (These statistics are averaged across the accounts of women and men since these differed slightly). The large majority of the couples had no reported partner violence. Although the specific form of violence was not measured in this survey, it did appear that much of the violence was not severe enough to cause serious injury. Earlier findings of high levels of mutual violence, and women being slightly more like to be the violent partner than men were replicated. Note, though, that the overall rates of IPV were lower than those reported in the earlier study by Straus et al. (1980). Anderson did find that, overall, women were more affected by any form of partner violence than men, showing higher rates than men of depression and substance abuse. This was the case regardless of whether the woman was the perpetrator of violence or the recipient or both.

Using these same NSFH data, Bookwala, Sobin, and Zdaniuk (2005) investigated the question of whether there were age differences in rates of IPV. They found that the highest rates of IPV existed in younger couples. In the 20–39-year-old age group, 9% of men and 10% of women reported having physical arguments in the previous year. Comparable rates were 4 and 6% for those aged 40–59 and 3 and 4% for those 60 and older. Thus, within this sample, age effects were greater than those for women as compared to men. Younger adults used more physical aggression than older couples. Overall rates of physical aggression were low, consistent with

Case Example #4

Leah and Andre do not live together, and are in an on and off relationship. Their relationship is characterized by jealousy, fueled by the close-knit urban community in which they live. They see each other around often, and hear from friends about the other's romantic and sexual escapades. Social services has been involved with the family repeatedly since Faith was born. The children were taken into care when Faith was six and Carson was four because of repeated and severe violence between the parents. Both Faith and Carson are intelligent, articulate children who speak casually about seeing their parents fight and hit each other. Faith stated that her mom says dad is a "nasty man-slut," and that her dad says mom is a "whore." When asked what happens when they get angry, Faith stated that mom will punch dad, and dad will pull mom's hair and they yell. Carson calmly spoke about the night that his mom had to go to the hospital because Andre got mad at her because she had a new boyfriend and he stabbed her in the arm with kitchen knife. The wound was superficial, but the incident was severe enough to remove the children…Both parents have a history of substance misuse; both drink regularly, Leah has misused prescription medication that she buys off the street while Andre has a history of crack use. Both claim that they never use around the children and neither feels that drugs have an effect on the violence. Leah and Andre both admit that there is violence between them, though each claims that the other starts it. Each also claims that the other is emotionally manipulative, giving affection and sex and then withholding it for no reason. However, both also state a desire to rekindle a stable relationship together and eventually marry.

Anderson's (2002) analyses of the same dataset. Men were more likely than women overall to report using calm discussion or keeping opinions to oneself during arguments while women of all ages reported higher rates of using heated arguments or shouting. Although these differences were statistically significant, the overall means were relatively similar. Other data did suggest a different story, though. Looking only at the small number of those reporting injuries from physical aggression from the partner, 71% of the younger group were women, and 87% of the 40–59-year olds were women. No injuries from IPV were reported for the oldest adults. Thus, women were more likely than men to report injury from partner violence.

Other large national samples have also been surveyed about IPV. Using a different nationally representative sample of over 3000 men and women between the ages of 15–54 sampled in 1990–1992, we (Williams & Frieze, 2005) found rates of partner violence comparable to those reported by Straus et al. Only married or cohabitating individuals were used in this analysis. A modified CTS scale was used, although partner violence questions were *not* limited to the last 12 months, as is done in the standard CTS. Overall, 18% of the sample reported ever experiencing or perpetrating some type of violence within their relationship with women (22%) more likely to report this than men (15%). These data allowed for comparisons of high and low severity violence as well as a comparison of those with no violence at all. In 5% of the couples, both used low levels of violence, while 4% reported using severe violence against each other. The large majority of the sample reported no IPV at all, as has been true in most of studies using non-shelter samples. Looking at asymmetrical patterns of violence, there were more situations of female violence being higher than male violence than the reverse. Three percent of men reported their partner used severe violence against them, and they were not violent while 2% of women reported they were victims of severe violence, while they were not violent themselves. Women employed outside the home were more often found to be perpetrators and more often involved in mutual IPV. Alcohol use was lowest in nonviolent couples. It was highest for men victimized by their female partner.

Caetano, Vaeth, and Ramisetty-Mikler (2008), drew on yet another national random sample of married [with a few cohabitating] couples. The sample was originally developed in 1995 and oversampled Black and Hispanic couples. Caetano and his colleagues contacted those in the original survey who were still together 5 years later. They developed a sample of about 1100 couples, with both partners being interviewed. Men were aged 52 on average, and women averaged 50. Most (87%) of the couples reported no IPV in the last year and 8% reported mutual violence. Close to 4% reported violence from the male partner only and 2% reported that the female partner was violent. On average, the couples who reported one or more violent acts in the last year committed two such acts, so the overall levels of violence were low. Age was one of the clearest correlates of IPV with less perpetration or victimization among the older individuals in the sample. Hispanic men were more likely than Blacks or Whites to use IPV, and Hispanic women were higher in reports of IPV victimization. Mutual violence was high in all groups, but especially among Blacks and Hispanics and was lowest in Whites.

The relatively high levels of IPV among Hispanic couples is consistent with other data reported about immigrant populations. For example, Vaughn, Salas-Wright, Cooper-Sadlo, Maynard, and Larson (2015) used a national U.S. sample to more closely examine IPV levels among different immigrant groups. Data were collected in 2004 to 2005. Analyses indicated that about 7% of native-born U. S. adults reported engaging in physical IPV in the last year. This behavior was more frequent in Latin American immigrants at 9%. All other immigrant groups were lower than the native-born population (3% of European immigrants, 4% of African immigrants and 6% of Asian immigrants). Across all samples, 53% of men and 47% of women reported engaging in IPV. Further information about the Latin American immigrants can be seen in a review by Gonzalez et al. (2018) who found that it was only those from Mexico who have consistently been found to have high rates of IPV.

The following case illustrates how relationship violence can occur over long periods of time and can have a mutual quality to it in which both adults are quick to anger and violence, and each blames the partner for the ongoing violence.

Some studies have combined those experiencing IPV in a dating relationship with those in a more committed relationship into one sample. In a large survey sponsored by the U.S. Department of Justice, Tjaden and Thoennes (2000) reported that nearly 25% of the women and 8% of the men in their nationally representative sample were physically assaulted or raped by a current or former spouse, cohabiting partner or dating partner at some time in their life. In an attempt to maximize disclosure, this survey used telephone interviews with female interviewers for the women in the sample, and both male and female interviewers for the men in the sample. Random telephone dialing was done to attain a random sample of about 8000 women and 8000 men aged 18 or older drawn from all 50 states and Washington, DC. Since the reported intimate partner violence in this survey is lower than in other national surveys, the authors discussed possible methodological differences, arguing their methodology was more valid.

When analyzed by race, Tjaden and Thoennes (2000) found the highest rates of victimization for women among American Indian or Alaska Natives (31%), and rates for those of Asian or Pacific Islander descent lowest (13%). Twenty-six percent of African American and 21% of White women reported having experienced IPV. For men, the highest rates of victimization were for the American Indian or Alaska Native group and for African American men (11% for both). Lowest rates were for Asian or Pacific Islander descent (3%). Seven percent of White men and 11% of African American men reported being victims of IPV. Reported physical assault by a partner was slightly higher for Non-Hispanic women (22% versus 21%) and men (8% versus 7%). When asked about injury from IPV, 42% of women and 20% of men reported some level of injury, and within this group, 28% of women and 22% of men said they had received medical care as a result of the IPV.

Combined data for married or cohabitating partners and dating couples was also used in Muftić, Finn, and March's, 2015 study of police data from North Carolina relating to IPV. Data were initially collected in 2002, with an 18 to 30-month follow-up. In this study, a sample of 1256 men and women were classified as being involved in an IPV incident. They were each classified as a victim, an offender, or a victim-offender. Only 4% of the men were classified as victims, while 70% of the women were defined as victims. Almost 30% of the men were labeled as victim-offenders, while about 25% of the women were in this group. In their conclusions, they pointed to this relatively large group involved in mutual violence who do not fit into the type of batterer-victim dichotomy described in Chap. 4. They further noted that both women and men in this group may need some of the services generally offered to victims, even though they are, themselves, violent. As reported in Chap. 8, many women seeking shelter as battered women do report also being violent toward their male partner. As Holmes et al. (2016) reported, in their sample of 227 women in battered women's shelters, 93% of the women said they had been violent toward their abusing partner.

One other type of general sample where IPV has been extensively studied is military families. Sparrow et al. (2018) reviewed and performed a meta-analysis of self-reported perpetration and victimization in 28 different studies. Most used some form of the CTS to measure IPV in primarily U.S. military personnel and their spouses or partners. Rates varied widely across studies, but overall, indicated similar rates of perpetration and victimization for women and men. Psychological forms of IPV were much higher than physical IPV.

In one of the largest studies of the U.S. population, Black et al. (2011) reported on an ongoing survey sponsored by the CDC about women's and men's experiences with violence. This survey is called the National Intimate Partner and Sexual Violence Survey or NISVS. For the data used in this report, telephone surveys were done to interview over 18,000 adults aged 18 or older in a nationally representative sample established through random telephone dialing. Data were collected in 2010. For questions about intimate partner violence, people were asked if a romantic or sexual partner had done any of a number of things to them. Severe violence included being hit with a fist or something hard, being kicked, being slammed against something, being hurt from chocking or having hair pulled, being beaten or burned, and being victimized with a knife or gun. Less severe violence included being slapped, pushed or shoved. More than 30% of women and 26% of men reported ever experiencing the less severe violence from an intimate partner. Overall percentages for those ever experiencing a form of *severe* violence were 24% for women and 14% for men. These rates were higher than in many of the earlier studies, especially for women.

As Black et al. acknowledged, their data did differ in several ways from that reported in other studies. This was especially notable in term of their lower reported rates for male than female victimization. They attributed this to the methodology used to try to maximize disclosure about sensitive issues. They also argued that their more detailed questions and clear association of experienced violence with a romantic or sexual partner may have affected their data. Depending on the specific data used, the response rate for the survey was about 30% which is considered an acceptable response rate, and is higher than reported in many studies, but is low enough to indicate that many who were initially asked to respond to the survey declined to participate. As in any research, there is always the question of how those who did not participate might differ from those who did.

Analysis of a 2015 administration of the NISVS by CDC using the new IPV items and a similar methodology was reported by Smith et al. (2018). Drawing on data from a sample of about 10,000, the pattern of men perpetrating more serious violence than women replicated with 21% of women and 15% of men being victimized. Data for being victimized by being slapped, pushed or shoved was higher and equal for men and women at 29%. Combining across both serious and less serious violence, victimization by one or both types was reported by 31% of both women and men. Other data indicated that 36% of women and 34% of men were victimized by psychological aggression at some point in their lives.

5.1.1.1 Summary of Findings for Married and Cohabitating Couples

As this brief review of the large national surveys on IPV indicates, it is clear that rates of violent behavior with a partner vary across studies. They are also dependent on the specific questions asked and the methodology used to ask these questions. There is no question that some women do use violence against their partners, as some men do. Whether men or women are more likely to perpetrate violence is unclear. It should also be kept in mind that the large majority of the *violence* reported in these studies is often mild and may not produce injury. Much of it is mutual (Straus, 2015). As this research suggests, although IPV does occur in adult couples, all of the studies report that the large majority of the population does not report using any of the violent acts associated with IPV.

5.1.2 IPV in College Students

There is now a large body of IPV research using college student samples. This population is often used since it is readily available to university or college-based researchers and inexpensive to survey. Data from this group tends to indicate higher levels of physical aggression of women than men toward dating partners. For example, in one of the early college student sample studies using a modified version of the CTS, we (Bookwala, Frieze, Smith, & Ryan, 1992) found the 58% of the female psychology students sampled admitted to using some act of physical aggression against a current date or last dating partner at least once, while 55% of the men made similar admissions. Many of these reported acts were pushes or slaps or other forms of relatively mild aggression. Suspecting that the men might be minimizing their aggression, we also asked what types of physical aggression the students had received from their current partner. Forty-two percent of the women said their date had used some form of physical aggression against them and 48% of the men said this had happened to them. Much of this reported physical aggression appeared to be less serious forms of "violence" such as slapping or pushing.

If one compares the rates of perpetration and victimization in the Bookwala et al. data, one finds that these percentages do not match. This discrepancy suggests that women and men differed in their perceptions of what they classified as partner violence. For example, while 58% of the women reported they had used violence against their male partner, only 48% of the men said their female partner had been violent towards them. Women reported more aggression overall both as perpetrators and as victims in dating relationships. The sample did not include actual couples, though, so we have no way of knowing how well actual partners would have matched in their ratings.

In a later study by Luthra and Gidycz (2006), again using a sample of college students taking psychology classes, 25% of women and 10% of men reported using some type of physical aggression against a dating partner. Again, the large majority of these acts were mild forms of violence such as throwing something, pushing or shoving. Some of the factors most strongly associated with using these behaviors were having a partner who had used physical aggression (indicating mutual violence) and using alcohol. This was true for both women and men. It should be noted, though, that the overall levels of IPV were lower in this study than in earlier studies.

Similar patterns are seen in more recent student samples, with women reporting more use of physically aggressive behaviors than men. Edwards et al. (2015) surveyed over 6000 college students between the ages of 18 and 24 from 10 New England universities. This study included students from many different types of classes, so it was not limited to psychology classes, as many studies are. Nearly 30% of the men and 13% of the women said they had received some form of physical aggression from a heterosexual dating partner in the last 6 months. Using the more common sample of college students in a variety of psychology courses, Elmquist et al. (2016) reported 15% of men and 19% of women reported using some form of physical aggression against a dating partner. Reasons for the lower percentages of IPV in later years are not clear. Frieze notes, though, that in later unpublished studies of the same type of sample used in the Bookwala et al. (1992) studies of Pittsburgh psychology students, much lower reported levels of IPV were found.

Other forms of IPV have been examined in college students. Marganski and Melander (2015) asked about use of social media such as Facebook or Twitter to harass a current or former partner. In this study 73% of the total sample of men and women reported experiencing this type of harassment from a partner while 23% reported being the victim of physical aggression and 53% reported psychological aggression. Social media victimization was most strongly associated with psychological aggression. Gender differences were not directly reported, but overall, gender was a significant predictor of physical aggression victimization, with men more often reporting this than women, consistent with the pattern seen in most other college samples of women perpetrating more IPV than men.

Expanding on the issue of social-media-related dating abuse, Reed, Tolman, and Ward (2016) asked a group of 307 college students with dating experience who were enrolled in an introductory psychology course about negative experiences with social networking as they related to a dating partner. Reports of monitoring behavior such as using a cell phone or computer to see where the partner was, who the partner was friends with and who the partner spoke with were quite common, with women reporting doing this more than men. (Such behaviors are often labeled as a form of stalking in other research, Sinclair & Frieze 2000). Many other types of harassing behavior using social networking were also reported. Men were more likely than women, though, to report pressuring their partner to take a sexually suggestive photo on their cell phone, and threating to send embarrassing information about her to others. Reported social media dating abuse was highly correlated with reports of psychological aggression, using a modified CTS measure. Similar types of behavior were found in a later study of adolescents aged 12 to 17 by this same research group (Reed, Ward, Tolman, Lippman, & Seabrook, 2018). Girls were again higher than boys in surveillance behavior, while boys engaged in more hostile or threatening digital abuse.

5.1.2.1 Summary of College Student Samples

As this brief survey indicates, college student samples surveyed with measures such as the CTS continue to report more physically and psychologically aggressive behavior of women than men with dating partners. The large majority of the physical IPV found in these studies would not be considered severe and involved behavior such as slapping or pushing. It does appear that the reported violent behavior has decreased over the last 30 years, which might indicate a real decrease or might be a reporting bias as increased publicity has made such behavior less acceptable (see Chap. 1). Other data indicate that both male and female college students are less accepting of male partner violence than the same behaviors done by women (Sylaska & Walters, 2014). Finally, in response to the implication that college women may be more involved in perpetration of IPV than non-college women of the same age, Coker, Follingstad, Bush, and Fisher (2016) used an on-line volunteer sample of women aged 18–24 living in the U.S. to directly compare those enrolled in college with those who had never attended college. No significant differences were found between these two groups of young women, with the non-college women reporting somewhat higher rates of all forms of IPV perpetration than the college women. Thus, the high rates found in the college samples may reflect behavior in this age group rather than their status as college students. As discussed below, Johnson, Giordano, Manning, and Longmore (2015) also reported a drop in IPV for adults older than 24, supporting the conclusion that physical IPV is higher in younger than somewhat older samples.

5.1.3 IPV in Younger Adolescents

Many studies done with younger, non-college samples make it clear that IPV exists in younger dating couples. In one demonstration of this, Cui, Gordon, Ueno, and Fincham (2013) used a nationally representative sample of high school students in grades 7 through 12 drawn from 132 middle schools and high schools in the U.S. The original data were collected in 1994–1995. Three other waves of data from the same students allowed the researchers to study changes over time in patterns of IPV. In the sample used by Cui et al., the partners were now aged between 24 and 32 in Wave IV of data collection in 2007–2008. Although only victimization data were collected in the first wave, perpetration was added in later waves. Violence was measured somewhat differently in different waves. Overall, boys and men reported more victimization from a partner than girls and women did. Consistent with this finding, girls and women reported higher rates than men of perpetration against a partner. The longitudinal data allowed the researchers to determine if IPV persisted over time. As expected, early IPV victimization was related to higher levels of IPV victimization and perpetration in later years. As noted in many of the studies discussed in this chapter, much IPV is mutual, so those victimized in adolescence may have often been involved in mutually violent relationships. Not being able to test this directly was noted as a limitation of the study by the researchers.

As with other samples, the way the violence questions are asked can greatly affect the resulting data and conclusions drawn (see Box 5.1). Since 1999, the U.S. Centers for Disease Control have been surveying high school students throughout the U.S. to assess health risk behaviors in a survey called the national Youth Risk Behavior Survey. As Vagi, Olsen, Basile, and Vivolo-Kantor (2015) discussed, the questions relating to dating violence were changed in 2013. The original item summarized the CTS questions by asking "During the past 12 months, did your boyfriend or girlfriend ever hit, slap, or physically hurt you on purpose? (p. 475). This item was reworded to more clearly focus on more serious types of IPV and to separate the effects of sexual and other forms of physical violence. The new items were "During the past 12 months, how many times did someone you were dating or going out with physically hurt you on purpose? (Count such things as being hit, slammed into something, or injured with an object or weapon)." The new sexual question was: "During the past 12 months, how many times did someone you were dating or going out with force you to do sexual things that you did not want to do? (Count such things as kissing, touching, or being physically forced to have sexual intercourse)." (p. 476). Until these items were changed, about 9% of girls and 9% of boys said they had been victims of IPV from a dating partner, based on the older wording of the question. In 2013, percentages changed, with 7% of girls and 4% of boys reporting physical victimization, 8% of girls and 3% of boys reporting sexual victimization, and 6% of girls and 3% of boys reporting both physical and sexual victimization. Thus, overall percentages of IPV were higher than in the earlier surveys, and girls were more often victims than boys for both types of violence. Victimization rates increased from Grade 9–12 and were higher in Black and Hispanic students than in Whites (Vagi et al., 2015). Of course, it is impossible to know how much these changes in reported violence patterns were related to the change in wording of the IPV items and how much reflected true changes in levels of violence over time in this adolescent population.

Using another sample of adolescents, Johnson et al. (2015) were interested in the question of how age was related to IPV perpetration. They drew on a sample of adolescents and young adults from a larger study called the Toledo Adolescent Relationships Study, drawn originally from enrollment records for students in the

7th, 9th and 11th grades in one county in Ohio. Data were included from the original sample in 2001 as well as from follow-ups through 2012. Those who answered that they had thrown something, pushed, shoved or grabbed, slapped, or hit a present or former partner were assigned to the IPV perpetration group. Overall, for boys or men, 13% were in this group for ages 13–16, 19% from 17 to 20, 15% for 21 to 24, and 10% for 25 to 28 years of age. The data for girls and women was described as "similar..but consistently higher with a peak of 29% for ages 21–24 years" (p. 716). Thus, it appears that the typical undergraduate ages had the highest levels of partner violence, although it was not clear if the length of time respondents were in a dating or other relationship was considered. Study participants were asked to describe violence in their current or most recent relationship. Overall, two of the best predictors of perpetration were lack of trust in the partner and jealousy.

In yet another national survey of teens aged 12–18, Taylor and Mumford (2016) drew a sample from an adult panel used for other research to locate parents of adolescents. The adult sample was primarily white and highly educated, so it was not a representative sample. Adults in the sample with a child of the appropriate age were asked to have the child complete an on-line survey. Only those with dating experience were used in the final sample of over 1800 teens. Questions asked about their victimization as well as about their own perpetration of IPV. Overall, reported rates of physical and sexual IPV were similar to those found in the CDC studies, and reported rates of perpetration and victimization were similar. No significant gender differences emerged. Taylor and Mumford further noted that most of the IPV was mutual. In addition to the physical and sexual questions, they also included questions about psychological violence. Again, most was mutual, with over half the girls and boys in the sample reporting this type of IPV.

More recently, in a major study of all types of partner aggression in high school students, Choi, Weston, and Temple (2017) surveyed a sample of over 900 ninth and tenth grade students at seven public high schools in Texas. To be included in the sample, the student had to agree that they had "begun dating, going out with someone, or had a boyfriend/girlfriend" (Choi et al., 2017, p. 856). The sample was divided into five different groups: Nonviolence, not reporting receiving any type of abuse (41%); Emotional and verbal abuse, with high scores for both receiving and perpetrating these types of abuse (31%); Sexual abuse victimization (12%); Psychological and physical violence perpetration and victimization (9%); and those being physically abused, and using and receiving emotional abuse (8%). Overall, emotional and verbal abuse were most commonly received from and given to a dating partner. More students reported being sexually abused than being sexual abusers. Reports of giving and receiving physical abuse were very similar. Female students were more likely than male students to be in all of the other groups than in the nonviolence group or the sexual abuse group. Thus, the girls were more likely than boys to be both perpetrators and victims, based on their self reports. Relative to the nonviolent group, those in all the other groups except the sexual abuse group had higher rates of anxiety, depression and hostility. Study authors suggested this may represent underreporting of this behavior, since students were warned that reports of forced sex could potentially be reported to authorities.

5.1.3.1 Summary

Although we did not attempt to provide a detailed review of the many studies on adolescent violence, it does not appear that levels of reported IPV perpetration or victimization are higher in this group than in older groups of adults. As in other age groups, rates of IPV vary greatly across studies, as do the specific measures used. As with older couples, most forms of IPV are mutual in adolescent samples. Studies yield differing conclusions about whether boys or girls are more likely to be perpetrators.

5.1.4 Studies of IPV among Sexual Minorities

Although the initial research on IPV and battered women focused on heterosexual couples, published research made it very clear by the 1990s that sexual minority couples also engaged in aggressive behavior toward each other. In a review of this literature, Burkea and Follingstad (1999) discussed 19 different studies published in preceding years that documented IPV within gay and lesbian couples. None of these studies used a national or even a local random sample, and instead relied on methods of identification of these groups through contacting relevant groups or advertising. Thus, all the samples would be described as convenience samples (see Chap. 1 for more information on samples). Difficulties in reaching these samples were discussed in Messinger's (2017) book. Reported rates of IPV across the studies varied greatly, but it was clear that IPV existed in both lesbian and in gay male couples. Since then, research has become more sophisticated, and continues to document IPV within sexual minority couples, including transgender and other sexual minority groups as well as gays and lesbians.

Although the national Tjaden and Thoennes' (2000) study, using a national representative sample that was discussed earlier, did not ask directly about sexual orientation, they did ask about living as part of a couple with a same-sex partner. Looking at gender within that group (about 1% of the women and men in the entire sample), sexual assault and rape rates were higher in the same-sex cohabitating women, and physical assault was higher in the same-sex cohabitating men. Rates of partner rape in the same-sex men were too low for statistical analysis. However, Tjaden and Thoennes further noted that both women and men were more likely to be victimized by a male partner than a female partner. [This study also reported higher victimization for women than men in heterosexual (cisgender) couples].

The NISVS CDC data from 2010 allowed for study of sexual minorities (Walters, Chen, & Breiding, 2013). Overall, for women, rates of reported severe physical violence ever received from an intimate partner were 24% for heterosexual women, 29% for lesbian women, and 49% for bisexual women. For men, these values were 14% for heterosexual men and 16% for gay men. Data for bisexual men were not computed because of a small sample size for this group. For both heterosexual and bisexual women, the large majority of perpetrators for partner violence were men.

The majority of bisexual men and heterosexual men reported that women were the perpetrators of the IPV they received. Rates of psychological aggression were much higher than rates for physical forms of IPV for all groups and followed similar incidence patterns as other forms of IPV. As noted earlier, psychological forms of IPV appear to be higher than for physical aggression for heterosexual couples, as well.

5.1.4.1 Lesbian Couples

Higher rates of psychological or emotional violence in lesbians than in heterosexual women have since been reported in many different studies. Badenes-Ribera, Frias-Navarro, Bonilla-Campos, Pons-Salvador, and Honterde-i-Bort (2015) did a meta-analysis of 14 U.S. studies published between 1990 and 2013. Overall, much higher rates of psychological/emotional aggression were reported among lesbian couples with 43% of women reporting they had ever received this from their partner, and 27% saying they had ever done this to a partner. These data did indicate experiences with any current or previous partner. Reported rates were lower for all types of IPV in the current partnership.

The following two cases involved lesbian women in a relationship characterized by IPV, with similar dynamics to those seen in heterosexual couples. These cases also illustrate how each partner in an abusive relationship might describe the violence differently. In these reports, each described the partner as the controlling partner. This relationship also indicated how fear of escalation of the violence might prevent the abused partner from seeking help from the police. Note that "Bebe" is the nickname for Lettie [Case 10] who came in for help a week after Elaine.

Case Example #9

Elaine is a 28 year old single African-American woman with four children. Only two of the children are with her; the other two are with their father. Elaine was referred to county mental health services for ongoing counseling by the Battered Women's Shelter. Elaine has lived in Sacramento for 3 years; before that, she was living in Oakland. While in Oakland—5 years ago—her husband was killed, she was very depressed after his untimely death and made one suicide attempt by overdosing. Following the suicide attempt, Elaine sought counseling and this helped her tremendously—she got back on her feet, worked for a while as a domestic for a wealthy family and managed to save money, get her kids back (they had been removed for a while by child protective services) and, overall, was doing well. Then a friend introduced her to a woman named Bebe. Bebe had a young child and had her own problems and attached herself to Elaine in a very dependent demanding fashion—began calling her at work and the family she worked for became angry about Bebe's constant calls but instead of Elaine telling Bebe not to call, she quit her job and moved in with Bebe and they both then moved to Sacramento. Bebe became more controlling, Elaine ended up taking care of Bebe's child along with her own children when Bebe got high on drugs and Bebe began almost terrorizing Elaine and her children and this eventually accelerated into Bebe beating Elaine physically and abusing Elaine's children almost daily. The beatings got worse but Elaine was afraid to call the police because she felt even if Bebe was jailed, when she got out of jail, Elaine would suffer worse beatings. Finally, last Friday, Bebe beat Elaine with a wooden chair, and Elaine tried to defend herself with a knife. Elaine didn't stab Bebe but did manage to get her children and leave. A community service worker referred Elaine to the shelter and to mental health services. Elaine states the apartment where she lives with Bebe is in Elaine's name and her furniture is still there but she is too afraid to go back. Currently, her plans are to stay at the shelter until she can get a new place, enroll her children in the school nearby and friends will provide her with furniture once she gets a new place. She is clear that she is not going back to Bebe and wants to start her life over. Since counseling helped her in the past, she is very anxious to start again. One issue she wants to have resolved is whether she is gay or straight and she feels very confused about this. She supports herself currently with welfare and all of her family and friends are in Oakland.

Case Example #10

Lettie is a 26 year old single black female referred to county mental health services by the Women's Center. For the past 3 years, Lettie has been involved in a live-in gay relationship with a woman named Elaine (see Case 9). Approximately a week ago, Elaine left Lettie and, with her two children, Elaine went to the Battered Women's Shelter asking for placement there, claiming that Lettie had beaten her and was threatening her, adding that she—Elaine—was planning to permanently sever the relationship and wanted to "start a new life". Lettie states that she has been devastated by Elaine's leaving and relates a description of their relationship quite different from what Elaine related to me when I saw her earlier in the week. Essentially, Elaine describes Lettie as the villain and she as the victim and Lettie describes Elaine as the villain and she as the victim—the actual events and problems described are approximately the same but the roles of the actors are reversed. Lettie has one child—a 6 year old boy—and Elaine has two children. Lettie states she has been gay for 13 years but her relationship with Elaine is the longest and most committed relationship she has had with a woman. They moved all over the Bay area and Oakland before finally settling in Sacramento. Lettie feels she has sacrificed for Elaine—giving up jobs (Lettie is a certified welder) and so forth—to follow her but feels Elaine has not appreciated this. She states that throughout their relationship Elaine has abused her—both physically and emotionally. Lettie states that

Elaine has a bad temper, gets easily insulted and seems to try to provoke Lettie into physical fights. When questioned about who starts the fights, Lettie admitted that both of them seem to mutually provoke each other. Elaine also lies about her to others—for example, Lettie states that Elaine has told others that Lettie uses drugs but Lettie denies any drug use except for an occasional beer—Lettie claims she has been the one who has primarily cared for the children—both hers and Elaine's—but Elaine claims the opposite. Lettie states that Elaine has punched holes in the walls of the apartment and currently is arguing with the landlady about paying for the damages. Why has Lettie stayed all this time? She says she has stayed because she loves Elaine and her children. But now she doesn't know what to do—she states she feels worse now than she has ever felt in her life. Last night she felt like killing herself (Elaine had left a loaded gun in the house) but she controlled herself because of her little boy. Currently, she says she is in control but has planned to stay in a motel tonight to avoid any temptation to harm herself. She was managing fairly well, but Elaine called her last night and began complaining about all their problems and this set Lettie off into a deep depression. She states she has no history of any suicide attempts, or even ideation. At this point she is planning to stay in Sacramento but wants very much to get involved in some counseling to get her life sorted out and figure out what she is going to do at this point.

Lettie's family is all in the San Francisco Bay Area. She describes herself as basically a loner and says she really has no friends locally in Sacramento—also that Elaine has turned their neighbors against Lettie and "her talk" has eliminated the possibility for friends she might have had.

5.1.4.2 Gay Male Couples

There have been very few studies specifically looking at male couples. One recent study of men in New York City having sex with men who were contacted through an anonymous internet app asked about different types of IPV victimization from an "intimate sexual partner" (Duncan et al., 2018, p. 3). The sample was a convenience sample recruited through ads on the app website. Overall, 38% of the men reported some type of IPV, with emotional IPV most often reported (24%). Other forms of IPV included physical (10%) and sexual (11%). The emotional category included financial abuse where the partner took over a bank account, isolation caused by the partner isolating him from others, and intimidation by the sexual partner. Thus, it appears that these relationships were not necessarily a single sexual encounter and involved more long-term partnerships.

The following case example from our files illustrates emotional abuse in a same-sex gay relationship:

Donald, age 32, has been in a committed relationship with Darren for over 10 years. Donald says that he and Darren will often get into arguments over money which leads to each accusing the other of overspending. These arguments sometimes escalate to where one partner will threaten to leave the other and then the other partner threatens suicide. Recently, Donald had had enough and told Darren that they should consider a trial separation. Darren threatened to kill himself if Donald left and then began to berate Donald for all the things he has done wrong during their relationship. The argument ended when Darren grabbed a knife to cut himself and Donald called the police.

Raghavan, Beck, Menke, and Loveland (2019) used a sample from a clinic offering services to gays and lesbians to examine emotional abuse in male-male couples more directly. The total sample included 135 men, but there was a good deal of missing data for some questions. When asked about their worst fight, more than half of the group mentioned some type of controlling behavior. Examples of this included being given no autonomy by the partner, intimidation, punishment, and other forms of dominance behavior. Many of the men also mentioned that physical violence was present along with the controlling behavior, but not all of them showed this association.

5.1.4.3 Trans Couples

Another sexual minority group are those assigned as female at birth who are in the process or have completed a transition to male, and birth-assigned males transitioning to female. Cook-Daniels (2015) described some of the issues these transgendered individuals face, and the ways in which a partner might exploit these as a form of abuse. King, Restar, and Operario (2019) provided a more formal analysis of IPV in trans populations, drawing on a study of almost 24,000 adults who were surveyed in 2015. The sample was generated from referrals from clinics servicing this population around the U.S. The sample included trans women (34%), trans men (31%) and nonbinary individuals who reported having a romantic or sexual partner. Psychological abuse was most frequently mentioned (42%), followed by physical abuse (40%), stalking (18%) and forced sex (22%). Thirty percent of the sample reported some form of trans-related abuse. Trans men reported being a victim of all forms of IPV more often than trans women.

5.1.4.4 Comparisons within Sexual Minority Couples and with Heterosexual Couples

In one study that was able to compare lesbians, gay men and those who were bisexual with transgendered women and men, Langenderfer-Magruder, Whitfield, Walls, Kattari, and Ramos (2016) reported on a large survey done in Colorado in 2011. The sample of 1139 individuals was drawn from a statewide anonymous survey of LGBT Health. [Respondents were volunteers]. Overall, 10% of the sample were transgender, while the rest were LBG. In responding to a single question asking if they had ever experienced IPV or dating violence, 20% of the LGB group said they had, and 31% of the transgroup agreed that they, too, had experienced IPV as either a perpetrator or a victim. Another single question asked if the IPV or dating violence was reported to the police. Twenty-six percent of the LGB group and 18% of the transgender group said they had reported to the police.

All of the studies described so far have involved sexual minority adults. There have also been some studies of sexual minority adolescents. Using a large sample of high school students in the state of Massachusetts, Martin-Storey (2015) was able to identify a sample of different types of sexual minorities and compare them with the heterosexual sample. Data were collected in 2003, 2005, 2007 and 2009. Looking only at those above the age of 13 who reported going on a date, there were 5368 girls and 5078 boys in the total sample. Among the girls, 57 identified as lesbian, 306 as bisexual and 97 as unsure. For the boys, 83 were gay, 82 were bisexual, and 69 were unsure. These individuals were classified as representing sexual minorities. Two questions asked about having been hurt physically or sexually by a date. Combining these items, sexual minority girls and boys reported higher rates of IPV victimization than those classified as heterosexual. Lesbian and bisexual girls had higher rates of victimization than gay and bisexual boys. Martin-Storey noted that these data were consistent with other reported data for similar samples. Those who rated themselves as unsure about their sexual orientation were intermediate between the two groups already described.

In one of the few national samples of sexual minority adolescents, Olsen, Vivolo-Kantro, and Kann (2017) analyzed data from the CDC's national Youth Risk Behavior Survey from 2015. This on-going survey assesses high school students throughout the U.S. in grades 9–12. Questions address many health issues, including IPV. Students identifying themselves as gay or lesbian or bisexual were compared as a group to those identifying as heterosexual or "straight." The girls in the LGB group made up about 13% of the total female sample responding to partner violence questions. The comparable percentage was 4% for boys. Analyses indicated higher rates of physical and sexual IPV among the LGB group than among the heterosexual boys and girls. No differences were found in a comparison of the male and female LGB samples.

Studies of IPV in sexual minorities have been critiqued for not clearly separating different sexual minorities (Reuter, Sharp, & Temple, 2015). In an investigation that attempted to remedy this, Reuter et al. (2015) surveyed high school students from five Houston-area school districts for a study on teen dating violence with an original sample and a 2 year follow-up. Only those who identified themselves as dating at the time of the follow-up were included in the analysis. Those who identified as "completely heterosexual" were included in the heterosexual group, while those identifying as "mostly heterosexual," "bisexual," "mostly homosexual," "completely homosexual," or "not sure" (p. 13) were categorized as part of a sexual minority group. Eighty-one percent of the sample identified as "completely heterosexual," with "mostly heterosexual" (7%) and "bisexual" (5%) being the next largest categories within the sample. Many more of the female (26%) than male (9%) students were classified as sexual minority. Overall, the (primarily female) sexual minority group reported more dating violence victimization and perpetration than the heterosexual group. However, perpetration rates did not differ for the females and males in the sexual minority groups. Perpetration rates were highest for the bisexual group.

Whitton, Dyar, Mustanski, and Newcomb (2019) provided other information about a sample of individuals assigned as female at birth, who were classified as sexual or gender minorities when sampled between the ages of 16 and 32. The sample of 352 young adults included 94 lesbians, 132 bisexuals, 36 queer, 62 pansexual, and 18 others. Extensive data were collected about a number of forms of IPV including minor and severe psychological abuse, cyber abuse, and severe physical and sexual IPV. Minor psychological abuse was quite common, reported in 64 to 70% within the various sexual minority groups. Much of the IPV of all types of mutual.

Although samples of sexual minority groups are often too small to allow for comparisons across groups, this is not always the case. [As the Whitton et al. data indicated, a large number of different sexual minority groups can be identified within the larger group, which is rarely more than 15% of a general sample]. Using a large convenience sample to investigate IPV in a lesbian and bisexual sample from Chicago, Steele, Everett, and Hughes (2017) replicated other studies of sexual minority groups in finding that rates of IPV victimization were higher for the Black and Latina women than White women. This race effect persisted even after controlling for SES and experiences of child sex abuse. Higher levels of education independently predicted lower levels of IPV.

5.1.4.5 Summary

As Reuter et al. (2015) pointed out, although the body of research on intimate partner violence among sexual minorities is growing, results may be difficult to generalize because of a lack of precision about the specific type of sexual minority groups within the sample. As with research on heterosexual couples, researchers also rely on very different measures of IPV across studies. Sampling can also be an issue, and some studies rely on highly selected samples such as those involved with a GLBT organization. One group about which almost nothing about IPV is known is the trans population (Walker, 2015).

5.2 Motives for Intimate Partner Violence

Chapter 2 discusses research and theory about causes of aggression and violence generally. Here, we focus specifically on correlational data showing potential causal factors for IPV and on self-reports from women and men about why they have been violent toward an intimate partner. In a major review of the literature, Birkley and Eckhardt (2015) reported on a meta-analysis of 61 studies of married, cohabitating and dating couples to see what consistent findings emerged about characteristics of those engaging in IPV. The most common correlations of IPV against a partner were anger, hostility, and other negative emotions. Those higher in these variables tended to engage in more severe IPV. (Note that this suggests that IPV is similar to other types of aggression, as discussed in Chap. 2). Overall, there were *no* significant differences in motives between women and men as perpetrators, or for the type of sample or type of relationship in terms of these correlates with IPV. Similar conclusions can be found in Larsen and Hamberger's (2015) review of data on perpetrators.

In another review, again failing to find major gender differences in motives for violence, although noting some, Neal and Edwards (2017) published a review of studies published from 1986 through 2014 examining the question of *why* women and men engage in IPV. Looking at studies of men and women identified as being violent toward a partner and being asked to participate in a Batterer Intervention Program (see Chap. 9 for more information about these programs), they noted little difference in the motives expressed by the women and by the men in these programs. Self-defense was often mentioned by the women, as well as by the men. Other motives were acting out of anger or frustration, and having difficulty in communicating with the partner. However, in a number of studies with this type of sample, women, more than men, reported that they had been violent in retaliation for previous violence from the partner. Men more often said they were punishing their female partner for something she had done. Men were more likely than women to blame their IPV on being drunk or affected by some other drug. Some studies identified protection of children as a reason for women to be violent, but this was not a common finding.

Looking at the broader sample of studies, many of which examined dating couples (typically college students), other motives were also identified. Perpetrators mentioned motives such as wanting to punish the partner or responding to something the partner said that seemed threatening. Victims offered somewhat different motives. These included the violent partner being drunk, being jealous, or upset at their jealousy. Victims also mentioned that the violence appeared to be a response to their refusal of sexual advances (Neal & Edwards, 2017).

Going beyond the survey studies, one can find more detailed qualitative studies of IPV motivation. For example, Cornelius, Bell, Wyngarden, and Shorey (2015) noted that several earlier studies had proposed that both men and women might be engaging in physically aggressive behavior toward dating partners because it was not punished by their partners, or was even rewarded. In a direct test of these ideas, they asked college *women* who reported they had been violent with a partner about what exactly had happened after their most recent use of physical aggression toward a partner. Interview data were coded using standard qualitative techniques. Data indicated that almost all the women said that the most immediate effect of their violence was that it stopped the conflict that they had been having with their partner. The partner was reported as expressing shock, upset or anger at her and sometimes responded with his own aggression. Some of the women said they felt bad about their violence afterwards, but others mentioned feeling calmer, less distressed or more emotionally connected to their partner. Many women said that their aggression led to her male partner being more likely to do what she wanted.

Overall, these data suggested that the women's violence had been reinforced by their dating partner.

Anger and provocation from the partner were the most commonly reported motives for IPV perpetration in an internet volunteer sample of women aged between 18 and 35 (Llorens, Salis, O'Leary, & Hayward, 2015). Other common responses were poor communication and jealousy. The women were also asked why they did *not* engage in physical aggression during their most recent conflict with their partner. Common responses were feeling it was inappropriate, that violence was never OK, that females should not be aggressive, or that they were not personally aggressive. For more information relating to attitudes about the acceptability of IPV, see Box 5.3.

Box 5.3: Cyber Aggression: Anther Type of Partner Aggression

The importance of social media in the lives of young adults appears to have led to the use of this means of communication as a method perpetrating dating IPV (Reed et al., 2018). Examples of this include monitoring where someone is, expressing hostility, and pressuring for sexual behavior. Reed et al. (2018) asked a sample of 703 ninth and 12th grade students in Michigan with dating experience about using social mediate to humiliate or threaten a dating partner, monitoring the partner's behavior and engaging in unwanted distribution of sexual images. Girls were more likely to report trying to monitor the behavior of a partner, while sexual coercion was more reported by boys. Much of the behavior was mutual, though. Other forms of cyber aggression against a dating partner were reported by Smith et al. (2018) using a sample of adolescents in Quebec, Canada. Sharing personal information about the partner to others, blackmailing the partner, or insulting the partner were some of the most common forms of this type of cyber violence. Again, much of the behavior was mutual within the couple.

Although most of the more recent work has examined motives for IPV in women, Elmquist et al. (2016) directly compared the reasons that men gave for using violence against a partner as compared to the reasons women gave in their sample of psychology students. They asked how often each of a long list of possible motives was a reason for them using physical aggression against their partner. For both women and men, one of the most commonly rated motives was self-defense, along with proving love for the partner, not being able to communicate in words, and because it was seen as sexual arousing or was identified as playful violence. Differences across genders were not statistically significant for the rated motives.

In another study of young adults drawn from interviews with a general community sample, Giordano, Copp, Longmore, and Manning (2015) reported that jealousy appeared to be a major factor, especially for male violence, with the violent party being jealous himself, or reacting violently to an accusation of being interested in someone else. In addition, the researchers argued that for young adults, concerns about economic factors and about time spent with friends might also generate arguments that led to violence. They argued that these themes generated anger on the part of the violent partner, leading to IPV.

5.2.1 Summary

At these studies suggest, there are a variety of reported motives for engaging in IPV. Both women and men reported similar types of motives. Anger and jealousy were commonly mentioned motives across studies. High use of alcohol is also commonly reported in both male and female perpetrators (see Larsen & Hamberger, 2015 for a review of this literature). Based on reports of perpetrators, it also appeared that there were not always negative consequences of IPV for the relationship or for the person who was demonstrating physical violence toward his or her partner. However, these conclusions are based primarily on reports of perpetrators about why they are violent with their partners and may omit factors they are not aware of or that put them in a negative light.

5.3 Effects of IPV Victimization

As mentioned above, reports about motives of women and men engaging in IPV may imply that they believe such behavior is acceptable (Ybarra & Langhinrichsen-Rohling, 2019), and possibly even beneficial to the relationship. However, a large body of work about the effects of IPV victimization indicates that both those victimized by IPV, as well as the perpetrators demonstrate negative effects of this behavior. This is true for female, as well as male victims, although it appears the consequences of victimization may be greater for women than men.

5.3.1 Mental and Physical Health Effects of IPV

Many studies have indicated that victims of IPV experience a variety of negative mental and physical health outcomes. Such outcomes are consistent with the reports of battered women discussed in Chap. 4. Evidence for physical and emotional reactions to IPV victimization can be seen in a national sample of U.S. adults surveyed in 2005 to 2007 (Blosnich & Bossarte, 2009). Health measures included self-reports of poor mental health, poor physical health, and low satisfaction with life. All three measures were associated with IPV victimization for those with same-sex and with other-sex partners. Overall, female victims reported poorer mental health than male victims, and male victims reported poorer physical health than female victims.

In the large national CDC survey discussed earlier (Black et al., 2011), many negative physical health outcomes were found to be significantly more likely for those who had experienced any form of IPV including physical aggression, rape or stalking as compared to those who had never had these experiences. For women, this list included higher rates of asthma, irritable bowel syndrome, diabetes, frequent headaches, chronic pain, difficulty sleeping, activity limitations and overall poor physical and mental health. Similar findings were seen for male victims, although differences between IPV victims and non-victims were not as great. Significant differences were found for frequent headaches, chronic pain, difficulty sleeping, activity limitations, and poor physical and mental health. Thirty-five percent of female victims reported activity limitations and 30% reported chronic pain. Somewhat fewer male victims (30%) reported activity limitations, and 24% reported chronic pain. Difficulty sleeping was seen in 38% of women and men. These three health issues were the most commonly reported health concerns for the IPV victims.

Black et al. (2011) also reported on emotional reactions of IPV victims. For women the most common was feeling fearful (26%) or concerned for their own safety (22%) followed by experiencing at least one PTSD symptom (22%, see Chap. 3 for more information on PTSD). Injury was reported by 15% of the women, and missing at least 1 day of work or school by 10%. For men, on 5% said they felt fearful or concerned for their safety. About 5% reported experiencing some form of PTSD and 4% reported injury. Also, 4% said they had missed a least 1 day of work or school. Overall 81% of women and 35% of the men reported at least one type of emotional impact from their IPV victimization.

Mental health effects can also been seen for dating violence IPV. In a national survey of high school students conducted by the CDC, Vagi et al. (2015) found that higher percentages of male (21%) and female (38%) victims of physical IPV reported seriously considering attempting suicide. These rates were more than double those for students not victimized by IPV. Victim rates were also significantly higher for actually making a suicide plan or attempting suicide, as well as using alcohol, binge drinking, or using cocaine. Other analyzes found that being the victim of a combination of both severe physical violence and sexual assault from a dating partner had the most serious health consequences for both girls and boys in high school.

Using the same CDC dataset collected in 2010 (see Black et al., 2011), Walters et al. (2013) looked specifically at not only the incidence of IPV within sexual minority populations (data discussed earlier in this chapter), but also at the impact of IPV broadly defined to include physical violence, stalking, or rape victimization. Female sexual minorities were compared to adolescent women dating men. Data for men were not reported due to small sample sizes. Overall, while 28% of heterosexual women reported some effect of their victimization by a partner, 34% of lesbian women and 57% of bisexual women reported some impact. Looking at individual types of impact, 22% of heterosexual women, 20% of lesbians and 46% of bisexual women reported PTSD symptoms. Feeling fearful was quite high for bisexual women (53%) compared to other groups of women.

5.3.2 Alcohol and Substance Abuse and IPV

A number of studies discussed in this discussed in this book have noted an association of IPV with alcohol use. Testa and Derrick (2014) examined this relationship more directly in a daily diary study 120 married and cohabiting couples in Buffalo, New York. Couples were recruited to participate in a study of alcohol use, but were also asked questions about IPV. Ages ranged from yearly 20s to 40s. They completed surveys for 56 days. Analysis of the data indicated that both women and men were more likely to engage in physical and psychological IPV on the days they also drank alcohol. Acts of psychological aggression occurred on less than 10% of the days in the study, while physical IPV occurred less than 1% of the days.

Alcohol misuse and dating violence was the focus of a study conducted by Singh et al. (2015). The sample was drawn from adolescents aged 14–20 seeking assistance in an emergency department who were identified as misusing alcohol. About ¼ of this group reported dating violence in the last year, either as perpetrators, as victims, or both. Overall, a higher proportion of girls than boys reported any of these forms of dating violence. Those involved with dating violence were significantly more likely to abuse other drugs, to be depressed, to have thought about suicide, and to have used psychiatric services. There were no significant differences between IPV perpetrators and victims.

A number of investigators have examined substance abuse and IPV within sexual minority samples. Lewis et al. (2015) used an online convenience sample of over 400 self-identified lesbians to ask about alcohol and IPV. A group reporting mutual IPV with their female partner (n = 54) was compared with those reporting no IPV within their lesbian relationship (n = 360). Overall, the mutual violence group was higher in alcohol consumption and alcohol problems, as well as rumination about their lives and generally negative affect than the nonviolent comparison group. A tested formal model indicated that being higher in emotional distress was associated with drinking alcohol as a coping mechanism (which in turn related to having alcohol-related problems). These problems in turn were associated with the presence of mutual couple violence.

In a broad review of existing research, Buller, Devries, Howard, and Bacchus (2014) summarized major findings across 18 studies of men who have sex with men. Within this sample, IPV victimization was associated with depression as well as substance use. They were also more likely to be HIV positive. Studies reviewed were primarily based on U.S. samples, but also included a Canadian, a Chinese, and a South African sample. Most of these studies used convenience samples.

As Goldenberg, Jadwin-Cakmak, and Harper (2018) pointed out, based on their review of the literature, levels of IPV within the LGBTQ population tend to be higher than for those involved with other-sex partnerships. One group about which relatively little is known are transgender and gender nonconforming adolescents and young adults. This group is often exposed to nonviolent and violent harassment from others. Their data from 131 individuals identified as transgender or gender nonconforming who were aged 16 to 24 [taken from a convenience sample from

14 U.S. cities] indicated that 45% of the sample had experienced physical or sexual IPV. Further analysis indicated that the IPV group compared to those who had not experienced IPV were much more depressed. They were also more likely to have been involved with sex work, had been homeless more often, were more likely to have been jailed, and had higher rates of substance abuse. Given all these negative life indicators, it was difficult to determine the specific causes of higher depression. They urged that more research be done on "transphobic stigma" (p. 22), and how this might contribute to poor mental and physical health.

Finally, in one of the most recent studies examining the relationship of dating IPV, substance abuse and sexual minority status, Rostad, Clayton, Estefan, and Jones (2019) were able to use data from CDC's National Youth Risk Behavior surveys of U.S. high schools. Students could label themselves as "heterosexual (i.e., straight), gay or lesbian, bisexual, or not sure" (p. 3). Reports of dating violence (both physical and sexual IPV) among all who had dating partners were highest for sexual minority males and bisexual females. Higher rates of substance abuse were related to IPV levels in these groups. When this was statistically factored out, rates of dating IPV were more similar across all groups, although there were still somewhat higher rates of IPV in the sexual minority groups. The authors noted that their finding of relatively low rates of IPV in lesbian couples was not consistent with earlier reported findings. They did not have a clear explanation for this difference.

5.3.2.1 Summary

Many of those who have experienced IPV from a partner appear to experience a variety of negative responses. This can be seen in adolescents involved in dating violence as well as in adult heterosexual couples. Studies have identified health issues as well as psychological or emotional reactions. Alcohol use and substance abuse appear to be coping mechanisms associated with stress resulting from victimization (see Chap. 4 for more on coping). Alcohol and other substance abuse as well as IPV rates are generally reported as being higher among sexual minority couples. Effects of IPV are seen in both female and male victims, although women and girls report more consequences. It should also be noted that not all IPV victims do report these negative reactions. Research data generally shows that the majority of IPV victims do not report any of the reactions studied.

5.4 Critiques of Research on Female Violence: Are Women Really as Likely to Perpetrate IPV as Men?

As this review has demonstrated, many studies of IPV indicate that women and adolescent girls can be as violent toward their partner or even more violent than men and boys. This is especially the case for researchers using the Conflict Tactics Scale to measure IPV (see Box 5.1). However, many researchers rejected this conclusion, especially during the 1980s and 1990s. Many still do (e.g., DeKeseredy, 2011; Johnson, 2015). With the publication of a meta-analysis of published research on IPV based primarily on the CTS measure, Archer (2000) hoped to resolve the issue of women's involvement in perpetration of IPV. His data further reinforced the idea that women were as likely as men or even more likely to engage in IPV, although he did note that women accounted for 62% of the injuries inflicted by IPV. (Many of the studies used in the analysis were based on college student samples, and U.S. data.)

The idea that men and women are equally violent in terms of perpetrating IPV is often labeled as the gender symmetry or asymmetry question, where "symmetry" is taken to mean that women and men are equally violent in partnerships (Hamby, 2017, p. 148). Debates and public and private discussion of this issue can be quite emotional, as Sheehy (2016) found was demonstrated in the many quite angry reactions she received to her book on women who kill their partners. Although her book drew on her legal experiences with women who had killed their partners, often out of desperation, Sheehy was attacked by many who saw her research as justifying women's violence against men. She details how she received such attacks particularly from those identifying themselves as men associated with the men's rights movement, and notes that these attacks included personal threats of violence against her for making these arguments.

The following case illustrates how men can be victims of physical, emotional, and sexual violence. However, shame, self-rationalization (e.g. it's not that bad, just "man up" and ignore it), and the belief that no services exist for men may prevent a male victim from reporting his experience. This case also illustrates how undocumented immigrants experiencing IPV may be especially fearful of reporting out of a fear of deportation. [Given these issues, we recommend that practitioners should make contact with immigrant rights groups who can provide information on where to obtain support, including how to apply for the right to stay in the U.S.]

Case Example #5

Juanita and Pedro moved to the U.S. 15 years ago. Both have become fluent in English, and while their son is a natural-born U.S. citizen, neither have made efforts to obtain citizenship. When asked why, they state they are afraid to let the government know of their presence lest they face potential deportation. Both parents work very long hours at various informal jobs. Vicente is a model student and a well-liked, well-behaved boy by all accounts from the school and acquaintances. Social services became involved when it was alleged that Vicente often is alone overnight and even for full weekends when his parents are working. When Vicente was interviewed at school, he also disclosed that his mother often gets very angry when she is stressed, and that she takes it out on both Vicente and Pedro. She will slap and punch Pedro during arguments. Vicente stated that while Pedro will yell as much as Juanita, he never uses physical violence. Vicente stated that his mom still spanks him on his bare bottom with a belt or extension cord, but that it doesn't happen as much as when he was younger. Vicente states he thinks his mom hits him less because he tries very, very hard to be good in school. Pedro's account of fights with Juanita fits with Vicente's. Pedro states that he does not hit back because he grew up in a very violent household in which he was afraid of his father. Additionally, Pedro fears that if he hits back, it will come to the attention of police and risk deportation. Pedro was embarrassed to talk about the hitting, and feels that there is no point in looking for help, not only because of the risk of deportation, but because he assumes there is no help for men. Juanita admitted in her interview that she sometimes hits Pedro, but claims she doesn't do it very often. Juanita also says she has told Pedro he can hit her back, which Vicente says he has heard as well. Juanita denied ever using an instrument to hit Vicente, though she admits she still spanks his bare bottom when he is bad because it will embarrass him and shame him into behaving. Neither adult wanted to leave the home; each stated they still love each other, would have no place to go, and would lose their son. The family were transferred to in-home services for long-term support.

Although some researchers in the late twentieth century acknowledged that battered women could be violent, empirical evidence of female IPV was generally interpreted (by Frieze as well as by other feminist researchers at that time) as these battered women fighting back against an abusive batterer (e.g., Frieze & Browne, 1989; or Saunders, 2002). But, as more data emerged, it became clear that such an explanation would not explain many of the reported frequencies of female violence within couples. Much of these data came from studies of dating couples, often within college student samples, as well as evidence of violence within same-sex couples as discussed earlier in this chapter. Many other explanations were advanced to either explain why this was happening, or to question the basis of the reported data.

In one of the many discussions of this conflict within the literature, Anderson (2013) discussed several hypotheses that might explain why women would engage in IPV at rates as high or higher than those of men. First was what she called the "Lara Croft" hypothesis (p. 315) that women feel empowered now because of having higher status than in the past. This idea is generally supported by reference to cross-cultural data indicating higher rates of female perpetration of IPV in societies where women have more economic and political equality (Archer, 2006). Twenge (2001) presented data on women's rises in assertiveness over the twentieth century, which would be consistent with this argument. Anderson argued, though, that this would imply that as women's status has risen in the U.S., their rates of IPV should have also risen, and that there is no data supporting this conclusion.

A second argument related to the finding that there is now less social approval of men battering their wives than in the past, leading to men underreporting their violence (see Felson, 2002, and Box 5.4 for ideas of chivalry and social disapproval of male violence against women). This possibility of the data showing high levels of female violence not being accurate because of underreporting by violent men was not discounted as an explanation. There does appear to be the general pattern of women and girls reporting more often than men or boys that they have exhibited some type of physical or emotional aggression against a partner. It is also the case that women report more violence overall in couple relationships than men do, and report themselves as perpetrators more than men identify a women as the perpetrator. Frieze (2005) suggests several reasons this might be the case. First there is some evidence that when asked about experiences related to aggression, men tend to focus more on male-male violence, while women focus on couple violence. Thus, when asked about how often they engage in various violent acts toward a female partner, men may simply not remember. Second, given the social disapproval associated with male violence toward women (Felson, 2002), men may be embarrassed to describe their own violent actions more than women.

Box 5.4: Changing Attitudes About IPV?

As discussed in Chap. 1, violent abuse of one's partner is no longer seen as socially acceptable behavior in the United States. In his book discussing gender and violence, Felson (2002) argued that U.S. society generally supported the idea that men should not display aggression toward women, and, instead, should be protective of women. He described this as a norm of chivalry. He further suggested that such norms might account for findings of higher levels of IPV in women toward men than in men toward women. Community studies have found supporting evidence that men's perpetration of IPV is viewed more harshly than women's (Sorenson & Taylor, 2005).

More recent studies report that these norms of chivalry still exist today in college students (Bradley, 2015; Hammock, Richardson, Lamm, Taylor, & Verlaque, 2017). In addition, Hammock and her colleagues found that there was greater disapproval of physical violence than psychological aggression within intimate partner relationships. Both studies found that male perpetrators were perceived more negatively than female perpetrators. Bradley examined a situation in which one used violence against someone who had hit them without justification. Further supporting the idea of chivalry, there was more disapproval of men using retaliatory violence against a woman than women retaliating against a man. Retaliation within different types of relationships was also examined in this study. Men were more accepting of women's retaliation against a husband than women were. Researchers argued that one explanation for their findings was that women's violence was seen as less serious than that of men.

Scenario studies have also been done to investigate view of IPV within sexual minorities. Crittenden, Policastro, and Eigenberg (2017) used a large sample of college students to examine this issue. Results indicated more disapproval of male than female violence regardless of the sexual orientation of the couple. In one of the few studies using scenarios with a sample other than college students, Russell (2017) reported on a study that drew on police officers as her sample. Data indicated that male violence was also rated as more serious than female violence within heterosexual couples by the police sample. Other data examined attitudes about gay and lesbian couples. Men's IPV toward a female partner was seen as the most dangerous. Heterosexual women and gay men using IPV were seen as least likely to harm their partners.

Some studies have indicated that women, too, may have negative views of their violence toward a male partner and report feeling shame. Weiss, Duke, Overstreet, Swan, and Sullivan (2016) administered a survey about IPV and feelings of shame to a volunteer sample of community women recruited for a study about women's relationships with men in their lives. The sample consisted of 369 women who reported engaging in physical IPV toward their male partner. Shame was assessed with items such as "I would be embarrassed if anyone found out about my abuse towards my partner" or "I do not tell people that I am sometimes abusive towards my partner" (p. 430). Shame scores were correlated with both IPV perpetration and victimization, and were especially high for the women with alcohol or drug use problems. Perhaps this shame relates to a general sense that intimate partner violence is not acceptable behavior?

A third argument was that violent men are not likely to participate in national studies, and thus, couples in which the male is the violent partner are not represented in their true proportions. Anderson discounts this argument, noting that attempts to examine this issue directly often fail to account for high rates of mutual couple IPV, a finding from many of the studies discussed earlier in this chapter. One might also argue that couples in which the woman is the violent partner may also be reluctant to participate in studies of marital dynamics.

A fourth hypothesis was that because of less physical ability to inflict injury, women need to engage in more acts of violence to achieve the same effect, or that women's violence is not taken as seriously as men's. Anderson (2013) suggested that this idea had merit but needed further empirical testing. [A later qualitative study discussed earlier by Lehrner and Allen (2018) does find support for the idea of women's violence not being taken seriously among college students.] Anderson concluded her analysis by indicating that it was more important to consider why IPV happens at all than to try to determine whether men or women do it more.

Other critiques of Straus et al. (1980) as well as of other national survey data indicating higher rates of female perpetration of IPV have focused on measurement concerns, especially as related to the use of the CTS (e.g., Brush, 1990). In an important paper published in 2017, Hamby addressed the methodological issues in some detail. Hamby was involved in a major redrafting of the CTS, resulting in the CTS2 (see Straus, Hamby, Boney-McCoy, & Sugarman, 1996). She discussed the development of the CTS2 in some detail in this paper and noted many critiques of this scale as well as of the original CTS. It has become clear that gender differences in IPV perpetration depend greatly on the particular measures used to assess IPV. Issues such as intentions related to violent acts as well as resulting harm are key to understanding apparently violent behavior, and these were not generally examined in large survey studies and were not assessed in the revised CTS.

Straus himself (Winstok & Straus, 2016) has published relatively recent papers noting the controversy his early work has generated, and arguing that the reality is that although both women and men do engage in acts of violence against martial or intimate partners, the reality is that the most typical situation is that both parties are violent within a couple classified as involved with IPV. Looking only at situations in which one partner engages in physical forms of IPV, Winstok and Straus argued that it was more likely that it is only the man who was violent, although there are some couples where only the woman was violent. Consistent with Archer's (2000) meta-analysis, it is also the case that more women are injured by IPV than men.

In response to these concerns about the CTS, researchers at the CDC have now developed a revised measure of IPV that separates serious from less serious violence. Some of the initial reports of data using this scale were reported earlier in the chapter (Black et al., 2011; Smith, Zhang, et al., 2018). Our guess is that as more researchers become familiar with this revised scale, some of the disagreements in the field will diminish. These data do clearly indicate that men are more likely to engage in serious IPV, but men and women engage at relatively equal rates in lower levels of IPV,

5.5 Summary

This chapter extends the work reviewed in Chap. 4 on battered women by examining IPV research based on community samples of adults as well as studies of college students and adolescents. Samples have also been extended beyond heterosexual couples to include a variety of sexual minorities. Much of this research is based on surveys, often using the CTS or some modified version of this scale, to measure intimate partner violence (IPV). The CTS measures how often people use various forms of physical aggression toward their partners. These behaviors range from quite severe violence to very mild forms of physical aggression that may not cause an injury or even pain. Much reported IPV has been found to consist of these less violent behaviors. Although the expression of some form of physical violence toward the partner is the primary measure of IPV seen in these studies, other types of IPV such as forced sexual behavior and psychological abuse can also be found.

One of the common findings of this research is that IPV is not limited to battered women and their abusive husbands or male partners. Instead, this work consistently indicates the women, too, use all forms of IPV, as do sexual minorities. This occurs in dating couples as well as in older couples who are married or living together. Although studies based on CTS-like measures often report that women are more likely than men to perpetrate IPV, newer studies using different measures of IPV do sometimes indicate that men are more often perpetrators, and the women are more often victimized by IPV. This is especially true when looking at the most serious forms of violence. It is also clear that the large majority of IPV within couples occurs in couples where both engage in often low levels of IPV. Incidence rates of IPV vary by age, as well as by race or ethnicity, but conclusions about exact rates are difficult because measures of IPV vary so much across samples. Samples drawn from general populations systematically indicate that the majority of couples use no physical violence at all. Rates of psychological or emotional aggression are higher than those for physical IPV, although both forms of IPV are correlated.

Reported motives for engaging in IPV are similar for women and men. Often mentioned reasons for violence include anger and jealousy. Being intoxicated from alcohol or drugs is another commonly identified motive. Research on the impact of IPV on victims indicates that IPV can be associated with a large variety of physical and mental health problems. In general, these consequences are higher for women than men. Psychological IPV can have more serious consequences than physical forms of IPV.

Discussions attempting to understand why so many of the CTS-based studies indicate higher levels of IPV perpetration in women than men suggest that measurement issues may be a major explanation, one supported by evidence of higher levels of male violence in recent studies using different measures that focus more on serious violence. Many studies have indicated that women experience serious injury from IPV more than men, data that was difficult to correlate with the higher reported rates of female than male perpetration of IPV.

References

Anderson, K. L. (2002). Perpetrator or victim? Relationships between intimate partner violence and well-being. *Journal of Marriage and the Family, 64*, 851–886. https://doi.org/10.1111/j.1741-3737.2002.00851.x3

Anderson, K. L. (2013). Why do we fail to ask "why" about gender and intimate partner violence? *Journal of Marriage and the Family, 75*, 314–318. https://doi.org/10.1111/jomf.12001

Archer, J. (2000). Sex differences in aggression between heterosexual partners: A meta-analytic review. *Psychological Bulletin, 126*, 651–680. https://doi.org/10.1037//0033-2909.126.5.651

Archer, J. (2006). Cross-cultural differences in physical aggression between partners: A social role analysis. *Personality and Social Psychology Review, 10*, 133–153. https://doi.org/10.1207/s15327957pspr1002_3

Arriaga, X. B., & Schkeryantz, E. L. (2015). Intimate relationships and personal distress: The invisible harm of psychological aggression. *Personality and Social Psychology Bulletin, 41*, 1332–1344. https://doi.org/10.1177/0146167215594123

Badenes-Ribera, L., Frias-Navarro, D., Bonilla-Campos, A., Pons-Salvador, G., & Honterde-i-Bort, H. (2015). Intimate partner violence in self-identified lesbians: A meta-analysis of its prevalence. *Sexuality Research & Social Policy, 12*, 47–59. https://doi.org/10.1007/s13178-014-0164-7

Birkley, E. L., & Eckhardt, C. I. (2015). Anger, hostility, internalizing negative emotions, and intimate partner violence perpetration: A meta-analytic review. *Clinical Psychology Review, 37*, 40–56. https://doi.org/10.1016/j.cpr.2015.01.002

Black, M. C., Basile, K. C., Breiding, M. J., Smith, S. G., Walters, M. L., Merrick, M. T., et al. (2011). *The National Intimate Partner and Sexual Violence Survey (NISVS): 2010 Summary Report*. Atlanta, GA: National Center for Injury Prevention and Control, Centers for Disease Control and Prevention.

Blosnich, J. R., & Bossarte, M. (2009). Comparisons of intimate partner violence among partners in same-sex and opposite-sex relationships in the United States. *American Journal of Public Health, 99*, 2182–2184. https://doi.org/10.2105/AJPH.2008.139535

Bookwala, J., Frieze, I. H., Smith, C., & Ryan, K. (1992). Predictors of dating violence: A multivariate analysis. *Violence and Victims, 7*, 297–311.

Bookwala, J., Sobin, J., & Zdaniuk, B. (2005). Gender and aggression in marital relationships: A life-span perspective. *Sex Roles, 52*, 797–806. https://doi.org/10.1007/s11199-00504200-1

Bradley, M. S. (2015). Gender and the acceptance of retaliatory violence among acquaintance, dating and marital relationships. *Violence and Victims, 30*, 377–392. https://doi.org/10.1891/0886-6708.VV-D-13-00169

Brush, L. (1990). Violent acts and injurious outcomes in married couples: Methodological issues in the National Survey of Families and Households. *Gender & Society, 4*, 56–67. https://doi.org/10.1177/089124390004001005

Buller, A. M., Devries, K. M., Howard, L. M., & Bacchus, L. J. (2014). Associations between intimate partner violence and health among men who have sex with men: A systematic review and meta-analysis. *PLOS Medicine, 11*(3), 1–12. e1001609. https://doi.org/10.1371/journal.pmed.1001609

Bumpass, L. L., & Sweet, J. A. (1989). National estimates of cohabitation. *Demography, 26*, 615–625. https://doi.org/10.2307/2061261

Burkea, L. K., & Follingstad, D. R. (1999). Violence in lesbian and gay relationships: Theory, prevalence, and correlational factors. *Clinical Psychology Review, 19*, 487–512. https://doi.org/10.1016/S0272-7358(98)00054-3

Caetano, R., Vaeth, P. A. C., & Ramisetty-Mikler, S. (2008). Intimate partner violence victim and perpetrator characteristics among couples in the United States. *Journal of Family Violence, 23*, 507–518. https://doi.org/10.1007/s10896-008-9178-3

Choi, H. J., Weston, R., & Temple, J. R. (2017). A three-step latent class analysis to identify how different patterns of teen dating violence and psychosocial factors influence mental health. *Journal of Youth and Adolescence, 46*, 854–866. https://doi.org/10.1007/s10964-016-0570-7

Coker, A. L., Follingstad, D. R., Bush, H. M., & Fisher, B. S. (2016). Are interpersonal violence rates higher among young women in college compared with those never attending college? *Journal of Interpersonal Violence, 31*, 1413–1429. https://doi.org/10.1177/0886260514567958

Cook-Daniels, L. (2015). Intimate partner violence in transgender couples: "Power and control" in a specific cultural context. *Partner Abuse, 6*, 126–139. https://doi.org/10.1891/1946-6560.6.1.126

Cornelius, T. L., Bell, K. M., Wyngarden, N., & Shorey, R. C. (2015). What happens after I hit? A qualitative analysis of the consequences of dating violence for female perpetrators. *Violence and Victims, 30*, 393–416. https://doi.org/10.1891/0886-6708.VV-D-13-00058

Crittenden, C. A., Policastro, C., & Eigenberg, H. M. (2017). Attitudes toward dating violence: How does sexual identity influence perceptions among college students? *Journal of Aggression, Maltreatment & Trauma, 26*, 804–824. https://doi.org/10.1080/10926771.2017.1328473

Cui, M., Gordon, M., Ueno, K., & Fincham, F. D. (2013). The continuation of intimate partner violence from adolescence to young adulthood. *Journal of Marriage and the Family, 75*, 300–313. https://doi.org/10.1111/jomf.12016

DeKeseredy, W. S. (2011). *Violence against women: Myths, facts, controversies*. Toronto, CA: University of Toronto Press.

Duncan, D. T., Goedel, W. C., Stults, C. B., Brady, W. J., Brooks, F. A., Blakely, J. S., et al. (2018). A study of intimate partner violence, substance abuse, and sexual risk behaviors among gay, bisexual, and other men who have sex with men in a sample of geosocial-networking smarthphone application users. *American Journal of Men's Health, 12*, 292–301. https://doi.org/10.1177/1557988316631964

Edwards, K. M., Sylaska, K. M., Barry, J. E., Moynihan, M. M., Banyard, V. L., Cohn, E. S., et al. (2015). Physical dating violence, sexual violence, and unwanted pursuit victimization: A comparison of incident rates among sexual-minority and heterosexual college students. *Journal of Interpersonal Violence, 30*, 580–600. https://doi.org/10.1177/0886260514535260

Elmquist, J., Wolford-Clevenger, C., Zapor, H., Febres, J., Shorey, R. C., Hamel, J., et al. (2016). A gender comparison of motivations for physical dating violence among college students. *Journal of Interpersonal Violence, 31*, 186–203. https://doi.org/10.1177/0886260514555130

Felson, R. B. (2002). *Violence and gender reexamined.* Washington, DC: American Psychological Association Press.

Frieze, I. H. (2005). *Hurting the one you love: Violence in relationships.* Pacific Grove, CA: Thompson/Wadsworth.

Frieze, I. H., & Browne, A. (1989). Violence in marriage. In L. Ohlin & M. Tonry (Eds.), *Family violence* (pp. 163–218). Chicago: University of Chicago Press.

Giordano, P. C., Copp, J. E., Longmore, M. A., & Manning, W. D. (2015). Contested domains. Verbal "amplifiers," and intimate partner violence in young adulthood. *Social Forces, 94*, 923–951. https://doi.org/10.1093/sf/sov055

Goldenberg, T., Jadwin-Cakmak, L., & Harper, G. W. (2018). Intimate partner violence among transgender youth: Associations with intrapersonal and structural factors. *Violence and Gender, 5*, 19–25. https://doi.org/10.1089/vio.2017.0041

Gonzalez, F. R., Benuto, L. T., & Casas, J. B. (2018). Prevalence of interpersonal violence among Latinas: A systematic review. *Trauma, Violence & Abuse*, 1–14. https://doi.org/10.1177/1524838018806507

Hamby, S. (2017). A scientific answer to a scientific question: The gender debate on intimate partner violence. *Trauma, Violence & Abuse, 18*, 145–154. https://doi.org/10.1177/1524838015596963

Hammock, G. S., Richardson, D. S., Lamm, K. B., Taylor, E., & Verlaque, L. (2017). The effect of gender of perpetrator and victim on perceptions of psychological and physical intimate partner aggression. *Journal of Family Violence, 32*, 357–365. https://doi.org/10.1007/s10896-016-9850-y

Hines, D. A., & Douglas, E. M. (2018). Influence of intimate terrorism, situational couple violence, and mutual violent control on male victims. *Psychology of Men & Masculinity, 19*, 612–623. https://doi.org/10.1037/men0000142

Holmes, S. C., Johnson, N. L., Rojas-Ashe, E. E., Ceroni, T. L., Fedele, K. M., & Johnson, D. M. (2016). Bidirectional violence in survivors of intimate partner violence residing at shelters. *Journal of Interpersonal Violence*, 1–24. https://doi.org/10.1177/0886260516670183

Johnson, H. (2015). Degendering violence. *Social Politics, 22*, 390–410. https://doi.org/10.1093/sp/jxv021

Johnson, W. L., Giordano, P. C., Manning, W. D., & Longmore, M. A. (2015). The age-IPV curve: Changes in the perpetration of intimate partner violence during adolescence and young adulthood. *Journal of Youth and Adolescence, 44*, 708–726. https://doi.org/10.1007/s10964-014-0158-z

Jones, R. T., Browne, K., & Chou, S. (2017). A critique of the revised Conflict Tactics Scales-2 (CTS-2). *Aggression and Violent Behavior, 37*, 83–90. https://doi.org/10.1016/j.avb.2017.08.005

King, W. M., Restar, A., & Operario, D. (2019). Exploring multiple forms of intimate partner violence in a gender and racially/ethnically diverse sample of transgender adults. *Journal of Interpersonal Violence*, 1–22. https://doi.org/10.1177/0886260519876024

Langenderfer-Magruder, L., Whitfield, D. L., Walls, N. E., Kattari, S. K., & Ramos, D. (2016). Experiences of intimate partner violence and subsequent police reporting among lesbian, gay, bisexual, transgender, and queer adults in Colorado: Comparing rates of cisgender and transgender victimization. *Journal of Interpersonal Violence, 31*, 855–871. https://doi.org/10.1177/0886260514556767

Langhinrichsen-Rohling, J. (2005). Top 10 greatest "hits": Important findings and future directions for intimate partner violence research. *Journal of Interpersonal Violence, 20*, 108–118. https://doi.org/10.1177/0886260504268602

Larsen, S. E., & Hamberger, L. K. (2015). Men's and women's experiences of IPV Part II: A review of new developments in comparative studies in clinical populations. *Journal of Family Violence, 30*, 1007–1030. https://doi.org/10.1007/s10896-015-9730-x

Lehrner, A. & Allen, N. E. (2018). A qualitative investigation of the role of gender in young women's dating violence in the United States. *Violence Against Women, 24*, 1697–1717. https://doi.org/10.1177/1077801218754408

Lewis, R. J., Padilla, M. A., Milletich, R. J., Kelley, M. L., Winstead, B. A., Lau-Barraco, C., et al. (2015). Emotional distress, alcohol use, and bidirectional partner violence among lesbian women. *Violence Against Women, 21*, 917–938. https://doi.org/10.1177/1077801215589375

Llorens, N. G., Salis, K. L., O'Leary, D. K., & Hayward, J. (2015). Aggression against a dating partner. *Journal of Family Violence, 31*, 75–83. https://doi.org/10.1007/s10896-015-9750-6

Luthra, R., & Gidycz, C. A. (2006). Dating violence among college men and women. *Journal of Interpersonal Violence, 21*, 717–731. https://doi.org/10.1177/0886260506287312

Marganski, A., & Melander, L. (2015). Intimate partner violent victimization in the cyber and real world: Examining the extent of cyber aggression experiences and its association with in-person dating violence. *Journal of Interpersonal Violence*, 1–25. https://doi.org/10.1177/0886260515614283

Martin-Storey, A. (2015). Prevalence of dating violence among sexual minority youth: Variation across gender, sexual minority identity and gender of sexual partners. *Journal of Youth and Adolescence, 44*, 211–224. https://doi.org/10.1007/s10964-013-0089-0

Messinger, A. M. (2017). *LGBTQ intimate partner violence: Lessons for policy, practice, and research*. Oakland, CA: University of California Press.

Muftić, L. R., Finn, M. A., & March, E. A. (2015). The victim-offender overlap, intimate partner violence, and sex: Assessing differences among victims, offenders, and victim-offenders. *Crime & Delinquency, 61*, 899–926. https://doi.org/10.1177/0011128712453677

Neal, A. M., & Edwards, K. M. (2017). Perpetrators' and victims' attributions for IPV: A critical review of the literature. *Trauma, Violence & Abuse, 18*, 239–267. https://doi.org/10.1177/1524838015603551

Olsen, E., Vivolo-Kantro, A., & Kann, L. (2017). Physical and sexual teen dating violence victimization and sexual identity among U.S. high school students, 2015. *Journal of Interpersonal Violence*, 1–20. https://doi.org/10.1177/0886260517708757

Raghavan, C., Beck, C. J., Menke, J. M., & Loveland, J. E. (2019). Coercive controlling behaviors in intimate partner violence in male same-sex relationships:A mixed-methods study. *Journal of Gay & Lesbian Social Services, 31*(3), 370–395. https://doi.org/10.1080/10538720.2019.1616643

Rathus, J. H., & Feindler, E. L. (2004). *Assessment of partner violence: A handbook for researchers and practitioners*. Washington, DC: American Psychological Association. https://doi.org/10.1037/10685-000

Reed, L. A., Tolman, R. M., & Ward, L. M. (2016). Snooping and sexting: Digital media as a context for dating aggression and abuse among college students. *Violence Against Women, 22*, 1556–1576. https://doi.org/10.1177/1077801216630143

Reed, J. H., Ward, L. M., Tolman, R. M., Lippman, J. R., & Seabrook, R. C. (2018). The association between stereotypical gender and dating beliefs and digital dating abuse perpetration in adolescent dating relationships. *Journal of Interpersonal Violence*, 1–25. https://doi.org/10.1177/0886260518801933

Reuter, T. R., Sharp, C., & Temple, J. R. (2015). An exploratory study of teen dating violence in sexual minority youth. *Partner Abuse, 6*, 8–28. https://doi.org/10.1891/1946-6560.6.1.8

Rostad, W. L., Clayton, H. B., Estefan, L. F., & Jones, M. M. (2019). Substance use and disparities in teen dating violence victimization by sexual identity among high school students. *Prevention Science*, 1–10. https://doi.org/10.1007/s11121-019-01049-7

Russell, B. (2017). Police perceptions in intimate partner violence cases: The influence of gender and sexual orientation. *Journal of Crime and Justice, 41*, 193–205. https://doi.org/10.1080/0735648X.2017.1282378

Ryan, K. M. (2013). Issues of reliability in measuring intimate partner violence during courtship. *Sex Roles, 69*, 131–148. https://doi.org/10.1007/s11199-012-0233-4

Ryan, K. M., & Mohr, S. (2005). Gender differences in playful aggression during courtship in college students. *Sex Roles, 53*, 591–601. https://doi.org/10.1007/s11199-005-7144-6

Saunders, D. G. (2002). Are physical assaults by wives and girlfriends a major social problem? *Violence Against Women, 8*, 1424–1448. https://doi.org/10.1177/107780102237964

Sheehy, E. (2016). Defending battered women in the public sphere. *International Journal for Crime, Justice and Social Democracy, 5*, 81–95. https://doi.org/10.5204/ijcjsd.v5i2.309

Sinclair, H. C., & Frieze, I. H. (2000). Initial courtship behavior and stalking: How should we draw the line? *Violence and Victims, 15*, 23–40. https://doi.org/10.1007/s1119-005-4203-4

Singh, V., Epstein-Ngo, Q., Cunningham, R. M., Stoddard, S. A., Chermack, S. T., & Walton, M. A. (2015). Physical dating violence among adolescents and young adults with alcohol misuse. *Drug and Alcohol Dependence, 153*, 364–368. https://doi.org/10.1016/j.drugalcdep.2015.05.003

Smith, K., Cenat, J. M., Lapierre, A., Dion, J., Herbert, M., & Cote, K. (2018). Cyber dating violence: Prevalence and correlates among high school students from small urban areas in Quebec. *Journal of Affective Disorders, 234*, 220–223. https://doi.org/10.1016/j.jad.2018.02.043

Smith, S. G., Zhang, X., Basile, K. C., Merrick, M. T., Wang, J., Kresnow, M., et al. (2018). *The National Intimate Partner and Sexual Violence Survey (NISVS): 2015 Data Brief – Updated Release*. Atlanta, GA: National Center for Injury Prevention and Control, Centers for Disease Control and Prevention.

Sorenson, S. B., & Taylor, C. A. (2005). Female aggression toward male intimate partners: An examination of social norms in a community-based sample. *Psychology of Women Quarterly, 29*, 78–96. https://doi.org/10.1111/j.1471-6402.2005.00170.x

Sparrow, K., Dickson, H., Kwan, J., Howard, L., Fear, N., & MacManus, D. (2018). Prevalence of self-reported violence victimization among military personnel: A systematic review and meta-analysis. *Trauma, Violence, & Abuse*, 1–24. https://doi.org/10.1177/1524838018782206

Stark, E. (2007). *Coercive control: How men entrap women in personal life*. New York, NY: Oxford University Press.

Steele, S. M., Everett, B. G., & Hughes, T. L. (2017). Influence of perceived femininity, masculinity, race/ethnic, and socioeconomic status on intimate partner violence among sexual-minority women. *Journal of Interpersonal Violence*, 1–23. https://doi.org/10.1177/0886260516683176

Straus, M. A. (1979). Measuring intrafamily conflict and violence: The Conflict Tactics (CT) Scales. *Journal of Marriage and the Family, 41*, 75–88. https://doi.org/10.2307/351733

Straus, M. A. (2015). Dyadic concordance and discordance in family violence: A powerful and practical approach to research and practice. *Aggression and Violent Behavior, 24*, 83–94. https://doi.org/10.1016/j.avb.2015.04.011

Straus, M. A., Gelles, R. J., & Steinmetz, S. K. (1980). *Behind closed doors: Violence in the American family*. New York, NY: Doubleday.

Straus, M. A., Hamby, S., Boney-McCoy, S., & Sugarman, D. (1996). The revised Conflict Tactics Scales (CTS2): Development and preliminary psychometric data. *Journal of Family Issues, 17*, 283–316. https://doi.org/10.1177/019251396017003001

Sylaska, K. M., & Walters, A. S. (2014). Testing the extent of the gender trip: College students' perceptions of and reactions to intimate partner violence. *Sex Roles, 70*, 134–145. https://doi.org/10.1007/s11199-014-0344-1

Taylor, B. G., & Mumford, E. A. (2016). A national descriptive portrait of adolescent relationship abuse: Results from the National Survey on Teen Relationships and Intimate Violence. *Journal of Interpersonal Violence, 31*, 963–988. https://doi.org/10.1177/0886260514564070

Testa, M., & Derrick, J. L. (2014). A daily process examination of the temporal association between alcohol use and verbal and physical aggression in community couples. *Psychology of Addictive Behaviors, 28*, 127–138. https://doi.org/10.1037/a0032988

Tjaden, P., & Thoennes, N. (2000). *Extent, nature and consequences of intimate partner violence: Findings from the National Violence Against Women Survey*. Washington, DC: National Institute of Justice.

Twenge, J. M. (2001). Changes in women's assertiveness in response to status and roles: A cross-temporal meta-analysis, 1931–1993. *Journal of Personality and Social Psychology, 81*, 133–145. https://doi.org/10.1037/0022-3514.81.1.133

Vagi, K. J., Olsen, E. O., Basile, K. C., & Vivolo-Kantor, A. M. (2015). Teen dating violence (physical and sexual) among US high school students: Findings from the 2013 National Youth Risk Behavior Survey. *JAMA Pediatrics, 169*(5), 474–482. https://doi.org/10.1001/jamapediatrics.2014.3577

Vaughn, M. G., Salas-Wright, C. P., Cooper-Sadlo, S., Maynard, B. R., & Larson, M. (2015). Are immigrants more likely than native-born Americans to perpetrate intimate partner violence? *Journal of Interpersonal Violence, 30*(11), 1888–1904. https://doi.org/10.1177/0886260514549053

Walker, J. K. (2015). Investigating trans people's vulnerabilities to intimate partner violence/abuse. *Partner Violence, 6*, 107–125. https://doi.org/10.1891/1946-6560.6.1.107

Walters, M. L., Chen, J., & Breiding, M. J. (2013). *The National Intimate Partner and Sexual Violence Survey (NISVS): 2010 findings on victimization by sexual orientation*. Atlanta, GA: Centers for Disease Control and Prevention.

Weiss, N. H., Duke, A. A., Overstreet, N. M., Swan, S. C., & Sullivan, T. P. (2016). Intimate partner aggression-related shame and posttraumatic stress disorder symptoms: The moderating role of substance abuse problems. *Aggressive Behavior, 42*, 427–440. https://doi.org/10.1002/ab.21639

Whitton, S. W., Dyar, C., Mustanski, B., & Newcomb, M. E. (2019). Intimate partner violence experiences of sexual and gender minority adolescents and young adults assigned female at birth. *Psychology of Women Quarterly, 43*(2), 232–249. https://doi.org/10.1177/0361684319838972

Williams, S. L., & Frieze, I. H. (2005). Patterns of violent relationships, psychological distress, and marital satisfaction in a national sample of men and women. *Sex Roles, 52*, 771–784. https://doi.org/10.1007/s11199-005-4198-4

Winstok, Z. (2013). From a static to a dynamic approach to the study of partner violence. *Sex Roles, 69*, 193–204. https://doi.org/10.1007/s11199-013-0278-z

Winstok, Z., & Straus, M. A. (2016). Bridging the two sides of a 30-year controversy over gender differences in perpetration of physical partner violence. *Journal of Family Violence, 31*, 933–935. https://doi.org/10.1007/s10896-016-9896-x

Woodin, E. M., Sotskova, A., & O'Leary, K. D. (2013). Intimate partner violence assessment in an historical context: Divergent approaches and opportunities for progress. *Sex Roles, 69*, 120–130. https://doi.org/10.1007/s11199-013-0294-z

Ybarra, M. L., & Langhinrichsen-Rohling, J. (2019). Linkages between violence-associated attitudes and psychological, physical,and sexual dating abuse perpetration and victimization among male and female adolescents. *Aggressive Behavior, 45*, 622–634. https://doi.org/10.1002/ab.21856

Chapter 6
Child Maltreatment: Physical, Emotional and Sexual Abuse of Children and Child Neglect

Maltreatment of children can take many forms. In this chapter, we review what researchers can tell us about physical abuse of children by their parents, as well as parental neglect, and sexual abuse by parents. The chapter first focuses on physical and psychological abuse as well as neglect, and then turns to sexual abuse of children by parents. Like intimate partner violence discussed earlier in Chaps. 4 and 5, societal views of violence of directed by parents toward children have become less accepting (Holden, Brown, Baldwin, & Caderao, 2014; See Chap. 1).

6.1 Defining Child Abuse and Neglect or Child Maltreatment

Definitions of child abuse and neglect vary. Based on legal codes, "The Child Abuse Prevention and Treatment Act (CAPTA), (P.L. 100–294) defined child abuse and neglect as, at a minimum: *Any recent act or failure to act on the part of a parent or caretaker which results in death, serious physical or emotional harm, sexual abuse or exploitation; or an act or failure to act, which presents an imminent risk of serious harm.*" (Children's Bureau, 2019, p. viii). According to the Centers for Disease Control and Prevention (CDC, 2019), "child maltreatment includes all types of abuse and neglect of a child under the age of 18 by a parent, caregiver, or another person in a custodial role (e.g., clergy, coach, teacher). There are four common types of child abuse: Physical Abuse, Sexual Abuse, Emotional Abuse, and Neglect." For more detailed definitions, see Box 6.1.

I. H. Frieze et al., *Dynamics of Family and Intimate Partner Violence*,
https://doi.org/10.1007/978-3-030-42608-8_6

Box 6.1: Definitions of Child Abuse and Neglect

There are a number of definitions offered for child maltreatment. For example, the U.S. Department of Justice, Office for Victims of Crime (2019, p. 4) offers these definitions:

Emotional abuse: A pattern of behavior that impairs a child's emotional development or sense of self-worth. This may include constant criticism, threats, or rejection, as well as withholding love, support, or guidance. Emotional abuse is often difficult to prove and, therefore, child protective services may not be able to intervene without evidence of harm to the child. Emotional abuse is almost always present when other forms are identified.

Neglect: Child neglect is the most common type of child abuse. Since children are dependent upon others to provide their basic necessities of life, deprivation can result in nutritional neglect, abandonment, inadequate supervision, medical/dental neglect, inadequate or inappropriate housing, inadequate or insufficient clothing, neglect of personal hygiene, educational neglect, and/or failure to protect the child from abuse. In cases of neglect, intent is not a necessary criterion. For example, caregivers may not have the intention to provide inadequate supervision but could nevertheless be neglectful if they leave their 1-year-old child alone in a bathtub.

Substantiated abuse or neglect: This term indicates that the child abuse or neglect reported to child protective services has been the subject of a civil investigation and found to be a case of abuse or neglect at a particular legal standard (most often preponderance of the evidence). This is sometimes called a "founded" case of abuse/neglect. It is important to note that this level of evidentiary proof is much lower than the criminal standard of "beyond a reasonable doubt." This allows a mere preponderance of the evidence (the lower standard) to be used to demonstrate that a child has been injured and/or is at substantial risk and is in need of protective intervention.

Sexual abuse: Child sexual abuse refers to the sexual assault of a child or certain other forms of touching or fondling of a child for the sexual stimulation and gratification of the adult perpetrator. While less obvious than sexual assault, sexual abuse may include making sexual propositions, forcing a child to watch sex acts, unwanted hugs, touches, and pinches, and may include tickling. Also, age is often a factor in the law that determines if child sexual assault is aggravated (e.g., sexual assault of a younger child)."

In a more detailed examination, one can find these definitions:

Physical abuse is causing physical injury to or otherwise harming a child. The parent or caretaker may not have intended to hurt the child; the injury may have resulted instead from excessive discipline or physical punishment.

Child neglect is failure to provide for a child's basic needs. Neglect can be divided into several types: physical neglect, medical neglect, inadequate supervision, emotional neglect, and educational neglect. For more information on types of neglect, visit Information Gateways' webpage on the Identification of Neglect at https://www.childwelfare.gov/pubs/focus/acts.

Sexual abuse includes fondling a child's genitals, intercourse, incest, rape, sodomy, exhibitionism, and commercial exploitation through prostitution or the production of pornographic materials. Many experts believe that child sexual abuse is the most underreported form of child maltreatment.

Emotional abuse (psychological, verbal, or mental) includes acts or omissions by parents or caregivers that have caused, or could cause, the symptoms listed below. In some cases, the acts alone, without any harm evident in the child's behavior or condition, can warrant intervention by Child Protective Services (e.g., practices such as confining a child to a dark closet or a cage). Children who have been abused and/or neglected are harmed physically, behaviorally, and emotionally. For example:

- A neglected child may look undernourished and/or may have sleep disorders or untreated injuries. He or she may beg or steal food, have poor hygiene, or be involved in promiscuity, drugs, or delinquency. As a result, the child may have poor self-esteem, emotional issues, or social problems.
- A physically abused child may have questionable injuries such as bruises, welts, burns, fractures, cuts, or scrapes. As a consequence of the abuse, the child may be uncomfortable with physical contact, frightened of parents or other adults, afraid to go home, or act aggressively or withdrawn.
- Most physical indicators of child sexual abuse are identified through a doctor's examination. Behavior that may signal child sexual abuse includes inappropriate knowledge of sex, highly sexualized play, unexplained fear of a specific person or place, nightmares, or withdrawal. A sexually abused child may have low self-confidence, feel shame or guilt, or appear depressed or anxious.
- Behaviors that indicate emotional abuse include conduct disorders, extreme behaviors, cruelty, and delinquency. Often, an emotionally abused child will experience delays in development.

The consequences of child abuse and neglect can be serious and long term. Abused and neglected children may experience a lifelong pattern of depression, anxiety, low self-esteem, inappropriate or troubled relationships, or a lack of empathy.

Office for Victims of Crime. Technical Training and Assistance Center (2019). *Training Unit 9. Child Abuse and Neglect.* Washington, DC: U.S. Department of Justice. https://www.ovcttac.gov/

In this chapter, our focus is the maltreatment by parents. As explained in more detail later in the chapter, it can be seen that it is not uncommon for more than one type of abuse or neglect to occur within a family. Thus, child abuse and neglect may occur in families with parental partner abuse (IPV). Observation of parental IPV has been shown to be traumatic for the child. Some classify this as another form of child maltreatment (see Chap. 8). In a review of research on the effects of child exposure to parental IPV, Carlson, Voitch, Brown, and Holmes (2019) demonstrate the many negative effects of this exposure on the child. Another form of emotional abuse is maltreatment of family pets. McDonald et al. (2015) argued that exposing children to abuse of the family pet can be quite traumatic for the child (McDonald et al. 2015). Chapter 7 describes this type of abuse in more detail. Researchers continue to expand their thinking about other behaviors that constitute child maltreatment. For example, Harman, Kruk, and Hines (2018) argued that parental alienation was a common, but largely ignored form of emotional abuse. This was defined as a parental figure using a variety of strategies to harm the relationship of a child with the other parent.

The reality of child abuse and neglect can be seen in our case files. Case 17 demonstrates a situation of extreme neglect and abuse of a child to the point that death was imminent. It shows how one child may be singled out for abuse and neglect while other children in the home are adequately cared for. The case notes make it clear how important it was for the neighbor to take action and call the police after seeing the starving boy, saving his life.

Case Example #17

For years, a seven-year-old boy was beaten, starved and neglected by his mother and grandparents. The child was only allowed to eat small amounts of tuna and eggs and resorted to eating insects to stay alive. If he tried to get other food, the three adults would beat him with a belt or force him to take cold showers. Although he was confined to his home, with neighbors not even knowing he existed, 1 day he managed to escape and was seen by a neighbor who was walking her dog. The neighbor described him as looking like a "human skeleton", as he weighed only 25 pounds and was only days away from death. The neighbor called police who called child protective services. The child was taken to the hospital and his mother and grandparents were arrested on multiple charges of child abuse and neglect including unlawful restraint of a minor, aggravated assault, child endangerment, medical neglect, false imprisonment and criminal conspiracy.

The boy's three siblings—one brother and two sisters—appeared to not have been abused and were all healthy, although they were also removed from the home by child protective services to ensure their safety. The motive for the victim's abuse, according to the investigating detective, appeared to be that the adult family members simply did not like him. One year ago, the mother removed him from school to homeschool him, although it was unclear if any schooling actually occurred.

One of the doctors from the local children's hospital said this was the worst case of childhood starvation, abuse and neglect that she had ever seen and the best medicine for him was providing him with kindness and nutritious food. During hospitalization, the boy gained 24 pounds and, when released, was placed in foster care. The child's mother and grandparents remain in jail awaiting trial.

6.2 Societal Attitudes About Physical and Emotional Maltreatment of Children

In the United States, formal organizations to help children growing up in abusive families began in the nineteenth Century. One of the first such organizations was the New York Society for the Prevention of Cruelty to Children, founded in 1875. A number of other groups worked on this issue in the years following. Such efforts eventually led to the U.S. Government providing funding to the states to help protect and care for neglected children as part of the Social Security Act of 1935. Individual states took on this role and by 1970, most states had established protective services for children when there was evidence of high levels of physical abuse or neglect (Chaffin, 2006). According to Chaffin (2006), these efforts were followed by an interest in the medical profession to diagnose or identify when such abuse existed. International concerns about child abuse and protecting children from physical and mental violence can also be seen in statements from the United Nations as well as other organizations (Miller-Perrin & Perrin, 2018).

Given these types of societal efforts to assist children who are not being properly cared for, it is clear that physical abuse and neglect of children has not been considered to be acceptable behavior by many people in U.S. society for many years. However, defining what people mean by abuse or neglect is not as simple as one would hope. Through much of the twentieth as well as into the twenty-first century, many people in the United States were unclear about when slapping or spanking a child was abusive (Rohner & Melendez-Rhodes, 2019). Since a spanking was expected to hurt, most people would not have considered it to be *abuse* for a parent to physically hurt his or her child, as long as there was not serious injury and the intent was to teach the child proper behavior. Many believed that children should be disciplined, and many felt that discipline could and should include physical punishment such as spanking. Such behavior was quite common and continues to occur regularly, although it has become less frequent (Straus, Douglas, & Medeiros, 2014). For example, Taylor and colleagues reported that 65% of 3-year-olds were spanked by parents in the previous month (Taylor, Lee, Guterman, & Rice, 2010). Miller-Perrin and Perrin (2018) have also argued that use of physical punishment is still relatively common in the U.S., citing data from many different studies. They suggest that the parents own personal experiences of being physically punished as children contribute to the continuation of this practice by many parents.

Researchers continue to argue that parental attitudes about use of physical punishment as a way to discipline children are related to religious teachings, especially those held by conservative Protestant Christians (e.g., Perrin, Miller-Perrin, & Song, 2017). Judeo-Christian teachings suggest there is a spiritual duty for parents to teach their children respect and obedience to authority as well as encouraging values such as honesty and doing things for others (Mahoney, 2005). Conservative or Fundamentalist Christian views expect parents to use physical punishment to make sure children learn appropriate behavior. Several verses from the Old Testament Bible mention this. For example, "He who spares the rod hates his son, but he who loves him is careful to discipline him" (Proverbs 23:24, cited from p. 515 in Perrin et al., 2017). Empirical tests of this view can be found in two major reviews by Mahoney and her colleagues. Looking at data from the 1980s and 1990s, Mahoney et al. (2002) found that more religious parents during this period placed a higher value on the obedience of their children than non-religious parents did. The more religious parents also were more likely to believe in the acceptability of corporal punishment and reported using spanking as a form of discipline more than less religious parents. A later review by Mahoney (2010) of the period from 1999 to 2009 indicated that studies from this somewhat more recent survey indicated that conservative Protestant parents continued to be believe that spanking was necessary to gain obedience from children and did not believe there were negative effects of doing this.

Several meta-analyses have been done to address the question of whether there is evidence that spanking of children has negative effects (e.g., Ferguson, 2013; Gershoff & Grogan-Kaylor, 2016). Generally, spanking is defined as using one's open hand to strike the child in the buttocks or arms or legs. This is often differentiated from "corporal punishment" which involves more extreme aggression such as striking the face, hitting the child with an object or severe shaking or pushing of the child (Ferguson, 2013, p. 196). Ferguson argued that previous studies of the effects of spanking often included other forms of corporal punishment, and thus did not provide clear evidence about spanking. In his meta-analysis of 45 previous studies, he attempted to separate these two types of physical discipline as well as to examine other moderating factors. Overall, no clear evidence was found in this study that spanking had negative effects on children, and only small negative effects were found for corporal punishment. However, a later, even more extensive meta-analysis done by Gershoff and Grogan-Kaylor (2016) did find evidence of negative effects of spanking, with more aggression and other antisocial behavior as well as more mental health concerns and more negative relationships with parents in children exposed to spanking as compared to other children. They did caution, though, that their review did not allow them to directly assess causation, only associations between variables. But, increasingly, the research community views spanking as harmful. A number of researchers joined in a paper published in 2017 to argue that spanking should be designated as an "adverse childhood experience" (Afifi et al., 2017, p. 24), noting the abundance of evidence of negative effects of spanking. However, the debate continues with Rohner and Melendez-Rhodes (2019) providing evidence that parental rejection of children may mediate or moderate the effects of spanking.

6.3 How Common Is Child Maltreatment by Parents?

In practice, it is not always straightforward to determine whether physical abuse of a child has occurred or not (U.S. Department of Justice, 2014). Other forms of child maltreatment may be even more ambiguous than physical abuse, although extreme forms of abuse or neglect are clear. In response to this ambiguity, the Office of

Juvenile Justice and Delinquency Prevention offers a manual to help recognize physical abuse in children and distinguishing this from accidental injuries. Certain types of injuries are noted that are often associated with abuse. Such injuries require careful investigation, as discussed in Chap. 9. Defining and measuring emotional abuse and neglect is even more complex (Slep, Heyman, & Snarr, 2011). Slep and her colleagues argued that this type of abuse can be even more damaging that physical abuse and neglect, as do others (e.g., Campbell & Hibbard, 2014).

Other cases of abuse may relate to differences in underlying values. For example, Case #21 below illustrates the challenges faced by health care providers when a family's religious beliefs are not consistent with what is believed by health care providers to be a child's best interests. It also shows the complexity of some medical neglect cases and the role that the legal system must play in cases when a child is not old enough to make their own decisions.

Case Example #21

Six year old Daniel was diagnosed with acute lymphoblastic leukemia (ALL). Although ALL had a survival rate of about 85% with chemotherapy, his parents refused to take him for treatment. Jim and Diane were Christian Scientists who did not believe in using medicine and wanted to rely on spiritual healing through prayer. Daniel's life was believed to be in grave danger from infection without treatment so an emergency removal order was issued. However, Jim and Diane hid Daniel outside their home and he could not be located by Child Protection workers. In the meantime they hired a lawyer to file a lawsuit against the county, stating that their freedom of religion was being violated. The case was rushed through the system and the courts sided with the county, since the minor child could not make his own decision about whether or not he wanted treatment. Jim and Diane were threatened with arrest if they did not turn over Daniel to authorities. They finally conceded although they claimed that their prayers were working to heal him. Daniel was retrieved from the home of church members and he presented as very medically frail. He was transferred to a foster care home with a woman who had medical training, and he started chemotherapy 2 days later. He received 3 months of intensive treatment and was prescribed a daily mediation to be taken for 2 years as maintenance. He also needed to attend hospital appointments every 6 weeks for 2 years to receive intravenous medication.

His parents visited him frequently throughout his chemotherapy treatment. They agreed to give him his maintenance drugs and take him to his appointments, so he was allowed to return home. After a year of regularly taking Daniel to appointments and giving him his oral medication, the case was closed.

In addition to difficulties in determining if abuse has occurred, data on the frequency of various forms of child maltreatment is difficult to obtain for other reasons. Data can come from reports of children, or from adults recalling what they experienced as children, as well as from parents reporting on their own behavior towards their children, or from social welfare agencies who investigate suspected child maltreatment (see Chap. 9). Often, conclusions drawn from one type of sample may differ from what other sources report. In addition, these sources typically are drawn from a relatively small area, so they may not generalize to other parts of the U.S., or to other regions in the world. (For this reason, we focus on U.S. data in this book). Although such limitations need to be considered, there are national U.S. data available. According to 2017 data from the Children's Bureau of the U.S. Department of Health and Human Services (2019), overall rates of child maltreatment were determined to be 9.1 per 1000 children based on a formal investigation done by staff at Child Protective Services (CPS). These rates have remained relatively stable since 2013. The largest category of abuse was neglect (75%), followed by physical abuse (18.0%), sexual abuse (9.0%) and other types of abuse (7%). It was estimated that 1720 children died that year from abuse and neglect (2.3 per 1,000,000 children). These data come from formal reports of abuse to state agencies. The national incidence data from CPS also provides information on perpetrators of child maltreatment. The majority of perpetrators are parents of the child (78%). The remaining cases involve the partner of mother or father, other relatives, foster parents, or child care providers. Women are more likely to be the abusers than men (54 versus 45% of perpetrators).

Another strategy for determining how common child abuse is involves surveying children directly. Finkelhor and his colleagues did this initially in 2008 (Finkelhor, Turner, Ormrod, & Hamby, 2009), in 2011 (Finkelhor, Turner, Hamby, & Ormrod, 2011), and again in 2013–2014 (Finkelhor, Turner, Shattuck, & Hamby, 2015). Looking at the most recent survey, data were collected using a representative sample of U.S. telephone numbers. A sample of 4000 children aged 0–17 were interviewed (caretakers answered questions for those from 0 to 9 years of age) about their exposure to all forms of violence, crime and abuse. Rates of reported *physical abuse* by a caretaker for children of all ages in the last year was 5%, and was 18% over their lifetime for the 14–17 year olds in the sample. Caretaker *emotional abuse* rates were 9% for the full sample in the last year and 24% for those 14–17 over their lifetime. Comparable rates for *neglect* were 5% and 18%. There were very few reported gender differences, and these most recent rates were quite similar to those in the 2011 study.

As can be seen, these data from two very different sources yield quite different pictures of the frequency and type of abuse that children experience. Similar sampling issues have been found for reports of intimate partner violence, as discussed in Chap. 5. It is interesting to note that another large national survey in the U.S. also found that 8% of adults reported being physically abused as children, a percentage similar to that reported in the Finkelhor et al. (2009) study (Sugaya et al. 2012). One interpretation of these sample differences is that when samples are based on confirmed reports of child protective services they may reflect what gets reported to CPS. This may suggest that many cases of abuse are never reported to formal government agencies (see Chap. 9).

6.4 Short and Long-Term Effects for the Child

Physical child maltreatment has the immediate effect for the child of dealing with the pain and possibly long-term suffering resulting from the injuries received. These may be relatively minor, but can be quite severe. Some children do die of their injuries inflicted by a parent. Although physical injury is often the focus when discussing child abuse, neglect is more common and can more often result in death. Severe neglect can result in death for the child, and is the most frequent reason for a child to die from maltreatment, accounting for 75% of the cases. Physical abuse accounts for 42% of fatalities, with some children experiencing both. The large majority of fatalities (72%) are for children aged 3 or younger. Boys are more likely to experience a fatality from maltreatment than girls (Children's Bureau, 2019). In addition to these physical consequences of maltreatment, there are a number of correlates of maltreatment relating to mental and physical health, as well as effects on behavior. These are briefly reviewed below.

Emotional abuse is typically associated with all of the other forms of child maltreatment. For example, emotional abuse might include fears about future injury. A number of other emotional or psychological effects of child maltreatment victimization have also been documented in the research literature (Sugaya et al., 2012). There are also behavioral consequences (e.g., Tallieu, Brownridge, Sareen, & Afifi, 2016).

6.4.1 Psychological, Behavioral and Health Effects of Child Maltreatment

In his detailed review article in the *Annual Review of Psychology*, Cicchetti (2016) argued that maltreatment of a child not only has negative effects on the child during infancy and childhood, but also initiates "a negative developmental cascade that continues throughout the life course" (p. 188), undermining normal developmental processes. He reviewed studies showing that physically abused infants have been observed showing increased rates of fear, anger and sadness. In their preschool years, maltreated children appeared to show increased sensitivity to anger-related cues in others, leading to problems with peer relations as they got older. Other evidence indicated that school-age children who were physically abused in earlier years were more verbally and physically aggressive toward others. Maltreatment more generally was associated with higher distractibility, over activity, and poorer concentration. Cicchetti also reviewed extensive literature demonstrating problems for maltreated children in developing normal patterns of attachment to their (abusive) caretaker, feeling they are somehow unacceptable to others, or feeling that significant others are not trustworthy. Feelings of shame were found to be especially associated with neglect. In concluding, Cicchetti noted that some children were found to be highly resilient, and appeared to be able to overcome the effects of their parental maltreatment. Possible biological factors that might help explain this resilience were explored in Cicchetti's review.

Following Cicchetti's analysis in 2016, Jaffee (2017) reviewed the research on later effects of child maltreatment in the *Annual Review of Clinical Psychology*, with a focus on mental health problems. As she noted, most of the research has relied on self-reports, often for events occurring many years earlier. For this reason, she selected studies for review where the maltreatment had been substantiated by Child Protective Services records. Based on an extensive review of the published literature, Jaffee concluded there was clear evidence that maltreated children are at increased risk for higher rates of externalizing problems, not only in childhood and adolescence, but also in adulthood. This can be seen in higher crime rates and other antisocial behavior in maltreated children. Higher use of drugs and alcohol have also been reported, although Jaffee suggested that these data were not as clear. Internalizing problems such as depression, anxiety and PTSD have also been found for maltreated children throughout their lives. As Jaffee pointed out, some of these long-term consequences of child maltreatment may have a biological component.

Longitudinal data are especially helpful in identifying long-term effects of child neglect and abuse. A number of longitudinal studies have reported such data in relatively recent years. Cohen, Menon, Shorey, Le, and Temple (2017) offer this type of data in an analysis of Wave 4 of an on-going study using a community sample. The initial sample were freshman or sophomore students in a Houston area high school. They completed a survey asking them about earlier experiences of abuse and neglect. They continued to complete surveys for the next 2 years. Analyses indicated that the experience of earlier emotional abuse showed a strong association with later depression. There were also significant correlations for depression and emotional neglect and physical neglect. Post-traumatic stress disorder (PTSD, See Chap. 3) was also most strongly associated with emotional abuse, as was anxiety. Overall trauma scores were highest for emotional neglect and sexual abuse.

Widom, Czaja, Kozakowski, and Chauhan's (2018) longitudinal sample had been found to have been abused or neglected as children and were surveyed again near the age of 40 to investigate relationship problems and attachment to romantic partners as adults. The sample also contained a matched comparison group used for the initial childhood data. A scale measuring anxious attachment was found to be associated with higher levels of earlier physical abuse or neglect. Anxious attachment is defined as worrying about whether the partner loves you or wants to stay with you. Higher levels of anxious attachment in turn predicted higher levels of general anxiety, as well as depression and lower levels of self esteem.

In another study based on a very long-term longitudinal sample, Raby et al. (2018) initially sampled a set of 267 high-risk pregnant mothers, collecting data about their first child several different times over their childhood and into their adult years with the last testing at age 34. They compared those experiencing early abuse or neglect at or before the age of 5 with those who were abused later in their middle childhood or adolescent years. Those abused at an early age were found to have poorer peer interactions and later romantic relationships beginning in kindergarten. Such findings are consistent with the attachment data reported by Widom et al. (2018). Raby et al. also examined academic competence, again finding lower levels beginning in kindergarten and continuing through adulthood for the early abuse group. Effects of those abused at later ages appeared to be less consistent. These findings are consistent with an earlier study by Currie and Widom (2010) who found that those with documented histories of abuse or neglect as children were more likely to be unemployed, had lower earnings, fewer assets and lower levels of education as adults at the age of 41.

Drawing from the Fragile Families data, Hunt, Slack, and Berger (2017) were able to relate behavioral data at age 9 for a sample of over 3000 children to several forms of earlier child maltreatment occurring at the age of 5 or even younger. Children who had experienced emotional or physical abuse or neglect were found to be more likely to have problems with externalizing behavior (aggressiveness or rule breaking) as well as internalizing behavior (anxiety, depression or withdrawal).

In an analysis of the underlying dynamics that might lead to these types of externalizing and internalizing behaviors, Craig and Moretti (2018) administered surveys to a sample of pre-teens and teenage boys and girls drawn from a population found to be experiencing serious behavior problems. They argued that callous-unemotional (CU) features, or an indifference to or lack of responsiveness to other people's emotions, have been found to be associated with aggressive and antisocial behavior, especially in boys and men. CU was believed to result from early experiences of child maltreatment including neglect as well as emotional and physical abuse. Such experiences led to hyperarousal in the child, and repression of feelings as a coping response. In this study, as predicted, the researchers found higher levels of anxiety as well as CU features in the boys and girls who had experienced the highest levels of maltreatment.

In yet another longitudinal study, Proctor et al. (2017) used the LONGSCAN database to investigate reasons for the commonly reported tendency for adolescents who had been maltreated as children to abuse alcohol and marijuana. As they predicted, they found evidence that this type of substance abuse was predicted by earlier externalizing behavior at age 8. This pattern was especially evident for those who had been physically abused.

Johnson and his colleagues (2017) used data from the Minnesota Longitudinal Study of Risk and Adaptation (also used in the Raby et al., 2018 study) to examine the long-term effects of abuse and neglect in childhood on physical health in adulthood. Children followed from birth were asked a number of questions about their health status in their late 30's. Childhood abuse and neglect were associated with lower self ratings of overall health and more reports of a number of specific health problems. Neglect was most associated with health problems.

6.4.2 Learning to Be a Parent and the Cycle of Abuse

As discussed in Chap. 2, a major mechanism of learning is role modeling. We learn about how to be a parent from observations of our own parents. This suggests that if one's own mother or father is abusive to you or to your siblings, you may come to model this behavior with your own children. This pattern has been labeled as the *cycle of abuse*. Widom (1989) is associated with the development of this theory that abusive parents have learned to be abusive from their observations of their own parents in childhood. She has published many studies examining this theory. In 2015, she and two colleagues published a follow-up of her early 1989 *Science* paper, again in *Science* (Widom, Czaja, & DuMont, 2015). In this follow-up, they note that much research has been done testing the cycle of violence theory but not all of it has found support for the idea that being abused as a child leads to one abusing their own children. They offer new findings from their longitudinal data. Initially, a comparison of children identified as abused was done with a matched sample of children not identified by (CPS). (Findings indicated that 11% of the comparison group reported some form of maltreatment.) Children were initially interviewed in 1967 through 1971, and again when they reached the age of 29. The children of these 29 year-olds were also interviewed. Abuse was determined by CPS reports as well as by self reports of adults and their children. There was evidence that those originally neglected by their parent or parents were more likely to neglect their own children, but evidence supporting the cycle of abuse was not found for physical abuse. These was also an effect for the abuse cycle for sexual abuse, although not as clear as that for neglect. These associations were seen in CPS data as well as in the self reports of parents and children. Their data further indicated that those who had been determined originally by CPS to have been abused were more likely to have had their own children assessed by CPS, suggesting that other parental abuse may not be as likely to come to the attention of CPS. In concluding their report, Widom et al. (2015) remind the reader that the original sample was predominately from a lower SES group and might not be representative of a broader U.S. sample.

Researchers continue to investigate the cycle of abuse. A special section of *Development and Psychopathology* published in 2019 included several papers reporting on recent findings. In a meta analysis of 142 studies, Madigan et al. (2019) found evidence of some relationship of transmission of abuse from one generation to another. These effects were greatest for emotional abuse, followed by physical abuse, and sexual abuse at similar levels. Neglect showed the lowest probability of being repeated across generations. Methodological issues in the examined studies were examined and did affect the results they found.

Specific types of parenting behavior found to be correlated with early experiences of child maltreatment in girls were investigated in another meta-analysis in the special section (Savage, Tarabulsy, Pearson, Collin-Vezina, & Gagne, 2019). A total of 32 studies were analyzed, looking at three types of parenting behavior. The category of Negative Parenting was found to be most likely in the abusive mothers, but the relationship was small. This consisted of using corporal punishment, making critical or mean statements, being insensitive to the child, over controlling, rejecting, or threatening, or neglectful. Thus, physical and emotional abuse as well as neglect were included in the set of negative parenting behavior. Positive parenting was predicted to be predictive of non-abuse, but was not found to have strong effects.

In their introduction to this section of *Development and Psychopathology*, Alink, Cyr, and Madigan (2019), outline the expanded version of the cycle of theory. In addition to modeling the abusive behavior of one's parents, other mechanisms that may operate to perpetuate abusive parenting through multiple generations include not being attentive to one's own children and interpreting ambiguous behavior in the child in a more negative way; having insecure attachment to their children; not responding well to stress because of bad early experiences; and developing depression or other psychopathology because of bad early experiences. Alink et al. further noted evidence that having strong emotional attachment to some other adult might reduce negative effects of early maltreatment.

6.4.3 Children's Observations of Parental Interactions

Children learn about parenting from observations of their parents. They also learn how adult couples interact. Along with observations about how couples behave, children exposed to parental IPV may also be learning to be violent, perhaps modeling the aggressive behavior of their parents. Using a sample of 1399 children from the National Survey of Child and Adolescent Well-Being who were living with their biological mother, Holmes, Yoon, and Berg (2017) found the young children who had observed violence between their parents were also more violent themselves in interactions with peers. Other data using a community sample of adults in their 20's indicated that those abused as children or who had witnessed IPV in their parents were more accepting of partner violence under a number of specific circumstances than those who had not had these childhood experiences (Copp, Giodano, Longmore, & Manning, 2016).

In a systematic review of 19 studies examining the relationship of childhood exposure to parental IPV and later violence in the adult relationships of these exposed children, Kimber and her colleagues (2018) found 19 relevant studies. Sixteen of these studies showed an association of childhood exposure and adult IPV. However, they noted methodological problems in many of these studies and urged further research. Similar conclusions were drawn by Godbout et al. (2017) in a meta-analysis of men who had been victimized by maltreatment as children and their later perpetration of IPV against a female partner. The correlation found was 0.19, which was significant, but is low enough to suggest that this relationship does not always occur. Jung et al.'s (2019) study analyzed data from a sample of abused and neglected children contacted years later at the age of 36. Exposure to parental IPV was found in this study to be predictive of later IPV for these now 36 year olds. Early physical and emotional child abuse experiences were also found to be related to later adult IPV.

There may be other effects of young children being exposed to violent fighting of their parents. In a study examining language development of 3 year old children, Peterson, Riggs, Guyon-Harris, Harrison, and Huth-Bocks (2019) examined the children of a group of mothers who were followed over time. The mothers were determined to be at risk for IPV when initially surveyed prenatally. In a later survey when the children were 3 years of age, they were able to determine that language development of the children was related to maternal education levels and the presence of a stimulating home environment, as has often been reported. If the mother had experienced IPV, however, language development was reduced but only for those children with more educated mothers or for those with a stimulating home environment. When the mothers were less educated or the environment was not positive, there was no effect of IPV exposure, suggesting that these factors alone led to lower levels of language proficiency.

6.5 Characteristics of Abusive and Neglectful Parents

A number of possible explanations have been proposed for why some parents are abusive toward or neglectful of their children (Mulder, Kuiper, van der Put, Stams, & Assink, 2018; Thornberry et al., 2014). These include mental illness or other emotional or cognitive factors in the parents to abuse. Others indicate that child maltreatment can be a reaction to stress or to the child being difficult. Several of the major theories are briefly discussed below. Some of the theories and empirical research studies focus on a specific form of parental maltreatment of children, while others are more general. Evidence has been found that the types of predictive factors that have been found in parents who are emotionally abusive and are similar to factors predicting those who are physically abusive (Campbell & Hibbard, 2014). Sexual abuse also shares some common causal factors with other types of maltreatment, but differs in a number of ways from other types of child maltreatment. This type of abuse is discussed in more detail later in the chapter.

At one time, the assumption was made by many people that parents who abuse their children must be mentally ill, but formal research indicated that this was not the case for the majority of abusing parents (Emery, 1989). As this chapter will demonstrate, there do appear to be many relatively stable characteristics that are found to be associated with abusive parents, but mental illness is not a typical explanation. However, in a meta-analysis of studies from around the world examining predictors of neglect, Mulder et al. (2018) did find a statistically significant effect of parental mental illness being correlated with parental neglect. Also predicting parental neglect were a number of other factors such as parental criminality, and the parents themselves having been neglected as children. Other evidence for parental psychopathology can be seen in studies showing that depressed mothers are more likely to neglect their children (Shanahan, Runyan, Martin, & Kotch, 2017).

Most of the more recent research on parental abuse of children examines other factors in the parents. In an exploratory study, Thornberry et al. (2014) used data from a longitudinal study which repeatedly assessed a sample of 1000 adolescents in public schools in Rochester, New York beginning in 1988. In the most recent data collection, the sample were aged 29–31. The goal of the study was to determine what risk factors that were apparent in adolescence were later associated with being a parent of a child determined by CPS to have been abused (see Chap. 9 for details of the CPS process). Of the 816 in the sample of adults in their late 20s or early 30s, 12.5% had been found to have abused a child at least once. Nearly 90% of those who had engaged in the abuse were found to be neglectful, while 25% had been physically abusive and 7% sexually abusive. More than a third of them had engaged in 2 or more forms of maltreatment or abuse. Having been abused themselves as children was a significant predictor of their abusing their own children, as was being aggressive toward others, and not feeling attached to their children. Growing up in a family characterized by low parental education and poverty was also a risk factor for later child abuse. As discussed earlier, the fact that abusive parents were themselves abused or neglected as children relates to the cycle of abuse theory (Widom, 1989). Other factors such as cognitive distortions and a number of stress factors in the lives of the parents have also been examined in some detail.

Although most of the theoretical work on abusive parents examines patterns of learned behavior, there is some evidence for a genetic contribution. In a complex study done by researchers in the Netherlands, the role of genetic factors in child maltreatment were examined (Pittner et al., 2019). Data were collected for physical child abuse as well as emotional abuse and emotional neglect, using a Dutch low SES sample. Their analyses indicated that there was evidence for heritability of emotional abuse, but not for physical or emotional neglect. Although researchers did not offer a theory about why only emotional abuse showed genetic contributions, they did suggest that it was important to look at various forms of child maltreatment separately. One explanation that might be offered is that the underlying genetic factor related to an inability to understand the perspective of the child, making emotionally abusive interactions more likely.

6.5.1 Child Maltreatment by Mothers and Fathers

In looking at child maltreatment by parents, conclusions about whether mothers or fathers are the abusers vary depending on the type of data examined. Most U.S. studies indicate that mothers are more likely to physically abuse children than men (Children's Bureau, 2019). Of course, mothers typically spend more time with children than fathers. In a detailed analysis of types of child maltreatment, long-time researcher Straus (developer of the widely used Conflict Tactics Scale to measure partner and parent-child violence) and his colleague Douglas (Straus & Douglas, 2017) differentiated maltreatment by mothers only, fathers only, and both mothers and fathers. They reported that 22% of physical abuse was done only by the father, 45% only by the mother, and 25% by both. Similar findings were provided by Straus and Douglas for use of corporal punishment, using data from the Fragile Families Study (19% father-only, 36% mother-only, and 45% by both mothers and fathers). In other data from a number of other countries, they found that physical abuse of girls was almost twice as likely to be mother-only in North America than abuse of boys. For boys, 29% was father-only and 52% was both parents, with mothers lower at 19%. No specific data from the United States was discussed for other types of child maltreatment in the Straus and Douglas paper.

6.5.2 Cognitive and Emotional Responses of Parents to Children

Difficulties in relating to peers and lack of empathy have been identified as reactions of maltreated children in response to their abuse (Craig & Moretti, 2018). Perhaps because of this, other data suggests that parents who are abusive also demonstrate distortions in perceptions of children's behavior and a lack of empathy. Evidence for this was seen in a study by Rodriguez and Tucker (2015) who surveyed mothers of 6–9 year olds in the community and their children. Those whose scores indicated they had a high potential for being abusive parents (using the CAPI measure) also tended to be lower in empathy toward the child and made negative attributions about why a child would misbehave. It appeared that the mothers believed that their child was purposefully misbehaving, and they felt they were punishing the child for this. In a follow-up study, Rodriguez (2018) asked mothers of elementary school age children that she recruited from the community to complete a number of surveys including three measures that attempted to determine if a parent was at risk for being abusive. A combined score based on these three measures indicated those most at risk for abuse were more likely to believe that their child often misbehaved, and that the child deserved discipline for this. They also expressed more anger at their children. (Note that these studies did not measure actual abusive behavior).

In another study that did have measures of actual physical abuse, Young et al. (2018) asked parents of injured children to list three words that described their infant. Parents determined to have been physically abusive [as compared to those whose child appeared to have been accidentally injured, based on medical judgment] were more likely to use negative words in describing their child. These data can be compared to findings of Lorber and Stuart (2018) who observed mothers recruited from the community interacting with their 2–3-year old children in the laboratory. Although they hypothesized that negative expectations of the mothers about their children would be associated with harsh discipline of the children, they did not find this to be the case. Instead, negative expectations were associated with lax discipline. They explained this by suggesting that because of their negative experiences in the past, the mothers had given up on being able to discipline their children. Lorber and Stuart also noted that abusive behavior was unlikely to be observed in a laboratory setting where the mothers knew they were being observed.

These conflicting findings do raise questions about the importance of parental expectations as a predictor of child maltreatment. Most of the studies reporting this association have used questionnaires that involved self-reports of parents about *potentially* abusive behaviors, not about actual behavior. Perhaps some parents are willing to report a negative attitudes and behaviors on a hypothetical questionnaire, while others are more likely to only report positive attitudes and behaviors? Clearly, more research is needed to better understand the actual relationship between cognitions and abusive behavior.

6.5.3 Parental Stress

Higher levels of parental stress have often been reported as a predictor of various forms of child maltreatment, including use of severe corporal punishment (Garcia, Ren, Esteraich, & Raikes, 2017; Lee, Perron, Taylor, & Guterman, 2011). This stress can arise from violence within the parental couple to having a child who is difficult to care for to factors outside the immediate family. For example, life is more difficult and stressful when there is less money available to the family. Low income is often associated with neglect and other forms of child maltreatment (Shanahan et al., 2017). In a longitudinal study allowing for a direct test of the effects of income levels, Berger, Font, Slack, and Waldfogel (2017) demonstrated a reduction of CPS involvement for families who experienced a rise in income levels. This study was done using data from the Fragile Families database.

Other work suggests an interaction between the characteristics of the parent and the child's behaviors. Very violent or hostile children may be more difficult for parents to handle. Children and adolescents identified as having the tendency to be aggressive and hostile are more likely to be abused (Ehrensaft et al., 2003). One can imagine that having such a child would be difficult on the parent. It is also likely that hostility and aggression in the parent and in the child would interact to make their joint interactions more volatile and abusive. Children with mental or physical problems or chronic illness are especially difficult for parents (Pinquart, 2017). Perhaps because of this, children with disabilities are especially vulnerable to abuse within the home as well as from their peers (Crowley, 2016).

Children also act differently at different ages, and parents may respond differently to different aged children. Younger children are more often physically abused than older children, perhaps because they require more work from parents (McQuillan, Bates, Staples, & Deater-Deckard, 2019; Starr Jr., 1988). As Haskett, Neupert, and Okado (2014) explained in interpreting the data from a study of 4–7 year old children, the children's behavior may have been changing during this period when they were entering formal school programs. The parents may have been reacting to these changes in the children. Although this might explain higher levels of abuse for the children when they were younger, no direct data were collected to test this hypothesis in this study.

6.5.3.1 Parental IPV as a Form of Stress

As already discussed, there is clear evidence that when there are violent interactions between the mother and father (IPV), it is not uncommon to find evidence of child maltreatment as well (Chiesa et al., 2018 or see Chaps. 8 and 9). In their meta-analysis investigating this issue, Chiesa et al. (2018) found that IPV was associated with physical and psychological abuse of children as well as with neglect. There were also lower levels of positive parenting in couples with IPV. As Nomaguchi, Johnson, Minter, and Aldrich's (2017) detailed analysis of the relationship between mother-father aggression and styles of parenting indicated, parents have less involvement with their children and poorer parenting styles when also engaged in violence with each other. Grasso et al. (2016) pointed out that parental IPV was also linked to parental *psychological* abuse of children.

Lapierre et al. (2018) interviewed children privately and in focus groups to determine their views about the IPV between their parents. The children reported that when their mother was assaulted, she might become angry and less patient with them. She often cried. The children also observed that their mothers seemed more attentive and that the family was in a better situation with their abusive father [or the male partner of their mother] left the family. In their Discussion of their findings, Lapierre et al. noted that the children who participated in the study were quite willing to share their feelings about the IPV and felt they had not had many opportunities to talk about this with others. They further state that "…children see their victimization as being inextricably linked to their mothers' victimization" (p. 1033).

6.5.3.2 Parental Substance Abuse

Perhaps related to higher levels of stress, alcoholism and drug use in parents have often been associated with higher levels of abuse (Kelley, Brovo, Braitman, Lawless, & Lawrence, 2016). Noting the large body of work indicating that parental substance abuse was a risk factor for verbal and physical child abuse, Kelley and her colleagues analyzed data from 61 couples involved in a behavioral couples therapy program for treatment of their drug or alcohol abuse. These couples were recruited for the program through notices in the community and offered 12 free counseling sessions. Couples with IPV were excluded. After involvement in the program, both mothers and fathers reported greater couple satisfaction and reduced *potential* for child abuse. A scale with items such as "A child needs very strict rules" was used to assess potential child abuse; actual abuse was not directly measured.

A more direct test of the association of parental substance abuse and child abuse was reported by Kepple (2018), using data from the National Survey of Child and Adolescent Well-being. A sample of caregivers of over 2000 children sampled between 1999 and 2004 was used for the analysis. Child abuse was assessed based on self reports of the caregivers about their own aggressive actions using the Conflict Tactics Scale (see Chap. 5 for more information on this scale). All forms of substance abuse in the caregivers were found to be associated with physical abuse, emotional abuse and neglect. Contrary to what was predicted, reduced use of alcohol and drugs did not predict lowered physical or emotional abuse, but did predict lower levels of neglect.

The following case from our files provides an example of a mother experiencing high levels of stress. She admited abusing a drug for weight loss which led to mood swings and irritability at her children. She was emotionally and physically abusive toward the children. (For more information on this case, see the Appendix).

Case Example #16
Karen, a 28 year old married white female with three children, came to the crisis clinic asking to see a counselor. Upon evaluation, Karen began to cry stating that she feels completely overwhelmed and doesn't know what to do. Karen's three children include Tevine, aged 8; Casey aged 7; and Mikey aged 4½. Karen's husband, Andy, works for a chemical company and was recently transferred from the town of Tracy to a much smaller town, Linden. Karen was quite happy living in Tracy because she had friends and family there, but hates living in Linden because she is very isolated, is stuck in the house all day with the kids (her husband uses their only car for work) and it is getting to her to the point she yells and screams at the kids "all the time". Karen states that her children "act like brats" and recently she hit Casey so hard she was afraid she broke his arm. The crisis clinic social worker advised Karen that she is obligated to make a report to CPS (Child Protective Services), but Karen didn't seem bothered by that, stating she would actually like to have a CPS social worker come out to her house and help her learn how to handle the kids better.

During the intake evaluation, Karen revealed additional information that provided more depth to understanding her difficulties managing her children and her depressed feelings. Recently, Karen has been experiencing flashbacks of incidents when she was sexually abused as a child by three male relatives. These flashbacks have caused her considerable distress. In addition, Karen said that controlling her weight has been a long-time issue for her and she has used amphetamines to keep her weight under control and this contributes to her mood swings, especially irritability with her children. The outpatient therapist referred Karen to the AMAC (Adults Molested as Children) group for targeted group therapy and to Weight Watchers to learn healthier ways of managing her weight.

Karen has been experiencing a number of psychosocial stressors during the past year. It is difficult to determine whether her depressive symptoms are related to these stresses, underlying dysthymic disorder, or chronic post traumatic stress disorder. The question of whether her use of street drugs to obtain energy has been a means of self-medication needs to be explored.

More recent studies, though, have begun to question this direct association of parental substance abuse and child abuse. Capaldi, Tiberio, Pears, Kerr, and Owen (2019) used data originally obtained from fathers of 283 boys with a history of delinquency to further examine these relationships in a longitudinal study across three generations. The boys [G2] were originally aged 9–10, and they were again surveyed at the age of 37–38. Children of these men [G3] were also assessed. There was clear evidence that the G2 men who had been severely abused as children were more likely to abuse their own [G3] children. However, those receiving no abuse or only moderate abuse as children showed no significant differences in how likely they were to abuse their children. The G2 men who had been severely abused were also more likely to be substance abusers when they grew up. Wives of the G2 men were also surveyed about their backgrounds, and those G2 wives who had been severely abused as girls were more likely to abuse their [G3] children. When other factors were controlled, there was no effect of G2 men or women who were substance abusers to also be abusive of their children. In attempting to explain these findings, Capaldi and her colleagues argued that spanking was quite common when the G2 women and men were children. Spanking would be typically defined as moderate abuse, using modern coding, and perhaps because of this, the long-term effects of this moderate abuse were not transmitted to their children. The lack of a direct effect of substance abuse was also unexpected. The researchers do identify many limitations of their data and urge that others attempt to replicate their findings.

In another study that also raised questions about a direct effect of parental substance abuse on children, Orsi, Brown, Knight, and Shillington (2018) used a sample of families identified as abusive by CPS to see if those where the parents were found to be abusing drugs or alcohol differed from those who did not. Children in this sample were between the aged of 6 and 12. Several measures of well-being in the children were used. No significant differences were found among the children in these well-being measures when the group with substance abusing parents was compared with the group whose parents did not abuse drugs or alcohol. Like the Capaldi et al. (2019) conclusions, Orsi et al. were surprised not to find a substance abuse effect. They, too, suggest that further replication is needed.

Further evidence that this well-established connection between parental substance abuse and child abuse might be questioned comes from a study of CPS records (Victor et al., 2018). Victor and his team used statistical modeling to examine records of CPS investigations from over 100,000 investigations between 2009 and 2013. In doing this analysis, they looked at cases where it was judged that there was a preponderance of evidence that abuse had occurred. When all other potential indicators of abuse were controlled, CPS workers were 17% more likely to judge abuse had occurred if they also noted parental substance abuse. They also judged abuse was more likely if there were evidence of parental violence, although this was not as big an effect as that for substance abuse. Inadequate housing was also found to be predictive of abuse substantiation. Victor and his colleagues conclude that CPS workers may assume that abuse is occurring when parents are substance abusers, without other supporting evidence.

6.6 Incest and Sexual Abuse of Children

The general classification of *child sex abuse* (CSA) is quite broad and includes a diverse set of behaviors (see Hines, Malley-Morrison, & Dutton, 2012). As Mathews and Collin-Vezina (2019) discuss, there are many issues involved in what should be labeled as CSA. One question is who is defined as a *child*. They suggested that simply using the legal definition may not be appropriate for an older individual who mentally is similar to a child, and cannot offer true consent to sex. In addition, an adolescent (technically considered a child) who is physically mature may be quite capable of agreeing to a sexual encounter. Another consideration involves what is considered to be a sexual act. For example, is filming or watching a naked sleeping child, who is not aware of this happening, a sexual act that should be labeled as child sex abuse? This would not be labeled as sexual for the child, but it might be for the person watching or filming. Mathews and Collin-Vezina argued that sexual play among young children should *not* be considered as CSA. A parenting bathing a child and cleaning her genitals should also be excluded as an example of CSA. They also explorde in detail what is meant by *abuse*. These are important considerations. In the review below, we rely on the definition of the researcher presenting the study.

Although earlier in the chapter, the different forms of child maltreatment within the family were listed as physical abuse, emotional abuse, neglect and sexual abuse, the major emphasis so far has been on the first three. Some researchers separate *incest* or abusive sex within families from other types of child sex abuse. Technically, incest refers to sexual contact between biologically related family members, such as parents and children or even siblings. Others living in the household, such as step-parents are often included in this category of incest. This type of CSA is the focus of this section. However, many of the studies cited do not differentiate between sex abuse done by family members from that done by others who might even be strangers. Studies that do focus specifically on incest are noted. As Assink et al. (2019) concluded based on a meta-analytic review of 72 relevant studies, CSA (defined broadly) is often found in the same household as other forms of child maltreatment. It is often found in households with IPV. So, even the broader conceptualization of CSA appears to have links to other forms of family child maltreatment.

The following case example illustrates how some families normalize incest and see it as a way to teach children about sex. The case also shows how youth who experience sexual abuse may then perpetrate abuse against younger children with a sexual abuse history contributing sometimes to aggressive or destructive behaviors in youth.

Case Example #18

13 year old Shannon was referred to Child Protective Services by her teacher after Shannon put her hands inside the front of an 8 year-old boy's pants and rubbed herself against him at a school assembly. During a meeting with Shannon's parents, her stepfather Dave reported that he has fondled her breasts and has purchased lingerie that he expected her to model for him. He also watched online pornography with Shannon. Dave did not think these behaviors were a problem, and stated: "I am the only father she has and the only man she has in her life so it is my job to teach her how to be a woman." Shannon's

mother, Julie, agreed with this behavior and shared that her own father treated her and her sisters the same way. Julie and Dave viewed the response toward Shannon touching the younger boy and the investigation as an overreaction. Neither had any interest in attending parenting classes and repeatedly said this was all a 'private family matter'. There was no evidence that 10 year old Layla had experienced any abuse and while it was thought that she was at high risk for future perpetration a case could not be opened for her.

It was determined to be unsafe for Shannon to remain in her home since her parents believed their actions were appropriate. Since sexual abuse was prevalent in her extended family, kinship care options were not explored. It emerged that Shannon had a history of sexually acting out with younger boys so she was placed in Multidimensional Treatment Foster Care. After an incident where she slapped her foster mother, Shannon was transferred to a Residential Treatment Facility (RTF) where she received individual and group therapy. Her parents were encouraged to participate in family therapy with a future goal of reunification but they only attended one session. Shannon spent 15 months in the RTF but after running away and setting a small fire in a common room she was transferred to a juvenile detention center. She was eventually returned to her mother's care after Dave was arrested and sentenced to 5 years in prison for a drug-related charge.

6.6.1 *Prevalence of Child Sex Abuse and Incest*

Given the complexities of defining what we mean by child sex abuse, it is not surprising that it has been very difficult to determine how common this is. Very few incest cases are reported to authorities (Azzopardi, Eirich, Rash, MacDonald, & Madigan, 2018; Hines et al., 2012). Definitional issues as well as differences in the samples used can lead to quite different estimates. Not surprisingly, clinical samples (of people seeking help for emotional problems) and samples from battered women's shelters yield much higher estimates than other samples.

One study explicitly separated parental child sex abuse from other forms of child sex abuse. Data came from criminal cases in Canada (Giroux, Chong, Coburn, & Connolly, 2018). Giroux and her colleagues coded information relating to 3430 allegations of CSA between 1986 and 2012. Comparing cases involving children aged 11 or younger with those aged 12–17, a number of differences were seen based on the age of the victim. For the younger children, 35% of the offenders were parents, while 22% of the offenders of the older children were parents. Comparable percentages were seen for other family members who were accused: 27% versus 17%. Thus, the majority of offenders of the young children (62%) were family members, while this was true for only 39% of offenders of the adolescents. Strangers rarely were accused of CSA (3% for young children and 12% for adolescents). The offending tended to last longer for the younger children and more often involved actual vaginal or anal penetration for the older children. Parental abuse is most often addressed in the remainder of the chapter. Other forms of sexual abuse within the family, such as sibling abuse, are considered in more detail in Chap. 7.

Findings from the Canadian data were replicated in a meta-analysis of studies of CSA published between 1986 and 2013 (Ventus, Antfolk, & Salo, 2017). Most of the 62 studies included in the analysis relied on US samples, and about half came from clinical settings. CSA abuse occurring within the family tended to begin at an earlier age for the child victim, and persisted longer. Targets were more often girls than boys. Family offenders were less often labeled as pedophiles (those with a general sexual interest in children) than were non-family members who offenced.

In another Canadian study, Macmillan, Tanaka, Duku, Vaillancourt, and Boyle (2013) analyzed data from the Ontario Child Health Study about all forms of CSA. Data collection began in 1983 and followed the sample of 1928 children into adulthood. About 20% of the initial sample were described as "living in poverty" (p. 17). Males reported more child *physical* abuse than females (34% versus 22%), but females reported more child sexual abuse (22% versus 8%). Those living in families with less income as children had higher levels of physical and sexual abuse.

6.6.2 Father-Child Incest

One type of child sex abuse that has received a good deal of media and research attention is father-daughter sex contact. Data is limited here, as for other situations of child maltreatment, since many of these situations are not reported to others. The following case illustrates father-daughter sexual abuse which was long-lasting, cutting across multiple victims over many years. The incest was kept secret in the family for an extensive period of time. However, once one of the victims reported the abuse, the abuse stopped and all the daughters who were victimized were able to access help and the perpetrator was punished. It also illustrates the extensive trauma that sexual abuse causes and how victims within a family can serve as social support for each other during the process of recovery.

Case Example 14

Janet is a 25 year-old white female who came to the crisis clinic, at the referral of a local judge, for an appointment with an outpatient therapist for counseling. Janet is married, has a 4 year old daughter and is currently pregnant. Janet revealed that she and her three sisters have a history of extensive sexual abuse from their biological father occurring over the course of many years. The abuse was a well-kept family secret until the oldest sister left home; she then confided in Janet and her twin sister Becky about her own abuse and then they admitted that they had also been abused by their father. The oldest sister Katie, was abused from age 8 on, with her father forcing her to have intercourse with him 3–4 times a week. Janet states she was fondled but never had sexual intercourse with her father, although Becky did. The lid was blown off the whole thing when the youngest sister Edie, now 15 years old, was approached by her father for intercourse after he had insisted on taking nude photos of her. Edie then rode her bike over to the judge's home (the judge is a long-time family friend) and told her about what was going on. The judge was furious, called child protective services, and insisted that Edie be removed from the home. Edie is now living with Janet. The father was arrested and taken to the police station, however the older sisters could not press charges because their abuse occurred too long ago. Edie's mother insisted that Edie forgive her father which infuriated Edie and she no longer wants to go home to her mother even though the father is now living in a different town while the criminal case is working its way through the court. Currently, both parents are attending an incest perpetrators group. Janet and Edie wish to obtain counseling together because Edie is afraid to come without her sister present because she would like to deny the whole thing, yet at the same time, knows she needs help. Janet is, for the first time, feeling truly enraged and feels she and her sister both need help- the older sisters are living elsewhere. I contacted one of our clinical psychologists who specializes in treating victims of sexual abuse and she agreed to see both sisters next Friday. Both sisters are also interested in attending our incest survivors group.

Using a very different type of sample and data collection, Stroebel et al. (2012) analyzed anonymous data from women who volunteered to respond to a web-based study on "Effects of Recalled Family Attitudes and Childhood Sexual Experiences on Adult Sexual Attitudes and Adjustment." The sample was recruited from students, faculty, staff and individuals in the surrounding communities from several colleges in the mid-Atlantic region of the U.S. Thus, the sample was quite diverse. Within the larger sample of over 15,000 women, only 19 said their father had been a sexual partner and described him as an *abuser*. This group was compared with 241 women reporting engaging in sexual behavior before the age of 18 with an adult male partner other than their father. [Although technically this group experienced CSA, most described their experiences as consensual]. Having been sexually involved with their fathers was associated with higher levels of depression than the other CSA group. Both CSA groups were more sexually active as adolescents and young adults and were more likely to have acted as prostitutes than other women in the sample. The women reporting incest (sex with their father) were the most likely of all three groups to report feeling distant from their families. Many of the incest group also reported not telling their current partner about this earlier experience with their father. Often the initial sexual contacts, such as being asked to touch their father's genitals, began at quite a young age. A typical age was 5 years old when this first occurred.

6.6.3 *IPV and Incest*

One pattern of incest that we have identified in our own studies of violent marriages occurs in the types of relationships we have labeled as battering situations (see Chap. 4). These clinical impressions have also been written about by others (Herman, 2012). In this type of marriage, the man is quite violent toward his wife. As she is exposed to continuing emotional abuse from her partner, her self esteem drops, and she develops more and more physical problems along with other evidence of emotional distress. Because of the abuse, she may have little ability to be closely involved with her children, and she may express her distress by being violent toward them. At the same time, the violent husband may also be violent toward the children.

Growing up in this type of family, the children may not feel loved or close to either parent. As the daughter reaches puberty and her body develops, her father may find her very attractive. She reminds him of his wife when she was younger and more attractive. The father, feeling that his wife is not fulfilling him sexually, turns to his now adolescent daughter, and begins to be very loving toward her, essentially courting her. The daughter responds to this attention, feeling loved for the first time. Over time, he becomes more and more aggressive in his sexual requests, eventually seeking sexual intercourse with her. If the wife finds out, she may feel powerless to do anything, because of fears for her own safety. The daughter may not seek help, enjoying the attention and thinking her mother is just being jealous.

As this situation evolves, the father begins to treat the daughter as a second wife. He becomes very jealous of her and may begin to be violent towards her. She may realize that this situation is not normal and may feel guilty for her loving feelings toward her father. As she tries to date boys her own age, she begins to fear her father's anger. She may become pregnant or acquire a sexually transmitted disease.

Finally, the situation becomes too difficult for her to cope with. She may run away from home, perhaps marrying a boy she has been seeing secretly. Or, she may turn to prostitution to support herself on the street. Another possibility is disassociation or even the development of a split personality. None of these alternatives are good ones for her. She may seek outside help, but generally only if she fears her father will begin to sexually assault a younger sister.

These clinical impressions are consistent with some of the few published empirical studies of those who have been convicted of incest offending. All these studies involve male offenders, since it is quite rare for women to be CSA offenders. (For some data on the very small number of female offenders, see Weinsheimer, Woiwod, Coburn, Chong, & Connolly, 2017). In a major review, Pullman, Sawatsky, Babchishin, McPhail, and Seto (2017) analyzed existing literature to determine if fathers convicted of incest differed from other non-biologically related child sex offenders in the family, such as step-fathers. One finding was that the biological fathers appeared to be less likely to have had other prior sex offenses and appeared to have different motives for engaging in CSA. Seto, Babchishim, Pullman, and McPhail (who included several of the same researchers in the Pullman et al. study) (2015) reported on another meta-analysis of studies on CSA offenders, comparing incest offenders to non-related offenders. Looking at 118 studies done primarily in the US and Canada, Seto et al. found that the incest offenders were more likely to have had a personal history of experiencing some form of child maltreatment, including CSA. They were less likely to have had prior sex offenses and less likely to have a sexual interest in children or young adolescents generally. In a study done in England, Pemberton and Wakeling (2009) interviewed different types of CSA offenders about their motives for doing this. Based on these interviews, the incest offenders were more likely to make comments such as "it's my right" or "she's mine to do what I want with" (p. 295). They also blamed their wives for not giving them sex and expressed the idea that they deserved sexual access to their children because of all the things they had done for them.

6.6.4 Memory of Child Sexual Experiences

When attempting to find out about sexual experiences of children, researchers often decide to ask adults about their experiences as children, rather than interviewing children themselves. One reason for not asking the children directly is that researchers don't want to upset children. Another factor is that parents will generally be present when researchers interview children, and children may not want to discuss sexual experiences in front of parents, especially if parents are the perpetrators. Even when the parents are not present, parents must give permission for their children to be interviewed.

Such concerns mean that *adult memories* of childhood experiences become very important in the research. Memories of events that happened many years ago can be unreliable. But, memories of child sexual abuse may be especially unreliable because one of the responses to this type of traumatic event may be to repress some or all of the memory (Goodwin et al., 2019; Harris et al., 2015). Such memories may stay repressed forever, but they can also emerge at some later point in the person's life (see Goodman et al., 2003). These are often called *recovered memories* although Goodwin and her colleagues (2019) more recently suggest the term *lost memories*. Such memories of child sex experiences may be triggered by a later sexual experience or some other event that reminds them of the earlier trauma. Forgetting of and later memory recovery for emotional and physical child abuse, as well as other traumatic events can also occur.

Some researchers have argued that these recovered memories may be inaccurate, labeling them *false memories* (Freyd, 1992). Freyd's controversial paper further claimed that such false memories can be created by therapists who persuade clients that they have had early traumatic forced sex experiences and need to bring them to awareness so they can be dealt with. Research on memory does show that our memories are not always accurate (Loftus, 1997). Discussion of recovered memories and false memories continues into the twenty-first century (Dodier, 2018). Several researchers have investigated this idea of false memories, looking to see how often therapists have been involved in helping clients recover memories of child sex. As Patihis and

Pendergrast (2019) note, although therapists are aware of the possibility of creating false memories, many feel that it is important to help their clients if they suspect that repression of earlier trauma is creating difficulties for the client, and that the client needs to aided in recovering these memories. So, it makes sense that therapists may use a variety of techniques to help clients recover memories that they have reason to believe have been repressed. But, use of techniques such as guided imagery (imaging the abuse) or hypnosis has been shown to create new "memories" that have been shown in controlled studies to be false memories (McNally, 2003). Therapists have to be very careful in working with clients who may have repressed memories (see Box 6.2).

Box 6.2: Creating False Memories

Laboratory studies have established that entire memories can be created by providing people with vivid, but false, details of a situation they had experienced at an earlier time (Hymen & Billings, 2010). It is estimated that such false memories can be established in 15–30% of those exposed (Patihis & Pendergrast, 2019). There is also evidence of false memories in the literature dating back to the 1880s. These relate to highly improbable events such as alien abductions or past lives. Such memories can be quite vivid, and once established, are fully believed to be true by the recipient.

Although some people believe memories are actually like recordings of actual situations, this is not generally the case. Most people remember only certain aspects of past events, with most details being vague if recalled at all. When someone else "reminds" us about a plausible detail, we are likely to see this as true and incorporate it into our own memory. If this reminder refers to something that never actually happened, we have gained a false memory.

Loftus (e.g., 1997) has done many laboratory studies demonstrating how false memories can be created. In their commentary about the report of Patihis and Pendergrast's (2019) research on the many recovered memories occurring in therapy and counseling, Loftus and Teitcher (2019) noted that there are many possible risks of the therapist presenting this idea of repressed memories to a client. Given the data that the large majority of those reporting finding recovered memories in counseling also had therapists who told them about the idea of repressed memories, it is possible that many of these recovered memories are actually false memories created through the suggestions of the therapist. One consequence of these recovered memories is negative effect they have on family relations (Patihis & Pendergrast, 2019). Loftus and Teitcher (2019) argued that it might be better if the few actual repressed true memories remain repressed, giving their article the title, "Invasion of the Mind Snatchers." They went on to cite data about lawsuits involving many of those reporting the repressed and now recovered memories who developed a variety of negative outcomes such as suicide attempts, self-mutilation and hospitalization (Loftus, 1997).

In a survey of 2500 US adults aged 20 and older recruited through the Amazon Mechanical Turk system, Patihis and Pendergrast (2019) asked about experiences relating to recovered memories in therapy. (About half of the original sample were included—those who had had therapy or counseling). They were asked if "During the course of counseling or therapy, did your therapist ever discuss the possibility that you might have been abused as a child but had repressed the memories?" (p. 9). They were also asked if they came to remember being abused as a child when they had no previous memory of this. Of those 1082 who did report having been in therapy, 20% said the therapist had discussed having a repressed memory of childhood abuse and 11% said they came to remember earlier abuse. Memories were most likely for emotional abuse, then physical abuse, sexual abuse, and neglect. After the memory of the abuse 43% reporting initially cutting off contact with family members, but about 10% of this group later re-established the family contact. Only 98% of those in therapy who had a recovered memory had also reported that this was an issue that had been raised by the therapist.

Goodwin, Gonzalves, and Wolpe (2019) responded to the Patihis and Pendergrast (2019) study by noting that there is clear evidence adults may not report (or remember) abuse documented in CPS records. In their earlier studies, Goodwin and her colleagues have found clients who explicitly noted that they had forgotten earlier child sexual abuse because it was so "horrible or frightful" (p. 30). Others reported that they did not think it was important. However, Lynn, Merckelbach, and Polizzi (2019) question these basic ideas arguing that there is no good evidence that traumatic memories are repressed. Research continues on these controversial issues.

6.7 Effects of Child Sex Experiences

There are a number of studies that examine the consequences for those victimized by CSA, although most rely on self-reports that do not identify whether the sexual abuse occurred within the home and might be considered incest. It does appear that abuse by those outside the family is relatively uncommon, though, so much of this abuse is probably within the home or by related family members. A further complication in identifying specific effects of child *sex* abuse is that it is so often occurring in situations where other types of child maltreatment are also victimizing the children (Lewis, McElroy, Harlaar, & Runyan, 2016; Turner, Taillieu, Cheung, & Afifi, 2017). These associations can be seen in many empirical studies. For example, using a national database (the 2004–2005 National Epidemiological Survey on Alcohol and Related Conditions) of US men aged 20 or older, Turner et al. (2017) examined how CSA in boys related to other forms of child maltreatment. CSA designation was based on self-reports of the men about childhood experiences. Only 1% of the sample reported being victimized by CSA, but not having any other experiences of child maltreatment. Emotional abuse, physical abuse and exposure to parental IPV were the most commonly associated with CSA. Thus, it appears that boys who were sexually abused were also abused in other ways within their homes, although the data were not collected in a form that indicated where the abuse occurred. A number of mental health disorders, including major depression and other mood disorders, anxiety, substance abuse and suicide attempts were all higher in the men who had experienced CSA as compared to men who had no CSA experience. In other studies, the reported effects of those experiencing CSA and other forms of child maltreatment are generally more negative than if there is no CSA, but thus may be at least partially a result of the many forms of victimization occurring rather than any specific effects related to sexual child abuse.

Additional concerns in understanding the effects of CSA were identified in an early paper by Spaccarelli (1994). The effects of CSA need to be assessed within a broader framework of other types of abuse that the child may be experiencing. The family may change in many ways once incest is identified. For example, a common consequence of reported incest is martial separation. The break-up of the family unit (and loss of other family relationships) may also contribute additional stress beyond the sexual abuse itself especially if the child victim is blamed for breaking up the family. In some cases, the victimized child and other siblings may be placed in foster care (see Chap. 9). Since allegations of sexual abuse require legal action, the abused child may need to testify. Such testimony may create additional stress for the child and other family members (Elmi, Daignault, & Herbert, 2018). Other difficulties arise from the loss of social contacts with friends after the disclosure (Bi et al., 2019). As Schreier, Pogue, and Hansen (2017) point out, issues arising from disclosure of CSA, especially incest occurring within the family, may also cause difficulties for siblings of the abused child which can further add to on-going problems within the family.

6.7.1 Effects Seen in Sexually Abused Children and Adolescents

Emotional and behavioral problems for children who have been sexually abused are similar to those associated with other forms of child maltreatment (Vachon, Krueger, Rogosch, & Cicchetti, 2015). These include both internalizing and externalizing emotions and behavior. In a summer-camp program for low-income children between the ages of 5 and 13, Vachon and his colleagues found that similar patterns were seen in the children exposed to neglect or to physical or emotional abuse. The small number of children also reporting sexual abuse were also exposed to other forms of child maltreatment and could not be differentiated as a separate group.

Running away from home may be an extreme form of coping with continuing sexual abuse in the family. Trying to live on his or her own creates a whole new set of difficulties for the sexually abused child (Spaccarelli, 1994). Benoit-Bryan (2011) reported on a national sample of 15,000 adolescents in grades 7–12 who were followed for 15 years. Within this group, 10% of girls and 7% of boys ran away from home before they turned 18. Verbal abuse, physical abuse and sexual abuse were all more likely in those who ran away. Surveys indicated that 17% of those exposed to CSA were runaways as compared to 8% of those not exposed.

CSA does has some unique consequences, though. Along with possible injury or sexually-transmitted infections that might result in either girls or boys (Fix, Assini-Meytin, & Le, 2019). Pregnancy is another consequence of incest involving intercourse for adolescent girls. The effects of pregnancy can be seen in the following cases from our files. The following two cases involve situations in which the incest resulted in a pregnancy. In Case 19, the 12-year-old abused child's mother denied that her husband was the father of her daughter's unborn child, stating that if he is, then it is the child's fault. Case 15 illustrates how incest between a biological father and daughter can be sustained over many years, leading to producing two children, and occurs with the daughter's mother's full knowledge but no efforts on the mother's part at intervening to stop it. The case also illustrates how knowing that one is the product of incest can be significantly traumatic for a child and can complicate existing behavior problems;

Case Example #19

The Campos family emigrated from Mexico 5 years ago to find better job opportunities. Rodrigo speaks English well but Ofelia does not. Rodrigo works full time but Ofelia stays home as she has ongoing health complications from lupus. The family was reported to Children's Protective Services by the family doctor after he discovered that Miranda was 6 months pregnant. Miranda reported that Rodrigo has been fondling her since she was 8 years old and he started having intercourse with her about a year ago. She stated that Rodrigo is the father of her baby. Ofelia denied that this could be true but said "if it is, it is Miranda's fault". Criminal charges were filed against Rodrigo but he fled back to Mexico. Ofelia said she wanted nothing more to do with her daughter and did not want her to return to their home. She was very upset that her husband left and blamed Miranda for all of her troubles. Oscar and Frieda claimed to be unaware of the abuse that occurred in their household.

Miranda was placed in foster care until her baby was born. The baby was adopted from birth and Miranda went to live with her aunt. She was referred to individual and group counselling but her aunt failed to get her to her appointments. Miranda began engaging in self-injurious behavior and started drinking heavily. Her aunt did not feel she could handle the care of Miranda any longer and she was sent to a residential treatment facility.

Case Example #15

Peter is a 12 year-old boy who was the victim of an attempted sexual assault involving two other boys who tried to force the victim into oral copulation. Peter was examined by a physician at the county hospital emergency room and released with a referral to county mental health services for evaluation. Upon evaluation Peter is alert, cooperative, and somewhat philosophical about the event although he states he has been harassed by other boys over the same thing but this is the first time actual attempted assault has occurred. He attributes this to the fact that he is the smallest kid in his class and some of the other boys taunt him as being "gay". Although Peter seems to have come through the incident without too much trauma, he should be observed over the next couple days for any further signs of trauma reaction, depression or anxiety. We recommend consultation with County Mental Health Children's Services.

Information from Children's Services consultation:

Peter's mother, Gloria Smith, describes Peter as basically uncontrollable: he becomes violent, angry, and has hit his mother on several occasions. In the past, Peter has run away and has gotten into fights at school; subsequently, he was put into a special education program. Peter is described as a bright child that now gets good grades, however, has been in special education programs since the third grade. What seems to have precipitated Mrs. Smith to bring in her son was the incident of attempted sexual assault, as described above, but also another traumatic incident that occurred approximately 3 weeks ago. Peter's biological father, who is also Mrs. Smith's biological father, had been drinking and shared the secret that he is Peter's real father. Peter began to scream at his father and, since this revelation, has been angry at his mother and has voiced how much he hates her, stating that he wishes he was dead.

Mrs. Smith reported that her father had made sexual advances for several years with her mother's full knowledge, adding that her mother accused her of lying when she asked for help. She admitted that during her pregnancy that she became very depressed and was contemplating having an abortion or giving the child up for adoption and that it took her a long time to develop an attachment to Peter as a baby. Peter's early years were normal and he had a good kindergarten year, however, he began to demonstrate behavior problems in first grade and, in third grade, was placed in special education. Mrs. Smith reports that the incest with her father occurred for many years before her pregnancy and continued for many years after Peter's birth, in fact, she has another child, age nine, who is also fathered by her biological father. The incestuous relationship did not stop until Mrs. Smith ran away from home and got married to the first man who asked her. She describes her husband as being a kind man with her children and they have formed a close relationship with him. She reported that she has had two "nervous breakdowns" and subsequently received therapy for herself as well as for her son.

6.7.1.1 Early Sexual Activity with Others

Children who are sexually abused may begin to sexually abuse other children. This may begin before adolescence, even before the age of 6. It may continue into adolescence (Dillard & Beaujolais, 2019). In one of the early studies of this issue, Burton, Nesmith, and Badten (1997) asked clinicians to respond to a series of questions about sexually aggressive children who they were seeing in their practices. On average, these children were between 4 and 6 years of age when the first evidence of their sexual activity was discovered, although many did not start therapy until several years later. Nearly 80% of the sample were boys. The most common behaviors reported were vaginal penetration of a girl with a finger, other genital contact or simulated sexual intercourse. More than 70% of the client children were known to have been sexually abused themselves. Forty-four percent had described sexual abuse from a father, foster father, or other father figure, and 16% had described sexual abuse from their mother, foster mother or mother figure. Many had a parent who had been sexually abused himself or herself, so there was evidence of a cycle of sexual abuse that is similar to the cycle of physical violence described earlier in the chapter.

In a more recent study, Wamser-Nanney, Sager, and Campbell (2019) review literature since the Burton et al. (1997) paper, noting that sexual behavior problems are still assumed by many to be a symptom of CSA. They acknowledge this association, but further note that not all CSA victims exhibit these sexual behavior problems, and some children with these behaviors have no evidence of earlier CSA. In attempting to identify what might explain why some children do and others don't exhibit early sexual behavior, a sample of 161 children aged 6–17 who were in treatment programs for their identified CSA experiences and their mothers were surveyed. Although the supportiveness of the mother and her blame of the child for the CSP or her doubts about whether it really happened were hypothesized to be major predictors, the data did not clearly support these predictions.

6.7.2 Long-Term Effects of CSA Seen in Adults

A number of studies have demonstrated that the effects of CSA seen in children continue into adulthood and manifest themselves in terms of psychopathology, as well as in terms of physical health and other symptoms. Perez-Fuentes et al. (2013) surveyed more than 34,000 adults aged 18 or older in a national U.S. sample. Those reporting earlier experiences of CSA were found to be higher in a number of psychiatric diagnoses, as well as in suicide attempts. It was also noted that most had other forms of child maltreatment as well as CSA. In another study drawing on health data from an HMO, Felitti et al. (2019) asked HMO patients to respond to a mailed survey about adverse childhood experiences. There was a response rate of 71%, yielding a final usable sample of 8056 adults. HMO health data indicated that reports of psychological, physical and sexual abuse in childhood as well as evidence of living in a dysfunctional household with IPV or substance abuse were so highly related that it was not feasible to examine independent effects of these experiences. Overall, the more of these experiences one had, the more likely it was that they were alcoholic, used illicit drugs, and had a sexually transmitted disease. In addition, adverse childhood experiences were related to heart disease, cancer, strokes, chronic bronchitis and diabetes. The authors conclude by pointing out how these effects relate to a higher death rate for those growing up in abusive households and argue for more effective interventions for such families.

Other adult effects of earlier experiences of CSA can be seen in specific sexual behaviors. Some male CSA survivors do commit sexual offenses as adults, although the large majority do not. Examining the specific forms of sexual offenses in a sample of 498 male adolescents judged to have committed sexual offenses, Morais, Alexander, Fix, and Burkhart (2018) compared those with and without a prior history of CSA. Those who had experienced CSA were more likely to offend against another male than those without CSA experiences (42% versus 25%). The CSA survivors also offended against a younger victim (age 8.2 versus 9.4) but this effect was not statistically significant. The CSA group also had higher scores on depression and PTSD.

Other research has indicated that adult CSA survivors may experience difficulty in their romantic and sexual relationships (Gauthier et al., 2018). Sexual functioning may be lowered, along with sexual satisfaction. Gauthier and his colleagues hypothesized that one reason for these sexual difficulties might relate to non-disclosure of their childhood sexual abuse to a martial partner. This was investigated in a sample of community volunteers who had been in a relationship at least 6 months and who had reported CSA experiences in the larger study of negative childhood experiences. The final sample of 70 adults was 86% women with an average duration of 5 years within their relationships who had disclosed their CSA history to their partner. Analyses indicated that those reporting that the partner responded positively to the disclosure rated their sexual and relationship satisfaction higher. Being stigmatized or treated differently after disclosure was associated with lower relationship and sexual satisfaction.

Perhaps related to relationship difficulties, child maltreatment and CSA have been linked to early pregnancy and motherhood for girls, as well as to other sexual risk behaviors such as having a large number of sexual partners and not consistently using contraceptive protection (Noll et al., 2018). Using data from a longitudinal study of adolescent girls, Noll and her colleagues investigated these associations and found that CSA was significantly associated with all these effects. Earlier physical abuse was correlated with risky sexual behaviors but not with early pregnancy or motherhood. Neglect showed much lower correlations with these behaviors. In their discussion, they suggested that CSA may be especially predictive because it could lead to maladaptive scripts for sexual behavior because of earlier coercion or reward for sexual activity as well as feeling powerless in sexual relationships.

This theme of feelings of powerless in issues relating to sexuality was also seen in a study of mother-child relationships (Linde-Krieger & Yates, 2018). Looking at mothers of preschoolers, Linde-Krieger and Yates found that mothers who had themselves experienced CSA later felt helpless, especially in dealing with their own daughters. In asking these mothers about their own mothers, those with CSA also were likely to report that their mothers had also demonstrated a helpless state of mind about parenting when they were 6 years old. Links between these variables were not significant in predicting the mothers interactions with their sons. The researchers argued that feelings of vulnerability for her young daughter related to the vulnerabilities these women experienced when they were children. Cross et al.'s (2016) study of mothers who had themselves experiences CSA having less warm feelings about their daughters than their sons is consistent with the Linde-Krieger and Yates data.

6.8 Resilience in Survivors of Child Maltreatment: Not all Abused Children Become Abusive as Adults

The discussion so far could easily lead to the conclusion that growing up in an abusive or violent household will automatically result in children growing up to be violent and abusive toward their own intimate partner as well as to any children they might have. This is not necessarily the case. As Dutton (1998) pointed out in one of the classic books on these issues, even though the probability of being violent towards one's own spouse is higher for abused children, not all of them followed this pattern. One study estimated that 40% of the child abuse victims grew up to become abusive themselves. Thus, the majority of abused children do not become abusive as adults. This may reflect the fact that the pathway is indirect and other factors may intervene to break the cycle of violence. Dutton (1998) cited evidence that having one supportive parent or other adult may overcome the effects of the hostile environment in which physically abused children live. Another possibility mentioned was that someone exposed to repeated abuse may learn to emotionally disengage, a process called *dissociation*. Such reactions may create other psychological problems, but they may stop the cycle of violence (Dutton, 1998).

In a major review of articles published in English from samples in many countries, Meng, Fleury, Xlang, Li, and D'Arcy (2018) identified 44 studies noting resilience to the general effects of child maltreatment of all types. The age of those looked at varied across the studies, but the overall conclusion was that there was evidence in children, adolescents and adults of less depression, PTSD, alcohol abuse, suicide attempts and other psychological problems in those who demonstrated resilience. Other studies identified protective factors. The most often cited was social support, although a variety of others were noted. Some of these functioned differently for boys and girls. Early maltreatment experiences were seen as especially difficult to recover from.

St-Laurent, Dubois-Comtois, Milot, and Cantinotti (2019) conducted a direct test of continuity of abuse and resilience by comparing abused mothers who were involved with Child Protective Services with their own children with a group of mothers selected from a high-risk sample who had no association with CPS. The study drew on a sample from Quebec, Canada. All forms of child maltreatment were included in the maltreatment groups, except child sexual abuse. Data indicated that in the sample of 193 mother-child dyads, mothers were maltreated in 74% of the dyads, but only 40% of the maltreated mothers were found to be abusive toward their own children, indicating a relatively high rate for those able to break the cycle of violence. Continuing the cycle of violence was associated with IPV for the mother, along with lack of family support, high levels of stress, and having been neglected as a child.

There is also evidence of resilience after experiencing child sexual abuse. In a systematic review of the literature from many counties, Domhardt, Munzer, Fegert, and Goldbeck (2015), a team of German researchers, found levels of normal functioning reported for 10–53% of the sample exposed to CSA across 37 studies. The CSA survivors included both adolescents and adults, mostly female. Resilience was measured in varying ways across the studies. Education levels [and perhaps associated knowledge about sexuality] was found to be especially protective. Those who were optimistic and had positive beliefs about their own ability to control their current environments were more often resilient. These are factors associated with higher levels of coping generally, as discussed in Chap. 3.

IPV exposure in childhood has been identified as a source of trauma independent of other forms of child maltreatment, although it is typically associated with physical and emotional child abuse. Some do show evidence of resilience to this IPV exposure (Carlson et al., 2019). Coping strategies such as being able to calm oneself or find other ways not to react have been shown to be effective, according to Carlson et al.'s review of this literature. Having friends one can turn to was also identified as protective, especially for adolescents. Anderson and Bernhardt's (2019) qualitative study of 29 adult daughters of battered women adds to this list. Coping processes such as distancing oneself from the abusive family, and wanting to break the cycle of violence and finding ways to do this were cited by the women interviewed.

6.9 Summary

As this chapter has indicated, when children are abused by their parents or caretakers, there is often a pattern of both emotional and physical abuse. Sexual abuse may also be part of the experiences of these abused children as well as exposure to IPV in their parents. The abuse can last over a period of years. Because of this, it is generally impossible, in practice, to clearly separate the effects of different types of child abuse within the family. To further complicate the research on child abuse, especially child sex abuse, many studies do not identify the relationship of the perpetrator to the maltreated child. So, abuse by parents cannot not be readily separated from abuse by acquaintances or even strangers, even though parental abuse appears to be more traumatic than sexual contact from others. Given these limitations, it is clear that there are many effects on the child victimized by child maltreatment. Effects can also be seen in adults. Effects of exposure to parental IPV have been associated with long term effects on how one interacts with an intimate partner as well as with other symptoms of trauma exposure such as PTSD. These effects may vary depending on the age of the exposed child (Carlson et al., 2019). In spite of these many reported effects, there is evidence that some children are able to function normally as teens or adults. Social support appears to be a major predictor of this resilience, along with other factors generally associated with good coping skills.

References

Afifi, T. O., Ford, D., Gershoff, E. T., Merrick, M., Grogan-Kaylor, A., Ports, K. A., et al. (2017). Spanking and adult mental health impairment: The case for the designation of spanking as an adverse childhood experience. *Child Abuse & Neglect, 71*, 24–31. https://doi.org/10.1016/j.chiabu.2017.01.014

Alink, L. R. A., Cyr, C., & Madigan, S. (2019). Introduction to the special section. The effect of maltreatment experiences on maltreating and dysfunctional parenting: A search for mechanisms. *Development and Psychopathology, 31*, 1–7. https://doi.org/10.1017/S0954579418001517

Anderson, K. M., & Bernhardt, C. (2019). Resilient adult daughters of abused women: Turning pain into purpose. *Violence Against Women*, 1–21. https://doi.org/10.1177/1077801219842946

Assink, M., van der Put, C. E., Meeuwsen, M. W. C. M., de Jong, N. M., Oort, F. J., Stams, G. J. M., et al. (2019). Risk factors for child sex abuse victimization: A meta-analytic review. *Psychological Bulletin, 145*, 459–489. https://doi.org/10.1037/bul0000188

Azzopardi, C., Eirich, R., Rash, C. L., MacDonald, S., & Madigan, S. (2018). A meta-analysis of the prevalence of child sexual abuse disclosure in forensic settings. *Child Abuse & Neglect, 93*, 1–14. https://doi.org/10.1016/j.chiabu.2018.11.020

Benoit-Bryan, J. (2011). *Executive summary of the runaway youth longitudinal study 2011*. Chicago, IL: National Runaway Switchboard.

Berger, L. M., Font, S. A., Slack, K. S., & Waldfogel, J. (2017). Income and child maltreatment in unmarried families: Evidence from the earned income tax credit. *Review of Economics of the Household, 15*, 1345–1372. https://doi.org/10.1007/s11150-016-9346-9

Bi, S., Rancher, C., Johnson, E., Cook, K., McDonald, R., & Jouiles, E. N. (2019). Perceived loss of social contact and trauma symptoms of adolescents who have experienced sexual abuse. *Journal of Child Sexual Abuse, 28*, 333–344. https://doi.org/10.1080/10538712.2018.1544599

Burton, D. L., Nesmith, A. A., & Badten, L. (1997). Clinician's views on sexually aggressive children and their families: A theoretical exploration. *Child Abuse & Neglect, 21*, 157–170. https://doi.org/10.1016/s0145-2134(96)00141-x

Campbell, A. M., & Hibbard, R. (2014). More than words: The emotional maltreatment of children. *Pediatric Clinics of North America, 61*(5), 959–970. https://doi.org/10.1016/j.pcl.2014.06.004

Capaldi, D. M., Tiberio, S. S., Pears, K. C., Kerr, D. C. R., & Owen, L. D. (2019). Intergenerational associations in physical maltreatment: Examination of mediation by delinquency and substance use, and moderated mediation by anger. *Development and Psychopathology, 31*, 73–82. https://doi.org/10.1017/S0954579418001529

Carlson, J., Voitch, L., Brown, J. C., & Holmes, M. (2019). Viewing children's exposure to intimate partner violence through a developmental, social-ecological, and survivor lens: The current state of the field, challenges, and future directions. *Violence Against Women, 25*, 6–28. https://doi.org/10.1177/1077801218816187

CDC. (2019). Retrieved from https://www.cdc.gov/violenceprevention/childabuseandneglect/index.html?CDC_AA_refVal=https%3A%2F%2Fwww.cdc.gov%2Fviolenceprevention%2Fchildmaltreatment%2Findex.html

Chaffin, M. (2006). The changing focus of child maltreatment research and practice within psychology. *Journal of Social Issues, 62*(4), 663–684. https://doi.org/10.1111/j.1540-4560.2006.00482.x

Chiesa, A. E., Kallechey, L., Harlaar, N., Ford, C. R., Garrido, E. F., Betts, W. R., et al. (2018). Intimate partner violence victimization and parenting: A systematic review. *Child Abuse & Neglect, 80*, 285–300. https://doi.org/10.1016/j.chiabu.2018.03.028

Children's Bureau. (2019). *Child maltreatment 2017*. Washington, DC: U.S. Department of Health & Human Services, Administration for Children and Families, Administration on Children, Youth and Families. Available from https://www.acf.hhs.gov/cb/research-data-technology/statistics-research/child-maltreatment

Cicchetti, D. (2016). Socioemotional, personality and biological development: Illustrations from a multilevel developmental psychopathology perspective on child maltreatment. *Annual Review of Psychology, 67*, 187–211. https://doi.org/10.1146/annurev-psych-122414-033259

Cohen, J. R., Menon, S. V., Shorey, R. C., Le, V. D., & Temple, J. R. (2017). The distal consequences of physical and emotional neglect in emerging adults: A person-centered. Multi-wave, longitudinal study. *Child Abuse & Neglect, 63*, 151–161. https://doi.org/10.1016/j.chiabu.2016.11.030

Copp, J. E., Giodano, P. C., Longmore, M. A., & Manning, W. D. (2016). The development of attitudes toward intimate partner violence: An examination of key correlates among a sample of young adults. *Journal of Interpersonal Violence, 34*, 1–31. https://doi.org/10.1177/0886260516651311

Craig, S. G., & Moretti, M. M. (2018). Primary and secondary callous-unemotional features in youth: The role of emotion regulation. *Development and Psychopathology, 31*, 1–12. https://doi.org/10.1017/S0954579418001062

Cross, D., Kim, Y. J., Vance, L. A., Robinson, G., Jovanovic, T., & Bradley, R. (2016). Maternal child sex abuse is associated with lower maternal warmth towards daughters but not sons. *Journal of Child Sex Abuse, 25*, 813–826. https://doi.org/10.1080/10538712.2016.1234532

Crowley, E. P. (2016). *Preventing abuse and neglect in the lives of children with disabilities*. New York, NY: Springer.

Currie, J., & Widom, C. S. (2010). Long-term consequences of child abuse and neglect on adult economic well-being. *Child Maltreatment, 15*, 111–120. https://doi.org/10.1177/1077559509355316

Dillard, R., & Beaujolais, B. (2019). Trauma and adolescents who engage in sexually abusive behavior: A review of the literature. *Journal of Child Sexual Abuse, 28*, 629–648. https://doi.org/10.1080/10538712.2019.1598528

Dodier, O. (2018). A bibliometric analysis of the recovered memory controversy in the 21st century. *Applied Cognitive Psychology*, 1–14. https://doi.org/10.1002/acp.3498

Domhardt, M., Munzer, A., Fegert, J. M., & Goldbeck, L. (2015). Resilience in survivors of child sexual abuse: A systematic review of the literature. *Trauma, Violence, & Abuse, 16*, 476–493. https://doi.org/10.1177/1524838014557288

Dutton, D. G. (1998). *The abusive personality: Violence and control in intimate relationships*. New York, NY: Guilford.

Ehrensaft, M. K., Cohen, R., Brown, J., Smailes, E., Chen, H., & Johnson, J. G. (2003). Intergenerational transmission of partner violence: A 20-year prospective study. *Journal of Consulting and Clinical Psychology, 71*, 741–753. https://doi.org/10.1037/0022-006x.71.4.741

Elmi, M. H., Daignault, I. V., & Herbert, M. (2018). Child sex abuse victims as witnesses: The influence of testifying on their recovery. *Child Abuse & Neglect, 86*, 22–32. https://doi.org/10.1016/j.chiabu.2018.09.001

Emery, R. E. (1989). Family violence. *American Psychologist, 44*, 321–328. https://doi.org/10.1037/0003-066x.44.2.321

Felitti, V. J., Anda, R. F., Nordenberg, D., Williamson, D. F., Spitz, A. M., Edwards, V., et al. (2019). Relationship of childhood abuse and household dysfunction to many of the leading causes of death in adults: The adverse childhood experiences (ACE) study. *American Journal of Preventive Medicine, 56*(6), 774–786. https://doi.org/10.1016/j.amepre.2019.04.001

Ferguson, C. J. (2013). Spanking, corporal punishment and negative long-term outcomes: A meta-analytic review of longitudinal studies. *Clinical Psychology Review, 33*(1), 196–208. https://doi.org/10.1016/j.cpr.2012.11.002

Finkelhor, D., Turner, H. A., Hamby, S. L., & Ormrod, R. K. (2011). *Poly-victimization: Children's exposure to multiple types of violence, crime, and abuse. OJJDP Juvenile Justice Bulletin - NCJ235504* (pp. 1–12). Washington, DC: US Government Printing Office.

Finkelhor, D., Turner, H., Ormrod, R., & Hamby, S. L. (2009). Violence, abuse, and crime exposure in a national sample of children and youth. *Pediatrics, 124*(5), 1411–1423. https://doi.org/10.1542/peds.2009-0467

Finkelhor, D., Turner, H., Shattuck, A., & Hamby, S. L. (2015). Prevalence of childhood exposure to violence, crime, and abuse. *Journal of the American Medical Association Pediatrics, 169*(8), 746–754. https://doi.org/10.1001/jamapediatrics.2015.0676

Fix, R. L., Assini-Meytin, L. C., & Le, P. D. (2019). Gender and race informed pathways from childhood sexual abuse to sexually transmitted infections: A moderated mediation analysis using nationally representative data. *Journal of Adolescent Health*, 1–7. https://doi.org/10.1016/j.jadohealth.2019.02.015

Freyd, P. (1992). How do we know we are not representing pedophiles? *False Memory Syndrome Newsletter, 1*, 1.

Garcia, A. S., Ren, L., Esteraich, J. M., & Raikes, H. H. (2017). Influence of child behavioral problems and parenting stress on parent-child conflict among low-income families: The moderating role of maternal nativity. *Merrill-Palmer Quarterly, 63*, 311–339. https://doi.org/10.13110/merrpalmquar1982.63.3.0311

Gauthier, L. D., Vaillancourt-Morel, M., Rellini, A., Godbout, N., Charbonneau-Lefebvre, V., Desjardins, F., et al. (2018). The risk of telling: A dyadic perspective on romantic partners' responses to child sexual abuse disclosure and their associations with sexual and relationship satisfaction. *Journal of Marital and Family Therapy., 45*, 480–493. https://doi.org/10.1111/jmft.12345

Gershoff, E. T., & Grogan-Kaylor, A. (2016). Spanking and child outcomes: Old controversies and new meta-analysis. *Journal of Family Psychology, 30*, 453–469. https://doi.org/10.1037/fam0000191

Giroux, M. E., Chong, K., Coburn, P. I., & Connolly, D. A. (2018). Differences in child sex abuse cases involving child versus adolescent complainants. *Child Abuse & Neglect, 79*, 224–233. https://doi.org/10.1016/j.chiabu.2018.02.011

Godbout, N., Vaillancourt-Morel, M., Bigras, N., Briere, J., Hebert, M., Runtz, M., & Sabourin, S. (2017). Intimate partner violence in male survivors of child maltreatment: A meta-analysis. *Trauma, Violence & Abuse*, 1–15. https://doi.org/10.1177/1524838017692382

Goodman, G. S., Ghetti, S., Quas, J. A., Edelstein, R., Alexander, K., Cordon, I., & Jones, D. (2003). A prospective study of memory for child sexual abuse. *Psychological Science, 14*, 113–118. https://doi.org/10.1111/1467-9280.01428

Goodwin, G. S., Gonzalves, L., & Wolpe, S. (2019). False memories and true memories of childhood trauma: Balancing the risks. *Clinical Psychological Science, 7*, 29–31. https://doi.org/10.1177/2167702618797106

Grasso, D. J., Henry, D., Kestler, J., Nieto, R., Wakschlag, L. S., & Briggs-Gowan, M. J. (2016). Harsh parenting as a potential mediator of the association between intimate partner violence and child disruptive behavior in young children. *Journal of Interpersonal Violence, 31*, 2102–2126. https://doi.org/10.1177/0886260515572472

Harman, J. J., Kruk, E., & Hines, D. A. (2018). Parental alienating behaviors: An unacknowledged form of family violence. *Psychological Bulletin, 144*, 1275–1299. https://doi.org/10.1037/bul0000175

Harris, L. S., Block, S. D., Ogle, C. M., Goodman, G. S., Augusti, E., Larson, R. P., et al. (2015). Coping style and memory specificity in adolescents and adults with histories of child sex abuse. *Memory, 24*, 1078–1090. https://doi.org/10.1080/09658211.2015.1068812

Haskett, M. E., Neupert, S. D., & Okado, Y. (2014). Factors associated with 3-year stability and change in parenting behavior of abusive parents. *Journal of Child and Family Studies, 23*(2), 263–274. https://doi.org/10.1007/s10826-013-9729-y

Herman, J. L. (2012). *Father–daughter incest*. Cambridge, MA: Harvard University Press.

Hines, D. A., Malley-Morrison, K., & Dutton, L. B. (2012). *Family violence in the United States: Defining, understanding, and combating abuse*. Thousand Oaks, CA: Sage.

Holden, G. W., Brown, A. S., Baldwin, A. S., & Caderao, K. C. (2014). Research findings can change attitudes about corporal punishment. *Child Abuse & Neglect, 38*, 902–908. https://doi.org/10.1016/j.chiabu.2013.10.013

Holmes, M. R., Yoon, S., & Berg, K. A. (2017). Maternal depression and intimate partner violence exposure: Longitudinal analyses of the development of aggressive behavior in an at-risk sample. *Aggressive Behavior, 43*, 375–385. https://doi.org/10.1002/ab.21696

Hunt, T. K. A., Slack, K. S., & Berger, L. M. (2017). Adverse childhood experiences and behavioral problems in middle childhood. *Child Abuse & Neglect, 67*, 391–402. https://doi.org/10.1016/j.chiabu.2016.11.005

Hymen, I. E., & Billings, F. J., Jr. (2010). Individual differences and the creation of false childhood memories. *Memory*, 1–20. https://doi.org/10.1080/741941598

Jaffee, S. R. (2017). Child maltreatment and risk for psychopathology in childhood and adulthood. *Annual Review of Clinical Psychology, 13*, 525–551. https://doi.org/10.1146/annurev-clinpsy-032816-045005

Johnson, W. F., Huelsnitz, C. O., Carlson, E. A., Roisman, G. I., Englund, M. M., Miller, G. E., & Simpson, J. A. (2017). Childhood abuse and neglect and physical health at midlife: Prospective, longitudinal evidence. *Development and Psychopathology, 29*, 1935–1946. https://doi.org/10.1017/S095457941700150X

Jung, H., Herrenkohl, T. I., Skinner, M. L., Lee, J. O., Klika, J. B., & Rousson, A. N. (2019). Gender differences in intimate partner violence: A predictive analysis of IPV by child abuse and domestic violence exposure during early childhood. *Violence Against Women, 25*, 903–924. https://doi.org/10.1177/1077801218796329

Kelley, M. L., Brovo, A. J., Braitman, A. L., Lawless, A. K., & Lawrence, H. R. (2016). Behavioral couples treatment for substance use disorder: Secondary effects on the reduction of risk for child abuse. *Journal of Substance Abuse Treatment, 62*, 10–19. https://doi.org/10.1016/j.jsat.2015.11.008

Kepple, N. J. (2018). Does parental substance use always engender risk for children? Comparing incidence rate ratios of abusive and neglectful behaviors across substance use behavior patterns. *Child Abuse & Neglect, 76*, 44–55. https://doi.org/10.1016/j.chiabu.2017.09.015

Kimber, M., Adham, S., Gill, S., McTavish, J., & MacMillan, H. L. (2018). The association between child exposure to intimate partner violence (IPV) and perpetration of IPV in adulthood—A systematic review. *Child Abuse & Neglect, 76*, 273–286. https://doi.org/10.1016/j.chiabu.2017.11.007

Lapierre, S., Côté, I., Lambert, A., Buetti, D., Lavergne, C., Damant, D., et al. (2018). Difficult but close relationships: Children's perspectives on relationships with their mothers in the context of domestic violence. *Violence Against Women, 24*, 1023–1038. https://doi.org/10.1177/1077801217731541

Lee, S. J., Perron, B. E., Taylor, C. A., & Guterman, N. B. (2011). Paternal psychosocial characteristics and corporal punishment of their 3-year-old children. *Journal of Interpersonal Violence, 26*(1), 71–87. https://doi.org/10.1177/0886260510362888

Lewis, T., McElroy, E., Harlaar, N., & Runyan, D. (2016). Does the impact of child sexual abuse differ from maltreated but non-sexually abused children? A prospective examination of the impact of child sexual abuse on internalizing and externalizing behavior problems. *Child Abuse & Neglect, 51*, 31–40. https://doi.org/10.1016/j.chiabu.2015.11.016

Linde-Krieger, L., & Yates, T. M. (2018). Mothers' history of child sexual abuse and child behavior problems: The mediating role of mothers' helpless state of mind. *Child Maltreatment, 23*, 376–386. https://doi.org/10.1177/1077559518775536

Loftus, E. F. (1997). Repressed memory accusations: Devastated families and devastated patients. *Applied Cognitive Psychology, 11*(1), 25–30. https://doi.org/10.1002/(SICI)1099-0720(199702)11:1<25::AID-ACP452>3.0.CO;2-J

Loftus, E. F., & Teitcher, J. (2019). Invasion of the mind snatchers: A nation full of traumatic memories. *Clinical Psychological Science, 7*, 25–26. https://doi.org/10.1177/2167702618797107

Lorber, M. F., & Stuart, J. (2018). Mothers' attitudes as organizers of discipline practices and related anticipatory processes. *Journal of Child and Family Studies, 27*, 4091–4102. https://doi.org/10.1007/s10826-018-1222-1

Lynn, S. J., Merckelbach, H., & Polizzi, C. P. (2019). Reflections on recovered memories: Comment on Patihis and Pendergrast (2019). *Clinical Psychological Science, 7*, 22–24. https://doi.org/10.1177/2167702618795700

Macmillan, H. L., Tanaka, M., Duku, E., Vaillancourt, T., & Boyle, M. H. (2013). Child physical and sexual abuse in a community sample of young adults: Results from the Ontario Child Health Study. *Child Abuse & Neglect, 37*, 14–21. https://doi.org/10.1016/j.chiabu.2012.06.005

Madigan, S., Cyr, C., Eirich, R., Fearon, R. M. P., Ly, A., Rash, C., et al. (2019). Testing the cycle of maltreatment hypothesis: Meta-analytic evidence of the intergenerational transmission of child maltreatment. *Development and Psychopathology, 31*, 23–51. https://doi.org/10.1017/S0954579418001700

Mahoney, A., Pargament, K. I., Tarakeshwar, N., & Swank, A. B. (2002). Religion in the home in the 1980s and 90s: Meta-analyses and conceptual analyses of links between religion, marriage, and parenting. *Journal of Family Psychology, 15*, 559–596. https://doi.org/10.1037/1941-1022.S.1.63

Mahoney, A. (2005). Religion and conflict in marital and parent-child relationships. *Journal of Social Issues., 61*, 689–706. https://doi.org/10.1111/j.1540-4560.2005.00427.x

Mahoney, A. (2010). Religion in families, 1999-2009: A relational spirituality framework. *Journal of Marriage and the Family, 72*, 805–827. https://doi.org/10.1111/j.1741-3737.2010.00732.x

Mathews, B., & Collin-Vezina, D. (2019). Child sexual abuse: Toward a conceptual model and definition. *Trauma, Violence & Abuse, 20*, 131–148. https://doi.org/10.1177/1524838017738726

McDonald, S. E., Collins, E. A., Nicotera, N., Hageman, T. O., Ascione, F. R., Williams, J. H., et al. (2015). Children's experiences of companion animal maltreatment in households characterized by intimate partner violence. *Child Abuse & Neglect, 50*, 11–127. https://doi.org/10.1016/j.chiabu.2015.10.005

McNally, R. J. (2003). Progress and controversy in the study of posttraumatic stress disorder. *Annual Review of Psychology, 54*, 229–252. https://doi.org/10.1146/annurev.psych.54.101601.145112

McQuillan, M. E., Bates, J. E., Staples, A. D., & Deater-Deckard, K. (2019). Maternal stress, sleep, and parenting. *Journal of Family Psychology, 33*, 349–359. https://doi.org/10.1037/fam0000516

Meng, X., Fleury, M., Xlang, Y., Li, M., & D'Arcy, C. (2018). Resilience and protective factors among people with a history of child maltreatment: A systematic review. *Social Psychiatry and Psychiatric Epidemiology, 53*, 453–475. https://doi.org/10.1007/s00127-018-1485-2

Miller-Perrin, C., & Perrin, R. (2018). Physical punishment of children by US parents: Moving beyond debate to promote children's health and well-being. *Psicologia: Reflexão e Crítica, 31*, 1–7. https://doi.org/10.1186/s41155-018-0096-x

Morais, H. B., Alexander, A. A., Fix, R. L., & Burkhart, B. R. (2018). Childhood sexual abuse in adolescents adjudicated for sexual offenses: Mental health consequences and sexual offending behaviors. *Sexual Abuse, 30*, 23–42. https://doi.org/10.1177/1079063215625224

Mulder, T. M., Kuiper, K. C., van der Put, C. E., Stams, G. J. M., & Assink, M. (2018). Risk factors for child neglect: A meta-analytic review. *Child Abuse & Neglect, 77*, 198–210. https://doi.org/10.1016/j.chiabu.2018.01.006

Noll, J. G., Guastaferro, K., Beal, S. J., Schreier, H. M. C., Barnes, J., Reader, J. M., et al. (2018). Is sexual abuse a unique predictor of sexual risk behaviors, pregnancy, and motherhood in adolescence? *Journal of Research on Adolescence., 29*, 967–983. https://doi.org/10.1111/jora.12436

Nomaguchi, K., Johnson, W. L., Minter, M. D., & Aldrich, L. (2017). Clarifying the association between mother-father relationship aggression and parenting. *Journal of Marriage and the Family, 79*, 161–178. https://doi.org/10.1111/jomf.12354

Office for Victims of Crime. Technical Training and Assistance Center. (2019). *Training unit 9. Child abuse and neglect*. Washington, DC: U.S. Department of Justice. https://www.ovcttac.gov/

Orsi, R., Brown, S. M., Knight, K. E., & Shillington, A. M. (2018). Remaining home: Well-being outcomes and co-occurring parental substance use following a maltreatment investigation in middle childhood. *Children and Youth Services Review, 84*, 118–124. https://doi.org/10.1016/j.childyouth.2017.11.022

Patihis, L., & Pendergrast, M. (2019). Reports of recovered memories of abuse in therapy in a large age-representative U.S. national sample: Therapy type and decade comparisons. *Clinical Psychological Science, 7*, 3–21. https://doi.org/10.1177/2167702618773315

Pemberton, A. E., & Wakeling, H. C. (2009). Entitled to sex: Attitudes of sex offenders. *Journal of Sexual Aggression, 15*(3), 289–303. https://doi.org/10.1080/13552600903097212

Perez-Fuentes, G., Olfson, M., Villegas, L., Morcillo, C., Wang, S., & Blanco, C. (2013). Prevalence and correlates of child sexual abuse: A national study. *Comprehensive Psychiatry, 54*, 16–27. https://doi.org/10.1016/j.comppsych.2012.05.010

Perrin, R., Miller-Perrin, C., & Song, J. (2017). Changing attitudes about spanking using alternative biblical interpretations. *International Journal of Behavioral Development, 41*, 514–522. https://doi.org/10.1177/0165025416673295

Peterson, C. C., Riggs, J., Guyon-Harris, K., Harrison, L., & Huth-Bocks, A. (2019). Effects of intimate partner violence and home environment on child language development in the first 3 years of life. *Journal of Developmental & Behavioral Pediatrics, 40*, 112–121. https://doi.org/10.1097/DBP.0000000000000638

Pinquart, M. (2017). Parenting stress in caregivers of children with chronic physical condition—A meta-analysis. *Stress and Health, 34*, 197–207. https://doi.org/10.1002/smi.2780

Pittner, K., Van Ijzendoorn, M. H., Alink, L. R. A., Buisman, R. M., Compier-De Block, L. H. C. G. C., Van Den Berg, L. J. M., et al. (2019). The genetic and environmental etiology of child maltreatment in a parent-based extended family design. *Development and Psychopathology, 31*, 157–172. https://doi.org/10.1017/S0954579418001608

Proctor, L. J., Lewis, T., Roesch, S., Thompson, R., Litrownik, A. J., English, D., et al. (2017). Child maltreatment and age of alcohol and marijuana initiation in high-risk youth. *Addictive Behaviors, 75*, 64–69. https://doi.org/10.1016/j.addbeh.2017.06.021

Pullman, L. E., Sawatsky, M. I., Babchishin, K. M., McPhail, I. V., & Seto, M. (2017). Differences between biological and sociolegal incest offenders: A meta-analysis. *Aggression and Violent Behavior, 34*, 228–237. https://doi.org/10.1016/j.avb.2017.01.003

Raby, K. L., Roisman, G. I., Labella, M. H., Martin, J., Fraley, R. C., & Simpson, J. A. (2018). The legacy of early abuse and neglect for social and academic competence from childhood to adulthood. *Child Development, 90*, 1–18. https://doi.org/10.1111/cdev.13033

Rodriguez, C. M. (2018). Predicting parent-child aggression risk: Cognitive factors and their interaction with anger. *Journal of Interpersonal Violence, 33*, 359–378. https://doi.org/10.1177/0886260516629386

Rodriguez, C. M., & Tucker, M. C. (2015). Predicting maternal physical child abuse risk beyond distress and social support: Additive role of cognitive processes. *Journal of Child and Family Studies, 24*, 1780–1790. https://doi.org/10.1007/s10826-014-9981-9

Rohner, R. P., & Melendez-Rhodes, T. (2019). Perceived parental acceptance—Rejection mediates or moderates the relation between corporal punishment and psychological adjustment: Comment on Gershoff et al. (2018). *American Psychologist, 74*, 500–502. https://doi.org/10.1037/amp0000437

Savage, L., Tarabulsy, G. M., Pearson, J., Collin-Vezina, D., & Gagne, L. (2019). Maternal history of childhood maltreatment and later parental behavior: A meta-analysis. *Development and Psychopathology, 31*, 9–21. https://doi.org/10.1017/S0954579418001542

Schreier, A., Pogue, J. K., & Hansen, D. J. (2017). Impact of child sexual abuse on non-abused siblings: A review with implications for research and practice. *Aggression and Violent Behavior, 34*, 254–262. https://doi.org/10.1016/j.avb.2016.11.011

Seto, M. C., Babchishim, K. M., Pullman, L. E., & McPhail, I. V. (2015). The puzzle of intrafamilial and exrafamilial offenders with child victims. *Clinical Psychology Review, 39*, 42–57. https://doi.org/10.1016/j.cpr.2015.04.001

Shanahan, M. E., Runyan, D. K., Martin, S. L., & Kotch, J. B. (2017). The within poverty differences in the occurrence of physical neglect. *Children and Youth Services Review, 75*, 1–6. https://doi.org/10.1016/j.childyouth.2017.02.014

Slep, A. M. S., Heyman, R. E., & Snarr, J. D. (2011). Child emotional aggression and abuse: Definitions and prevalence. *Child Abuse & Neglect, 36*, 268. https://doi.org/10.1016/j.chiabu.2011.07.002

Spaccarelli, S. (1994). Stress, appraisal, and coping in child sexual abuse: A theoretical and empirical review. *Psychological Bulletin, 116*, 340–362. https://doi.org/10.1037/0033-2909.116.2.340

Starr Jr., R. (1988). Physical abuse of children. In V. B. Van Hasselt, R. L. Mossison, A. S. Bellack, & M. Hersen (Eds.), *Handbook of family violence* (pp. 119–155). New York, NY: Plenum. https://doi.org/10.1007/978-1-4757-5360-8_6

St-Laurent, D., Dubois-Comtois, K., Milot, T., & Cantinotti, M. (2019). Intergenerational continuity/discontinuity of child maltreatment among low-income mother-child dyads: The roles of childhood maltreatment characteristics, maternal psychological functioning, and family ecology. *Development and Psychopathology, 31*, 189–202. https://doi.org/10.1017/S095457941800161X

Straus, M. A., & Douglas, E. M. (2017). Concordance between parents in perpetration of child mistreatment: How often is it by father-only, mother-only, or by both and what difference does it make? *Trauma, Violence, & Abuse*, 1–12. https://doi.org/10.1177/1524838017717742

Straus, M. A., Douglas, E. M., & Medeiros, R. A. (2014). *The primordial violence: Spanking children, psychological development, violence, and crime*. New York, NY: Routledge/Taylor & Francis Group.

Stroebel, S. S., O'Keefe, S. L., Beard, K. W., Kuo, S., Swindell, S. V. S., & Kommer, M. J. (2012). Father-daughter incest: Data from an anonymous computerized survey. *Journal of Child Sexual Abuse, 21*, 176–199. https://doi.org/10.1080/10538712.2012.654007

Sugaya, L., Hasin, D. S., Olfson, M., Lin, K.-H., Grant, B. F., & Blanco, C. (2012). Child physical abuse and adult mental health: A national study. *Journal of Traumatic Stress, 25*(4), 384–392. https://doi.org/10.1002/jts.21719

Tallieu, T. L., Brownridge, D. A., Sareen, J., & Afifi, T. O. (2016). Childhood emotional maltreatment and mental disorders: Results from a nationally representative adult sample from the United States. *Child Abuse & Neglect, 59*, 1–12. https://doi.org/10.1016/j.chiabu.2016.07.005

Taylor, C. A., Lee, S. J., Guterman, N. B., & Rice, J. C. (2010). Use of spanking for 3-year-old children and associated intimate partner aggression or violence. *Pediatrics, 126*(3), 415–424. https://doi.org/10.1542/peds.2010-0314

Thornberry, T. P., Matsuda, M., Greenman, S. J., Augustyn, M. B., Henry, K. L., Smith, C. A., et al. (2014). Adolescent risk factors for child maltreatment. *Child Abuse & Neglect, 38*, 706–722. https://doi.org/10.1016/j.chiabu.2013.08.009

Turner, S., Taillieu, T., Cheung, K., & Afifi, T. O. (2017). The relationship between childhood sexual abuse and mental health outcomes among males: Results from a nationally representative United States sample. *Child Abuse & Neglect, 66*, 64–72. https://doi.org/10.1016/j.chiabu.2017.01.018

United States Department of Justice. (2014). *Recognizing when a child's injury or illness is caused by abuse*. Washington, DC: U.S. Department of Justice, Office of Juvenile Justice and Delinquency Prevention.

Vachon, D. D., Krueger, R. F., Rogosch, F. A., & Cicchetti, D. (2015). Assessment of the harmful psychiatric and behavioral effects of different forms of child maltreatment. *JAMA: Psychiatry, 72*(11), 1135–1142. https://doi.org/10.1001/jamapsychiatry.2015.1792

Ventus, D., Antfolk, A., & Salo, B. (2017). The associations between abuse characteristics in child sexual abuse: A meta-analysis. *Journal of Sexual Aggression, 23*, 167–180. https://doi.org/10.1080/13552600.2017.1318963

Victor, B. G., Grogan-Kaylor, A., Ryan, J. P., Perron, B. E., & Gilbert, T. T. (2018). Domestic violence, parental substance misuse and the decision to substantiate child maltreatment. *Child Abuse & Neglect, 79*, 31–41. https://doi.org/10.1016/j.chiabu.2018.01.030

Wamser-Nanney, R., Sager, J. C., & Campbell, C. L. (2019). Maternal support as a predictor of children's sexualized behaviors following childhood sexual abuse. *Child Maltreatment, 24*, 36–44. https://doi.org/10.1177/1077559518786821

Weinsheimer, C. C., Woiwod, D. M., Coburn, P. I., Chong, K., & Connolly, D. A. (2017). The unusual suspects: Female versus male accused in child sexual abuse cases. *Child Abuse & Neglect, 72*, 446–455. https://doi.org/10.1016/j.chiabu.2017.09.003

Widom, C. S. (1989). The cycle of violence. *Science, 244*(4901), 160–166. https://doi.org/10.1126/science.2704995

Widom, C. S., Czaja, S. J., & DuMont, K. A. (2015). Intergenerational transmission of child abuse and neglect: Real or detection bias? *Science, 347*(6229), 1480–1485. https://doi.org/10.1126/science.1259917

Widom, C. S., Czaja, S. J., Kozakowski, S. S., & Chauhan, P. (2018). Does adult attachment style mediate the relationship between childhood maltreatment and mental and physical health outcomes? *Child Abuse & Neglect, 76*, 533–545. https://doi.org/10.1016/j.chiabu.2017.05.002

Young, A., Pierce, M. C., Kuczor, K., Lorenz, D. J., Hickey, S., Berger, S. P., et al. (2018). Are negative/unrealistic parent descriptors of infant attributes associated with physical abuse? *Child Abuse & Neglect, 80*, 41–51. https://doi.org/10.1016/j.chiabu.2018.03.020

Chapter 7
Other Forms of Family Violence: Elder Abuse, Sibling Abuse, and Animal Cruelty

In earlier chapters in this book, we have reviewed the research on intimate partner violence (Chaps. 4 and 5) and child abuse and neglect (Chap. 6). Although these are the most extensively studied forms of violence and abuse within families and within close relationships, they are not the only types of abuse that occur in these settings. This chapter reviews three types of additional abuse within the family that may co-occur with child maltreatment and intimate partner violence: abuse of older adults, abuse between siblings, and cruelty to household pets and their relationship to intimate partner violence (IPV). There is less discussion in the academic literature about these topics than those covered in other chapters, although there is a growing body of work on each of these, especially abuse of older adults.

In this chapter, we focus on how each of these three types of abuse operate within the family setting. It is clear that elder abuse can also occur within nursing homes or other institutional settings (e.g., Macko & Valcarce, 2018; Roberto, 2016), but discussion of these situations is beyond the score of this book. It does appear that the majority of maltreatment of older adults is not done by a family member (Amstadter et al., 2010). Similarly, it is not unusual for children who are *not* living together (or in the same family) to bully and physically attack each other (e.g., Coyle, Demaray, Malecki, Tennant, & Klossing, 2017; Tucker, Finkelhor, Turner, & Shattuck, 2014), but again, peer harassment is not an issue covered in this book. Animal cruelty, too, occurs in many ways in our society (e.g., Hoffer & Hargreaves-Cormany, 2017), but our focus here is on how this abuse of household pets can be a part of other forms of intimate partner violence and abuse. As will be discussed, each of these additional forms of abuse often co-occurs with other types of abuse discussed in other chapters.

I. H. Frieze et al., *Dynamics of Family and Intimate Partner Violence*,
https://doi.org/10.1007/978-3-030-42608-8_7

7.1 Elder Abuse and Maltreatment of Older Adults

In the following case taken from newspaper accounts, a severe case of physical abuse of a vulnerable older adult within the family is demonstrated. Given her age, Mrs. Girdish was probably unable to defend herself physically. She was at the mercy of her daughter. Fortunately, a good Samaritan was willing to call in a tip to the local area Agency on Aging. Fortunately, this meant that help and protection were subsequently provided. Without such intervention, Mrs. Girdish might have eventually died from the physical abuse and neglect inflicted by her daughter. For more information about investigations of suspected elder abuse see Chap. 9.

Published Case Example

Helen Girdish, 92, had lived independently in her rural farmhouse for years. Then her 64-year-old daughter, Barbara, moved in with her to "lend a hand". Six months later, the Washington County Area Agency on Aging, located in Western Pennsylvania, received an anonymous tip that an elderly woman at a certain address was being abused. The following day, an agency caseworker made a home visit.

When the caseworker knocked on the door, Barbara Girdish answered, but would not allow the caseworker entry to the home, telling the caseworker to get off her property. Concerned, the caseworker called the police. When officers arrived at the home, they told Barbara that they had to see her mother in person to check on her well-being and what they found was shocking. Helen Girdish was lying partially clothed on an old mattress, and she was covered from head to toe with bruises, cuts and scrapes. Police discovered that Mrs. Girdish had suffered multiple beatings at the hands of her daughter and they immediately arranged for medical hospitalization. The daughter was subsequently charged with multiple felonies including aggravated assault, unlawful restraint, simple assault and harassment and a charge of neglect of a care-dependent person. Barbara Girdish denied all charges, stating she "did the best I could" and remains in jail awaiting trial (Brawshaw, 2016; Kane, 2016).

It is clear that abuse of older adults is an important issue in the United States. Elder abuse has also been identified as an ongoing issue in other countries around the world (Roberto, 2016). The U.S. Census Bureau (2011) reported that 13% of the U.S. population was aged 65 or older with the older population projected to grow to 83.7 million by 2050. Unfortunately, some of these older adults will suffer from some form of abuse and/or exploitation at the hands of family members. Lachs and Pillemer (2015) provided detailed descriptions of the many types of injuries experienced by older adults in their guide for written for physicians on how to recognize physical elder abuse. They also outlined signs of neglect, including malnutrition and lack of cleanliness. After their review of the literature, Lacks and Pillemer concluded that at least 10% of older adults in the United States experience some form of abuse every year. As Whitaker (2018) explained, elder abuse can be physical, but is often psychological or financial. He outlined some of the ways in which the U.S. Department of Justice is fighting against this behavior.

7.1.1 Vulnerability in Older Adults

Older adults are at greater risk for abuse than younger adults for a number of reasons. Physically, they may be more prone to injuries from any type of assault than younger adults. [An example of this can be seen in a national study of those injured by crimes of all types involving assault. Those over 65 were more likely to require medical attention for their injuries than crime victims under the age of 65 (Bachman, Lachs, & Meloy, 2004).] Poor health can also be a risk factor, especially for neglect (Burnes et al., 2015). Another factor for older adults may be that they are not as likely to be living with a caregiver who is committed to them. In their random sample of New York state adults aged 60 or older, Burnes et al. (2015) noted that those who were not living with a spouse or other intimate partner were more likely to experience some form of abuse (See CDC, 2018b for further information).

Another major risk factor is cognitive impairment, which is more likely in older adults (Dong, Chen, & Simon, 2014). More than 5.5 million adults aged 65 or older are believed to be suffering from Alzheimer's disease (National Institute on Aging, 2020). Higher rates of physical and emotional abuse, as well as neglect have been reported for older adults with dementia (Dong et al., 2014). Research has shown that as dementia progresses, so does risk of all forms of elder abuse. Older adults with cognitive impairment living at home often depend on their abuser for care and may not be able to report this abuse to Adult Protective Services (Cooney, Howard, & Lawlor, 2006). This can be because they are not mentally able to do this, or it may be a result of the helplessness they feel because of their dependency on the abuser (Bornstein, 2019).

Many older adults need some form of assistance in daily living because of physical or mental limitations or both. Most older adults with long-term care needs rely on partners, other family members and sometimes on friends to provide assistance. The willingness of these people to provide needed care often determines whether older adults can remain in their home or must live in an assisted living facility. In fact, 50% of older adults who have a long-term care need but no family available to care for them are in nursing homes, while only 7% who have a family caregiver available are in institutional settings (Family Caregiver Alliance, 2017).

Case Example from our Files
The situation involves Ms. M., an older woman living in her home, who increasingly needs physical help due to arthritis and diabetic complications. After inviting her nephew to live with her to "help out", Ms. M. complains to her personal care aide that her nephew demands access to her money (financial exploitation) but that she cannot deny him because without him she would not be able to manage in her home. Ms. M. absolutely does not want to live in a nursing facility. The nephew is observed being verbally abusive to his aunt by the home health nurse and is reported to Adult Protective Services (APS). The APS social worker visits and assesses Ms. M's situation. Ms. M. admits that she is being exploited and that she doesn't like how her nephew behaves but refuses to admit anything in court or give access to any records. She is fully capacitated cognitively and able to make such decisions independently. APS stays in contact with her by phone on a monthly basis for the better part of a year seeing if she wishes to change her mind. At 13 months, she reveals that she may want to talk again because she is in terrible pain. Her nephew has been taking her oxycodone for last 2 months, and she cannot live in all this pain.

This case example from Mulvaney's (2016) clinical work illustrates how older adults often want to remain in their own home and will do whatever it takes to avoid a nursing facility placement. As older adults become more physically challenged due to chronic illness, in this case diabetic complications and arthritis, they need assistance and may turn to a family member to move in with them to help with activities of daily living. They continue to need help from their caregiver and may not seek outside assistance even when that relative becomes abusive. In this case, Ms. M. put up with verbal abuse and financial exploitation. It was only when her physical pain became unbearable due to her nephew stealing her pain medication that she finally reached out for help from APS. Even when abused, many older adults needing someone to take care of them may not seek help or even report the abuse, since they wish to remain in their home (Jackson, 2017).

7.1.2 Identifying Abuse of the Older Victim

As discussed in Chap. 9, the process of identifying any form of family abuse or violence is difficult. Much abuse is never identified. Even when reported to the police, or other agencies such as Adult Protective Services (APS), the report may not be formally investigated. The investigation itself often leads to distress within the family and estrangement of the elder adult and from other members of the family who are concerned about the person accused of abuse (Labrum & Solomon, 2015). When the abuse is confirmed, this can have other consequences for the older person. One of the most serious of these is that those found to be abused in their home setting may be forced to enter assisted living, or be given a financial or legal guardian (Jackson, 2017).

One study estimated that only one out of every 25 cases of elder abuse was reported to authorities (Lifespan of Greater Rochester, 2011). Unlike the situation for battered women, older adults very rarely make a formal report to authorities about the abuse they are receiving. An older person may not want others to know about the abuse either because of embarrassment, or believing he or she is somehow responsible for what is happening. Realistic fears of punishment from the abuser may also keep someone from reporting abuse. Others may be concerned that there is no real help available. For many, there are concerns about being removed from the home and placed in a senior care facility if abuse is confirmed (Jackson, 2017; Roberto, 2016). Because of these factors, it may be difficult for abused older people to freely tell APS about what has been happening to them. When suspected elder abuse is suspected and reported by a concerned neighbor or someone else with knowledge of the situation, the abuse may not be confirmed by the older adult. Box 7.1 outlines some of the steps that can be taken by the APS staff member investigating the complaint to facilitate disclosure to APS by the older person.

Box 7.1: What the Social Worker or Other Professional Should Do if Elder Abuse is Suspected

Create a Safe Environment for Discussion. Remove any intimidating factors that may hinder the older adult from having an open discussion. This may mean moving to another room or asking to speak to the client and the caregiver separately. Recall that most abusers are well known to the victim and many live in the same home.

Use or Establish a Trusting Relationship. If you have not already done so, create a trusting relationship with the older adult. It is important to achieve mutual respect and develop a bond. This will allow the older adult to let down defenses and speak in confidence about fears, concerns, wants and desires that will assist you in developing a resolution to their situation. Recall that if you are a Mandated Reporter (p. 16) you should have informed the person of this in an early meeting or visit so the person can make informed choices about what he or she wishes to tell you.

Engage in Discussion about the Suspected Abuse. Using soft, non-confrontational and non-judgmental words helps to set the person at ease. NEVER begin by saying, "Has someone been abusing, hitting, or threatening you?" This could cause the older adult to feel very uncomfortable by adding additional pressure to an existing stressful, degrading and embarrassing situation.

Use "I" statements and give examples and choices. You might say, "I've seen people with bruises on their arms; sometimes they come from people bumping in to things, falling down, or someone grabbing them or pushing them.

Which one happened to you?" Another example could be stated as, "Sometimes people get angry when caring for someone; does this happen to you?" Remember every time you get a person to answer, "yes," to a question it opens a door for further discussion.

Pay attention to verbal and nonverbal communication. Use observation statements such as, "I notice when I start talking about your daughter you become nervous or stop talking. Why is that?"

Determine Your Next Course of Action. Deciding what course of action to take next should be based on the severity of the situation. The degree of risk and the presence of imminent danger for the older adult will determine the next course of action. Please refer to the Reporting Section (p. 13) for additional guidance. It is also a good idea to consult with your supervisor and/or administrator before making a report or to get additional ideas about the appropriate way to proceed.

Educate the Client and Possibly the Caregiver about Elder Abuse and Next Steps. Depending upon the situation, this step may occur before step four. If you have determined that the person is not being abused but is at risk for abuse, then education and prevention efforts are very important. Please see the section on Prevention (p. 10) for more information on what you will discuss with the client.

If you suspect abuse, see if you can empower the client to report it him or herself. This is beneficial because it will encourage the older adult to regain a sense of dignity, increase self-esteem, autonomy and confidence. In the event the older adult does not wish to report it, you must then file the report (p. 13) with Adult Protective Services. You will find information on making a report in the next section.

As the older adult and/or caregiver may become angry, assess for and assure your own safety. For the sake of the helping relationship, it is often best to let the older adult know that you are the person making the report and that this is necessary to fulfill your duties as a Mandated Reporter (p. 16). This may minimize the sense of betrayal and possible mistrust in the relationship. If the older adult does not want to submit a report, inform the consumer you will continue to follow-up and leave your business card if they need to contact you.

(Belinger, Davis, & Fulmore, 2010, pp. 11–12) (*permission has been obtained for this material*)

Even if a formal report is made, professionals and paraprofessionals working with older adults may not be adequately trained to detect signs of abuse and the report may not be taken seriously (Gallione et al., 2017). In a national study, Breckman et al. (2018) found that 30% of their sample reported knowing a relative, friend or neighbor who had experienced some form of elder abuse. About 60%

further stated that they had tried to help in some way, but many found their attempts to assist to be ineffective. It was not clear in this study if a formal report was filed with APS by those knowing about the abuse of an older adult.

7.1.3 Types of Elder Abuse within a Family Setting

Abuse of older adults can take many forms. Box 7.2 shows the detailed definitions for types of maltreatment of elders published by the U.S. government through the Centers for Disease Control website. As can be seen, this abuse can be physical violence, unwanted sexual contact, emotional abuse, neglect, or financial abuse. Similar definitions for IPV or child abuse can also be seen on the CDC website. For elder abuse, there is the addition of the category of financial abuse. As also occurs with other types of abuse within the family, many of the abused older adults experience more than one form of abuse, a situation labeled as polyvictimization (Ford & Delker, 2018). Heisler (2017) argued that greater awareness of polyvictimization was especially important for those providing services for older adults since multiple types of services may be needed.

Box 7.2: Defining Elder Abuse

According to the Centers for Disease Control (2018a): Elder abuse is an intentional act, or failure to act, by a caregiver or another person in a relationship involving an expectation of trust that causes or creates a risk of harm to an older adult. (An older adult is defined as someone age 60 or older.) Forms of elder abuse are below.

- **Physical Abuse:** the intentional use of physical force that results in acute or chronic illness, bodily injury, physical pain, functional impairment, distress, or death. Physical abuse may include, but is not limited to, violent acts such as striking (with or without an object or weapon), hitting, beating, scratching, biting, choking, suffocation, pushing, shoving, shaking, slapping, kicking, stomping, pinching, and burning.
- **Sexual Abuse or Abusive Sexual Contact:** forced or unwanted sexual interaction (touching and non-touching acts) of any kind with an older adult. This may include forced or unwanted:
  - Completed or attempted contact between the penis and the vulva or the penis and the anus involving penetration
  - Contact between the mouth and the penis, vulva, or anus
  - Penetration of the anal or genital opening of another person by a hand, finger, or other object
  - Intentional touching, either directly or through the clothing, of the genitalia, anus, groin, breast, inner thigh, or buttocks

These acts also qualify as sexual abuse if they are committed against a person who is not competent to give informed approval.

- **Emotional or Psychological Abuse:** verbal or nonverbal behavior that results in the infliction of anguish, mental pain, fear, or distress. Examples include behaviors intended to humiliate (e.g., calling names or insults), threaten (e.g., expressing an intent to initiate nursing home placement), isolate (e.g., seclusion from family or friends), or control (e.g., prohibiting or limiting access to transportation, telephone, money or other resources).
- **Neglect:** failure by a caregiver or other responsible person to protect an elder from harm, or the failure to meet needs for essential medical care, nutrition, hydration, hygiene, clothing, basic activities of daily living or shelter, which results in a serious risk of compromised health and safety. Examples include not providing adequate nutrition, hygiene, clothing, shelter, or access to necessary health care; or failure to prevent exposure to unsafe activities and environments.
- **Financial Abuse or Exploitation:** the illegal, unauthorized, or improper use of an older individual's resources by a caregiver or other person in a trusting relationship, for the benefit of someone other than the older individual. This includes depriving an older person of rightful access to, information about, or use of, personal benefits, resources, belongings, or assets. Examples include forgery, misuse or theft of money or possessions; use of coercion or deception to surrender finances or property; or improper use of guardianship or power of attorney.

Source: Centers for Disease Control (2018a). Elder abuse: Definitions. https://www.cdc.gov/violenceprevention/elderabuse/definitions.html [Retrieved August 2, 2018].

Data on the prevalence of elder abuse may be inconsistent across studies due to differences in operational definitions of abuse, limitations imposed by the type of data used and samples employed, and because of methodological differences across studies (Roberto, 2016). Many have argued that studies that rely on formal reports to APS also underestimate the extent of the problem. Many cases are not included in research studies, because they have not come to the attention of APS (Dong, Chen, Chang, & Simon, 2013; see Chap. 9). Even community studies (which may include cases not reported to APS) are probably incomplete. An additional complication is that abused elders may not want to alert others to the abuse even on an anonymous survey. Older adults with cognitive impairment or dementia may not able to participate in a community survey and thus would not be a part of the sample either.

We provide some data here from a few major studies, but the percentages reported in these studies do vary greatly. Acierno et al. (2010), in a national U.S. study of 5777 older adults, found that 1 in 10 respondents reported emotional, physical, sexual, neglect or financial abuse in the past year with neglect and financial exploitation as the most common types reported. In another study of the prevalence and risk factors for elder abuse and neglect in a random sample in New York State. Data were collected in 2009 from a sample of 4156 adults aged 60 or older who lived in the community and were determined to be "cognitively intact" (Burnes et al., 2015, p. 1907). Burnes et al. (2015) found the past-year prevalence of emotional abuse was 1.9%, physical abuse was 1.8%, and neglect was 1.8% with an overall abuse prevalence rate of 4.6%. Friedman, Santos, Liebel, Russ, and Conwell (2015) in a longitudinal study of elder abuse among older adults receiving home visiting nursing found neglect to be the most common form of maltreatment followed by psychological abuse and financial exploitation. Finally, Laumann, Leitsch, and Waite (2008) examined the prevalence of elder abuse in a nationally representative study, and reported that verbal abuse was the most common form of maltreatment followed by financial exploitation and physical abuse.

7.1.4 General Effects of Elder Abuse

As Roberto (2016) summarized in her review of the literature, older adults suffering from abuse may experience a variety of reactions in addition to physical injury, including declines in physical health as well as psychological well-being. She argued that the negative impact of sexual abuse may be especially traumatic, although this type of maltreatment has received little research attention. Psychological abuse may have quite negative effects, even though the older adult experiencing this may not even recognize this is happening.

Using data from the earlier National Elder Mistreatment Study, Acierno, Hernandez-Tejada, Anetzberger, Loew, and Muzzy (2017) examined people identified originally at age 60 to determine how they were doing 8 years later. They compared those identified as abused in the earlier study with those who had not been abused on four different outcomes: overall health, post-traumatic stress disorder, depression and generalized anxiety. These negative outcomes were 200 to 700 times more likely for the abused group. However, these long term negative effects were much reduced for abused elders who currently had good social support. Social support was measured with a scale containing items such as having someone they felt made them feel wanted, someone available if they needed help and someone who could give good advice. Other studies have indicated that those older adults with more than one type of abuse (polyvictimization) were likely to have worse outcomes than those with less abuse (Ford & Delker, 2018). Chapter 3 reviews the research on these and other reactions of people of all ages to victimization of all types.

7.1.5 Financial Exploitation

A special form of elder abuse involves taking money or other assets from the older adult. It may be the most common form of elder abuse (Williams, Racette, Hernandez-Tejada, & Acierno, 2017). One estimate was that annual losses because of financial exploitation of older adults in the U.S. were nearly $3 billion. This exploitation can take many forms. It can involve cashing checks sent to the older person or using their ATM card without their permission. Forging a signature on a financial document is another example (Wood & Lichtenberg, 2017). As Peterson et al. (2014) explained, although someone can experience financial abuse at any age, older adults may be more at risk for a number of reasons. First, they often have more money and other financial resources than younger people. They may be less well educated about money and have poorer mathematical skills generally. Wood and Lichtenberg (2017) demonstrated this empirically using a sample of 395 community dwelling older adults. Low mathematical literacy was a risk factor for financial exploitation while higher levels of mathematical skills were protective. Perhaps because having low mathematical skills, the older person may not even be aware of money being taken. Cognitive declines and Alzheimer's disease may also result in older adults being more vulnerable, since they may not have a good understanding of their finances (Lichtenberg, 2016).

Peterson et al. (2014), in a study using a sample of 4156 community-dwelling, cognitively-intact individuals aged 60 and older, identified a number of factors associated with risk for financial exploitation. A greater risk for such abuse was most common with older adults "traditionally considered to be economically, medically and sociodemographically vulnerable" (p. 1615). One of these demographic factors was being African-American and another was living in poverty. Other factors were the presence of numerous non-spousal household members, and having one or more impairments in activities of daily living. In another study based on a Pittsburgh sample, Beach, Schulz, Castle, and Rosen (2010) also found being African American was the most significant predictor of financial exploitation.

Although there is relatively little research that directly addresses this issue, it is believed that those with disadvantaged status in the U.S., such as low income individuals, migrant and seasonal farmworkers and their families, the homeless, and many racial and ethnic minority groups, may have relatively high rates of other forms of elder abuse as well (Jervis et al., 2016). Jervis and her colleagues discuss why research is lacking on these groups. One issue is lack of trust within these groups. Ways to overcome this research barrier are outlined.

7.1.6 *Neglect*

Like other forms of abuse, neglect can take many forms, including being completely abandoned by a caretaker (Rzeszut, 2017). In an analysis of data from the National Elder Mistreatment Study, Williams et al. (2017) found that neglect was a close second in prevalence to financial exploitation for a national sample of older U.S. adults living in the community. For those reporting any type of abuse, 34% reported neglect. These numbers do vary, though, depending on the definitions used. In their survey of New York State older residents, Burnes et al. (2015) reported that 2% of their sample had signs of neglect. Lower levels of neglect were found for those identifying as Hispanic than for other racial or ethnicity groups. They argued that this reflected a strong cultural value within Hispanics to take care of other family members.

One form of neglect of older adults is self-neglect (Dong, 2017). This occurs when someone is not able to provide proper food, water, clothing, shelter or personal hygiene for him or herself. Recognition of this situation by a family member or someone else who observes this may result in a report to APS. There has been relatively little research on this issue, but Dong suggests that older adults lacking financial resources or having cognitive impairment are more likely to self-neglect . Even when identified by APS, the older adult may resist any attempt to provide aid since this might require moving to some type of assisted living. One might argue that an extreme form of self-neglect is suicide. Fowler, Jack, Lyons, Betz, and Petrosky (2018), reporting on national U.S. data, noted that older white men had the highest rates of suicide among all groups within the U.S. Their suicide was often associated with prior depression.

7.1.6.1 Effects of Neglect

Effects of neglect can be malnutrition or other, sometimes serious, health consequences as seen in the case of Helen Girdish, described earlier in the chapter. One consequence of caretaker or self-neglect that may not be well-known is dental disease. This can also result from physical abuse or from lack of routine dental treatment. Petti (2018) outlined some of the specific dental issues that dentists might identify, arguing that dentists should routinely screen for evidence of neglect or other abuse. He did note, though, that accusations of abuse need to be carefully supported, since some people tend to avoid getting treatment for dental problems because of worry about having this reported to APS.

7.1.7 Physical Abuse

Another form of elderly abuse is physical assault. This was reported by 2% of Burnes et al.'s (2015) New York sample. Williams et al. (2017) also found that rates of physical abuse were relatively low relative to other forms of elder abuse. Physical abuse was often done either by a spouse or intimate partner, who is often a caregiver (Burnes et al., 2015). Physical abuse can also occur between adult children and older parents. An analysis of police reports and other legal documents indicated that physical violence against an older parent was generally precipitated by an argument, often involving confrontation about the abuse with the abuser (Rosen et al., 2016).

In 2010, the CDC and National Institute of Justice collaborated to collect national data on physical and emotional abuse from intimate partners. Rosay and Mulford (2017) reported on data from this national U.S. survey as it related to abuse of older adults. A total of 2185 individuals aged 70 or older who were involved in an intimate partner relationship were used as the sample. Twelve percent reported psychological or emotional abuse, 1.1% reported physical abuse and 0.7% reported sexual abuse. Overall, 14% of this older population reported some type of abuse in the last year, with some experiencing multiple forms of abuse. About ¼ of this reported abuse was done by an intimate partner. This can be a continuation of earlier IPV within the relationship or it can arise later in the relationship. Cheung, Tiwari, and Wang (2015) describe two case studies of IPV in older Chinese couples where the husbands engaged in violence toward their wives that demonstrate the dynamics of IPV among older adults.

7.1.7.1 Effects of Physical Abuse

Physical elder abuse can have a devastating impact. As in the case of Helen Girdish, described at the beginning of this chapter section, common physical consequences of elder abuse include welts, wounds, and other injuries (bruises, lacerations, dental and head injuries, broken bones, pressure sores); persistent physical pain and soreness; poor sleep; increased vulnerability to developing new illnesses (including sexually transmitted diseases); exacerbation of pre-existing health and mental health conditions; and increased risks for premature death (Lachs & Pillemer, 2015). Even experiencing modest abuse can increase the risk of subsequent death by 300% (Dong et al., 2009; Salari & Maxwell, 2016). As Salari and Maxwell noted, frail older individuals may be injured more severely than younger adults when assaulted by a partner.

7.1.8 Emotional or Psychological Abuse

Reported rates for emotional or psychological abuse are relatively low. For example, Burnes et al. (2015) found rates of emotional abuse of 2% of their New York sample. It was generally higher for those with cognitive impairments. A spouse or intimate partner was most likely the abuser (31%) although an adult child was nearly as likely to do this (30%). There is evidence that these rates are higher in some groups than others. In their comparison of African American older adults with other groups, Beach et al. (2010) found psychological abuse was more common for African Americans. The most commonly reported form of psychological abuse was being screamed at or yelled at. A caretaker stomping out of the room after an argument, or saying something deliberately hurtful were also relatively common forms of reported psychological abuse. Reported rates of 16% for African Americans and 7% for other groups in the Beach et al. study were much higher than found in the Burnes et al. (2015) study. This discrepancy in rates probably reflects the differing definitions of this type of abuse used in the two studies. The Burnes et al. only considered "very serious" (p. 1907) emotional abuse.

7.1.8.1 Effects of Emotional Abuse

The effect of being psychologically abused by a family member or intimate partner as an older adult is similar to the effects of experiencing this type of abuse at a younger age (see Chaps. 3, 4 and 6). Psychologically abused older adults may experience emotional distress, symptoms of depression, and post-traumatic stress. These effects can be quite upsetting. Research data indicated that verbal abuse resulted in a greater decline in mental health status than physical abuse alone (Dong et al., 2009; Fulmer, Rodgers, & Pelger, 2014; Mouton, Rodabough, Rovi, Brzyski, & Katerndahl, 2010).

7.1.9 Sexual Abuse

A final form of elder abuse that has received very little research attention is sexual abuse (Bows, 2017). It is included, though, in the CDC's listing of types of elder abuse (see Box 7.1). In a review of published literature, Bows stated that sexual abuse was a rare form of elderly abuse, but that it did occur. Women were most often the victims, but victimization was occasionally reported for men (typically in nursing facilities). Although findings were not consistent across studies, it did appear that most sexual abuse of older adults was done by a spouse or intimate partner. For women, vaginal injury was more common after forced sex than for younger female victims.

7.1.10 Perpetrators of Elder Abuse

7.1.10.1 Family Caregivers of Older Adults

In considering who is most likely to abuse an older adult within a family setting, we first consider who the informal caregivers are for older adults who need some assistance in daily living or who want a family member to live with them. Women, usually spouses or adult daughters, provide the bulk of informal care to older adult relatives who have long-term care needs, but other family members may also assume this role.

For some of these informal and unpaid caregivers, the experience may be difficult and stressful, especially if they do not have the resources or skills to provide the help needed. For example, some caregivers may suffer physical abuse from the individual they are caring for, especially for an older adult with dementia, making the situation even more difficult for the caregiver (Isham, Hewison, & Bradbury-Jones, 2017). Violence against the caregiver is one of the strongest predictors of nursing home placement (Wharton & Ford, 2014).

Case Example from our Files

Mr. A is an older married gentleman who has a slowly progressing Alzheimer's type dementia. He is a retired pastor, and his wife and family have only known him as a gentle and patient person. His wife is his primary caregiver. Mr. A has become increasingly angry and combative in response to his losses and inability to function, reverting back to temperament which his brother says he showed as a young man. His wife has promised to take care of him at home and is committed to caring for him. Initially she hides from the family that he is hitting her and how afraid of him she is. One day, he breaks his wife's arm. At this point, he must be admitted to a nursing facility where he remains combative and angry. He is excessively medicated (aka, chemically restrained) by the nursing home staff in order to "manage" his aggressive behavior.

In this situation from Mulvaney's case files, the client's wife was committed to caring for her husband in their home, but his combative and violent behavior, as a result of his advancing dementia, led to an unsafe and unmanageable situation. This resulted in a nursing home placement where the client was heavily medicated as a means of controlling his aggression. Antipsychotic medications may be used for such purposes and can sometimes, unfortunately, lead to adverse outcomes in older adults with dementia (Bonner et al., 2015; Dennis et al., 2017).

Although caring for someone can be stressful, at the same time, there can be positive experiences associated with caregiving, and for most family caregivers, these often outweigh the negative experiences (Brown & Brown, 2014; Roth, Fredman, & Haley, 2015). Roth et al. (2015), in a detailed review of the existing literature, argued that the large majority of studies have *not* shown a general negative effect of caregiving for an older adult in the family. They further argue that the media have given much more attention to those few studies that do show negative effects.

7.1.10.2 Characteristics of those Who Abuse Older Adults

Stress related to the demands of taking care of an older relative has often been identified as one of the factors that can lead to the caregiver becoming abusive toward the older person being cared for (Brown & Brown, 2014; Roth et al., 2015). Abusers do tend to have other predisposing factors in addition to the stress of caregiving though. Some elder abuse is done by a violent partner, continuing or reversing an earlier pattern of IPV as one person becomes more dependent on the other.

For adult children, earlier experiences with parental abuse as children can be predictive of their later physically abusing an aged parent (Campbell Reay & Browne, 2001; Storey, 2019). Witnessing of IPV in parents as a child is also predictive if later abuse of one of these parents as an older adult (Storey, 2019). As described in Box 7.3, such maltreatment of parents by children can begin when the children are young or later as adolescents.

Box 7.3: Abuse of Parents by Children

As discussed in Chap. 6, there appears to be a cycle of violence such that children who are abused or witness IPV in their parents may grow up to be abusive to their own children, perpetuating a pattern of child abuse across generations. A similar pattern exists for those who witness parental IPV who may then engage in IPV with their own partners as adults. There is data indicating that another aspect of this transmission of violent behavior across generations may also apply to abuse of older adults in the family. O'Hara et al. (2019) provided data on the high numbers of adolescents who become involved in the criminal justice system because of violence toward a parent or caregiver. They described some of the therapeutic interventions they had been developing to work with these violent adolescents. Gabriel et al. (2018) reported on an interview study of UK parents and children about why children and adolescents might engage in physical or verbal abuse against their parents. Some of the explanations noted were that the children were angry about earlier or current abuse. Another explanation of abuse of the mother was that the son was modeling behavior seen in his abusive father.

The following example from our files demonstrates another type of situation where an adult child becomes abusive to his parents. They live in a family with violence among multiple members of the family. It also shows how drug use might elevate risk for abuse.

Case Example #22

Initial contact and presenting problem: Mark is a 19 year old unemployed single white male brought to the psychiatric health facility inpatient unit for evaluation by the local city police. Mark has a history of phencyclidine (PCP) use and was released from jail only 4 days ago after an 8 day stay on charges of "driving under the influence"—he goes to court next week. Tonight Mark got into an argument with his stepfather and his mother (all three had been drinking since early afternoon), Mark pulled a knife and threatened to kill them and when police arrived, he had already cut himself and was threatening to kill himself, stating he has nothing to live for. Upon evaluation Mark is extremely agitated and labile, so the police were asked to stand by during the mental health evaluation. Mark was subsequently hospitalized on the basis of danger to self and others.

Follow up family meeting: One week later, after Mark was sufficiently detoxed from the PCP and alcohol, a meeting was convened with Mark, his stepfather and his mother. When confronted about the incident with the knife, Mark denied he intended to hurt anyone, i.e. "I was just messing around". This precipitated an argument amongst the three family members, escalating to the point that the stepfather was asked to step out in the hallway while the social worker attempted to intervene with Mark and his mother. Mother states that her husband hits her but then admitted that she has thrown hot coffee at him and once hit him over the head with a frying pan. Mark states both of his parents have threatened him and it seems like alcohol plays a major role in the numerous incidents of violence that have occurred. Mark says he uses drugs and "sometimes does stuff" because he is frustrated over not having a job; mother says she drinks because Mark won't get a job and she gets frustrated. The stepfather, once he rejoined the conversation, blames both his wife and Mark for his violence "if they'd shape up, I wouldn't have to smack them". None of the family members is interested in getting counseling, and blame each other for all their troubles.

Many abusers have been found to have mental illness of some type. This might take the form of bipolar, major depression, or schizophrenia related disorders (Labrum & Solomon, 2015). Labrum, Solomon, and Bressi (2015) recruited a national sample of 217 women via an online survey to explore the rates of abuse of older women by a relative with a psychiatric disorder. Findings showed 15% of survey respondents experienced physical abuse in the past 6 months, 20% experienced financial abuse, and 42% experienced psychological abuse committed by their relative with a psychiatric disorder.Using data from the National Elder Mistreatment Study, Labrum and Solomon (2018) examined the victim, perpetrator and interaction characteristics in cases of elder abuse committed by a relative with substance abuse and/or mental health conditions. Findings showed that of 622 incidents of psychological elder abuse, 34% of the perpetrators had these characteristics. Further analysis indicated that the abusers with mental health issues were more likely to be have had a history of troubles with the police. They were also more likely to be living with the older person being abused and were often unemployed. These data were interpreted as indicating that the abusers were financially dependent on the older person, a finding reported in other studies. Emotional abuse for these perpetrators was also associated with their having fewer friends.

7.1.11 *Interventions for Preventing and Reducing Abuse of Older Adults*

Interventions to prevent and reduce the occurrence of elder abuse have been developed at the community level and at the provider level. Such interventions generally address social isolation and enhancement of social support, providing education about elder abuse, using multidisciplinary teams to address the complex nature of elder abuse, and enhancing the effectiveness of adult protective services agencies.

Community interventions aimed at enhancing an older adult's social support is one avenue for preventing elder abuse. Such interventions typically focus on increasing the individual's mental and emotional resilience in dealing with stress and have been shown to lower the risk of abuse (Cooper & Livingston, 2016). An example of such a program is "Eliciting Change in At-Risk Elders (ECARE)" (Mariam, McClure, Robinson & Yang, 2015). Through a partnership with local law enforcement, ENCARE helps suspected victims of elder abuse and self-neglect by (1) building alliances between the older adult and his/her family members, (2) connecting the older adult to programs providing services designed to reduce the risk for future abuse; and (3) using motivational interviewing techniques to help resolve ambivalence the older adult may have about reporting abuse and making other challenging life changes. Mariam, et al. (2015), in an evaluation of ECARE effectiveness, found that the factors associated with elder abuse decreased during the intervention process.

Providing education about elder abuse at the community level can help dispel myths (for example, if an older adult is really being abused, they would leave) and change attitudes about the abuse of older adults which may then impact individual behavior. One study showed that education interventions can alter attitudes toward and tolerance for elder abuse. However, such education efforts must continue over time to maintain such gains (Hayslip, Reinberg, & William, 2015).

Because situations involving elder abuse are often complex, and no single professional or community resource is sufficient in terms of expertise and resources, multidisciplinary teams involving physicians, social workers, law-enforcement, attorneys, and other community stakeholders may be involved in protecting the abused older adult and providing interventions to resolve the situation effectively (Connolly, Brandl & Breckman, 2014; Lachs & Pillemer, 2015).

Adult Protectives Services (APS) organizations also play a significant role in providing professional intervention. Where APS agencies are housed varies across states and localities and there also are variations in how services are provided. In an effort to support Adult Protective Service Agencies, enhance elder abuse response, and encourage consistency in the interventions provided, the Administration on Community Living (ACL) in collaboration with the U.S. Department of Health and Human Services produced a document entitled Final National Voluntary Consensus Guidelines for State Adult Protective Services Systems in 2016 which outlines best practices for APS services.

7.2 Sibling Abuse

In this section, we discuss another form of violence and abuse within the family, that of abusive or aggressive behavior between siblings. Many have suggested that sibling violence is the most common form of family violence in the United States, surpassing both child abuse and IPV (Finkelhor, Turner, Shattuck, & Hamby, 2015; Morrill, 2017). Although fighting among siblings may not be taken seriously by many people, there is clear evidence that such violence can result in high levels of trauma (Perkins, Spira, & Key, 2018). Such trauma may persist over the life course, and might even result in elder abuse when the formerly abused sibling becomes the caretaker of an aged parent (Perkins et al., 2018).

Case Example from our Files

An elementary school teacher called in a report of suspected child abuse to children's protective services. A CPS worker visited the school to assess whether 10-year-old Kelsey was being abused at home. The worker immediately noticed that Kelsey had a series of bruises, both new and in the process of healing, up and down her arms. She also had some fresh scratches on her neck. After assuring Kelsey that her purpose was not to get anyone in trouble but to make sure Kelsey was safe, the CPS worker asked the girl who had been hurting her. Reluctantly and tearfully, she blurted out, "John always hurts me. He beats me up and breaks my stuff. He even comes into my room at night after I have gone to bed and holds a pillow over my face. I hate him!". The worker consults her notes and sees that the child's stepfather is named John. "So your dad has been hurting you?", she asks. Kelsey looks puzzled and replied, "No, I said John—my big brother!".

This case from our personal files describes a situation encountered by Fusco when she was a new and unexperienced CPS worker (names were changed for anonymity). Further investigation in the above case revealed that Kelsey was being physically and emotionally abused by her stepbrother who was 6 years older than she was. The parents were not aware of this abuse and considered the children's physical interactions to be "roughhousing" even though their daughter was much younger and smaller than her brother. In fact, they frequently had John babysit his younger sister and viewed her complaints about her brother as a form of retaliation because he had limited her access to snacks and television when he was in charge. The parents, who were a married, educated, middle-class couple, were outraged that their family was being investigated by CPS, and they vehemently denied any abuse was taking place. As the research discussed below indicates, this story is not an unusual one.

Before describing the dynamics of sibling violence and abuse, we first look briefly at the general family context in which this sibling abuse may or may not occur. Sibling relationships are important throughout one's life (Greif & Woolley, 2016). As Dirks, Persram, Recchia, and Howe (2015) explained, sibling relationships contribute in many ways to children's development. These are frequent and involuntary relationships that involve sharing living space. Children tend to spend more time with siblings than with anyone else, including parents. Children tend to model behavior they observe in their older brothers and sisters. Sibling interactions teach children how social relationships function. These relationships may have very strong positive aspects as well as potentially destructive conflict. On the positive side, siblings engage in mutual play, sharing of toys as well as secrets. They also show affection to one another and comfort one another. If these relationships are close, warm interactions, they can be protective when problems arise with others (Harper, Padilla-Walker, & Jensen, 2014). Older children may take on a supportive parental-type role with a younger sibling (Callaghan, Alexander, Fellin, & Sixsmith, 2016).

At the same time, some physical violence and other forms of aggression are quite common in siblings, especially in younger children. Although parents may be concerned about this, and may worry about an older sibling hurting a younger brother or sister (Tucker & Finkelhor, 2017), there appears to be a general acceptability of siblings hitting or using other violence against each other (Hardy et al., 2009). In one demonstration of this, using a sample of college students asked to rate the acceptability of various types of sibling aggression, Hardy and her colleagues found that an older sibling hitting a younger sibling was rated as close to being completely acceptable. Gender of the siblings involved did not affect these ratings. The majority of the study participants indicated being both victims and perpetrators of both verbal and physical sibling aggression in their own childhoods.

The case below provides an example of emotional abuse along with physical abuse between brothers. It also illustrates how parents often ignore or minimize sibling violence. For additional information about this case, see Case #27 in the case Appendix.

Case Example #27
Melanie and Johnathan own a number of franchised restaurants and are a very wealthy family. They live in an exclusive neighborhood and their children attend a private day school. The school contacted social services out of concern about the relationship between Anthony and Lewis. Though the boys are in different classes and different years, they have often been seen around school arguing, and Lewis was caught with two of his friends holding down and giving Anthony a "swirly," putting his face in the toilet of the boys' room and flushing it…When the boys were interviewed separately, Anthony stated that his life is horrible and it is because of Lewis. Lewis has stolen his money, often hits him, threatens him, and teases him relentlessly by calling him a "girl" and a "faggot."…Lewis says that Anthony is just a crybaby and is always trying to get him in trouble with their parents….The Elwoods were very concerned about the involvement of social services, and while they engaged a lawyer to sit in on meetings, were willing to cooperate with interviews. Melanie stated she knows that the boys don't often get along, but that they love each other and will grow out of their difficulties. Johnathan stated that the boys are competitive as he would expect them to be, they are both bright and full of potential and that competition prepares them for attending an elite college and eventually entering the business world. Both parents deny that there is excessive physical violence between the boys and both deny there is any kind of emotional abuse… Ongoing in-home services were provided to the family, including extensive counseling both separately and together for Anthony and Lewis.

As discussed in Chap. 6, children raised in homes where one or both parents are violent experience a number of negative outcomes as a result of this experience. It appears that one of these consequences is an increased level of sibling violence (Piotrowski, Tachie, & Cameranesi, 2017). As mentioned in Chap. 6, one effect of parental IPV seen in their children is higher levels of aggressiveness in those children, either because of modeling or other factors. Some of this aggression may be directed towards siblings. Research has indicated that both sibling physical and verbal aggression were increased when children were exposed to parental IPV (Piotrowski et al., 2017). Sibling aggression occurs as well in children not exposed to parental violence and in families with no other form of violence. However, rates are even higher in families where other forms of interpersonal aggression occurs.

7.2.1 Prevalence

Unfortunately, there are no standard definitions of sibling violence or aggression. Since there is no agreement about the terminology used to describe this violence, researchers interchangeably use the terms *violence, aggression, conflict*, and *abuse*.

While sibling *sexual* abuse is actionable by child welfare agencies, physical violence often is not (see Chap. 9). One reason for this may be that since young children engage in some type of physical aggression so often, many consider this to be normal behavior and would not classify it as abuse or even as abnormal. Even sibling sexual contact (such as *playing doctor)* may be considered as normal childhood behavior, so it can be difficult to determine when these incidents cross the line to abuse.

An early examination of sibling physical violence came from Gelles and Straus's (1979) work on the National Family Violence Study. This study utilized a representative national sample. They explored the presence of sibling violence in families that had two or more children between the ages of 3–17 living at home. Their results showed that four out of five children reported using some type of violence against a sibling during the past year, with more than half reporting serious physical violence such as kicking, biting, punching, hitting with an object, or beating up a sister or brother. These high levels of sibling physical violence were found in homes with and without parental IPV.

Subsequent studies have continued to indicate high levels of sibling aggression, although the reported percentages are often lower. Button and Gealt (2010) examined sibling violence using the Delaware Secondary School Student Survey. The survey is administered annually to all eighth and eleventh grade classrooms in all public schools within the state of Delaware. The Button and Gealt (2010) study included only those who lived with a sibling, creating a total sample size of 8122 students. More than 40% of the students reported some type of sibling aggression during the past school year. The most common form was shoving pushing, and slapping (32%) followed by verbal abuse (31%). They also found that a high percentage of youth who reported sibling violence also reported both child maltreatment by a caregiver (72%) and/or witnessing domestic violence (55%) in their home.

Tucker et al. (2013) investigated the question of whether some of the reported sibling aggression was reactive, responding to aggression directed toward them by a brother or sister. A sample of 8th and 12th grade students were surveyed about aggression involving the sibling closest in age. In this study, 25% of the boys and girls in the sample reported using some form of aggression against a sibling. Data indicated that boys were more likely than girls to initiate the sibling aggression, although initiation was reported by both boys and girls. These same students were surveyed again 4 years later, now averaging the age of 21 (Tucker, Sharp, Van Gundy, & Rebellon, 2019). Those who had reported earlier sibling aggression now reported less warmth and emotional engagement with that sibling, and were less likely to provide emotional support to that sibling. Thus, the earlier aggression appeared to be related to having a poorer relationship as this sample entered adulthood.

In one of the more recent national surveys, Finkelhor et al. (2015) reported on data from a national study done by the CDC every 3 years since 2008 on children's experiences with all types of violence. Looking at the 2014 data, 4000 children between the ages of 0 and 17 were surveyed by telephone. Children aged 10 and older were questioned directly, but a caregiver provided information for younger children. One category in the survey was "assault by a juvenile sibling" (Finkelhor et al., 2015, p. 748). Overall 21% of boys and 23% of girls reported experiencing such a sibling assault in the last year. Brother to brother assault was reported by

26% of the sample and sister to sister by 12%. Boys were somewhat more likely than girls to be aggressors and to be aggressed against. When analyzed by age, those aged 6–9 were most likely to have been assaulted by a sibling, at a rate of 31% in the last year. Rates were lower for younger and for older children. Since this survey was done several times, researchers were able to look at national trends over time for exposure to all types of violence. Their overall data table indicated that experiences with violence for the children surveyed had declined between 2008 and 2014 in nearly every category *except* sibling violence, which showed a very small increase. Thus, although violence in general may be decreasing in the U.S. over time (see Chap. 1), this does not appear to be true for sibling aggression, at least in recent years. Note, though, that the reported percentages in the more recent studies are much lower than those in the earlier Gelles and Straus (1979) study.

7.2.2 Forms of Sibling Aggression

Sibling aggression falls into three main categories. First is physical violence, which can range from pushing and shoving to using weapons against a sibling. Second is emotional abuse, which includes teasing and name-calling that has a negative psychological effect upon the recipient. Both types of sibling abuse may occur in the family. Research has indicated that physical and emotional sibling abuse are highly correlated (Piotrowski & Cameranesi, 2018). Third, and perhaps the most complex form of sibling aggression is sexual violence directed toward a sibling. This is further discussed in a later section below.

7.2.2.1 Physical Violence

Sibling violence is defined as a pattern of aggression toward a sibling with the intent to cause harm and gain power and control (Caffaro & Conn-Caffaro, 1998). As mentioned earlier, society does not tend to identify the often low-level physical violence against a sibling as deviant and often normalizes this behavior (Gelles & Comell, 1985). People often attribute sibling violence to sibling rivalry, and it is typically viewed as a something that children will eventually grow out of with no negative consequences (Eriksen & Jensen, 2009). There is evidence that both U.S. and Canadian parents often believe sibling aggression to be beneficial to social development, believing that it may help children learn how to successfully manage conflicts in their future extrafamilial relationships (DeKeseredy & Ellis, 1997; Gelles & Comell, 1985). The result is that sibling violence is rarely perceived as a problem and goes both unreported and unaddressed.

Physical aggression occurs in children not exposed to parental IPV as well as in those whose parents are violent toward one another. In a study of families recruited through newspaper ads, Piotrowski and Cameranesi (2018) observed sibling pairs in a waiting room while their mothers were being interviewed. They found that 27% of the children engaged in physical aggression with a sibling in the group with parental IPV, while this was true for 20% of those whose parents were not violent toward one another. They further noted that much of the sibling violence they observed or as reported by the mother was mutual—siblings tended to fight back when assaulted by a brother or sister.

Empirical research examining sibling violence often relies on a measure called the Conflict Tactics Scale (see Chaps. 5 and 6), which asks about specific acts of physical aggression ranging from pushing or slapping to assault with a weapon. Standard scoring of this measure leads to classifying any of these acts as *violent*, and makes no assessment of intent or injury (Khan & Cooke, 2013). Khan and Cooke argued that researchers needed to consider the severity of sibling aggression, and proposed a new scale that did this. Using a sample of adolescents identified as violent offenders from Great Britain, they found that severe sibling violence most frequently involved forceful punching, kicking or biting. They did note, though, that even among the sample using such severe violence, most often there was no injury or only minor injury in the child who was assaulted.

Other data indicate that sibling violence can be extreme, and may, in a few rare cases, result in homicide (Peck & Heide, 2012). Peck and Heide (2012) analyzed arrest records in the U.S. from 1976 to 2007, looking at details of cases involving arrests of juveniles for sibling homicide. Over this period, these homicides averaged about 100 per year. The most common pattern was brother to brother, followed by brother to sister, sister to sister, with sister to brother least common. Guns were often used. These sibling homicide arrests were most common in the South, especially for brother-to-brother homicide. Sibling homicide was least common in the Northeastern part of the country and in the West. Over the time period studied, there was an overall decline in these cases. Other data looking at homicide among siblings of all ages indicated that it is more likely that adult men perpetrate homicide against an adult brother rather than children killing a sibling (Bourget & Gagne, 2006).

7.2.2.2 Emotional or Psychological Abuse

This abuse can take the form of intimidation, belittling, destroying possessions, and even harming pets (Wiehe, 2000). Another form of emotional sibling abuse is bullying. Skinner and Kowalski (2013) asked college students to describe instances in which they had been bullied by a sibling or they themselves bullied a brother or sister. Teasing was the most commonly noted form of bullying, followed by being physically abused or being excluded or ignored by the sibling. More than half of the students saw sibling bullying as acceptable and 85% felt it was something to be expected. Eighty five percent indicated they had done this themselves. Not surprisingly, the narratives describing the bullying behavior indicated that perpetrators of sibling bullying saw less negative impact than did the recipients of the bullying. Other forms of emotional abuse identified by Morrill (2017) were threats to hurt one's pet, threats to or actually destroying possessions, or being told that no one in the family cares about him or her. Vandalism or stealing of property was one of the most common forms of sibling aggression directed against young siblings (Tucker, Finkelhor, Shattuck, & Turner, 2013).

7.2.2.3 Impact of Physical or Emotional Sibling Aggression

As noted, definitions of sibling aggression vary widely. Some forms of sibling aggression may not have long-term effects, but there is clear evidence of some children experiencing a variety of psychological and behavioral effects both in childhood, adolescence and adulthood as a result of some form of sibling abuse (Greif & Woolley, 2016; Morrill, 2017). While the effects of sibling violence look similar to those of child abuse by a parent or caregiver (see Chap. 6), some scholars have argued that the impact of sibling violence is likely worse since it involves not only abuse from the sibling, but parents who fail to protect the victim from harm (Green, 1984). As discussed earlier, it can be difficult to interpret specific effects of sibling abuse since they often co-occur within a family with other forms of violence as well.

Some studies do indicate clear negative consequences of sibling aggression. Analyses from a large national probability sample of 3599 children and adolescents (Tucker et al., 2014) revealed that sibling violence in the past year was associated with significantly more mental health problems. Mental health status was measured with the Trauma Symptom Checklist for children. This measure included scores for anger, depression, anxiety, dissociation and post-traumatic stress. This association of being the recipient of sibling aggression and decreased mental health was apparent for both mild and severe forms of sibling abuse as well as for those who had experienced just one type of sibling violence. Those who experienced multiple types showed even greater negative effects. While physical peer aggression is sometimes thought of as more damaging, their data showed that sibling psychological and emotional violence were equally harmful. A later analysis of these same data (van Berkel, Tucker, & Finkelhor, 2018) found that these effects of sibling aggression on mental health could be seen even if the effects associated with child abuse or neglect were factored out. The long term effects of sibling aggression over and above these other effects of abuse were also manifested in higher rates of delinquency.

Others have also reported negative effects of sibling aggression. In a longitudinal study of children who had experienced sibling bullying at the age of 12, Bowes, Wolke, Joinson, Lereya, and Lewis (2014) surveyed these same children at the age of 18. Compared to their peers who had not been bullied, those who had experienced sibling bullying were twice as likely to report depression, self-harm and anxiety. Effects were stronger for those who experienced this bullying more often.

In another large survey mentioned earlier that was done in Delaware, Button and Gealt (2010) surveyed students in the 8th and 11th grade. Overall, 42% of students said they had experienced some form of violence or other abuse from a sibling, with shoving, pushing and slapping being the most common. This was twice the rate of reported parental violence experienced by the students. Those reporting sibling violence were found to be more likely to also report using tobacco, alcohol or marijuana. They also reported more delinquent behavior such as stealing from a store, cheating on a test, or destroying property of others. Such effects were stronger for those experiencing more serious violence from siblings. Violent behavior towards others was also higher for those reporting physical or emotional aggression from siblings than for those not reporting any sibling violence.

Other effects of experiencing sibling abuse have also been reported. College students with a history of sibling violence victimization showed lower self-esteem and social competence than their peers (Morrill-Richards & Leierer, 2010). Adolescents have been found to run away from home if they want to get away from abusive siblings (Morrill, 2017). Those experiencing sibling abuse may also have difficulties in developing close relationships with others as adolescents or adults (Morrill, 2017).

7.2.3 Sexual Abuse by Siblings

In a review of literature on sibling sexual abuse written for the nursing profession, Yates (2017) argued that there were three types of sibling sexual interactions discussed in the literature. First, is sexual play among siblings that may be mutually initiated and may have no harmful effects. This tends to have a playful quality and is a form of gathering information about the nature of the genitals. When such activity goes beyond this type of normal childhood activity, it can become harmful. The difficulty, according to Yates, is that defining the line between normal sexual play and harmful or abusive sexual activity is not a clear process. As he notes, even studies that have attempted to examine this is have found wide differences of opinion about what is and is not acceptable (see Box 7.4). A third category of sibling sexual activity that is definitely labeled as abusive would include behavior that is forced or coerced in some way or activity between siblings who vary widely in age. Such abuse is quite traumatic as is coerced sex from a parent (see Chap. 6). (See DiClemente & Ricks, 2015, for more discussion of differentiating abusive sexual activity between siblings and what they describe as "harmless sex play", p. 595).

Box 7.4: Common Sexual Experiences of Children

Although direct observational studies of childhood sexual activity are difficult since such behavior is often hidden, there is a growing consensus that it is quite common for children in the U.S. to engage in a variety of activities that might be labeled as *sexual.* Although many parents are uncomfortable with children seeing them naked, or engaging in sex with each other, this is quite common for children in many countries, and there is no evidence that such experiences have negative consequences. Children often see each other without clothes, as well. It is also common for even very young children to touch their genitals and even to engage in what appears to be masturbation, although boys do not ejaculate. Children may also show their genitals to other children, beginning at the age of 2, and may touch the genitals of other children. If parents disapprove of this type of activity, children learn to do this when the parents do not see it occurring. Children may also feel guilty for doing this if they know adults do not approve. But, there is no evidence that such sexual exploration has negative effects when done voluntarily (LeVay, Baldwin, & Baldwin, 2015).

Another method of determining the types of behaviors associated with sibling sexual *abuse* can be seen in Krienert and Walsh's (2011) analysis of U.S. national data compiled from incidents reported to the police or other legal authorities. As discussed further in Chap. 9, sexual assault is a crime and such behavior is more likely to be reported to police when discovered than other forms of family violence. The most common behavior in these data was forceful fondling, followed by forcible rape, forcible sodomy, and sexual assault with an object. Both girls and boys were more likely to be assaulted by an older brother than someone closer in age, but this was not always the case. Far more sisters than brothers were victimized. Other forms of sibling sexual abuse were suggested by Morrill (2014a, 2014b). Her analysis included children forced by siblings to watch pornography, forced exposure of genitals and sexual harassment. Victims of all of these acts were found to suffer long term negative effects.

In an attempt to better understand the dynamics of sibling sexual abuse, McDonald and Martinez (2017) conducted an on-line survey of adults who had experience with "sibling abuse" (p. 878) either as victims or as perpetrators. The survey was advertised widely, and asked for adults to volunteer to participate. The final sample included 33 people who reported having sexual contact with a sibling. Thirty of these were women. Although detailed information about the nature of the sexual activity was not provided, many of the victims indicated that the sexual activity had continued over a period of years, although for some it was a one-time experience. In the large majority of cases, the abuser was an older, typically male, sibling. There were a few cases of abuse from a younger sibling, and some cases of a sister being the abuser. A typical pattern was that the children lived in a family where they were physically abused or neglected by their parents. In some cases, the father was also sexually abusive to the daughter. Even when the children told their parents about the sexual abuse they were receiving from their siblings, the parents did nothing to stop this and occasionally encouraged it. Most of the victims believed that their abuser had, himself, been sexually abused at some earlier period. Some mentioned that he had learned about sexual activity through viewing pornography. These perceptions have been supported by empirical research (e.g., Latzman, Viljoen, Scalora, & Ullman, 2011). Morrill (2017) described very similar family dynamics in her chapter on the many forms of sibling abuse already described.

A very different picture emerges from another on-line survey of students, staff, faculty and community residents in 3 campus communities. Stroebel et al. (2013) reported on cases of brother-sister sexual activity, based on a sample of 40 cases. The total sample of 1521 men and women had volunteered to participate in a study of childhood sexual experiences. Within this group were the 19 cases of father-daughter incest described in detail in Stroebel et al. (2012), where the methodology of the study is also described in detail. Looking at the 40 women who described sexual activity with a brother, the large majority of the cases involved voluntary sexual touching and looking at each other's genitals (Stroebel et al., 2013). The brother was typically older, and the activity began when the sister was a preteen. A number of mental health measures were used, but the brother-sister activity did not appear to have statistically-significant negative effects when the sample was compared to a control group. Findings here could well be related to the very different way in which the study was described to potential study participants. No mention of *abuse* was used, only the reference to *sexual activity*. This study suggested that some types of sexual interactions between siblings did not appear to result in measurable negative outcomes for the participants. This conclusion is considered controversial, with ongoing debate about whether this can occur or not.

7.3 The Relationship of Animal Cruelty to Intimate Partner Violence

Case Example from our Files

Five year old Mary loved her 3-month old kitten, Smoky. Mary's grandmother's cat had recently had a litter of eight kittens and Mary was allowed to choose one of the kittens to keep, so she chose Smoky because of his beautiful gray fur and green eyes. Smoky was like a puppy, following close behind Mary as she played outside. One morning, Mary decided to take Smoky across the street to her friend Danny's house to play. While crossing the street, Mary looked up and saw David, the neighborhood "mean boy", riding his bike towards her. David speeded up, turned his bike to the side and then deliberately rode his bike over Smoky, killing him. Mary was devastated. She picked up Smoky's lifeless body and went home crying to her mother. Later that afternoon, Mary's mother went to David's home to tell his parents what he had done. She knocked on the door and David' mother, Susan, answered. Mary's mother could see that Susan had two black eyes and her arm was in a sling. Susan admitted that David's father had gotten drunk and beaten her 2 days ago. Susan begged Mary's mother not to tell anyone what had happened to her or what David had done "or it will just make things worse". The year was 1957, and there were no services, no shelter for abused women in their small town and calls to police about such things were typically brushed off as "private family business". Many years later, Mary's mother heard that David had been arrested and jailed for abusing his girlfriend.

This case vignette illustrates a number of issues relevant to how cruelty to animals can manifest and how such cruelty may co-exist with intimate partner violence. The teenage boy who killed Mary's kitten was known to all the neighbors as a "mean boy" because he had bullied other children (in one case, pushing another child down an abandoned water well), and he seemed to take pleasure in doing so. Mary's mother discovered that David's father had abused his mother. In this case, there was little to no help for the family, unlike today, when many communities do have help available for victims of IPV (see Chap. 8). Many regions now also provide family interventions to help adolescents who engage in antisocial behavior, including bullying and animal cruelty.

In this last section of the chapter, we discuss another form of family aggression, animal abuse. As with elder abuse and sibling abuse, cruelty to and killing of animals occurs in many different contexts (Hoffer & Hargreaves-Cormany, 2017). Our focus is again how the dynamics of animal cruelty contribute to and interact with other forms of family violence and aggression. But, first we briefly look at the broader issues relating to human interactions with animals and all types of animal abuse.

7.3.1 The Role of Pets in People's Lives

As Amiot and Bastian (2015) discussed, nonhuman animals have been associated with humans for thousands of years. Although these animals have many roles in human life, some animals become pets and are typically considered by their owners as part of the family. These become very special animals. It is estimated that about 2/3 of families in the U.S. have pets and spend more than $55 billion every year on their welfare. Relationships with pets have been found to be especially important to children. Adults, too, can be highly attached to a pet. Animals are increasingly being used as comfort animals, or in various forms of therapy (Amiot & Bastian, 2015). Jalongo's (2018) book on dogs discusses animal support for humans in more detail.

Social science research relating to animal abuse and its relationship to other forms of abuse has existed for many years. Cultural anthropologist Margaret Mead (1901–1978) was the first scholar to address the issue of cruelty to animals as a pathological behavior in childhood which, without appropriate cultural sanctions, may evolve into aggressive and violent behavior in adolescence and adulthood toward both animals and people (Mead, 1964). Tacit parental approval of cruelty to animals and/or a lack of consistent cultural taboos against killing or torturing animals were seen as critical elements by Mead (1964) in elevating the risk that a child will engage in such behavior. Mead noted how a cycle of violence can develop in children if certain cultural restrictions regarding the treatment of animals are absent. She emphasizes that in every culture children are taught which creatures they may or may not kill and how, and which creatures are to be protected, loved, or simply left alone. Such cultural parameters are sometimes, however, neglected.

More recent research has examined these relationships more closely. Attachment to pets can be used by an abuser as a form of control. Newberry (2017) examined online forums where IPV survivors share their stories. Common themes that emerged related to the importance of the bond with companion animals for IPV survivors and how abuse or threats of abuse toward companion animals is often used as a strategy by abusers to control their human victims. Animal abuse and IPV is also the focus of Taylor and Fraser's (2019) book. These authors come from New Zealand and Australia, so these issues are of concern in many countries.

7.3.2 What Is Animal Cruelty or Neglect?

Animal cruelty, animal maltreatment and animal abuse are interchangeable terms that may be defined as human behavior that causes medically unnecessary pain, suffering, distress and/or death of an animal (Ascione, 1993, p. 228). This definition includes both abuse, such as hitting and injuring a dog with a stick. It also includes serious neglect of animals one is caring for such as not providing food to a housebound cat (Onyskiw, 2007). Abuse of animals is recognized in the U.S. as a crime and statistics on this are reported nationally as is the case for other crimes (see Chap. 1). Burchfield (2016) analyzed reports of animal crimes in Chicago between 2003 and 2013. She found that 90% of these reports involved cases of neglect and 10% related to using animals to fight one another for illegal profit. Arrests occurred for only 28% of these reported crimes. Conviction rates were not reported. The majority of individuals engaged in criminal animal cruelty, looking at both children and adults, are male (Hoffer & Hargreaves-Cormany, 2017).

Other studies have indicated that those who abuse animals tend to either not care about animals, feel that animals should be used in ways that help humans, and/or feel that animals should be mastered by humans (Alleyne & Parfitt, 2017). This same review of published literature further noted that there was a pattern of people who were cruel to animals having other antisocial traits as well. Animal abuse was also associated with low levels of empathy, and with negative experiences during childhood.

7.3.3 Relationship of Animal Cruelty to Intimate Partner Violence

The types of animal cruelty related to other forms of family violence differ from these reported animal crimes, and often are never reported to authorities. They generally involve cruelty to household pets. According to the Humane Society of the United States (2017), dogs are the most common U.S. household pet, and dogs are the species suffering the most abuse within the family, although cats are also often targeted. The Humane Society reports that animal abuse and domestic violence show a clear correlation with 71% of pet-owning women who were victimized by domestic violence reporting that their attacker also abused or threatened to abuse their pets.

Many studies have found that women abused by an intimate partner report that their pets have been threatened and/or harmed by the abusive partner. Specific numbers vary depending on how the sample is determined. In a study of men arrested for partner abuse, 41% admitted physically abusing an animal at least once since the age of 18. More than half of these men also indicated they had threatened to abuse an animal (Febres et al., 2014). In a later study, Barrett, Fitzgerald, Stevenson, and Cheung (2017) surveyed 86 women receiving services from battered women's shelters in Canada. They were asked about how their partners treated family pets. Sixty-four percent of the women had pets. Among this group, 53% reported that their partner had frequently or severely injured their pets. This abuse of pets was especially likely for those who had themselves received higher levels of partner abuse from the pet abuser.

The linking of pet abuse to IPV can also be seen in studies of battered women and their concerns about safety for their pets. Campbell, Thompson, Harris, and Wiehe (2018) analyzed over 3000 reports of police responding to calls for help with IPV. One of the questions asked victims was whether the abuser had ever abused, tortured or killed any household pets. Three percent of the victims answered that this form of several animal abuse had occurred. Typically, the identified abuser was male (96%), and in his 20's. Pet abuse was associated with higher levels of abuse, and those reporting this had happened were observed to be more likely than other victims to be afraid (63% versus 42%), apologetic (15% versus 5%) or nervous (48% versus 33%). The large majority of those victims reporting pet abuse also expressed concerns that their pet would be killed by their abuser if left at home with them gone. These researchers noted, though, that the percentage of their sample reporting pet abuse was relatively small as compared to other studies. They attributed this to the victims not wanting to disclose this information to the police for a variety of reasons. They further noted that 28% of their sample refused to answer the question about pet abuse. This group was included with those answering "no" to the question.

In a further exploration of why pet abuse may occur along with other forms of IPV, as part of a larger study, Collins et al. (2018) interviewed a sample of 103 women receiving services from a domestic violence shelter who had pets. Among these women, 75% said their abusing partner had threatened to harm a companion animal and 66% said the partner had actually harmed the animal. As they explained in more detail what had happened, many of the women felt that this was done as a form of retaliation against them because they had done something their partner did not want them to do. Sometimes the abusive partner threatened to hurt the pet unless the woman did something he wanted. In other cases, the pet abuse appeared to be in reaction to jealousy over the woman's caring for her pet or pets more than for him. Sometimes the pets were hurt for doing something themselves that the abuser did not like, such as chewing on his shoe or not coming when called. Another situation in which reported pet abuse occurred was when a dog attempted to protect the woman from her abuser. The women also noted that their children sometimes abused the pets, attributing this to their copying what their abuser had done earlier. Many of the women also noted that fears about what might happen to their pets kept them from leaving their abuser.

Other research has indicated that women experiencing IPV may delay seeking help because of concern for the safety of their pets (Hageman et al., 2018). In interviews with staff at agencies working with IPV, Hageman and her colleagues found that the women victims they worked with often expressed concerns about their pets. In further discussion, they agreed that it was important that there be safety planning for pets as part of the services offered victims of IPV and that questions about whether this was needed should be in the in-take screening for shelters and other agencies. Having facilities for pets at shelters was seen as a high priority.

Steps are being taken to address these needs. The Animal Welfare Institute https://awionline.org/content/animals-family-violence reported that the 2018 Farm Bill was passed by the U.S. Congress. This bill established a grant program to allow battered women to better meet the need for assistance with pets. It also includes pets and service and emotional support animals in federal laws pertaining to stalking, orders for protection from abuse, and restitution.

Although the large majority of studies on animal cruelty and IPV focus on men who are abusive to female partners, and also display maltreatment of pets in the home, Alleyne and Parfitt (2017), in a review of published studies on animal abusers, found that there are some cases identified in the literature of female IPV perpetrators who also abuse pets. The association of IPV and pet abuse was much more common for men than women, though.

7.3.4 Effects in Children of Observing Cruelty to Pets

Children in the family can be quite affected by observations of an older man [perhaps their father] who abuses their mother, and who also harms or kills a family pet. McDonald et al. (2017) asked a small sample of mothers receiving services relating to IPV about their children's exposure to cruelty to pets. In depth interviews indicated that children were often quite upset by this. Some of them described situations in which the abusive man was able to force the child to do something by using threats of hurting or killing a pet. This would suggest that animal cruelty is used coercively not only toward a woman partner, but also toward children living in the home. In another study by this team of researchers, McDonald et al. (2015) further noted that children sometimes reacted to threats towards pets by taking proactive action to hide the pet from the potential abuser. An additional theme found in the interviews was that children sometimes saw other children in the home abusing a pet.

Bright, Huq, Spencer, Applebaum, and Hardt (2018) analyzed data from a large sample of juvenile offenders referred for delinquent behavior in the state of Florida between 2005 and 2014. Analyses of these records indicated that about 1% of these youth indicated they had engaged in animal cruelty. The large majority of this smaller group were boys, and were often younger when first arrested than other juvenile offenders. Animal cruelty was also strongly associated with coming from a household where there were other forms of violence, and had often been physically or sexually abused themselves. Experiences of emotional abuse and neglect were also associated with the youth having been cruel to animals.

McDonald et al. (2017) have also found evidence that exposure to animal maltreatment in the home affects children in many ways. Data came from women receiving services related to IPV. This exposure was most often associated with the children developing internalizing problems such as anxiety and depression. Exposure was also correlated significantly with behavior problems in the child. It may also lead to the child being less emotional and more callous and uncaring generally.

7.4 Summary

This chapter addresses three additional types of family or partner maltreatment. These include elder abuse and neglect, sibling aggression, and pet abuse and its relationship to IPV. Looking first at abuse of older adults, this can take the form of physical violence, emotional abuse, financial abuse or neglect. Neglect is probably the most common form of elder abuse within the family setting, especially if self-neglect is included. Older adults are at greater risk of abuse from a family member for a number of reasons. A major factor appears to be not wanting to be placed in an assisted living or nursing care facility, and being willing to accept an abusive caretaker to avoid this. Effects of abuse for the older adult can range from injury, loss of money, emotional distress, and health issues resulting from neglect. Of course, most caregivers of dependent older adults are not abusive. Those who are may have their own mental health issues, and may have been abused themselves as children, perhaps by the now elderly parent.

Sibling aggression is quite common, and many people perceive this as normal behavior. It tends to be more common in families with parental IPV or where child maltreatment occurs. Children in these families may be modeling the aggressive behavior they observe in their parent. Like other forms of family violence, sibling aggression can be physical or emotional, and may include sexual abuse.

Pets are very important to many people, and abusers may threaten or actually harm pets as a form of controlling their partner. Battered women may hesitate leaving their abusive partner if they fear that their pet may be harmed or even killed if left in the home. Shelters are beginning to respond to this need and are starting to offer emergency housing for pets. Children can be quite negatively affected when a pet they love is abused.

References

Acierno, R., Hernandez, M. A., Amstadter, A. B., Resnick, H. S., Steve, K., Muzzy, W., et al. (2010). Prevalence and correlates of emotional, physical, sexual, and financial abuse and potential neglect in the United States: The National Elder Mistreatment Study. *American Journal of Public Health, 100*(2), 292–297.

Acierno, R., Hernandez-Tejada, M. A., Anetzberger, G. J., Loew, D., & Muzzy, W. (2017). The National Elder Mistreatment Study: An 8-year longitudinal study of outcomes. *Journal of Elder Abuse & Neglect, 29*, 254–269. https://doi.org/10.1080/08946566.2017.1365031

Alleyne, E., & Parfitt, C. (2017). Adult-perpetrated animal abuse: A systematic literature review. *Trauma, Violence & Abuse, 20*, 1–14. https://doi.org/10.1177/1524838017708785

Amiot, C. E., & Bastian, B. (2015). Toward a psychology of human-animal relations. *Psychological Bulletin, 141*(1), 6–47. https://doi.org/10.1037/a0038147

Amstadter, A. B., Cisler, J. M., McCauley, J. L., Hernandez, M. A., Muzzy, W., & Acierno, R. (2010). Do incident and perpetrator characteristics of elder mistreatment differ by gender of the victim? Results from the National Elder Mistreatment Study. *Journal of Elder Abuse & Neglect, 23*(1), 43–57. https://doi.org/10.1080/08946566.2011.534707

Animal Welfare Institute. (n.d.), https://awionline.org/content/animals-family-violence

Ascione, F. R. (1993). Children who are cruel to animals: A review of research and implications for developmental psychopathology. *Anthrozoös, 6*(4), 226–247. https://doi.org/10.2752/089279393787002105

Bachman, R., Lachs, M., & Meloy, M. (2004). Reducing injury through self-protection by elderly victims of violence: The interaction effects of gender of victim and the victim/offender relationship. *Journal of Elder Abuse and Neglect, 16*(4), 1–24. https://doi.org/10.1300/J084v16n04_01

Barrett, B. J., Fitzgerald, A., Stevenson, R., & Cheung, C. H. (2017). Animal maltreatment as a risk marker of more frequent and severe forms of intimate partner violence. *Journal of Interpersonal Violence*, 1–26. https://doi.org/10.1177/0886260517719542

Beach, S. R., Schulz, R., Castle, N. G., & Rosen, J. (2010). Financial exploitation and psychological mistreatment among older adults: Differences between African Americans and non-African Americans in a population-based survey. *The Gerontologist, 50*(6), 744–757. https://doi.org/10.1093/geront/gnq053

Belinger, E., Davis, C., & Fulmore, C. (2010, April). *Elder abuse: What professionals need to know*. Retrieved from: https://www.socialwork.pitt.edu/downloads/Elder%20Abuse%20Project.pdf

Bonner, A. F., Field, T. S., Lemay, C. A., Mazor, K. M., Andersen, D. A., Compher, C. J., et al. (2015). Rationales that providers and family members cited for the use of antipsychotic medications in nursing home residents with dementia. *Journal of the American Geriatrics Society, 63*(2), 302–308. https://doi.org/10.1111/jgs.13230

Bornstein, R. F. (2019). Synergistic dependencies in partner and elder abuse. *American Psychologist, 74*, 713–724. https://doi.org/10.1037/amp0000456

Bourget, D., & Gagne, P. (2006). Fratricide: A forensic psychiatric perspective. *Journal of the American Academy of Psychiatry Law, 34*(4), 529–533. Retrieved from https://www.semanticscholar.org/

Bowes, L., Wolke, D., Joinson, C., Lereya, S. T., & Lewis, G. (2014). Sibling bullying and risk of depression, anxiety, and self-harm: A prospective cohort study. *Pediatrics, 134*(4), 1032–1039. https://doi.org/10.1542/peds.2014-0832

Bows, H. (2017). Sexual violence against older people: A review of the empirical literature. *Trauma, Violence and Abuse, 19*, 1–17. https://doi.org/10.1177/1524838016683455

Brawshaw, G. (2016, June 6). Daughter's hearing postponed. Observer-Reporter. Retrieved from: https://observer-reporter.com/news/localnews/daughter-s-hearing-postponed/article_b11dc3f9-0308-5b60-b30b-047cac7bdef0.html

Breckman, R., Burnes, D., Ross, S., Marshall, P. C., Suitor, J. J., Lachs, M. S., et al. (2018). When helping hurts: Nonabusing family, friends, and neighbors in the lives of elder mistreatment victims. *The Gerontologist, 58*(4), 719–723. https://doi.org/10.1093/geront/gnw257

Bright, M. A., Huq, M. S., Spencer, T., Applebaum, J. W., & Hardt, N. (2018). Animal cruelty as an indicator of family trauma: Using adverse childhood experiences to look beyond child abuse and violence. *Child Abuse & Neglect, 76*, 287–296. https://doi.org/10.1016/j.chiabu.2017.11.011

Brown, R. M., & Brown, S. L. (2014). Informal caregiving: A reappraisal of effects on caregivers. *Social Issues and Policy Review, 8*(1), 74–102. https://doi.org/10.1111/sipr.12002

Burchfield, K. B. (2016). The sociology of animal crime: An examination of incidents and arrests in Chicago. *Deviant Behavior, 37*(4), 368–384. https://doi.org/10.1080/01639625.2015.1026769

Burnes, D., Pillemer, K., Caccamise, P. L., Mason, A., Henderson, C. R., Berman, J., et al. (2015). Prevalence of and risk factors for elder abuse and neglect in the community: A population-based study. *Journal of the American Geriatrics Society, 63*(9), 1906–1912. https://doi.org/10.1111/jgs.13601

Button, D. M., & Gealt, R. (2010). High risk behaviors among victims of sibling violence. *Journal of Family Violence, 25*(2), 131–140. https://doi.org/10.1007/s10896-009-9276-x

Caffaro, J. V., & Conn-Caffaro, A. (1998). *Sibling abuse trauma: Assessment and intervention strategies for children, families, and adults*. New York, NY: Haworth Press.

Callaghan, J., Alexander, J., Fellin, L., & Sixsmith, J. (2016). Children's experiences of domestic violence and abuse: siblings' accounts of relational coping. *Clinical Child Psychology and Psychiatry, 21*(4), 649–668. https://doi.org/10.1177/1359104515620250

Campbell Reay, A. M., & Browne, K. D. (2001). Risk factor characteristics in carers who physically abuse or neglect their elderly dependents. *Aging and Mental Health, 5*(1), 56–62. https://doi.org/10.1080/13607860020020654

Campbell, A. M., Thompson, S. L., Harris, T. L., & Wiehe, S. E. (2018). Intimate partner violence and pet abuse: Responding law enforcement officers' observations and victim reports from the scene. *Journal of Interpersonal Violence*, 1–20. https://doi.org/10.1177/0886260518759653

Centers for Disease Control. (2018a). Elder abuse: Definitions. Retrieved August 2, 2018 from: https://www.cdc.gov/violenceprevention/elderabuse/definitions.html

Centers for Disease Control. (2018b). Elder abuse: Risk and protective factors. Retrieved August 2, 2018 from: https://www.cdc.gov/violenceprevention/elderabuse/riskprotectivefactors.html

Cheung, D., Tiwari, A., & Wang, A. (2015). Intimate partner violence in late life: A case study of older Chinese women. *Journal of Elder Abuse & Neglect, 27*(4), 428–437. https://doi.org/10.1080/08946566.2015.1092903

Collins, E. A., Cody, A. M., McDonald, S. E., Nicotera, N., Ascione, F. R., & Williams, J. H. (2018). A template analysis of intimate partner violence survivors' experiences of animal maltreatment: Implications for safety planning and intervention. *Violence Against Women, 24*(4), 452–476. https://doi.org/10.1177/1077801217697266

Connolly, M. T., Brandl, B., & Breckman, R. (2014). *The Elder Justice Roadmap: A Stakeholder Initiative to Respond to an Emerging Health, Justice, Financial and Social Crisis*. Retrieved from: http://vawnet.org/material/elder-justice-roadmap-stakeholder-initiative-respond-emerging-health-justice-financial-and

Cooney, C., Howard, R., & Lawlor, B. (2006). Abuse of vulnerable people with dementia by their carers: Can we identify those most at risk? *International Journal of Geriatric Psychiatry, 21*(6), 564–571. https://doi.org/10.1002/gps.1525

Cooper, C., & Livingston, G. (2016). Intervening to reduce elder abuse: challenges for research. *Age and Ageing 45*(2), 184–185. https://doi.org/10.1093/ageing/afw00

Coyle, S., Demaray, M. K., Malecki, C. K., Tennant, J. E., & Klossing, J. (2017). The associations among sibling and peer-bullying, social support and internalizing behaviors. *Child & Youth Care Forum, 46*(6), 895–922. https://doi.org/10.1007/s10566-017-9412-3

DeKeseredy, W. S., & Ellis, D. (1997). Sibling violence: A review of canadian sociological research and suggestions for further empirical work. *Humanity and Society, 21*(4), 397–411. https://doi.org/10.1177/016059769702100405

Dennis, M., Shine, L., John, A., Marchant, A., McGregor, J., Lyons, R. A., et al. (2017). Risk of adverse outcomes for older people with dementia prescribed antipsychotic medication: A population based e-cohort study. *Neurology and Therapy, 6*(1), 57–77. https://doi.org/10.1007/s40120-016-0060-6

DiClemente, R. J., & Ricks, J. M. (2015). Sibling incest. In T. P. Gullotta, R. W. Plant, & M. A. Evans (Eds.), *Handbook of adolescent behavioral problems: Evidence-based approaches to prevention and treatment* (2nd ed., pp. 595–608). New York, NY: Springer.

Dirks, M. A., Persram, R., Recchia, H. E., & Howe, N. (2015). Sibling relationships as sources of risk and resilience in the development and maintenance of internalizing and externalizing problems during childhood and adolescence. *Clinical Psychology Review, 42*, 145–155. https://doi.org/10.1016/j.cpr.2015.07.003

Dong, X. (2017). Elder self-neglect: Research and practice. *Clinical Interventions in Aging, 12*, 949–954. https://doi.org/10.2147/CIA.S103359

Dong, X., Chen, R., Chang, E. S., & Simon, M. (2013). Elder abuse and psychological well-being: a systematic review and implications for research and policy—a mini review. *Gerontology, 59*(2), 132–142. https://doi.org/10.1159/000341652

Dong, X., Chen, R., & Simon, M. A. (2014). Elder abuse and dementia: A review of the research and health policy. *Health Affairs, 33*(4), 642–649. https://doi.org/10.1377/hlthaff.2013.1261

Dong, X., Simon, M., Mendes de Leon, C., Fulmer, T., Beck, T., & Hebert, L. (2009). Elder self-neglect and abuse and mortality risk in a community-dwelling population. *Journal of the American Medical Association, 302*(5), 517–526. https://doi.org/10.1001/jama.2009.1109

Eriksen, S., & Jensen, V. (2009). A push or a punch: Distinguishing the severity of sibling violence. *Journal of Interpersonal Violence, 24*(1), 183–208. https://doi.org/10.1177/0886260508316298

Family Caregiver Alliance. (2017). *Women and caregiving: Facts and figures*. Retrieved from: https://www.caregiver.org/women-and-caregiving-facts-and-figures

Febres, J., Brasfield, H., Shorey, R. C., Elmquist, J., Ninnemann, A., Schonbrun, Y. C., et al. (2014). Adulthood animal abuse among men arrested for domestic violence. *Violence Against Women, 20*(9), 1059–1077. https://doi.org/10.1177/1077801214549641

Finkelhor, D., Turner, H. A., Shattuck, A., & Hamby, S. L. (2015). Prevalence of childhood exposure to violence, crime, and abuse: Results from the national survey of children's exposure to violence. *JAMA Pediatrics, 169*(8), 746–754.

Ford, J. D., & Delker, B. C. (2018). Polyvictimization in childhood and its adverse impacts across the lifespan: Introduction to the special issue. *Journal of Trauma & Dissociation, 19*(3), 275–288.

Fowler, K. A., Jack, S. P. D., Lyons, B. H., Betz, C. J., & Petrosky, E. (2018). *Surveillance for violent deaths—National Violent Death Reporting System, 18 States, 2014*. U.S. Department of Health and Human Services: Centers for Disease Control.

Friedman, B., Santos, E. J., Liebel, D. V., Russ, A. J., & Conwell, Y. (2015). Longitudinal prevalence and correlates of elder mistreatment among older adults receiving home visiting nursing. *Journal of Elder Abuse & Neglect, 27*(1), 34–64. https://doi.org/10.1080/08946566.2014.946193

Fulmer, T., Rodgers, R. F., & Pelger, A. (2014). Verbal mistreatment of the elderly. *Journal of Elder Abuse & Neglect, 26*(4), 351–364. https://doi.org/10.1080/08946566.2013.801817

Gabriel, L., Tizro, Z., James, H., Cronin-Davis, J., Beetham, T., Corbally, A., et al. (2018). "Give me some space": Exploring youth to parent aggression and violence. *Journal of Family Violence, 33*, 161–169. https://doi.org/10.1007/s10896-017-9928-1

Gallione, C., Molin, A. D., Cristina, F. V. B., Ferns, H., Mattioli, M., & Suardi, B. (2017). Screening tools for identification of elder abuse: A systematic review. *Journal of Clinical Nursing, 26*(15–16), 2154–2176. https://doi.org/10.1111/jocn.13721

Gelles, R. J., & Comell, C. P. (1985). *Intimate violence in families*. Beverly Hills, CA: Sage.

Gelles, R. J., & Straus, M. A. (1979). Violence in the American family. *Journal of Social Issues, 35*(2), 15–39. https://doi.org/10.1111/j.1540-4560.1979.tb00799.x

Green, A. H. (1984). Child abuse by siblings. *Child Abuse & Neglect, 8*(3), 311–317. https://doi.org/10.1016/0145-2134(84)90072-3

Greif, G. L., & Woolley, M. E. (2016). *Adult sibling relationships*. New York, NY: Columbia University Press.

Hageman, T. O., Langenderfer-Magruder, L., Greene, T., Williams, J. H., St. Mary, J., McDonald, S. E., et al. (2018). Intimate partner violence survivors and pets: Exploring practitioners' experiences in addressing client needs. *Families in Society, 99*(2), 134–145. https://doi.org/10.1177/1044389418767836

Hardy, M., Beers, B., Burgess, C., & Taylor, A. (2009). Personal experience and perceived acceptability of sibling aggression. *Journal of Family Violence, 25*(1), 65. https://doi.org/10.1007/s10896-009-9270-3

Harper, J. M., Padilla-Walker, L. M., & Jensen, A. C. (2014). Do siblings matter independent of both parents and friends? Sympathy as a mediator between sibling relationship quality and adolescent outcomes. *Journal of Research on Adolescence, 26*(1), 101–114. https://doi.org/10.1111/jora.12174

Hayslip, B., Reinberg, J., & William, J. (2015). The impact of elder abuse education on young adults. *Journal of Elder Abuse & Neglect, 27*(3). https://doi.org/10.1080/08946566.2014.1003264

Heisler, C. J. (2017). Moving forward: Recommendations for advancing late-life polyvictimization practice, policy, and research. *Journal of Elder Abuse & Neglect, 29*(5), 351–363. https://doi.org/10.1080/08946566.2017.1388013

Hoffer, T. A., & Hargreaves-Cormany, H. (2017). Animal cruelty offenders. In V. B. Van Hasselt & M. L. Bourke (Eds.), *Handbook of behavioral criminology* (pp. 81–95). Cham: Springer. https://doi.org/10.1007/978-3-319-61625-4_6

Humane Society of the United States. (2017). *Animal cruelty laws by state: Is it a crime to abuse an animal?* Retrieved March 20, 2017 from: http://www.dopplr.com/animal-cruely-laws/

Isham, L., Hewison, A., & Bradbury-Jones, C. (2017). When older people are violent or abusive toward their family caregiver: A review of mixed-methods research. *Trauma, Violence & Abuse*, 1–12. https://doi.org/10.1177/1524838017726425

Jackson, S. L. (2017). Adult protective services and victim services: A review of the literature to increase understanding between these two fields. *Aggression and Violent Behavior, 34*, 214–227. https://doi.org/10.1016/j.avb.2017.01.010

Jalongo, M. R. (Ed.). (2018). *Children, dogs and education: Caring for, learning alongside, and gaining support from canine companions*. New York, NY: Springer.

Jervis, L. L., Hamby, S., Beach, S. R., Williams, M. L., Maholmes, V., & Castille, D. M. (2016). Elder mistreatment in underserved populations: Opportunities and challenges to developing a contemporary program of research. *Journal of Elder Abuse & Neglect, 28*(4–5), 301–319. https://doi.org/10.1080/08946566.2016.1245644

Kane, K. (2016, May 27). Daughter charged with repeatedly beating elderly mother in Washington County. *Pittsburgh Post-Gazette*. Retrieved from: http://www.post-gazette.com/local/washington/2016/05/27/Daughter-charged-with-assaulting-elderly-mother-in-Washington-County-girdish/stories/201605270212

Khan, R., & Cooke, D. J. (2013). Measurement of sibling violence: A two-factor model of severity. *Criminal Justice and Behavior, 40*(1), 26–39. https://doi.org/10.1177/0093854812463349

Krienert, J. L., & Walsh, J. A. (2011). Sibling sexual abuse: An empirical analysis of offender, victim, and event characteristics in National Incident-Based Reporting System (NIBRS) data, 2000–2007. *Journal of Child Sexual Abuse, 20*(4), 353–372. https://doi.org/10.1080/10538712.2011.588190

Labrum, T., & Solomon, P. L. (2015). Physical elder abuse perpetrated by relatives with serious mental illness: A preliminary conceptual social–ecological model. *Aggression and Violent Behavior, 25*, 293–303. https://doi.org/10.1016/j.avb.2015.09.006

Labrum, T., & Solomon, P. L. (2018). Elder mistreatment perpetrators with substance abuse and/or mental health conditions: Results from the national elder mistreatment study. *Psychiatric Quarterly, 89*(1), 117–128. https://doi.org/10.1007/s11126-017-9513-z

Labrum, T., Solomon, P. L., & Bressi, S. K. (2015). Physical, financial, and psychological abuse committed against older women by relatives with psychiatric disorders: Extent of the problem. *Journal of Elder Abuse & Neglect, 27*(4–5), 377–391. https://doi.org/10.1080/08946566.2015.1092902

Lachs, M. S., & Pillemer, K. A. (2015). Elder Abuse. *New England Journal of Medicine, 373*(20), 1947–1956. https://doi.org/10.1056/NEJMra1404688

Latzman, N. E., Viljoen, J. L., Scalora, M. J., & Ullman, D. (2011). Sexual offending in adolescence: A comparison of sibling offenders and nonsibling offenders across domains of risk and treatment need. *Journal of Child Sexual Abuse, 20*(3), 245–263. https://doi.org/10.1080/10538712.2011.571233

Laumann, E. O., Leitsch, S. A., & Waite, L. J. (2008). Elder mistreatment in the United States: Prevalence estimates from a nationally representative study. *The Journals of Gerontology: Series B, 63*(4), S248–S254. https://doi.org/10.1093/geronb/63.4.S248

LeVay, S., Baldwin, J., & Baldwin, J. (2015). *Discovering human sexuality* (3rd ed.). Sunderland, MA: Sinauer Associates, Inc..

Lichtenberg, P. A. (2016). Financial exploitation, financial capacity, and Alzheimer's disease. *American Psychologist, 71*, 312–320. https://doi.org/10.1037/a0040192

Lifespan of Greater Rochester, Inc., Weill Cornell Medical Center of Cornell University, & New York City Department for the Aging. (2011). *Under the Radar: New York State Elder Abuse Prevalence Study*. Retrieved from: http://ocfs.ny.gov/main/reports/Under%20the%20Radar%2005%2012%2011%20final%20report.pdf

Macko, M. S., & Valcarce, B. (2018). Using the false claims to combat fraud by personal care homes. Elder justice. *Department of Justice Journal of Federal Law and Practice, 66*, 129–136.

McDonald, S. E., Collins, E. A., Maternick, A., Nicotera, N., Ascione, F. R., & Williams, J. H. (2017). Violence survivors' reports of their children's exposure to companion animal maltreatment: A qualitative study. *Journal of Interpersonal Violence*. https://doi.org/10.1177/0886260516689775

McDonald, S. E., Collins, E. A., Nicotera, N., Hageman, T. O., Ascione, F. R., Williams, J. H., et al. (2015). Children's experiences of companion animal maltreatment in households characterized by intimate partner violence. *Child Abuse & Neglect, 50*, 11–127. https://doi.org/10.1016/j.chiabu.2015.10.005

McDonald, S. E., Dmitrieva, J., Shin, S., Hitti, S. A., Graham-Bermann, S. A., Ascione, F. R., et al. (2017). The role of callous/unemotional traits in mediating the association between animal abuse exposure and behavior problems among children exposed to intimate partner violence. *Child Abuse & Neglect, 72*, 421–432. https://doi.org/10.1016/j.chiabu.2017.09.004

McDonald, C., & Martinez, K. (2017). Victims' retrospective explanations of sibling sexual violence. *Journal of Child Sexual Abuse, 26*(7), 874–888. https://doi.org/10.1080/10538712.2017.1354953

Mariam, L. M., McClure, R., Robinson, J. B., Yang, J. A. (2015). Eliciting change in at-risk elders (ECARE): evaluation of an elder abuse intervention program. *Journal of Elder Abuse and Neglect, 27*(1), 19–33. https://doi.org/10.1080/08946566.2013.867241

Mead, M. (1964). Cultural factors in the cause and prevention of pathological homicide. *Bulletin of the Menninger Clinic, 28*(1), 11.

Morrill, M. (2014a). Sibling sexual abuse: An exploratory study of long-term consequences for self-esteem and counseling considerations. *Journal of Family Violence, 29*, 205–213. https://doi.org/10.1007/s10896-013-9571-4

Morrill, M. (2014b). Sibling sexual abuse: An exploratory study of long-term consequences for self-esteem and counseling considerations. *Journal of Family Violence, 29*(2), 205–213. https://doi.org/10.1007/s10896-013-9571-4

Morrill, M. (2017). Sibling abuse. In V. B. Van Hasselt & M. L. Bourke (Eds.), *Handbook of behavioral criminology* (pp. 351–364). Cham: Springer. https://doi.org/10.1007/978-3-319-61625-4_6

Morrill-Richards, M., & Leierer, S. J. (2010). The relationship between sibling maltreatment and college students' sense of well-being. *Journal of College Counseling, 13*(1), 17–30. https://doi.org/10.1002/j.2161-1882.2010.tb00045.x

Mouton, C. P., Rodabough, R. J., Rovi, S. L. D., Brzyski, R. G., & Katerndahl, D. A. (2010). Psychosocial effects of physical and verbal abuse in postmenopausal women. *The Annals of Family Medicine, 8*(3), 206–213. https://doi.org/10.1370/afm.1095

Mulvaney, E. (2016). *Older adult case examples*. (Unpublished manuscript, University of Pittsburgh).

National Institute on Aging, U.S. National Institute of Health. (retrieved 2020). *Alzheimer's-disease fact sheet*. https://www.nia.nih.gov/health/alzheimers-disease-fact-sheet

Newberry, M. (2017). Pets in danger: Exploring the link between domestic violence and animal abuse. *Aggression and Violent Behavior, 34*, 273–281. https://doi.org/10.1016/j.avb.2016.11.007

O'Hara, K. L., Duchschere, J. E., Shanholtz, C. E., Reznik, S. J., Beck, C. J., & Lawrence, E. (2019). Multidisciplinary partnership: Targeting aggression and mental health problems of adolescents in detention. *American Psychologist, 74*(3), 329–342. https://doi.org/10.1037/amp0000439

Onyskiw, J. E. (2007). The link between family violence and cruelty to family pets. *Journal of Emotional Abuse, 7*(3), 7–30. https://doi.org/10.1080/10926798.2007.10766830

Peck, J. H., & Heide, K. M. (2012). Juvenile involvement in fratricide and soricide: An empirical analysis of 32 years of U.S. arrest data. *Journal of Family Violence, 27*(8), 749–760. https://doi.org/10.1007/s10896-012-9456-y

Perkins, N. H., Spira, M., & Key, J. E. (2018). Intergenerational transmission of physical and emotional sibling violence: A potential connection to elder abuse. *Families in Society, 99*(3), 256–268. https://doi.org/10.1177/1044389418782429

Peterson, J. C., Burnes, D. P. R., Caccamise, P. L., Mason, A., Henderson, C. R., Wells, M. T., et al. (2014). Financial exploitation of older adults: A population-based prevalence study. *Journal of General Internal Medicine, 29*(12), 1615–1623. https://doi.org/10.1007/s11606-014-2946-2

Petti, S. (2018). Elder neglect—Oral diseases and injuries. *Oral Diseases, 24*(6), 891–899. https://doi.org/10.1111/odi.12797

Piotrowski, C. C., & Cameranesi, M. (2018). Aggression by children exposed to IPV: Exploring the role of child depressive symptoms, trauma-related symptoms, & warmth in family relationships. *Child Psychiatry & Human Development, 49*(3), 360–371. https://doi.org/10.1007/s10578-017-0755-7

Piotrowski, C. C., Tachie, R., & Cameranesi, M. (2017). Aggression in children exposed to intimate partner violence: A comparison of maternal, sibling, and observer perspectives. *Journal of Interpersonal Violence*, 1–22. https://doi.org/10.1177/0886260517741624

Roberto, K. A. (2016). The complexities of elder abuse. *American Psychologist, 71*(4), 302–311. https://doi.org/10.1037/a0040259

Rosay, A. B., & Mulford, C. F. (2017). Prevalence estimates and correlates of elder abuse in the United States: The National Intimate Partner and Sexual Violence Survey. *Journal of Elder Abuse & Neglect, 29*, 1–14. https://doi.org/10.1080/08946566.2016.1249817

Rosen, T., Bloemen, E. M., LoFaso, V. M., Clark, S., Flomenbaum, N. E., Breckman, R., et al. (2016). Acute precipitants of physical abuse: Qualitative analysis of legal records from highly adjudicated cases. *Journal of Interpersonal Violence*, 1–25. https://doi.org/10.1177/0886260516662305

Roth, D. L., Fredman, L., & Haley, W. E. (2015). Informal caregiving and its impact on health: A reappraisal from population-based studies. *The Gerontologist, 55*(2), 309–319. https://doi.org/10.1093/geront/gnu177

Rzeszut, S. M. (2017). The need for a stronger definition: Recognizing abandonment as a form of elder abuse across the united states. *Family Court Review, 55*(3), 444–457. https://doi.org/10.1111/fcre.12295

Salari, S., & Maxwell, C. D. (2016). Lethal intimate partner violence in later life: Understanding measurements, strengths, and limitations of research. *Journal of Elder Abuse & Neglect, 28*(4–5), 235–262.

Skinner, J. A., & Kowalski, R. M. (2013). Profiles of sibling bullying. *Journal of Interpersonal Violence, 28*(8), 1726–1736. https://doi.org/10.1177/0886260512468327

Storey, J. E. (2019). Risk factors for elder abuse and neglect: A review of the literature. *Aggression and Violent Behavior*. https://doi.org/10.1016/j.avb.2019.101339

Stroebel, S. S., O'Keefe, S. L., Beard, K. W., Kuo, S.-Y., Swindell, S. V. S., & Kommor, M. J. (2012). Father–daughter incest: Data from an anonymous computerized survey. *Journal of Child Sexual Abuse, 21*(2), 176–199. https://doi.org/10.1080/10538712.2012.654007

Stroebel, S. S., O'Keefe, S. L., Beard, K. W., Kuo, S.-Y., Swindell, S., & Stroupe, W. (2013). Brother–sister incest: Data from anonymous computer-assisted self interviews. *Journal of Child Sexual Abuse, 22*(3), 255–276. https://doi.org/10.1080/10538712.2013.743952

Taylor, H., & Fraser, H. (2019). *Companion animals and domestic violence*. Cham: Palgrave Macmillan. https://doi.org/10.1007/978-3-030-04125-0_1

Tucker, C. J., Cox, G., Sharp, E. H., Van Gundy, K. T., Rebellon, C., & Stracuzzi, N. F. (2013). Sibling proactive and reactive aggression in adolescence. *Journal of Family Violence, 28*(3), 299–310. https://doi.org/10.1007/s10896-012-9483-8

Tucker, C. J., & Finkelhor, D. (2017). The state of interventions for sibling conflict and aggression: A systematic review. *Trauma, Violence & Abuse, 18*(4), 396–406. https://doi.org/10.1177/1524838015622438

Tucker, C. J., Finkelhor, D., Shattuck, A. M., & Turner, H. (2013). Prevalence and correlates of sibling victimization types. *Child Abuse & Neglect, 37*(4), 213–223. https://doi.org/10.1016/j.chiabu.2013.01.006

Tucker, C. J., Finkelhor, D., Turner, H., & Shattuck, A. M. (2014). Sibling and peer victimization in childhood and adolescence. *Child Abuse & Neglect, 38*(10), 1599–1606. https://doi.org/10.1016/j.chiabu.2014.05.007

Tucker, C. J., Sharp, E. H., Van Gundy, K. T., & Rebellon, C. (2019). Perpetration of sibling aggression and sibling relationship quality in emerging adulthood. *Personal Relationships*, 1–11. https://doi.org/10.1111/pere.12288

U.S. Census Bureau. (2011). The Older Population: 2010. Retrieved from: https://www.census.gov/prod/cen2010/briefs/c2010br-09.pdf

van Berkel, S. R., Tucker, C. J., & Finkelhor, D. (2018). The combination of sibling victimization and parental child maltreatment on mental health problems and delinquency. *Child Maltreatment, 23*(3), 244–253. https://doi.org/10.1177/1077559517751670

Wharton, T. C., & Ford, B. K. (2014). What is known about dementia care recipient violence and aggression against caregivers? *Journal of Gerontological Social Work, 57*(5), 460–477. https://doi.org/10.1080/01634372.2014.882466

Whitaker, M. G. (2018). Introduction (to issue on Elder Abuse). *Department of Justice Journal of Federal Law and Practice, 66*(7), 1–2. https://www.justice.gov/usao/resources/journal-of-federal-law-and-practice

Wiehe, V. R. (2000). Sibling abuse. In H. Henderson (Ed.), *Domestic violence and child abuse resource sourcebook* (pp. 409–492). Detroit, MI: Omnigraphics.

Williams, J. L., Racette, E. H., Hernandez-Tejada, M. A., & Acierno, R. (2017). Prevalence of elder polyvictimization in the United States: Data from the National Elder Mistreatment Study. *Journal of Interpersonal Violence*, 1–16. https://doi.org/10.1177/0886260517715604

Wood, S., & Lichtenberg, P. A. (2017). Financial capacity and financial exploitation of older adults: Research findings, policy recommendations and clinical implications. *Clinical Gerontologist, 40*(1), 3–13. https://doi.org/10.1080/07317115.2016.1203382

Yates, P. (2017). Sibling sexual abuse: Why don't we talk about it? *Journal of Clinical Nursing, 26*(15–16), 2482–2494. https://doi.org/10.1111/jocn.13531

Chapter 8
Interventions with Family Violence Survivors: Assistance for Abused Women and Children

Experiencing violence within your own family can have devastating long-term effects, and many child and adult victims need counselling and support. This chapter discusses some of the treatments or interventions used for battered women and for the children exposed to intimate partner violence (IPV). In addition, we review some of the treatments used for children or adults who had been exposed to child abuse or neglect. Chap. 4 provides a more general discussion of intimate partner violence (IPV), including the impact on women who are abused, and Chap. 6 describes contributing factors to and outcomes of child maltreatment.

The interventions described in this chapter are drawn from the most current evidence-based practices used across the U.S. at the time of this writing. While it is acknowledged that women perpetrate violence against men, and that partner violence occurs within same-sex relationships (see Chap. 5 and Box 8.1), the IPV interventions in this chapter are focused on female survivors of male violence and their children. This is the survivor group most likely to seek help. The term *survivor* is used in this chapter, since that is the common usage in the intervention literature. Other sections of the book use the term *victim*, again reflecting the common usage in the more theoretical literature.

8.1 Intimate Partner Violence

Women who have been victimized by their partners report both mental health problems, including depression, anxiety, and PTSD, and physical health problems, such as frequent headaches, hypertension, and diabetes (see Chap. 4). There are a number of services available for these women (see the internet listing of the National Domestic Violence Hotline at https://www.thehotline.org/help/, which includes a detailed listing of these resources). An important resource is emergency housing shelters (often referred to as battered women's shelters or domestic violence shelters) whose primary mission is assisting the female survivors of IPV. These shelters

I. H. Frieze et al., *Dynamics of Family and Intimate Partner Violence*,
https://doi.org/10.1007/978-3-030-42608-8_8

Box 8.1: Assistance for Male IPV Survivors and Others Who Violate the Assumption that IPV Survivors are Women Abused by Men

The large majority of options for those who experience violence or other abuse from a partner are only available for women. Men are sometimes the victim of IPV perpetrated by a male or by a female partner (see Chap. 5 or Hines & Douglas, 2018). However, the shelter system established for battered women may not provide any assistance for male victims. In a national sample of 302 men who had experienced physical violence from a female partner in the past year, Douglas and Hines (2011) found that the men rated domestic violence service agencies as the least helpful. Some of the men were made fun of by the agency staff they spoke with or were accused of being the batterer in the relationship. They found most help from family and friends or from mental health or medical service providers. In a follow-up study, Douglas worked with an international group from Australia, Canada, England and the U.S. (Douglas, Hines, Dixon, Celi, & Lysova, 2018) to establish web-based focus groups for this hard to reach population of men experiencing assault from a female partner. In both studies, the sample was recruited through ads placed with various agencies and hotlines as well as referrals from the Domestic Abuse Helpline for Men and Women, a national helpline specializing in male survivors of IPV.

As Perry and O'Neal (2015) explained, those in same-sex partnerships are another group that may resist seeking help for a variety of reasons (such as fears about outing). Both men and women in same-sex relationships who are survivors of IPV may find that shelters or other domestic violence service agencies are not welcoming. Similar findings were reported in a PhD dissertation by Frierson (2014) who provided qualitative data from a small sample of African American men abused by male partners. Friends were cited as being most helpful when they sought help for the abuse. Yerke and DeFeo (2016) argue that similar issues exist for transgendered individuals.

typically encourage the woman to leave her partner and offer a variety of services to assist her in doing this. However, only a relatively small percentage of IPV survivors go to these shelters and many of the women who do ask for assistance from a shelter do return to their abusive partners after being at the shelter (Grossman & Lundy, 2011). Many women continue to live in violent relationships, often because they lack the resources to leave or want to remain with their partner for any of a number of reasons. (A more detailed discussion of factors that contribute to women's leaving an abusive partner or staying with him can be found in Chap. 4). The women who stay with an abuser cope with the daily stress of maintaining their safety and physical and emotional well-being. There are also services available in many locations for these women. In this chapter, some of the resources for women who want to leave as well as for those who stay are discussed.

Case Example #7 illustrates how an abused woman might seek safety with relatives. When this doesn't work out, a shelter may serve as the best available option. This case also illustrates a common pattern in which after an episode of abuse, the victim seeks safety at a shelter but leaves after only a brief stay, returning to the abuser after he apologizes and promises to change. After multiple episodes of this cycle, the victim finally makes a commitment to leave and stay at the shelter for a sufficient length of time to obtain the assistance she needs to leave the abuser.

Case Example #7
Julie states that her husband kicked her out of the house 2 days ago and she has no place to go and is, essentially, homeless. Her sister-in-law took her in to stay with her family but her husband (Julie's brother-in-law) says he wants Julie to leave because his brother will get too upset. Julie's husband drinks heavily on a daily basis, beats her up regularly and she doesn't know what to do. Julie presents as an attractive young woman who is upset and desperate. Her speech is pressured, affect is somewhat labile in presentation, there is no evidence thought disorder, and she denies suicidal or homicidal ideation. Julie has stayed at the battered women's shelter before but has never been willing to stay longer than overnight. When I inquired as to why she doesn't stay longer at the shelter, she says that she has always contacted her husband, he apologizes and promises never to hit her again and so she returns home. Things are good for a couple weeks or so but then his drinking escalates and inevitably he abuses her again. Julie realizes she needs to do more than what she has done so far to change her situation, including staying at the shelter and getting counseling, so I called the shelter and she talked with them on the phone and agreed to go there and commit to staying for a few days. Her sister-in-law agreed to drive her over.

The following case from our case notes also demonstrates this pattern of going to a shelter, returning to an abuser, and then again seeking emergency at a later time.

Case Example
Tammy has been admitted to the shelter for the third time in an 18 month period. She feels embarrassed to have returned, especially since she swore she would never go back to her abusive boyfriend after the last shelter stay. Her caseworker assured her that it is very difficult to leave, and many women use the shelter multiple times. The caseworker pointed out to Tammy that the last time she came in she had a black eye and a sprained wrist. This time Tammy left her boyfriend when she knew the violence was about to escalate, and therefore avoided physical injury.

8.1.1 Shelters for Women Experiencing IPV

Probably the best-known intervention for female survivors of IPV is battered women's shelters (Augusta-Scott, Scott, & Tutty, 2017). In the following sections, we first discuss these shelters and the services they provide. Box 8.2 discusses the development of these shelters. Next, several of the types of formal treatment or intervention programs offered at shelters, as well as at other agencies, are described. In addition to providing housing, a number of services are offered at shelters including counseling and support groups for the women and any children they bring with them. They may provide assistance in finding new housing and employment for the women as well as connecting them to other social services (Sullivan & Virden, 2017). Some women survivors of IPV may seek emergency shelter at a battered woman's shelter, with the intention of returning to their abusive partner when he calms down (Fisher & Stylianou, 2019). Based on residents' own assessments, the desire for personal safety was a major factor in their coming to the shelter (Sullivan & Virden, 2017).

Although services vary, shelters offer case management, individual and group counseling, drug and alcohol treatment services, and legal assistance. The shelter staff often work with women to help them understand the dynamics of IPV, often by using a conceptual framework such as the Power and Control Wheel (see the National Domestic Violence Hotline website for more information). These formal services are complemented by informal opportunities to talk with other shelter residents throughout the normal course of a day. Most shelters provide an advocate to

Box 8.2: History of Battered Women's Shelters

The women's liberation movement of the 1960s paved the way for the recognition of IPV as a significant social issue. Husbands' abuse of their wife was not considered a serious problem before this (Barner & Carney, 2011). Grassroots efforts of women's organizations led to the development of a shelter system where women could find safe haven from abusive partners (Fisher & Stylianou, 2019). The early shelters were often little more than a bedroom in a house that provided emergency shelter. As these shelters became more widespread, more and more women began requesting services. This developmental process can be seen in more detail in the case study of the transitions of one of the early shelters in Massachusetts (Fleck-Henderson, 2017).

Eventually, federal funding for shelters was established in 1984, as part of the funding for the Victims of Crime Act (Barner & Carney, 2011). Shelter funding has increased substantially since that time, and public attitudes have become more negative about violence against women, particularly since the passage of the Violence against Women Act (VAWA) in 1994 and again in 2013. The bill is due to be reconsidered by Congress. Thus, levels of future funding have not yet been determined by the time of this writing (Viebeck, 2018).

help women navigate the details of leaving their abusive partner. Women often need support around challenges such as negotiating a leave from work, finding employment, obtaining health care, or communicating with their children's school about a change in residence. Shelter residents are given information about their legal rights and are assisted in obtaining protection orders and legal assistance if they choose to pursue criminal justice remedies (Wood, Heffron, Voyles, & Kulkarni, 2017). Because of limited resources, domestic violence shelters usually have time limits on the length of stay. This can range from 30 days to more than a year. However, many women only stay for a short time (Fisher & Stylianou, 2019).

Additionally, shelter-based counseling services provide women and their children with an opportunity to address the impact of violence on their lives. Women usually have the opportunity for individual counseling sessions in addition to group counseling with other survivors in the shelter. Counseling services vary by agency and may be more psychoeducational or more therapeutically focused. However, most programs use a feminist framework for service delivery and a common theme is often an exploration of IPV from the perspective of power, control, and gender inequality.

Shelters provide safety and support for the women who take advantage of them, but can be a difficult environment to live in. Living at a shelter requires a willingness to accept collective living with strangers and offers little privacy. Shelter residents sometimes have private bedrooms, but in others there are shared bedrooms, bathrooms and kitchens. To our knowledge, there are no shelters available for male survivors of IPV (See Box 8.1) (Sullivan & Virden, 2017). Shelters typically establish a number of rules of conduct that the women seeking shelter are required to follow. These rules for may prohibit contact with valued friends or family members, which many women find upsetting and can undermine important sources of social support (Fisher & Stylianou, 2019). Other rules may relate to contact with the abuser, how they interact with their children in the shelter, not smoking, rules about using the kitchen, and participation in offered services (Wood et al., 2017). In a qualitative study of how women responded to these types of rules, Wood and her colleagues reported that several of the women they interviewed complained that all the rules brought back too many memories of rules established by their abusers. They also complained about rules requiring daily testing for drugs. Curfew rules interfered with employment for some of the shelter residents.

8.1.2 Assessments of Shelter Services

Assessments of shelter services and other counseling programs for IPV survivors are generally positive (Koss, White, & Lopez, 2017). This can be seen in ratings by residents themselves. For example, in a study of 215 programs in 8 different states, Sullivan and Virden (2017) found that on average the residents agreed that they had received help at the shelter with learning about their options and choices, and that they had gained a better understanding about the dynamics of domestic violence. They also positively rated safety planning for the future for themselves and their children as well as gaining emotional support from other survivors. This positive assessment of shelters can also be found through a formal review of the existing published research. Trabold, McMahon, Alsobrooks, Whitney, and Mittal (2018) found evidence for a positive impact of the type of empowerment-focused assistance provided at shelters for IPV survivors, as well as safety-planning in their systematic review of the published literature.

Others have noted some negative effects of shelters. Both Stylianou, Counselman-Carpenter, and Redcay (2018) and Goodwin, Banyard, Woulfe, Ash, and Mattern (2016) found evidence that rules about limiting contact with others outside the shelter led to losing important social support that IPV survivors had relied on before coming to the shelter. As Stylianou et al. explained, both family members and friends had provided encouragement to the women as well as financial help and assistance in caring for children. Although, overall the women in their sample were positive about the shelter experience, they wished they had been allowed to have visitors. Focus groups for women in shelters organized by Goodwin et al. (2016) led to recommendations that shelters focus more on helping the women build stronger social networks and assist with this after the survivors left the shelter.

Sullivan (2018), who has been involved with shelter programs for many years (e.g., Sullivan et al., 1992; Sullivan 2011), offered a conceptual model guiding the services they offered. She labeled this as a "Social and Emotional Well-Being Framework" (p. 123). The model was developed in collaboration with the National Resource Center on Domestic Violence who convened three national meetings of experts to discuss and refine this model. Underlying this model was the idea that domestic violence survivors suffer from a loss of economic, social, and interpersonal resources as well as a reduced sense of self. Shelter services were designed to reduce these losses and add resources back for the women they serve. Doing this allows the women and their children to improve their overall quality of life. She argued that there were 8 basic services that led to these positive outcomes:

1. Providing information about adult and child survivors' rights, options and experiences.
2. Safety planning in a way that is individualized to each survivors own experiences.
3. Building skills the survivor identifies as needed.
4. Offering encouragement, empathy and respect to the survivor through staff being non-judgmental and respectful of differences among survivors.
5. Providing supportive counseling to survivors through individual counseling, support groups, casual conversations with staff or other means.
6. Increasing access for survivors to community resources and opportunities.
7. Increasing social support and community connections for survivors.
8. Having staff who are engaged with the community and involved in social change to hold those who are violent accountable and promote justice. Also included in this aspect of shelters is support for organizations that provide adequate resources and opportunities for all community members (Sullivan, 2018).

8.1.3 Suggestions for Additional Services for Shelters

A number of studies have made suggestions for additional services that might be offered at shelters (or other agencies for IPV survivors). Given the data indicating that IPV survivors tend to have poorer physical health than comparison groups (Kamimura, Christensen, Tabler, Ashby, & Olson, 2014; Chap. 4), more emphasis on health care issues would be beneficial. In order to better understand these needs, Ferranti, Lorenzo, Munoz-Rojas, and Gonzalez-Guarda (2018) interviewed 10 service providers who worked with survivors of IPV at an agency in South Florida as well as 122 female IPV survivors. Many health needs were identified, including the need for general physical exams and education about basic hygiene and nutrition. Education about sexual issues and chronic disease management were also mentioned. The IPV survivors explained that deficiencies in these areas were partially due to lack of health insurance and difficulties in transportation. Immigrants were sometimes fearful about getting medical help, and then being forced to leave the country. In other research, Mantler, Jackson, and Walsh (2018) found evidence that programs have been developed to enhance dental care, test for HIV, or do routine health examinations for the women in shelters and their children (Ragavan et al., 2018). More attention needs to be given to treating substance abuse issues (Weaver, Gilbert, El-Bassel, Resnick, & Noursi, 2015). Ragavan et al. (2018) outlined a series of workshops they developed to offer to female IPV survivors living in transitional housing as they left their abusive partner and prepared to move to a more permanent situation. These workshops focused on health education topics, but their evaluation assessment indicated that many of the women treated some of the sessions as support groups, as they discussed the workshop topics with other survivors.

Although offered in some shelters, legal assistance was also identified as an important service needed by IPV survivors (Lee & Backes, 2018). Lee and Backes offered suggestions for how services such as civil counsel in divorce, custody and protective order proceedings might be made more available for IPV survivors. An important question is how such legal services can be paid for.

Renzetti and Follingstad (2015) suggested that encouraging the shelter residents to work in a garden might be therapeutic. Having the women do gardening provided physical activity, gave them contact with nature, and allowed for opportunities for social contact, as well as providing a calming activity. An evaluation of such a program in Kentucky indicated that staff felt the program was beneficial to the residents, although they had been skeptical at first.

Greater attention to developing appropriate rules for shelter residents is a continuing suggestion (Fisher & Stylianou, 2019). Gregory, Nnawulezi, and Sullivan (2017) suggested that greater attention to rule-making at shelters might lead to greater feelings of empowerment for shelter residents. Other suggestions about enhancing empowerment at shelters can be seen in Nnawulezi, Sullivan, and Hacskaylo (2018) as well as Kulkarni (2018).

8.1.4 *Survivor Assistance for those Who Choose to Stay with the Abusive Partner*

While law enforcement, mental health professionals, and advocates often want women to leave their violent partner, the reality is most women stay in these relationships. Research shows that less than half of women leave their abusive partners, and those who do leave frequently return to them at least once (see Chap. 4). The following case from our files provides an example of the type of type of women who might need services other than shelters.

Case Example

Angela has lived with her abusive husband for 9 years. She has been attending a support group for the past 6 months. Angela shares that she loves her husband and has no desire to leave him. She says that the 'in between times', when he is in good spirits and they are getting along well, fill her with great happiness. Angela and her husband both like to travel, go hiking, and attend classical music concerts. Their two sons are in middle school and love playing sports with their father. She says that in the past she always hid the abuse from everyone because she feared judgment. After she disclosed the abuse to her trusted family doctor, he threatened to stop seeing her as a patient if she stayed with her spouse. Angela was happy to find the group where she can receive support around coping with the abuse and protecting her children from violence exposure, but does not feel pressured to leave her husband. She reports that meeting the other women in the group has made her feel less alone.

Case #12 provides an example of an immigrant couple who remain together in spite of Felipe's abuse of Itzel. This example illustrates how a woman can become trapped in a violent relationship due to lack of resources or access to viable alternatives. In this particular situation, the victim's lack of English fluency kept her isolated, vulnerable to maltreatment and unable to seek help. Although the victim, Itzel, disclosed the occurrence of violence soon after it happened, she subsequently retracted her disclosure due to coercion by the abuser and fear of losing financial support and possibly her children as the result of child welfare involvement, which served to keep her from leaving. For more details on this case, see the full Case #12 in the Appendix.

Case Example #12

Itzel and Felipe migrated to the U.S. for work 3 years ago. Itzel did office cleaning before she was pregnant with Francisco. Felipe used to do itinerant agricultural work, but took full-time employment in a restaurant kitchen when Itzel became pregnant. Felipe speaks English well enough to communicate and take care of day to day needs, whereas Itzel cannot speak, write, or understand English at all. Because of this, Felipe has full control of the family's shared checking account and makes all of the family's business decisions. The family became known to social services when a downstairs neighbor called to say that there is often shouting and banging around upstairs, often accompanied by Francisco crying. When the family were interviewed, Itzel had a visible bruise on her neck and cheek. Felipe denied that he has ever been physically violent, and stated Itzel's injury was from a fall in which she hit her face on the coffee table. Felipe also states that Itzel doesn't want to take care of the finances and isn't interested in taking English classes. Itzel claimed in her interview that Felipe has become increasingly angry due to a combination of financial stress and changes in their relationship since Francisco was born. Itzel states Felipe has always had a temper, but he didn't start hitting her until after Francisco was born. He has also told Itzel that, despite their small income, she cannot work.

Even when women leave the relationship, they may continue to struggle with the psychological effects of their experiences in the abusive relationship. These long term reactions can be seen in the following example from our case notes:

Case Example

Dani was in a relationship with Hector for several years. He was her high school boyfriend and after she got pregnant during her senior year, they got married. Hector began abusing her verbally and physically during her pregnancy and things escalated after the baby's birth. When Dani's son was 3 years old, he was injured during an argument. After this, Dani moved out and filed for divorce. Dani came to see her therapist on the day the divorce was finalized. She reported feeling hopeless, depressed, and anxious. "I thought today would be a day for celebration but I just feel defeated", she said. "I am happy to be single again, but I do not think I will ever feel free from Hector. I still get nervous a lot, and I had to leave a restaurant the other day because a man at the next table was raising his voice to his family. I worry that Hector will show up at my job or my apartment building and make trouble. I fear that he will not return our son after their weekends together, not because he wants our son, but to punish me. I feel like I will always be haunted by Hector."

Other women may stay with an abusive partner for financial reasons. The following clinical case example (described in more detail in the Appendix) illustrates how Andrea, a victim of domestic violence may call for help with genuine concern for their own and their children's well-being, but may recant these statements out of fear of losing the financial and other support provided by the abuser. Fighting in the couple centered on the behavior of Andrea's daughter, Caitlyn, aged 15. In this case, when the victim and her abuser insisted on staying together, despite social services' concerns. The decision was made to provide safety planning followed by in-home intensive services to the family to reduce future harm.

Case Example #13

The Jackson family recently moved to a new city. Andrea called the police the night that they moved in to their rental home, alleging that George was hitting her. A check with the family's previous county of residence found two child welfare reports of fighting between the adults, though both times were unclear as to who began the fight and what actually happened. Both reports were closed because there had been no evidence of physical fighting. When interviewed, Andrea alleged that George was upset about Caitlyn's behavior. Caitlyn has begun to engage in self-cutting, which Andrea is concerned about but feels, from her own negative experiences with therapy, that it is best to ignore the behavior rather than reward it with attention by going to therapy. George is angry about this, as he and Andrea have young twins who are exposed to Caitlyn's behavior...An argument about Caitlyn's behavior began when George said she needs to get therapy..., and Andrea took offense to this. The argument escalated to dishes being thrown, at which point Andrea called the police. George admitted he threw a plate, but was not aiming for Andrea. He also noted that all of the children were in bed, and thus did not see anything. Caitlyn stated in her interview that she has heard them yelling at each other, but has never seen anyone hitting. Caitlyn said she hated George... George was asked to leave, and Andrea agreed to keep him away from the home until the investigation was completed. However, an unannounced visit found that George was back in the home. When asked why she allowed him to return, Andrea said they cannot live without George's salary, and that the plate-throwing fight had been a misunderstanding. Andrea and George insisted they would stay together. Despite social services' concern, the courts did not find enough risk to justify removing the children if George refused to leave.

As Grossman and Lundy (2011) discuss more formally, despite the importance of shelters as a source of safety and other services for women abused by a partner, not all of these women are able to go to a shelter because of limited resources or availability as seen in the cases presented here. Some women may select other options for immediate safety or for help in leaving a partner. This may be because they do not want to explain to others that they are survivors of partner violence. Immigrant women may be concerned about language difficulties, and, if undocumented, they may fear being deported. Male survivors do not have an option of going to a shelter. Thus, shelters do not provide services to the majority of IPV survivors for a variety of reasons. The most common alternative option is staying with friends or family. If they have the financial ability to do so, some may choose to go to a hotel.

In a study of 70 state-funded domestic violence centers in the state of Illinois, Grossman and Lundy (2011) surveyed women using these services to compare those who first sought assistance at a shelter to those who relied on other services. Overall, those who initially went to a shelter were younger, less educated, and more likely to be African American. Shelter residents were also more often single rather than married. They were more likely to be survivors of physical than of emotional abuse, although physical abuse was the most common type of abuse for both groups. Other analyses indicated those going to shelters did receive higher levels of assistance.

8.1.4.1 Safety Planning

One type of service available to those who remain with their abusive partners or return to them after a shelter stay is safety planning. In a qualitative analysis of how this process occurs, Logan and Walker (2018) conducted focus groups with staff of shelters, as well as rape crisis centers, child protective services, and law enforcement agencies. Several major strategies emerged from these discussions: Determining what the risks and needs were for the survivor in terms of physical and emotional concerns, helping the survivor create a safe space by focusing on her strengths, and providing resources and referrals as needed. A number of common safety concerns centered around substance abuse in the survivor as well as the abuser; issues relating to guns and whether the survivor should get a gun; stalking by the abuser; and threats made to others such as friends or family members. The staff members also noted that there were no accepted protocols relating to safety planning.

Safety planning may be needed if a survivor seeks assistance at family court. Stylianou (2018) presented detailed information on this process as it occurred in a victim-service agency in the northeastern U.S. that served five different family courts. When IPV survivors sought help from the courts, they were directed to the agency and met privately with a family court advocate. Stylianou was able to access recordings of actual meetings and analyzed what survivors were asked about in terms of their immediate physical and emotional risks and how they were guided into a discussion of how they could enhance their personal safety in the future to minimize the risk of revictimization. These services were available to both female and male survivors.

When a sample of women seeking protection from abuse orders (see Chaps. 4 and 9) were asked what strategies they had used in the past to protect themselves from abuse from their partner, the most common responses were keeping money and other valuables hidden, working out an escape plan, and keeping important phone numbers that could be used if help was needed. Letting friends and family know about the abuse and seeking their assistance if needed was also frequently mentioned. Many tried to placate their abuser by keeping things quiet in the home, doing whatever he asked, trying not to cry when being abused, and sleeping separately (Parker, Gielen, Castillo, Webster, & Glass, 2016).

Safety planning might also be improved for immigrant women if cultural factors specific to different nationality groups are considered. Sabri et al. (2018) discussed some of the particular problems of immigrant women experiencing IPV. She argued that immigrant and refugee women were at high risk for IPV and often have difficulty in finding appropriate services.

In 2015, Eden and her colleagues developed a website that provided personalized safety planning for abused women as well as providing information about available resources. The website was advertised widely in the community through posters and online ads. A formal evaluation of the program was done through comparing the experiences of half the women provided the personalized assistance to another randomly assigned group who also received a list of resources, but only received very general safety planning information. The group with the personalized information did report feeling more supported by the program and felt more confident about their own safety planning. This website was further developed and expanded to four different states by many in the original research team (Glass et al., 2017). A similar control group was used for an assessment of the expanded website. A Spanish as well as an English language version of the website was tested, with data collected a year after the initial use of the website. Those with the personalized website were found to be more likely to have left their abuser a year later than the comparison group, and reported that more of the safety behaviors they had tried had been helpful. Overall, though, there were no significant differences in the personalized and comparison group in depression or PTSD. These data do suggest that using on-line resources may be a very useful way of providing safety planning for abused women, especially for those who have not sought help at a shelter or other agency. Safety planning through the use of a phone app has also been developed for those exposed to violence within a lesbian relationship (Bloom, Gielen, & Glass, 2016).

On-line training has also been developed for service providers. As Chap. 10 explains, many of those working at shelters to assist battered women have not received much formal education about intimate partner violence. Etherington and her colleagues (2017) in Canada provided information about a program they have developed and tested to serve these helpgivers. A 4 week course was provided to those working in shelters in Ontario, Canada. Topics covered included feminist views of IPV and understanding risk factors for IPV, as well as practical concerns such as record keeping. They also offered guidance about networking among those taking the course.

8.1.5 Evidence-Based Interventions for Female IPV Survivors

While there are many interventions currently being utilized with family violence survivors, this chapter will primarily focus on those which have been evaluated and shown to be effective in published research studies. The types of services discussed may be offered at shelters, but may also be done in community centers providing services of survivors of IPV (Arroyo, Lundahl, Butters, Vanderloo, & Wood, 2017). For more information about trauma and ideas about treatment generally, see Chap. 3.

The idea of *evidence-based practice* had its origins in the medical field. Historically, medicine was based more on intuition and anecdotal experience (Guyatt et al., 1992). Credit has been given to Florence Nightingale for moving the field toward more scientific rational for medical decision making in the nineteenth century. When she practiced nursing during the Crimean War, she noticed a connection between poor sanitary conditions in the hospital and rising death rates among wounded soldiers (McDonald, 2001). Nightingale's subsequent efforts to sanitize hospitals led to dramatic drops in patient mortality (Baker, 1983). Her process of identifying, critically appraising, and summarizing the best available data was a precursor of modern standards for evidence-based practice. Since then, this evidence-based approach to decision making has become widely accepted by not only the medical community, but by allied professions such as public health, psychology, and social work. Current practices that are considered to be evidence-based have been tested through an experimental or quasi-experimental research design to show effectiveness. These treatment programs are offered through shelters or other community agencies.

8.1.5.1 Community Advocacy Project (CAP)

Advocacy has long been recognized as essential to the well-being of women in violent relationships (Allen, Larsen, Trotter, & Sullivan, 2013). After they leave the shelter, they may continue to have assistance by staff known as advocates. Staff advocates play an important role in accompanying and supporting women as they navigate legal, medical, and social systems that can help protect them from future abuse as well as providing continuing assistance for those women who leave their partners (see Chap. 10 for more information about the advocates). As Allen et al. (2013) explained, this continuing role for advocates was developed in response to requests from the domestic violence survivors for more long-term assistance. Sullivan and Bybee's (1999) research demonstrated the importance of an advocacy program for battered women's safety and quality of life. They developed the Community Advocacy Project (CAP) to standardize this important process.

CAP provides advocacy and individually tailored assistance to women who have been physically and/or emotionally abused by intimate partners. The program also recognizes the needs of children who may have been exposed to the violence in their homes. CAP's objectives of eliminating or reducing the risk of future abuse and improving participants' quality of life are premised on women gaining empowerment and coping skills, obtaining social support, and recognizing and using community resources. CAP is delivered by trained, supervised paraprofessionals who work as advocates with women and their children to help them obtain needed community resources and social support, after the women leave a shelter-based program. The program is designed to be short term but intensive, involving 4–6 h per week for 10 weeks. Advocates are trained to help women obtain community resources they might need and provide support. CAP begins with discussions of safety and moves through five phases.

The first phase of CAP is assessment (Sullivan, 2011). The advocate gathers important information regarding the needs and goals of each participant and her child. The participant, not the advocate, guides the direction and activities of the intervention by identifying issues that are important to her. Next is the implementation phase. During this phase the advocate and the participant actively work together to generate, mobilize, and access community resources. Women often need resources such as legal assistance, housing, employment, education, transportation, child care, social support, and/or material goods. For children, advocacy focuses on participating in recreational activities (e.g., joining a sports team or a Boys and Girls Club), receiving help with school work, or obtaining needed material goods. The third phase is monitoring, when the advocate checks in with the participant regularly to determine whether her identified needs have been satisfied. The fourth phase is the secondary implementation. This is when alternate strategies for meeting the clients' needs are generated, in the event that community resources have not been effective. Finally, the termination phase occurs during the last few weeks of the intervention, when the advocate focuses even more intensively on the transfer of skills and knowledge to the participant, ensuring that she no longer needs the advocate at the end of the intervention.

The effectiveness of CAP has been tested in randomized control trials. Sullivan and Bybee (1999) randomly assigned 278 women living in a domestic violence shelter to either CAP or a control group upon shelter exit. Women in the CAP received 10 weeks of advocacy and support. Both groups were interviewed immediately upon leaving the shelter and six additional times across a 2 year period. Both groups had retention rates of more than 90% across the length of the study. Women in the CAP intervention group reported both short- and long-term benefits (Sullivan & Bybee, 1999). These women were more likely to have left their abusive partner and reported less psychical and psychological abuse than the control group women. The women who received CAP reported decreased depression and greater social support. Experimental group women also reported a greater overall quality of life than control group women, and these gains persisted over the 2 year time period of the study.

Subsequent studies included children along with their mothers. Sullivan, Bybee, and Allen (2002) recruited 80 women with at least one child between the ages of 7 and 11 (if multiple children were in this age range, one was randomly selected for the study). Families were randomly assigned to CAP for 16 weeks or to a control group and followed for a total of 8 months. Results indicated that in addition to improvements in the mothers' well-being, children showed positive gains after being in CAP. The CAP children reported greater feelings of self-competence, including self-worth. They also reported less exposure to violence than the control group children.

Allen and Sullivan have continued to work with the CAP program. In a more recent study, Allen et al. (2013) analyzed qualitative data from the survivors during the first 5 years of the program to determine which aspects of the program were viewed as most helpful. A common theme was the good relationship between the domestic violence survivor and the advocate. The emotional support and non-judgmental approach provided by the advocate were seen as crucial. The experience of setting personal goals in collaboration with the advocate was also commonly mentioned. The responses were summarized as supporting the importance of the "strengths-based, survivor-centered, emotionally supportive, action-oriented advocacy" (p. 13), all of which were part of the underlying assumptions guiding the development of the CAP program.

8.1.5.2 Cognitive Trauma Therapy for Battered Women (CTT-BW)

Cognitive Trauma Therapy for Battered Women (CTT-BW) is an intervention designed to address posttraumatic stress in battered women (see Chap. 4 for more discussion of post-traumatic stress disorder or PTSD), especially when they have been physically or sexually abused (Kubany & Watson, 2002). The intervention includes elements from existing treatments for PTSD: (1) psychoeducation about PTSD, (2) stress management including relaxation training, (3) self-monitoring of maladaptive thoughts and speech, and (4) talking about the trauma. A unique aspect of CTT-BW is its inclusion of systematized procedures for both assessing and correcting dysfunctional beliefs and reducing negative self-talk related to guilt and shame, in particular. Correcting erroneous guilt-related beliefs is accomplished through a highly systematic step-by-step format (Kubany & Manke, 1995). Negative thought and speech habits are addressed directly by teaching women to recognize them and then make adjustments accordingly (Kubany, 1998). CTT-BW also includes modules for addressing issues faced by many women in a male-dominated society in which women's needs are sometimes considered less important than the needs of men, and in which women are often vulnerable to exploitation by men. These modules focus on self-advocacy and empowerment and include self-advocacy strategies, assertive communication skill building, managing unwanted contacts with former partners, and identifying potential perpetrators and avoid re-victimization (Box 8.2).

In spite of this past federal funding, many shelters have struggled financially to remain open. Much of the federal money is used for services other than shelters. Many shelters rely on private donations and other sources of funding. Thousands of survivors and their children are turned away annually due to lack of space or other resource limitations (Koss et al., 2017).

Kubany, Hill, and Owens (2003) tested the effectiveness of CTT-BW in a randomized control trial with 37 ethnically diverse women who had recently been abused by a partner. To be eligible to participate in the study, women had to be out of the relationship for at least 30 days with no desire to reconcile and had to meet the following additional criteria: (1) no physical or sexual victimization by anyone in the prior 30 days; (2) diagnosis for partner abuse -related PTSD (3) reported moderate to high levels of abuse-related guilt; (4) no current alcohol or drug abuse; and (5) no diagnosis of schizophrenia or bipolar disorder. Women were randomly assigned to receive either immediate or delayed treatment. Thirty two women completed treatment. Due to the small sample size of this feasibility study, they were unable to test possible group differences between women who received treatment initially and those in the delayed treatment group. Within group improvements, however, were promising. IPV survivors showed significant reduction of PTSD symptoms post treatment, and these improvements were maintained at a 3 month follow up. This outcome was found regardless of whether the investigators included only women who completed treatment or women who received parts of the intervention.

A larger follow up study was completed with 127 women (Kubany et al., 2004). Again, women were randomly assigned to receive either immediate or delayed treatment. Data were collected at the end of 11 sessions, 3 months post treatment, and 6 months post treatment. More than 90% of women showed no PTSD symptomology at the end of treatment. They also showed significant reductions in depressive symptomology. The intervention significantly reduced participants' guilt and increased their self-esteem. Improvements were maintained at 3- and 6 month follow-up assessment points.

In a more recent study investigating the effectiveness of cognitive trauma therapy for battered women, Allard, Norman, Throp, Browne, and Stein (2018) recruited women experiencing IPV through ads and flyers, offering them free therapy. Levels of PTSD were assessed before and after treatment. The trauma-focused therapy was again found to be effective in reducing PTSD symptoms. In the therapy program, they specifically focused on reducing the guilt that many of the women were experiencing. As they explained, many battered women blame themselves for the violence as a means of trying to control how often they are abused. If they identify something they do that leads to violence, they may then believe they can reduce it (see Frieze, 1979, for an early presentation of this idea). Allard et al. argued that it was important in the treatment of the survivors that this guilt be discussed and that the women learn they are not responsible for the violence. Their treatment was effective in reducing this guilt.

In another trauma-focused treatment offered to women in the community, Trabold, O'Malley, Rizzo, and Russell (2018) used cognitive-based theory to help women survivors to accomplish changes in their thoughts and behavior. This was delivered over 10 h-long group sessions at a community-based agency offering services to IPV survivors. Interviews were conducted with 15 of the women in this program. The women were quite positive about the therapy, noting that it helped them identify their own strengths, to feel less guilty about the violence, and to generally feel better emotionally. The group discussion was seen as giving them ideas about how to better cope with their abusive partner.

8.1.5.3 Helping to Overcome PTSD with Empowerment (HOPE)

HOPE is an intervention for battered women with PTSD that is based on cognitive-behavioral therapy principles (Johnson & Zlotnick, 2009). HOPE involves nine to twelve 60–90 min individual sessions conducted twice per week over roughly 8 weeks in the program. HOPE is unique in that it is delivered to women while they are living in domestic violence shelters. The intervention involves three stages of recovery: (1) re-establishing safety and a sense of self-care; (2) remembering and mourning; and (3) reconnecting with people, meaningful activities, and other aspects of life. The treatment prioritizes women's safety and focuses heavily on empowerment.

HOPE is client-driven, and therapists focus on helping women develop skills needed to reach their self-identified personal goals. Later sessions focus on building cognitive and behavioral skills to manage PTSD symptoms. There are optional modules that address common co-occurring issues such as dealing with substance abuse and managing grief. The HOPE session structure is the same for each session: (a) checking in regarding safety and progress on accomplishments; (b) agenda setting; (c) discussion of module-specific information; and (d) negotiating accomplishments for the next session. A hierarchy of target behaviors was developed to guide the content of treatment within and across sessions: (1) immediate physical and emotional risks, (2) PTSD symptoms, behaviors, and cognitions that interfere with achieving shelter and treatment goals and quality of life, and (3) goals and safety after leaving the shelter. This hierarchy determines the order of specific modules over the course of therapy and prioritizes safety issues within each session.

Johnson and Zlotnick (2006) evaluated the effectiveness of HOPE with 18 participants living in a shelter. While women only needed to show subthreshold PTSD symptoms to receive the intervention, 15 of the women in the study met full criteria for PTSD. Women were assessed while in the shelter, 1 week after leaving the shelter, and at 3 and 6 months post-shelter. There average length of shelter stay was 20 days for the participants with an average of seven sessions completed. Results showed that women reported a reduction of PTSD symptoms and depression, and more effective use of resources compared to shelter entry.

A larger evaluation of HOPE was conducted by Johnson, Zlotnick, and Perez (2011). Seventy women living in two domestic violence shelters were randomized to receive HOPE or to standard shelter services. Those randomized to the control condition were provided referrals for treatment in the community upon leaving the shelter. All participants were assessed for follow-up 1 week, 3 months, and 6 months after leaving the shelter. Participants received a maximum of 12 sessions of HOPE while in shelter over roughly 8 weeks. Sessions were offered bi-weekly and lasted approximately 60–90 min. While there was no difference in PTSD rates overall between the treatment and experimental groups, women who received HOPE showed significant improvement over time on depression severity, empowerment, and social support compared to the control condition women. The HOPE group was also less likely to report partner abuse 6 months after leaving the shelter.

Johnson has continued to work on the development of the HOPE treatment program, and published a description of HOPE + SSSs which was specifically designed to be used for women who were residents of a shelter (Johnson, Johnson, Perez, Palmieri, & Zlotnick, 2016). The added SSSs referred to the additional standard shelter services that the women were also receiving. Follow-up assessments of 30 women were done. A comparison group of 30 women who only received the standard shelter treatment was also used in the study. Analyses indicated lowered PTSD scores for the HOPE+SSSs group as compared to the SSSs group. The HOPE+ group also showed more improvement in terms of lowered depressive symptoms, more gains in personal and social resources, and increased feelings of empowerment over the 6-month follow-up.

8.1.5.4 Other Therapies for Survivors of IPV

There are a number of other therapies offered for female survivors of IPV. Many of these are short-term. Arroyo and her colleagues provide a systematic review of some of these (Arroyo et al., 2017). Many are specialized, treating immigrant women, or working on substance abuse along with IPV victimization, for example. Overall, it was clear that short-term therapies can be effective, leading to declines in PTSD, general distress, and depression, and increased general life functioning. Positive, but more moderate effects were found for feelings of safety, emotional well-being, substance abuse, and re-occurrence of IPV.

8.1.6 Assessment of Treatments or Interventions for IPV Survivors

Trabold, McMahon, et al. (2018) published a systematic review of the literature (looking at U.S. studies as well as those done in other countries) looking across many different types of treatment for female survivors of IPV. Overall, they found evidence that treatments often reduced re-victimization, although the evidence was mixed, with some studies failing to find this effect. Evidence for decreased levels of depression showed short-term effects, but not long-term lowering of depression in the IPV survivors. Similarly mixed results were seen for lowering of PTSD symptoms. Results were most positive for psychological well-being, with most studies showing improvements in this measure. In assessing their findings, Trabold et al. noted that much of the therapy offered was short-term, and perhaps survivors needed more sessions than they often received. Key elements of the more successful interventions identified by these researchers were a focus on altering distorted self-thinking of the survivors, along with assistance in problem-solving for those leaving their abusers. Cognitive and CBT interventions appeared to be effective in treating psychological distress and PTSD. None of the treatments provided clear evidence of long-term reductions in depression for the survivors. Trabold et al. concluded by critiquing the quality of much of the research demonstrating the effectiveness of different treatments.

Although the treatments described earlier tend to be longer-term, they are sometimes offered as short-term treatment. Arroyo et al's. (2017) review of IPV survivor treatment programs indicated that short-term cognitive behavioral therapies specifically targeted toward IPV survivors, such as CTT-BW appeared to be most effective of the short-term treatments. Therapies administered to individuals were more effective than group therapies. Those receiving more treatments fared better than less extensive treatment. Arroyo et al. concluded that there was evidence that these short-term therapies could be quite effective, although they noted that often their findings were based on a small number of studies for each of the treatments included in the study. Long term effects were not assessed in this review.

8.2 Children Exposed to IPV and Survivors of Child Abuse and Neglect

There are several ways in which children or adolescents develop trauma and PTSD that relate directly to the types of family violence discussed in this book. One is through exposure to IPV in their parents or caregivers. Many children grow up in homes where IPV is present. These children are frequently exposed to the violence; they hear it, see it, and sometimes get caught in the middle of it (Fusco & Fantuzzo, 2009). They experience some of the same symptoms as abused and neglected children (Fusco, 2017; McTavish, MacGregor, Wathen, & MacMillan, 2016). These children may be identified at a battered women's shelter. They may also be identified by CPS (see Chap. 9) when acting out in inappropriate ways at school. An example of this can be seen in the description of Emma in the cases below from our case files.

Case Example

Emma, 10 years old, was referred to therapeutic services after she was caught damaging school property. Emma's parents, Mary and Don, had recently separated and were in the process of divorce. Don was physically abusive to Mary and verbally abusive to both Mary and Emma. In the 6 months since Mary and

Emma left the family home Emma had become hostile and defiant toward her mother, and she was having problems with her peers at school. Mary was angry with Emma for being disruptive and could not understand why she was not happier to be away from her abusive father. Emma said she was angry that she had to leave her house, her neighborhood, and her dog. It was recommended that Emma and her mother engage in therapy together so that they could work on their issues related to the abuse they experienced, and strengthen their parent-child bond.

Eight-year old Basim's story below illustrates how children exposed to IPV may imitate such violence or casually disclose it to others, such as a teacher. Sometimes, as illustrated here, such situations are complicated by cultural issues around gender roles and norms. In this case, long-term in-home services were seen as the most appropriate intervention.

Case Example #3

Basim's school called with concern that his behavior is increasingly violent, and seems to be particularly directed toward his mother. Most recently Basim had asked his mother to take him to McDonalds after school for dinner because he prefers American food and didn't want to eat his mom's more traditional cooking. When Nur refused, Basim began hitting and kicking her. The principal and guidance counselor both spoke with Nur and found that she has been experiencing this quite a lot, and is concerned that Basim is copying his father's behavior. Nur states that he often shoves and slaps her, though she has never been bruised by him. Basim has told female teachers and staff that he doesn't have to listen to them because he is going to be a man, and they are only women. Social services began an investigation into the family.

Neglect is the most common form of child maltreatment followed by physical abuse. This can take for form of physical, emotional or sexual child maltreatment. Sexual maltreatment within the family is often referred to as incest. Details about these types of abuse can be found in Chap. 6. Case #18 illustrates how incest can occur and continue because some families normalize incest and justify it as a way to teach children about sex. Children who experience sexual abuse sometimes respond by perpetrating abuse against younger children. In addition, a sexual abuse history may contribute to aggressive or destructive behaviors in youth.

Case Example #18
13 year old Shannon was referred to Child Protective Services by her teacher after put her hands inside the front of an 8 year-old boy's pants and rubbed herself against him at a school assembly. During a meeting with Shannon's parents, her stepfather Dave reported that he has fondled her breasts and has purchased lingerie that he expected her to model for him. He also watched online pornography with Shannon. Dave did not think these behaviors were a problem, and stated: "I am the only father she has and the only man she has in her life so it is my job to teach her how to be a woman." Shannon's mother, Julie, agreed with this behavior and shared that her own father treated her and her sisters the same way. Julie and Dave viewed the response toward Shannon touching the younger boy and the investigation as an overreaction. Neither had any interest in attending parenting classes and repeatedly said this was all a 'private family matter'.

It was determined to be unsafe for Shannon to remain in her home since her parents believed their actions were appropriate. Since sexual abuse was prevalent in her extended family, kinship care options were not explored. It emerged that Shannon had a history of sexually acting out with younger boys so she was placed in Multidimensional Treatment Foster Care. After an incident where she slapped her foster mother, Shannon was transferred to a Residential Treatment Facility (RTF) where she received individual and group therapy. Her parents were encouraged to participate in family therapy with a future goal of reunification but they only attended one session. Shannon spent 15 months in the RTF but after running away and setting a small fire in a common room she was transferred to a juvenile detention center. She was eventually returned to her mother's care after Dave was arrested and sentenced to 5 years in prison for a drug-related charge.

8.2.1 Therapeutic Programs for Maltreated Children and their Parents

When a family is identified as abusing or neglecting a child, a caseworker is assigned to work with the family (see Chap. 9). As Larrieu (2018) explained, when it appears that the child is experiencing trauma, and that the parent may be receptive to addressing that trauma, the family may be referred to some type of specialized treatment. This treatment may occur at the agency, at a specialized clinic, or in the home of the family. A number of different treatment programs used in these cases are outlined below. As will be seen, there are a large number of these programs. We briefly discuss some of the most well-known of these programs at this point in time.

8.2.1.1 Parent-Child Interaction Therapy

Parent–child interaction therapy (PCIT) was developed for children with conduct problems and their families in the 1970s, but evolved for use with families experiencing maltreatment (Eyberg, 2005). PCIT is an evidence-based dyadic behavioral intervention for children ages 2–7 and their caregivers. The focus is on decreasing child externalizing behaviors and increasing child-parent attachment. This manualized intervention is rooted in social learning theory and attachment theory, and it occurs in two stages: (1) a focus on enhancing the parent –child relationship, referred to as child-directed interaction; and (2) a focus on improving child compliance, known as parent-directed interaction. PCIT involves using therapists to teach parents skills and coach them as they practice implementation. This coaching is performed using wireless communication and one-way mirrors (Hembree-Kigin & McNeil, 1995). The average number of recommended sessions is 14 conducted in 1 or 2 h.

The evidence base for PCIT is robust (e.g., Eisenstaadt, Eyberg, McNeil, Newcomb, & Funderbunk, 1993; Eyberg, 1988) and positive gains in child behaviors has been sustained for as many as 6 years post treatment (Hood & Eyberg, 2003; Lieneman, Brabson, Highlander, Wallace, & McNeil, 2017). When used with families where maltreatment has occurred, the emphasis is more on parenting behaviors than on child externalizing problems (Herschell & McNeil, 2005). While child behavior problems do not need to be in the clinical range when working with these families, externalizing problems are still central to this model (Thomas & Zimmer-Gembeck, 2012). In a review of the existing research with families who received PCIT as a result of child maltreatment, varying degrees of effectiveness were found (Batzer, Berg, Godinet, & Stotzer, 2018). PCIT was found to reduce maltreatment recidivism more than other models, and to significantly reduce child behavior problems. However, the results on whether negative parenting behaviors decreased and positive parenting behaviors increased was equivocal, with one study showing only a 5% improvement in parental sensitivity (Thomas & Zimmer-Gembeck, 2011). There is also evidence that PCIT might improve child-parent attachment in families with physical abuse but not with other types of maltreatment (Chaffin et al., 2004).

8.2.1.2 Child Parent Psychotherapy

CPP is a dyadic relationship-based treatment for parents and young children that helps restore normal developmental functioning after experiences of violence and trauma (Lieberman, Ippen, & Van Horn, 2006). This intervention focuses on restoring attachment bonds that are negatively affected by violence, establishing a sense of safety and trust within the parent-child relationship, and addressing the co-constructed meaning of the event or trauma shared by parent and child. Sessions focus on parent-child interactions to support and foster health coping, affect regulation, and increased appropriate reciprocity between parent and child. Parent guidance on development, behavioral management, crisis intervention, and case management are provided as needed in an unstructured way. Recommended intervention is 50 weekly session of 60–90 min.

An evaluation of CPP was conducted with mother–child dyads referred for services. Some were referred because of problematic behavior of the maltreated child in school. Other families were referred because of CPS concerns about the mother's parenting skills. Seventy-five mothers and their preschool-aged children were randomized to receive CPP or case management plus community referral for individual treatment. The perpetrator of the IPV was no longer living in the home, and children who had been physically or sexually abused were excluded from the sample. The CPP group had weekly hour long sessions with a therapist for up to 50 weeks. Families attended an average of 32 CPP sessions. Data from a 6 month follow-up indicated that children in the CPP group showed decreased traumatic stress and fewer behavior problems than the control group children. Mothers also showed a reduction in PTSD and reported better overall functioning than women who received only case management. Lieberman and her colleagues did note that improvements were found in both groups over time, although they were stronger for the CPP group. A later reanalysis of the original data indicated that CPP was also effective in helping children exposed to other forms of trauma in addition to IPV as well as leading to more positive outcomes in their mothers (Ippen, Harris, Van Horn, & Lieberman, 2011).

CPP has also been used as an intervention for maternal neglect by Toth and Manly (2019; Toth, Sturge-Apple, Rogosch, & Cicchetti, 2015). This treatment was developed to help mothers better understand how earlier experiences of mothers with abuse or neglect when they were children might affect their interactions with their children as mothers. This was predicted to help build stronger mother-child relationships and well as giving mothers a more positive image of their children. In one of the more recent of these studies, Toth et al. (2015) identified a sample of families with 13 month infants being served by Child Protective Services for child neglect, as well a comparison group of 52 families being served by the Department of Human Services for poverty-related needs where there was no evidence of child maltreatment. Within the group identified as neglectful, 44 of the families were assigned to receive CPP, another 34 families received a form of therapy relating to parenting style (PPI), and 27 families served as a control group, receiving only the usual services. Data collection included a 1-year follow-up. Analyses indicated that parental stress associated with negative views of children decreased over time for the CPP group, while increasing for the other groups in the study. The researchers attributed this increase in stress for the comparison group to the fact that the initial ratings were taken when the children were infants. They argued that children became more difficult for parents to manage as they got older. Other forms of stress associated with parenting decreased for the PPI group, but there were no significant differences for the CPP group.

Larrieu (2018) discussed how CPP was currently being implemented within the child welfare system. She argued that it incorporated trauma informed care and helped promote safety for children previously identified as being abused. CPP treatment was also described as helping parents and children to learn adaptive coping strategies. This may suggest that CPP treatment now incorporates aspects of some of the other treatment programs described below.

8.2.1.3 Trauma Focused Cognitive Behavioral Therapy (TF-CBT)

TF-CBT is an evidence-based treatment approach developed to help children ages 3–18 and their families cope with traumatic events, such as experiencing child sexual abuse (Cohen & Mannarino, 2017; Cohen, Mannarino, & Deblinger, 2017). It has now been tested in at least 20 randomized controlled trials for many types of trauma involving children, including sexual, physical or emotional abuse or neglect as well as exposure to IPV. This type of treatment has also been used for those exposed to community violence, serious accidents and natural or other disasters. Although the therapy is not intended to treat the traumatic experiences themselves, it does address trauma-related mental health problems as well as other PTSD symptoms.

The intervention incorporates both learning and cognitive theories to help individuals recognize and address cognitive distortions that may develop after traumatic experiences. For example, children who have lived in homes with IPV often develop maladaptive beliefs such as blaming themselves for the abuse, feeling powerless in their lives, and fearing that people will treat them differently than other children. They may show post-traumatic stress symptomology including intrusive thoughts, avoidance of people, places, or things, and physical and emotional hyperarousal, which can contribute to emotional and behavioral problems. The assumption is that when children are able to recognize distorted beliefs and attributions that arise from trauma they are better able to change negative emotions and behaviors. Their treatment program was designed to address these issues.

TF-CBT involves child and (nonoffending) parent psychosocial therapy for children and youth with emotional/behavioral difficulties associated with trauma. Parents, including foster parents for abused or neglected children, may be frustrated by behavior problems in the children and are taught about why the children may be acting in these ways. The treatment enables the parents to become more supportive and may also lead to improvements in sibling relationships as well as general family functioning. The treatment also addresses trauma-related symptoms of the parents. Parents are offered guidance on how to appropriately respond to their children's needs and offer emotional support to them. Some hourly sessions as split between the child and the parents, while conjoint sessions include both parents and children together, with a brief private meeting with the child and then with the parents before the conjoint session. Typically, treatment duration is 12 to 15 session, but may be extended for more complex trauma.

There are eight core components of TF-CBT. These components include: (1) Psychoeducation about the nature of the child's traumatic experiences; (2) Parenting Skills that are taught to parents, often using role-playing to help parents implement these skills; (3) Relaxation skills individualized to the child and parent; (4) Affective modulation skills training children to express emotions through enjoyable games and other interactive activities and educating parents to assist children in doing this; (5) Cognitive coping skills including connecting thoughts, feelings, and behaviors related to the trauma; (6) Trauma narrative development and processing; (7) In-vivo exposure to reduce anxiety relating to trauma reminders; (8) Conjoint parent-child sessions to practice skills and enhance trauma-related discussions; and (9) Enhancing personal safety and optimal development through providing safety and social skills training as needed. The strength of the therapeutic relationship is very important to this intervention, and clinicians must show a high level of sensitivity, flexibility, and creativity as they work with families.

Many studies have been published by Cohen and Mannarino and other colleagues demonstrating the effectiveness of TF-CBT beginning in 1996 (summarized in Cohen & Mannarino, 2017). Declines in PTSD symptoms and improvements in social behaviors for children have been demonstrated in these studies. Other researchers are also using this treatment protocol. For example, Goldbeck, Muche, Sachser, Tutus, and Rosner (2016), compared TF-CBT to non-treatment for children aged 7–17 in eight German outpatient clinics. The children had been exposed to a variety of different types of trauma. The TF-CBT children showed significantly fewer PTSD symptoms than those on the waiting list. After treatment 45% of the children no longer met PTSD diagnostic criteria. This was also true for 29% of those who were on the waiting list, but did not get treatment (indicating that symptoms do sometimes disappear over time without treatment). The treatment appeared to be most effective for the younger children with fewer PTSD symptoms.

In another randomized controlled trial, Cohen, Mannarino, and Iyengar (2011) provided TF-CBT to a sample of 64 children who had been exposed to partner violence. The sample was recruited from a shelter for women experiencing IPV, Mothers and children receiving 8 sessions of TF-CBT were compared to a group of 60 children receiving child-centered therapy for 8 sessions, the standard treatment for the shelter. Children in the TF-CBT group had significantly greater declines in hyperarousal and avoidance, symptoms of PTSD. There were no differences in other PTSD symptoms such as trauma-related thoughts. Researchers suggested this was not unexpected since many had continued contact with their abusive father. It was also noted that there was a relatively high drop-out rate within both groups.

In a more recent study, Stewart, Orengo-Aguayo, Cohen, Mannarino, and de Arellano (2017), working with Cohen and Mannarino, experimented with providing TF-CBT to a small sample of 15 traumatized youth aged 7–16 through videoconferencing. Five had experienced sexual abuse, one had physical abuse, another had witnessed abuse of a sibling, and others had multiple traumas. It was not clear if any had been exposed to parental IPV. After treatment, there were declines in PTSD symptoms. Although the sample was small, the researchers suggested that this type of service delivery would be helpful for those who are not able to received face-to-face treatment due to living in rural areas or who are unable to come for other reasons.

8.2.1.4 Alternatives for Families: A Cognitive-Behavioral Therapy

AF-CBT also incorporates cognitive-behavioral techniques to work with family conflict, coercion or aggression, including physical child abuse (Kolko et al., 2012). It is designed to increase the well-being and safety of children in families with high levels of physical and verbal aggression. As in CF-CBT, both children and their caregivers participate in individual and joint sessions. A website explaining this type of therapy and providing additional information can be found at https://www.afcbt.org .

These risks include coercive parenting practices, anger hyperarousal, negative child attributions, and family conflict. The consequences include, but are not limited to, child aggression, poor interpersonal skills/functioning, and emotional distress. Thus, the intervention incorporates methods designed to address specific child, caregiver, and family adjustment problems commonly documented among such families in the research literature.

AF-CBT treatment duration varies by severity, scope of problems, frequency of sessions, and level of family motivation. Some families may complete the work in 3 months while others might require as much as a year of the intervention. The treatment settings have included outpatient mental health clinics, schools, homes, and residential treatment facilities. AF-CBT draws from several theoretical perspectives including behavioral, learning, cognitive, and family systems.

There are three phases of the intervention. Phase I, Engagement and Psychoeducation, focuses on assessing family needs, enhancing motivation, and providing information. Phase II, Individual Skill Building and Processing of Conflict, involves developing emotional regulation in both children and caregivers, using cognitive restructuring to address child and caregiver attributions related to the abuse, and teaching alternative strategies to coercive, hostile, and abusive parenting. Phase III, Family Applications, includes the active participation of the caregiver–child dyads in communication training, clarification about the caregivers' responsibility for abusive behaviors, family problem solving, relapse prevention strategies, and development of aftercare plans if needed.

In one of the earliest demonstrations of the effectiveness of AF-CBT, Kolko (1996) evaluated the effectiveness of CBT approaches in maltreated children compared to standard family therapy. Fifty-five physically abused children were randomly assigned to each treatment modality. After roughly 19 weeks of treatment, children receiving CBT showed greater improvements in child abuse risk and lower rates of internalizing and externalizing behaviors. Other published studies further supporting AF-CBT include Kolko et al. (2012) and Kolko, Herschell, Baumann, Hart, and Wisniewski (2018).

8.2.1.5 Project Support

Project Support was designed to be implemented when families were transitioning from a battered women's shelter to a new home independent of the perpetrator of violence (Jouriles et al., 2001). The goal of Project Support was to reduce externalizing behavior problems which were frequently seen in children who had been exposed to IPV. In addition to targeting the child's behaviors, this intervention focused on developing the mothers' ability to appropriately address and cope with these problems in their children. The intervention was developed for children between the ages of 4 and 9 exhibiting clinical levels of conduct problems.

Families involved in Project Support received in-home services focused on two primary aims: teaching appropriate child management skills and providing emotional and instrumental support to mothers (McDonald, Jouriles, & Skopp, 2006). A Project Support manual discusses specific skills and includes both vignettes for practice role plays and homework assignments to demonstrate learning of the skills. The child management skills component includes 12 skills such as listening to your child, praising them, and appropriate ways to reprimand them. Skills are presented in a sequence that begins with a focus on improving the quality of the mother–child relationship and increasing prosocial child behavior, and then builds on these to focus on the reduction of problematic behavior. The program involves weekly sessions of 60–90 min with a trained therapist. Sessions last an average of 20 weeks.

An evaluation of the effectiveness of Project Support studied 36 mother-child dyads after leaving a domestic violence shelter (McDonald et al., 2006). To be eligible to participate in the study, mothers had to report the occurrence of at least one physically violent act from a male partner during the previous 12 months and have at least one child aged 4–9 who met Diagnostic and Statistical Manual of Mental Disorders (see Chap. 4) criteria for oppositional defiant disorder or conduct disorder. If women had more than one child in this age range the youngest child was selected. The family could not be returning to live with the abusive partner. Dyads were randomly assigned to either receive Project Support or services as usual.

Families in the intervention group received weekly sessions for up to 8 months post shelter exit (McDonald et al., 2006). The average number of sessions for the experimental group families was 23. Comparison group families were contacted monthly for up to 16 months and were encouraged to access local services. Both groups received in-home follow up assessments 24 months after leaving the shelter. Findings revealed that the children who received Project Support showed a significant decrease in conduct problems, internalizing problems, and externalizing problems compared to the control group. Mothers in the experimental group engaged in fewer aggressive parenting practices and were less likely to have returned to their abusive partners than mothers in the control group.

A subsequent evaluation randomized 66 mother-child dyads into Project Support or a control group after exiting a domestic violence shelter (Jouriles et al., 2009). Families were assessed on six occasions over 20 months, following their departure from the shelter. Mother-child dyads assigned to Project Support received weekly home visits for up to 8 months that included training in child management skills. Children in families receiving the Project Support intervention, compared with those in the control group, exhibited greater reductions in conduct problems. Mothers in Project Support displayed greater reductions in inconsistent and harsh parenting behaviors and psychiatric symptoms than mothers in the control group. Changes in mothers' parenting and psychiatric symptoms accounted for a sizable proportion of Project Support's effects on child conduct problems at the end of treatment. Project Support has continued to be used to assist mothers whose children have been exposed to IPV (e.g., McDonald, Dodson, Rosenfield, & Jouriles, 2011).

Aspects of Project Support have been expanded to be available for community members and labeled as the Change A Life program (Sargent, McDonald, Vu, & Jouriles, 2016). Goals of this expanded program were to educate the broader community about the consequences of children's exposure to IPV through an interactive internet program. Within this program, there was an emphasis on directly helping these children, providing specific suggestions about how this would be done.

8.2.1.6 Multisystemic Therapy

MST-CAN is for families with serious clinical needs who have come to the attention of Child Protective Services (CPS) due to physical abuse and/or neglect. MST-CAN clinicians work on a team of three therapists, a crisis caseworker, a part-time psychiatrist who can treat children and adults, and a full-time supervisor (Swenson, Henggeler, Taylor, & Addison, 2009; Swenson & Schaeffer, 2018). Each therapist carries a maximum caseload of four families. Treatment is provided to all adults and children in the family. Services are provided in the family's home or other convenient places. Extensive safety protocols are geared towards preventing re-abuse and placement of children and the team works to foster a close working relationship between CPS and the family. Empirically-based treatments are used when needed and include functional analysis of the use of force, family communication and problem solving, Cognitive Behavioral Therapy for anger management and PTSD, clarification of the abuse or neglect, and Reinforcement Based Therapy for adult substance abuse.

An evaluation of MST-CAN was conducted with 86 youth and the custodial parent who was indicated in a CPS report of physical abuse (Swenson, Schaeffer, Henggeler, Faldowski, & Mayhew, 2010). All youth in the study were between ages 10 and 17 and had a CPS case opened within the previous 90 days. Families were excluded if: (a) youth was currently or previously enrolled in an MST project, (b) the child had been removed from the home and there was no plan for family reunification; and (c) children or their parents experienced psychosis. Self-report measures were administered individually and separately for the youth and parent in their home at five time points (baseline, 2, 4, 10, and 16 months).

In a more recent follow-up paper, Swenson and Schaeffer (2018) discussed the history of MST-CAN treatment and noted that it was used not only for treating children and youth who have experienced physical abuse from their caregivers, but also for those experiencing neglect. As Henggeler and Schaeffer (2016) explained, MST, more generally, has been used to treat youth with serious antisocial behavior who are at risk for out-of home placement. Both the troubled young adult and their family are involved in this treatment.

8.2.1.7 SafeCare®

SafeCare is an in-home parenting program that targets risk factors for child maltreatment, with a particular focus on neglect. Parents are taught (1) how to interact in a positive manner with their children, to plan activities, and respond appropriately to challenging child behaviors; (2) to recognize hazards in the home in order to improve the home environment; and (3) to recognize and respond to symptoms of illness and injury, in addition to keeping good health records (Guastaferro, Lutzker, Graham, Shanley, & Whitaker, 2012).

SafeCare typically provides 18–22 weeks of training to parents with children from birth to age 5 who have experienced child maltreatment. Trained home visitors conduct 60- to 90-min weekly or biweekly home visits focusing on three modules: (1) parent-child/parent-infant interactions, (2) infant and child health, and (3) home safety. All SafeCare modules include baseline assessments and observations of parental knowledge and skills, parent training, and follow-up assessments to monitor change. Each module typically involves one assessment session and five training sessions. During the parent trainings, SafeCare home visitors explain the rationale for a particular concept, model the concept, have the parent practice the steps, and then provide feedback. SafeCare home visitors are not required to meet specific education requirements.

An evaluation involved families assigned to SafeCare compared to a matched control group of families receiving standard family preservation services (Gershater-Molko, Lutzker & Sherman, 2002). The experimental group received approximately 24 weeks of SafeCare services. Follow ups at 12, 24, and 36 months after the beginning of services showed that the SafeCare group had significantly fewer re-reports of child maltreatment across time.

In a later study, Chaffin, Hecht, Bard, Silovsky, and Beaskley (2012) evaluated the effectiveness of SafeCare by randomizing 2175 families with reported child neglect to receive either SafeCare or standard CPS services for 6 months. Cases were followed for 6 years after treatment to measure recidivism rates. Families receiving SafeCare showed greater compliance with treatment plans, and demonstrated significantly lower re-abuse rates than the control group families.

More recently, Gallitto, Romano and Drolet (2018) further examined SafeCare by asking 30 caregivers in Canada about their experiences while participating in the program. Neglect was the primary type of maltreatment identified in the sample, but there were also some families with exposure to IPV or where children had been physically abused. Overall, comments from the caregivers were positive about how the program helped them improve parenting skills. The health module was seen as most helpful, noting that it provided needed information about how address illness or injury in their children. Other modules were also cited as being helpful in helping them learn to better take care of their children.

8.2.2 Other Programs for Maltreated Children

Other programs have worked with preschool children to provide supportive and enriched environments, with benefits in school achievement as well as lower levels of criminal activity reported as outcomes (Niolon et al., 2017). Another sample that has been targeted is children with aggressive behavior who have been placed in juvenile detention. Psychologists argue that many of these children have a history of experiencing violence in their families. O'Hara, Suchschere, Shanholtz, Reznik, and Beck (2019) review some of the issues raised by these children and how these might be best addressed. Other treatments are being developed for men who were abused as children by a parent (Hopton & Huta, 2013) or sexually abused by a sibling (Caffaro, 2017).

8.2.3 Comparing Treatments for Children and their Families

Given the large number of treatment protocols developed to assist child survivors of physical abuse or neglect, or children exposed to IPV in their parents or caretakers, a number of formal reviews have been done to try to determine which of these programs are most effective. Our focus in this chapter has been on those which are evidence-based, so all these treatments have been shown to have demonstrated positive outcomes for parents or children or both. Some types of treatment do appear to be more effective than others. Overall, cognitive behavioral therapy has received the most endorsement for all of these troubled children. For example, Dorsey et al. (2017) did a formal review of treatments for child and adolescent trauma. They determined that treatment involving CBT, either for the child alone, for the child and the parent, or in a group setting achieved a *well-established* designation. None of the other treatments were as highly rated.

In another review of treatments, a German study (Ehring et al., 2014) examined treatments used for adults who had experienced physical or sexual child abuse and were experiencing PTSD symptoms as adults in a formal meta-analysis. Only studies meeting standards for evidence-based treatment were included. The large majority of these studies were TF-CBT treatment studies. Their conclusion was that trauma-focused CBT treatment was effective in lowering PTSD symptoms in adult survivors. They were also more effective than CBT treatment that was not trauma-focused. Similar conclusions were reached in a report by Benuto and O'Donohue (2015) who did a formal review of 7 different meta-analyses examining treatment for children or adolescents identified as survivors of sexual abuse. Overall, CBT, especially TF-CBT was the most effective treatment for lessening symptoms of PTSD, either for the individual child or for the family. They noted that there was no clear benefit for having the offending parent participate in the treatment. Longer treatments tended to be more effective. Play therapy was identified by one study as especially helpful for social functioning. They also identified a number of issues that should be addressed in future studies to enable one to draw clearer conclusions about the efficacy of different treatments. Often the details of the therapy offered were not included in the published reports, which would be very useful information. They also noted that most of the total of 77 studies included in the meta-analyses did not have randomized controls.

Some reviews have specifically examined programs for children exposed to IPV. Two researchers from Germany and the Netherlands evaluated treatment programs from many countries, with the majority being from the U.S. (Anderson & van Ee, 2018). Their analysis indicated that programs in which mothers and children work together and separately were the most effective. These programs showed reductions in PTSD and in conduct problems for the children while the mothers were rated as having improvements in parenting skills and lowered anxiety and depression. By combining individual and combined treatments, Anderson and van Ee suggested that this allowed the children time to talk openly about their experiences as well as engaging in therapeutic activities. For the mother, private sessions allowed them to focus on herself and not have to be concerned about how her child was reacting. The combined sessions to work together and aided communication between them in a healing environment. They did note that long-term treatment requirements of some of the types of interventions were difficult to put into practice. Austin, Shanahan, Barrios, and Macy (2017) have also published a review of program for mothers who were survivors of IPV and their children. In this systematic review of 19 different interventions, they found there was no clear evidence about which were most effective, especially given the limitations in published studies which were often based on small samples or incomplete research designs. They also noted that many of the programs were not conducted as planned, with many modifications as programs were put into practice.

8.3 Summary

This chapter described evidence-based interventions for women who are survivors of IPV and children who have experienced exposure to IPV and/or child maltreatment. For women, battered women's shelters offer physical safety from abuse as well as many other services for the women and their children. However, many women never seek services from shelters, and turn instead to other sources of help, as do men since the shelters are generally receptive only to female survivors of abuse from a male partner. One of the services often offered at the shelters is referral to one of the formal treatment programs described in the chapter.

A variety of treatment options are available for the women and their children. These may be offered in the shelter or through other domestic violence agencies. Other treatments are discussed for children exposed to trauma either through witnessing partner violence in their parents or caretakers, and those personally abused by their caretakers physically, emotionally or sexually, or those who have been neglected. Again, a variety of different treatment options are available for these children. The interventions described in this chapter have been shown to improve outcomes in women and children. Most often cited as being effective are treatments associated with cognitive-behavioral therapy. For children, treatments involving both children and the non-abusing parent, who have separate sessions as well as sessions together appear to be most effective.

References

Allard, C. B., Norman, S. B., Throp, S. R., Browne, K. C., & Stein, M. B. (2018). Mid-treatment reduction in trauma-related guilt predicts PTSD and functioning following cognitive trauma therapy for survivors of intimate partner violence. *Journal of Interpersonal Violence, 33*(23), 3610–3629. https://doi.org/10.1177/0886260516636068

Allen, N. E., Larsen, S., Trotter, J., & Sullivan, C. M. (2013). Exploring the core service delivery proceses of an evidence-based community advocacy program for women with abusive partners. *Journal of Community Psychology, 41*, 1–18. https://doi.org/10.1002/jcop.21502

Anderson, K., & van Ee, E. (2018). Mothers and children exposed to intimate partner violence: A review of treatment interventions. *International Journal of Environmental Research and Public Health, 15*, 1955. https://doi.org/10.3390/ijerph15091955

Arroyo, K., Lundahl, B., Butters, R., Vanderloo, M., & Wood, D. S. (2017). Short-term interventions for survivors of intimate partner violence: A systematic review and meta-analysis. *Trauma, Violence, & Abuse, 18*, 155–171. https://doi.org/10.1177/1524838015602736

Augusta-Scott, T., Scott, K., & Tutty, L. (Eds.). (2017). *Innovations in interventions to address intimate partner violence*. New York, NY: Routledge.

Austin, A. E., Shanahan, M. E., Barrios, Y. V., & Macy, R. J. (2017). A systematic review of interventions for women parenting in the context of intimate partner violence. *Trauma, Violence, & Abuse, 20*, 1–22. https://doi.org/10.1177/1524838017719233

Baker, F. (1983). Quality assurance and program evaluation. *Evaluation & the Health Professions, 6*, 149–160.

Barner, J. R., & Carney, M. M. (2011). Interventions for intimate partner violence: A historical review. *Journal of Family Violence, 26*, 235–244. https://doi.org/10.1007/s10896-011-9359-3

Batzer, S., Berg, T., Godinet, M. T., & Stotzer, R. L. (2018). Efficacy or chaos? Parent–child interaction therapy in maltreating populations: A review of research. *Trauma, Violence, & Abuse, 19*, 3–19.

Benuto, L. T., & O'Donohue, W. (2015). Treatment of the sexually abused child: Review and syntheses of recent meta-analyses. *Children and Youth Services Review, 56*, 52–60. https://doi.org/10.1016/j.childyouth.2015.06.009

Bloom, T., Gielen, A., & Glass, N. (2016). Developing an app for college women in abusive same-sex relationships and their friends. *Journal of Homosexuality, 63*, 855–874. https://doi.org/10.1080/00918369.2015.1112597

Caffaro, J. (2017). Treating adult survivors of sibling sexual abuse: A relational strengths-based approach. *Journal of Family Violence, 32*, 543–552. https://doi.org/10.1007/s10896-016-9877-0

Chaffin, M., Hecht, D., Bard, D., Silovsky, J. F., & Beaskley, W. H. (2012). A statewide trial of the SafeCare home-based services model with parents in child protective services. *Pediatrics, 129*, 509–515. https://doi.org/10.1542/peds.2011-1840

Chaffin, M., Silovsky, J., Funderburk, B., Valle, L., Brestan, E., Balachova, T., et al. (2004). Parent-child interaction therapy with physically abusive parents: Efficacy for reducing future abuse reports. *Journal of Consulting and Clinical Psychology, 72*, 500–510.

Cohen, J. A., & Mannarino, A. P. (2017). Evidence-based intervention: Trauma-focused cognitive behavioral therapy for children and their families. In D. M. Teti (Ed.), *Parenting and family processes in child maltreatment and intervention* (pp. 91–105). Cham: Springer. https://doi.org/10.1007/978-3-319-40920-7_6. (2015).

Cohen, J. A., Mannarino, A. P., & Deblinger, E. (2017). *Treating trauma and traumatic grief in children and adolescents* (2nd ed.). New York, NY: Guilford Press.

Cohen, J. A., Mannarino, A. P., & Iyengar, S. (2011). Community treatment of posttraumatic stress disorder for children exposed to intimate partner violence. *Archives of Pediatric Adolescent Medicine, 165*(1), 16–21. https://doi.org/10.1001/archpediatrics.2010.247

Dorsey, S., McLaughlin, K. A., Kerns, S. E. U., Harrison, J. P., Lambert, H. K., Briggs, E. C., et al. (2017). Evidence base update for psychosocial treatments for children and adolescents exposed to traumatic events. *Journal of Clinical Child & Adolescent Psychology, 46*(3), 303–330. https://doi.org/10.1080/15374416.2016.1220309

Douglas, E. M., & Hines, D. A. (2011). The helpseeking experiences of men who sustain intimate partner violence: An overlooked population and implications for practice. *Journal of Family Violence, 26*, 473–485. https://doi.org/10.1007/s10896-011-9382-4

Douglas, E. M., Hines, D. A., Dixon, L., Celi, E. M., & Lysova, A. V. (2018). Using technology to conduct focus groups with a hard-to-reach population: A methodological approach concerning male victims of partner abuse in four English-speaking countries. *Journal of Interpersonal Violence*, 1–24. https://doi.org/10.1177/0886260518799459

Eden, K. B., Perrin, N. A., Hanson, G. C., Messing, J. T., Bloom, T. L., Campbell, J. C., et al. (2015). Use of online safety decision aid by abused women: Effect on decisional conflict in a randomized controlled trial. *American Journal of Preventative Medicine, 48*(4), 372–383. https://doi.org/10.1016/j.amepre.2014.09.027

Ehring, T., Welboren, R., Morina, N., Wicherts, J. M., Freitag, J., & Emmelkamp, P. M. G. (2014). Meta-analysis of psychological treatments for posttraumatic stress disorder in adult survivors of childhood abuse. *Clinical Psychology Review, 34*, 645–657. https://doi.org/10.1016/j.cpr.2014.10.004

Eisenstaadt, T., Eyberg, S., McNeil, C., Newcomb, K., & Funderbunk, B. (1993). Parent-child interaction therapy with behavior problem children: Relative effectiveness of two stages and overall treatment outcome. *Journal of Clinical Child Psychology, 22*, 42–51.

Etherington, N., Baker, L., Ham, M., & Glasbeek, D. (2017). Evaluating the effectiveness of online training for a comprehensive violence against women program: A pilot study. *Journal of Interpersonal Violence*, 1–24. https://doi.org/10.1177/0886260517725734

Eyberg, S. (1988). Parent-child interaction therapy: Integration of traditional and behavioral concerns. *Child and Family Behavior Therapy, 10*, 33–46.

Eyberg, S. (2005). Tailoring and adapting parent-child interaction therapy to new populations. *Education and Treatment of Children, 28*, 197–201.

Ferranti, D., Lorenzo, D., Munoz-Rojas, D., & Gonzalez-Guarda, R. M. (2018). Health education needs of intimate partner violence survivors: Perspectives from female survivors and social service providers. *Public Health Nursing, 35*, 118–125. https://doi.org/10.1111/phn.12374

Fisher, E. M., & Stylianou, A. M. (2019). To stay or to leave: Factors influencing victims' decisions to stay or leave a domestic violence emergence shelter. *Journal of Interpersonal Violence, 34*, 785–811. https://doi.org/10.1177/0886260516645816

Fleck-Henderson, A. (2017). From movement to mainstreat: A battered women's shelter evolves (1976-2017). *Affilia: Journal of Women and Social Work, 32*, 476–490. https://doi.org/10.1177/0886109917718230

Frierson, D.T. (2014). The fear of being judged: African American gay men and intimate partner violence: A qualitative study. Washington, DC: Howard University, School of Social Work PhD dissertation.

Frieze, I. H. (1979). Perceptions of battered wives. In I. H. Frieze, D. Bar-Tal, & J. S. Carroll (Eds.), *New approaches to social problems: Applications of attribution theory* (pp. 79–108). San Francisco, CA: Jossey-Bass.

Fusco, R. A. (2017). Socioemotional problems in children exposed to intimate partner violence: Mediating effects of attachment and family supports. *Journal of Interpersonal Violence, 32*(16), 2515–2532. https://doi.org/10.1177/0886260515593545

Fusco, R. A., & Fantuzzo, J. W. (2009). Domestic violence crimes and children: A population-based investigation of direct sensory exposure and the nature of involvement. *Children and Youth Services Review, 31*, 249–256. https://doi.org/10.1016/j.childyouth.2008.07.017

Gallitto, E., Romano, E., & Drolet, M. (2018). Caregivers' perspectives on the SafeCare programme: Implementing an evidence-based intervention for child neglect. *Child & Family Social Work, 23*, 307–315. https://doi.org/10.1111/cfs.1241

Gershater-Moko, RM, Lutzker, JR, and Sherman, JA (2002). Intervention in child neglect: an applied behavioral perspective. *Aggression and Violent Behavior, 7*, 103–124.

Glass, N. E., Perrin, N. A., Hanson, G. C., Bloom, T. L., Messing, J. T., Clough, A. S., et al. (2017). The longitudinal impact of an internet safety decision aid for abused women. *American Journal of Preventive Medicine, 52*(5), 606–615. https://doi.org/10.1016/j.amepre.2016.12.014

Goldbeck, L., Muche, R., Sachser, C., Tutus, D., & Rosner, R. (2016). Effectiveness of trauma-focused cognitive behavioral therapy for children and adolescents: A randomized controlled trial in eight German mental health clinics. *Psychotherapy and Psychosomatics, 85*, 159–170. https://doi.org/10.1159/000442824

Goodwin, L. A., Banyard, V., Woulfe, J., Ash, S., & Mattern, G. (2016). Bringing a network-oriented approach to domestic violence services: A focus group exploration of promising practices. *Violence Against Women, 22*, 64–89. https://doi.org/10.1177/1077801215599080

Gregory, K., Nnawulezi, N., & Sullivan, C. M. (2017). Understanding how domestic violence shelter rules may influence survivor empowerment. *Journal of Interpersonal Violence*, 1–22. https://doi.org/10.1177/0886260517730561

Grossman, S. F., & Lundy, M. (2011). Characteristics of women who do and do not receive onsite shelter services from domestic violence programs. *Violence Against Women, 17*, 1024–1045.

Guastaferro, K. M., Lutzker, J. R., Graham, M. L., Shanley, J. R., & Whitaker, D. J. (2012). SelfCare: Historical perspective and dynamic development in evidence-based scaled-up model for the prevention of child maltreatment. *Psychosocial Intervention, 21*, 171–180. https://doi.org/10.5093/in2012a17

Guyatt, G., Cairns, J., Churchill, D., Cook, D., Haynes, B., Hirsh, J., et al. (1992). Evidence-based medicine: A new approach to teaching the practice of medicine. *Journal of the American Medical Association, 268*, 2420–2425.

Hembree-Kigin, T. L., & McNeil, C. B. (1995). *Parent–child interaction therapy*. New York, NY: Plenum Press.

Henggeler, S. W., & Schaeffer, C. M. (2016). Multisystemic therapy: Clinical overview, outcomes, and implementation research. *Family Process, 55*, 514–528. https://doi.org/10.1111/famp.12232

Herschell, A., & McNeil, C. (2005). Theoretical and empirical underpinnings of parent-child interaction therapy with child physical abuse populations. *Education and Treatment of Children, 28*, 142–162.

Hines, D. A., & Douglas, E. M. (2018). Influence of intimate terrorism, situational couple violence, and mutual violent control on male victims. *Psychology of Men and Masculinity, 19*, 612–623. https://doi.org/10.1037/men0000142

Hood, K., & Eyberg, S. (2003). Outcomes of parent-child interaction therapy: Mother's reports of maintenance three to six years after treatment. *Journal of Clinical and Adolescent Psychology, 32*, 412–419.

Hopton, J. L., & Huta, V. (2013). Evaluation of an intervention designed for men who were abused in childhood and are experiencing symptoms of posttraumatic stress disorder. *Psychology of Men & Masculinity, 14*, 300–313. https://doi.org/10.1037/a0029705

Ippen, C. G., Harris, W. W., Van Horn, P., & Lieberman, A. F. (2011). Traumatic and stressful events in early childhood: Can treatment help those at highest risk? *Child Abuse & Neglect, 35*, 504–513. https://doi.org/10.1016/j.chiabu.2011.03.009

Johnson, D. M., Johnson, N. L., Perez, S. K., Palmieri, P. A., & Zlotnick, C. (2016). Comparison of adding treatment of PTSD during and after shelter stay to standard care in residents of battered women's shelters: Results of a randomized clinical trial. *Journal of Traumatic Stress, 29*, 365–373. https://doi.org/10.1002/jts.22117

Johnson, D. M., & Zlotnick, C. (2006). A cognitive—Behavioral treatment for battered women with PTSD in shelters: Findings from a pilot study. *Journal of Traumatic Stress, 19*, 559–564.

Johnson, D. M., & Zlotnick, C. (2009). HOPE for battered women with PTSD in domestic violence shelters. *Professional Psychology: Research and Practice, 40*, 234–242.

Johnson, D. M., Zlotnick, C., & Perez, S. (2011). Cognitive behavioral treatment of PTSD in residents of battered women's shelters: Results of a randomized clinical trial. *Journal of Consulting and Clinical Psychology, 79*, 542–551.

Jouriles, E. N., McDonald, R., Rosenfield, D., Stephens, N., Corbitt-Shindler, D., & Miller, P. C. (2009). Reducing conduct problems among children exposed to intimate partner violence: A randomized clinical trial examining effects of project support. *Journal of Consulting and Clinical Psychology, 77*(4), 705–717. https://doi.org/10.1037/a0015994

Jouriles, E. N., McDonald, R., Spiller, L., Norwood, W. D., Swank, P. R., Stephens, N., et al. (2001). Reducing conduct problems among children of battered women. *Journal of Consulting and Clinical Psychology, 69*(5), 774–785. https://doi.org/10.1037/0022-006X.69.5.774

Kamimura, A., Christensen, N., Tabler, J., Ashby, J., & Olson, L. M. (2014). Prevalence of intimate partner violence and its impact on health: Female and male patients using a free clinic. *Journal of Health Care for the Poor and Underserved, 25*, 731–745. https://doi.org/10.1353/hpu.2014.0105

Kolko, D. J. (1996). Individual cognitive behavioral treatment and family therapy for physically abused children and their offending parents: A comparison of clinical outcomes. *Child Maltreatment, 1*, 322–342. https://doi.org/10.1177/1077559596001004004

Kolko, D. J., Baumann, B. L., Herschell, A. D., Hart, J. A., Holden, E. A., & Wisniewski, S. R. (2012). Implementation of AF-CBT by community practitioners serving child welfare and mental health: A randomized trial. *Child Maltreatment, 17*, 32–46. https://doi.org/10.1177/1077559511427346

Kolko, D. J., Herschell, A. D., Baumann, B. L., Hart, J. A., & Wisniewski, S. R. (2018). AF-CBT for families experiencing physical aggression or abuse served by the mental health or child welfare system: An effectiveness trial. *Child Maltreatment, 23*, 319–333. https://doi.org/10.1177/1077559518781068

Koss, M. P., White, J. W., & Lopez, E. C. (2017). Victim voice in reenvisioning responses to sexual and physical violence nationally and internationally. *American Psychologist, 72*, 1019–1030. https://doi.org/10.1037/amp0000233

Kubany, E. S. (1998). Application of cognitive therapy for trauma-related guilt (CT-TRG) with a Vietnam veteran troubled by multiple sources of guilt. *Cognitive and Behavioral Practice, 4*, 213–244.

Kubany, E. S., Hill, E. E., & Owens, J. A. (2003). Cognitive trauma therapy for battered women with PTSD: Preliminary findings. *Journal of Traumatic Stress, 16*, 81–91.

Kubany, E. S., Hill, E. E., Owens, J. A., Iannce-Spencer, C., McCaig, M. A., Tremayne, K. J., et al. (2004). Cognitive trauma therapy for battered women with PTSD (CTT-BW). *Journal of Consulting and Clinical Psychology, 72*, 3–11.

Kubany, E. S., & Manke, F. P. (1995). Cognitive therapy for trauma-related guilt: Conceptual bases and treatment outlines. *Cognitive and Behavioral Practice, 2*, 27–61.

Kubany, E. S., & Watson, S. B. (2002). Cognitive trauma therapy for formerly battered women with PTSD: Conceptual bases and treatment outlines. *Cognitive and Behavioral Practice, 9*, 111–127.

Kulkarni, S. (2018). Intersectional trauma-informed intimate partner violence (IPV) services: Narrowing the gap between IPV service delivery and survivor needs. *Journal of Family Violence., 34*, 55–64. https://doi.org/10.1007/s10896-018-0001-5

Larrieu, J. A. (2018). Introducing evidence-based trauma treatment in preventive services: Child-parent psychotherapy. In V. C. Strand & G. Sprang (Eds.), *Trauma responsive welfare systems* (pp. 147–164). New York, NY: Springer.

Lee, J. G., & Backes, B. L. (2018). Civil legal aid and domestic violence: A review of the literature and promising directions. *Journal of Family Violence, 33*, 421–433. https://doi.org/10.1007/s10896-018-9974-3

Lieberman, A. F., Ippen, C. G., & Van Horn, P. (2006). Child-parent psychotherapy: 6-month follow-up of a randomized controlled trial. *Journal of the American Academy of Child and Adolescent Psychiatry, 45*, 913–918. https://doi.org/10.1097/01.chi.0000222784.03735.92

Lieneman, C. C., Brabson, L. A., Highlander, A., Wallace, N. M., & McNeil, C. B. (2017). Parent–child interaction therapy: Current perspectives. *Psychology Research and Behavior Management, 10*, 239–256.

Logan, T. K., & Walker, R. (2018). Looking into the day-to-day process of victim safety planning. *Journal of Family Violence, 33*, 197–211. https://doi.org/10.1007/s10896-018-9951-x

Mantler, T., Jackson, K. T., & Walsh, E. J. (2018). Integration of primary health-care services in women's shelters: A scoping review. *Trauma, Violence & Abuse*, 1–14. https://doi.org/10.1177/1524838018781105

McDonald, L. (2001). Florence nightingale and the early origins of evidence-based nursing. *Evidence-Based Nursing, 4*, 68–69.

McDonald, R., Dodson, M. C., Rosenfield, D., & Jouriles, E. N. (2011). Effects of a parenting intervention on features of psychopathy in children. *Journal of Abnormal Child Psychology, 39*, 1013–1023. https://doi.org/10.1007/s10802-011-9512-8

McDonald, R., Jouriles, E. N., & Skopp, N. A. (2006). Reducing conduct problems among children brought to women's shelters: Intervention effects 24 months following termination of services. *Journal of Family Psychology, 20*(1), 127–136. https://doi.org/10.1037/0893-3200.20.1.127

McTavish, J. R., MacGregor, J. C. D., Wathen, C. N., & MacMillan, H. L. (2016). Children's exposure to intimate partner violence: An overview. *International Review of Psychiatry, 28*, 504–518. https://doi.org/10.1080/09540261.2016.1205001

Niolon, P. H., Kearns, M., Dills, J., Rambo, K., Irving, S., Armstead, T., et al. (2017). *Preventing intimate partner violence across the lifespan: A technical package of programs, policies, and practices*. Atlanta, GA: National Center for Injury Prevention and Control. Retrieved from: https://www.cdc.gov/violenceprevention/pdf/ipv-technicalpackages.pdf

Nnawulezi, N., Sullivan, C. M., & Hacskaylo, M. (2018). Examining the setting characteristics that promote survivor empowerment: A mixed method study. *Journal of Family Violence*, 1–14. https://doi.org/10.1007/s10896-018-0016-y

O'Hara, K. L., Suchschere, J. E., Shanholtz, C. E., Reznik, S. J., & Beck, C. J. (2019). Multidisciplinary partnership: Targeting aggression and mental health problems of adolescents in detention. *American Psychologist, 74*, 329–342. https://doi.org/10.1037/amp0000439

Parker, E. M., Gielen, A. C., Castillo, R., Webster, D. W., & Glass, N. (2016). Intimate partner violence and patterns of safety strategy use among women seeking temporary protective orders: A latent class analysis. *Violence Against Women, 22*, 1663–1681. https://doi.org/10.1177/1077801216631436

Perry, M. M., & O'Neal, E. N. (2015). Help-seeking behavior among same-sex intimate partner violence victims: An intersectional argument. *Criminology, Criminal Justice Law & Society, 16*, 51–67. E-ISSN 2332-886X.

Ragavan, M., Bruce, J., Bair-Merritt, M., Lucha, S., Maya-Silva, J., Stebbins, E., et al. (2018). Building a novel health curriculum for survivors of intimate partner violence residing at a transitional housing program. *Violence Against Women, 24*(3), 266–285. https://doi.org/10.1177/1077801217697206

Renzetti, C. M., & Follingstad, D. R. (2015). From blue to green: The development and implementation of a therapeutic horticulture program for residents of a battered women's shelter. *Violence and Victims, 30*, 676–690. https://doi.org/10.1891/0886-6708.VV-D-14-00091

Sabri, B., Nnawulezi, N., Njie-Carr, V. P. S., Messing, J., Ward-Lasher, A., Alvarez, C., et al. (2018). Multilevel risk and protective factors for intimate partner violence among African, Asian, and Latina immigrant and refugee women: Perceptions of effective safety planning interventions. *Race and Social Problems, 10*, 348–365. https://doi.org/10.1007/s12552-018-9247-z

Sargent, K. S., McDonald, R., Vu, N. L., & Jouriles, E. N. (2016). Evaluating an online program to help children exposed to domestic violence: Results of two randomized controlled trials. *Journal of Family Violence, 31*, 647–654. https://doi.org/10.1007/s10896-016-9800-8

Stewart, R. W., Orengo-Aguayo, R. E., Cohen, J. A., Mannarino, A. P., & de Arellano, M. A. (2017). A pilot study of trauma-focused cognitive-behavioral therapy delivered via telehealth technology. *Child Maltreatment, 22*, 324–333. https://doi.org/10.1177/1077559517725403

Stylianou, A. M. (2018). Family court survivor-centered practice: A qualitative study of advocate-IPV survivor safety planning interactions. *Journal of Family Violence*, 1–15. https://doi.org/10.1007/s10896-018-0020-2

Stylianou, A. M., Counselman-Carpenter, E., & Redcay, A. (2018). "My sister is the one that made me stay above water": How social supports are maintained and strained when survivors of intimate partner violence reside in emergency shelter programs. *Journal of Interpersonal Violence*, 1–24. https://doi.org/10.1177/0886260518816320

Sullivan, C. M. (2011). *The community advocacy project instructor manual*. East Lansing, MI: Michigan State University.

Sullivan, C. M. (2018). Understanding how domestic violence support services promote survivor Well-being: A conceptual model. *Journal of Family Violence, 33*, 123–131. https://doi.org/10.1007/s10896-017-9931-6

Sullivan, C. M., & Bybee, D. I. (1999). Reducing violence using community-based advocacy for women with abusive partners. *Journal of Consulting and Clinical Psychology, 67*, 43–53.

Sullivan, C. M., Bybee, D. I., & Allen, N. E. (2002). Findings from a community-based program for battered women and their children. *Journal of Interpersonal Violence, 17*, 915–936.

Sullivan, C. M., Tan, C., Basta, J., Rumptz, M., & Davidson, W. S. (1992). An advocacy intervention program for women with abusive partners: Initial evaluation. *American Journal of Community Psychology, 20*, 309–332.

Sullivan, C. M., & Virden, T. (2017). Interrelationships among length of stay in a domestic violence shelter, help received, and outcomes achieved. *American Journal of Orthopsychiatry, 87*, 434–442. https://doi.org/10.1037/ort0000267

Swenson, C. C., Henggeler, S. W., Taylor, I. S., & Addison, O. (2009). *Multisystemic therapy and neighborhood partnerships: Reducing adolescent violence and substance abuse (reprinted paperback ed.)*. New York, NY: Guilford.

Swenson, C. C., & Schaeffer, C. M. (2018). A multisystemic approach to the prevention and treatment of child abuse and neglect. *International Journal on Child Maltreatment: Research, Policy and Practice, 1*, 97–120. https://doi.org/10.1007/s42448-018-0002-2

Swenson, C. C., Schaeffer, C. M., Henggeler, S. W., Faldowski, R., & Mayhew, A. (2010). Multisystemic therapy for child abuse and neglect: A randomized effectiveness trial. *Journal of Family Psychology, 24*, 497–507. https://doi.org/10.1037/a0020324

Thomas, R., & Zimmer-Gembeck, M. J. (2011). Accumulating evidence for parent–child interaction therapy in the prevention of child maltreatment. *Child Development, 82*, 177–192.

Thomas, R., & Zimmer-Gembeck, M. J. (2012). Parent–child interaction therapy: An evidence-based treatment for child maltreatment. *Child Maltreatment, 17*, 253–266.

Toth, S. L., & Manly, J. T. (2019). Developmental consequences of child abuse and neglect: Implications for intervention. *Child Development Perspectives, 13*(1), 59–64. https://doi.org/10.1111/cdep.12317

Toth, S. L., Sturge-Apple, M. L., Rogosch, F. A., & Cicchetti, D. (2015). Mechanisms of change: Testing how preventive interventions impact psychological and physiological stress functioning in mothers in neglectful families. *Development and Psychopathology, 27*, 166–1674. https://doi.org/10.1017/S0954579415001017

Trabold, N., McMahon, J., Alsobrooks, S., Whitney, S., & Mittal, M. (2018). A systematic review of intimate partner violence interventions: State of the field and implications for practitioners. *Trauma, Violence & Abuse*, 1–15. https://doi.org/10.1177/1524838018767934

Trabold, N., O'Malley, A., Rizzo, L., & Russell, E. (2018). A gateway to healing: A community-based brief intervention for victims of violence. *Journal of Community Psychology, 46*, 418–428. https://doi.org/10.1002/jcop.21948

Viebeck, E. (December 22, 2018). Violence against women act expires with government shutdown. *The Washington Post*. https://www.washingtonpost.com/powerpost/violence-against-women-act-to-expire-with-government-shutdown/2018/12/21/b66f600a-0557-11e9-b5df-5d3874f1ac36_story.html?noredirect=on&utm_term=.45f68a786d7d

Weaver, T. L., Gilbert, L., El-Bassel, N., Resnick, H. S., & Noursi, S. (2015). Identifying and intervening with substance-using women exposed to intimate partner violence: Phenomenology, comorbidities, and integrated approaches within primary care and other agency settings. *Journal of Women's Health, 24*, 51–56. https://doi.org/10.1089/jwh.2014.4866

Wood, L., Heffron, L. C., Voyles, M., & Kulkarni, S. (2017). Playing by the rules: Agency policy and procedure in service experience of IPV survivors. *Journal of Interpersonal Violence*, 1–26. https://doi.org/10.1177/0886260517716945

Yerke, A. F., & DeFeo, J. (2016). Redefining intimate partner violence beyond the binary to include transgender people. *Journal of Family Violence, 31*, 975–979. https://doi.org/10.1007/s10896-016-9887-y

Chapter 9
Societal Responses to Abuse in the Family: Programs to Prevent Future Violence

This chapter examines the situation relating to *treatment* of those who engage in one of three major forms of partner or family violence discussed throughout this book. We first examine intimate partner violence and battering. Next is a discussion of physical and then sexual child abuse in the home. We briefly discuss elder abuse. More discussion of abuse of older adults in the family can be found in Chap. 7. We italicize the word *treatment* above because the clients or targets of this treatment are, in many cases, those who have committed a crime. Offenders rarely volunteer for help. Thus, the first step is to identify those who commit this violence. Although jail terms are sometimes the result when one is determined to have engaged in partner or family violence, increasingly the focus has been on trying to change the offending behavior through some type of formal program or to remove the violent individual to protect others in the household. Sometimes the victim or target of the abuse is moved to another living situation for protection. As will be discussed, many of these programs have not received clear evidence of effectiveness. Because of this, there is an increased emphasis on very basic educational programs that may prevent people from ever engaging in partner or family violence (Niolon et al., 2017).

9.1 Intimate Partner Violence: *Treatment* for Batterers

As discussed in Chaps. 4 and 5, partner violence can take many forms. In this section of the chapter, we focus on couples who live together. In most cases, these couples consist of a man and a woman, but other types of couples are briefly mentioned. Since most of the procedures for dealing with offenders (labeled as *batterers*, although the physical abuse may be relatively mild in some cases) address physical violence, we do not include discussion of emotional or psychological abuse, although these are often correlated with physical abuse (see Chap. 4). Sexual assault is briefly discussed at the end of this section, as is homicide. In both cases, procedures are generally quite different from the situation for less serious physical IPV. Accusations of sexual abuse or

I. H. Frieze et al., *Dynamics of Family and Intimate Partner Violence*,
https://doi.org/10.1007/978-3-030-42608-8_9

homicide involve criminal investigations and legal prosecution, with a jail term resulting if the offender is found guilty. An overview of the process for identifying physical IPV offenders and others who are violent to family members and societal responses to their offenses can be seen in Box 9.1.

Box 9.1: Societal Responses to Violence or Neglect among family members

Target of Violence	Intimate Partner or Spouse	Child of Parent or Caretaker	Older Person in the Family
How is Violence Discovered?	Police called for help with active violence	Reporting by designated professional or others for physical abuse or neglect	Reporting by designated professional or others. Sometimes by the abused person
Consequences of report	Arrest of violent partner. Could be both. Court action to determine who offended	Investigation by child protective services to see if abuse or neglect present	Investigation by Adult Protective Services and police
Long term consequences for offender(s)	Mandatory attendance at educational programs	Continuing CPS home visits, parent training or other program, mental health or counseling services if needed	Jailing or served with a restraining order
Consequences for victim(s)	May be referred to shelter for battered women or victim program for men	Child placed in foster care if determined necessary. Court action may be needed	Older person placed in nursing home or separated from abusive caretaker
Homicide or sexual assault	Jail for offender	Jail for offender	Jail for offender

Data come from published reports and personal clinical experiences of authors.

9.1.1 Identification of Offenders

When someone calls the police for assistance with partner violence (IPV), the violent offender is identified when the police arrive. This is typically the way that these offenders enter treatment programs. Many states now have laws requiring arrest for the violent partner. This is a clear change from the situation before the 1980s, when it was argued that police did not take partner violence seriously and arrests were not common (Feder & Henning, 2005). However, note that it is necessary that either the victim or someone else call the police for the IPV perpetrator to be identified. If no police report is made, the partner violence may be hidden (see Chaps. 4 and 5), and it is unlikely for the offender to seek counseling or other help.

There have been attempts to identify those who are abusive to their partner through screening by health providers. However, in practice, few clinicians do this type of screening. There are a number of reasons that have been identified that contribute to a lack of effectiveness for this type of screening. Clinicians have reported fears of offending patients, personal discomfort with the issue of partner violence, lack of time, and lack of knowledge about how to respond if IPV is identified (Paterno & Draughon, 2016). Sometimes, however, a patient is seen in a medical setting with injuries severe enough that it is likely that the patient has been abused. In such cases, inquiry about abuse is more likely to happen as illustrated in the following case example.

This case illustrates how victims of intimate partner violence are often seen in the emergency room when they sustain injuries that must be treated. This opens an opportunity for emergency personnel to identify the presence of abuse and arrange for help. The abused individual may even make a suicide gesture or attempt, as Rose did, either to force access to help or as an act of desperation. Emergency room contact is often a time when victims are most motivated to seek help as they are safe in that environment, the most recent violence may be severe, and transportation to a shelter for battered women (see Chap. 8) can usually be safely arranged.

Case Example #8

Rose is a 44 year old married white female who was brought to a rural community hospital emergency room by her husband, Tom. Tom told the ER doctor that his wife had taken pills in a suicide attempt. Rose denied this, stating that her husband lies all the time. Later, however, when talking with the crisis social worker, Rose admitted that she had taken the pills because she had felt hopeless about the situation with her husband. She didn't want to die, but just wanted to "go to sleep and escape" the physical and emotional pain she was experiencing.

Upon evaluation by the crisis social worker, Rose presented as alert, completely oriented, although she thought today is February 4th when it was actually December 14th. Rose states that her husband has abused her for 15 years of her 18 year marriage and that she wants help. She has a large hematoma on her forehead and is complaining of severe stomach pain - her husband had kicked her in the stomach. Rose states that Tom has, over the years, broken both of her wrists, broken both her legs, cracked her ribs and given her multiple black eyes, cuts, and abrasions. Up until now she hoped he would change and stop the violence if she were a "better wife" but realizes now that hope is futile and she is motivated to get help. Rose agreed to go to the Battered Women's Shelter and I contacted them and they agreed to accept her once she is completely medically stable and ready for discharge. Rose told the social worker that she felt better after talking.

Even if a victim of partner violence is identified as such by medical staff, the offenders are not required to or even necessarily asked to seek help. In the case of Rose, her husband Tom brought her to the emergency room, but the medical staff did not attempt to call the police about his violence. By the time the social worker arrived at the ER, Tom had left. It appears that the focus of medical screening and treatment was on helping the victim to find needed help when IPV was identified, rather than attempting to get the offender into some type of batterer treatment program. As will be discussed, the primary way that those who abuse their partners are encouraged to end their violence is through formal programs they may be required to attend after a call to the police. Unfortunately, since many battered women (or men) do not seek police assistance (see Chaps. 4 and 5), the offenders may never be identified.

9.1.2 When is Police Assistance Sought?

The U.S. Department of Justice summarized data from the National Crime Victimization Survey (see Chap. 1) indicating that police were involved for almost 60% of the women victimized by IPV and slightly more than 50% of the men victimized by IPV between 2006 and 2015. In 80% of these incidents, it was the victim who called the police (Reaves, 2017). Although police calls were sometimes made by neighbors or even strangers witnessing IPV, this was not common, since partner violence typically does not occur in public locations. The most common reason for not calling the police in the NCVS was that the IPV was seen as a personal matter. However, about a quarter of the women who were victimized said that fears of reprisal kept them from calling.

Analyses of data before the 1980s indicated that few, if any, cases were ever reported to any type of authorities. Once legal attention was directed to the situation of intimate partner violence in the 1980s, reporting rates began to rise (Buzawa, Buzawa, & Stark, 2017). However, as these authors explain, statistics about rates of reporting are often questioned, since the methodology used has a strong effect on the reported rates of victim calls for help from the police.

The following is an example of a clinical case in which the police were called by concerned neighbors. It illustrates the pathways a perpetrator and victim move through in accessing help, how multiple systems of care can become involved with a family in which there is intimate partner violence - once law enforcement becomes involved - and the nature of follow-up care following a crisis for both the victim and the perpetrator.

Case Example #6

John is a 36 year-old married white male with five children who was brought to the crisis clinic for evaluation by Sheriff's deputies and a Department of Public Assistance (DPA) worker. John's wife, Karen, was seen 4 days prior by one of the clinic social workers for evaluation of depression. John has abused Karen off and on throughout the 8 years of their marriage, but last Saturday he almost killed her. Because of the violence in the home, the five children were removed last year and placed in the Dependent Children's Home by Child Protective Services and are currently in foster care. John reports that he injured his back in an auto accident 4 years ago and, because his back is still bad, John says nobody will hire him so he must work privately in a body shop he constructed in his garage. The shop, however, has been losing business and the family's finances are in a squeeze. This past Saturday, John and Karen were having a yard sale. John was working in his body shop and told Karen to keep the people at the yard sale out of his way; she started to argue with him so he attacked and beat her; he broke a broom over her head and was about to ram the broken end through her but stopped in time. Karen immediately left, went to the hospital for treatment of her injuries, and then went to the local battered women's shelter. Karen refused to press charges against John and never has after previous incidents of abuse. In John's words, though: "If somebody did to me what I do to her, I'd have him thrown in jail or kill him." Karen is now staying with a friend. This morning the DPA worker tried to reach Karen in order to discuss the situation with the children, but found out she was gone because of the recent incident of abuse. The DPA worker then attempted to make a home visit to talk to John, but neighbors said he was being held at the sheriff's department. According to the neighbors, they called the sheriff after they observed the abuse going on in the yard, and when John admitted to the deputies that he had beaten his wife, they threw him in the squad car and brought him to the crisis clinic. The DPA worker then met them there. Upon evaluation, John initially threatened suicide (said he wanted to blow his brains out), but as the interview progressed, he said that if he could get some help, he would promise to get rid of his gun at home and could postpone any harm to himself.

One reason for not calling for assistance with IPV when being assaulted is the belief that no real help is available (Cerulli et al., 2015). In a study examining data from the National Crime Victimization Survey from 1996 through 2012, Xie and Lynch (2017) found that 12% of those who did report to the police further noted that the police did not respond, so such fears may be reasonable, at least for some IPV victims. Others may decide not to call for police assistance if they don't want their partner to be arrested (Cerulli et al., 2015). Embarrassment about being a victim of partner violence can be another reason that women do not call the police. Such embarrassment is particularly a factor for male victims. Some people argue that men should never allow themselves to be assaulted by a woman, and if they are, they should not let others know. Such attitudes may keep a male victim from seeking help. Young, Cook, Smith, Turtletaub, and Hazlewood (2007) found that this bias against men calling for assistance when assaulted by a female partner was still present in the U.S. at the time of their study. These ideas about male victimization may not be as strong now as they were in the twentieth century, but there does not appear to be empirical data demonstrating this.

Now, let's look at a case example which describes a situation involving a male victim of partner violence (see Chap. 5). Shame, self-rationalization (e.g. it's not that bad, just "man up" and ignore it), and the belief that no services exist for men, may prevent a male victim from reporting his experience. This particular case also demonstrates how undocumented immigrants, male or female, may be especially reluctant to report partner violence because of fear that contact with the police could lead to identifying their immigration status and result in deportation. In such situations, our advice is that those in this situation should be encouraged to make contact with immigrant rights groups who can provide information on where to obtain support, including how to apply for the right to stay in the United States.

Case Example # 5

Juanita and Pedro moved to the U.S. 15 years ago. Both have become fluent in English, and while their son is a natural-born U.S. citizen, neither have made efforts to obtain citizenship. When asked why, they state they are afraid to let the government know of their presence lest they face potential deportation. Both parents work very long hours at various informal jobs. Vicente is a model student and a well-liked, well-behaved boy by all accounts from the school and acquaintances. Social services became involved when it was alleged that Vicente often is alone overnight and even for full weekends when his parents are working. When Vicente was interviewed at school, he also disclosed that his mother often gets very angry when she is stressed, and that she takes it out on both Vicente and Pedro. She will slap and punch Pedro during arguments. Vicente stated that while Pedro will yell as much as Juanita, he never uses physical violence. Vicente stated that his mom still spanks him on his bare bottom with a belt or extension cord, but that it doesn't happen as much as when he was younger. Vicente states he thinks his mom hits him less because he tries very, very hard to be good in school. Pedro's account of fights with Juanita fits with Vicente's. Pedro states that he does not hit back because he grew up in a very violent household in which he was afraid of his father. Additionally, Pedro fears that if he hits back, it will come to the attention of police and risk deportation. Pedro was embarrassed to talk about the hitting, and feels that there is no point in looking for help, not only because of the risk of deportation, but because he assumes there is no help for men. Juanita admitted in her interview that she sometimes hits Pedro, but claims she doesn't do it very often. Juanita also says she has told Pedro he can hit her back, which Vicente says he has heard as well. Juanita denied ever using an instrument to hit Vicente, though she admits she still spanks his bare bottom when he is bad because it will embarrass him and shame him into behaving. Neither adult wanted to leave the home; each stated they still love each other, would have no place to go, and would lose their son. The family were transferred to in-home services for long-term support.

The likelihood of reporting IPV also depends on race or ethnicity. For example, Black women are more likely than other groups to report to the police as victims of partner violence, while Black men are the least likely group to report their victimization from partner violence (Buzawa et al., 2017). Reporting issues for immigrant Latina women were the focus of a quantitative study by Pitts (2014). Using a sample of 568 women born in Latin America who had immigrated to Los Angeles and who had sought services in an agency offering a shelter and other services for Latina battered women, Pitts found that overall only 40% of the women had ever reported the violence to the police. Statistical analysis indicated that the most important predictors of reporting were higher levels of education for the women, having witnesses to the violence, and having children. Pitts speculated that wanting to protect her children was an important concern of battered mothers. The data on the presence of witnesses was interpreted by the researchers as an indicator that the abused woman was not able to deny that the violence had occurred.

Reporting differences also relate to sexual orientation or identity. Miles-Johnson (2013) noted that those who identified as LGBTI (described as being lesbian, gay, bisexual, transsexual or intersex) were less likely to report being the victim of another's assault. These data were based on surveys of people leaving bars in Australia. Researchers attributed the reporting differences to concerns of the victims that they might suffer negative consequences as a result of bringing themselves to the attention of the police. Although partner violence victimization was not directly assessed in this study, it is likely that similar concerns about negative and unintended consequences of reporting might exist for immigrant Hispanic or LGBTX victims. Aside from fears of deportation or having one's sexual orientation made public, others may feel that the arrest of the violent partner could have negative consequences when this person returned to the home (Novisky & Perlata, 2015).

The following are two related case examples from the appendix which illustrate how intimate partner violence can occur in same-sex relationships with many similar dynamics to such violence in heterosexual relationships. Case #9 describes the situation for one of the partners in the relationship and Case #10 describes the situation of the other partner in the relationship and illustrates how each partner in an abusive relationship may describe the violence differently. In these cases, each participant described the other as the controlling abusive partner. The cases also illustrate how fear of the violence getting worse may prevent an abused partner from involving the police and how an abused partner may stay due to continuing to love the abuser and her children.

Case Example #9

Elaine is a 28 year old single African-American woman with four children. Only two of the children are with her; the other two are with their father…a friend introduced her to a woman named Lettie. Lettie had a young child and had her own problems and attached herself to Elaine in a very dependent demanding fashion—began calling her at work and the family she worked for became angry about Lettie's constant calls but instead of Elaine telling Lettie not to call, she quit her job and moved in with Lettie and they both then moved to Sacramento. Lettie became more controlling, Elaine ended up taking care of Lettie's child along with her own children when Lettie got high on drugs and Lettie began almost terrorizing Elaine and her children and this eventually accelerated into Lettie beating Elaine physically and abusing Elaine's children almost daily. The beatings got worse but Elaine was afraid to call the police because she felt even if Lettie was jailed, when she got out of jail, Elaine would suffer worse beatings. Finally, last Friday, Lettie beat Elaine with a wooden chair, and Elaine tried to defend herself with a knife. Elaine didn't stab Lettie but did manage to get her children and leave. A community service worker referred Elaine to the shelter and to mental health services. Elaine states the apartment where she lives with Lettie is in Elaine's name and her furniture is still there but she is too afraid to go back. Currently, her plans are to stay at the shelter until she can get a new place, enroll her children in the school nearby and friends will provide her with furniture once she gets a new place. She is clear that she is not going back to Lettie and wants to start her life over. Since counseling helped her in the past, she is very anxious to start again. One issue she wants to have resolved is whether she is gay or straight and she feels very confused about this. She supports herself currently with welfare and all of her family and friends are in Oakland.

Case Example #10

Lettie is a 26 year old single black female referred to county mental health services by the Women's Center. For the past 3 years, Lettie has been involved in a live-in gay relationship with a woman named Elaine. Approximately a week ago, Elaine left Lettie and, with her two children, Elaine went to the Battered Women's Shelter asking for placement there, claiming that Lettie had beaten her and was threatening her, adding that she—Elaine—was planning to permanently sever the relationship and wanted to "start a new life". Lettie states that she has been devastated by Elaine's leaving and relates a description of their relationship quite different from what Elaine related to me when I saw her earlier in the week. Essentially, Elaine describes Lettie as the villain and she as the victim and Lettie describes Elaine as the villain and she as the victim—the actual events and problems described are approximately the same but the roles of the actors are reversed. Lettie has one child—a 6 year old boy—and Elaine has two children. Lettie states she has been gay for 13 years but her relationship with Elaine is the longest and most committed relationship she has had with a woman. They moved all over the Bay area and

Oakland before finally settling in Sacramento. Lettie feels she has sacrificed for Elaine—giving up jobs (Lettie is a certified welder) and so forth—to follow her but feels Elaine has not appreciated this. She states that throughout their relationship Elaine has abused her—both physically and emotionally. Lettie states that Elaine has a bad temper, gets easily insulted and seems to try to provoke Lettie into physical fights. When questioned about who starts the fights, Lettie admitted that both of them seem to mutually provoke each other. Elaine also lies about her to others—for example, Lettie states that Elaine has told others that Lettie uses drugs but Lettie denies any drug use except for an occasional beer—Lettie claims she has been the one who has primarily cared for the children—both hers and Elaine's—but Elaine claims the opposite. Lettie states that Elaine has punched holes in the walls of the apartment and currently is arguing with the landlady about paying for the damages. Why has Lettie stayed all this time? She says she has stayed because she loves Elaine and her children. But now she doesn't know what to do—she states she feels worse now than she has ever felt in her life. Last night she felt like killing herself (Elaine had left a loaded gun in the house) but she controlled herself because of her little boy. Currently, she says she is in control but has planned to stay in a motel tonight to avoid any temptation to harm herself. She was managing fairly well, but Elaine called her last night and began complaining about all their problems and this set Lettie off into a deep depression. She states she has no history of any suicide attempts, or even ideation. At this point she is planning to stay in Sacramento but wants very much to get involved in some counseling to get her life sorted out and figure out what she is going to do at this point.

Lettie's family is all in the San Francisco Bay Area. She describes herself as basically a loner and says she really has no friends locally in Sacramento – also that Elaine has turned their neighbors against Lettie and "her talk" has eliminated the possibility for friends she might have had.

9.1.3 Police Responses to Partner Violence

When someone is assaulted by a partner, they may call the police to make the assault stop. Others may fear future victimization and feel that the police making an arrest may make the violence stop in the future (Ward-Lasher et al., 2018). Reviewing the literature, Ward-Lasher et al. concluded that arrest may result in an end to future violence, but can also have the reverse effect of increasing future violence. Xie and Lynch's (2017) analysis of NCVS data indicated that calling the police for help was associated with a 34% reduction in the risk of repeated IPV, but whether or not an arrest was made showed no association with future IPV victimization.

Although the U.S. Department of Justice reported that the majority of police calls were responded to quite quickly (Reaves, 2017), a call to the police for assistance may not always be answered (Stout & Kennedy, 2017). Police may find IPV situations to be dangerous for them, and some express frustration over repeated calls from the same individuals. They may fail to respond for other reasons, as well. Although it is clear that calls about intimate partner violence are more attended to than in the past, the police response is sometimes determined by a formal assessment of how lethal the situation is likely to be (Klein, 2012). These assessments may be done by police screeners when the call is received, or by police officers who respond to the call by going to the home (Buzawa et al., 2017).

9.1.3.1 The Decision to Arrest

States vary across the United States in terms of how they request that police address calls for IPV assistance. Some have policies that require that the violent partner be arrested if there is clear evidence of this violence. These are known as mandatory arrest policies. Since it is common for a partner to fight back if assaulted, the mandatory arrest policies have resulted in both partners being arrested (Hirschel, McCormack, & Buzawa, 2017). In response to this, states have sometimes moved to a rule that only the primary aggressor be arrested. In an analysis of the effects of this modification of arrest policies, Hirschel and his colleagues found that there were fewer arrests made of either partner, as well as reducing dual arrests.

In their review of the literature, Ward-Lasher, Messing, Cimino, and Campbell (2018) noted that even when these mandatory arrest policies are in place, police may not make an arrest. This also happens in states with policies stating that arrest is preferred but not required, or where arrest is discretionary. Often the victim requests that an arrest is not made, and many argue that that victims should have this power. Others, in trying to protect the victim, refer to the fact that a victim may fear retaliation and that the arrest should be made in spite of a victim request not to (Ward-Lasher et al., 2018). In some cases, it is not possible to make the arrest if the offender has left after the call for help was made (Thorndike, 2015).

Arrests may be affected by the presence of children. Swerin, Bostaph, King, and Gillespie (2018) analyzed 345 police reports of IPV in the Northwestern U.S. in 2013. Women were the offenders in 18% of the cases. Children, often under the age of 6, were present in 47% of the cases. Police generally did not interact specifically with the children, but when children were there, they were less likely to make an arrest. There was evidence, though, that they made more efforts to ensure the victim was safe at the time and did more follow-up with the victim afterward.

When the assault is determined to be relatively minor, the victim may be directed to a counselor or battered women's shelter rather than the police responding directly. Such referrals for the victim can also occur in addition to arrest of the offender (Klein, 2012). Police may even provide transportation to a battered women's shelter for a female victim. If the victim is a man, shelters are not an option, and the police may not respond at all if they determine that the situation is not dangerous (Buzawa et al., 2017).

Many more men are arrested than women. When women are arrested, some report that they were acting in self-defense, while others said they were driven to violence after a period of verbal and physical abuse from their partner. All blamed their violence on earlier experiences of growing up in a violent home (Li et al., 2015). Sometimes both partners are arrested (Young et al., 2007). Once arrested, the offender may be released through court action but is requested to attend a *Batterer Intervention Program.* The nature of these programs is explained later in the chapter.

9.1.3.2 Lethality Assessment

One assessment that police make is called a Lethality Assessment Program (LAP) to determine if there is a risk for homicide when a call is made relating to intimate partner violence. A field trial of the Maryland Network Against Domestic Violence LAP was done in Oklahoma (Messing et al., 2015). Questions asked of the victim included whether the offender had ever used a weapon or threatened to do so against the victim, or threatened killing the victim. Other questions concerned behaviors such as the offending being jealous or unemployed. Answers to these questions affect the behavior of police called about a current act of IPV. Messing and her colleagues also found in follow-up interviews that those responding to the LAP were more likely to take protective action against future violence and to reduce risk of future violence.

Although the LAP appeared to be useful, police were not always happy about having to do this formal assessment. Based on a qualitative assessment of police officers in Canada done in 2014, Ballucci, Gill, and Campbell (2017) found that police were not always supportive of these formal assessments. Some argued that the formal list of questions meant that their own knowledge gained over many personal experiences with IPV calls were discounted and that the questions did not always tap into specific factors they felt were relevant for the couple they were working with. It was noted that the questions were especially inappropriate when the offender was female and the victim male. Collecting the data took time, and many expressed frustration that the data might not be used in the present situation or even placed where it could be used for future calls. Grant and Cross-Denny (2017) noted similar concerns in their interviews with police in Connecticut. They also pointed to situations where the victim of partner violence did not cooperate in answering the formal questions associated with the lethality assessment protocol. They did find evidence that police were concerned about partner violence, but with the dangerous environment in which they worked, they did not see the formal assessment as necessary or helpful.

9.1.3.3 Other Factors Relating to the Police Response

Many have analyzed the decisions made by police and arguing that these may be biased in various ways. In one detailed but older analysis of what happens after these arrests, Henning and Renauer (2005) found that prosecutors often rejected arrests of women who were identified as the violent partner. According to their data relating to female domestic offenses gathered in 2000 in Tennessee, prosecutors rejected 47% of the cases, and judges dismissed another 16%. They concluded that the criminal justice system treated women arrested for partner violence more leniently than men. In another study done by Henning with a different colleague (Feder & Henning, 2005), also in Tennessee, cases involving arrests of both the male and female partner were examined. They found that male and female victims of those arrested reported similar levels in severity of abuse experienced, although the criminal justice system data indicated higher levels of severity for the male arrestees. Also, the men arrested had a more serious history of previous partner violence as well as other forms of antisocial behavior.

9.1.4 Consequences of Arrest for Partner Violence: Batterer Intervention Programs

Police policies relating to IPV calls changed greatly over the 20th century. As Hazelwood (2007) discussed in her analysis of the criminal justice response to partner violence, this evolved in the late 20th century from a pattern of nonintervention, to attempts to mediate, to the current situation of mandatory arrest policies in many states. Now, increasing numbers of communities require arrest of perpetrators of partner violence, and a growing number of programs have been developed to work with those arrested (Morrison et al., 2016). [See Box 9.2 for discussion of programs in other countries]. Often attendance at such programs, typically labeled as *batterer intervention programs* (BIPs), is mandated for those arrested. Those arrested can be male or female partners. In some situations, both members of the couple are arrested (Babcock et al., 2016).

Box 9.2: Violence Perpetrator Programs in Other Countries
Changes in legal practices to address the problems relating to partner violence began in the United States in the 1980s. Since that time, programs attempting to change the behavior of those who are violent to partners or other family members as well as a system of shelters or supports for victims have been developed in many other countries around the world (Hamel, 2016). However, there is little published literature about these programs.

In Sub-Saharan Africa, the legal system is not effective in identifying or prosecuting perpetrators, so the major focus is prevention (McCloskey, Boonzaier, Steinbrenner, & Hunter, 2016). McCloskey and her colleagues report that there are some effective programs for high school students to teach them about problems relating to partner violence. Other programs work at the community level to try to educate people about partner violence. Evidence for their effectiveness is not as strong, and many men and women in these African countries still accept or even encourage physical punishment for wives who are not submissive to their husbands.

There is also evidence of high levels of partner violence in Latin America and the Caribbean, and a number of programs have been designed to lower these levels (Santovena & Silva, 2016). However, formal data relating to their effectiveness or even to details about how they function are difficult to obtain. In a survey of programs from a number of countries in this region, Santovena and Silva conclude that these programs need clearer guidelines and need to be more closely tied to the particular type of perpetrator. It appears that there are many more programs for victims than for perpetrators.

The process by which the identified violent partner is handled by the legal system may not be straightforward. Police can potentially take a number of actions once they respond to a call (Xie & Lynch, 2017). In their NCVS data, about 25% of the calls resulted in arrests. Arrest decisions are affected by beliefs within the local community and the associated court system. An example of the role of these beliefs can be seen in a study done in Salt Lake City. Mirchandani's (2006) interview of the staff associated with a domestic violence court there indicated that there was a strong feminist bias among court personnel in that location. During the interviews, many of those working within the courts strongly argued that men need to take responsibility for their violence toward a wife or partner and appeared to see men as responsible for the large majority of IPV cases. The female victims in these cases were told the violence was not their fault and that the men needed to understand this. Many of the judges were women, as were many of the prosecuting lawyers. Although these conclusions were based on one particular city, other locations appear to have a similar pattern of considering men to be the more violent partner in most situations (Young et al., 2007). Thus, offending men are more likely to be ordered to attend a formal treatment program (BIP) than offending women in many locations.

In their comprehensive review of BIPs, Babcock et al. (2016) identified and examined evidence of effectiveness of over 3000 such programs in the United States. Unfortunately, the empirical evidence supporting their effectiveness was not found to be strong. As Morrison et al. (2016) pointed out in their review of these programs, others have also questioned the quality of these programs, as did Babcock et al. (see Madden et al., 2019). We return to this issue after examining some of these programs.

9.1.4.1 Examining How BIPs Operate

In an attempt to better understand the overall nature of batterer intervention programs in the U.S. and Canada, Cannon, Hamel, Buttell, and Ferreira (2016) sent a survey to directors of over 3000 programs they were able to identify in these two countries. Responses were received from about 20% of these, yielding a sample of 238 programs for their analysis. About half of the programs in the sample were identified as being part of a larger social service or counseling agency, somewhat less than a third were identified as an independent private practice and another quarter of programs were associated with a battered women's shelter. Programs ranged from 8 to 78 weeks, with an average of 30 weeks. Groups of 10 people were most typical. Slightly less than half the programs required that the facilitator had at least a bachelor's degree, while a master's degree was required for another 47%. Less than 4% required a doctoral level degree for the facilitator. This suggests that many of the existing programs may not have formally trained facilitators.

Cannon's et al.'s survey asked for very detailed information about the nature of the programs offered. They first looked at the most common content across all the many different programs. They found that the educational topics included in at least 80% of the programs covered the effects of violence on children, the effects of IPV on the victims, the power and control tactics people generally use within couples, and the nature of gender roles within couple relationships and how these relate to IPV. Programs also included training of relevant skills. Specific skills included in at least 80% of programs included communication skills, conflict management and conflict resolution skills, helping clients to learn to manage and control their emotions, more specifically to change violence-related and irrational thoughts, and general coping skills. Other types of content that were used by smaller numbers of programs included the theoretical basis of the Duluth model (36%), followed by CBT (Cognitive Behavioral Therapy) which was mentioned by 29% of the programs.

9.1.4.2 Programs for Male Batterers

Much of the BIP focus is on programs for men who abuse their female partners. One of the more cited models for assisting batterers to stop their abusive behavior is the Duluth Model Batterer Intervention Program (Aaron & Beaulaurier, 2017; Babcock et al., 2016). This model focuses on patriarchal societal beliefs and how these contribute to male violence against female partners. Participants are taught about these beliefs in group sessions.

In a formal analysis of the outcomes a Duluth model program, Herman , Rotunda, Williamson, and Vodanovich (2014) analyzed data from male batterers who were required by the courts to participate in the program. A total of 103 of these men actually completed the program, and 53 dropped out. Thus, many of the men dropped out before completing the program. Looking only at those completing the program, over one third of these men were found to have committed some type of violent crime in the follow-up period of 9 years. These data were compared with recidivism rates of the group not completing the full Duluth program, and no differences were found between the two groups. These data did not provide any clear evidence supporting the Duluth model. The authors noted that their lack of good data supporting the effectiveness of the Duluth program was consistent with other published studies also failing to provide support for this type of program for male batterers.

In another attempt to evaluate the Duluth programs, Morrison et al. (2016) published a preliminary report of a major study to better understand the content of these programs as well as the clients and the professionals who work with them. In this initial 2016 report, they have analyzed data from two programs that focused on male batterers with female partners. They used an ethnographic approach with interviews of the therapists or other care providers associated with those programs, who we refer to as *facilitators*. One of the first issues identified by Morrison's group was the lack of information available to these facilitators about the mental health or other background for the men referred to the programs. They were forced to rely almost entirely on what the men themselves told them. In some cases, they were able to talk to the female partners of the men in the programs, but this was not always possible. When facilitators did speak with the abused partners, they complained that they were not able to tell the men in later sessions what the abused partner had told them. Another difficulty was that the facilitators were not able to effectively monitor the behavior of the men in the program. Thus, rules about the men not using violence while in the program could not be enforced. Finally, many facilitators lacked formal training. They reported that the pay was quite low and trained professionals typically had other, higher paying options and did not tend to opt for these types of positions. Some of these data and other elaborations can be found in Morrison et al. (2017, 2018).

As Babcock et al. (2016) explained, these Duluth-model programs are not based on any standard therapeutic models. Other programs for batterers do build on formal types of therapeutic interventions, typically a cognitive-behavioral therapy (CBT) model. In a CBT program, participants are taught about how their thinking about themselves and their partners might be distorted in ways that increase conflict and the potential for violence. Techniques for anger management may rehearsed in the group setting. Lee and DiGiuseppe (2018) provided a review and meta-analysis of therapies for anger management generally. Many use CBT techniques, and these were found to be the most effective for many types of anger. Unfortunately, as they noted, they found no evidence that these therapies were being used for BIPs. As explained below, CBT theory-based programs have been successfully used for couples.

Adding to the negative views of BIPs for male batterers, Aaron and Beaulaurier (2017) also pointed to the growing concern about their effectiveness. Some judges have stopped referring batterers to them and many programs have closed or have been experiencing reduced funding. Aaron and Beaulaurier argued that having effective programs for batterers is essential for the safety of battered women and that new programs are needed to better target particular types of batterers and asked that researchers work to help develop such programs.

Many have suggested that a major concern about BIPs is the lack of training for the facilitators of these programs. In particular, Cannon et al. (2016) noted that treatment providers did not appear to be sufficiently knowledgeable about the empirical data on partner violence and abuse (see Chaps. 4 and 5). High levels of mutual violence, in particular, were identified as an issue that needed to be more widely understood by those attempting to help batterers stop their abuse. Cannon et al. also noted, though, that although the empirical data are not strongly supportive of the male batterer intervention programs, the facilitators themselves were very satisfied with the job they were doing.

9.1.4.3 Programs for Female Batterers

As Fraehlich and Ursel (2014) explained, police departments in the United States and Canada have generally adopted policies that require that anyone committing violent acts against a partner must be arrested, when there is a call for police assistance. Such policies began to be instituted in the 1980s. The original intent of these policies was to require arrests of male batterers as a means of protecting battered women. However, the reality is that even the most severely battered women do fight back, at least on some occasions. Women also initiated partner violence outside of the context of immediate self-defense, and there are cases when the woman is the most violent partner in the relationship (see Chap. 5). Since women may be violent, even if only fighting back, police may be confronted with a situation in which both parties in the couple have engaged in physical IPV. The mandatory arrest policies have, therefore, led to arrests of both men and women. In their study of IPV arrests in Winnipeg, Canada, Fraehlich and Ursel examined court records from September 1999 to September 2005. A total of more than 17,000 cases were in these files, and women were arrested in about 3000 of them. In order to better understand the consequences when women were arrested for partner abuse, a sample of 2736 cases was established that involved one female offender and one male victim, who was a partner of the woman. The researchers noted that a smaller proportion of women were arrested in the more recent cases as the police moved toward a policy of only arresting the *primary* aggressor in situations when both partners engaged in violence. Before this change, if there was any evidence of mutual violence, both partners were arrested. Looking at the final sample of arrested women, many of the women were not prosecuted by the courts after their arrest. This was a lower percentage of prosecution than experienced by the arrested men, suggesting some leniency of the courts for women accused of partner violence. Detailed data were presented about the variables associated with arrests and with prosecution in the courts.

Others have also noted the arrests of women for partner violence, and further pointed out that most of the batterer intervention programs are based on a model of male violence against women based on underlying patriarchy. Such logic is not helpful for explaining why women might be violent toward a male partner (Dowd & Leisring, 2008). Thus, there is a need for new programs intended for women who batter or otherwise use physical aggression against their male partner. In an analysis of 23 existing studies looking at motives for female violence, Bair-Merritt et al. (2010) found that the primary motives for these women were anger, wanting to get the partner's attention, self-defense, retaliation and "coercive control" (p. 185). Although coercive control would imply that these women might have been classified as *batterers* (see Chap. 4), the authors noted that the actual data did not always support this interpretation since the female-initiated violence was rarely severe. The other motives that were identified do support the idea that programs based on very different ideas about the causes of violence are needed.

Following this earlier research, Tutty, Babins-Wagner, and Rothery (2017), in an attempt to better understand the women arrested for partner violence, compared a group of these women to the female partners (designated as the survivor group) of men arrested for partner violence in Calgary, Canada. Both groups were participating in formal programs designed for both types of women. Analyses comparing these two groups of women indicated there were relatively few differences for a number of psychological measures. In both groups, the women reported their male partners as being more violent than they were, although there were higher levels of overall violence in the survivor group. Over the course of the 14-week program, both groups showed improvements in depression, stress and general distress. However, the survivor group showed more improvement on these measures than the women arrested for their own abuse.

Others have also attempted to develop BIPs for women. Dowd and Leisring (2008) listed a number of characteristics of programs for female offenders that they considered essential. These included safety planning for the women. They noted that in most cases, the violent women were in relationships with mutual violence and their own safety was something that had to be considered since they might also be victims of partner violence. It was also recommended that the women should be taught to manage conflict. This would be helpful in lessening the possibility of escalation of conflicts in the future. Other content might include education about the costs and consequences of their own aggressive behavior. A number of skills relating to emotional regulation were also seen as important. These included basic emotional education about how emotions function in daily life, teaching the women to be more aware of when they were experiencing emotional arousal, explaining how anger and gender expectations were socialized in families, and discussing how their reactions to negative events in their relationships might be modified. A number of general relationship skills were included: Communication skills, assertiveness and negotiation, and characteristics of healthy relationships. Skills relating to stress management and ways of coping were included. As needed, other aspects that might be added included parenting skills and dealing with substance abuse issues. These guidelines were not directly translated, though, into a specific treatment program that could be formally evaluated.

9.1.4.4 Programs for Violent Couples and Other BIP Models

In comparing their more recent findings to those from earlier studies, Cannon et al. (2016) noted that their more recent data suggested there was *less* reliance now on the Duluth model for BIPs. Those working to develop BIPs appeared to be trying to find other, possibly more effective, models such as working with violent couples together. Recent data on the possibly greater effectiveness of couples counseling rather than working only with the identified violent partner have not yet been incorporated into the many programs across the U.S. and Canada, though. As Messing et al. (2015) pointed out, most of the traditional BIPs may not be appropriate for couples who wish to continue to be together.

Others, too, have advocated for couples' programs. Noting the lack of data demonstrating a high level of effectiveness for either programs for male or for female batterers, Stith, McCollum, and Smith (2012) argued that programs for couples would be a better fit to our current understanding of the dynamics of family violence. There is clear evidence that the majority of couples experience at least some level of mutual violence rather than being in a relationship with one-sided violence. They also pointed to the growing evidence that both women and men experience negative mental health consequences from partner violence, either as perpetrators or victims of this violence, or both. Another issue that suggests that both the woman and the man in the violent couple need to be treated together is the high frequency of co-occurring substance abuse. For example, many violence incidents involve alcohol in either or both of those in the couple. (See Chaps. 4 and 5 for more discussion of these issues).

Stith et al. (2012) reviewed a number of couples' programs for those involved with IPV. They pointed to evidence that these programs were effective in reducing violence, and that many of the participants were more positive about such couples' focused programs than they were about programs aimed at only the identified violent partner. An example of one of these was developed by Bradley, Friend, and Gottman (2011). Rather than the exclusive focus on violence seen in many BIPs, this program grew out of more than 30 years of work by Gottman and his colleagues to develop healthy relationships in couples (CHRP, Creating Healthy Relationships Program). Data from a randomized design where half the sample experienced the program and the others had no treatment indicated higher satisfaction and reductions of conflict in the treatment group.

In a later paper on this model (Bradley, Drummey, Gottman, & Gottman, 2014), the team evaluated 115 couples with mutual violence. They again assigned half of their sample to a no-treatment group. However, results did *not* indicate that there were changes over time in self-reported violence within the treatment couples. There was evidence, though, of less negative behavior in men in the treatment group, using a measure based on observations of belligerence, domineering, anger and defensiveness, but the differences for women were not statistically significant. Thus, formal evidence for this type of couples' treatment is mixed, at best.

Others have criticized the couples approach, and the cognitive-behavioral therapy model (CBT) often incorporated. Barner and Carney (2011) found that the outcomes from traditional BIPs were no worse than those associated with CBT. Murphy,

Eckhardt, Clifford, Lamotte, and Meis (2017) reported that in their comparison of individual couple treatment as compared to group therapy with couples, the group approach appeared to be more effective, possibly because of social support from others in the group, and seeing others able to reduce their violence. In their comprehensive review of evaluation studies published since 1990, Eckhardt et al. (2013) found that although CBT principles were increasingly being incorporated into all the BIP programs, there was still no convincing evidence that any of these programs were effective in ending or even reducing partner violence. They did note, though, that programs providing services for victims of partner violence (discussed in Chap. 8) appeared to have much better evidence of having a positive impact than those for the violent member(s) of the couple.

9.1.4.5 Programs for LGBTX Couples

As discussed in Chap. 5, gay couples also experience partner violence. Many do not seek help, and when they do, the police may not be helpful (Calton, Cattaneo, & Gebhard, 2016). Using data from a 2011 statewide survey asking about health issues for LGBTQ individuals in Colorado, Langenderfer-Magruder, Whitfield, Walls, Kattari, and Ramos (2016) analyzed data relating to police calls for lesbians and gays and for transgender individuals. They reported that 31% of those identified as transgender had experienced IPV, and within this group, 18% had reported this to the police. For lesbians and gay men, 20% reported IPV, and 26% of this group had called the police. Even if police assistance was sought, very few BIP programs addressed this type of couple. As Ford, Slavin, Hilton, and Holt (2012), pointed out, the LGBT community is not well served by the police or by other social agencies when problems with IPV arise. A published description of one program is the Virginia Anti-Violence program which has a general mission of promoting LGBTQ community health and safety through a variety of educational programs for the society generally as well as specifically for those identified as LGBT or Q (Strickler Jr. & Drew, 2015). As is often true for other types of partner violence (see Chap. 8), much of the focus of this program is on help for victims. Calton et al. (2016) describe some of the issues for these victim populations in seeking help for IPV.

9.1.4.6 Overall Assessment of Batterer Intervention Programs

As already noted, the data supporting batterer intervention programs is not encouraging. There have been questions about implementation (e.g., Wagers, Pate, & Brinkley, 2017), as well as about the basic theory underlying the widely used Duluth model (Cantos & O'Leary, 2014). In their NCVS data that looked generally at IPV victims, Xie and Lynch (2017) found that just reporting the IPV to the police had the greatest impact on a lowered chance of revictimization within the couple, and appeared to be more important than participation in any type of BIP. When the victim received services, this was more impactful than the BIP, which works with the offender, as others have also noted. In a review of programs to intervene when dating violence was identified, Jennings et al. (2017) found only modest evidence of effectiveness in these programs as well.

One reason for the lack of supporting data for BIPs is that programs tend to have low response rates in surveys of the programs. When data is available, there is a high dropout rate for participating batterers. As Jackson (2003) pointed out in her review of these programs, one explanation for the poor data on program effectiveness is that the measures used to assess how well the program is doing may be flawed. In these assessments, it is not clear what the desired outcome is. Is it merely having some reduction in the amount of violence or is it necessary that the violence be stopped completely? Hammett, Karney, and Bradbury (2018) observed the effects of changes in aggression levels (as measured by the CTS scale) over time in a general sample of couples. When aggression levels dropped there was better marital functioning. Increases in aggression levels were associated with worsened communication levels and greater stress. Levels of aggression in husbands was even more predictive of couple outcomes than aggression levels in wives.

If violence reduction is the goal of a couples BIP, what is the appropriate comparison group to be used for statistical comparisons? In clinical studies, a procedure of random assignment is used so that one group gets the treatment being assessed and another group gets no treatment or a placebo. For batterers mandated to attend a batterer intervention program, it would not be ethical to assign no treatment. So, the batterers need to be given some type of program. Another difficulty is that most programs are eclectic and do not rigidly follow a defined model, making it hard to compare across programs or even know what exactly is being assessed.

Perhaps more targeted programs are needed? As noted earlier, programs designed for male batterers may be especially *ineffective* for women who are the identified violent member of the couple. Another issue underlying all the programs is that offenders may differ in terms of how willing they are to make changes. Some studies have found that BIPs are largely ineffective for those forced to participate and having no desire to change (Alexander, Morris, Tracy, & Frye, 2010). Other batterer characteristics may also be important. For example, Welland and Ribner (2010) argued that programs for Latino immigrant men needed to include culturally appropriate content, including parenting skills for men, ideas about appropriate gender roles, spirtuality and discussion of discrimination toward immigrants. Montalvo-Liendo, Matthews, Gilroy, Nava, and Gangialla (2018) explore these issues further in a qualitative study of Mexican origin men who about women.

9.1.5 Other Forms of Partner Violence

9.1.5.1 Marital Rape

Although partner violence may include rape and other forms of sexual assault, and generally these do not occur outside the context of other forms of partner violence (Frieze, 1983), most states in the United States now consider forced sex within marriage to be a crime. This has not always been the case (Jackson, 2015). Before the 1970s, there was a general assumption that because agreement to sexual contact was assumed as a typical part of marriage, there was no such thing as *marital* rape. As awareness of rape as a social problem grew, more and more states began to include forced sex within marriage to be criminal acts, especially when a couple was separated. By 2007, 30 states included marital rape in their criminal codes, while others had various marital rape exemptions (Jackson, 2015). Since then, several states still exempt a rape verdict for a married couple. Falk (2015) discussed some of these cases, focusing on one in Ohio. Falk concluded that in general, now, when there is an accusation of marital rape, and laws are present to criminalize this, the rapist is tried within the court system and possibly jailed if found guilty.

9.1.5.2 Homicide

Whether intended, or occurring without prior intent in an act of violence against a partner, the violence can lead to death. When homicide occurs, there is a formal criminal process and a police investigation to determine the guilty party in the homicide and the circumstances under which it occurs. Campbell, Webster, and Glass (2009) estimate there are at least twice as many men who kill their female partner or ex-partner as women who kill a partner or former partner. Predictive factors for homicide include a history of partner violence, a relationship breakup, mental illness, drug use, and the presence of firearms. When the person is found to be guilty, a jail sentence is the typical outcome.

A number of studies have examined the situation in which a battered woman kills her abuser, possibly in self-defense. An important issue here is whether or not the woman will be formally prosecuted (Follingstad, Rogers, Welling, & Priesmeyer, 2015). When this occurs, the woman will typically be jailed while awaiting the outcome of her trial. There have been attempts to argue that when a battered woman has committed murder against her abuser, she should be excused because her actions can be seen as retaliation for past abuse, regardless of the circumstances of the murder. Fallingstad and her colleagues argue that this type of defense has rarely been successful. When law students completing a course in Criminal Law were surveyed about their decision-making in regard to whether to prosecute a battered woman accused of killing her partner, most *did support* prosecution, especially in cases where the man killed was not seen as a *bad* person.

One very unfortunate form of partner homicide is a situation where a male abuser kills his female partner, and then commits suicide (see opening vignette, Chap. 4) (Salari & Sillito, 2015). Generally, there has been a history of previous partner violence in these cases, but not always One situation in which this appears to occur is in response to the female partner leaving her male abuser. Cases were identified where he reacted to her leaving by searching for her and stalking her even when she had made extreme efforts to hide.

Although it is very rare for women to kill an intimate partner, it does happen. The case described below is one example:

Case Example #2

"Joyce" is a 22-year-old single African-American woman who, under extreme stress, came to the crisis clinic with her 4 year old daughter for help because of trauma flashbacks and periods of dissociation. Joyce tells the crisis worker that a little over 2 years ago, she started going out with a man named "George". Their relationship went well at first, and so she allowed him to move with her (her other child, a 2-year-old boy, is his biological child). Soon, however, George started beating Joyce frequently and severely. Once he beat her breasts so badly they got infected and she had to have surgery. Joyce finally kicked George out of the house, but he continued to come around and abuse her – he would follow her in parks and on the street, and then would attack her. Sometimes she was successful in pressing charges and having him put in jail, but recently the police had been unwilling to act on her complaints.

Joyce tried to get help from every resource she could think of including the police (repeatedly), the local district attorney, and Haven House∗ (the local domestic violence shelter), but got nowhere. The situation had progressed to the point that George was calling her constantly and threatening that he was going to kill her. Joyce developed ulcers, couldn't sleep, had problems concentrating and lost weight. When she was able to fall asleep, Joyce reported having nightmares related to the abuse. George had also beaten Joyce's two children, and the children began having nightmares, flashbacks of the abuse, angry outbursts and showed fear toward adult men in general. Finally, in desperation, Joyce borrowed a gun from her sister, and after a particularly brutal beating in which George poked Joyce's eye in with a stick (she required many stitches), she finally went out, found George sitting on a park bench, and after much deliberation, walked up and shot him. She then went to a pay phone and turned herself in to the police. Joyce states that for the first time—sitting in jail - she felt safe.

George did not die from the gunshot wound and was still recovering in the county hospital when Joyce came to the crisis clinic for help…

9.1.6 Prevention of Partner Violence Through Community Educational Programs

The Centers for Disease Control have developed a public document that reports on a large variety of programs developed to help prevent all types of partner violence and concludes by discussing prevention through educational programs targeted to many different audiences rather than attempting to work with violence perpetrators directly (Niolon et al., 2017). Thus, the focus is on prevention of violence before it occurs. They further suggest that these types of educational programs may also have beneficial effects on preventing other forms of interpersonal violence such as child abuse.

The first programs described fall under the heading of programs to "Teach Safe and Healthy Relationship Skills" (Niolon et al., 2017, p. 13). This is classified as a primary prevention approach, since it teaches attitudes that could serve to lower the frequency of partner violence. They further argue that such programs can also have beneficial effects on other forms of interpersonal violence. Two targets are identified—youth and couples. Several specific programs are discussed, with supporting evidence based on long-term follow-ups. Over a period of years, there was less reported partner violence for each of the programs for teenagers, especially that perpetrated by the men. Programs for couples were also described, and again were found to reduce reported partner violence in follow-up studies.

Another set of programs were based on the belief that if influential adults and peers were taught about positive relationship expectations and learned about the harmful effects of physical and psychological violence in couples, there would be an overall lowering of partner violence within the communities where these programs were done. One set of programs worked with men and boys. An example was a program with male high school athletes and their coaches (Miller et al., 2013). Follow up data indicated less social approval for partner violence, as well as lower levels of reported physical, sexual and psychological aggression. Another set of programs attempted to work with a broader community such as a school or workplace to teach attitudes that would discourage all types of violence, including partner violence. Reported effectiveness of these programs was mixed, however, especially as relating to reducing levels of reported partner violence.

Overall, there does appear to be more support in the research literature for educational programs being more effective in preventing IPV than the direct intervention seen in the BIPs discussed earlier (Fox & Shjarback, 2016). Many different types of prevention programs are being developed, many using quite innovative techniques. Dill-Shackleford, Green, Scharrer, Wetterer, and Shackleford (2015) reported on using theatre to demonstrate myths about partner violence, addressing both physical and psychological abuse. The plays were shown to a general audience at a university theatre. Another type of approach that has been suggested involves working with faith-based communities (Choi, Elkins, & Disney, 2016). Choi and her colleagues suggest that education within these groups may be especially important for preventing partner violence in immigrant populations. Another example of this approach can be seen in work done in Minneapolis with faith-based communities within African American populations. In this project, focus group discussions were held with lay and secular leaders to discuss better ways of helping people to better understand and address potential issues with partner violence (Raymond, Spender, Lynch, & Clark, 2016).

9.2 Child Physical and Emotional Abuse and Neglect: Identification and Treatment for Parental Abusers

The situation for mothers or fathers who neglect or physically or psychologically abuse their children is quite different from procedures for those who physically abuse an adult partner. In this section, we review the various steps in identifying parents who abuse or neglect a child, and then discuss what the *treatments* or punishments are for those found to be abusers. As briefly discussed at the end of this section, this process is quite different for sexual abuse of a child or when a child dies, as it is for partner rape or homicide.

Child abuse was recognized as a serious problem by U.S. society long before partner violence was labeled as a social problem (see Chap. 6). Some of the first formal laws relating to identification of parents abusing their children were passed in the United States in the 1960s (Mathews & Kenny, 2008). In response to concerns about identifying those engaging in child physical or other abuse or neglect, laws were developed in the United States, as well as many other countries, *requiring* that people who might have knowledge of abused children or their parents report their concerns to designated authorities (Mathews & Bross, 2015). Once such laws were in place, societal institutions were developed to identify and address those found to be offenders.

Identification of child abusers is a complex process as discussed in more detail below. One issue with such reporting is that people's personal definitions of abuse may differ. Although more common and more often fatal, neglect is even more difficult to define than abuse (Proctor & Dubowitz, 2014). Emotional abuse and neglect are even more complex and open to varying interpretations (Glaser, 2011; Runyan, 2015). See Box 9.1 for an outline of the process of addressing physical child abuse.

Once a report is made to Child Protective Services (CPS), a formal investigation is done to determine if there is merit in the report and if there is evidence that one or both parents are abusive or neglectful (Cross, Goulet, Helton, Lux, & Fuller, 2015). If abuse is confirmed, the next step in this process is the decision about what services are needed to assist the child and the abusing adult(s). Cases of neglect are often referred to other agencies if determined to be related to very low income for the family. For other forms of abuse, mental health or other services are offered for family members under the guidance of CPS. Typically, a monitoring system is also set up, and CPS case workers begin a regular monitoring of the family to make sure the abuse did not occur again.

In addition to having programs for assistance of the identified abusive families, another possibility is that the identified child may be removed from the custody of the abusive parent and placed in foster care. This occurs when it is believed that there is a high level of risk for the identified child and requires legal action by family courts. These steps in the identification are discussed in more detail in the next sections of the chapter.

9.2.1 Identification of Offenders

9.2.1.1 Reporting of Suspected Abuse

Like the situation for those who are violent or abusive to an adult partner, parents who abuse children rarely come forward requesting treatment or other assistance. Since children are not likely to report being victimized by their parents (in contrast to the situation for victims of partner violence), an important first step in lessening or ending parental abuse of children is the identification of abusive or neglectful parents by the broader society. This almost always means that someone else has to suspect abuse and report it to the appropriate authorities.

Laws about reporting child abuse vary across countries as well as across states within the United States (Korbin & Krugman, 2014). These laws specify what type of abuse needs to be reported, how these reports should be done, and what categories of people are required to make such reports. Generally, those mandated by these laws to report possible child maltreatment are professionals who come in contact with children through their work, and who are seen as having some level of knowledge or expertise about the characteristics of abused children. They may be able to make such reports anonymously, meaning that accused parents are not informed about who made the report or why. In other states, reporters are identified. The types of maltreatment that are suspected that must be reported vary, but generally include physical, sexual and psychological abuse as well as neglect or being abandoned (a form of very serious neglect). Suspected abuse by parents or adult caregivers is always included in laws governing mandatory reporting, but sometimes abuse by other family members or people outside the family must also be reported. Definitions of abuse have changed over time, and are believed to be more inclusive in more recent time periods. For example, infants born to mothers using illegal drugs or otherwise affected by illegal drugs are now sometimes reported as being potentially abused. Some states also mandate reporting of cases when an infant was affected by alcohol use by the mother during pregnancy. Children in homes where they are exposed to violence in the parental couple have to be reported in some states. As described above, the first step in the identification process is a formal report made to Child Protective Services (CPS) of a suspected case of child abuse. Once this report is made, CPS staff must decide whether or not to investigate, do a formal investigation if this is the decision, and if abuse is determined, to determine the appropriate response based on the level of risk for the child. The following case illustrates how a referral to Child Protective Services can be perceived by the abusive parent as a positive mechanism for obtaining help.

Case Example # 16
Karen, a 28 year old married white female with three children, came to the crisis clinic asking to see a counselor. Upon evaluation, Karen began to cry stating that she feels completely overwhelmed and doesn't know what to do. Karen's three children include Tevine, aged 8; Casey aged 7; and Mikey aged 4½. Karen's husband, Andy, works for a chemical company and was recently transferred from the town of Tracy to a much smaller town, Linden. Karen was quite happy living in Tracy because she had friends and family there, but hates living in Linden because she is very isolated, is stuck in the house all day with the kids (her husband uses their only car for work) and it is getting to her to the point she yells and screams at the kids "all the time". Karen states that her children "act like brats" and recently she hit Casey so hard she was afraid she broke his arm. The crisis clinic social worker advised Karen that she is obligated to make a report to CPS (Child Protective Services), but Karen didn't seem bothered by that, stating she would actually like to have a CPS social worker come out to her house and help her learn how to handle the kids better.

Karen indicates that she had a complete hysterectomy 3 years ago and was told she must take hormones but she has not filled her prescription because she can't afford it. As a result, she has chronic severe hot flashes and mood swings. She has decided to go back to her family doctor and get the hormones and has an appointment to see the doctor today. The crisis clinic social worker spoke with her husband Andy, who seems to understand what is going on but admits when he comes home at night he doesn't respond to her needs like he should because he wants his own needs met. Both Karen and Andy are very amenable to the idea of counseling.

9.2.2 Differences in Who Reports the Abuse

There is evidence that reports of possible abuse are more likely to come from some types of mandated reporters than others. In an analysis of national U.S. data form 2010, Kesner and Dever (2015) analyzed the reports made by different types of professionals mandated to report possible abuse or neglect. The largest group of reports (30%) came from police or other law enforcement staff. Forty-four percent of these reports were substantiated. Many of reports (29%) came from people working in educational settings, but only 19% of these were substantiated. Staff in social service agencies made 20% of the reports, with 29% of these being classified as abuse or neglect. Those working in medical settings submitted 13% of the reports and 33% of these were substantiated. An additional 8% of the reports of possible abuse came from those working in mental health settings; 19% were substantiated. Reasons why some types of reporters appeared to be more accurate than others in identifying abuse were not discussed. Kesner and Dever noted that many of the abused or neglected children identified in this study had already been identified previously in earlier reports. They further noted that there were more cases of potential neglect reported than of physical abuse, especially by those working in social service agencies.

As Ho, Gross, and Bettencourt (2017) explained, as mandatory reporting laws have been refined in many states, the group of professionals now under the requirement of mandated reporting of suspected child abuse or neglect includes health care providers, law enforcement staff, social service staff, teachers, childcare providers and mental health providers. In a number of states, this list has been expanded to include anyone who might have knowledge of child abuse (called "Universal Mandatory Reporting," Ho et al., p. 709). However, in a formal assessment of the effects of these expanded reporting requirements using a national data set from 2013, Ho et al. found that although the total numbers of reports did rise with universal reporting, many of the reports were not confirmed with formal investigation. A negative consequence of broadening the types of people making formal reports to CPS was that the staff needed to engage in more formal investigations, all of which are time consuming. Overall, only 13% of reports were confirmed. Of these confirmed reports 84% came from identified professionals and 16% from others. Thus, encouraging others to report suspicions of child abuse did not appear to be beneficial to the process of identifying abusive parents, and may cause problems because of an expansion in the number of allegations filed.

9.2.2.1 Investigation of Reports of Suspected Abuse

The process of investigating a complaint can be quite time consuming and difficult. In an analysis of national U.S. data in 2011, Cross et al. (2015) determined that about 61% of the initial reports of suspected maltreatment that were made to CPS resulted in a formal investigation. Reasons for not doing a formal investigation varied, but often related to a lack of information about how to find the parents, a lack of jurisdiction or other technical reasons. The decision to investigate as well as the outcome of the investigation varied widely across states and individual CPS offices. Smith and Donovan's (2003) interviews of caseworkers doing these investigations demonstrated the complexities of this process. One issue that emerged from these data was that there were few formal guidelines for how these investigations should be done. Often, quite subjective judgments were made about what constituted abuse.

In a very ambitious study, Putnam-Hornstein, Needell, King, and Johnson-Motoyama (2013) analyzed both the reports made and the investigations of these reports. Their sample of potential cases included all children born in California in 2002. Any reports filed for these children up to the age of 5 were examined. Data are summarized in Box 9.3. Specific comparisons were made for White as compared to

Black children. Looking first at cases where children were reported to CPS as potentially being abused, it was clear that a much higher rate of Black than White children were investigated for abuse. Overall, 38% of all the cases that were investigated were substantiated by CPS. The rate of substantiation was much higher for Blacks than Whites. The same pattern of higher rates for the Black children was seen for children who were removed from the parents found to be abusive and placed in foster care. Overall, this was the outcome for 42% of the cases determined to be abuse, but rates of Black children placed in foster care were higher than for Whites. Thus, these data imply a clear racial bias in the reporting process. To investigate this further, Putnam-Hornstein and her colleagues further analyzed the data looking only at those children born to mothers receiving public health insurance. They argued that this was the best indicator they had for identifying children in low SES families. Looking only at the children in the low SES group, the racial differences tended to disappear. Overall, there were much higher rates of reporting, substantiation of abuse and placement in foster care for the lower SES children, regardless of race. These data suggest that what appears to be a higher rate of child abuse within Black families may, instead, be a result of more of these families living in poverty. Chap. 6 discusses some of the reasons that parents may experience high levels of stress that might affect their parenting behavior when there are serious concerns about money in the family.

Box 9.3: Reporting of Child Abuse and Neglect

	Total population	White	Black
% of all children referred for abuse	14%	13%	30%
% substantiated overall	–	5%	12%
% placed in foster care	2%	2%	6%
	Children of Mothers with Public Health Insurance		
% referred to CPS	–	38%	41%
% substantiated	–	18%	17%
% placed in foster care	–	9%	10%

Based on data from Putnam-Hornstein et al. (2013) who analyzed data from all birth records of 531,035 children born in California in 2002 and then used this to look at Child Protective Services data for children up to the age of 5.

Victor and his colleagues (2018) identified another potential bias in the investigative process. After noting the high levels of parental substance abuse and IPV found in other studies of families identified as abusive of children and families where an abused child was placed in foster care, Victor et al. used data from a statewide child welfare agency to better understand the role of parental substance and IPV in the parents or caretakers when neither had a direct relationship to the suspected abuse or neglect. The final sample included over 150,000 alleged perpetrators who were investigated by CPS, but neither IPV nor substance abuse was mentioned in the initial complaint. Outcomes of these investigations were either no evidence of abuse, weak evidence or strong evidence of abuse. Only in cases of strong evidence, was the family determined to have substantiated child abuse. Analysis of the data indicated that when substance abuse was identified in the family, the odds of the family being determined to be abusive were more than three times higher that if there was no substance. The presence of IPV nearly doubled the odds of a determination of abuse. When both were present, the odds were nearly five times higher. Thus, in spite of the face that there was no evidence that these issues of substance abuse or partner violence in the parents were directly related to how they interacted with the children, the mere presence of these factors led to caseworkers being more likely to decide that the family was abusive.

Because of these types of limitations, many attempts have been made to improve and formalize the investigative process. In one such example, Camasso and Jagannathan (2013) proposed a formal mathematical approach for the investigations. However, our personal assessment was that this type of very formal approach would not solve problems relating to the types of definitional and subjective judgements required. They would also have little effect when there were external pressures on the agency and the caseworkers doing the investigation that might impact the decisions made.

9.2.3 *Responding to a Determination that Child Maltreatment is Present*

Just as the reporting process varies across regions within the United States, so does the process of determining what to do if abuse is verified. The circumstances of the family and the child have to be considered (Font & Maguire-Jack, 2015). Decisions depend on specific agency factors such as whether or not there has been recent publicity about a particular case of highly abusive parenting. The overall case load of the CPS office may also be a factor. The first basic decision is whether or not the maltreated child should remain with the abusive family.

9.2.3.1 Protection for the Abused Child

If a parent is determined to be highly neglectful or abusive, there is a very real potential danger for the child. Damashek, Drass, and Bonner (2014) noted that 1500 children died in the United States in 2011 because of some form of child maltreatment. In a more detailed analysis of deaths of children in the state of Oklahoma that were associated with child maltreatment, they found that about half of these deaths were due to inadequate supervision of the child by the parent leading to a fatal accident. Other deaths were directly caused by the parents and were classified as homicides. Overall, more boys than girls were homicide victims. Deaths relating to inadequate supervision tended to occur more for somewhat older children (4 as compared to 2 years of age) and for children living in homes with 3 as compared to 2 children. The most common cause of death was drowning, often related to lack of supervision of bathing. Death is the worst outcome, of course, but serious injuries may also result from neglect or physical abuse (see Chap. 6).

9.2.3.2 Removing the Child From the Home: Placement in Foster Care

Once a determination is made that the situation is abusive, the first question is whether the parents are willing to work with CPS to improve the situation for the child. Glaser (2011) pointed to concerns if the caregiver was not willing to cooperate or was unable to make necessary changes. In such situations, it may be necessary to remove the child from these caregivers and place her or him in alternative housing. In their 2011 data, foster care placement varied from a low of 2–14% of the cases investigated (in California) to a high of 28% (in Hawaii) (Cross et al., 2015). Although removing the abused child from the parents and placing her or him with other, typically paid caregivers or foster parents, is sometimes determined to be the best way to protect the child from future abuse, this is generally not a desired outcome. Clinical psychologists are sometimes asked to assess the child's mental health, and testify in court in formal custody hearings.

Sometimes, a child is placed temporarily in foster care, when there is a question about the best long-term option for that child. When this occurs, the birth parent[s] are encouraged to have regular visits with the child, but these are done under the supervision of an employee of CPS (Saini, Van Wert, & Gofman, 2012). This supervised visitation is often a stressful situation for the social worker (who needs to observe the patterns of interaction between the child and the parent) and for the parent who knows she is being observed. Such visits are necessary, though, for the parent and child to maintain emotional bonds and to ease reunification if this is the final decision made.

There is a clear desire to find a permanent solution for the child as soon as possible (Aguiniga et al., 2015; Brown & Ward, 2014). Without permanent caregivers, the child may have difficulty in developing attachment with the current caregiver. Strong child-parent attachment is believed to be necessary for developing good relationships throughout one's life and are especially important for infants. A permanent caregiver is more likely to understand the needs of the child and help the child develop a sense of trust in the world. Aguiniga and her colleagues (2015) worked with a program that involved training some of the CPS staff to assist in helping foster children find a permanent placement. They provided data about what types of placements were developed in a sample of 311 cases. The most typical situation was that the child was reunited with his or her birth family, although this tended to be least likely to happen if the parent was using drugs or had serious mental health difficulties. Permanent placement with some other family member, or with the temporary foster caregiver was the next most common outcome. Although adoption was often believed to be an excellent situation, this was relatively rare, especially for older children and for African American children.

In a related study of adoption as a permanent solution for foster children, Scott, Lee, Harrell, and Smkith-West (2013) analyzed barriers to adoption among family caregivers who had assumed legal guardianship in the state of Florida. Such a placement was seen as preferable to placement with a non-family member. One benefit was that continuing contact between the child and the birth parent was facilitated when the child was living with a family member. Often, these caregiving family members reported not wanting to move to formal adoption of the child. This was primarily for financial reasons, and because of concerns about pressure from other family members and/or the birth parents not to do a formal adoption. In a review of the published literature, Hegar and Maria Scannapieco (2017) argued that adoption or guardianship by family members led to more beneficial outcomes for the children placed by CPS, even if the abusive parent was living in the same household. They pointed to evidence that there was evidence that the percentage of such placements was increasing, suggesting that others, too, perceived this type of placement as a good option.

Many have critiqued the system of foster care for a variety of reasons (e.g., Wildeman & Waldfogel, 2014). As Villodas et al. (2016) have found, many of the children placed in foster care show evidence of post-traumatic stress (see Chap. 3) as a result of their prior experiences of being abused by their parents. Their placements can be unstable, possibly because their PTSD may result in them being difficult children for the foster parents. Sometimes the foster parents find it impossible to care for these traumatized children. This creates a situation where this is a need to assign a different foster parent when problems appear. The lack of stability in their placement is associated with continuing mental health difficulties for the children. In a very careful analysis of the data on children in foster care as compared to children living with abusive or neglectful parents, Wildeman and Waldfogel (2014) concluded that both groups suffer from a variety of problems including higher rates of mental health problems and homelessness as adults, lower rates of educational attainment, and poorer employment histories. There was no clear evidence that foster care led to better or to worse outcomes for these already troubled children, especially if their birth parents continued to be abusive.

9.2.3.3 Underlying Goals of Child Protective Services

As society has worked to address child abuse, a number of different strategies have been attempted. These have changed over time. Current national priorities in the U.S. today are probably best found in publications of U.S. government agencies. In a non-technical publication, the U.S. Centers for Disease Control (https://www.cdc.gov/violenceprevention/pdf/essentials_for_childhood_framework.pdf) outline three major goals in their publication on Essentials for Childhood: Steps to Create Safe, Stable, Nurturing Relationships and Environments (2014). These goals are safety for the child (defined as freedom from fear and security from physical or psychological harm); stability (predictability and consistency in the child's social, emotional and physical environment; and nurturing (having a caregiver who is sensitive to and meets the needs of the child).

As Whitt-Woosley and Sprang (2014) explained, since the Adoption and Safe Families Act was adopted.in 1997, federal policy mandated that the protection of the child from future abuse should be the most important concern for CPS. This was a change from earlier views that family preservation was the primary goal, to be achieved if at all possible. This law was passed in response to reports of children who were returned to their abusive families and then continued to be abused (or even killed). Another concern was that when children were removed from the family and assigned to foster care, they often lived in very unstable situations because of the need to continually seek family reunification. Case workers, though, have personal views on these issues. As Fluke, Corwin, Hollinshead, and Maher (2016) found, it was the newer child welfare staff who were most concerned about child safety, while the older, more experienced staff saw family preservation as more important.

9.2.4 Working With the Abusive Families

Once the decision has been made that one or more children in a family are being maltreated, either through physical abuse or neglect, and CPS chooses not to place the children in foster care, the child welfare system works with the abusive families to improve the conditions and create a safer situation for the maltreated child or children (Stephens, Gopalan, Acri, Bowman, & McKay, 2018). Working with these families can be quite difficult. As Stephens and her colleagues explained, the parents may be angry with the investigation process and with the whole role of CPS. Once the case workers begin to make recommendations about what must be done to better protect the children, parents may resent these requests. They may feel forced to comply, since there is the threat that the children could be taken away if they don't cooperate. This can lead to a feeling of helplessness in the parents. In describing this situation, Stephens et al. stressed the importance of working cooperatively with parents, and seeing their role as providing social support to help them become better parents. At the same time, they noted that case workers often have a large number of families they work with, and may not have sufficient time to develop this supportive approach. As Chap. 10 explains, often case workers have limited training for their difficult jobs. Many experience burnout and other negative reactions to their jobs. The fact that many CPS staff work with families from different cultures or racial groups may also create barriers to communication between case workers and the families they work with (Brown, Hansen, & Saxe, 2018).

Along with providing advice themselves, CPS staff often recommend that the parents and children enter some type of formal program. Some of these are briefly described below. These programs are discussed in more detail in Chap. 8, since the focus of many of these programs is not only helping the parents gain parenting skills, but also helping the traumatized children. As Brown et al. (2018) explained, participation in these programs is mandatory for the parents and children, making these mental health programs function differently than they normally would as voluntary programs. The CDC publishes information providing details about how various programs might be implemented (Fortson, Klevens, Merrick, Gilbert, & Alexander, 2016).

9.2.4.1 Programs for Parents of Abused Children

There are many types of programs. Once a parent is determined to be abusive, they may be asked to participate in a parenting program being conducted by a local hospital or social service agency. These may be designed to help mothers or, sometimes both parents, develop skills to enable them to interact with their children in a positive way, and, in this way, prevent future child abuse (Baker, Brassard, Schneiderman, Donnelly, & Bahl, 2011). Some programs even target *potentially* abusive mothers. These programs have been used to prevent child fatalities, and include education about safe ways of interacting with children (Krugman & Lane, 2014). All of the programs require participating parents to confront their abusive behavior (Brown et al., 2018).

SafeCare is a home-based program intended to work with parents of very young children who are neglecting their children (Proctor & Dubowitz, 2014). Parents are taught about how to manage children in nonabusive ways, as well as being given information about household management and home safety. Information about how children develop over time is also provided. This program has received some supporting data, and is often used in conjunction with other services. Rosenblum et al. (2017) outline another similar program that provides parenting skills for abusive mothers called MomPower. Other programs are discussed in Chap. 8.

Programs for parents may be incorporated into BIPs. As discussed in Chap. 6, there is clear evidence indicating a relationship between partner violence between the parents and negative effects on children. In response to such concerns about the effects of IPV on the children of the violent couple, a number of programs have been developed to assist the female victims of partner battering and their children (e.g., Macy, Rizo, Guo, & Ermentrout, 2013). In many cases, the women are mandated to attend such programs when the violent male partner is arrested, or when they, themselves are arrested for partner violence. One such program is called MOVE (Mothers Overcoming Violence through Education and Empowerment) (Turner, Gilbert, Hendricks, & Demaree, 2006). This program included both safety training for the mothers as well as teaching parenting skills. The sessions also served as a support-group for the mothers.

In an assessment of a MOVE program, 73 women either referred by Child Protective Services or by the courts involved in an IPV case were assessed to determine if participation in the program led to reductions of partner violence (Macy et al., 2013).

Data indicated that 3 months after completion of this 13 session intervention, there were reported reductions in male partner violence as well as in violent of the woman toward her partner. [However, rates of violence were slightly higher at the 3 month follow-up before they declined by the end of the 13th session of the program]. The researchers noted that the sample of women in the program were generally highly educated, with 70% having some post-secondary education. About half of the women identified their race as African American or Black.

9.2.4.2 Other Responses to Child Abuse

Ideas about providing more safety for the abused child in other ways are being developed. In one example of this, Nelson-Dusek, Rothe, Roberts, and Pecora (2017) report on a program that goes beyond the immediate family, and asks for involvement of other family members and friends in assisting in ensuring the safety of the children. The parent (generally the mother) was asked to work out a plan for the future safety of her child and to think about who could be called upon for help among family and friends. Parents often interpreted this as thinking about who they could call on if they were feeling frustrated by their children. Doing this planning was seen as difficult but necessary by the participating parents. Very preliminary data were collected to determine how well this program would work. Difficulties in finding families to participate were noted, although those who did get involved in this pilot program had positive comments.

9.2.4.3 How Effective are Programs Treating Child Abuse Offenders?

Overall, the evidence supporting the effectiveness of any the types of programs discussed above is mixed, at best. Unfortunately, few of these programs have been tested in a randomized, controlled study (Batzer, Berg, Godinet, & Stotzer, 2018). Existing evaluation data does not indicate strong effects, at least in preventing future abuse (Euser, Alink, Stoltenborgh, Bakermans-Kranenburg, & van Uzendoorn, 2015: Finkelhor, 2018). Studies have indicated that sometimes the abuse gets worse over time after the family enters a treatment program if the child remains with the abusive parent (Yampolskaya, Greenbaum, Brown, & Armstrong, 2015). Many programs do show positive effects for some families, but none are completely effective in completely overcoming parental abuse or neglect in all the participating families (Fortson et al., 2016).

There are a number of reasons for lack of evidence-based treatments for parents who maltreat their children. Haskett, Neupert, and Okado (2014) outlined some of the complexities in evaluating parenting programs. First, parental behavior changes over time and may be dependent on personal issues in the lives of the parents. Their empirical data also indicated that parental behavior often became more abusive once CPS was involved in working with the parents. Second, programs may not target important issues beyond physical abuse or neglect. In a review of ten apparently evidence-based parenting programs identified by SAMSHA, Baker et al. (2011) found that none of these dealt adequately with issues relating to psychological maltreatment of children by caregivers and urged that this be given more attention. Special issues arise when parental neglect is not intentional, but is related to poverty in the family (Mathews & Kenny, 2008).

Another type of family that appears to be at risk for child maltreatment is military families (Milner, 2015). As Milner described, military families may be forced to relocate frequently, making it difficult to develop close relationships with others outside the family. The nature of being in the military is associated with high levels of stress for the active duty member as well as other members of the family. These families have also had high rates of partner violence. In response to these concerns, the military Family Advocacy Program (FAP) has been working to provide a number of services to their families. One is general education about all forms of family violence. In addition, FAP staff do investigations of suspected abuse and encourage others on the base to report suspicions of abuse. If abuse is verified, they work with abusing parents to develop better parenting skills. In some cases, the active duty parent may be separated from the military if the abuse is severe, so there is an added incentive for these parents to end or change their abusive behavior before it is reported. Perhaps as a result of these programs, the rates of reported child maltreatment and the rates of substantiated reports are both lower than in the general U.S. population (Milner, 2015).

9.2.4.4 Should Child Protection Goals Be Changed?

As noted above, current policy is that the protection of the abused child from physical harm should be the most important goal of CPS, but it does not appear that we do a good job of meeting this goal in the U.S. In an analysis of programs for addressing child abuse in England and Australia, as well as in the U.S., Broadhurst and Mason (2017) argued that the strong focus on protecting the abused child in all these countries may have been misguided. As they point out, data indicate that many children who are removed from the home are upset by this and often make strong efforts to reunite with their birth family as adults. Policies encouraging removal of children may also create many difficulties for the offending parents. They often experience grief over the loss of a child, and the mother may become pregnant again as a response to this grief. Court documents related to the removal of the child become lasting evidence of their failure as parents. Whitt-Woosley and Sprang (2014) further build on these arguments supporting making greater attempts to help families found to be abusive to function in less abusive ways. They note that many of the criteria used to determine that a child should be removed are much more likely to apply to poorer families, creating a basic injustice.

Other goals for CPS have been suggested by other researchers. Hart and Glaser (2011) argue that increased attention should be given to emotional abuse as well as to physical abuse and neglect. Wald (2014) further broadened these program aims to suggest that another goal should be to help children develop social and academic skills they will need as successful adults. Methods for achieving this goal are not as clear. Other goals mentioned by Wald such as helping children lead happy and healthy lives may be less widely accepted and may be goals that require societal changes rather than relying solely on parents.

9.3 Child Sexual Abuse: Identification and Treatment for Parental Abusers

9.3.1 Identification of Parents Who Sexually Abuse Children

As has been discussed, when there is a suspicion of physical abuse or neglect of a child, CPS investigates these complaints. If confirmed, a program is developed to either remove the maltreated child from the home, or work with the abusive family members to lessen the abuse. However, suspected child abuse is treated quite differently by agencies in the U.S. (see Box 9.1). Suspicions of sexual abuse from parents or siblings may be reported by any of those mandated to also report physical abuse or neglect. Or it may be reported by the child who is being victimized. When there is suspected sexual abuse within the home, a criminal process is initiated, and there is a police investigation rather than a CPS investigation. Evidence is presented in a court case, and if found guilty, the abuser is jailed (Heger, 2014).

Since there may be less physical evidence of sexual abuse than of other forms of child maltreatment, it may be difficult to determine if sexual abuse has occurred. As Heger (2014) explains, a medical exam is generally required, although this may not provide definitive evidence. There is rarely injury in the genital region that would clearly demonstrate abuse. There is also limited information about the *normal* appearance of the genitals in young children which might allow the examiner to see if there were clear abnormalities or evidence of genital sexual activity. If there is evidence of the child having a sexually transmitted infection, or being pregnant, this is seen as relatively clear evidence, but this is not common.

Generally, the child's testimony about what has occurred is needed to substantiate suspected sexual abuse. As discussed in Chap. 6, there was a period when investigators used leading questions that led to children accusing a parent or caregiver of abuse that apparently never happened. As a result of this, new interviewing techniques have been developed to avoid such leading questions so that the child's testimony is more reliable.

Possibly because of the resulting criminal prosecution, when children disclose abuse, the results are not always positive for the child. There may also be emotional trauma for siblings or others in the family (Schreier, Pogue, & Hansen, 2017). Looking at data from a clinical sample of adults seeking treatment at an outpatient trauma clinic for earlier sexual abuse as children, Swingle et al. (2016) found that that majority of their sample did not disclose the abuse as children. When they did tell someone, it was most often a parent. In the majority of cases, disclosure was not met with supportive action, and often the abuse continued. The large majority of the sample also reported that there was partner violence in their household. As discussed in Chap. 4, a battered wife may not feel she can do anything to stop sexual abuse from the partner who is abusing her, and, thus, may not be willing to do anything for the child who reports this to her.

Sexual abuse may not be reported or investigated at the time the abuse is happening. The following case illustrates how sexual abuse, even abuse that is long-lasting and cuts across many victims, can be kept "secret" in the family for an extensive period of time. However, if just one of several victims reports the abuse, those victimized in the family can access help and the perpetrators punished and provided with help. This case also demonstrates the extensive trauma that sexual abuse causes for the victims and how victims within a family can serve as positive social support for each other.

Case Example #14

Janet is a 25 year-old white female who came to the crisis clinic, at the referral of a local judge, for an appointment with an outpatient therapist for counseling. Janet is married, has a 4 year old daughter and is currently pregnant. Janet revealed that she and her three sisters have a history of extensive sexual abuse from their biological father occurring over the course of many years. The abuse was a well-kept family secret until the oldest sister left home; she then confided in Janet and her twin sister Becky about her own abuse and then they admitted that they had also been abused by their father. The oldest sister Katie, was abused from age 8 on, with her father forcing her to have intercourse with him 3–4 times a week. Janet states she was fondled but never had sexual intercourse with her father, although Becky did. The lid was blown off the whole thing when the youngest sister Edie, now 15 years old, was approached by her father for intercourse after he had insisted on taking nude photos of her. Edie then rode her bike over to the judge's home (the judge is a long-time family friend) and told her about what was going on. The judge was furious, called child protective services, and insisted that Edie be removed from the home. Edie is now living with Janet. The father was arrested and taken to the police station, however the older sisters could not press charges because their abuse occurred too long ago. Edie's mother insisted that Edie forgive her father which infuriated Edie and she no longer wants to go home to her mother even though the father is now living in a different town while the criminal case is working its way through the court. Currently, both parents are attending an incest perpetrators group. Janet and Edie wish to obtain counseling together because Edie is afraid to come without her sister present because she would like to deny the whole thing, yet at the same time, knows she needs help. Janet is, for the first time, feeling truly enraged and feels she and her sister both need help- the older sisters are living elsewhere. I contacted one of our clinical psychologists who specializes in treating victims of sexual abuse and she agreed to see both sisters next Friday. Both sisters are also interested in attending our incest survivors group.

9.3.2 What Happens to the Convicted Abuser and the Rest of the Family?

If there is evidence that the suspicions of sexual abuse have merit, these cases have a formal court process, and if convicted, the offender is typically jailed. Once jailed, some type of treatment programs may be offered, but this is not always the case. The length of jail time depends on assessments of the likelihood of recidivism. After release from jail, any sex offender involved with children has to register as a sex offender, and various requirements regarding housing and contact with children are present (Grossi, 2017).

While in jail, the offender may be required to attend a program for sex offenders. As Finklehor (2009) discussed, many of these programs for sexual abuse offenders were directed at all types of convicted child sex offenders. Sexual abuse within the family was a relatively small group within this larger group. Thus, specific data on family sexual abusers were not readily available. In a more recent international review of the offender literature, Langstrom et al. (2013) also noted this limitation. Many of the programs involved group therapy, using cognitive-behavioral principles. Both Finkelhor and Langstrom et al. concluded that the data supporting the effectiveness of these programs was limited.

Given the lack of demonstrated effectiveness in the existing sex offender programs, both Finklehor (2009) and Langstrom et al. (2013) have pointed to educational programs for children as a preventive method of addressing this issue. As Del Campo and Fávero (2019) found after reviewing 70 studies examining these programs, these tend to be administered through schools. They typically provide knowledge to children about the issue of child sex abuse, and educate children about their right to have control over their own bodies. They encourage children to report attempts to abuse them sexually. Such programs appear to be helpful to the children exposed to them, although there is little formal evaluation data.

When a family member, often the father, is convicted of child sex abuse, there are often problems for the remaining family members (Vaughan-Eden, 2014). The mother may be upset about the jailing of the father, and may blame the abused child for this. At the same time, CPS staff often wonder why the mother did not report the abuse earlier or stop it from happening. Negative assessments of the mother, the non-offending parent, may lead to removal of the child victim, as well as other children, from the home. Other mothers may blame themselves for not being aware of the abuse and protecting their children. This might also have negative effects on the dynamics of the family (Vaughan-Eden, 2014).

9.4 Child Homicide or Death From Neglect: Identification and Treatment for Parental Abusers

As is the case for sexual abuse, when a child dies, a criminal process is initiated, and there is a police investigation rather than a CPS investigation. Evidence is presented in a court case, and if found guilty, the abuser is jailed (Krugman & Lane, 2014). Although these cases are not common, they do occur. According to the United States Department of Health and Human Services (2017), it was estimated that 1670 children died from physical abuse or neglect in the U.S. in 2015. The largest group of deaths was for children 1 year old or younger. Boys were more likely to die than girls. Rates were highest for African-American children and lowest for Hispanic children. About 70% of those who died had suffered from neglect, while 44% had experienced physical abuse. (Some had experienced both). More than 75% of these deaths were caused by parents of the children.

Looking at a smaller sample, Whitt-Woosley, Sprang, and Gustman (2014) compared a set of 50 families under the supervision of CPS with another 15 families from this same agency where there was a child fatality and compared this group with 35 families who had experienced a near-fatal event. Both types of families were compared to CPS families where no fatality had occurred. One major finding was that the fatal or near-near fatal aggressor was much more likely to be a male, whereas the majority of abusers in the non-fatal child maltreatment were mothers. The fatal group was also associated to a higher degree than the comparison group with partner violence (see Chaps. 4 and 6) as well as to previous violence toward the child.

In another analysis based on reports of 135 case workers who had experienced the death of a child in their case load, Douglas (2013) reported that these deaths occurred in families that they had been closely monitoring. Thus, this sample consists only of families already under the supervision of CPS. Many of the children died because of neglect or lack of parental supervision. In 36% of the total group of cases in which a child died, the mother was determined to be the offender, while the father was the offender in 20%. Step fathers were responsible in 19% of the cases. Other family members were blamed in the other cases. Family characteristics included parental unemployment or other major negative life events that probably added to parental stress. Many of the families were seen as socially isolated. Mental health issues in the parents were also noted. When infants had died, there was more likelihood of parental alcohol or substance abuse. When the deceased child was older, the parents were more likely to have reported the child as being "difficult." The case workers did note that these families had not taken advantage of the many social services available to them.

Jaffe, Campbell, Olszowy, and Hamilton (2014) identified one special risk factor for fathers who kill a child in their review of their own research in Canada. It appears that some fathers who are physically abusive toward their female partner may have been motivated by anger at the mother, especially when she was trying to leave the abusive relationship. (As noted earlier, this situation may also result in his killing of the mother). One of the distinctive signs of a potential child homicide by the father was found to be prior threats to kill a child (Jaffe et al., 2014).

Although not common, women were more likely than men to be acquitted for homicide because of insanity (Ferranti, McDermott, & Scott, 2013). This was true for 18 or the 47 women in the sample. The one man who had killed his child targeted his adult child. Both the men and the women in this study were hospitalized in a facility for the criminally insane for their homicide offense.

9.5 Abuse of the Older Adults in Family Settings

Abuse of older adults can take the form of physical, sexual, or emotional abuse or neglect of adults aged 60 or older (Beach, Carpenter, Rosen, Sharps, & Gelles, 2016; Roberto, 2016; Teresi et al., 2016, see Chap. 7). Neglect (not providing needed care) is another form of abuse, and is the most commonly found. One form of neglect is abandonment, which might involve leaving an older person at a hospital or other location with no information about who the person is or how to contact family (Rzeszut, 2017). Unlike other forms of family abuse, financial abuse is also considered to be a form of abuse and is one of the most common forms of elder abuse. Financial exploitation is especially difficult to detect and prosecute since it requires a psychological assessment of the decision-making ability of the potentially abused elder (Gibson & Greene, 2013). Although any of these forms of abuse can occur in nursing homes or other institutional settings, the focus here is on the perpetrators of elder abuse occurring within the family setting.

The abuser in a family setting is most often the partner or spouse or an adult child of the older person (Bernal, 2017). It might be another family member as well. As Beach and his colleagues point out (Beach et al., 2016), the partner abuse of an older adult can either be a continuation of earlier partner abuse, or it can be initiated when one partner is caring for the other or becomes cognitively impaired. Cognitive impairment in the partner can lead to sexual demands that cause injury or to forced sex may occur. Another pattern sometimes seen is that a formerly battered woman may herself become abusive as her male partner becomes frail.

9.5.1 Reporting and Investigating Suspected Elder Abuse

The situation for elder abuse is similar in many ways to that of child abuse. Although abuse may be reported by the older person her or himself, this is relatively rare (Jackson, 2017). Laws vary by state, but most now require reporting of suspected elder abuse by a large group of professionals such as health care providers or employees of financial institutions who might gain knowledge of abuse through their work (Crandall et al., 2016). Reports may be made to Adult Protective Services or to the police. States vary in terms of the procedure that needs to be following in making a report (Mukherjee, 2011). After a report is made, as in the situation for reports of child maltreatment, the agency staff need to make a determination about whether a formal investigation is needed. If so, the investigation is done and a decision is made about what needs to be done.

As Jackson and Hafemeister (2015) and Jackson (2017) explained, there are a number of reasons that many cases of elder abuse are not identified nor reported. One reason for this is that people doing investigations, and the applicable state laws, may have varying definitions about what constitutes abuse. In addition, the maltreatment is often hidden from others. Many older adults who are living at home may have little regular contact with those outside the family. Another reason is that even those states with reporting requirements for various groups may not enforce them (Bernal, 2017). Thus, there may not be a strong incentive to report, especially if one is not certain whether abuse is actually occurring or not. Sometimes a report is made only when the observer is concerned about very serious harm to the older person.

Evidence of physical harm of an elderly person is not always clear. Carney (2015) provides some of the indicators that medical staff might use. In a study of five hospitals with trauma centers, Friedman, Avila, Rizvi, Partida, and Friedman (2017) found that only 57% of the 111 cases of physical trauma to a person aged 60 or older were reported to Adult Protective Services or to the police. Many of the cases involved someone who had been brought to the hospital for earlier trauma, implying a long-term pattern of physical abuse. Crandall et al. (2016) argued that many of the mandated reporting professionals are not well trained to recognize signs of elder abuse which may explain these hospital data.

The outcome of an investigation may be that the abusing caretaker is asked to move away, and a restraining order is issued requiring them not to go back to the home of the abused older adult. Unfortunately, this outcome may not be seen as desirable for the older adult, who values the caretaking of the accused offender. Another possibility is that the older adult determined to be abused is removed to a nursing home (Jackson, 2017). This may be more likely when the older adult has been judged to have reduced cognitive capacity. Given the possibilities of these undesirable outcomes, the potentially victimized older adult may refuse to have an investigation done after a report is made, which is possible in some states, but not all (Jackson, 2017).

Those determined to have committed elder abuse may be prosecuted and jailed if found to be guilty. One group of abusers that have been largely ignored, and who are likely to be the worst offenders are those with serious mental illness (Labrum & Solomon, 2015). Research suggests that although most of those who are mentally ill are not violent, this group are from 2 to 8 times more likely to be violent than others in the general population, and much of their violence occurs within the home. This violence may be directed at any family member or close associate, but might include older members of the family. Labrum and Solomon argued that older adults might be especially likely targets of those with serious mental illness, and that such individuals need to be identified and given treatment before serious violence occurs. Once they have been violent, these offenders may be institutionalized in a hospital for the criminally insane.

9.5.2 Societal Responses to Confirmed Reports of Elder Abuse

Attitudes about elder abuse have changed in major ways since the 1950s (Jackson, 2016, 2017). With increasing life spans and more and more older widows living alone, and often in poverty, many people became concerned and urged that the government take some action. Protective legislation was included in the Older American's Act of 1965 to help needy those who were seen as not being able to take care of themselves. Jackson (2016) argued that these efforts led to high levels of institutionalization of older adults, which many saw as an undesirable outcome. As the issue of child abuse gained attention in the 1970s, physicians and others argued that some of the older members of the population were also being abused by their caretakers. Corresponding to the battered women's movement with advocacy for arresting partner batterers, there was increasing demand that those who abused a dependent older adult should be arrested and punished.

Social services have continued to respond to cases of elder maltreatment and to develop preventative programs. Just as there are attempts to identify parents at risk for child abuse, there are also programs that attempt to prevent or help caretakers deal with elder abuse (Hattery & Smith, 2017). Such programs are targeted to an adult child of an older parent or other relative. Physicians may refer these adult children to an existing program or suggest institutionalization of the older adult when this person is brought for a medical checkup. However, such programs are much less common than those available for potentially abusing parents of young children (Moore & Browne, 2017). Hattery and Smith argue that older adults are not seen as being as needy as young children. This may be changing, though. As part of the Patient Protection and Affordable Care Act passed by Congress in 2010, some funding was made available to improve the government response to suspected abuse of the elderly (DeLiema, Navarro, Moss, & Wilber, 2016). However, Teresi et al. (2016) argued that much more research is needed on the prevention of elder abuse. They outline a number of ways such programs might be developed based on models from child abuse or partner violence programs.

9.6 Conclusions

As discussed, there is both a social services approach and a criminal justice approach toward perpetrators of each of the major forms of family violence discussed in this chapter. Unfortunately, programs to try to *cure* these perpetrators and keep them from being physically abusive or highly neglectful have not been highly successful. It appears that prevention may be more successful. It is interesting and reassuring to note that reports of confirmed cases of both physical and sexual child abuse have been gradually declining in the U.S. since the early 1990s (Sedlak & Ellis, 2014). However, there has been no similar major decline in reported cases of neglect. Neglect is the largest category of all forms of child abuse and maltreatment now as it was in 1993. But, neglect of a child may be more related to lack of ability to provide adequate care and may not be as affected by underlying attitudes. Evidence of attitude change can also be seen in regards to the acceptability of spanking as a form of discipline. Although once widely accepted, attitudes of the general public (Ryan, Kalil, Ziol-Guest, & Padilla, 2016) and among professionals working with children (Taylor, Fleckman, & Lee, 2017) have shown large declines in the view of this practice which has been linked to child abuse.

9.7 Summary

This chapter discusses issues relating to the identification of family violence offenders and the many ways in which U.S. society attempts to either work with offenders to help end partner violence or abuse of a child or an older person in the home. In some cases of extreme violence or neglect, sexual abuse, or homicide, the offender is sent to jail if found by the courts to have committed the crime.

Looking first at partner violence, the most typical situation is that the offender is identified when the abused partner calls for police assistance. Although it is impossible to know for sure, it appears that a relatively small proportion of battered spouses or partners do seek police assistance, so in many cases, nothing is done to stop offenders. When police are called, they do not always respond, and if they do go to the location of the on-going abuse, they may not arrest the offender. Arrests can involve both partners if there is mutual fighting occurring. Once arrested, present practice is that the violent party (or parties) are released from jail relatively quickly, but are expected to participate in a batterer intervention program (BIP). These programs take many forms, and none have strong evidence of being effective at stopping partner violence. Other forms of partner abuse, such as rape or homicide, typically result in arrest and criminal prosecution, with jail terms as a likely consequence if found guilty. Since BIP participation does not appear to stop partner violence, the CDC now recommends that general education programs to help people understand that violence should not be tolerated. Preventing violence or stopping it when first done may be a better long-term solution to problems of partner violence than trying to change batterer behavior.

The chapter next turns to the issues surrounding child abuse or neglect. Here, the situation is quite different and many types of professionals are mandated by law to report any suspicions of child abuse or neglect. Such reports are made to Child Protective Services (CSP) which typically, but not always, do a formal investigation of the family to determine if maltreatment is occurring. If this determination is made, the family may be offered any needed mental health or other services and education to help find better ways for the parents to interact with the child. If the child appears to be in serious danger of harm, the child may be removed from the family on a short-term basis and may eventually be placed in permanent foster care or offered to other families for adoption. Abusing parents and children are often asked to participate in some form of family therapy. They are also monitored by CPS.

Issues relating to identifying offenders for elder abuse and the results of these investigations for perpetrators are next discussed. Both criminal prosecution and removal of an offending person may occur if elder abuse is found to be happening.

Although evidence for the effectiveness of any of the reported programs for getting any of these types of perpetrators to end their abusive behavior is not strong, there is evidence that work on changing societal attitudes can be effective if continued over many years.

References

Aaron, S. M., & Beaulaurier, R. L. (2017). The need for new emphasis on batterers intervention programs. *Trauma, Violence & Abuse, 18*(4), 425–432. https://doi.org/10.1177/1524838015622440

Aguiniga, D. M., Madden, E. E., & Hawley, A. (2015). Exploratory analysis of child protection mediation permanency placement outcomes. *Children and Youth Services Review, 50*, 20–27. https://doi.org/10.1016/j.childyouth.2014.12.021

Alexander, P. A., Morris, E., Tracy, A., & Frye, A. (2010). Stages of change and the group treatment of batterers: A randomized clinical trial. *Violence and Victims, 25*, 571–587. https://doi.org/10.1891/0886-6708.25.5.571

Babcock, J., Armenti, N., Cannon, C., Lauve-Moon, K., Buttell, F., Ferreira, R., et al. (2016). Domestic violence perpetrator programs: A proposal for evidence-based standards in the United States. *Partner Abuse, 7*, 355–460. https://doi.org/10.1891/1946-6560.7.4.355

Bair-Merritt, M. H., Crowne, S. S., Thompson, D. A., Sibinga, E., Trent, M., & Campbell, J. (2010). Why do women use intimate partner violence? A systematic review of women's motivations. *Trauma, Violence & Abuse, 11*, 178–189. https://doi.org/10.1177/1524838010379003

Baker, A. J. L., Brassard, M. R., Schneiderman, M. S., Donnelly, L. J., & Bahl, A. (2011). How well do evidence-based universal parenting programs teach parents about psychological maltreatment?: A program review. *Child Abuse & Neglect, 35*(10), 855–865. https://doi.org/10.1016/j.chiabu.2011.05.013

Ballucci, D., Gill, C., & Campbell, M. A. (2017). The power of attitude: The role of police culture and receptivity of risk assessment tools in IPV calls. *Policing, 11*, 242–257. https://doi.org/10.1093/police/pax018

Barner, J. R., & Carney, M. M. (2011). Interventions for intimate partner violence: A historical review. *Journal of Family Violence, 26*, 235–244. https://doi.org/10.1007/s10896-011-9359-3

Batzer, S., Berg, T., Godinet, M. T., & Stotzer, R. L. (2018). Efficacy or chaos? Parent-child interaction therapy in maltreating populations: A review of research. *Trauma, Violence & Abuse, 19*(1), 3–19. https://doi.org/10.1177/1524838015620819

Beach, S. R., Carpenter, C. R., Rosen, T., Sharps, P., & Gelles, R. (2016). Screening and detection of elder abuse: Research opportunities and lessons learned from emergency geriatric care, intimate partner violence, and child abuse. *Journal of Elder Abuse & Neglect, 28*, 185–216. https://doi.org/10.1080/08946566.2016.1229241

Bernal, R. (2017). Do I really have to?: An examination of mandatory reporting statutes and the civil and criminal penalties imposed for failure to report elder abuse. *The Elder Abuse Journal, 25*, 133–137. Retrieved from: https://heinonline.org/HOL/LandingPage?handle=hein.journals/elder25&div=10&id=&page=

Bradley, R. P. C., Drummey, K., Gottman, J. M., & Gottman, J. S. (2014). Treating couples who mutually exhibit violence or aggression: Reducing behaviors that show a susceptibility for violence. *Journal of Family Violence, 29*, 549–558. https://doi.org/10.1007/s10896-014-9615-4

Bradley, R. P. C., Friend, D. J., & Gottman, J. M. (2011). Supporting healthy relationships in low-income, violent couples: Reducing conflict and strengthening relationship skills and satisfaction. *Journal of Couple and Relationship Therapy, 10*, 97–116. https://doi.org/10.1080/15332691.2011.562808

Broadhurst, K., & Mason, C. (2017). Birth parents and the collateral consequences of court-ordered child removal: Towards a comprehensive framework. *International Journal of Law, Policy and the Family, 31*, 41–59. https://doi.org/10.1093/lawfam/ebw013

Brown, A., Hansen, S., & Saxe, G. N. (2018). System change designed to increase safety and stabilization for traumatized children and families: Trauma systems therapy. In V. C. Strand & G. Sprang (Eds.), *Trauma responsive welfare systems* (pp. 87–104). New York: Springer.

Brown, R., & Ward, H. (2014). Cumulative jeopardy: How professional responses to evidence of abuse and neglect further jeopardize children'slife changes by being out of kilter with time-frames for early childhood development. *Children and Youth Services Review, 47*, 260–267. https://doi.org/10.1016/j.childyouth.2014.09.017

Buzawa, E. S., Buzawa, C. G., & Stark, E. D. (2017). *Responding to domestic violence: The integration of criminal justice and human services* (5th ed.). Los Angeles, CA: Sage.

Calton, J. M., Cattaneo, L. B., & Gebhard, K. T. (2016). Barriers to help seeking for lesbian, gay, bisexual, transgender, and queer survivors of intimate partner violence. *Trauma, Violence & Abuse, 17*, 585–600. https://doi.org/10.1177/1524838015585318

Camasso, M. J., & Jagannathan, R. (2013). Decision making in child protective services: A risky business? *Risk Analysis, 33*, 1636–1649. https://doi.org/10.1111/j.1539-6924.2012.01931.x

Campbell, J. C., Webster, D. W., & Glass, N. (2009). The danger assessment: Validation of a Lethality Risk Assessment Instrucment for intimate partner femicide. *Journal of Interpersonal Violence, 24*, 653–674. https://doi.org/10.1177/0886260508317180

Cannon, C., Hamel, J., Buttell, F., & Ferreira, R. J. (2016). A survey of domestic violence perpetrator programs in the United States and Canada: Findings and implications for policy and intervention. *Partner Abuse, 7*, 226–276. https://doi.org/10.1891/1946-6560.7.3.226

Cantos, A. L., & O'Leary, K. D. (2014). One size does not fit all in treatment of intimate partner violence. *Partner Abuse, 5*, 204–236. https://doi.org/10.1891/1946-6560.5.2.204

Carney, A. (2015). Indicators of abuse in the elderly ICU patient. *Critical Care Nursing Quarterly, 38*, 293–297. https://doi.org/10.1097/CNQ.0000000000000069

Cerulli, C., Kothari, C., Dichter, M., Marcus, S., Kim, T. K., Wiley, J., et al. (2015). Help-seeking patterns among women experiencing intimate partner violence: Do they forgo the criminal justice system if their adjudication wishes are not met? *Violence and Victims, 30*, 16–31. https://doi.org/10.1891/0886-6798.VV-D-13-00064

Choi, Y. J., Elkins, J., & Disney, L. (2016). A literature review of intimate partner violence among immigrant populations: Engaging the faith community. *Aggression and Violent Behavior, 29*, 1–9. https://doi.org/10.1016/j.avb.2016.05.004

Crandall, M., Duncan, T., Mallat, A., Greene, W., Violano, P., Christmas, A. B., et al. (2016). Elder abuse: Paucity of data hampers evidence-based injury prevention. *Journal of Trauma Acute Care Injury, 81*, 603–605. https://doi.org/10.1097/TA.0000000000001132

Cross, T. P., Goulet, B., Helton, J. J., Lux, E., & Fuller, T. (2015). What will happen to this child if I report? Outcomes of reporting child maltreatment. In B. Mathews & D. C. Bross (Eds.), *Mandatory reporting laws and identification of severe child abuse and neglect* (pp. 417–442). New York, NY: Springer.

Damashek, A., Drass, S., & Bonner, B. L. (2014). Child maltreatment fatalities related to inadequate caregiver supervision. *Journal of Interpersonal Violence, 29*, 1987–2001. https://doi.org/10.1177/0886260513515951

Del Campo, A., & Fávero, M. (2019). Effectiveness of programs for the prevention of child sexual abuse: A comprehensive review of evaluation studies. *European Psychologist.*. Advance online publication. https://doi.org/10.1027/1016-9040/a000379

DeLiema, M., Navarro, A. E., Moss, M., & Wilber, K. H. (2016). Prosecutors' perspectives on elder justice using an Elder Abuse Forensic Center. *American Journal of Criminal Justice, 41*, 780–795. https://doi.org/10.1007/s12103-015-9321-7

Dill-Shackleford, K. E., Green, M. C., Scharrer, E., Wetterer, C., & Shackleford, L. E. (2015). Setting the stage for social change: Using live theatre to dispel myths about intimate partner violence. *Journal of Health Communication, 20*, 969–976. https://doi.org/10.1080/10810730.2015.1018622

Douglas, E. M. (2013). Case, service and family characteristics of households that experience a child maltreatment fatality in the United States. *Child Abuse Review, 22*, 311–326. https://doi.org/10.1002/car.2236

Dowd, L., & Leisring, A. A. (2008). A framework for treating partner aggressive women. *Violence and Victims, 23*, 249–263. https://doi.org/10.1891/0886-6708.23.2.249

Eckhardt, C. I., Murphy, C. M., Whitaker, D. J., Sprunger, J., Dykstra, R., & Woodard, K. (2013). The effectiveness of intervention programs for perpetrators and victims of intimate partner violence. *Partner Abuse, 4*, 196–231. https://doi.org/10.1891/1946-6560.4.2.196

Euser, S., Alink, S. R. A., Stoltenborgh, M., Bakermans-Kranenburg, M. J., & van Uzendoorn, M. H. (2015). A gloomy picture: a meta-analysis of randomized controlled trials reveals disappointing effectiveness of programs aiming at preventing child maltreatment. *Bio Med Central, 15*, 1068. https://doi.org/10.1186/s12889-015-2387-9

Falk, P. J. (2015). Husbands who drug and rape their wives: The injustice of the martial rape exemption in Ohio's sexual offenses. *Women's Rights Law Reporter, 36*, 265–309. Retrieved from HeinOnline at http://heinonline.org/HOL/Page?handle=hein.journals/worts36&div=17&g_sent=1&casa_token=&collection=journals#

Ferranti, J., McDermott, B. E., & Scott, C. L. (2013). Characteristics of female homicide offenders found not guilty by reason of insanity. *The Journal of the American Academy of Psychiatry and the Law, 41*, 516–522.

Feder, L., & Henning, K. (2005). A comparison of male and female dually arrested domestic violence offenders. *Violence & Victims, 20*, 153–171. https://doi.org/10.1891/0886-6708.2005.20.2.153

Finkelhor, D. (2018). Screening for adverse childhood experiences (ACEs): Cautions and suggestions. *Child Abuse & Neglect, 85*, 174–179. https://doi.org/10.1016/j.chiabu.2017.07.016

Finklehor, D. (2009). The prevention of childhood sexual abuse. *The Future of Children, 19*, 169–194. https://doi.org/10.1353/foc.0.0035

Fluke, J. D., Corwin, T. W., Hollinshead, D. M., & Maher, E. J. (2016). Family preservation or child safety? Associations between child welfare workers' experience, position, and perspectives. *Children and Youth Services Review, 69*, 210–218. https://doi.org/10.1016/j.childyouth.2016.08.012

Follingstad, D. R., Rogers, M. J., Welling, S. N., & Priesmeyer, F. J. (2015). Decisions to prosecute battered women's homicide cases: An exploratory study. *Journal of Family Violence, 30*, 859–874. https://doi.org/10.1007/s10896-015-9725-7

Font, S. A., & Maguire-Jack, K. (2015). Decision-making in child protective services: Influences at multiple levels of the social ecology. *Child Abuse & Neglect, 47*, 70–82. https://doi.org/10.1016/j.chiabu.2015.02.005

Ford, C. L., Slavin, T., Hilton, K. L., & Holt, S. I. (2012). Intimate partner violence prevention services and resources in Los Angeles: Issues, needs, and challenges for assisting lesbian, gay, bisexual, and transgender clients. *Health Promotion Practice, 14*, 841–849. https://doi.org/10.1177/1524839912467645

Fortson, B. L., Klevens, J., Merrick, M. T., Gilbert, L. K., & Alexander, S. P. (2016). *Preventing child abuse and neglect: A technical package for policy, norm, and programmatic activities*. Atlanta, GA: National Center for Injury Prevention and Control, Centers for Disease Control and Prevention. Retrieved from: https://www.cdc.gov/violenceprevention/pdf/can-prevention-technical-package.pdf

Fox, K. A., & Shjarback, J. A. (2016). What works to reduce victimization? Synthesizing what we know and where to do from here. *Violence and Victims, 31*, 285–319. https://doi.org/10.1891/0886-6708.VV-D-14-00146

Fraehlich, C., & Ursel, J. (2014). Arresting women: Pro-arrest policies, debates and developments. *Journal of Family Violence, 29*, 507–518. https://doi.org/10.1007/s10896-014-9605-6

Friedman, L. S., Avila, S., Rizvi, T., Partida, R., & Friedman, D. (2017). Physical abuse of elderly adults: Victim characteristics and determinants of revictimization. *Journal of the American Geriatrics Society, 65*, 1420–1426. https://doi.org/10.1111/jgs.14794

Frieze, I. H. (1983). Investigating the causes and consequences of marital rape. *Signs: Journal of Women in Culture and Society, 8*(3), 532–553. https://doi.org/10.1086/493988

Gibson, S. C., & Greene, E. (2013). Assessing knowledge of elder financial abuse: A first step in enhancing prosecutions. *Journal of Elder Abuse & Neglect, 25*, 162–182. https://doi.org/10.1080/08946566.2013.751820

Glaser, D. (2011). How to deal with emotional abuse and neglect—Further development of a conceptual framework (FRAMEA). *Child Abuse & Neglect, 35*, 866–875. https://doi.org/10.1016/j.chiabu.2011.08.002

Grant, T. M., & Cross-Denny, B. (2017). Lethality assessment protocol: Police perceptions of a domestic violence intervention. *Criminal Justice Review, 42*(4), 1–16. https://doi.org/10.1177/0734016817699967

Grossi, L. M. (2017). Sexual offenders, violent offenders, and community reentry: Challenges and treatment considerations. *Aggression and Violent Behavior, 34*, 59–67. https://doi.org/10.1016/j.avb.2017.04.005

Hamel, J. (2016). Editorial: Domestic violence perpetrator programs around the world. *Partner Abuse, 7*, 223–225. https://doi.org/10.1891/1946-65560.7.3.223

Hammett, J. F., Karney, B. R., & Bradbury, T. N. (2018). Longitudinal effects of increases and decreases in intimate partner violence. *Journal of Family Psychology, 32*, 343–354. https://doi.org/10.1037/fam0000351

Hart, S. N., & Glaser, D. (2011). Psychological maltreatment—maltreatment of the mind: A catalyst for advancing child protecting toward proactive primary prevention and promotion of personal well-being. *Child Abuse and Neglect, 35*, 758–766. https://doi.org/10.1016/j.chiabu.2011.06.002

Haskett, M. E., Neupert, S. D., & Okado, Y. (2014). Factors associated with 3-year stability and change in parenting behavior of abusive parents. *Journal of Child and Family Studies, 23*, 263–274. https://doi.org/10.1007/s10826-013-9729-y

Hattery, A., & Smith, E. (Eds.). (2017). *The social dynamics of family violence* (2nd ed.). Boulder, CO: Westview Press.

Hazelwood, L. (2007). Systems considerations in working with court-ordered domestic violence offenders. In J. Hamel & T. L. Nicholls (Eds.), *Family interventions in domestic violence: A handbook of gender-inclusive theory and treatment* (pp. 341–361). New York, NY: Springer.

Hegar, R. L., & Maria Scannapieco, M. (2017). Foster care to kinship adoption: The road less traveled. *Adoption Quarterly, 20*, 83–97. https://doi.org/10.1080/10926755.2016.1149535

Heger, A. H. (2014). Child sexual abuse: The history, current state of the art and the challenges for the future: A pediatric perspective. In J. E. Korbin & R. D. Krugman (Eds.), *Handbook of child maltreatment* (pp. 81–97). New York, NY: Springer. https://doi.org/10.1007/978-94-007-7208-3_4

Henning, K., & Renauer, B. (2005). Prosecution of women arrested for intimate partner violence. *Violence and Victims, 20*, 361–376. https://doi.org/10.1891/vivi.20.3.361

Herman, K., Rotunda, R., Williamson, G., & Vodanovich, S. (2014). Outcomes from a Duluth Model Batterer Intervention Program at completion and long term follow-up. *Journal of Offender Rehabilitation, 53*, 1–18. https://doi.org/10.1080/10509674.2013.861316

Hirschel, D., McCormack, P. D., & Buzawa, E. (2017). A 10-year study of the impact of intimate partner violence primary aggressor laws on single and dual arrest. *Journal of Interpersonal Violence*, 1–35. https://doi.org/10.1177/0886260517739290

Ho, G. W. K., Gross, D. A., & Bettencourt, A. (2017). Universal mandatory reporting policies and odds of identifying child physical abuse. *American Journal of Public Health, 107*, 709–716. https://doi.org/10.2105/AJPH.2017.303667

Jackson, A. I. (2015). State contexts and the criminalization of marital rape across the United States. *Social Science Research, 51*, 290–306. https://doi.org/10.1016/j.ssresearch.2014.10.001

Jackson, S. (2003). Analyzing the studies. In S. Jackson, L. Feder, D. R. Forde, R. C. Davis, C. D. Maxwell, & B. G. Taylor (Eds.), *Batterer intervention programs: Where do we go from here? NIJ Special Report*. Washington, DC: National Institute of Justice.

Jackson, S. L. (2016). Guest Editorial. The shifting conceptualization of elder abuse in the United States: From social services, to criminal justice, and beyond. *International Psychogeriatrics, 28*, 1–8. https://doi.org/10.1017/S1041610215001271

Jackson, S. L. (2017). Adult protective services and victim services: A review of the literature to increase understanding between these two fields. *Aggression and Violent Behavior, 34*, 214–227. https://doi.org/10.1016/j.avb.2017.01.010

Jackson, S. L., & Hafemeister, T. L. (2015). The impact of relationship dynamics on the detection and reporting of elder abuse occurring in domestic settings. *Journal of Elder Abuse & Neglect, 27*, 121–145. https://doi.org/10.1080/08946566.2015.1008085

Jaffe, P. G., Campbell, M., Olszowy, L., & Hamilton, L. H. A. (2014). Paternal filicide in the context of domestic violence: Challenges in risk assessment and risk management for community and justice professionals. *Child Abuse Review, 23*, 142–153. https://doi.org/10.1002/car.2315

Jennings, W. G., Okeem, C., Piquero, A. R., Sellers, C. S., Theobald, D., & Farrington, D. P. (2017). Dating and intimate partner violence among young persons ages 15-30: Evidence from a systematic review. *Aggression and Violent Behavior, 33*, 107–125. https://doi.org/10.1016/j.avb.2017.01.007

Kesner, J. E., & Dever, B. V. (2015). An inter-reporter analysis of mandated child maltreatment reporting in the USA. In B. Mathews & D. C. Bross (Eds.), *Mandatory reporting laws and identification of severe child abuse and neglect* (pp. 61–76). New York, NY: Springer.

Klein, A. R. (2012). Lethality assessments and the law enforcement response to domestic violence. *Journal of Police Crisis Negotiations, 12*, 87–102. https://doi.org/10.1080/15332586.2012.720175

Korbin, J. E., & Krugman, R. D. (Eds.). (2014). *Handbook of child maltreatment*. New York, NY: Springer. https://doi.org/10.1007/978-94-007-7208-3

Krugman, S. D., & Lane, W. G. (2014). Fatal child abuse. In J. E. Korbin & R. D. Krugman (Eds.), *Handbook of child maltreatment* (pp. 99–114). New York, NY: Springer. https://doi.org/10.1007/978-94-007-7208-3_5

Labrum, T., & Solomon, P. L. (2015). Physical elder abuse perpetrated by relatives with serious mental illness: A preliminary conceptual social-ecological model. *Aggression and Violent Behavior, 25*, 293–303. https://doi.org/10.1016/j.avb.2015.09.006

Langenderfer-Magruder, L., Whitfield, D. L., Walls, N. E., Kattari, S. K., & Ramos, D. (2016). Experiences of intimate partner violence and subsequent police reporting among lesbian, gay, bisexual, transgender, and queer adults in Colorado: Comparing rates of cisgender and transgender victimization. *Journal of Interpersonal Violence, 31*(5), 855–871. https://doi.org/10.1177/0886260514556767

Langstrom, N., Enebrink, P., Lauren, E., Lindblom, J., Werko, S., & Hanson, R. K. (2013). Preventing sexual abusers of children from reoffending: systematic review of medical and psychological interventions. *BMJ, 347*(f4630). https://doi.org/10.1136/bmj.f4630

Lee, A. H., & DiGiuseppe, R. (2018). Anger and aggression treatments: a review of meta-analyses. *Current Opinion in Psychology, 19*, 65–74. https://doi.org/10.1016/j.copsyc.2017.04.004

Li, S., Levick, A., Eichman, A., & Chang, J. C. (2015). Women's perspectives on the context of violence and role of police in their intimate partner violent arrest experiences. *Journal of Interpersonal Violence, 30*, 400–419. https://doi.org/10.1177/0886260514535100

Macy, R. J., Rizo, C. F., Guo, S., & Ermentrout, D. M. (2013). Changes in intimate partner violence among women mandated to community services. *Research in Social Work Practice, 23*, 624–638. https://doi.org/10.1177/1049731513490810

Madden, K., Tai, K., Schneider, P., Evaniew, N., Ghert, M. A., & Bhandari, M. (2019). What happens to intimate partner violence studies registered on clinicaltrials.gov? A systematic review of a clinical trials registry. *Trials, 20*, 288. https://doi.org/10.1186/s13063-019-3412-6

Mathews, B., & Bross, D. C. (Eds.). (2015). *Mandatory reporting laws and identification of severe child abuse and neglect*. New York, NY: Springer.

Mathews, B., & Kenny, M. C. (2008). Mandatory reporting legislation in the United States, Canada, and Australia: A cross-jurisdictional review of key features, differences, and issues. *Child Maltreatment, 13*, 50–63. https://doi.org/10.1177/1077559507310613

McCloskey, L. A., Boonzaier, F., Steinbrenner, S. Y., & Hunter, T. (2016). Determinants of intimate partner violence in Sub-Saharan Africa: A review of prevention and intervention programs. *Partner Abuse, 7*, 277–315. https://doi.org/10.1891/1946-6550.7.3.277

Messing, J. T., Campbell, J., Webster, D. W., Brown, S., Patchell, B., & Wilson, J. S. (2015). The Oklahoma Lethality Assessment study: A quasi-experimental evaluation of the Lethality Assessment Program. *Social Service Review, 89(3)*. https://doi.org/10.1086/683194

Miles-Johnson, T. (2013). LGBTI variations in crime reporting: How sexual identity influences decisions to call the cops. *SAGE Open*, 1–15. https://doi.org/10.1177/2158244013490707

Miller, E., Tancredi, D. J., McCauley, H. L., Decker, M. R., Virata, M. C. D., Anderson, H. A., et al. (2013). One-year follow-up of a coach-delivered dating violence prevention program: a cluster randomized controlled trial. *American Journal of Preventive Medicine, 45*(1), 108–112. https://doi.org/10.1016/j.amepre.2013.03.007

Milner, J. S. (2015). Child maltreatment in United States military families. *Child Abuse & Neglect, 47*, 102–113. https://doi.org/10.1016/j.chiabu.2015.05.008

Mirchandani, R. (2006). "Hitting is not manly." Domestic violence court and the re-imagination of the patriarchal state. *Gender & Society, 20*, 781–804. https://doi.org/10.1177/0891243206292002

Montalvo-Liendo, N., Matthews, D. W., Gilroy, H., Nava, A., & Gangialla, C. (2018). Men of Mexican origin who abuse women: A qualitative study. *Journal of Transculural Nursing, 29*, 457–464. https://doi.org/10.1177/1043659618766215

Moore, C., & Browne, C. (2017). Emerging innovations, best practices, and evidence-based practices in elder abuse and neglect: A review of recent developments in the field. *Journal of Family Violence, 32*, 383–397. https://doi.org/10.1007/s10896-016-9812-4

Morrison, P. K., Cluss, P. A., Miller, E. P., Fleming, R., Hawker, L., Bicehouse, T., et al. (2017). Elements needed for quality batterer intervention programs: Perspectives of professionals who deal with intimate partner violence. *Journal of Family Violence, 32*, 481–491. https://doi.org/10.1007/s10896-016-9835-x

Morrison, P. K., Hawker, L., Cluss, P. A., Miller, E., Fleming, R., Bicehouse, T., et al. (2018). The challenges of working with men who perpetrate partner violence: Perspectives and observations of experts who work with batterer intervention programs. *Journal of Interpersonal Violence*, 1–23. https://doi.org/10.1177/0886260518778258

Morrison, P. K., Hawker, L., Miller, E. P., Cluss, P. A., George, D., Fleming, R., et al. (2016). The operational challenges for batterer intervention programs: Results form a 2-year study. *Journal of Interpersonal Violence*, 1–23. https://doi.org/10.1177/0886260516662307

Mukherjee, D. (2011). Organizational structures of elder abuse reporting systems. *Administration in Social Work, 35*, 517–531. https://doi.org/10.1080/03643107.2011.614532

Murphy, C. M., Eckhardt, C. I., Clifford, J. M., Lamotte, A. D., & Meis, L. A. (2017). Individual versus group cognitive-behavioral therapy for partner-violent men: A preliminary randomized trial. *Journal of Interpersonal Violence*, 1–23. https://doi.org/10.1177/0886260517705666

Nelson-Dusek, S., Rothe, M. I., Roberts, Y. H., & Pecora, P. J. (2017). Assessing the value of family safety networks in child protective services: Early findings from Minnesota. *Child & Family Social Work, 22(4)*, 1–9. https://doi.org/10.1111/cfs.12354

Niolon, P. H., Kearns, M., Dills, J., Rambo, K., Irving, S., Armstead, T., et al. (2017). *Preventing intimate partner violence across the lifespan: A technical package of programs, policies, and practices*. Atlanta, GA: National Center for Injury Prevention and Control, Centers for Disease Control and Prevention. Retrieved from: https://www.cdc.gov/violenceprevention/pdf/ipv-technicalpackages.pdf

Novisky, M. A., & Perlata, R. L. (2015). When women tell: Intimate partner violence and factors related to police notification. *Violence Against Women, 21*, 65–86. https://doi.org/10.1177/1077801214564078

Paterno, M. T., & Draughon, J. E. (2016). Screening for intimate partner violence. *Journal of Midwifery & Women's Health, 61*, 370–375. https://doi.org/10.1111/jmwh.12443

Pitts, K. M. (2014). Latina immigrants, interpersonal violence, and the decision to report to the police. *Journal of Interpersonal Violence, 29*, 1661–1678. https://doi.org/10.1177/0886260513511700

Proctor, L. J., & Dubowitz, H. (2014). Child neglect: Challenges and controversies. In J. E. Korbin & R. D. Krugman (Eds.), *Handbook of Child Maltreatment* (pp. 27–61). New York, NY: Springer. https://doi.org/10.1007/978-94-007-7208-3_2

Putnam-Hornstein, E., Needell, B., King, B., & Johnson-Motoyama, M. (2013). Racial and ethnic disparities: A population-based examination of risk factors for involvement with child protective services. *Child Abuse & Neglect, 37*, 33–46. https://doi.org/10.1016/j.chiabu.2012.08.005

Raymond, J. L., Spender, R. A., Lynch, A. O., & Clark, C. J. (2016). Building Nehemiah's Wall: The North Minneapolis faith community's role in prevention of intimate partner violence. *Violence and Victims, 31*, 1064–1079. https://doi.org/10.1891/0886-6708.VV-D-14-00156

Reaves, B. A. (2017). *Police response to domestic violence, 2006-2015*. Washington, DC: Bureau of Justice Statistics, U.S. Department of Justice. NCJ 250231.

Roberto, K. A. (2016). The complexities of elder abuse. *American Psychologist, 71*, 302–311. https://doi.org/10.1037/a0040259

Rosenblum, K. L., Muzik, M., Morelen, D. M., Alfafara, E. A., Miller, N. M., Waddell, R. M., et al. (2017). A community-based randomized controlled trial of Mom Power parenting intervention for mothers with interpersonal trauma histories and their young children. *Archives of Women's Mental Health, 20*, 673–686. https://doi.org/10.1007/s00737-017-0734-9

Runyan, D. K. (2015). Who is maltreated and how mandated reporting might help. In B. Mathews & D. C. Bross (Eds.), *Mandatory reporting laws and identification of severe child abuse and neglect* (pp. 27–32). New York, NY: Springer. https://doi.org/10.1007/978-94-017-9685-9_2

Ryan, R. M., Kalil, A., Ziol-Guest, K. M., & Padilla, C. (2016). Socioeconomic gaps in parents' discipline strategies from 1988 to 2011. *Pediatrics, 138*. https://doi.org/10.1542/peds.2016-0720

Rzeszut, S. M. (2017). The need for a stronger definition: Recognizing abandonment as a form of elder abuse across the United States. *Family Court Review, 55*, 444–457.

Saini, M., Van Wert, M., & Gofman, J. (2012). Parent-child supervised visitation within child welfare and custody dispute contexts: An exploratory comparison of two distinct models of practice. *Children and Youth Services Review, 34*, 163–168. https://doi.org/10.1016/j.childyouth.2011.09.011

Salari, S., & Sillito, C. L. (2015). Intimate partner homicide-suicide: Perpetrator primary intent across young, middle and elder adult categories. *Aggression and Violent Behavior, 26*, 26–34. https://doi.org/10.1016/j.avb.2015.11.004

Santovena, E. E. E., & Silva, T. D. (2016). Domestic violence intervention programs for perpetrators in Latin America and the Caribbean. *Partner Abuse, 7*, 316–352. https://doi.org/10.1891/1946-6560.7.3.316

Schreier, A., Pogue, J. K., & Hansen, D. J. (2017). Impact of child sexual abuse on non-abused siblings: A review with implications for research and practice. *Aggression and Violent Behavior, 34*, 254–262. https://doi.org/10.1016/j.avb.2016.11.011

Scott, D. L., Lee, C., Harrell, S. W., & Smkith-West, M. B. (2013). Permanency for children in foster care: Issues and barriers for adoption. *Child & Youth Services, 34*, 290–307. https://doi.org/10.1080/0145935X.2013.826045

Sedlak, A. J., & Ellis, R. T. (2014). Trends in child abuse reporting. In J. E. Korbin & R. D. Krugman (Eds.), *Handbook of child maltreatment* (pp. 3–23). New York, NY: Springer. https://doi.org/10.1007/978-94-007-7208-3_1

Smith B. D., & Donovan S., E. F. (2003). Child welfare practice in organizational and institutional context. *Social Service Review, 77*(4), 541–563. https://doi.org/10.1086/378328

Stephens, T., Gopalan, G., Acri, M. C., Bowman, M., & McKay, M. M. (2018). Culturally relevant, trauma-informed engagement strategies for child welfare workers: Moving beyond compliance to engagement with families experiencing high levels of exposure to trauma and stress. In V. C. Strand & G. Sprang (Eds.), *Trauma responsive welfare systems* (pp. 67–86). New York, NY: Springer.

Stith, S. M., McCollum, E. E., & Smith, D. (2012). Systemic perspectives on intimate partner violence treatment. *Journal of Marital and Family Treatment, 38*, 220–240. https://doi.org/10.1111/j.1752-0606.2011.00245.x

Stout, K. R., & Kennedy, M. A. (2017). Police as educators: Support for possible responses to intimate partner violence calls. *Justice Policy Journal, 14*, 1–20.

Strickler Jr., E., & Drew, Q. (2015). Starting and sustaining LGBTQ antiviolence programs in a southern state. *Partner Abuse, 6*, 78–106. https://doi.org/10.1891/1946-65560.6.1.78

Swerin, D. D., Bostaph, L. G., King, L. L., & Gillespie, L. K. (2018). Police response to children present at domestic violence incidents. *Child Maltreatment, 23*, 417–425. https://doi.org/10.1177/1077559518778795

Swingle, J. M., Tursich, M., Cleveland, J. M., Gold, S. N., Tolliver, S. F., Michaels, L., et al. (2016). Childhood disclosure of sexual abuse: Necessary but not necessarily sufficient. *Child Abuse and Neglect, 62*, 10–18. https://doi.org/10.1016/j.chiabu.2016.10.009

Taylor, C. A., Fleckman, J. M., & Lee, S. J. (2017). Attitudes, beliefs, and perceived norms about corporal punishment and related training needs among members of the "American Professional Society on the Abuse of Children.". *Child Abuse & Neglect, 71*, 56–68. https://doi.org/10.1016/j.chiabu.2017.04.009

Teresi, J. A., Burnes, D., Skowron, E. A., Dutton, M. A., Mosqueda, L., Lachs, M. S., et al. (2016). State of the science on prevention of elder abuse and lessons learned from child abuse and domestic violence prevention: Toward a conceptual framework for research. *Journal of Elder Abuse & Neglect, 28*, 263–300. https://doi.org/10.1080/08946566.2016.1240053

Thorndike, B. (2015). Police response time to domestic violence calls and its effects. (2015). *Boise State University Theses and Dissertations*. Retrieved from: https://scholarworks.boisestate.edu/td/915

Turner, S., Gilbert, A., Hendricks, A., & Demaree, J. (2006). *Growing beyond conflict: The path to building safer families parent group curriculum*. San Diego, CA: Chadwick Center for Children & Families, Children's Hospital and Health Center.

Tutty, L. M., Babins-Wagner, R., & Rothery, M. A. (2017). Women in IPV treatment for abusers and women in IPV survivor groups: Different or two sides of the same coin? *Journal of Family Violence*. https://doi.org/10.1007/s10896-017-9927-2

U.S. Department of Health & Human Services, Administration for Children and Families, Administration on Children, Youth and Families, Children's Bureau. (2017). *Child Maltreatment 2015*. Retrieved from http://www.acf.hhs.gov/programs/cb/research-data-technology/statistics-research/child-maltreatment.

Vaughan-Eden, V. (2014). Nonoffending mothers of sexual abused children. In J. E. Korbin & R. D. Krugman (Eds.), *Handbook of child maltreatment* (pp. 431–441). New York, NY: Springer. https://doi.org/10.1007/978-94-007-7208-3_23

Victor, B. G., Grogan-Kaylor, A., Ryan, J. P., Perron, B. E., & Gilbert, T. T. (2018). Domestic violence, parental substance misuse and the decision to substantiate child maltreatment. *Child Abuse & Neglect, 79*, 31–41. https://doi.org/10.1016/j.chiabu.2018.01.030

Villodas, M. T., Cromer, K. D., Moses, J. O., Litrownik, A. J., Newton, R. R., & Davis, I. P. (2016). Unstable child welfare permanent placements and early adolescent physical and mental health: The roles of adverse childhood experiences and post-traumatic stress. *Child Abuse & Neglect, 62*, 76–88. https://doi.org/10.1016/j.chiabu.2016.10.014

Wagers, S. M., Pate, M., & Brinkley, A. (2017). Evidence-based best practices for batterer intervention programs: A report from the field on the realities and challenges batterer intervention programs are facing. *Partner Abuse, 8*, 409–428. https://doi.org/10.1891/1946-6560.8.4.409

Wald, M. S. (2014). Beyond maltreatment: Developing support for children in multiproblem families. In J. E. Korbin & R. D. Krugman (Eds.), *Handbook of child maltreatment* (pp. 251–280). New York, NY: Springer. https://doi.org/10.1007/978-94-007-7208-3_13

Ward-Lasher, A., Messing, J. T., Cimino, A. N., & Campbell, J. C. (2018). The association between homicide risk and intimate partner violence arrest. *Policing: A Journal of Policy and Practice*, pay004. https://doi.org/10.1093/police/pay004

Welland, C., & Ribner, N. (2010). Culturally specific treatment for partner-abusive Latino men: A qualitative study to identify and implement program components. *Violence and Victims, 25*(6), 799–813. https://doi.org/10.1891/0886-6708.25.6.799

Wildeman, C., & Waldfogel, J. (2014). Somebody's children or nobody's children? How the sociological perspective could enliven research on foster care. *Annual Review of Sociology, 40*, 599–618. https://doi.org/10.1146/annurev-soc-071913-043358

Whitt-Woosley, A., & Sprang, G. (2014). When rights collide: A critique of the Adoption and Safe Families Act from a justice perspective. *Child Welfare, 93*, 111–134.

Whitt-Woosley, A., Sprang, G., & Gustman, B. D. (2014). Lives at risk: Uncovering factors associated with fatal child maltreatment. *Children and Youth Services Review, 47*, 307–313. https://doi.org/10.1016/j.childyouth.2014.10.007

Xie, M., & Lynch, J. P. (2017). The effects of arrest, reporting to the police, and victim services on partner violence. *Journal of Research in Crime and Delinquency, 54*, 338–378. https://doi.org/10.1177/0022427816678035

Yampolskaya, S., Greenbaum, P. E., Brown, C. H., & Armstrong, M. I. (2015). Heterogeneity in trajectories of child maltreatment severity: A two-part growth mixture model. *Violence and Victims, 30*, 916–932. https://doi.org/10.1891/0886-6708.VV-D-13-00114

Young, C., Cook, P., Smith, S., Turtletaub, J., & Hazlewood, L. (2007). Domestic violence: New visions, new solutions. In J. Hamel & T. L. Nicholls (Eds.), *Family interventions in domestic violence: A handbook of gender-inclusive theory and treatment* (pp. 601–619). New York, NY: Springer.

Chapter 10
Examining the Service Provider: Challenges (and Successes) in Assisting Victims of Violence and the Need for Self-Care

This chapter addresses the experiences of the people who are paid or volunteer to assist the victims of family violence. As other chapters in this book have explained, victims of family violence experience a range of psychological reactions to the abuse they have received, as well as having concerns about physical injury and psychological abuse in the future. Helping these victims is essential for their well-being. Such help is provided by staff in public and private agencies, as well as by counselors, who may or may not have formal academic training in their area of practice. These staff may work in Child Protective Services or in Adult Protective Services (see Chap. 9). Assistance may also be provided by paid and unpaid staff as victim advocates or shelter staff in shelters for battered women and by those who work as private counselors or as staff in mental health centers (see Chap. 8).

At least some of the staff who work in these fields have had personal experience as survivors of some form of family or partner abuse including when they were children (Frey, Beesley, Abbott, & Kendrick, 2017; Lee, Pang, Lee, & Melby, 2017). This pattern of experiencing a high level of experience with abuse or neglect as children has been seen in a survey of MSW students at a social work program in the U.S. (Thomas, 2016). One reason these students and staff may select this field is that being able to help others with similar issues may be empowering for them and/or a way to pay forward the help that they received. Some students in social work explicitly express feelings of being called to help others (Newell & Nelson-Gardell, 2014). However, although many are drawn to the idea of being able to help other people with personal problems, such as being victimized by some type of violence in their family or from a romantic partner, Our work has indicated that the reality is that those who choose to work in this field may find it more challenging than expected (Kanno & Newhill, 2009). Perhaps because of this, as will be discussed, turnover is relatively high for those who provide services to those victimized by family or partner violence (Kim, 2011).

In this chapter, we explore some of the frustrations and difficulties that caregivers of those who are victimized may experience, keeping in mind that the negative responses to these work situations are not universal and not all caregivers experience these negative reactions to their work. We focus on those who provide services

I. H. Frieze et al., *Dynamics of Family and Intimate Partner Violence*,
https://doi.org/10.1007/978-3-030-42608-8_10

relating to child abuse and neglect, intimate partner violence (IPV), or abuse or neglect of older adults. We first examine data on the backgrounds of such service providers, and the nature of what they do within these three fields. We also outline some of the commonly experienced problems faced by service providers, and then describe some of the negative and positive reactions to these problems. Finally, we conclude with advice about what can be done in the workplace, and how service providers need to take care of themselves through various forms of self-care. To illustrate these issues, we include a real-life case example from one of the authors'(Newhill) practice experience at the beginning of her career. This case will be divided into excerpts connected to the different topics addressed in this chapter.

10.1 Who Are the Providers of Services?

As discussed earlier in Chaps. 8 and 9, those who provide assistance in some way to victims of family violence are quite diverse. Looking first at education levels, one can find a wide range of educational attainment among this group. Formal educational training can include Ph.D. degrees in Clinical or Counseling Psychology, although this is relatively rare. Some of these staff have a Masters degree in Social Work (MSW degree) or Counseling (MA degree in Psychology or Counseling). Others may have only a bachelor's degree in social work (BSW degree), or in other fields (often in psychology, but not necessarily). A small number are not college graduates at all and may serve as volunteers. Thus, the amount of training varies greatly, and, as will be discussed, this can have an impact on job turnover and negative reactions to the challengies faced in their work as service providers.

Knowledge about child abuse, intimate partner violence (IPV), elder abuse and/or other forms of family violence would be expected to be greater for those educated in the field of social work than those earning degrees in other fields. Both of these groups would have more knowledge than who are not college graduates. Information about the dynamics of family violence would *not* be expected within the typical curriculum for non-social work fields, although relevant course work might exist at some institutions. Looking at textbooks within different fields outside of social work, one can find a few books in psychology (e.g., Barnett, Miller-Perrin, & Perrin, 2010; Frieze, 2005) and sociology (Hattery & Smith, 2017) that discuss family violence, but there are relatively few of these textbooks. Thus, the majority of those working in child welfare, adult protective services or battered women's shelters most likely have little, if any, formal education related directly to their work. Many service providers, particularly those in child welfare or mental health resource coordination, are provided with some agency-based training. However, such training may vary in terms of coverage (Morazes, Benton, Clark, & Jacquet, 2010).

Understanding of the dynamics of family violence also varies across service providers, and may not depend on the level of formal education. It may even be lacking for those with degrees in social work. For example, in a survey of MSW programs across the United States, Vacca (2016) found that none of them offered a special concentration or certificate in Domestic Violence. For her MSW thesis, Vacca surveyed the students in her program to see how knowledgeable they were about issues related to IPV, with a focus on psychological abuse. She found very low levels of knowledge among the students. Individual courses addressing domestic violence, IPV and/or family violence are offered in some schools of social work (e.g. the University of Texas at Austin and the University of Pittsburgh). Such courses are usually elective, though, and not all students are able to or interested in taking such a class.

The following is the first part of the case based on Newhill's own experiences which illustrates how a service provider may be hired for a social work type position with highly demanding and challenging work responsibilities, but equipped with only a bachelor's degree in a related but distinctly different field.

The Case of Ethel – Part 1

After graduating from college with a bachelor's degree in sociology and philosophy, I was hired by a public community mental health agency serving a rural two county area to develop and administer a 24-h mobile crisis service. I had no background in crisis work, social work or mental health services, but I figured this job would be better than continuing to work as a waitress. With only a small budget to work with, I hired volunteers from the community to respond to the crisis calls, covering the service 24 h a day, 7 days a week. These volunteers had at least an associate's degree or bachelor's degree in a social science field and some were graduate students from the local university. We did not have offices where we could see clients needing help. We met our clients in crisis in their homes or at the local emergency room. One day, when I was on call, I received a telephone call from a woman who said she was concerned about her next door neighbor, Ethel, because she had not seen her outside for many weeks, Ethel did not answer her door or telephone, and the neighbor smelled a foul odor emanating from under the door.

10.1.1 Helping Children and their Families Who Have Experienced Abuse and Neglect

As discussed in Chap. 8, staff in child welfare offices and, more specifically, in Child Protective Services (CPS), investigate situations in which there is an accusation of child abuse or neglect. If abuse is substantiated during this investigation, the CPS or child welfare staff continue to work with the abusive family members. This may involve finding a placement for the abused or neglected children in foster care. If the abused children remain with their parents, than the staff monitor the families to ensure that the abuse does not continue and that the abused child is safe.

They may help parents improve their parenting skills. Child welfare services may assist the families with getting access to other services such as food stamps, behavioral health care or other types of services (Edwards & Wildeman, 2018).

In doing this work, child welfare staff at first rely on any training they have received earlier or on their own personal experiences. Workplace training may provide some additional help, but this may not occur for some time. Perhaps because of this, practices of the agencies may not follow scientifically-based recommendations. Beginning in 2010, Horwitz and her colleagues (2014) surveyed a national U.S. sample of 92 child welfare agencies to determine if evidence-based procedures were being used in helping families. Unfortunately, they concluded that often this was not done in about a quarter of the agencies. (Other research examines some of the difficulties in implementation of the findings of social work research; see Palinkas, He, Choy-Brown, & Hertel, 2017, for example). Only 16% of the case worker staff in the agencies in the Horwitz et al. sample had MSW degrees. Those with a BSW degree were more common at 29%. Far more likely (53%) was that staff held a BA degree or less, in a field different than social work. It was further noted that these agencies had difficulty filling vacant case worker positions and had to rely on the available workforce to fill vacancies.

Perhaps because of the lack of staff training and the difficulties of the job, turnover is high. The fact that pay is often low adds to this turnover. Evidence for high turnover can be seen in data from a national survey of case workers done by Edwards and Wildeman (2018). Their data relied on case records of the National Child Abuse and Neglect System from 2003 through 2015. Each caseworker in the data had a unique identifier, making it possible to track how long various caseworkers were actually working within the CPS system between 2003 and 2015. Over 140,000 unique caseworkers were identified, working in 46 states. Data indicated that between 14% and 22% of caseworkers left the system every year. The median caseworker in their database entered cases within the system a total of 1.8 years, indicating relatively short tenure for more than half of the caseworkers.

A number of studies have documented the concerns of CPS staff. As Stephens, Gopalan, Acri, Bowman, and McKay (2018) explained, there is often a fundamental conflict between these staff and the parents they work with. Parents may feel that CPS wants to take their children away and may feel quite hostile towards them. This may make them resistant to complying with the things staff ask them to do. These tensions create a difficult work environment.

In another study, Tavormina and Clossey (2017) interviewed CPS workers in a rural area about their daily job duties. A consistent theme was that there were frequent emergencies that the CPS staff needed to address. The nature of these crises was highly variable. A crisis in their caseload might involve a father discovering that the abusive mother was using prescription drugs at dangerous levels. Another crisis example might be a report of children in one of their families observing the father being violent to the mother, and the children being quite upset. Such situations require immediate action on the part of the caseworker. Such problems occurred on a daily basis. Part 2 of the Case of Ethel illustrates how turnover in front line positions, in this case volunteers, results in increased job responsibilities for paid staff who themselves may feel overwhelmed, underpaid and underprepared for the work they must do.

The Case of Ethel – Part 2

The call from Ethel's neighbor was worrisome and I knew I needed to respond right away. However, I was exhausted because I had been up for most of the night fielding crisis calls because the two volunteers who would have been on call had quit, stating that they were not prepared for doing this kind of work. I had begun having similar feelings myself but, for now, I had to go out to Ethel's house to see what was going on. Ethel lived in a tiny village about a half hour from our town which could be reached only by a winding hilly two lane road. It was late winter, and I knew from experience that this road could be icy and treacherous.

When asked about how they viewed their jobs in another study, caseworkers were found to be relatively negative in a study based on quantitative and qualitative data from a sample of child welfare workers in Florida (Radey & Stanley, 2018). As these authors noted, the job is clearly a demanding one that involves decisions about the physical and emotional wellbeing of many children as well as their abusive family members. Caseworkers often noted how stressful and demanding the work was for them, especially with the high caseloads they were assigned. Adding to their discontent, caseworkers explained that theirs was not a well-paid job, sometimes creating personal financial problems for them. Others have also noted that high workloads contributed to the high rates of leaving for child welfare agency staff (Griffiths, Royse, Culver, Piescher, & Zhang, 2017). To further complicate this discouraging work environment, many agencies have growing workloads as child welfare agencies have suffered funding cuts and fewer staff (Mignon, 2016). Workloads may also be high because so many caseworkers leave the field, and, as Palinkas et al. (2017) found, vacant positions are hard to fill. Child welfare caseloads have also been impacted by higher societal rates of parental and family substance use, particularly the increased use of opioids and methamphetamine resulting in an increase in cases of child neglect and need for foster care (Ghertner, Waters, Radel, & Crouse, 2018).

10.1.2 Helping Older Adults Who Are Abused or Neglected

As is the case for children who are abused or neglected, there are publically funded agencies that take charge when there is suspicion of abuse or neglect of an older adult (see Chap. 9). These agencies are called Adult Protective Services (APS). APS staff investigate notifications of potential abuse or neglect of adults. In addition to working with abused older adults, they might also work with anyone over 18 with physical, intellectual or psychological disabilities. Like other types of caregiving staff already discussed, APS staff may have high case loads, low salaries, and limited training or background in the situations they encounter in their jobs (Ghesquiere, Plichta, McAfee, & Rogers, 2018).

One aspect of APS work, elder abuse or neglect, is the focus of this section. If an elder abuse claim is confirmed, APS staff work with the older adult (and the family) to remedy the situation. This may involve helping the abused adult to move to some type of assisted living situation or to live with or be cared by a different family member. For an older adult living alone and displaying hoarding behavior or otherwise engaging in self-neglect, the APS staff member may work to help them remain at home by linking them to existing community resources and/or finding a family member who might help.

As is also the case for children experiencing abuse or neglect (see Chaps. 6 and 7), abused older adults are unlikely to report the abuse they are experiencing to authorities. Even if reported by someone else, the older individual may deny the abuse, making the APS investigation more difficult (DeLiema, Navarro, Enguidanos, & Wilber, 2015). As Jackson (2017) discusses, one of the special issues that APS staff must consider is that the potentially abused older adult may not want services of APS. Even if abuse or neglect is found, the person may wish to remain with the abuser, especially if this person is a family member. Unless the older adult is judged by the court system to be mentally incompetent, the person has the right to make decisions about how and where to live. Judgments about competence, personal freedom and self-determination may create difficult ethical issues for the caseworker and for the courts. An especially complex ethical issue relates to self-neglect, which is often an issue for APS (Day, 2016). Again, judgments about neglect can be subjective, and the APS staff member may have to consider ethical issues about when to attempt to remove the person from self-imposed behavior that appears to result in neglect of her or his physical needs.

Ghesquiere et al. (2018) conducted a survey of APS workers in a large urban area in 2015. The response rate of 78% was relatively high, giving a total sample of 321 APS workers. The majority of respondents had a Bachelor's degree (60%), 28% had a Master's degree, and 8% had less than a Bachelor's level of education. The median time working for APS was 6 years with the range from less than a year to 33 years of APS employment. Over 80% of the sample said they had been exposed to dangerously cluttered or dirty living spaces and/or had been yelled at or cursed by a client or a family member of the client during an investigation. Nearly 25% of the APS staff said they had been physically attacked by a client or family member, and even higher percentages reported being threatened. In spite of these negative experiences, many also saw positive aspects of their work. For example, 69% of respondents reported that they felt their work gave them a sense of personal accomplishment, and over half believed their talents were being well used. When asked about overall job satisfaction, 69% were somewhat satisfied or very satisfied, and 16% reported being very or somewhat dissatisfied.

The Case of Ethel – Part 3

I reached Ethel's house and surveyed the surroundings. The house seemed run-down, sagging to one side and needing a coat of paint. There was a weather-beaten sign out front that read "Smith Championship Yorkshire Terriers". Hmmm…I thought, maybe she breeds dogs. I walked up the splintered front steps and rang the doorbell; it didn't work. I knocked loudly and heard barking and what sounded like scratching at the door. Nobody came to the door even after repeated knocking. I went around to the side of the house and peered through a dirty window. Small creatures were scuttling about and I figured it was a mixture of small dogs and maybe rats. I saw what looked like a pair of human legs through the hallway. I went next door to the neighbor's and she tried calling Ethel but nobody answered (this was before the era of cell phones). I realized the only option was to call the sheriff's office to see if an officer could come out and pry the door open. The dispatcher I reached was not happy: "We don't like social work type calls; our job is to fight crime, but alright, I'll send an officer out—don't know how long it'll be though". I sat down on the one porch step that wasn't broken and waited for the sheriff, and I wondered once again why I was doing this job, especially given that my pay was so low I had to continue to live with my parents because I couldn't afford an apartment. Two hours later the officer arrived and tried to pry open the door—no luck. "Well, do you want me to break down the door? Your call" he said. I told him to go ahead and he kicked in the door. The smell of garbage, feces, and something dead hit us. "Put this orange oil under your nose" the officer said, handing me a small bottle, "It'll mask the odor." What seemed like dozens of emaciated tiny dogs ran up to us, pawing our legs. Dead dogs in various stages of decomposition covered the front hallway floor and as we peered into the room we could see an elderly woman, probably Ethel, sitting in a chair.

10.1.3 Helping Battered Women and their Children at Battered Women's Shelters

As discussed in Chap. 4, many battered women turn to battered women's shelters or intimate partner violence agencies (Wood, 2016) when they feel physically threatened by an abusive partner or if they need help in leaving their abusive relationship. They may bring children or even pets (see Chap. 7) with them when they seek shelter. The children and the pets may also be abused and may also need services. The women and their children and pets may stay at the shelter overnight, or for several days or even several weeks when there is room at the shelter. While there, a staff of caregivers, often called domestic violence advocates (Frey et al., 2017) offer various forms of assistance. These caregivers may be paid staff members or volunteers.

In addition to emergency shelter, services offered by shelters include personal counseling for the battered woman, legal advice relating to protection from abuse orders or filing formal assault charges, and assistance in locating appropriate social services, housing and a source of income if she wants to leave her partner (Burnett, Ford-Gilboe, Berman, Wathen, & Ward-Griffin, 2016). Burnett and her colleagues interviewed staff from four shelters in Ontario, Canada to get a better sense of the day-to-day work of these staff. One of the most common issues mentioned was the need to provide the many different types of assistance needed. Poverty was a common issue for many of the women wanting to leave their abusive situation. Attempting to set up a new household with limited income was challenging for the battered women and the staff attempting to help them do this. Other commonly cited problems were mental health issues and substance abuse in the women seeking shelter. In discussing their own work situation, staff complained of low pay and lots of turnover among staff.

A similar vision of the situation for staff working at battered women's shelters emerges from a study involving in-depth interviews of 19 shelter workers from nine different shelters in the southwest region of the U.S. (Merchant & Whiting, 2015). When asked about when they first started working at the shelter, a common theme was that the first few months were "eye opening…both personally and professionally" (p. 470). Many workers were surprised by the severity of violence they learned about, and by the fact that many of the women downplayed this violence. Other researchers have also discussed the need to provide careful supervision for social work students who begin a field placement working at a shelter for battered women, noting the possibility of indirect trauma for these students (Tarshis & Baird, 2018).

Many of the shelter staff have had personal experiences as a battered woman and now see themselves as survivors who want to help other battered women (Wood, 2016). Wood's interviews with shelter advocates indicated that many of them identified with their clients and that empathy for the battered women they worked with grew over time. However, for some, hearing about trauma experienced by other women brought back memories of their own experiences and created psychological difficulties for these advocates.

Merchant and Whiting's (2015) interviews asked about how more experienced advocates handled their work. Balancing all the different needs of the women seeking help was seen as a major concern by many of the staff. They also discussed the need not to try to be a hero in helping the women leave their abusers. A more satisfying goal was defined as learning to listen to the women and help them with their concerns.

As Frey et al. (2017) found in a study of advocates working at battered women's shelters and rape crisis centers, many had had personal experiences with traumas similar to those of the women they were assisting. When the advocate had worked through this personal trauma, often with the help of a good social support network, helping the client work through similar traumas sometimes led to posttraumatic growth and positive feelings in the advocate. Thus, the work could be highly satisfying for the advocate.

As this summary has suggested, the work situation for staff of battered women's shelters is much different than that of those working to assist abused and neglected children and their families, or older adults who are physically or otherwise abused or neglected. The victims of abuse have chosen to come to the shelter, so there are no issues relating to investigation of an abuse complaint for those working at battered women's shelters. The women seeking shelter are also free to leave, and there is often little follow-up after they leave. This, staff do not have the duty of continuing to monitor a potentially continuing abusive situation, and they do not interact with the abusers.

10.2 General Sources of Frustration in Caregivers for Family Violence Victims

Overall, national U.S. data indicated that the job category of "community and social services" (most of whom were described as "social workers" although they may or may not have had social work degrees) (Shockey, Zack, & Sussell, 2017, p. 1320) had the highest rates of mental distress across all of these large occupational groups. Others have also pointed out that social work is a "challenging profession" (Thomas, 2016, p.235). As Thomas went on to note, "social workers regularly witness oppression, injustice, poverty, and violence and provide services to persons who are traumatized, disenfranchised, and suffering" (p. 235). The work often requires working with many different types of people, each of whom has their own needs, and there may be no solutions to their problems that satisfy everyone. Although the staff positions are demanding, as already noted, many of the staff working with victims of family violence come to this job without a degree in social work, and often with a bachelor's degree in some related field. It does not appear that new staff have typically learned much about child abuse or neglect, elder abuse or IPV or domestic violence before accepting these staff positions.

The Case of Ethel – Part 4

Although Ethel was confused, clearly had not bathed or eaten for some time and had open sores on her legs, the sheriff opted to transport her in his car to the nearest hospital for evaluation rather than calling for an ambulance. While he did that, my next job was to call the animal control officers about the dogs. The animal control officers responded quickly, arriving on the scene in less than an hour. They surveyed the dogs and shook their heads. "I doubt any of these pups can be salvaged. We'll take them to the animal care and welfare shelter but it doesn't look good." I said I'd be willing to adopt one or two of them and the officer looked at me skeptically, "Well, give them a call in the next day or so", handing me a card. The outcome was that all three dozen dogs had to be euthanized. Ethel was hospitalized and finally provided with the care she needed. Later, I found out that she had an adult son living in the next county over. I was so furious about the whole situation that I called him, informed him about what happened with his mother and, although I was only 21 years old, and he was probably middle-aged, I read him the riot act for neglecting his mother. His only concern was whether he could salvage his mother's house somehow and get some money by selling it.

Research studies have identified a number of factors common to all three of the types of agencies and staff that we have been discussing in this chapter that may be reasons for the high dissatisfaction seen in those working in agencies relating to family violence. First, as noted, especially in child protective services, staff typically have high caseloads resulting in having little time to work as closely as many would like with the abused and neglected children and their families. To a lesser degree, this has also been noted in adult protective services and in battered women's shelters. Also seen across all these agencies is generally low pay for staff, which is probably related to the fact that many staff have not had formal training to prepare themselves for this type of work. Another factor common across all these staff is a lack of promotion opportunities or other types of job advancement (Johnco, Salloum, Olson, & Edwards, 2014).

Another source of frustration seen by staff is that their work may not be valued by the public. In a study of public child welfare agencies by Lawrence and her collaborators (Lawrence, Zeitlin, Auerbach, Chakravarty, & Rienks, 2018), a sample of 2910 staff responded to a series of items about how their work was viewed by others. Four different themes emerged when these data were factor analyzed. First was perceived general stigma associated with items such as "when people find out I am a child welfare worker, they seem to look down on me" (p. 7). Another set of items referred to a lack of understanding by others about the work. Items under the general heading of respect were another theme. A sample item, which was reverse coded, was "Most people respect you for your choice to work in child welfare" (p. 7). Finally, was the theme of blame, represented by items such as "Most people blame the child welfare worker when something goes wrong with a case" (p. 7). Overall, the more agreement with each of these themes, the more likely the staff members were to intend to leave their jobs. The theme with the highest level of agreement was lack of respect.

Other general types of dissatisfactions relate to frustration over not being able to help their clients, client aggression toward the caseworker, and having to spend too much time on paperwork. Each of these is examined briefly in this section. All of these issues can lead to a number of reactions in the staff member such as burnout and compassion fatigue described in more detail later in this chapter. There are steps that the practitioner can take to maintain psychological wellness and prevent burnout. These individual strategies are often referred to as self-care, and we will address this in the last section of the chapter.

10.2.1 Frustration over Not Being Able to Help the Client Victim

One common issue faced by those attempting to help those affected by family violence or neglect is the frustration that may arise from the fact that needed services may not be readily available for the individuals who could benefit from them.

This may be especially relevant in cases of neglect, when a basic issue is lack of financial and material resources to provide needed care (see Chap. 6). There may be other factors, too, in not being able to provide the assistance needed.

For example, in their qualitative study of CPS staff, Tavormina and Clossey (2017) found that one of the frequent themes emerging from their interviews was a sense of frustration and feeling powerless to help the families they worked with. One of the staff members noted that it was impossible to be non-emotional when a child was hurt. Another mentioned that when families needed help with obtaining housing, there was no way they could help with this.

Staff investigating situations when elder abuse was reported, but the older person and the family denied this when they tried to investigate, find this to be frustrating. Their own belief often was that the abuse was occurring, but without some type of clear evidence, nothing could be done (DeLiema et al., 2015). In other cases, it appeared that a lack of financial resources was a major reason that an older person was not being cared for adequately. With everyone having to be employed, sometimes there was no one to take on necessary caretaking duties. Such issues could not be resolved by the APS staff.

Looking specifically at the situation of someone who is victimized by IPV, the social worker or other professional mental health worker attempting to help the victim is likely to find that the victim will encounter the same problem again. Efforts to assist the client in ending the violence are rarely successful and sometimes the help that staff are able to offer is not viewed by the client as something they want. All these issues can be a source of frustration for the staff member.

10.2.2 Client Aggression toward the Service Provider

Data indicate that individuals providing social services of all kinds are at high risk for workplace violence (Kanno & Newhill, 2009; Newhill, 1996), with CPS staff at particular risk (Kim & Hopkins, 2017; Newhill & Wexler, 1997; Strolin-Goltzman, Kollar, Shea, Walcott, & Ward, 2016). These professional staff may be verbally abused, or even attacked physically by the victim or by the abuser or by other family members. They may also experience sexual harassment (see Box 10.1). Reports of property damage have also been reported by shelter staff, damage apparently done by clients staying at a shelter for battered women. For child welfare and elder abuse workers, the most dangerous situation appears to be home visits (Ghesquiere et al., 2018; Kim & Hopkins, 2017). There are a number of strategies that agencies can take to promote worker safety, which are discussed later in this chapter.

Box 10.1: Sexual Harassment and Social Work Students
Moylan and Wood (2016) sent surveys to a sample of BSW and MSW students in 40 different schools. Over 500 students completed the surveys. The sample was largely female (91%). Overall, 56% reported at least one experience of sexual harassment in their field placements. The most common responses related to being told offensive sexual stories or jokes (28%), and being treated differently "due to sex" (p. 411) (20%). Being stared at in a way that made them feel uncomfortable was experienced by 16% of the sample. No one reported an actual sexual assault or having someone offer better treatment in exchange for sex. Typically, the perpetrator was another staff member (42%), but almost as common was a client doing this (41%). Both male and female students reported incidents of sexual harassment at equal rates.

Kim and Hopkins (2017) developed a scale to measure personal safety concerns of child welfare workers. A random sample was contacted for administration of an on-line survey, with 57% of those contacted responding. Their responses indicated that about 40% said that they had left the home during a home visit because they felt uncomfortable, while 60% had ended a visit early because of feeling uncomfortable. More than half the sample reported meeting a client at a public place because of not wanting to go to the client's home due to safety concerns. In addition, half of the survey respondents reported wanting to decline an assignment because of the client having a past history of violence, and half said they wanted to decline an assignment because of the dangerousness of the neighborhood. However, less than 20% reported recommending that a case be closed because of a risk of violence. Thus, it appeared that the large majority of these workers were affected by personal safety concerns, but were still willing and able to do their assigned work.

High rates of experiences of client physical or psychological aggression were also reported in a Canadian study of CPS staff (Lamothe et al., 2018). In depth interviews were conducted with 30 CPS staff some of whom did fieldwork and others who worked at a residential treatment center. Violence levels were higher at the residential treatment center, but were experienced by both groups of CPS staff. Examples provided of psychological violence included name calling, while acts of physical violence included destroying the staff members property, hitting, kicking and biting. One staff member was stabbed with a knife by one of the children in the home she visited. Another was greeted by a client holding a shotgun. During the interviews, staff sometimes expressed shock at the violence, while others felt this was just part of the job. Most said they did not take the violence or aggression personally, but, at the same time, some expressed a need to be vigilant, as well as being discouraged or exhausted, or even overwhelmed in dealing with the violence.

Related issues arise for the staff at shelters for battered women as well as for social wok students working on IPV issues. Based on their review of the literature, Kanno and Newhill (2009) suggested that one reason for that violence was directed toward the victim advocate assisting battered women may be frustration on the part of the client that the violence and abuse she has been experiencing is not being helped at the shelter.

10.2.3 Too Much Paperwork

Another source of frustration expressed by the caregivers of those involved with family violence and abuse is the need to spend time doing paperwork to document the work being done. This is seen as taking time away from the important work they did with clients. Gibson, Samuels, and Pryce (2018) documented this concern in a qualitative study of 28 child welfare professionals in a Midwestern city. Many had been working in the child welfare field for many years and over half had degrees in social work. Individual interviews were done with this group who had volunteered to participate in a study of client well-being mandated and released by the U.S. Administration for Children, Youth and Families in 2010. This mandate outlined a need to show positive changes in well-being in clients served by child welfare services. In their discussions of this mandate, it was frequently noted that one factor that detracted from this mandate was the need to document their work by completing required forms during their workday. This paperwork was often described as overly time-consuming. A few of the study participants noted that writing reports about how they worked with clients was helpful in clarifying the work they were doing.

10.3 Job Reactions Experienced by Social Workers or Other Service Providers

Literature on those who work with victims of all types includes four major concepts that identify the types of reactions experienced by counselors and caseworkers in response to the stresses of their work: burnout, vicarious traumatization, secondary traumatic stress, and compassion fatigue. Each of these will be discussed below in this section. All of these are negative reactions experienced by social workers and others working in the human services fields. Not only do these reactions represent difficulties for the staff, but when mental health professionals experience any of these, there is a measurable result in poorer quality care of clients (e.g., Salyers et al., 2016). Fortunately, there is also evidence that some of the types of staff being discussed in this chapter find much satisfaction in their work in spite of the difficulties. A more positive reaction that has been labeled as compassion satisfaction may also occur.

Although all the service providers discussed in this chapter can sometimes experience stress in their jobs, it does appear that working in a child welfare agency is one of the more challenging assignments for helpgivers of those victimized by family violence (Leake, Rienks, & Obermann, 2017). For example, Kim (2011) compared registered social workers working in many different settings in California and noted that those in the child welfare agencies had the most negative reactions to their jobs. Dagan, Ben-Porat, and Itzhaky (2016) report a similar finding in a sample of social workers in Israel. In this study, the social workers working in child protective services reported highest levels of secondary trauma when compared to social workers in other types of jobs in Israel. Thus, there may be inherent difficulties for staff working with abused and neglected children and their families.

We discuss some of the research relating to burnout and compassion fatigue below. As will be seen, there is much overlap between these terms, but all are used in the research literature. A search on Psychinfo in 2017 identified that burnout was the concept cited most often. It first appeared in the mental health literature in 1978, followed by the other terms in 1995. The next most cited term was compassion fatigue, with vicarious traumatization least cited (Can, 2018).

10.3.1 Burnout

The idea of burnout has been in the published research literature for many years. As Maslach and Schaufeli (1993) explained, the term *burnout* became a popular research topic beginning in the mid-1970s. They argued that at that time, people in many professions were seeking personal fulfillment from their work and entered their jobs with high expectations for achieving this fulfillment. This was especially the case with those working in the human services field, who hoped to meet the needs of people looking to human services agencies to help them with the problems that might at one time have been addressed by relatives or neighbors. At the same time, many of the human service jobs were becoming more institutionalized and bureaucratic.

Some of the classic and most widely cited books on burnout were written by Cherniss (e.g., 1980, 1995). In his 1995 book, he wrote in the Preface that his work was with "human service professionals" who wanted to "serve others" and who "began their careers with enthusiasm and commitment, caring and compassion" (p. ix). The samples that were used in Cherniss' work were a group of social workers as well as poverty lawyers, public health nurses, high school teachers and psychologists. All were studied during their first year of work. He explains that in that first year, there was evidence that they "lost much of their idealism and commitment" (p. ix). His 1995 book outlines not only their experiences that first year, but also examined how this group had responded and changed 10 years later.

Cherniss (1995) outlined a number of issues that the human service professionals he was studying encountered. First was that although they largely felt they would be able to do their jobs well prior to entering the workplace, many found that they did not feel they had gotten the training they needed and did not have the background they felt they should have received. Another difficulty related to an expectation many had that their clients would be grateful for the help they offered them.

Given this expectation, they were quite disappointed when this did not happen. Instead the clients refused to follow the advice that they were being offered, and complained they were not getting the help they needed from the human service professionals. Expectations of having meaningful and interesting work were also violated when they found the work was often boring, and involved hours of clerical tasks.

Once they encountered this mismatch between their hopes and the actual job duties they had, these initially dedicated human service professionals began to change. As Cherniss explains, "they became less caring and committed. They began to see many of their clients as adversaries rather than as innocent victims of misfortune" (Cherniss, 1995, p. 37). They began to lower their own goals and began to blame their clients for their not being able to have the impact they expected to have on them. Others have also noted that blaming the client and becoming angry and frustrated were not uncommon feelings when efforts to help a client didn't work (Friedman, 2008). Such reactions were labeled as *burnout*. Cherniss explains in his books that as a result of this burnout, many left their profession, but others managed to remain by changing their approach to their work.

Many have written about the concept of burnout, and the definitions of this concept have varied across authors (Maslach & Schaufeli, 1993). One of the more widely cited definitions was provided by Pines (1993). As Pines outlined, "the unique characteristic of burnout…is the fact that burnout is always the end result of a gradual process of disillusionment in the quest to derive a sense of existential significance from work" (p. 40). She further explained that "burnout happens only in people who entered their professions with an expectation to derive from it a sense…of significance…who work over long periods of time in situations that are emotionally demanding" (p. 40).

10.3.1.1 Measurement of Burnout with the MBI

The most widely used scale to measure burnout was and still is the Maslach Burnout Inventory (MBI) that measured three dimensions: emotional exhaustion, depersonalization [of clients], and reduced feelings of personal accomplishment (Maslach & Jackson, 1981). However, critiques of this scale have been appearing in the published literature for many years. For example, Koeske and Koeske (1989) used a sample of 328 social workers identified as doing work that "involved direct contact with clients" (p. 133) in a set of five different studies to examine the reliability and validity of the scale. Although the data were supportive of the internal consistency reliability and the validity of the scale, other data indicated that the emotional exhaustion component of burnout was the most important in predicting negative outcomes in the workplace. In a later study, Kim and Kao (2014) conducted a formal meta-analysis of the published U.S. studies of child welfare workers and found a strong association between burnout as measured by the MBI and the intention to leave their job among the workers studied, supporting earlier ideas of Cherniss.

In spite of its wide usage, there have been critiques of the MBI. In a recent paper, Walters, Brown, and Jones (2018) noted that many empirical studies of social workers continue to use the MBI, in spite of its limitations. They suggested that the Copenhagen Burnout Inventory (CBI) measure developed in Europe (Borritz et al., 2005) was more appropriate for use with human service workers. This scale assumed that burnout would have emotional effects and measured these directly. There were three subscales in the CBI: General levels of distress, distress specifically related to one's work, and distress associated with work with clients (most associated with the MBI's emotional exhaustion component). A sample of U.S. social workers with BSW or MSW degrees were recruited and asked to complete the CBI in an on-line survey. The U.S. version was found to have good internal consistency and reliability for this sample of those with social work degrees. This suggests that the CBI may be a useful alternative scale for measuring different types of burnout.

10.3.1.2 Empirical Research Examining Burnout in Human Service Staff

In a systematic review of the published research literature from 1970 to 2014 from many countries (although with the majority from the U.S.), Lizano and Barak (2015) noted that many studies have documented burnout in human service workers and further document that these jobs were more likely to be associated with higher levels of burnout than found in other types of work. Emotional exhaustion was especially predictive of negative feelings about the job for human service workers, replicating the earlier replicating the earlier Koeske and Koeske study (see Koeske & Koeske, 1989). Emotional exhaustion was also found to often be related to depression and anxiety and other forms of emotional distress, as were other dimensions of burnout. In another study, Lazano and Barak (2015) empirically tested some of these relationships in a longitudinal study of child welfare workers in California, again finding that emotional exhaustion was the most important component of burnout. Emotional exhaustion was correlated with low levels of job satisfaction and also appeared to predict depersonalization of clients. Such data are consistent with the findings of Lazano and her colleagues.

Looking at a sample of victim advocates working with battered women as well as rape victims, Bemille and Williams (2011) used the MBI to assess burnout levels. Overall levels of burnout were only moderate in this sample of 194 advocates in a rural midwestern state within the U.S. Although all of the correlations were relatively low, there was evidence of higher burnout for those who worked more hours per week, perhaps reflecting physical exhaustion along with emotional exhaustion. Many of the advocates reported that the rewards of the job decreased stress levels for them, and these lower stress ratings were associated with lower levels of burnout.

Using a different approach, Boyas, Wind, and Ruiz (2015) used a sample of child welfare workers from a northeastern state to do a cluster analysis to better understand how different groups of these workers might differ. Three distinct patterns emerged. Levels of job stress were one of the variables that most differentiated the groups. The group highest in job stress were labeled as Leavers (24% of the group). Job stress was lowest in the Thrivers group (32% of the group), and intermediate in a Perservers group (44%). Job stress levels followed a similar pattern, being highest in the Leavers and lowest in the Thrivers. The MBI was used to assess emotional exhaustion and depersonalization, with the emotional exhaustion levels most important in differentiating the groups. Not surprising was the fact that Leavers were highest in intending to leave their jobs, and Thrivers being relatively low on this variable. However, overall, the Thrivers and Perserverers were not statistically different in terms of overall well-being measures. As the researchers pointed out, in spite of the large body of research documenting high levels of burnout and job dissatisfaction for child welfare workers, many of their sample appeared relatively satisfied with their work. They further noted that the Leavers group contained more of the youngest workers, suggesting that this group might not have developed the coping skills needed to function in this potentially stressful work.

Noting the limitations of the MBI, other research has utilized the CBI to measure burnout in a sample of child welfare workers (Leake et al., 2017). A sample of 2302 case workers and their supervisors responded to an invitation to participate in a workforce study. The large majority of this group held a bachelor's degree in a field other than social work. The CBI assesses distress associated with the workplace and associated with working with clients separately. These distress measures were equated with burnout in these two dimensions. This group of child welfare workers had higher scores for workplace-related distress than they did for client-related interactions. Based on comparisons of scores with other samples, the majority of the sample scored below the generally accepted cutoff for being identified as having client-related burnout, but above the cutoff for work-related burnout. These patterns were seen in case workers as well as supervisors. Additional analyses indicated that work-related burnout was more related to intending to leave the institution and to low levels of job satisfaction than client-related burnout. Leake and her colleagues suggested that their data supported the validity of the CBI with child welfare workers, and provided important information about the sources of distress for these workers.

10.3.2 Secondary Traumatic Stress, Compassion Fatigue and Compassion Satisfaction

Burnout is not the only response to the frustrations of social service work. Negative effects in service providers may be intensified as they listen to stories of the pain and fear experienced by victims of trauma, such as that produced by IPV. It is not uncommon for the staff to begin to experience these same feelings themselves. This reaction is called by a number of terms including "secondary traumatic stress" or "vicarious trauma" (Kanno & Newhill, 2009, p. 48). This creates many of the traumatic reactions (labeled as post traumatic stress disorder or PTSD) described in Chap. 3, but in this situation, they are being experienced by a care provider who did not personally experience the trauma, but learned about it from someone who did experience it directly.

Secondary traumatic stress (STS) was documented in a sample of victim advocates working with battered women by Benuto, Yang, Ahrendt, and Cummings (2018). As they explain, STS reactions are quite similar to those of posttraumatic stress disorder, discussed in Chap. 3, although STS is a result of indirect exposure to trauma through learning about trauma experienced by someone else (see Hensel, Ruiz, Finney, & Dewa, 2015, for a general discussion of STS). For the victim advocate, this would result from hearing about the experiences of the battered woman that led her to seek assistance at the shelter.

The term *compassion fatigue* is most associated with Charles Figley. Although Figley's early work examined the reactions of veterans and others exposed to traumatic events, over time he began to study those who have not personally experienced trauma, but who work with those who have. As he observed, these professional care providers also experience trauma (Figley, 1995). In his 1995 edited book, Figley writes: "The professional work centered on the relief of the emotional suffering of clients automatically includes absorbing information that is about suffering. Often it includes absorbing that suffering itself as well… I now refer to it as compassion fatigue" (Figley, 1995, p. 2). Like STS, compassion fatigue is also associated with PTSD symptoms.

Although the concept of compassion fatigue has been widely used in the literature, this construct has received criticism from other researchers, although many find this idea to be useful in explaining the reactions they have observed. In a review of 90 published papers in the nursing field, Sinclair, Raffin-Bouchal, Venturato, Mijovic-Kondejew, and Smith-MacDonald (2017) noted that many of these studies supported the prediction that there would be of high levels of compassion fatigue in nurses. As the same time, there were a number of studies evaluated in this review that raised questions about the nature of compassion fatigue, how it is measured, and how it develops. They concluded their review with a request that the concept be re-conceptualized. Coming from a health care administration framework, Gerard (2017) also raised concerns about the idea of compassion fatigue, suggesting that rather than having too much compassion, the symptoms associated with compassion fatigue might result from having too little compassion for those experiencing trauma in their lives.

Perhaps in response to concerns such as these, Figley has continued to develop theory in this area. In a recent paper with Ludick (Ludick & Figley, 2017), a model was presented that suggested connections between exposure to suffering, secondary traumatic stress, and compassion fatigue and resilience. The model also included variables such as self-care and empathy, as well as social support and personal traumatic memories of the caregiver. The revised model proposed how all of these concepts interact. Ludick and Figley (2017) argued that having some level of empathy and concern for the person experiencing trauma was necessary for having STS (see Box 10.2). They also suggested that STS was intensified if the person had memories of their own personal traumatic experiences. An additional step was added to the model of STS, arguing that if the caregiver experienced a sense of satisfaction in helping the traumatized person, the caregiver might have increased feelings of worth and purpose and might experience "compassion fatigue resilience" (p. 114). They also added the prediction that social support for the provider of care could lower STS. This new model appeared to address the types of concerns in the literature about the prevalence of compassion fatigue in service providers. Ludick and Figley invited others to more formally test their new model and suggested ways that researchers might test their new model.

Box 10.2: The Importance of Empathy
In the *Social Work* journal of the National Association of Social Workers, Wagaman, Geiger, Shockley, and Siegal (2015) discussed the importance for social workers of having empathy for their clients. Carl Rogers (1961) defined empathy as "accurate understanding of the [client's] world as seen from the inside. To sense the [client's] private world as if it were your own, but without losing the 'as if' quality—this is empathy" (p. 284). Gerdes, Lietz, and Segal (2011) suggest that empathy consists of four subjective components:

- affective responses
- self–other awareness
- perspective taking, and
- emotion regulation

In an empirical study to examine the association of empathy with burnout and compassion for social workers, Wagaman et al. (2015) identified and surveyed field instructors at a southwestern university. The 173 who responded had degrees in social work and worked in a variety of settings. Average scores for each of the four components of empathy listed above were between 4 and 5 on a 1–6 point scale. Burnout scores were relatively low and compassion satisfaction was high, on average. Burnout was most associated with an inability to regulate one's own emotions while compassion satisfaction was most associated with sharing the emotions of the client and being able to take the perspective of the client. The researchers concluded that better training is needed for social work students to learn how to develop their skills in empathy.

10.3.2.1 Empirical Research on Secondary Traumatic Stress, Compassion Fatigue and Related Variables

A number of studies looking a child welfare or CPS staff, APS staff and victim advocates at shelters for battered women have looked for evidence of STS, and compassion fatigue in these groups. As will be seen, there has been clear evidence that these reactions occur, but several studies also found evidence for some of the positive reactions included in the new Ludick and Figley (2017) model.

In 2016, Sorenson and her colleagues published a review of literature on compassion fatigue over the period from 2005 through 2015. After a systematic search,

43 articles were identified that met their search criteria, and involved samples of healthcare professionals. These studies indicated that there was often a high positive correlation between compassion fatigue and burnout, and that both of these were associated with less positive feelings about caring for others. Those working directly with patients reported higher levels of compassion fatigue overall. Both of these findings are consistent with the earlier models of burnout and compassion fatigue. Sorenson, Bolick, Wright, and Hamilton (2016) further noted that self-care, discussed below, was associated with lower levels of compassion fatigue.

Hunsaker, Chen, Maughan, and Heaston (2015) is an example of a study that examined both compassion fatigue and burnout in a sample of emergency department nurses. Correlated factors were quite similar for compassion fatigue and burnout. Compassion fatigue was defined as "emotional, physical, and spiritual exhaustion from witnessing and absorbing the problems and suffering of others" while suggesting that burnout involves feelings of hopelessness and apathy (p. 187). Nurses experiencing either of these were less effective in the workplace and had lower levels of patient satisfaction. Hunsaker et al. also suggested that it was important to better understand *compassion satisfaction*, which was defined as deriving satisfaction from one's work by helping others and being able to do one's work well. In their empirical research, analyses indicated that older nurses were higher on compassion satisfaction and lower on compassion fatigue and burnout. Perhaps this result related to high dropout from nursing for those with the negative reactions? Both compassion fatigue and burnout were correlated with low levels of manager support for the nurses.

Indirect evidence for both compassion fatigue and compassion satisfaction was seen in a qualitative study child protective services workers discussed earlier (Tavormina & Clossey, 2017). Although some of the CPS staff mentioned how seeing so many negative events in the families they worked with changed them, they also noted that their work led to them learning things about being a better parent, and to experiencing personal growth. These findings are consistent with the newer theories outlining how caregivers might experience positive reactions to their work, as well as negative reactions such as burnout or compassion fatigue. A study of APS workers discussed earlier (Ghesquiere et al., 2018) reported that in this group, although nearly all reported exposure to difficult work situations, only 23% reported burnout and 25% reported secondary traumatic stress, suggesting that the majority of those working with elder abuse did not experience the negative reactions describe earlier. Compassion satisfaction was relatively high in this sample, with only 20% having low scores on this measure.

Evidence for burnout, secondary traumatic stress *and* compassion satisfaction can be seen in a study of victim advocates working in domestic violence services (Kulkarni et al., 2013). Providers of services in two statewide domestic violence coalitions were recruited for this study. Overall means were relatively low for burnout and secondary traumatic stress. Means were high for compassion satisfaction. Similar findings can be seen in a later study of a similar sample. Cummings, Singer, Hisaka, and Benuto (2018) used a convenience sample of victim advocates to investigate the interrelationships of secondary trauma, burnout and compassion satisfaction. As expected, secondary traumatic stress and burnout were positively associated. There was evidence of positive reactions, though. Burnout was negatively related to compassion satisfaction. Mean levels for these variables were not reported for this sample of victim advocates.

Frey et al. (2017) recruited a sample of victim advocates working with women victimized by sexual assault or partner violence to directly explore some of positive aspects of their work for this sample. They found evidence of compassion satisfaction and a response they labeled as posttraumatic growth in their sample. Those who had worked longer as advocates were higher in compassion satisfaction, as were those feeling they were receiving good organizational support. Levels of compassion satisfaction were at the high end of the scale.

10.3.3 Summarizing Research on Reactions of Caregivers to their Work

As this review has outlined, there is clear evidence that some of those working in CPS and APS, as well as in shelters for battered women, do experience burnout, secondary traumatic stress, and compassion fatigue, although this is not true for all of these professional caregivers. This is true for all three of these groups. In spite of the many problems experienced by child welfare workers, Boyas et al. (2015) did find that even some of those in the field did manage to thrive and reported high levels of job satisfaction. These thrivers tended to be older and more experienced, suggesting that those with more negative reactions to the work are less likely to remain in this type of work.

10.4 Help for the Service Provider

As discussed, many of those working in CPS, APS or as service providers for those experiencing IPV do experience a variety of debilitating emotional reactions, including burnout, compassion fatigue and secondary traumatic stress. Perhaps for this reason, many quit their jobs, creating high turnover among this staff. Although recognition of the problems faced by those staff who attempt to assist those victimized by family violence is growing in response to works such as Newhill (2003) book on client violence toward social workers, much still needs to be done. Two types of responses have been proposed to assist the staff and create a better working environment. First, the service provider herself or himself can engage in practices known as *self-care* (see Box 10.3). Some of the ways in which people engage in self-care are briefly reviewed in this section. In addition there are a number of steps that can be taken by the organization. These, too, are discussed in this section.

Box 10.3: Advice on Self-Care and Avoiding Burnout

Based on her years as a clinical social worker and School of Social Work faculty member, co-author Newhill advises the following:

It is important to emphasize that burnout is a very common occupational hazard amongst helping professionals, because our work involves direct personal contact involving emotionally intense work with other people who are having serious personal problems, may be traumatized, and are suffering in ways that we may not be able to completely relieve. When one has worked in the same agency doing the same work for a long time, it is only human to develop feelings of boredom, frustration and "burnout". If not addressed, burnout only gets worse and can significantly impact the quality of services provided to clients. It can negatively affect one's performance as a professional and co-worker, and ultimately lead to job dissatisfaction. The good news is that there are many strategies that can prevent burnout and relieve it when it occurs.

The first strategy is to recognize burnout when it occurs. It is important that burnout be openly acknowledged and identified. The following are examples of strategies that can prevent and relieve burnout:

1. All licensed social workers must amass a certain number of continuing education (CE) credits to maintain their license. It is important to choose continuing education opportunities that can enhance skills, provide networking opportunities, and enhance the learning of new knowledge and skills. Avoid CE courses that are too elementary; instead, challenge yourself. Use your CE gained knowledge to start working with new client populations presenting new types of problems or try working in a new type of service environment.
2. If you are facing client situations that are frustrating, and you know you don't have the right skills to handle them, go to your supervisor for help and seek out training to gain the skills that you need to be successful in practice.
3. One learns something thoroughly when one teaches it. So, along with taking CE courses, volunteer to teach a CE course yourself—such experiences can incite new passion about your work. If there is a social work or counseling program in your area, inquire about teaching a course in the undergraduate or graduate programs. Teaching overlaps with but is different from practice and can provide a new and exciting experience.
4. Serving as an internship supervisor or field instructor is another wonderful way to gain new insights, and bring new energy to your work. You will find that teaching others and supervising them can bring enormous rewards and serve to prevent burnout and renew the excitement you originally felt about your work.
5. Volunteer in your community for something that has nothing to do with your regular job. You will meet new people and get the satisfaction of contributing to your community. This will also give you a break from your normal routine.

6. Be open to seeking psychotherapy for yourself. This can be an important part of learning to be a good therapist and service provider. It may also be useful for caseworkers who are often angry or frustrated by their work or who are depressed or anxious and don't know how to deal with such feelings.
7. Make sure that you take care of yourself. People who go into the helping professions are commonly the "caretakers" of their families and live lives of constant giving. This is wonderful, but the giver needs to be given to as well. Take all of your vacation time and use it in the way that will best "recharge" your emotional and personal "batteries". Take all your personal days, learn to say "no" diplomatically, and be assertive about fairness in workload distribution in your job.
8. Finally, get plenty of sleep, exercise, eat regular meals and build in down time – you deserve it!

10.4.1 Self-Care

Self-care is defined in various ways in the published literature. For example, Newell and Nelson-Gardell (2014) describe self-care as use of various strategies that enable the social worker to "maintain their own personal, familial, emotional, and spiritual needs while attending to the needs and demands of their clients" (p. 431). They include participation in spiritual activities, as well as obtaining personal psychotherapy as two self-care activities, along with healthy life activities such as exercise and having a healthy diet.

Lee et al. (2017) described self-care as engaging in behaviors promoting positive outcomes such as stress relief or engaging in a positive lifestyle. Both quantitative and qualitative data were collected from a sample of 254 child welfare professionals working in Iowa. First looking at the characteristics of their sample, they noted a relatively high level of these staff having personally experienced difficulties in childhood (ACE), as well as feeling moderate or somewhat high stress levels now in their work on average. Qualitative data suggested that time pressures from high caseloads and feelings of guilt for not finishing their work on time were major sources of the stress. The sample was also asked what they did to cope with work stress. Strategies were classified as positive (including taking action to get rid of the problem, or developing a strategy for what to do) or negative (denial of the problem, using alcohol or drugs or other methods to disengage from the stressful feelings). The most used strategies within the sample were denial of the problem or using alcohol or drugs, both negative coping strategies. As might be expected, use of negative coping strategies was associated with higher levels of stress than using positive strategies.

In an interview study of child welfare workers in Canada described earlier, Lamothe et al. (2018) reported that seeking and finding social support was a major form of coping for this group. They typically turned to colleagues when wanting social support.

This might occur when they wanted to talk about a troubling experience with someone they thought would understand. Sometimes they just wanted to vent. Others described turning to a supervisor for social support. Those who could not find a supportive coworker or supervisor were disappointed. In some of the interviews, caseworkers described being in an organizational culture where admitting that one was having trouble coping was frowned on and found this experience to be quite upsetting.

10.4.1.1 Self-Care Not Always Done

In is not clear how many of the caseworker staff engage in self-care. In an attempt to better understand this, Miller, Donohue-Dioh, Niu, and Shalash (2018) surveyed a convenience sample of 222 child welfare workers in one southeastern state. Within the sample, many did not rate their level of self-care very high, with the overall mean at the moderate level, indicating they *sometimes* did this. Data indicated that those who felt they were *not* doing well financially were less likely to be doing things to facilitate their self-care activities. A correlation was also found such that those who rated their physical health more favorably also rated their levels of self-care higher. Miller et al. conclude by noting that organizations need to do more to teach about and promote self-care.

As this review has suggested, those working in the caregiving roles discussed in this chapter may have great need of self-care, but it appears that many do not engage in this in an effective way. As Bloomquist, Wood, Friedmeyer-Trainor, and Kim (2015) found in a survey of 786 MSW graduates from over 200 programs, social workers who were asked how often they engaged in a long list of self-care activities, on average, they engaged at levels between sometimes (a few times a month) or rarely (once a month). Most common were eating well, sleeping regularly, laughing, spending time with those they enjoyed being with, chatting with coworkers, and setting limits with clients. When asked how much they valued self-care, ratings were quite high, as was the belief that self-care was effective in alleviating job-related stress. Newell and Nelson-Gardell (2014), suggest that training in self-care practices should be an essential part of social work education and outline ways in which this might be done.

10.4.1.2 Types of Self-Care

There are many types of self-self care. Box 10.2 presents some of our recommendations. Many others have offered advice on this. For example, Salloum, Kondrat, Johnco, and Olson (2015) discuss the benefits of trauma-informed self-care for those experiencing burnout or secondary trauma as a result of their work. This situation applies to all of the types of staff discussed in this chapter who work with those victimized by family violence. According to these authors, this type of self-care involves being aware of one's emotional responses to the workplace and engaging in positive coping strategies such as seeking help from supervisors, getting training relating to secondary trauma, balancing one's caseload, and finding a good work-home balance. Salloum et al. argue that trauma-induced self-care is especially important to child welfare workers.

Another technique for self-care increasingly used to increase health and well-being by a variety of professionals is mindfulness. Mindfulness continues to receive research attention with nearly 700 journal publications on this topic in 2016, a huge increase since the initial publication found by Baer (2018) in 1982. Mindfulness has its roots in early Buddhist texts, but researchers today define it in a number of different ways. Baer, Smith, Hopkins, Krietemeyer, and Toney (2006) analyzed some of the scales used at that time and found there were five basic dimensions of mindfulness in these scales: Nonreactivity to one's inner feelings [I watch my feelings without getting lost in them]; observation of one's inner perceptions or emotions [When I am walking, I deliberately notice the sensations of my body moving]; acting with awareness [I find it difficult to stay focused on what's happening in the present (reverse scored)]; labeling one's thoughts or feelings with words [I can usually describe how I feel at the moment in considerable detail]; and not judging oneself [I criticize myself for having irrational or inappropriate emotions (reverse scored)]. Further research (Baer et al., 2006) indicated that three of these dimensions were most important in predicting good psychological outcomes: being able to describe feelings or thoughts, being aware of them, and not reacting to them. As a result of these analyses, Baer et al. (2006) developed a widely used scale to for self-reported mindful behavior. Decker, Brown, Ong, and Stiney-Ziskind (2015) used all five of the Baer et al. dimensions to measure mindfulness in a sample of MSW students. As predicted, lower levels of mindfulness behavior were correlated with higher levels of compassion fatigue.

Paulson (2018) argued that mindfulness training has become an important intervention for social workers to use with clients. Summarizing the literature, Paulson reported that the effective use of mindfulness had been shown to be important for those in direct practice, allowing the social worker to be non-judgmental toward clients. It was also linked to reductions in compassion fatigue. However, he further noted that better teaching about mindfulness was needed in schools of social work since the skills were not always being properly taught.

10.4.2 Self-Care or Organizational Change?

As this chapter has documented, all of the service providers for those directly affected by family violence or neglect have high workloads, stressful jobs, and low pay. Bressi and Vaden (2017) suggest that the focus on helping these staff by asking them to engage in self-care may be misguided, since basic changes are needed in the agencies themselves to lessen workloads and make the jobs more manageable. Better supervision would also be helpful in alleviating burnout of compassion fatigue, according to Bressi and Vaden (2017). In addition, they note that the nature of self-care itself may need to change.

Critique of organizations. Personal self-care is stressed rather than professional self-care. Miller et al. (2018) also note that organizations need to do more.

10.4.3 Institutional Assistance

10.4.3.1 Encouraging Self-Care in Staff

In order to reduce some of the negative reactions in professional help-giving staff, training in self-care for the staff has been suggested as being helpful to them personally as well as making them more effective in their work. Such training can occur in school when staff are earning their degrees, but, as noted, many do not have degrees in social work where such training is most likely to occur. Thus, it is essential that the agencies themselves offer training in self-care. Since the stresses appear to be highest for those in child welfare work, these agencies, in particular need to offer such training (Miller et al., 2018). Miller and his colleagues also suggest that more training is needed for supervisors in these agencies. Encouraging staff members to join professional associations can also be beneficial since they, too, offer a variety of workshops for professional development. Social work associations, such as the National Association of Social Workers (NASW), provide continuing education programs both in-person and via webinars specifically in techniques of self-care.

In order to empirically test these recommendations, Salloum et al. (2015) anonymously surveyed a sample of 108 child welfare caseworkers and supervisors involved in a training program. Surveys were administered before and after the three training sessions conducted. Data analysis indicated that by the end of the training, those completing the survey rated themselves as having lower levels of burnout and higher levels of compassion satisfaction. No changes were found for ratings of secondary trauma stress. These data appear consistent with what might be predicted from Ludick and Figley's theoretical model discussed earlier.

10.4.3.2 Making the Workplace Safe

Another important service agencies can do is to enable safety planning for staff members, and to have developed procedures for making the workplace safe (Kim & Hopkins, 2015). As Kim and Hopkins discussed, this problem may be somewhat hidden since many of the staff working in CPS may underreport their experiences of violence from clients since they perceive this as an inevitable part of their work. Gathering systematic information about the incidence of violence may be a first step in reducing it.

Based on their work in identifying the types of client violence encountered by child welfare staff, Lamothe et al. (2018) suggested that the institution needs to not only identify safety concerns, but provide tangible evidence that they want to know about the concerns of workers and are interested in helping with these concerns. Supervisors play an important role in helping reduce caseworker concerns. By encouraging open discussion of client aggression among the staff, others can be made more aware and learn from these examples. On-going staff training was also recommended.

Strolin-Goltzman et al. (2016) outline some of the efforts that could and should be made by organizations where child welfare workers are employed. These include developing plans for a unified organizational response when a violent individual is present. Making sure the service providers have cell phones or other means of calling for help is one of these plans. Having an on-going relationship with law enforcement authorities is also suggested. Staff training in de-escalation techniques and recognition of dangerous situations is needed. Keeping careful records of past violence or other abuse in the workplace would be helpful for identifying future situations with a potential for abuse of staff workers.

Other advice for improving workplace safety can be seen in Box 10.4. Other strategies that might be useful relate to the de-escalation skills offered in training for police officers (Olivia, Morgan, & Compton, 2010). For example, the first duty of a police officer arriving at a crisis event to to secure the scene and make sure everyone in the situation is safe. This may involve removing someone who is disruptive. The police officer is asked to remain calm and speak slowly, using short sentences. The officer is expected to show he or she wants to understand the person in crisis and provide whatever help is possible. These skills are often taught using role-playing.

Box 10.4: Enhancing Safety in the Workplace

Co-author Newhill (2003) offers these suggestions for making the workplace safer for those who work with potentially violent clients:

1. When talking with a potentially violent client:
   - Try to appear calm and relaxed.
   - Speak in a non-judgmental manner.
   - Introduce yourself with your name, position and agency affiliation.
   - Begin the discussion by commenting in concrete terms about something obvious.
   - Empathize with the client's feelings and point of view. Show respect for the client.
   - Listen carefully to what the client says and allow them to tell their story.
   - Calmly and honestly state your own perceptions of the situation.
   - Never make promises you cannot keep.
   - It your find it difficult to remain calm, try to arrange a break.
   - Don't get pulled into arguments.
2. Setting the stage for a meeting with a potentially violent client in the office.
   - If meeting in the office, you should decide whether others should be present with you and the client to ensure safety and whether the office

door should be open or closed. When in doubt, decide on the approach that best promotes safety.
- Make sure everyone is sitting down; this mitigates perceptions of power imbalance.
- Make sure there are no heavy objects present that might be thrown or used as weapons.
- Remove any dangerous items from the client.
- Dress professionally.

3. When meeting with a client outside the office in the community:

- Notify a co-worker or supervisor about where you are going.
- Make sure your car or other transportation is in good working order.
- Make sure to park in a safe location, that can't be blocked by an angry client.
- When entering the home, know where the exits are and try to remain near them. Have your keys handy and be ready to leave if you need to.
- If there are any signs of imminent violence, LEAVE.
- Never conduct an interview in the kitchen because kitchens have objects that can be used to harm someone, such as knives.

10.5 Summary

This chapter addresses the experiences of staff at agencies whose mission it is to assist the victims of family violence. Those working in child protective services, or, more generally, at child welfare agencies work with reported or verified cases of child abuse and neglect. Staff at adult protective services, among other duties, work with situations of elder abuse. Staff at shelters for battered women work with the women who seek shelter, as well as with children and animals they bring with them. All of these jobs may involve high caseloads and difficult work situations. Although most of these staff have college degrees, few are trained in social work. Many have a bachelor's degree in another field, where their education has included very little information directly relevant to their work. Frustration is generated because the staff may feel they are not helping. They may experience aggression or even violence from clients or family members. Having to complete detailed reports and other paperwork is another source of frustration.

As a result of this workplace frustration, staff may experience burnout or compassion fatigue. This is especially for those in child welfare. Job turnover is very high in this area especially, but also for staff in adult protective services and battered women's shelters. However, in spite of these frustrations and difficult work settings, some staff find great satisfaction in their work. For those whose burnout is high, self-care of various types is often recommended. The agencies themselves may provide training in self-care, as helping to enhance safety for staff. Many have suggested that agencies need to do more of this.

References

Baer, R. (2018). Assessment of mindfulness by self-report. *Current Opinion in Psychology, 28*, 42–48. https://doi.org/10.1016/j.copsyc.2018.10.015

Baer, R. A., Smith, G. T., Hopkins, J., Krietemeyer, J., & Toney, L. (2006). Using self-report assessment methods to explore facets of mindfulness. *Assessment, 13*(1), 27–45. https://doi.org/10.1177/1073191105283504

Barnett, O., Miller-Perrin, C. L., & Perrin, R. D. (2010). *Family violence across the lifespan: An introduction* (3rd ed.). Thousand Oaks, CA: Sage.

Benuto, L. T., Yang, Y., Ahrendt, A., & Cummings, C. (2018). The secondary traumatic stress scale: Confirmatory factor analyses with a national sample of victim advocates. *Journal of Interpersonal Violence*, 1–20. https://doi.org/10.1177/0886260518759657

Bemiller, M., & Williams, L. S. (2011). The role of adaptation in advocate burnout: A case of good soldiering. *Violence Against Women, 17*(1), 89–110. https://doi.org/10.1177/107780121039392

Bloomquist, K. R., Wood, L., Friedmeyer-Trainor, K., & Kim, H. (2015). Self-care and professional quality of life: Predictive factors among MSW practitioners. *Advances in Social Work, 16*, 292–311. https://doi.org/10.18060/18760

Borritz, M., Bültmann, U., Rugulies, R., Christensen, K. B., Villadsen, E., & Kristensen, T. S. (2005). Psychosocial work characteristics as predictors for burnout: Findings from 3-year follow up of the PUMA study. *Journal of Occupational and Environmental Medicine, 47*(10), 1015–1025.

Boyas, J. F., Wind, L. H., & Ruiz, E. (2015). Exploring patterns of employee psychosocial outcomes among child welfare workers. *Child and Youth Services Review, 52*, 174–183. https://doi.org/10.1016/j.childyouth.2014.11.002

Bressi, S. K., & Vaden, E. R. (2017). Reconsidering self care. *Clinical Social Work Journal, 45*, 33–38. https://doi.org/10.1007/s10615-016-0575-4

Burnett, C., Ford-Gilboe, M., Berman, H., Wathen, N., & Ward-Griffin, C. (2016). The day-to-day reality of delivering shelter services to women exposed to intimate partner violence in the context of system and policy demands. *Journal of Social Service Research, 42*, 516–532. https://doi.org/10.1080/01488376.2016.1153562

Can, N. (2018). *Caring for beginning counselors: The relationship between empathy, supervisory working alliance, resilience, wellness, and compassion fatigue among counselors-in-training*. PhD dissertation. Counselor Education, Texas A & M University-Corpus Christi, Corpus Christi, Texas.

Cherniss, C. (1980). *Professional burnout in the human service organizations*. New York, NY: Praeger.

Cherniss, C. (1995). *Beyond burnout: Helping teachers, nurses, therapists, and lawyers recover from stress and disillusionment*. New York, NY: Routledge.

Cummings, C., Singer, J., Hisaka, R., & Benuto, L. T. (2018). Compassion satisfaction to combat work-related burnout, vicarious trauma, and secondary traumatic stress. *Journal of Interpersonal Violence*, 1–16. https://doi.org/10.1177/0886260518799502

Dagan, S. W., Ben-Porat, A., & Itzhaky, H. (2016). Child protection workers dealing with child abuse: The contribution of personal, social and organizational resources to secondary traumatization. *Child Abuse & Neglect, 51*, 203–211. https://doi.org/10.1016/j.chiabu.2015.10.008

Day, M. R. (2016). Self-neglect: Ethical considerations. *Annual Review of Nursing Research, 34*(1). https://doi.org/10.1891/0739-6686.34.8

Decker, J. T., Brown, J. L. C., Ong, J., & Stiney-Ziskind, C. A. (2015). Mindfulness, compassion fatigue and compassion satisfaction among social work interns. *Social Work & Christianity, 42*, 28–42.

DeLiema, M., Navarro, A., Enguidanos, S., & Wilber, K. (2015). Voices from the frontlines: Examining elder abuse from multiple professional perspectives. *Health & Social Work, 40*, e15–e24. https://doi.org/10.1093/hsw/hlv012

Edwards, F., & Wildeman, C. (2018). Characteristics of the front-line child welfare workforce. *Children and Youth Services Review, 89*, 13–26. https://doi.org/10.1016/j.childyouth.2018.04.013

Figley, C. R. (1995). Compassion fatigue as secondary traumatic stress disorder: An overview. In C. R. Figley (Ed.), *Coping with secondary traumatic stress disorder in those who treat the traumatized* (pp. 1–20). New York, NY: Routledge.

Frey, L. L., Beesley, D., Abbott, D., & Kendrick, E. (2017). Vicarious resilience in sexual assault and domestic violence advocates. *Psychological Trauma: Theory, research, practice, and policy, 9*, 44–51. https://doi.org/10.1037/tra0000159

Friedman, R.A. (2008). When all else fails, blaming the patient often comes next. *The New York Times,* October 21.

Frieze, I. H. (2005). *Hurting the one you love: Violence in relationships*. Belmont, CA: Thompson Wadsworth.

Gerard, N. (2017). Rethinking compassion fatigue. *Journal of Health Organization and Management, 31*, 363–368. https://doi.org/10.1108/JHOM-02-2017-0037

Gerdes, K. E., Lietz, C. A., & Segal, E. A. (2011). Measuring empathy in the 21st century: Development of an empathy index rooted in social cognitive neuroscience and social justice. *Social Work Research, 35*, 83–93. https://doi.org/10.1093/swr/35.2.83

Ghertner, R., Waters, A., Radel, L., & Crouse, G. (2018). The role of substance use in child welfare caseloads. *Children and Youth Services Review, 90*, 83–93. https://doi.org/10.1016/j.childyouth.2018.05.015

Ghesquiere, A., Plichta, S. B., McAfee, C., & Rogers, G. (2018). Professional quality of life of adult protective service workers. *Journal of Elder Abuse & Neglect, 30*, 1–19. https://doi.org/10.1080/08946566.2017.1352550

Gibson, K., Samuels, G., & Pryce, J. (2018). Authors of accountability: Paperwork and social work in contemporary child welfare practice. *Children and Youth Services Review, 85*, 43–52. https://doi.org/10.1016/j.childyouth.2017.12.010

Griffiths, A., Royse, D., Culver, K., Piescher, K., & Zhang, Y. (2017). Who stays, who goes, who knows? A state-wide survey of child welfare workers. *Children and Youth Services, 77*, 110–117. https://doi.org/10.1016/j.childyouth.2017.04.012

Hattery, A., & Smith, E. (2017). *The social dynamics of family violence* (2nd ed.). Boulder, CO: Westview.

Hensel, J. M., Ruiz, C., Finney, C., & Dewa, C. A. (2015). Meta-analysis of risk factors for secondary traumatic stress in therapeutic work with trauma victims. *Journal of Traumatic Stress, 28*, 83–91. https://doi.org/10.1002/jts.21998

Horwitz, S. M., Hurlburt, M. S., Goldhaber-Fiebert, J. D., Palinkas, L. A., Rolls-Ruetz, J., Zhang, J., et al. (2014). Exploration and adoption of evidence-based practice by US child welfare agencies. *Children and Youth Services Review, 39*, 147–152. https://doi.org/10.1016/j.childyouth.2013.10.004

Hunsaker, S., Chen, H., Maughan, D., & Heaston, S. (2015). Factors that influence the development of compassion fatigue, burnout, and compassion satisfaction in emergency department nurses. *Journal of Nursing Scholarship, 42*, 1876–1194. https://doi.org/10.1111/jnu.12122

Jackson, S. L. (2017). Adult protective services and victim services: A review of the literature to increase understanding between these two fields. *Aggression and Violent Behavior, 34*, 214–227. https://doi.org/10.1016/j.avb.2017.01.010

Johnco, C., Salloum, A., Olson, K. R., & Edwards, L. M. (2014). Child welfare workers' perspectives on contributing factors to retention and turnover: Recommendations for improvement. *Children and Youth Services Review, 47*, 397–407. https://doi.org/10.1016/j.childyouth.2014.10.016

Kalkarni, S., Bell, H., Hartman, J. L., & Herman-Smith, R. L. (2013). Exploring individual and organizational factors contributing to compassion satisfaction, secondary traumatic stress, and burnout in domestic violence service providers. *Journal of the Society for Social Work and Research, 4*, 114–130. https://doi.org/10.5243/jsswr.2013.8

Kanno, H., & Newhill, C. E. (2009). Social workers and battered women: The need to study client violence in the domestic violence field. *Journal of Aggression, Maltreatment & Trauma, 18*, 46–63. https://doi.org/10.1080/10926770802610632

Kim, H. (2011). Job conditions, unmet expectations, and burnout in public child welfare workers: How different from other social workers? *Children and Youth Services Review, 33*, 358–367. https://doi.org/10.1016/j.childyouth.2010.10.001

Kim, H., & Hopkins, K. M. (2015). Child welfare workers' personal safety concerns and organizational commitment: The moderating role of social support. *Human Service Organizations: Management, Leadership & Goverance, 32*(2), 10–115. https://doi.org/10.1080/23303131.2014.987413

Kim, H., & Hopkins, K. M. (2017). A validation study of the revised personal safety decision scale. *Research on Social Work Practice, 27*, 607–615. https://doi.org/10.1177/1049731515590483

Kim, H., & Kao, D. (2014). A meta-analysis of turnover intention predictors among U.S. child welfare workers. *Children and Youth Services Review, 47*, 214–223. https://doi.org/10.1016/j.childyouth.2014.09.015

Koeske, G. F., & Koeske, R. D. (1989). Construct validity of the Maslach burnout inventory: A critical review and reconceptualization. *Journal of Applied Behavioral Science, 25*, 131–144. https://doi.org/10.1177/0021886389252004

Kulkarni, S., Bell, H., Hartman, J. L., & Herman-Smith, R. L. (2013). Exploring individual and organizational factors contributing to compassion satisfaction, secondary traumatic stress, and burnout in domestic violence service providers. *Journal of the Society for Social Work and Research, 4*(2), 114–130. https://doi.org/10.5243/jsswr.2013

Lamothe, J., Couvrette, A., Lebrun, G., Yale-Soulière, G., Roy, C., Guay, S., et al. (2018). Violence against child protection workers: A study of workers' experiences, attributions, and coping strategies. *Child Abuse & Neglect, 81*, 308–321. https://doi.org/10.1016/j.chiabu.2018.04.027

Lawrence, C. K., Zeitlin, W., Auerbach, C., Chakravarty, S., & Rienks, S. (2018). Measuring the impact of public perceptions on child welfare workers. *Journal of Public Child Welfare, 13*, 401–418. https://doi.org/10.1080/15548732.2018.1508537

Leake, R., Rienks, S., & Obermann, A. (2017). A deeper look at burnout in the child welfare workforce. *Human Service Organizations: Management, Leadership & Governance, 41*, 492–502. https://doi.org/10.1080/23303131.2017.1340385

Lee, K., Pang, Y. C., Lee, J. A. L., & Melby, J. N. (2017). A study of adverse childhood experiences, coping strategies, work stress, and self-care in the child welfare profession. *Human Service Organizations: Management, Leadership & Governance, 41*, 389–402. https://doi.org/10.1080/23303131.2017.1302898

Lizano, E. L., & Barak, M. M. (2015). Job burnout and affective wellbeing: A longitudinal study of burnout and job satisfaction among public child welfare workers. *Children and Youth Services Review, 55*, 18–28. https://doi.org/10.1016/j.childyouth.2015.05.005

Ludick, M., & Figley, C. R. (2017). Toward a mechanism for secondary trauma induction and reduction: Reimagining a theory of secondary traumatic stress. *Traumatology, 23*(1), 112–123. https://doi.org/10.1037/trm0000096

Maslach, C. (1993). Burnout: A multidimensional perspective. In W. B. Schaufeli, C. Maslach, & T. Marek (Eds.), *Professional burnout: Recent developments in theory and research* (pp. 19–51). Washington, DC: Taylor & Francis.

Maslach, C., & Jackson, S. E. (1981). The measurement of experienced burnout. *Journal of Occupational Behavior, 2*, 99–113.

Maslach, C., & Schaufeli, W. B. (1993). Historical and conceptual development of burnout. In W. B. Schaufeli, C. Maslach, & T. Marek (Eds.), *Professional burnout: Recent developments in theory and research* (pp. 1–18). Washington, DC: Taylor & Francis.

Merchant, L. V., & Whiting, J. B. (2015). Challenges and retention of domestic violence advocates: A grounded theory. *Journal of Family Violence, 30*, 467–478. https://doi.org/10.1007/s10896-015-9685-y

Mignon, S. I. (2016). *Child welfare in the United States: Challenges, policy and practice.* New York, NY: Springer.

Miller, J. J., Donohue-Dioh, J., Niu, C., & Shalash, N. (2018). Exploring the self-care practices of child welfare workers: A research brief. *Children and Youth Services Review, 84*, 137–142. https://doi.org/10.1016/j.childyouth.2017.11.024

Morazes, J. L., Benton, A. D., Clark, S. J., & Jacquet, S. E. (2010). Views of specially-trained child welfare social workers: A qualitative study of their motivations, perceptions, and retention. *Qualitative Social Work, 9*(2), 227–247. https://doi.org/10.1177/1473325009350671

Moylan, C. A., & Wood, L. (2016). Sexual harassment in social work field placements: Prevalence and characteristics. *Affilia: Journal of Women and Social Work, 31*, 405–417. https://doi.org/10.1177/0886109916644643

Newell, J. M., & Nelson-Gardell, D. N. (2014). A competency-based approach to teaching professional self-care: An ethical consideration for social work educators. *Journal of Social Work Education, 50*, 427–439. https://doi.org/10.1080/10437797.2014.917928

Newhill, C. E. (1996). Prevalence and risk factors for client violence towards social workers. *Families in Society: The Journal of Contemporary Human Services, 77*, 488–495.

Newhill, C. E. (2003). *Client violence in social work practice: Prevention, intervention, and research.* New York, NY: Guilford.

Newhill, C. E., & Wexler, S. (1997). Client violence toward children and youth services social workers. *Children and Youth Services Review, 19*, 195–212.

Olivia, J. R., Morgan, R., & Compton, M. T. (2010). A practical overview of de-escalation skills in law enforcement: Helping individuals in crisis while reducing police liability and injury. *Journal of Police Crisis Negotiations, 10*, 15–29. https://doi.org/10.1080/15332581003785421

Palinkas, L. A., He, A. S., Choy-Brown, M., & Hertel, A. L. (2017). Operationalizing social work science through research-practice partnerships: Lessons from implementation science. *Research on Social Work Practice, 27*, 181–188. https://doi.org/10.1177/1049731516666329

Paulson, J. (2018). Developing competence with mindfulness-based interventions: Guidelines for clinical social workers. *Journal of Sociology and Social Work, 6*(1), 1–6. https://doi.org/10.15640/jssw.v6n1a1

Pines, A. M. (1993). Burnout: An existential perspective. In W. B. Schaufeli, C. Maslach, & T. Marek (Eds.), *Professional burnout: Recent developments in theory and research* (pp. 33–51). Washington, DC: Taylor & Francis.

Radey, M., & Stanley, L. (2018). "Hands on" versus "empty": Supervision experiences of frontline child welfare workers. *Children and Youth Services Review, 91*, 128–136. https://doi.org/10.1016/j.childyouth.2018.05.037

Rogers, C. (1961). *On becoming a person: A therapist's view of psychotherapy*. Cambridge, MA: Riverside.

Salloum, A., Kondrat, D. C., Johnco, C., & Olson, K. R. (2015). The role of self-care on compassion satisfaction, burnout and secondary trauma among child welfare workers. *Children and Youth Services Review, 49*, 54–61. https://doi.org/10.1016/j.childyouth.2014.12.023

Salyers, M. P., Bonfils, K. A., Luther, L., Firmin, R. L., White, D. A., Adams, E. F., et al. (2016). The relationship between professional burnout and quality and safety in healthcare: A meta-analysis. *Journal of General Internal Medicine, 32*, 475–482. https://doi.org/10.1007/s11606-016-3886-9

Shockey, T. M., Zack, M., & Sussell, A. (2017). Health-related quality of life among US workers: Variability across occupational groups. *American Journal of Public Health, 107*, 1316–1323. https://doi.org/10.2105/AJPH.2017.303840

Sinclair, S., Raffin-Bouchal, S., Venturato, L., Mijovic-Kondejew, J., & Smith-MacDonald, L. (2017). Compassion fatigue: A meta-narrative review of the healthcare literature. *International Journal of Nursing Studies, 69*, 9–24. https://doi.org/10.1016/j.ijnurstu.2017.01.003

Sorenson, C., Bolick, B., Wright, K., & Hamilton, R. (2016). Understanding compassion fatigue in healthcare providers: A review of current literature. *Journal of Nursing Scholarship, 48*, 456–465. https://doi.org/10.1111/jnu.12229

Stephens, T., Gopalan, G., Acri, M. C., Bowman, M., & McKay, M. M. (2018). Culturally relevant, trauma-informed engagement strategies for child welfare workers: Moving beyond compliance to engagement with families experiencing high levels of exposure to trauma and stress. In V. C. Strand & G. Sprang (Eds.), *Trauma responsive welfare systems* (pp. 67–86). New York, NY: Springer.

Strolin-Goltzman, J., Kollar, S., Shea, K., Walcott, C., & Ward, S. (2016). Building a landscape of resilience after workplace violence in public child welfare. *Children and Youth Services Review, 71*, 250–256. https://doi.org/10.1016/j.childyouth.2016.11.001

Tarshis, S., & Baird, S. L. (2018). Addressing the indirect trauma of social work students in intimate partner violence (IPV) field placements: A framework for supervision. *Clinical Social Work Journal, published on-line., 47*, 90–102. https://doi.org/10.1007/s10615-018-0678-1

Tavormina, M., & Clossey, L. (2017). Exploring crisis and its effects on workers in child protective services work. *Child & Family Social Work, 22*, 126–136. https://doi.org/10.1111/cfs.12209

Thomas, J. T. (2016). Adverse childhood experiences among MSW students. *Journal of Teaching in Social Work, 36*, 235–255. https://doi.org/10.1080/08841233.2016.1182609

Vacca, L. (2016). Psychological abuse: *A review of 2016 Southern Connecticut State University graduating MSW student's knowledge base.* Southern Connecticut State University MSW thesis.

Wagaman, M. A., Geiger, J. M., Shockley, C., & Siegal, E. A. (2015). The role of empathy in burnout, compassion satisfaction, and secondary traumatic stress among social workers. *Social Work, 60*, 201–209. https://doi.org/10.1093/sw/swv014

Walters, J. E., Brown, A. R., & Jones, A. E. (2018). Use of the Copenhagen burnout inventory with social workers: A confirmatory factor analysis. *Human Service Organizations: Management, Leadership & Goverance, 42*, 437–456. https://doi.org/10.1080/23303131.2018.1532371

Wood, L. (2016). "I look across from me and I see me": Survivors as advocates in intimate partner violence agencies. *Violence Against Women, 23*, 309–329. https://doi.org/10.1177/1077801216641518

Appendix: Case Vignettes from our Files

In this Appendix, we introduce the professionals whose clinical experiences we draw on throughout the book. These are followed by a number of short case vignettes based on the practice experiences of authors Christina Newhill, Rachel Fusco and special contributor, Allison Little. To provide a background context for these cases, we have described the location, settings and type of practice for each contributor below.

Introducing the Clinicians

Christina Newhill, Ph.D., LCSW

Christina Newhill holds an LSW (Licensed Social Worker) license in Pennsylvania and an LCSW (Licensed Clinical Social Worker) license in California. Her case examples are drawn from her practice experience in both states. In Pennsylvania, Christina worked for a year and a half as the Emergency Coordinator for one of Pennsylvania's Mental Health/Mental Retardation Programs. This program provided mental health and intellectual/developmental disability services for two relatively rural counties in Western Pennsylvania, and psychiatric emergency services were available for anyone in the two county area 24-h a day. In this position, Christina supervised and trained volunteer crisis staff and directly provided psychiatric emergency and crisis intervention services. The cases from that work all involved "field" visits in which Christina made visits in the community to help clients in crisis in their homes, in the county emergency rooms, and at the various psychiatric community services across the two county area. Some of these client situations involved violent incidents in close relationships among family and friends. The population served was primarily white, many were working class or poor and resources were few and far between.

In California, Christina worked as a licensed clinical social worker for 7 years with a county community mental health center in central California. A "crisis" is an event or situation that results in a person's need for immediate mental health

I. H. Frieze et al., *Dynamics of Family and Intimate Partner Violence*,
https://doi.org/10.1007/978-3-030-42608-8

intervention on the phone or in person in the clinic or in the community. This particular county was, at that time, mostly rural with much of the industry agricultural in nature. The county has always been racially and ethnically diverse with 58% of the population self-identifying as White non-Hispanic, 30% Hispanic or Latino of any race, 8% Black (African-American, Carribbean-American), 1% Native American, 12% Asian or Pacific Islander, 6% multi-racial, and 16% from other races or ethnicities. Clients served spoke multiple languages other than English including Spanish, Tagalog, Mon-Khmer or Cambodian, Vietnamese and Hmong as their first language and, thus, interventions sometimes were provided using an interpreter. The crisis clinic clinicians reflected this diversity during the time Christina worked there and included two bilingual Mexican-American male clinicians, one Asian-American male clinician, two white male clinicians and one white female clinician (Christina). There were two psychiatrists in the clinic; one was South Indian-American and one was Pakistani-American. The county was also home to many undocumented immigrants who were mostly from Mexico or Southeast Asia and worked as seasonal farm laborers. These individuals were not counted in the census figures above and, thus, the actual figures for these racial/ethnic groups was much higher than officially reported.

The Crisis Intervention Service phone line was available 24-h, 365 days a year, with a mental health clinician on call at all times. The goal of our service was to assist people in crisis to maintain their ability to function in the community to the fullest extent possible. Crisis services could be requested in person by appointment, on a walk-in basis, or by telephone and were/are provided throughout the community. Although the name of the clinic is Crisis Services, persons do not have to be in a "crisis" or an urgent condition to request our services. A triage evaluation by mental health professionals determines the level or urgency or crisis and the appropriate course of intervention. Following the triage evaluation, the crisis clinician refers the individual to appropriate resources including short term counseling provided in the crisis service, outpatient longer term counseling, evaluation for medication by the crisis psychiatrist, temporary out-of-home placement, acute inpatient care, adult or child protective services, or another community resource. A field clinician is assigned daily, to respond to community requests for crisis services, including mental health evaluations for temporary, involuntary psychiatric inpatient care in situations where the mental health consumer is a danger to self, danger to others or gravely disabled. Some of these situations involve violence between family members or other individuals in close relationships. The clinician assesses the individual's ability to maintain community functioning in the least restrictive environment and determines the most appropriate level of care for that person at that time. Hospitals providing medical care may call Crisis Services to request a crisis evaluation for any person at the hospital who has already been medically cleared (ready for medical discharge), and who may be a danger to self, others or gravely disabled due to a mental disorder.

Rachel Fusco, Ph.D., LSW

Rachel Fusco is a Licensed Social Worker (LSW) in Pennsylvania and Oregon and a former Licensed Clinical Social Worker (LCSW) in Texas. Her case examples draw on her practice experience in both Texas and Oregon. In Texas Rachel worked with Children's Protective Services (CPS) in a medium sized city. The population was primarily White and White Hispanic. Her first role with this agency was to investigate allegations of child abuse and neglect. Investigations involved interviews with alleged child victims, often in the school setting. Alleged perpetrators, family members, and other contacts were also interviewed as appropriate to establishing the facts of the case. This role also included determining whether a parent or guardian is able to provide adequate care, evaluating whether a child should be temporarily or permanently removed from his/her living situation, and placing children in out of home care when needed.

Rachel also provided in-home family preservation services at CPS. Family preservation services are family-focused, community-based crisis intervention services designed to maintain children safely in their homes and prevent separation of families whenever possible. Rachel provided intensive case management and weekly counselling sessions with families to help them develop parenting, problem solving, and stress management skills. Her caseload was largely composed of White Hispanic families, many of whom were new to the U.S., and some who were undocumented. The families were often struggling to reconcile their own cultural beliefs about physical punishment of children with U.S. laws and norms. Families commonly experienced intimate partner violence (IPV), mental health problems, and substance abuse issues in addition to child maltreatment.

After seeing the high percentage of CPS-involved families who were experiencing IPV, Rachel obtained a position with the Center for Battered Women. She was a social worker in their outreach center where she developed a program for children who were exposed to IPV. Mothers brought their children to the outreach center when they received their own therapy and support. The children ranged in age from 3 years old to 12 years old, and some of them had witnessed severe physical and sexual violence. A few children had seen their mother raped and one had witnessed the murder of her mother, and was now living with her aunt. Most of the children had spent time at the battered women's shelter and were experiencing poverty, housing instability, and food insecurity. Some were still living with the perpetrator of the violence. Rachel conducted group and individual therapy with these children, including art and play therapy. Many of the children were experiencing significant trauma symptomology, including hyperarousal and re-experiencing, which was frequently demonstrated through their art and play.

Rachel moved to Oregon where she worked at a residential treatment facility for adolescents who were diagnosed with emotional and behavioral problems. She was the lead therapist on a unit that housed ten girls of varying racial, ethnic, and socioeconomic backgrounds. The facility was in a medium-sized city but many girls were sent there from smaller communities that lacked adequate mental health resources, including American Indian reservations. Most of the girls had a history of child maltreatment and a few had experienced failed adoptions. Rachel worked with an interdisciplinary team that included a psychiatrist, a nurse, and an education specialist to develop treatment plans, and provided individual and group therapy. She also provided family therapy using a family systems perspective.

Allison Little, MSW

Allison Little has practiced as a social worker in multiple counties across North Carolina and in a suburban/urban county in London, England. Her case examples are drawn from practice experience in all of these locations. In North Carolina, Allison worked for 2 years in a medium sized city as an investigation and assessment social worker for the county child welfare agency. In this position, Allison investigated allegations of child abuse, neglect, and dependency made either by professionals involved with families or by non-professionals, such as friends, relatives, and neighbors. Investigations required interviews with alleged victim children and alleged perpetrators, as well as background checks and collateral community contacts in order to determine whether allegations should be dismissed and the case closed or the case should remain open and transferred to a long-term services social worker within the agency. A small number of these referrals led to the removal of children from parental care and placement in informal kinship or legally sanctioned foster care. A significant number of cases included concern about relationship violence as a primary or secondary referring issue; many also turned up these concerns in the process of investigation. While the majority of relationship violence allegations were based around concerns of men abusing female partners, many included concerns about other relationships, including women abusing male partners, abuse in same-sex relationships, abuse between siblings, and teenage children abusing their parents. The community served by this agency was majority White (about 85%) with smaller numbers of African American and Hispanic members (about 7% each). The community also included a small number of European immigrant families and a small but growing population identifying as two or more races (about 2%). After leaving this agency, Allison moved to work in the same position for 2 years at a very small child welfare agency in a rural county. Though the work and cases were similar, the population was less diverse at about 95% White and about 5% Hispanic.

Allison then spent 4 years working as a referral and assessment social worker in London, England in an urban/suburban Outer London borough. This position was essentially the same as the previous two positions in that it required accepting, screening, and responding to referrals of abuse, neglect, and dependency made either by professionals or non-professional community contacts. Though time frames, legal definitions, and policies differed from the U.S., the work was much the same. The greatest difference, however, was the great diversity within the agency and the community served. While the borough was majority White British (about 75%), the rest of the community was incredibly diverse, with about 5% describing themselves as White Other, and the remainder of the population representing about 15 racial and ethnic groups in small but significant percentages. The agency reflected community diversity, with social workers from over 20 countries. Interpreters were regularly needed for languages other than those spoken by the social workers. Referrals of maltreatment were often much the same as in the U.S., with the majority of relationship violence allegations concerning male abusers and female victims. Cultural differences in beliefs about roles and rights for women and girls versus men and boys sometimes influenced family violence, such as a father and brothers physically attacking a sister who wanted to date or a husband using violence to keep his wife from going out alone.

Finally, Allison spent 2 years back in North Carolina as a supervised visitation social worker in multiple North Carolina counties. Children who are removed from parents due to severe concerns about abuse or neglect are required to have regular visitation with parents both to maintain the family bond and to allow the agency to monitor progress on the case. The vast majority of these cases were based on substantiated concerns about parental substance abuse or family violence, with a significant number of families experiencing both. Cases in which family violence is the only or primary concern tend to exhibit severe physical and emotional violence resulting in physical injury or a substantial threat thereof. Case planning and management was focused on harm reduction, including safety planning with victim parents and mandated abuser treatment. The issue of separating the victim parent from his or her abuser is an especially difficult one in child welfare case management. The victim parent may not want to separate or may pretend to separate in order to regain custody or to end social services' involvement. The parent may genuinely want to separate, but may find life alone to be emotionally and financially difficult. Separating from an abuser can also be an extremely dangerous undertaking, placing the victim at risk of harm or death from violence. Yet, allowing vulnerable children to be exposed to an abuser is a serious risk in itself. Case planning and management for families with minor children in which violence is an issue requires careful, supervised, multi-level decision-making.

The Cases

Case #1 (Christina Newhill)

This Case Demonstrates

- How symptoms of serious mental illness can play a role in the occurrence of family violence;
- How repetitively violent/aggressive individuals with mental illness are most likely to target family members due to proximity and emotional involvement and attachment;
- How difficult it can be for a family to manage violence exhibited by a family member with serious mental illness and protect themselves, particularly when the individual may be resistant to accepting treatment.

Initial Contact and Presenting Problem

Fred is a 42 year-old single white male with paranoid schizophrenia who has received outpatient and inpatient services at the county mental health service for many years. Recently he has not been doing well in terms of his psychiatric status, and has been seen in the crisis clinic both during the day and at night several times over the past 2–3 weeks. Fred complains of smelling foul odors and fears he will lose control and kill his mother. Fred has felt rage toward his mother for years because he blames her for bringing him into this world with a disability. Fred has attacked his mother several times in the past and has injured her severely enough for her to require medical care and even, on one occasion, hospitalization. Fred's mother has never been willing to press charges against him, always insisting that he needs psychiatric treatment, not jail, however Fred is often unwilling to take prescribed medication or follow through with outpatient care. Many attempts have been made to secure stable housing for Fred so that he doesn't have to live with his mother but he always leaves such situations to go back home and his mother takes him in and allows him to live with her.

Recently, although he has been treated with extremely high doses of antipsychotic medications (prolixin and mellaril) he has continued to maintain only marginally. A stay at our transitional care facility was attempted this past week but Fred would not even get out of his car when he arrived there, stating there were foul odors in the air that would contaminate him and make him sexually impotent. Tonight he states that he cannot control himself any longer from killing his mother. Upon evaluation he is calm and fairly appropriate except when talking about mother whereupon he becomes agitated. He states that he cannot stand living with mother but also can't stay away so he believes that the only solution is to kill her, plus he feels she is influencing the increase of the foul odors that are bothering him.

We then received a telephone call from Fred's brother, John, who stated that yesterday Fred tried to rape John's wife (Fred's sister-in-law). According to John, his wife states that she hugged Fred and subsequently he threw himself on her, knocked her to the ground and tried to rape her. The family states that Fred refuses to come to the mental health service to see the psychiatrist. We called Fred, and he was calm and cooperative on the phone. He stated that he did not try to rape his sister-in-law but claimed that she is always hugging and kissing everyone and that when he tried "to give her a taste of her own medicine" and hug her back, she screamed rape. He says that the family is trying to get him "put away for good in the state hospital" so they can get their hands on his mother's house. He does not want to continue to take his medication and will only see the doctor if he ends up in jail and it is court ordered to treatment. He states he is now waiting for the sheriff to take him away, as his brother threatened to do. Outcome: Fred was taken by sheriff's deputies to the county mental health inpatient unit and hospitalized on the basis of danger to others and grave disability.

Case #2 (Christina Newhill)

This Case Demonstrates

- How even when an abused victim takes action and evicts the abuser from the home, the abuser may stalk and continue to assault the victim;
- How victims may seek help through all the appropriate channels but not receive the help needed;
- The profound physical and psychological toll that ongoing abuse can take on a mother and her children which led to post-traumatic stress disorder in both mother and children;
- How an individual who has been repeatedly victimized, has not been able to access help, and who fears for her life may use a violent action to fight back;
- How victims may view the only resort to be to cut all ties to their current life and "disappear".

Initial Contact and Presenting Problem

"Joyce" is a 22-year-old single African-American woman who, under extreme stress, came to the crisis clinic with her 4 year old daughter for help because of trauma flashbacks and periods of dissociation. Joyce tells the crisis worker that a little over 2 years ago, she started going out with a man named "George". Their relationship went well at first, and so she allowed him to move with her (her other child, a 2-year-old boy, is his biological child). Soon, however, George started beating Joyce frequently and severely. Once he beat her breasts so badly they got infected and she had to have surgery. Joyce finally kicked George out of the house, but he continued to come around and abuse her—he would follow her in parks and on the street, and then would attack her. Sometimes she was successful in pressing charges and having him put in jail, but recently the police had been unwilling to act on her complaints.

Joyce tried to get help from every resource she could think of including the police (repeatedly), the local district attorney, and Haven House∗ (the local domestic violence shelter), but got nowhere. The situation had progressed to the point that George was calling her constantly and threatening that he was going to kill her. Joyce developed ulcers, couldn't sleep, had problems concentrating and lost weight. When she was able to fall asleep, Joyce reported having nightmares related to the abuse. George had also beaten Joyce's two children, and the children began having nightmares, flashbacks of the abuse, angry outbursts and showed fear toward adult men in general. Finally, in desperation, Joyce borrowed a gun from her sister, and after a particularly brutal beating in which George poked Joyce's eye in with a stick (she required many stitches), she finally went out, found George sitting on a park bench, and after much deliberation, walked up and shot him. She then went to a pay phone and turned herself in to the police. Joyce states that for the first time—sitting in jail - she felt safe.

George did not die from the gunshot wound and was still recovering in the county hospital when Joyce came to the crisis clinic for help. The crisis worker called Haven House and they said they now had room for Joyce and her children (they didn't before, which is why they couldn't help her previously) and staff agreed to come down to the clinic immediately to pick them up. Joyce's sister had posted her bail. Joyce states that her nerves are so bad, she has had no sleep in days, and is at the end of her rope. The crisis worker referred her to the crisis psychiatrist for temporary medication (Joyce does not drink or use illicit drugs) and the doctor prescribed valium, 10 mg. twice a day.

Joyce states that she is planning to get some money together, get out of town and go somewhere secretly to disappear before George gets out of the hospital. As to what will happen with the court will remain to be seen.

Original DSM-III Diagnosis: Post Traumatic Stress Reaction.

Updated DSM-5 Diagnosis: Post Traumatic Stress Disorder with Dissociative Symptoms.

Case #3 (Allison Little)

Rashid family, Iranian immigrants to the U.S.
Father: Ali, age 29
Mother: Nur, age 28
Son: Basim, age 8
Daughter: Adila, age 5

This Case Demonstrates

- Domestic violence may become obvious because of children's behavior, including mimicking violence or casual disclosure.
- Financial concerns for the victim can be paramount when faced with the loss of a primary earner, especially when the victim parent does not work or is unable to hold employment providing a living wage.
- In situations where the victim parent chooses to leave with children, it is vital to support the parent in accessing any benefits that they may be entitled to. Food stamps, cash benefits, housing subsidies, Medicaid, child care subsidies, etc. all require documentation and take time and sometimes a great deal of effort to maintain. If the victim parent can safely obtain passports, birth certificates, and other vital documents upon choosing to leave, they should be encouraged to do so in order to begin this process.

The Rashid family migrated from Iran to U.S. for economic reasons shortly after Basim was born. Ali is an I.T. (Information Technology) specialist and felt that the U.S. would allow him greater opportunity to advance in his field. Nur left university to marry Ali and is a full time stay at home mom. The family speak Persian at home, though the parents and Basim speak English well enough to understand professionals. Adila has some language delays. Basim's school called with concern that his behavior is increasingly violent, and seems to be particularly directed toward his mother. Most recently Basim had asked his mother to take him to McDonalds after school for dinner because he prefers American food and didn't want to eat his mom's more traditional cooking. When Nur refused, Basim began hitting and kicking her. The principal and guidance counselor both spoke with Nur and found that she has been experiencing this quite a lot, and is concerned that Basim is copying his father's behavior. Nur states that he often shoves and slaps her, though she has never been bruised by him. Basim has told female teachers and staff that he doesn't have to listen to them because he is going to be a man, and they are only women. Social services began an investigation into the family. Ali reluctantly agreed to leave the home and stay with friends. Nur and her children hold American citizenship, so the social worker assisted Nur in applying for benefits. Nur was concerned because, even if Ali maintains support for the family and they are able to obtain benefits, their standard of living would drop. In particular, Nur was concerned that they would lose their apartment and that she and the children may have to stay in a shelter until they could obtain Section 8 housing benefit. Ali fully denied any violence, and stated that in fact Nur often yells at him and has slapped him in front of the children. Ali also denied that Basim is showing any behavior problems. Because of language delay, Adila could not be interviewed in English or with a Persian translator. When Basim was interviewed by the SW, he said his dad yells at his mom and tells her and everyone else what to do. When asked if anything else happens, Basim said his mom gets a smack, and mimicked a slapping motion. The family were found to be in need of services and transferred to long-term in-home services.

Case #4 (Allison Little)

Anderson family, biracial African American/White American
Mother: Leah, age 27 White American
Father: Andre, age 29 African American
Daughter: Faith, age 7 (biracial)
Son: Carson, age 5 (biracial)

This Case Demonstrates

- Relationship violence can occur over long periods of time in relationships where the adults do not live together, have children in common, and have inconsistent involvement with one another.
- Relationship violence can have a mutual quality in which both adults are quick to anger and violence. However, thorough assessment and separate interviews are vital: what initially appears to be mutual violence may be repeated victimization.

- Children who are exposed to repeated physical and emotional violence may act out in various ways, including physical aggression and emotional manipulation. Parents may share highly inappropriate information about one another with children because of a lack of boundaries, potentially because the adult lacks any appropriate confidantes.
- Both the victim and perpetrator of violence may exhibit problems with substance abuse. Even when appropriate services can be found for the perpetrator and victim, noncompliance may be an issue.

Leah and Andre do not live together, and are in an on and off relationship. Their relationship is characterized by jealousy, fueled by the close-knit urban community in which they live. They see each other around often, and hear from friends about the other's romantic and sexual escapades. Social services has been involved with the family repeatedly since Faith was born. The children were taken into care when Faith was six and Carson was four because of repeated and severe violence between the parents. Both Faith and Carson are intelligent, articulate children who speak casually about seeing their parents fight and hit each other. Faith stated that her mom says dad is a "nasty man-slut," and that her dad says mom is a "whore." When asked what happens when they get angry, Faith stated that mom will punch dad, and dad will pull mom's hair and they yell. Carson calmly spoke about the night that his mom had to go to the hospital because Andre got mad at her because she had a new boyfriend and he stabbed her in the arm with kitchen knife. The wound was superficial, but the incident was severe enough to remove the children. Both Faith and Carson have severe behavior problems. Faith has tantrums in which she screams, however she does not usually hit. Rather, Faith looks for ways to manipulate other people, including her brother, her parents, schoolmates, etc. She will cause fights by telling one person that another said something about them, or will find ways to casually goad Carson into violence by subtly teasing him. Carson is physically violent, he goes into rages in which he hits and kicks and curses. He often says things like "you have to listen to me, I'm in charge," and has such severe behavior issues that he is in a special day facility rather than school. Both parents have a history of substance misuse; both drink regularly, Leah has misused prescription medication that she buys off the street while Andre has a history of crack use. Both claim that they never use around the children and neither feels that drugs have an effect on the violence. Leah and Andre both admit that there is violence between them, though each claims that the other starts it. Each also claims that the other is emotionally manipulative, giving affection and sex and then withholding it for no reason. However, both also state a desire to rekindle a stable relationship together and eventually marry. The parents get weekly supervised visitations and are receiving counseling and drug services. Parental compliance with these services has been inconsistent, and the parents risk the permanent termination of their parental rights if this continues.

Case #5 (Allison Little)

Martinez family, Mexican Immigrants to the U.S.
Mother: Juanita, age 38
Father: Pedro, age 36
Son: Vicente, age 12

This Case Demonstrates

- While the majority of reported relationship violence is perpetrated by a male partner against a female partner, men can be victims of physical, emotional, and sexual violence as well.
- Shame, self-rationalization (e.g. it's not that bad, just "man up" and ignore it), and the belief that no services exist for men may prevent a male victim from reporting his experience.
- Undocumented migrants may be especially fearful of reporting out of a fear of deportation. Practitioners should make contact with immigrant rights groups who can provide information on where to obtain support, including how to apply for the right to stay in the U.S.
- Children experiencing family violence may sometimes respond by showing outwardly positive behaviors at school and with friends. This may be a method of coping, of receiving positive attention in a safe environment, or out of fear of provoking the abusive family member.

Juanita and Pedro moved to the U.S. 15 years ago. Both have become fluent in English, and while their son is a natural-born U.S. citizen, neither have made efforts to obtain citizenship. When asked why, they state they are afraid to let the government know of their presence lest they face potential deportation. Both parents work very long hours at various informal jobs. Vicente is a model student and a well-liked, well-behaved boy by all accounts from the school and acquaintances. Social services became involved when it was alleged that Vicente often is alone overnight and even for full weekends when his parents are working. When Vicente was interviewed at school, he also disclosed that his mother often gets very angry when she is stressed, and that she takes it out on both Vicente and Pedro. She will slap and punch Pedro during arguments. Vicente stated that while Pedro will yell as much as Juanita, he never uses physical violence. Vicente stated that his mom still spanks him on his bare bottom with a belt or extension cord, but that it doesn't happen as much as when he was younger. Vicente states he thinks his mom hits him less because he tries very, very hard to be good in school. Pedro's account of fights with Juanita fits with Vicente's. Pedro states that he does not hit back because he grew up in a very violent household in which he was afraid of his father. Additionally, Pedro fears that if he hits back, it will come to the attention of police and risk deportation. Pedro was embarrassed to talk about the hitting, and feels that there is no point in looking for help, not only because of the risk of deportation, but because he assumes there is no help for men. Juanita admitted in her interview that she sometimes hits Pedro, but claims she doesn't do it very often. Juanita also says she has told Pedro he can hit her back, which Vicente says he has heard as well. Juanita denied ever using an instrument to hit Vicente, though she admits she still spanks his bare bottom when he is bad because it will embarrass him and shame him into behaving. Neither adult wanted to leave the home; each stated they still love each other, would have no place to go, and would lose their son. The family were transferred to in-home services for long-term support.

Case #6 (Christina Newhill)

This Case Demonstrates

- How multiple systems of care can become involved with a family in which there is intimate partner violence;
- The important role of bystanders (i.e. neighbors) in mobilizing a critical intervention (police);
- The pathways a perpetrator and victim move through in accessing help;
- The nature of follow-up care following a crisis.

Initial Contact and Presenting Problem

John is a 36 year-old married white male with five children who was brought to the crisis clinic for evaluation by Sheriff's deputies and a Department of Public Assistance (DPA) worker. John's wife, Karen, was seen 4 days prior by one of the clinic social workers for evaluation of depression. John has abused Karen off and on throughout the 8 years of their marriage, but last Saturday he almost killed her. Because of the violence in the home, the five children were removed last year and placed in the Dependent Children's Home by Child Protective Services and are currently in foster care. John reports that he injured his back in an auto accident 4 years ago and, because his back is still bad, John says nobody will hire him so he must work privately in a body shop he constructed in his garage. The shop, however, has been losing business and the family's finances are in a squeeze. This past Saturday, John and Karen were having a yard sale. John was working in his body shop and told Karen to keep the people at the yard sale out of his way; she started to argue with him so he attacked and beat her; he broke a broom over her head and was about to ram the broken end through her but stopped in time. Karen immediately left, went to the hospital for treatment of her injuries, and then went to the local battered women's shelter. Karen refused to press charges against John and never has after previous incidents of abuse. In John's words, though: "If somebody did to me what I do to her, I'd have him thrown in jail or kill him." Karen is now staying with a friend. This morning the DPA worker tried to reach Karen in order to discuss the situation with the children, but found out she was gone because of the recent incident of abuse. The DPA worker then attempted to make a home visit to talk to John, but neighbors said he was being held at the sheriff's department. According to the neighbors, they called the sheriff after they observed the abuse going on in the yard, and when John admitted to the deputies that he had beaten his wife, they threw him in the squad car and brought him to the crisis clinic. The DPA worker then met them there. Upon evaluation, John initially threatened suicide (said he wanted to blow his brains out), but as the interview progressed, he said that if he could get some help, he would promise to get rid of his gun at home and could postpone any harm to himself.

Disposition

1. John was referred to the crisis clinic doctor for evaluation for medication due to John's complaints of feeling depressed, sleeping poorly over past few weeks, and poor appetite resulting in weight loss. He may not be truly depressed, rather, he may meet criteria for antisocial personality disorder. However, given his explosive temper and behavior, antidepressant medication could aid in helping him to maintain emotional balance and behavioral control;
2. John was given a follow-up appointment to return to crisis tomorrow morning 9:30 to see the crisis worker;
3. John made a contract that tonight he will call our emergency number if he feels he is losing control and might harm himself;
4. John was given an appointment in our outpatient clinic for 2 weeks from now. Once the current crisis abates, he may not need to continue on medication but would benefit from psychotherapy;
5. John agreed to allow me to inform the DPA worker about the disposition.

Follow-up Appointment Three Days Later

John is doing much better now. Taking 150 mg of imipramine is too strong, so the dose was decreased to 100 mg at night, which seems to be working, i.e. John is sleeping well, he has not been explosive, and feels much more stable. John subjectively states that he "feels good". John and Karen have discussed the problems they have been having and John feels that they are talking constructively for the first time. Wisely, they are remaining separated to avoid any recurrence of conflict. John seems motivated to pursue counseling (he is in the remorseful stage) To return to the crisis clinic 5/25 to see the psychiatrist. Return June 1 to see me. Has intake 6/9.

Follow-up Appointment Seven Days Later

John looks good and seems to be doing well, sleeping better and staying in control. John and Karen are now living together again but there have been no fights and John thinks the medication is helping him control his temper. The body shop business is still down and John has to go to the small claims court regarding a guy who "ripped him off" and didn't pay his bill for body work. There will be no change regarding the children's foster care until the outpatient therapist can verify that John is attending counseling.

Case #7 (Christina Newhill)

This Case Demonstrates

- How heavy alcohol abuse is often associated with intimate partner violence;
- How after an episode of abuse, the perpetrator may apologize and be contrite, promising to change but, without intervention, the abuse often occurs again;
- How the victim of abuse may try to leave multiple times before she makes a commitment to leave and/or get assistance.

Initial Contact and Presenting Problem

Julie is a 25 year old married white female with one child who was brought to the crisis clinic by her sister-in-law. Julie states that her husband kicked her out of the house 2 days ago and she has no place to go and is, essentially, homeless. Her sister-in-law took her in to stay with her family but her husband (Julie's brother-in-law) says he wants Julie to leave because his brother will get too upset. Julie's husband drinks heavily on a daily basis, beats her up regularly and she doesn't know what to do. Julie presents as an attractive young woman who is upset and desperate. Her speech is pressured, affect is somewhat labile in presentation, there is no evidence thought disorder, and she denies suicidal or homicidal ideation. Julie has stayed at the battered women's shelter before but has never been willing to stay longer than overnight. When I inquired as to why she doesn't stay longer at the shelter, she says that she has always contacted her husband, he apologizes and promises never to hit her again and so she returns home. Things are good for a couple weeks or so but then his drinking escalates and inevitably he abuses her again. Julie realizes she needs to do more than what she has done so far to change her situation, including staying at the shelter and getting counseling, so I called the shelter and she talked with them on the phone and agreed to go there and commit to staying for a few days. Her sister-in-law agreed to drive her over. *Disposition*: referred to Battered Women's shelter for placement and counseling

Case #8 (Christina Newhill)

This Case Demonstrates

- How victims of domestic violence are often seen in the emergency room when they sustain injuries that must be treated, which opens an opportunity for emergency personnel to identify the presence of domestic violence and arrange for help;
- Victims may make a suicide gesture or attempt either to force access to help or as an act of desperation;
- Emergency room contact is often a time when victims are most motivated to seek help as they are safe in that environment, the most recent violence may be severe, and transportation to a shelter is available;
- The forms in which severe abuse occurs and how it can be sustained over a long period of time before the victim seeks help.

Initial Contact and Presenting Problem

Rose is a 44 year old married white female who was brought to a rural community hospital emergency room by her husband, Tom. Tom told the ER doctor that his wife had taken pills in a suicide attempt. Rose denied this, stating that her husband lies all the time. Later, however, when talking with the crisis social worker, Rose admitted that she had taken the pills because she had felt hopeless about the situation with her husband. She didn't want to die, but just wanted to "go to sleep and escape" the physical and emotional pain she was experiencing.

Upon evaluation by the crisis social worker, Rose presented as alert, completely oriented, although she thought today is February fourth when it was actually December 14th. Rose states that her husband has abused her for 15 years of her 18 year marriage and that she wants help. She has a large hematoma on her forehead and is complaining of severe stomach pain - her husband had kicked her in the stomach. Rose states that Tom has, over the years, broken both of her wrists, broken both her legs, cracked her ribs and given her multiple black eyes, cuts, and abrasions. Up until now she hoped he would change and stop the violence if she were a "better wife" but realizes now that hope is futile and she is motivated to get help. Rose agreed to go to the Battered Women's Shelter and I contacted them and they agreed to accept her once she is completely medically stable and ready for discharge. Rose told the social worker that she felt better after talking.

Case #9 (Christina Newhill)

This Case Demonstrates

- How intimate partner violence can occur in same-sex relationships with similar dynamics to such violence in heterosexual relationships;
- How each partner in an abusive relationship may describe the violence differently (see Case 15), for example, each describing the other as the controlling partner;
- How fear of the violence getting worse may prevent the abused partner from involving the police.

Initial Contact and Presenting Problem

Elaine is a 28 year old single African-American woman with four children. Only two of the children are with her; the other two are with their father. Elaine was referred to county mental health services for ongoing counseling by the Battered Women's Shelter. Elaine has lived in Sacramento for 3 years; before that, she was living in Oakland. While in Oakland—5 years ago—her husband was killed, she was very depressed after his untimely death and made one suicide attempt by overdosing. Following the suicide attempt, Elaine sought counseling and this helped her tremendously—she got back on her feet, worked for a while as a domestic for a wealthy family and managed to save money, get her kids back (they had been removed for a while by child protective services) and, overall, was doing well. Then a friend introduced her to a woman named Bebe. Bebe had a young child and had her own problems and attached herself to Elaine in a very dependent demanding fashion—began calling her at work and the family she worked for became angry about Bebe's constant calls but instead of Elaine telling Bebe not to call, she quit her job and moved in with Bebe and they both then moved to Sacramento. Bebe became more controlling, Elaine ended up taking care of Bebe's child along with her own children when Bebe got high on drugs and Bebe began almost terrorizing Elaine and her children and this eventually accelerated into Bebe beating Elaine physically and abusing Elaine's children almost daily. The beatings got worse but Elaine was afraid to call the police because she felt even if Bebe was jailed, when she got out of jail, Elaine would suffer worse beatings. Finally, last Friday, Bebe beat Elaine with a wooden chair, and Elaine tried to defend herself with a knife. Elaine didn't stab Bebe but did manage to get her children and leave. A community service worker referred Elaine to the shelter and to mental health services. Elaine states the apartment where she lives with Bebe is in Elaine's name and her furniture is still there but she is too afraid to go back. Currently, her plans are to stay at the shelter until she can get a new place, enroll her children in the school nearby and friends will provide her with furniture once she gets a new place. She is clear that she is not going back to Bebe and wants to start her life over. Since counseling helped her in the past, she is very anxious to start again. One issue she wants to have resolved is whether she is gay or straight and she feels very confused about this. She supports herself currently with welfare and all of her family and friends are in Oakland.

Plan

- Cut off all utilities in her old apartment with Bebe because they are in Elaine's name
- Inform the landlady that she has moved out
- Go to legal aid for legal advice about the above in case she needs it
- Stay at the shelter with her children for now
- Call our 24-hr emergency number if needed
- Appointment for intake for outpatient counseling was set
- Return in the meantime to see the crisis clinic social worker for support

NOTE: "Bebe" is the nickname for Lettie [Case 10] who came in for help a week later.

Case #10 (Christina Newhill)

This Case Demonstrates

- How intimate partner violence can occur in same-sex relationships with similar dynamics to such violence in heterosexual relationships;
- How each partner in an abusive relationship may describe the violence differently (see Case 9), for example, each describing the other as the controlling partner;
- How an abused partner will stay due to loving the abuser and her children.

Initial Contact and Presenting Problem

Lettie is a 26 year old single black female referred to county mental health services by the Women's Center. For the past 3 years, Lettie has been involved in a live-in gay relationship with a woman named Elaine (see Case 9). Approximately a week ago, Elaine left Lettie and, with her two children, Elaine went to the Battered Women's Shelter asking for placement there, claiming that Lettie had beaten her and was threatening her, adding that she—Elaine—was planning to permanently sever the relationship and wanted to "start a new life". Lettie states that she has been devastated by Elaine's leaving and relates a description of their relationship quite different from what Elaine related to me when I saw her earlier in the week. Essentially, Elaine describes Lettie as the villain and she as the victim and Lettie describes Elaine as the villain and she as the victim—the actual events and problems described are approximately the same but the roles of the actors are reversed. Lettie has one child—a 6 year old boy—and Elaine has two children. Lettie states she has been gay for 13 years but her relationship with Elaine is the longest and most committed relationship she has had with a woman. They moved all over the Bay area and Oakland before finally settling in Sacramento. Lettie feels she has sacrificed for Elaine—giving up jobs (Lettie is a certified welder) and so forth—to follow her but feels Elaine has not appreciated this. She states that throughout their relationship Elaine has abused her—both physically and emotionally. Lettie states that Elaine has a bad temper, gets easily insulted and seems to try to provoke Lettie into physical fights. When questioned about who starts the fights, Lettie admitted that both of them seem to mutually provoke each other. Elaine also lies about her to others—for example, Lettie states that Elaine has told others that Lettie uses drugs but Lettie denies any drug use except for an occasional beer—Lettie claims she has been the one who has primarily cared for the children—both hers and Elaine's—but Elaine claims the opposite. Lettie states that Elaine has punched holes in the walls of the apartment and currently is arguing with the landlady about paying for the damages. Why has Lettie stayed all this time? She says she has stayed because she loves Elaine and her children. But now she doesn't know what to do—she states she feels worse now than she has ever felt in her life. Last night she felt like killing herself (Elaine had left a loaded gun in the house) but she controlled herself because of her little boy. Currently, she says she is in control but has planned to stay in a motel tonight to avoid any temptation to harm herself. She was managing fairly well, but Elaine called her last night and began complaining about all their problems and this set Lettie off into a deep depression. She states she has no history of any suicide attempts, or even ideation. At this point she is planning to stay in Sacramento but wants very much to get involved in some counseling to get her life sorted out and figure out what she is going to do at this point.

Lettie's family is all in the San Francisco Bay Area. She describes herself as basically a loner and says she really has no friends locally in Sacramento—also that Elaine has turned their neighbors against Lettie and "her talk" has eliminated the possibility for friends she might have had.

Case #11 (Allison Little)

McDowell family, White American
Daughter Lena, age 3
Mother Jane, age 27
Father Jason, age 30
Maternal Grandparents George and Ellen, age 60

This Case Demonstrates

- Victim parents may exhibit a genuine wish to leave their situation, but then change their mind. This may be out of fear, loyalty to the abuser, loneliness, or the experience of manipulation or intimidation.
- When children are involved in abusive situations, social services may mandate that a parent leave with the child or children and may remove the child or children if the parent cannot or will not do so.
- Parents may hide the status of the relationship with the abuser out of fear of losing their children.

The McDowell family have been known to social services for reports of domestic violence. Jane and Jason have one daughter together, though Jason has two sons who live with two other former partners in other towns, both of which who have occasional contact. Jane came into the office in August with bruising about her eyes, in tears, and explained that Jason had been hitting her again. The case had been opened and closed twice because there was no visible injury, Lena was too young to be interviewed, and the MGPs (maternal grandparents) agreed to spend more time with Jane and Lena. A safety plan was devised with Jane that she would obtain a restraining order and not make contact with Jason. Failure to do so would result in Lena's removal from Jane's care. Jane agrees, and Jason is required to leave the home. Jason is the sole earner, so a one-time emergency TANF (Temporary Assistance to Needy Families) payment was secured to pay rent, as well as money toward a title loan that Jason had taken out. Jason is a long distance delivery driver, so he is out of town for over a week at a time. Supervised visits are set up with SW attending twice per week. Jane is asked to work with local victims services, but does not want to. The case continues without incident for a month, at which point an anonymous relative calls to say Jane and Lena have disappeared. After contacting the transport company, Jason's truck is located on an interstate in the North Texas Panhandle. SW contacts the local sheriff's department and asks that the truck be pulled over and, if Jane and Lena are present, that Lena be taken into immediate protective custody to give time for SW's agency to file a petition. Jane and Lena are found on the truck, Lena is unharmed but Jane is badly injured. She has been beaten to the point of bruising and later reports sexual assault and experiencing a seizure from being struck in the head. Jason abandons the truck and disappears into a farm field. SW files a petition and is granted custody of Lena. The agency pays for two social workers to fly out and retrieve Jane and Lena. Despite Jane's and the Maternal Grandparents' request to place Lena with her MGPs, Lena is placed in agency foster care for safety. Jane reports that she had taken Lena to see Jason one night, and he forced them to stay until the next morning when he told them to get in his truck. Lena is distraught at the removal from her mother. Jason returns home and is immediately arrested by the local sheriff's department. He is unrepentant, and proudly reports that they had attended church together every Sunday and that Jane begged him to take the truck to Mexico so they could disappear together. Jason is eventually arraigned on charges including kidnapping, sexual assault, as well as damages and charges from his employer and is imprisoned. Contacts to his older sons and their mothers are met with denials that any violence ever took place. Lena is eventually reunited with her mother after 6 months in care.

Case #12 (Allison Little)

Zacapa family, Guatemalan immigrants to the U.S.
Mother: Itzel, age 24
Father: Felipe, age 29
Son: Francisco, age 6 months

This Case Demonstrates

- Lack of fluency in the dominant language can leave the victim adult isolated and vulnerable to maltreatment.
- Violence perpetrated by one adult against another in a family does not always mean that children are being physically abused. However, children remain at significant risk both because of the emotional harm of witnessing physical violence and the risk of accidental physical harm should they get caught between the adults. Older children may try to intervene, increasing the risk of harm.
- Emotional coercion and threats by the abuser, with or without physical violence, may be used to force the victim into sex.
- An initial disclosure may occur shortly after the violence has most recently occurred, when the victim is afraid and angry. However, the victim may retract because of coercion by the abuser and/or their extended family, fear of losing the abuser's financial and emotional support, or fear of child welfare involvement.

Itzel and Felipe migrated to the U.S. for work 3 years ago. Itzel did office cleaning before she was pregnant with Francisco. Felipe used to do itinerant agricultural work, but took full-time employment in a restaurant kitchen when Itzel became pregnant. Felipe speaks English well enough to communicate and take care of day to day needs, whereas Itzel cannot speak, write, or understand English at all. Because of this, Felipe has full control of the family's shared checking account and makes all of the family's business decisions. The family became known to social services when a downstairs neighbor called to say that there is often shouting and banging around upstairs, often accompanied by Francisco crying. When the family were interviewed, Itzel had a visible bruise on her neck and cheek. Felipe denied that he has ever been physically violent, and stated Itzel's injury was from a fall in which she hit her face on the coffee table. Felipe also states that Itzel doesn't want to take care of the finances and isn't interested in taking English classes. Itzel claimed in her interview that Felipe has become increasingly angry due to a combination of financial stress and changes in their relationship since Francisco was born. Itzel states Felipe has always had a temper, but he didn't start hitting her until after Francisco was born. He has also told Itzel that, despite their small income, she cannot work. This is even despite the fact that Itzel has a Spanish-speaking friend who would keep Francisco for her in exchange for errands around the house. Itzel states also that she knows Felipe has been seeing other women, he often stays out late and either comes home drunk, or not at all. Felipe has become upset about their decreasing sex life, and says that he takes care of Itzel and Francisco so she owes him. Itzel denies she has ever been physically forced to have sex, but states that Felipe will get very angry and threaten to withhold money. Itzel also states that Felipe will not allow her to take free English classes, because he says she will start meeting men behind his back. Felipe is a doting father to Francisco and has not done anything to hurt him, though he will yell at Itzel and hit her even if she is holding Francisco. Felipe was soon asked to leave the home for the duration of the investigation. When Itzel found out, she immediately recanted everything she had said, stated she did get a bruise from a fall, and that she was just so angry at Felipe for infidelity that she wanted to scare him. Itzel was advised that if she allows Felipe to move back in before services can be secured, that Francisco will be removed. The family were referred to intensive in-home services provided by a Spanish language family support agency.

Case #13 (Allison Little)

Jackson family, White American
Mother: Andrea, age 39
Father/Stepfather: George, age 41
Daughter: Caitlyn, age 15
Daughter: Telly, age 18 mos.
Son: George Jr., age 18 mos.

This Case Demonstrates

- Relationship violence between adults in a family can be difficult to assess because of conflicting accounts by the involved parties.
- Children may be fearful of getting adults in their family in trouble or may fear repercussion from other family members if they disclose having seen violence. Adults may make an effort to hide violence from their children.
- A victim of violence may call for help with genuine concern for their own and their children's well-being, but may recant these statements out of fear of losing the financial and other support provided by the abuser. Children may also be pressured to recant.
- A thorough safety assessment by multiple professionals is necessary to work with the victim parent in making a decision about staying in a relationship.

The Jackson family recently moved to a new city. Andrea called the police the night that they moved in to their rental home, alleging that George was hitting her. A check with the family's previous county of residence found two child welfare reports of fighting between the adults, though both times were unclear as to who began the fight and what actually happened. Both reports were closed because there had been no evidence of physical fighting. When interviewed, Andrea alleged that George was upset about Caitlyn's behavior. Caitlyn has begun to engage in self-cutting, which Andrea is concerned about but feels, from her own negative experiences with therapy, that it is best to ignore the behavior rather than reward it with attention by going to therapy. George is angry about this, as he and Andrea have young twins who are exposed to Caitlyn's behavior. Caitlyn's father lives out of state, and they have very little contact. An argument about Caitlyn's behavior began when George said she needs to get therapy, or go live with her dad, and Andrea took offense to this. The argument escalated to dishes being thrown, at which point

Andrea called the police. George admitted he threw a plate, but was not aiming for Andrea. He also noted that all of the children were in bed, and thus did not see anything. Caitlyn stated in her interview that she has heard them yelling at each other, but has never seen anyone hitting. Caitlyn said she hated George, but not because of the arguments, rather because she felt he wanted her to move away so Andrea would pay all her attention to him and the twins. George was asked to leave, and Andrea agreed to keep him away from the home until the investigation was completed. However, an unannounced visit found that George was back in the home. When asked why she allowed him to return, Andrea said they cannot live without George's salary, and that the plate-throwing fight had been a misunderstanding. Andrea and George insisted they would stay together. Despite social services' concern, the courts did not find enough risk to justify removing the children if George refused to leave. Intensive in-home services were provided to the family.

Case #14 (Christina Newhill)

This Case Demonstrates

- How sexual abuse, even abuse that is long-lasting and cuts across many victims, can be kept "secret" in the family for an extensive period of time;
- How if just one of several victims reports the abuse, the abuse will stop and all those victimized in the family can access help and the perpetrators punished and provided with help;
- The extensive trauma that sexual abuse causes;
- How victims within a family can serve as social support for each other.

Initial Contact and Presenting Problem

Janet is a 25 year-old white female who came to the crisis clinic, at the referral of a local judge, for an appointment with an outpatient therapist for counseling. Janet is married, has a 4 year old daughter and is currently pregnant. Janet revealed that she and her three sisters have a history of extensive sexual abuse from their biological father occurring over the course of many years. The abuse was a well-kept family secret until the oldest sister left home; she then confided in Janet and her twin sister Becky about her own abuse and then they admitted that they had also been abused by their father. The oldest sister Katie, was abused from age 8 on, with her father forcing her to have intercourse with him 3–4 times a week. Janet states she was fondled but never had sexual intercourse with her father, although Becky did. The lid was blown off the whole thing when the youngest sister Edie, now 15 years old, was approached by her father for intercourse after he had insisted on taking nude photos of her. Edie then rode her bike over to the judge's home (the judge is a long-time family friend) and told her about what was going on. The judge was furious, called child protective services, and insisted that Edie be removed from the home.

Edie is now living with Janet. The father was arrested and taken to the police station, however the older sisters could not press charges because their abuse occurred too long ago. Edie's mother insisted that Edie forgive her father which infuriated Edie and she no longer wants to go home to her mother even though the father is now living in a different town while the criminal case is working its way through the court. Currently, both parents are attending an incest perpetrators group. Janet and Edie wish to obtain counseling together because Edie is afraid to come without her sister present because she would like to deny the whole thing, yet at the same time, knows she needs help. Janet is, for the first time, feeling truly enraged and feels she and her sister both need help- the older sisters are living elsewhere. I contacted one of our clinical psychologists who specializes in treating victims of sexual abuse and she agreed to see both sisters next Friday. Both sisters are also interested in attending our incest survivors group.

Case #15 (Christina Newhill)

This Case Demonstrates

- How incest between a biological father and daughter can be sustained over many years, even producing two children, and occur with the daughter's mother's full knowledge but no efforts at intervening to stop it;
- How incest can adversely affect both the victim and the victim's child borne from the incestuous relationship;
- How knowing that one is the product of incest can be significantly traumatic for a child and can complicate existing behavior problems.

Initial Contact and Presenting Problem

Peter is a 12 year-old boy who was the victim of an attempted sexual assault involving two other boys who tried to force the victim into oral copulation. Peter was examined by a physician at the county hospital emergency room and released with a referral to county mental health services for evaluation. Upon evaluation Peter is alert, cooperative, and somewhat philosophical about the event although he states he has been harassed by other boys over the same thing but this is the first time actual attempted assault has occurred. He attributes this to the fact that he is the smallest kid in his class and some of the other boys taunt him as being "gay". Although Peter seems to have come through the incident without too much trauma, he should be observed over the next couple days for any further signs of trauma reaction, depression or anxiety. We recommend consultation with County Mental Health Children's Services.

Information from Children's Services Consultation

Peter's mother, Gloria Smith, describes Peter as basically uncontrollable: he becomes violent, angry, and has hit his mother on several occasions. In the past, Peter has run away and has gotten into fights at school; subsequently, he was put into a special education program. Peter is described as a bright child that now gets good grades, however, has been in special education programs since the third grade. What seems to have precipitated Mrs. Smith to bring in her son was the incident of attempted sexual assault, as described above, but also another traumatic incident that occurred approximately 3 weeks ago. Peter's biological father, who is also Mrs. Smith's biological father, had been drinking and shared the secret that he is Peter's real father. Peter began to scream at his father and, since this revelation, has been angry at his mother and has voiced how much he hates her, stating that he wishes he was dead.

Mrs. Smith reported that her father had made sexual advances for several years with her mother's full knowledge, adding that her mother accused her of lying when she asked for help. She admitted that during her pregnancy that she became very depressed and was contemplating having an abortion or giving the child up for adoption and that it took her a long time to develop an attachment to Peter as a baby. Peter's early years were normal and he had a good kindergarten year, however, he began to demonstrate behavior problems in first grade and, in third grade, was placed in special education. Mrs. Smith reports that the incest with her father occurred for many years before her pregnancy and continued for many years after Peter's birth, in fact, she has another child, age nine, who is also fathered by her biological father. The incestuous relationship did not stop until Mrs. Smith ran away from home and got married to the first man who asked her. She describes her husband as being a kind man with her children and they have formed a close relationship with him. She reported that she has had two "nervous breakdowns" and subsequently received therapy for herself as well as for her son.

Disposition: Peter will be seen in individual therapy as well as in sessions with his mother to work on their relationship. The primary issue at this time is to help Bruce to cope better with his feelings surrounding the disclosure of the identity of his biological father.

Case #16 (Christina Newhill)

This Case Demonstrates

- How a referral to Child Protective Services can be perceived as a positive mechanism for obtaining help
- How past abuse as a child can lead to an adult engaging in abusive behavior as a result of post-traumatic stress and depression
- How drug use can play a role in exacerbating psychosocial stress

Initial Contact and Presenting Problem

Karen, a 28 year old married white female with three children, came to the crisis clinic asking to see a counselor. Upon evaluation, Karen began to cry stating that she feels completely overwhelmed and doesn't know what to do. Karen's three children include Tevine, aged 8; Casey aged 7; and Mikey aged 4½. Karen's husband, Andy, works for a chemical company and was recently transferred from the town where they were living to a much smaller town. Karen was quite happy living in their former neighborhood because she had friends and family there, but hates living in the current town because she is very isolated, is stuck in the house all day with the kids (her husband uses their only car for work) and it is getting to her to the point she yells and screams at the kids "all the time". Karen states that her children "act like brats" and recently she hit Casey so hard she was afraid she broke his arm. The crisis clinic social worker advised Karen that she is obligated to make a report to CPS (Child Protective Services), but Karen didn't seem bothered by that, stating she would actually like to have a CPS social worker come out to her house and help her learn how to handle the kids better.

Karen indicates that she had a complete hysterectomy 3 years ago and was told she must take hormones but she has not filled her prescription because she can't afford it. As a result, she has chronic severe hot flashes and mood swings. She has decided to go back to her family doctor and get the hormones and has an appointment to see the doctor today. The crisis clinic social worker spoke with her husband Andy, who seems to understand what is going on but admits when he comes home at night he doesn't respond to her needs like he should because he wants his own needs met. Both Karen and Andy are very amenable to the idea of counseling.

Disposition

- Keep appointment with medical doctor for a new prescription for hormones
- Outpatient intake appointment set for tomorrow at 1:00 pm for Karen

Complicating Factors Revealed from Intake Evaluation

During the intake evaluation, Karen revealed additional information that provided more depth to understanding her difficulties managing her children and her depressed feelings. Recently, Karen has been experiencing flashbacks of incidents when she was sexually abused as a child by three male relatives. These flashbacks have caused her considerable distress. In addition, Karen said that controlling her weight has been a long-time issue for her and she has used amphetamines to keep her weight under control and this contributes to her mood swings, especially irritability with her children. The outpatient therapist referred Karen to the AMAC (Adults Molested as Children) group for targeted group therapy and to Weight Watchers to learn healthier ways of managing her weight.

Karen has been experiencing a number of psychosocial stressors during the past year. It is difficult to determine whether her depressive symptoms are related to these stresses, underlying dysthymic disorder, or chronic post traumatic stress disorder. The question of whether her use of street drugs to obtain energy has been a means of self-medication needs to be explored. It is also unclear as to the reason why she is experiencing flashbacks regarding her sexual abuse now and suspect that there are other precipitants which she has failed to reveal during the initial intake. The major problems at the present time appear to be her depressive symptomatology, unresolved feelings regarding her sexual abuse as a child, and impaired coping skills including hitting her child.

Intake Evaluation Short Term Goals Include

1. Positively engage and establish a therapeutic relationship.
2. Obtain additional information for diagnostic clarification.
3. Monitor of depressive symptomology.
4. Group preparation for joing the AMAC group.

Focus of Therapy Will be Directed Towards

1. Helping her understand the relationship between psychosocial stressors and depressive symptomology.
2. Explore alternative means of coping with stresses to help avoid hitting her children.
3. Understanding and working through her feelings of guilt, responsibility, and depression about her molest.
4. Working through feelings about her negative self-image, sexual identity and relationships with the opposite sex with subsequent enhancement of self-esteem.

Case #17 (Christina Newhill)

This Case Demonstrates

- Extreme neglect and abuse of a child to the point that death was imminent;
- How one child may be singled out for abuse and neglect while other children in the home are adequately cared for;
- That parents do not automatically love all of their children, in fact, a child may be actually disliked by parents and other family members with negative consequences for the child;
- The importance of "see something, tell someone", in which a neighbor's observation of the abused and neglected child's condition led to getting him help and saving his life;
- The complex nature of severe abuse and neglect and the consequences for a child's health.

For years, a 7-year-old boy was beaten, starved and neglected by his mother and grandparents. The child was only allowed to eat small amounts of tuna and eggs and resorted to eating insects to stay alive. If he tried to get other food, the three adults would beat him with a belt or force him to take cold showers. Although he was confined to his home, with neighbors not even knowing he existed, 1 day he managed to escape and was seen by a neighbor who was walking her dog. The neighbor described him as looking like a "human skeleton", as he weighed only 25 pounds and was only days away from death. The neighbor called police who called child protective services. The child was taken to the hospital and his mother and grandparents were arrested on multiple charges of child abuse and neglect including unlawful restraint of a minor, aggravated assault, child endangerment, medical neglect, false imprisonment and criminal conspiracy.

The boy's three siblings—one brother and two sisters—appeared to not have been abused and were all healthy, although they were also removed from the home by child protective services to ensure their safety. The motive for the victim's abuse, according to the investigating detective, appeared to be that the adult family members simply did not like him. One year ago, the mother removed him from school to homeschool him, although it was unclear if any schooling actually occurred.

One of the doctors from the local children's hospital said this was the worst case of childhood starvation, abuse and neglect that she had ever seen and the best medicine for him was providing him with kindness and nutritious food. During hospitalization, the boy gained 24 pounds and, when released, was placed in foster care. The child's mother and grandparents remain in jail awaiting trial.

Sources

1. "Police charge mom, grandparents of starving beaten child who ate insects to survive". (July 19, 2014). *Pittsburgh Post-Gazette*. Retrieved June 12, 2015 at: http://pittsburgh.cbslocal.com/2014/07/19/police-charge-mom-grandparents-of-starving-beaten-child-who-ate-insects-to-survive/
2. Jackson, C. (July 22, 2014). Starving child ate insects to stay alive. *Pittsburgh Post-Gazette*. Retrieved June 12, 2015 at: http://guardianlv.com/2014/07/starving-child-ate-insects-to-stay-alive-video/

Case #18 (Rachel Fusco)

Family: Allan
Parent(s): Dave (age 28) and Julie (age 33)
Target child: Shannon (age 13)
Other children in household: Layla (age10)

This Case Demonstrates

- Some families normalize incest and see it as a way to teach children about sex
- Youth who experience sexual abuse sometime perpetrate abuse against younger children.
- A sexual abuse history may contribute to aggressive or destructive behaviors in youth.

13 year old Shannon was referred to Child Protective Services by her teacher after put her hands inside the front of an 8 year-old boy's pants and rubbed herself against him at a school assembly. During a meeting with Shannon's parents, her stepfather Dave reported that he has fondled her breasts and has purchased lingerie that he expected her to model for him. He also watched online pornography with Shannon. Dave did not think these behaviors were a problem, and stated: "I am the only father she has and the only man she has in her life so it is my job to teach her how to be a woman." Shannon's mother, Julie, agreed with this behavior and shared that her own father treated her and her sisters the same way. Julie and Dave viewed the response toward Shannon touching the younger boy and the investigation as an overreaction. Neither had any interest in attending parenting classes and repeatedly said this was all a 'private family matter'. There was no evidence that 10 year old Layla had experienced any abuse and while it was thought that she was at high risk for future perpetration a case could not be opened for her.

It was determined to be unsafe for Shannon to remain in her home since her parents believed their actions were appropriate. Since sexual abuse was prevalent in her extended family, kinship care options were not explored. It emerged that Shannon had a history of sexually acting out with younger boys so she was placed in Multidimensional Treatment Foster Care. After an incident where she slapped her foster mother, Shannon was transferred to a Residential Treatment Facility (RTF) where she received individual and group therapy. Her parents were encouraged to participate in family therapy with a future goal of reunification but they only attended one session. Shannon spent 15 months in the RTF but after running away and setting a small fire in a common room she was transferred to a juvenile detention center. She was eventually returned to her mother's care after Dave was arrested and sentenced to 5 years in prison for a drug-related charge.

Case #19 (Rachel Fusco)

Family: Campos
Parent(s): Rodrigo (age 32) and Ofelia (age 27)
Target child: Miranda (age 12)
Other children in household: Oscar (age 11) and Frieda (age 10)

This Case Demonstrates

- Sometimes one child in the household is the target of the abuse.
- Sexual abuse can be linked with ongoing mental health problems such as self-injurious behavior.
- Children removed from their homes may end up placed in more restrictive settings if their initial problems are not adequately addressed.

The Campos family emigrated from Mexico 5 years ago to find better job opportunities. Rodrigo speaks English well but Ofelia does not. Rodrigo works full time but Ofelia stays home as she has ongoing health complications from lupus. The family was reported to Children's Protective Services by the family doctor after he discovered that Miranda was 6 months pregnant. Miranda reported that Rodrigo has been fondling her since she was 8 years old and he started having intercourse with her about a year ago. She stated that Rodrigo is the father of her baby. Ofelia denied that this could be true but said "if it is, it is Miranda's fault". Criminal charges were filed against Rodrigo but he fled back to Mexico. Ofelia said she wanted nothing more to do with her daughter and did not want her to return to their home. She was very upset that her husband left and blamed Miranda for all of her troubles. Oscar and Frieda claimed to be unaware of the abuse that occurred in their household.

Miranda was placed in foster care until her baby was born. The baby was adopted from birth and Miranda went to live with her aunt. She was referred to individual and group counselling but her aunt failed to get her to her appointments. Miranda began engaging in self-injurious behavior and started drinking heavily. Her aunt did not feel she could handle the care of Miranda any longer and she was sent to a residential treatment facility.

Case #20 (Rachel Fusco)

Family: Reynolds
Parent(s): Alison (age 29)
Target child: Eve (age 8)
Other children in household: None

This Case Demonstrates

- Emotional abuse often co-occurs with physical abuse.
- People with their own childhood abuse history may struggle with appropriate parenting.
- Children with a history of early maltreatment may develop emotional and behavioral problems.

The Reynolds family was referred to Child Protective Services by Eve's second grade teacher. The teacher reported that Eve wore a long sleeve shirt on a very hot day, and when she was encouraged to push her sleeves up, bruises were revealed up and down both of Eve's arms. Eve also has a very explosive temper and has been very aggressive toward other children. Alison reports that she is often rough with Eve, and grabs her, spanks her, and shakes her frequently. She admits that she is easily angered and says she has trouble dealing with Eve sometimes. Alison grew up in foster care and aged out of the system with no family support. She said that she lived in four different homes between the ages of 8 and 18, and never felt that any of the providers really cared about her. Alison reports that Eve's father was the first person who ever loved her, but her left when Eve was an infant. Allison says that they would still be together if it wasn't for Eve because he wanted her to get an abortion. She often tells Eve that her father is not around because he never wanted children. Alison also says that she had a tough time coping when Eve was a baby, and she would occasionally leave the child at home on her own for hours during the day.

Alison and Eve were referred to Parent Child Interaction Therapy (PCIT) to improve Alison's parenting skills, decrease Eve's behavioral problems, and develop their attachment bond. Intensive in-home services were also provided.

Case #21 (Rachel Fusco)

Family: Wilson
Parent(s): Jim (age 40) and Diane (age 36)
Target child: Daniel (age 6)
Other children in household: Alice (age 15), Ellen (age 12), Freddie (age 10), and Greg (age 8)

This Case Demonstrates

- Challenges when a family's religious beliefs are not in line with what is believed to be a child's best interests.
- The complexity of some medical neglect cases.
- The role that the legal system must play in cases when a child is not old enough to make their own decisions.

Six year old Daniel was diagnosed with acute lymphoblastic leukemia (ALL). Although ALL had a survival rate of about 85% with chemotherapy, his parents refused to take him for treatment. Jim and Diane were Christian Scientists who did not believe in using medicine and wanted to rely on spiritual healing through prayer. Daniel's life was believed to be in grave danger from infection without treatment so an emergency removal order was issued. However, Jim and Diane hid Daniel outside their home and he could not be located by Child Protection workers. In the meantime they hired a lawyer to file a lawsuit against the county, stating that their freedom of religion was being violated. The case was rushed through the system and the courts sided with the county, since the minor child could not make his own decision about whether or not he wanted treatment. Jim and Diane were threatened with arrest if they did not turn over Daniel to authorities. They finally conceded although they claimed that their prayers were working to heal him. Daniel was retrieved from the home of church members and he presented as very medically frail. He was transferred to a foster care home with a woman who had medical training, and he started chemotherapy 2 days later. He received 3 months of intensive treatment and was prescribed a daily mediation to be taken for 2 years as maintenance. He also needed to attend hospital appointments every 6 weeks for 2 years to receive intravenous medication.

His parents visited him frequently throughout his chemotherapy treatment. They agreed to give him his maintenance drugs and take him to his appointments, so he was allowed to return home. After a year of regularly taking Daniel to appointments and giving him his oral medication, the case was closed.

Case #22 (Christina Newhill)

This Case Demonstrates

- How violence can be an ongoing and pervasive element across relationships amongst multiple members in a family;
- The role of recreational drug use in elevating risk for abusive aggressive interactions among family members;
- The role of the police in intervening when violence occurs, identifying the current primary perpetrator or instigator of the violence, removing that individual from the family situation to prevent further violence from occurring, and applying for mental health care;
- Resistance to help and denial of responsibility on the part of the perpetrator and other family members.

Initial Contact and Presenting Problem

Mark is a 19 year old unemployed single white male brought to the psychiatric health facility inpatient unit for evaluation by the local city police. Mark has a history of phencyclidine (PCP) use and was released from jail only 4 days ago after an 8 day stay on charges of “driving under the influence”—he goes to court next week. Tonight Mark got into an argument with his stepfather and his mother (all three had been drinking since early afternoon), Mark pulled a knife and threatened to kill them and when police arrived, he had already cut himself and was threatening to kill himself, stating he has nothing to live for. Upon evaluation Mark is extremely agitated and labile, so the police were asked to stand by during the mental health evaluation. Mark was subsequently hospitalized on the basis of danger to self and others.

Follow Up Family Meeting

One week later, after Mark was sufficiently detoxed from the PCP and alcohol, a meeting was convened with Mark, his stepfather and his mother. When confronted about the incident with the knife, Mark denied he intended to hurt anyone, i.e. "I was just messing around". This precipitated an argument amongst the three family members, escalating to the point that the stepfather was asked to step out in the hallway while the social worker attempted to intervene with Mark and his mother. Mother states that her husband hits her but then admitted that she has thrown hot coffee at him and once hit him over the head with a frying pan. Mark states both of his parents have threatened him and it seems like alcohol plays a major role in the numerous incidents of violence that have occurred. Mark says he uses drugs and "sometimes does stuff" because he is frustrated over not having a job; mother says she drinks because Mark won't get a job and she gets frustrated. The stepfather, once he rejoined the conversation, blames both his wife and Mark for his violence "if they'd shape up, I wouldn't have to smack them". None of the family members is interested in getting counseling, and blame each other for all their troubles.

Case #23 (Christina Newhill)

This Case Demonstrates

- How the police are often called in domestic violence situations, including sibling to sibling violence, because they are the only 24-h free service with legal power that many families know about;
- How long-standing sibling conflict can lead to violence and suicidal behavior, particularly if parents do not intervene constructively;
- How the initial instigator of a violent episode isn't necessarily the individual who ultimately suffers the consequences, such as incarceration or being pushed out of a living situation;
- How parental responses may serve to escalate rather than help mitigate a conflict situation between siblings.

Stephanie is a 17 year old single African-American female brought to the crisis clinic by the police, accompanied by her mother. Mother called the police because Stephanie and her sister, Mary, were fighting. The police state they heard Stephanie threaten to kill Mary and cut off her legs. Stephanie claims that her sister attacked her with an asparagus knife and in defense, Stephanie threatened to kill Mary. Mother states both sisters threatened each other with Stephanie's sister making the first threat and then the mother threatened to hit both sisters with a lead pipe. The altercation occurred after Mary taunted Stephanie about not graduating high school, and called Stephanie a whore and other derogatory names. Stephanie calmed downed considerably in the crisis clinic social worker's office, telling the social worker that her sister always says mean things to her, mother doesn't understand her and the only person nice to her is her boyfriend. The conflict with her sister has been so upsetting to Stephanie that she has overdosed on aspirin three times during the past month. She denies any suicidal feelings at this time, and denies wanting to hurt sister now but her mother wants her out of the house. There is no evidence of mental disorder, just a long standing hostile relationship with her sister. Currently, Stephanie is living with her mother, stepfather and sisters and is looking for work. Stephanie's sister has pressed charges against her for assault, therefore, police transported Stephanie to juvenile hall.

Case #24 (Christina Newhill)

This Case Demonstrates

- How violence and aggression can be directed by an adult child toward a parent;
- An individual with an antisocial personality initiating a request for help;
- The types of intervention appropriate for a person with anger issues;
- The importance of "environmental manipulation", in this case, recommending the aggressor not live with the targeted victim.

Initial Contact and Presenting Problem

Jack is a 39 year old single white male referred to the crisis clinic by the emergency room at the county general hospital. He initially came to the hospital emergency room this afternoon requesting help for his violent temper. The patient presents with the statement "I need help with my temper." He also stated "I'm not very sociable. I become hostile. For years I've been losing my temper pretty bad." Jack has a history of incarceration in Juvenile Hall as a youth and CYA (California Youth Authority) commitment along with eight arrests as an adult (all in the last 2 years) including assault and battery, and receipt of stolen property.

Up until 2 years ago, Jack was running a dump truck business with some partners but claims they did some "dirty business deals" and got him implicated for misuse of funds, even though—according to him—he was innocent of any wrong doing. Jack ended up having to go to court; he avoided the potential legal problems, but lost the business and blames the local police for this. Since that time, he has had various jobs but nothing permanent has worked out. Now, Jack is unemployed and, because of lack of financial resources, is having to live with his mother. He states evenly that he hates his mother and would never live with her under any other circumstances but desperation drove him to ask her if he could live with her. He claims that his mother nags him constantly and brings up the past which aggravates him to the point he will explode and strike out at her aggressively—either verbally or physically. A few days ago he got so angry that he hit her with a shovel and came very close to killing her—he has also pulled her hair out and hit her. He states he has no homicidal feelings towards her in general- only when she pushes him "over the limit". The crisis clinic social worker strongly advised Jack to get out of that living situation but he says he has no use for people and as a result has burned all his bridges as far as other friends or relatives are concerned. He requested both "nerve medicine" and counseling—the crisis social worker advised him that medication issues could be discussed at an outpatient counseling intake appointment but doubted that would be appropriate for his problems. Jack does not seem to be a good candidate for insight oriented psychotherapy but he might benefit from a good confrontive group or a few sessions of good directive therapy. It is likely that Jack will control his temper and aggression only if he sees the consequence of his actions are sufficiently noxious. Diagnostic impression: Antisocial Personality Disorder.

Disposition

1. Appointment set for an outpatient counseling intake evaluation;
2. Short term goals include: (1) no medication; (2) Supportive therapy for reality control of behavior and safe ventilation of his anger;
3. Long term goals include the possibility of group therapy and of relocating away from his mother. Jack will be provided with directive help and introduction of healthier alternatives to expression of anger and acceptance of others in an attempt to become more sociable.

Case #25 (Christina Newhill)

This Case Demonstrates

- The vulnerability of elderly individuals who live alone.
- The importance of having someone who will regularly check in on such vulnerable older adults to make sure they are okay;
- Hoarding and medical self-neglect due to dementia and untreated type II diabetes;
- How neglect can take many forms, in this case, an adult child who paid little to no attention to his parent's health and well-being, allowing his parent's ill health to reach a crisis point;
- The role of the police in serving as first-line responders in checking on the well-being of elderly individuals living alone.

Initial Contact and Presenting Problem

Mrs. Jones is an 85-year-old widowed white woman who lived alone in her home in a neighborhood on the edge of the center of the city. She had lived in her present residence for 35 years with her husband and was widowed 5 years ago. She has three grown children, two of whom lived on the other side of the country and a son who lives in an adjacent county. Neighbors reported that she had little contact with any of her adult children. Mrs. Jones used to have occasional visitors and neighbors would see her go outside to retrieve her mail and sometimes take a walk around the block. Mrs. Jones's next door neighbor, however, realized that she had not seen Mrs. Jones for quite some time and so decided to check on her. When Mrs. Jones didn't answer the door, the neighbor called the police, asking them if they could come out and check on her. Police officers came out and, again, nobody answered the door but police smelled bad odors emitting under the door, were concerned about what might be going on and so forced the door open. When they saw the inside of the house, they called social workers affiliated with the local community mental health center to come out and meet them at the house. This is what the social worker and police officers saw: Inside the house papers and other debris were piled from the floor to the ceiling, filling the large entry hallway and living room. A small path had been formed from the door to the middle of the living room and at the end of the path was a small empty circle and in the middle of the circle, Mrs. Jones sat in a chair. Empty containers of canned goods were next to her along with a camp stove. When the social worker approached Mrs. Jones to introduce herself, Mrs. Jones stared at the social worker and then tried to speak but her words were barely audible and she seemed confused. She clearly had not bathed in a long time and open running sores could be seen on her swollen legs. Cockroaches and mouse droppings were visible everywhere. The social worker asked the police to call the paramedics who then transported Mrs. Jones to the nearest emergency room for evaluation. The social worker followed and discussed Mrs. Jones's situation with the emergency room doctor following examination. The doctor indicated that Mrs. Jones seemed to have advanced dementia, her body was ravaged by untreated Type II diabetes and her condition reflected severe neglect. The son who lived nearby was contacted and he admitted that he hadn't paid much attention to what was going on with his mother. The social worker insisted that he come to the hospital immediately, as certain decisions needed to be made about his mother's care. Reluctantly, he agreed, and arrived at the hospital an hour later. At this point, Mrs. Jones was referred to Aging Services for follow-up.

Case #26 (Allison Little)

Martin family, African American
Mother: Eleanor, age 41
Son: Samuel, age 15
Son: Jonas, age 12
Son: Elias, age 9

This Case Demonstrates

- Domestic violence between parents and teenage or young adult children may be the result of a sustained culture of violence in the family. Teenagers who physically fight with their parents sometimes report having received excessive discipline as a child.
- Substance abuse by both adults and teenagers and undiagnosed mental health conditions can play a significant role in parent/child family violence.
- It can be difficult for professionals to reconcile different narratives of violence in a home when parties give different accounts.
- Extended family or close friends can be valuable resources in finding a safe place for children and teenagers to go when there is mutual parent/child violence. However, it is important to work closely with social services and other professionals to ensure that any family placement is safe and appropriate. Extended family caregivers are often entitled to financial and other resource supports through social services if they formally take on long-term care of a child or children.
- Foster care or group home living may be a necessary alternative if no safe family placement can be made. If the juvenile is charged with a crime, he or she may be placed in a secure facility.

The Martin family had been known to social services historically because of violence between the mother, Eleanor, and 15-year old Samuel's father, who is now completely uninvolved with the family. The other children, Jonas and Elias, see their father on weekends at his home in an adjacent county, and were with their father when the following incident occurred.

The police were called by a neighbor when Samuel was seen scaling the outside of the building to get back into his third floor apartment at 1:30 am. Eleanor and Samuel began to yell at each other and a physical altercation ensued. When the police arrived, both Eleanor and Samuel had to be physically restrained. Samuel was so aggressive and angry that he was put in handcuffs and leg restraints, while Eleanor began to threaten the police and was stunned with a taser. Eleanor admitted to having consumed several alcoholic drinks that evening, as she does most days. Samuel's toxicology report later showed traces of cocaine and marijuana. Eleanor and Samuel each alleged the other began hitting first, and both had scratches and swelling from the fight. Samuel was placed in the care of social services while a home study was completed to assess the safety of a potential placement with grandparents. Samuel stated in his interview that he and his mom often yell at each other and that his mom has slapped him before, and this is the first time he has hit back. Eleanor was arrested and released with a warning for disturbing the peace. Eleanor alleged that Samuel often hits her, which he began doing once he had grown physically taller and stronger than his mother. Jonas and Elias remained in the full-time care of their father while Eleanor entered alcohol abuse treatment. Samuel was released into the care of his grandparents, who worked with social services to obtain mental health and substance abuse support services for Samuel.

Case #27 (Allison Little)

Elwood family, African American
Mother: Melanie, age 44
Father: Johnathan, age 46
Son: Anthony, age 14
Son: Lewis, age 12
Daughter: Sasha, age 5

This Case Demonstrates

- Because some level of inter-sibling violence and conflict is a normal part of child development and family life, abusive behavior may go unreported or may be rationalized by parents and other family members.
- Sibling violence can occur in families regardless of whether or not other family violence is occurring.
- Sibling abuse may be physical, emotional, sexual, or a combination thereof.
- Power differentials between siblings may go in unexpected directions, such as a younger sibling holding power over an elder sibling. Practitioners should consider a number of aspects including age, gender, physical and intellectual development, and what role a child plays in the family (e.g. the scapegoat, the golden child, the peacemaker). The abusive sibling may target only one sibling or may mistreat all of his or her siblings.
- Support services should be provided to all members of the family, not just to the siblings involved.

Mr. and Mrs. Elwood own a number of franchised restaurants and are a very wealthy family. They live in an exclusive neighborhood and their children attend a private day school. The school contacted social services out of concern about the relationship between Anthony and Lewis. Though the boys are in different classes and different years, they have often been seen around school arguing, and Lewis was caught with two of his friends holding down and giving Anthony a "swirly," putting his face in the toilet of the boys' room and flushing it. Lewis, though younger than Anthony, is a very good athlete and is already involved in weightlifting and other endurance sports. Anthony is a quieter child, has fewer friends, and often seems to be in the shadow of his younger brother. When the boys were interviewed separately, Anthony stated that his life is horrible and it is because of Lewis. Lewis has stolen his money, often hits him, threatens him, and teases him relentlessly by calling him a "girl" and a "faggot." Both boys are very dark skinned, so it is hard to see any bruising. However, Anthony pulled up his shirt and showed some swellings on his back and shoulders. Anthony stated he tries to hit back, but he is too slow and it only makes Lewis madder. Lewis has threatened to tell the whole school that Anthony is gay and has threatened to tell their parents that Anthony is molesting Sasha. Anthony stated Lewis told him he knows he can do this, because Sasha practically worships him and will say what he wants. On one particular occasion, Anthony states that Lewis took Anthony's phone and used it to download hardcore gay pornography, and then showed the phone to their parents. Anthony lost his phone for a month and his parents questioned him extensively. They did not believe Lewis had done this because they assumed Anthony had a password protected phone. Anthony states that Lewis is never like this with Sasha, in fact he is always being very nice to her, gives her things, and tells her bad things about Anthony so she will not like him. Lewis says that Anthony is just a crybaby and is always trying to get him in trouble with their parents. Lewis says his dad once told him privately that Lewis should be the older son, though Lewis stated he didn't want to tell Anthony that because it would make him upset. Lewis stated he loves his brother, and that everything is being exaggerated. The Elwoods were very concerned about the involvement of social services, and while they engaged a lawyer to sit in on meetings, were willing to cooperate with interviews. Melanie stated she knows that the boys don't often get along, but that they love each other and will grow out of their difficulties. Johnathan stated that the boys are competitive as he would expect them to be, they are both bright and full of potential and that competition prepares them for attending an elite college and eventually entering the business world. Both parents deny that there is excessive physical violence between the boys and both deny there is any kind of emotional abuse. Jonathan states that he never told Lewis he should be the oldest son, but would not be surprised if this is what Lewis feels since he is always coming out ahead of his brother. Ongoing in-home services were provided to the family, including extensive counseling both separately and together for Anthony and Lewis.

Case #28 (Christina Newhill)

This Case Demonstrates

- Drug and alcohol abuse as a complicating factor in an abusive relationship;
- Although an abusive partner is violent in the couple relationship, he may be a good parent for the couple's child and even handle challenges, such as a child's disability, well;
- How an abusive partner's jealousy may fuel controlling behavior and efforts to restrain the woman's options for friends and employment;
- The type of event that finally triggers a person to leave an abusive relationship;
- Challenges in learning how to be independent after one has left an abusive relationship and the strengths that emerge in someone who has been abused once they leave and are on their own.

Initial Contact and Presenting Problem

Barbara is a 25 year old divorced white woman referred to the Crisis Clinic by the Battered Women's Center and Shelter. Barbara presents as a thin shy young woman who could not make eye contact during the first half of the interview. Her speech was soft and hesitant; affect was sad. She denies suicidal ideation, however, once about a year ago when her husband was abusing her regularly, she threatened to cut herself with a pocket knife but her husband wrestled knife away from her.

Barbara relates a range of problems that she is struggling with. First of all, she has a drug problem which she readily admits she needs help with. About 3 years ago, Barbara used LSD heavily for 3 months, resulting in a lingering psychotic condition for which she was hospitalized and treated with antipsychotic medication and eventually stabilized, although last May (1 year ago) she had some recurrent visual hallucinations of "green phosphorescent Negro faces". She reports no psychotic symptoms at this time. Currently, Barbara is drinking alcohol to excess and smoking marijuana as often as she can afford it.

The other half of Barbara's problem set involves life situation problems. She was married for 3 years to a man who physically and emotionally abused her and was an alcoholic. Barbara and her former husband have a long history of marital discord with her citing his insane jealousy as being the primary difficulty in that he monitored her every move and was very controlling, including deciding who she could and could not associate with in terms of friends and family. She had a baby 16 months ago that has cerebral palsy due to birth trauma caused by use of forceps in the delivery, and the child's problems put added stress on the marriage. Although her husband abused Barbara, he was very loving towards the baby and actually was able to cope better with the child's problems than Barbara was, according to her, and so he now has custody. The last straw for her, in terms of the marriage, occurred 3 months ago when the husband slammed her against the wall and almost choked her to death. He now lives in another town in the county with the baby, and Barbara has her own apartment, surviving on small alimony payments. She is having a very difficult time learning to be independent and living on her own. She went straight from living with her parents to getting married and living with her husband and, until now, has never lived alone. She has no job skills but on her own has applied for Project Step and a job training program through the JTPA (Job Training Partnership Act) program. Barbara has three different job ideas she is interested in: secretarial work, graphic design and drafting. She took a drafting course a couple years ago, but couldn't complete it because heavy use of LSD impaired her thinking and she was hospitalized for injuries caused by her husband's abuse and missed too many classes as a result. Barbara states that her husband opposed her efforts to learn a trade. Barbara says that her future goals include obtaining an apartment without cockroaches and a car that doesn't break down. Along with what she is already doing to help herself, Barbara would also benefit from ongoing counseling at our mental health outpatient clinic as well as alcohol/drug counseling.

Disposition

1. Appointment for residential drug/alcohol rehabilitation treatment tomorrow;
2. Continue AA meetings at Women's the Center;
3. Continue pursuing job training
4. Followup appointment in crisis clinic on 6/11 Take appointment with outpatient clinic on 7/2.

Follow-up

On 6/4, Barbara called and said she will be going to 28-day RTC (Residential Treatment Center) drug and alcohol rehabilitation program, thus her outpatient counseling intake appointment was rescheduled for July 11th. Barbara will see the crisis clinic social worker when released from RTC for support until her intake. Shortly after completing rehab, Barbara succeeded in obtaining a full time job and has been working at the King's Table as a busgirl for the past month.

Index

I. H. Frieze et al., *Dynamics of Family and Intimate Partner Violence*,
https://doi.org/10.1007/978-3-030-42608-8

D

CPSIA information can be obtained
at www.ICGtesting.com
Printed in the USA
LVHW082109220520
656320LV00015B/154

9 783030 426064